SOVEREIGN DEBT MANAGEMENT

SOVEREIGN DEBT MANAGEMENT

Edited by

Rosa M. Lastra

Lee Buchheit

OXFORD
UNIVERSITY PRESS

OXFORD
UNIVERSITY PRESS

Great Clarendon Street, Oxford, OX2 6DP,
United Kingdom

Oxford University Press is a department of the University of Oxford.
It furthers the University's objective of excellence in research, scholarship,
and education by publishing worldwide. Oxford is a registered trade mark of
Oxford University Press in the UK and in certain other countries

First edition published in 2014

Impression: 1

Published in the United States of America by Oxford University Press
198 Madison Avenue, New York, NY 10016, United States of America

British Library Cataloguing in Publication Data
Data available

Library of Congress Control Number: 2013946772
Data available

ISBN 978–0–19–967110–6

Printed in Great Britain by
CPI Group (UK) Ltd, Croydon, CR0 4YY

To Lee Buchheit from his friends and colleagues

FOREWORD

This book radiates with the warmth of friendship for Lee Buchheit and the deep admiration for his work by the leading scholars, economists, and practitioners in the field of sovereign debt management. But the book is much more than a Festschrift. It is a definitive treatment of the field of sovereign debt crisis management, which has become one of the most difficult and crucial policy issues facing the global economy.

Such a comprehensive treatment would not have been possible without Lee Buchheit. More than anyone else, through his writing, speaking, advice-giving, and actually implementing policy, he has defined the field of sovereign debt crisis management, and has usefully identified its common elements across many different types of countries and periods of time.

I had the opportunity to work particularly closely with Lee Buchheit while I was Under Secretary for International Affairs at the US Treasury a decade ago. As the leading light in the field, he was the person to reach out to on sovereign debt problems. He gave sensible advice on broad reform issues, such as the introduction of collective action clauses into sovereign debt of emerging market countries. And he gave actionable solutions to really tough specific cases, such as the need to achieve a large write-down of Iraq's debt run up during Saddam Hussein's regime.

At the Treasury I saw him immerse himself into these difficult problems and come up with practical answers, as he has done many times before and since, most recently with his cogent analysis of the eurozone debt crisis. Indeed we at the Treasury took advantage of his generosity and consulted him so much that I later wrote in my book about that period that he was 'coming to Treasury so often that he seemed to be on the staff.' [1]

As Lee has patiently and clearly explained to me many times, there are several key common elements in sovereign debt crises, whether one is talking about those that began in emerging markets countries in the 1980s and continued through the 1990s, or those that began in some of the more advanced countries of Europe today.[2] You can see these elements in all the chapters of this book.

First is the *cause*, which Lee characterizes as 'excessively easy credit'. In the early 1980s crisis, the easy credit was caused by the huge revenue flows from the oil exporting countries into banks as oil prices surged with the oil shocks of the 1970s. These funds flowed from the banks and into the emerging markets in the form of loans to the governments, perhaps induced by the expectation that the IMF or the official sector would come to the rescue if repayments or sovereign defaults became a problem. The inflationary monetary policy by the Fed and other central banks which continued into the late 1970s helped to accommodate this excessively easy credit.

---

[1] John B. Taylor, *Global Financial Warriors: The Untold Story of International Finance in the Post-9/11 World* (New York: WW, Norton, 2007), 111.

[2] Lee C. Buchheit, 'The Eurozone Debt Crisis In Historical Perspective', 2 February 2011.

In the case of the eurozone crisis, fiscal and monetary policy was the underlying cause. Many eurozone countries were reluctant to follow the sensible fiscal policy as laid out in the Maastricht Treaty. The resort to deficits and the resulting growth of government debt was likely exacerbated by the setting of interest rates too low by the European Central Bank in 2003–05, which was in turn partly due to the low interest rates set by the Fed.

The second element in the typical sovereign debt crisis is what Lee Buchheit calls the *trigger*, something which makes it clear that the 'music has stopped' or will soon stop because of the realization that the government's debt has become too big to service or roll over. In the 1980s, the trigger was the decision by the Federal Reserve under Paul Volcker to end the inflationary policies and raise interest rates dramatically. As the later performance of the American economy in the 1980s and 1990s demonstrated, Volcker made the correct decision, but it had the short run consequence of significantly raising debt service and making roll over of debt in many emerging markets nearly impossible. In the case of the eurozone crisis, the trigger was the great recession and economic growth slowdown associated with the 2008 financial crisis. But in the absence of these triggers, most likely there would have been some other trigger.

Once the trigger is pulled, the third element of the story—the government policy response—comes into play, and this is usually the place where Lee Buchheit is called into the scene as well. Policymakers typically respond in a series of chaotic political decisions under a great deal of uncertainty in which they seem to have no good choices. Private sector lenders and sovereign borrowers both call for a bailout of some kind from the official sector, which consists of the large developed countries and the international financial institutions, especially the International Monetary Fund. The lenders and borrowers argue that a bailout is necessary to prevent a painful default or an equally painful restructuring of the sovereign debt. Either default or restructuring, they argue, would harm the people in the country as well as the individual investors and financial institutions who would suffer the write down. Those in favour of a bailout further argue that contagion to other countries will amplify these costs. Policymakers and politicians find it hard to resist such arguments, but they are urged to do so by those who say that the bailout will cause moral hazard, make future crises more likely, and that taxpayers should not be bailing out investors who took on too much risk.

The choice is often starkly put as painful bailout or painful default.

Frequently, public officials attempt to avoid this hard choice. They 'kick the can down the road' hoping that higher economic growth and more revenues will help resolve the sovereign's problem. But rarely does the delay tactic work, and, as Lee has argued many times, it usually makes the problem worse. The eventual adjustment—including a bout of severe austerity—is more difficult than it would have been if a prompt decision had been made. In the 1980s the initial calls for bailout were resisted, leading to a period when private sector lenders and sovereign borrowers tried to scramble to delay or prevent defaults and write-downs with new money loans from the banks. Eventually the 1980s debt crisis ended, but only when sovereign debt was restructured in the 1990s.

Lee Buchheit's long experience has given him unique insights and a special appreciation for the incentives that drive policymakers in these situations. That is why he is so often called on and listened to. There is a certain tragic inevitability to the process. When you brief him on the details of a particular sovereign debt case, and explain the positions of all the parties, and then listen to his reaction, you know you are talking to someone who has seen this movie before.

This experience is why Lee Buchheit has been so constructive in the ongoing quest for reform. In his view there is usually no need for a stark choice between bailout and chaotic default. Indeed in many cases, he argues, there are other options, especially if you prepare for them in advance. Putting collective action clauses into sovereign bonds is one way to prepare for a smooth, relatively painless restructuring with little or no contagion. When such clauses are part of the bond contract, sovereign borrowers and lenders can achieve an orderly restructuring of the debt. Thanks to Lee's strong support, collective action clauses were part of the reform process for emerging market debt a decade ago, and that has helped reduce the likelihood of governments mismanaging a bailout-default choice. For these reasons, the IMF exceptional access framework was revised to reduce the likelihood of bailouts in emerging markets, and that has led to more responsible fiscal and monetary policy in many emerging market countries, making them less prone to crises.

Ironically, the problems that faced emerging markets a decade ago have returned to plague Europe, and there is thus still much need for reform. Fortunately, Lee Buchheit and the other authors of the chapters in this book are on top of the problem. The analysis and recommendations found in their contributions are exactly what is needed to bring about such reform, and thereby begin to remove or at least mitigate this continuing source of economic turbulence in the world economy.

John B. Taylor
Stanford University
7 November 2013

PREFACE

The sovereign debt problems of emerging market countries in the last quarter of the twentieth century caused the international financial system to groan audibly. The sovereign debt problems of developed countries, in Europe and elsewhere, are having a remarkably similar effect in the first quarter of the twenty-first century. There now seems little doubt that excessive sovereign debt and its attendant economic, social, and political problems will constitute a major international challenge for the balance of this decade and beyond.

The idea for this volume germinated at a meeting of the International Monetary Law Committee (a standing committee of the International Law Association) in Rome in the autumn of 2011. From the outset, the goal was not only to commission a Festschrift; rather, the objective was to produce a general treatise on sovereign debt management, written by leading experts (lawyers, economists, and academics) with practical experience in lending, borrowing, regulating, analysing, restructuring, and litigating sovereign debt.

With this as its target, contributions were solicited to answer five broad questions, as follows.

(i) How, from whom, and for what purposes do sovereigns borrow money, and what are the symptoms of sovereign debt pathology?
(ii) How and with what consequences can unsustainable sovereign debt be restructured?
(iii) What legal remedies are available to the creditors of sovereign borrowers and what legal defences can be mustered by the sovereign defendants?
(iv) What factors can complicate the sovereign debt workout process?
(v) How might sovereign insolvencies be handled more efficiently in the future?

This book is also intended as a *liber amicorum* in honor of Lee Buchheit. Somewhat unusually, we asked Lee to serve both as a co-editor and contributor to a volume in his honour. He kindly agreed to do so. The rationale for our request was simple: for more than three decades, Lee's professional life has been congruent with the life of sovereign debt. Beginning in 1982 with the Latin American debt crisis, Lee has been involved—usually as counsel to the debtors—in most of the sovereign debt workouts of the last thirty years. Virtually every innovation in this field, from collective action clauses to exit consents to the *pari passu* debate, bears his distinctive mark. A treatise on sovereign debt management without a contribution from Lee would have been unthinkable. Therefore, as co-editor of this volume, I felt it appropriate to invite Lee to participate actively in a project that was always intended to recognize his lifetime contribution to this field.

Rosa María Lastra
London
15 August 2013

LEE BUCHHEIT: A BIOGRAPHICAL NOTE

Lee Buchheit was born in Pittsburgh, Pennsylvania, in 1950. His father, Charles R. Buchheit, Jr, was a businessman and his mother, Helen Wheeler Buchheit, a librarian. Lee has an elder brother, Carl L. Buchheit, living in San Raphael, California.

Lee's parents had met during the Second World War. Both were officers, his mother an officer in the US Army Nurse Corps. They had met briefly at Fort Sill, Oklahoma, a staging area for troops being sent to the European and Pacific theatres. Lee's father was bound for Europe; his mother, for the Pacific. They promised that, if they both survived the war, they would marry.

No doubt his parents' war-time experience was an influence on Lee's chosen profession as a teenager, which was to be a soldier. At the age of seventeen, he won a scholarship from the US Army, which paid tuition and expenses for four years, allowing him to attend any college in the United States that sponsored a Reserve Officer Training Corps (ROTC) programme. The advantage to this over attending the US Military Academy at West Point was that it allowed Lee a free choice to study what he wished, while the West Point curriculum laid a heavy emphasis on engineering.

Lee chose Middlebury College, which has a splendid location in Vermont's Champlain Valley, with the Green Mountains to the east and the Adirondacks to the west. Founded in 1800, Middlebury is a highly regarded liberal arts college. As a condition of his scholarship, Lee had to enlist in the army. This was at a time that the Vietnam War was becoming increasingly unpopular on American college campuses, leading to events such as the shooting by the Ohio National Guard of college students at Kent State University in May 1970. When he developed a medical condition in his third year, however, Lee had to leave the ROTC programme.

Philosophy was Lee's college major and his second choice of profession was to become an academic philosopher. However, one of his philosophy professors at Middlebury advised him to attend law school first and then to return to philosophy if he was still determined. So Lee enrolled in 1972 at the University of Pennsylvania Law School in Philadelphia. A private Ivy League school, Penn Law has a long and distinguished history, providing a home for the American Law Institute in its early years. Lee's grades meant an appointment as an editor of the *University of Pennsylvania Law Review*.

Rather than entering law practice immediately, Lee undertook a Diploma in International Law at Trinity College, Cambridge, during the academic year 1975–76. This is a degree awarded after a year of research informing a dissertation. The topic of Lee's thesis was the claims of secessionist groups to legitimacy under public international law. The thesis was an outstanding piece of work, which Yale University Press published in 1976 as *Secession: The Legitimacy of Self-Determination*. Lee chose to focus on six recent secessionist attempts: Katanga; the Kurds; Biafra; the Somalis; the Nagas; and Bangladesh. In outline, Lee argued that natural political units, deriving consent from their people, were the basis for understanding the issue. A review in the *Yale Law Review* by a young Japanese scholar criticized the focus on the legal prescriptions to be applied to claims to self-determination once made, rather than how the environmental conditions for such claims could be rectified beforehand. This seemed to miss the point, but chimed with the sentiment shared by proponents of the newly decolonized world, who strongly supported the inviolability of national borders.

The law firm of Cleary Gottlieb Steen & Hamilton was formed in 1946 as Cleary Gottlieb Friendly and Cox, with offices in New York and Washington DC. The Washington office was unusual at a time when larger, well-established New York firms did not have branches in the capital. The firm was also innovative in establishing a 'European office' in Paris as early as 1949, initially because it was counsel to the commercial and financial sections of the French Embassy in Washington. In a privately printed account of the firm's history in 1983, Leo Gottlieb explained that, unlike other American law firms, Cleary Gottlieb's foreign offices equipped themselves at an early stage to handle the whole job for their clients. The Paris office was followed by one in Brussels and one in London in 1971, because of London's importance as a centre for international finance.

Lee joined Cleary Gottlieb in 1976. He was absolutely certain that he never wished to work in New York City and so began in its Washington office, working in his first three years principally on litigation and regulatory matters. Half of his time was spent representing the then-nascent private courier industry in a vicious battle against the US Postal Service over the question of whether the latter's statutory monopoly on the carriage of letters precluded private couriers from offering a competing service for time-sensitive materials. In 1971, Lee moved to the London office. He tells the story that, on arrival, his fellow associate asked him a simple question: 'Loans or bonds?' Knowing nothing about either, he says that he bleated 'Loans'. So began his work on international syndicated loan agreements. At the time, it was the height of the frenzied effort by international banks to recycle the petrodollar deposits resulting from the two oil shocks of the 1970s. Much of this lending was destined for sovereign borrowers in emerging markets.

Returning to Washington DC in spring 1982, Lee almost immediately began work in the area that he made his own over the next thirty years. Mexico had declared a debt moratorium in mid-1982, when it was no longer able to repay the amounts borrowed on international markets. That triggered a debt crisis in other Latin American countries. Cleary Gottlieb represented Mexico in the process of debt restructuring and, because Mexico enjoyed the status of flagship country restructuring sovereign debt, many of other countries hired the firm as their international legal adviser. Lee explains his own involvement in characteristic fashion:

> It began for me with a telephone call from one of my colleagues in New York. I had just returned from drafting syndicated loans in London, I recall him saying, and therefore I must surely know how to restructure such instruments. Of course, I had no idea how to restructure the debt stock of a sovereign borrower but I quickly realized—and this is the delicious part—that no one else did either. Such a thing had not really been attempted since the last sovereign debt crisis in the 1930s. Thus, Cleary Gottlieb (and, by extension, me, as the junior lawyer on the Cleary team) were quite literally present at the creation of a new field of law and practice.

During his time in Washington, Lee resumed his legal writing, with a regular column on recent US legal developments for the *Business Law Review*.

US commercial banks are primarily based in New York City, so that was where Cleary Gottlieb's sovereign debt work was centred. Breaking a personal commandment never to practise in New York, Lee relocated north. By then, he had become the partner in charge of the firm's work for the Republic of the Philippines, and was commuting regularly to Manila and Tokyo. The Philippines had incurred large foreign debt and, in the mid-1980s, was faced with problems in servicing it. There were recommendations from within the country that there be a two-year moratorium, but through agreements with the International Monetary Fund (IMF) and the international commercial banks, the Philippines rescheduled its debt and entered the Brady Plan (named after the then US Treasury Secretary). In 1987, Lee relocated to manage the Hong Kong office. It shortened his commute to Manila and there, apart from debt restructuring, he worked on matters such as privatizations and project finance.

By now, Lee was becoming well known through his practice, but it was his contributions to the *International Financial Law Review* that established his reputation more widely in the international legal world. Between 1989 and 1992, he wrote a monthly column on sovereign debt management topics. Then, between 1992 and 1994, he published a series of articles, based on in-house seminars that he prepared as part of the firm's continuing legal education programme. Each was entitled 'How to...' and covered the negotiation of the standard clauses in international financial documentation. The articles were later collected in a book, now in its second edition, entitled *How to Negotiate Eurocurrency Loan Agreements*.

Ostensibly written as a practical work of instruction for harried young lawyers, Lee says that the book also seeks to overcome the temptation among them to view a document spilling out of the printer as a product of divine revelation, with the consequent reluctance to change it for fear of tinkering with some critical piece of text or to question it for fear of betraying one's neophyte status. In the book, the purpose and history of the specimen clauses in loan agreements are explained, along with the negotiating stances of the borrower and lender. But within the text is the distilled wisdom of the experienced practitioner and legal scholar, so that, in the process, the reader learns a great deal about the market background to Eurocurrency transactions. Characteristically, the discussion is clever and amusing. Consider this passage about the disaster clause, for example:

> Despite its colourful title, the Eurodollar disaster clause has nothing to do with floods or earthquakes or any other unpleasant acts that are routinely attributed to the deity. It refers instead to a situation in which lending banks are not able to fund themselves in the Euromarkets in the normal way. This, if you are a banker, is a disaster.

In 1991, Lee returned to Cleary Gottlieb's New York office from Hong Kong. The morning he arrived, one of his colleagues in Washington told him that the State of Kuwait had retained the firm to assist in a massive procurement programme. This was in anticipation of the removal of Saddam Hussein's troops from occupying their country. Lee led the finance team, which meant streamlining the process by which hundreds of letters of credit were to be issued to the suppliers of the goods and services to be purchased. The Government of Kuwait, still in exile, also arranged the largest ever sovereign loan in the Eurodollar market.

Over the following two decades in Cleary Gottlieb's New York office, Lee's practice increasingly concentrated on sovereign advisory work, which often led to other work for the governments. The Philippines continued to be a client through the mid-1990s; Ecuador began in 1992; Russia was a client during 1997–98; work with Uruguay spread over many years; work with Iraq started in 2004 and continues. More recently came work with Iceland in 2010 and with Greece in 2011. Sandwiched between these larger sovereign advisory assignments were debt workouts for countries such as Nigeria, Liberia, Guatemala, and Belize. About sovereign debt restructuring, Lee says this:

> [A] large sovereign debt restructuring is played out against a colorful backdrop of both domestic and international politics. The principal skill required of a sovereign debt restructurer is the ability to persuade perfectly sensible people to do something—reduce or stretch out their claims against a sovereign debtor—that no perfectly sensible person would ever think of doing. The required talents? An ability when speaking to creditors to slip effortlessly between an imperious tone ('Read This and Tremble') and a cooing, let-the-little-children-come-unto-me intonation. A sense of theater. And, when dealing with large creditor committees, a familiarity with the basic principles of animal husbandry.
>
> But in the spirit of Jean Jacques Rousseau, I will inject into these confessions an element of unvarnished truth. I was attracted to sovereign debt restructuring mainly because it appealed to my paladin instinct. The client—the sovereign borrower—will by definition be in the middle of a crisis, otherwise they wouldn't be talking to someone like you. Creditors will drip with hostility; citizens of the debtor country will groan under 'economic adjustment' measures; opposition politicians will chortle at their good fortune in being out of office at that moment. The client will have one friend in the world, you. To a certain type of lawyer, this is irresistible.

Following his thesis at Cambridge, Lee could well have become a full-time academic; instead, he turned to practice. But in many ways he never left the academy. Over the years, he has spent a great deal of time with students. Lee has shown an unparalleled enthusiasm and passion for teaching, generously sharing his time and his knowledge with generation after generation of students. The combination of wit, wisdom, erudition, and mastery of the English language make his lectures legendary. He has held a variety of appointments in leading law schools. He was an adjunct professor at the School for International and Public Affairs of Columbia University (1994–97), a visiting professor at Chuo University in Japan (1997–98), a lecturer on law at the Harvard Law School (2000), a visiting lecturer in law at the Yale Law School (2005), an adjunct professor of law at Duke University Law School (2006–07), and an adjunct professor of law at New York University Law School (2008). Importantly, for the University of London, he has been a visiting professorial fellow in the Centre for Commercial Law Studies at Queen Mary College since 1997. His skills as a lecturer are matched by his skills as a legal scholar. Lee has published some forty articles in books and leading law journals.

Lee never realized his ambition to become a professional philosopher, but summarizes his philosophy of life as follows:

> I have been for forty years a disciple of the 17th century Dutch philosopher Baruch Spinoza. Metaphysics aside, Spinoza's principal thesis was that superstition, fear and ignorance are the well-springs of most of the misery that our hapless species inflicts on itself. The problem, as Spinoza well knew, is that fear is an innate characteristic of featherless bipeds such as ourselves, ignorance our common inheritance and superstition the method by which we pretend to master the first and camouflage the second. The objective, Spinoza would say, is freedom, by which he meant emancipation in both an emotional and intellectual sense. Achieving that freedom requires both good luck and discipline. I have had plenty of the former in my life but less of the latter than I would like.

The latter is a typical understatement. One cannot have reached the heights that Lee has in legal practice, or made his contributions to the literature, without discipline. In 2010, he received the *International Financial Law Review*'s inaugural Lifetime Achievement Award for his contributions to international finance; in 2012, he was recognized in the US Innovative

Lawyers Report of the *Financial Times* as one of the ten most innovative individuals for his work on Greek debt restructuring; in 2012, an article in the *New York Times* referred to him as the 'philosopher king of sovereign debt'; in 2013, he was described by *The Guardian* newspaper as 'the fairy godmother to finance ministers in distress' and by the *Financial Times* as 'the doyen of sovereign debt restructurings'. No doubt, at this point, Lee would remind us of Spinoza: 'None are more taken in by flattery than the proud, who wish to be the first and are not.'

Sir Ross Cranston, FBA
Rosa María Lastra

APPROACHES TO SOVEREIGN DEBT RESOLUTION: RECENT DEVELOPMENTS

A book recognizing the work of Lee Buchheit would be incomplete without reflecting upon his vital contributions to the advancement of the recent work of the International Law Association (ILA) in sovereign debt resolution and a look forward to the completion of its ongoing projects. This short note will discuss important current events regarding sovereign debt, acknowledge the achievement of the Sovereign Insolvency Study Group, and provide an update on the pioneering work of the ILA's Sovereign Bankruptcy Working Group.

1. Current Events

Sovereign debt crises are very much back on centre stage and no longer primarily a developing country issue. This evolution can be significantly attributed to the global financial crisis and its spillover into the sovereign sector of some euro area member states which has posed a severe threat to global economic stability due to both the interconnectedness of the global economy and the accompanying risk of contagion.

Further, the uncertainty generated by the ongoing litigation between NML Capital et al and Argentina,[1] and the decisions taken to date by American courts, have given cause for alarm among a number of market participants (including trustees, paying agents, clearing systems, and infrastructure providers) as well as debtors and many in the official sector, together with various creditors who participated in Argentina's restructuring.

On 7 October 2013, the US Supreme Court decided not to hear an appeal from the Second Circuit's most recent decision of 23 August, which rejected an appeal from the trial judge's sweeping decision.[2] Argentina is expected to file a second petition in the coming months that the Supreme Court will review and decide again if it will hear the appeal. If the Supreme Court ultimately does not take the case, further uncertainty may result, potentially making participation in future restructurings less attractive for some creditors.

This legal uncertainty may open the door to reform, whether contractual or more treaty-based. As France has argued in its *amicus* brief to the US Supreme Courts, the Court of Appeal's decision jeopardizes the ability of sovereign debtors to achieve orderly and negotiated

---

[1] Supreme Court of the United States, '12-1494 – Republic of Argentina v NML Capital, Ltd, et al' (7 October 2013), online at Supreme Court of the United States <http://www.supremecourt.gov/Search.aspx?FileName =/docketfiles/12-1494.htm>.

[2] Supreme Court of the United States, '12-1494 – Republic of Argentina v NML Capital, Ltd, et al' (7 October 2013).

restructurings of their external debt.[3] This concern has been shared by the International Monetary Fund (IMF),[4] World Bank,[5] and the US Government.[6]

The present climate makes the ongoing work of the Sovereign Insolvency Study Group and Sovereign Bankruptcy Working Group very relevant to the international agenda.

2. The Prior Contributions of ILA Working Groups

As this volume so richly demonstrates, Lee Buchheit has a deep appreciation for academic debate and philosophy; he has brought this passion to the ILA's working groups on sovereign debt and has been a driving force behind its initiatives.

The Sovereign Insolvency Study Group was formed in 2008 to study the existing legal framework and to propose the broadest range of policy options, without regard to their political feasibility. The study group was not to favour any of the options, as this task was to be left to a successor group after receiving feedback and thoughts from interested parties on the merits of the policy options.

In August 2010, the Sovereign Insolvency Study Group chaired by Philip Wood published its report entitled 'State Insolvency: Options for the Way Forward' at The Hague Conference (2010).[7] This report described the existing regime for restructuring sovereign debt and compared the legal regimes for states and the private sector. The Sovereign Insolvency Study Group proposed four policy options without making recommendations. They were: first, leave it to the market (e.g. collective action clauses); second, introduce a limited provision for creditor voting with a stay on creditors as voted on by creditors; third, full bankruptcy regime by treaty so far as feasible; and fourth, reduce protections available to sovereign states.

In 2012, a successor working group was formed, the Sovereign Bankruptcy Working Group—again chaired by Philip Wood. This time the working group's mandate was to explore treaty-based and contractually-based options to resolve enduring sovereign issues.

At the initial meeting in London in January 2013, the Sovereign Bankruptcy Working Group selected an innovative and unusual format to enliven the debate; two 'teams' were created, with one to advocate a treaty-based approach and the other a purely contractual approach. These teams were to proceed in parallel, each defending and advocating its approach and highlighting deficiencies in the other. Membership is non-exclusive, and indeed many working group members have chosen to participate in both.

---

[3] Brief for the Republic of France as *Amicus Curiae* in support of the Republic of Argentina's petition for a writ of *certiorari* in *Republic of Argentina v NML Capital, Ltd., et al.*, Docket No. 12-1494 (26 July 2013).

[4] 'IMF Launches Discussion of Sovereign Debt Restructuring', *International Monetary Fund* (23 May 2013), online at International Monetary Fund <http://www.imf.org/external/pubs/ft/survey/so/2013/POL052313A.htm>.

[5] 'World Bank to Increase Support to Curb Vulture Fund Actions' *World Bank* (31 May 2007) online at The World Bank <http://web.worldbank.org/WBSITE/EXTERNAL/TOPICS/EXTFINANCIALSECTOR/0,,contentMDK:21353898~menuPK:282890~pagePK:64020865~piPK:149114~theSitePK:282885,00.html>.

[6] Brief for the United States of America as *Amicus Curiae* in support of the Republic of Argentina's petition for panel rehearing and rehearing *en banc* in *Republic of Argentina v NML Capital, Ltd., et al*, Docket No. 12-105-cv(L) (28 December 2012).

[7] Sovereign Insolvency Study Group, 'State insolvency: Options for the Way Forward' (Paper delivered at the International Law Association Hague Conference 2010), The Hague Conference Report 2010. Online at ILA <http://www.ila-hq.org/download.cfm/docid/0A7ACEAC-94A3-4B47-B9E642CF4BEA5D81>.

In April 2014 (to coincide with the next meeting of the ILA International Monetary Law Committee and the annual American Society of International Law meetings in Washington), it is planned to present the reports of each group in a moot court format before a panel of judges (probably) at the Georgetown University Law Centre. This format is intended to expose the two streams to challenge and get these ideas circulating and available to a broader audience.

3. The Path to Washington 2014

A. Working Group 1—the 'Treaty Team' (chaired by Lee Buchheit)

The Treaty Team's initial discussions canvassed a number of possible approaches. The broadest would be a new treaty replicating all aspects of a US Chapter 11 Bankruptcy, including some parts of Chapter 9; more modestly, amendments to several existing treaties; and finally, the most narrowly focused, amendments to the IMF Articles of Agreement.

For a number of reasons, the Treaty Team fairly quickly agreed that a minimalist treaty change was the most feasible approach, the leading candidate being the IMF Articles of Agreement due to its high degree of flexibility, and near-universal membership.

The principal reason for this choice seems fairly obvious. A maximalist proposal, however elegant and complete it might be, would likely lead to a losing argument as being unachievable, as experience with the sovereign debt restructuring mechanism (SDRM)[8] has shown. Even though the SDRM evolved significantly and was subsequently slimmed down, it undoubtedly bore the weight of its overly ambitious origins. Something straightforward and minimalist would be vital.

An amendment to the IMF Articles of Agreement requires 85 per cent support; only the United States would have the ability to independently veto the agreement.

The Treaty Team, under Lee Buchheit's guidance, has identified a number of key issues to consider for a statutory approach:

Independent assessment of debtor's financial condition The treaty needs to clarify which party makes the decisions about who enters the restructuring: the creditors or a subset of them, the debtor country, or the IMF. On one hand, the IMF has not in the past been particularly good at distinguishing between illiquidity and insolvency. On the other hand, debtors tend to delay the commencement of a restructuring until it is too late which leaves some creditors paid in full and others with nothing at all. A key advantage of the statutory approach is that even though debtors may not know the outcome with a treaty, they will know the process leads to effective restructuring, which may encourage debtors to come forward sooner.

Super-majority creditor control of process The concept 'super-majority' needs to be defined to lay out which creditors are included, and how other creditors, especially bilateral creditors (Paris Club), should be treated. Bilateral creditors, particularly the Paris Club, may applaud the effort for an efficient resolution, but will be reluctant to cede authority. Even though the statutory approach may not be able to compel bilateral actors, the Treaty Team

[8] See Sean Hagan, 'Designing a Legal Framework to Restructure Sovereign Debt' (2005) 36(2) Georgetown J Int'l L 299.

may need to look for a way to bring them in as the lack of coordination between private and bilateral actors has often led to greater disparity.

Automatic stay/asset immunization A treaty could include the domestic bankruptcy features of an automatic stay and/or asset immunization at some level. However, in deciding on its inclusion, the Treaty Team will consider whether the use of a statutory approach could mean that such a stay is not required because creditors will not commence a disruptive suit with little chance of profiting as a result of the new regime.

Dispute resolution mechanism The Treaty Team will examine whether the dispute resolution mechanism should be judicial or quasi-judicial. If the body is judicial, the team will need to determine what aspects it would be asked to rule on.

Due process considerations The Treaty Team may address which body should rule on the legitimacy of the underlying debts. A prominent belief is that a quasi-judicial body should not be asked to determine the validity of claims.

Supervisory function The treaty should determine which organization would oversee the regime, whether it is the IMF or a new body. Both of these options come with challenges. The IMF has an established international reputation, and a new body carries the threat of a new transnational bureaucracy.

Claim submission/verification process The statutory route would require some kind of claim verification process (e.g. Iraq claim verification process in its debt restructuring).

Master of ceremonies role The Treaty Team may propose a neutral, procedural arbiter to oversee the process.

The second part of each group's mandate is to challenge the other group's vision. In this instance, the Treaty Team will point out the deficiencies of the status quo. First, the contractual approach can only go so far, as many legacy debts do not have collective action clauses; time intensive negotiated resolutions further delay the restructuring process; and negotiated restructurings may result in inadequate debt relief.

Second, the contractual approach cannot 'de-fang' the holdouts. The *NML et al v Republic of Argentina* case[9] demonstrates a history of innovations and counter-innovations, leading to an ongoing cycle where contractual innovations are eventually circumvented. In contrast, a statutory approach may be able to end this disruptive cycle and provide a predictable process to restructure sovereign debt.

Third, the contractual tools would work better with a baseline statutory regime for the purposes of enforcement, process uniformity, and predictability.

These arguments and others will be refined in the Team's final report.

B. Working Group 2—the 'Contractual Team' (chaired by Deborah Zandstra)

The contractual regime is characterized by negotiations and contract, where insolvencies are resolved through existing voluntary methods. As such, the Contractual Team's overall argument is that the current system has worked well and the evolution in sovereign debt crisis resolution should be toward 'refinement' and 'improvement'. Therefore, a main focus

[9] *See* n. 1.

of the contractual approach is on mechanisms for a super-majority of bondholders to bind holdouts to new payment terms through collective action clauses.

At its first meeting in May 2013, the group began by reviewing recent developments in the contractual/voluntary/market-based approach of sovereign debt restructuring, including:

- the widespread adoption of the single series collective action clause in both New York and English law-governed bonds;[10]
- the adoption as of January 2013 of a new Euro area Model Collective Action Clauses with an aggregation feature to further facilitate sovereign debt restructuring;[11]
- the use of domestic legislation in Greece to facilitate the restructuring of Greek law governed debt, highlighting the different effective approaches available to sovereign debtors where domestic law instruments are issued;[12]
- the Institute of International Finance (IIF) established a Joint Public-Private Committee on Strengthening the Framework for Sovereign Debt Crisis Prevention and Resolution which published an Addendum to the Principles for Stable Capital Flows and Fair Debt Restructuring;[13]
- the UNCTAD (United Nations Conference on Trade and Development) published in April 2011 Principles on Promoting Responsible Sovereign Lending and Borrowing;[14]
- the UN-DESA (Department of Economic & Social Affairs) has established a UN Experts Group to explore how to improve the framework for restructuring sovereign debt in order to reduce the length of the negotiation processes and return countries to sustainable growth as quickly as possible, while preserving the delicate relationship between debtors and private capital flows;[15]
- the IMF, US Treasury, and industry bodies such as the International Capital Markets Association are studying ways to further facilitate orderly sovereign debt restructuring processes;[16] and
- the Paris Club is also trying to revisit its role, now that much of the Heavily Indebted Poor Countries (HIPC) work has been completed, and frame a future for itself in the context of this new thinking.[17]

---

[10] Group of Ten, *Report of the G-10 Working Group on Contractual Clauses* (12 September 2002), available online at Europa <http://europa.eu/efc/sub_committee/pdf/report_of_the_g-10_working_group_on_contractual_clauses.pdf>. The G-10 Working Group drafted a set of model clauses that formed a template for subsequent contract revisions in New York-law bonds.

[11] 'Euro area Model CAC 2012' (22 March 2013), available online at Europa Economic and Financial Committee <http://europa.eu/efc/sub_committee/cac/cac_2012/>.

[12] Committee on Foreign & Comparative Law, 'Governing Law in Sovereign Debt – Lessons from the Greek Crisis and Argentina Dispute of 2012', *New York City Bar Association* (February 2013), available online at <http://www2.nycbar.org/pdf/report/uploads/20072390-GoverningLawinSovereignDebt.pdf>.

[13] Joint Committee on Strengthening the Framework for Sovereign Debt Crisis Prevention and Resolution, 'Principles for Stable Capital Flows and Fair Debt Restructuring & Addendum' (October 2012), available online at IIF <http://www.iif.com/emp/principles/>.

[14] UNCTAD, 'Principles on Promoting Responsible Sovereign Lending and Borrowing' (10 January 2012), available online at UNCTAD <http://www.unctad.info/upload/Debt%20Portal/Principles%20drafts/SLB_Principles_English_Doha_22-04-2012.pdf>.

[15] 'Expert Group Meeting on Sovereign Debt Restructuring', *Financing for Development* (18 May 2012), online at United Nations <http://www.un.org/esa/ffd/msc/2012Egm_debt/>.

[16] e.g. 'ICMA Sovereign Bond Consultation Paper' (23 November 2010), available online at International Capital Market Association <http://www.icmagroup.org/resources/Sovereign-Debt-Information/>.

[17] Hugh Carnegy, '"Rich country" creditors seek emerging markets lender accord', *Financial Times* (23 October 2013), available online at Financial Times <http://www.ft.com/intl/cms/s/0/0fbfae36-3bd6-11e3-b85f-00144feab7de.html#axzz2iec47jxa>.

In addition, the Contractual Team recognized that any contractual approach cannot stand alone and must be complemented by a number of key facets. First, cross-border inter-connectedness of financial markets has magnified the problems of collective action, however, collective action clauses still represent a very substantive tool for restructuring that needs to be adjusted to national legal settings.

Second, contractual proposals need to go hand-in-hand with crisis resolution mechanisms (including crisis funding) and additional surveillance mechanisms for sovereign debtors. Third, contractual enhancements need to be combined with stronger capital and liquidity frameworks and firewalls to stop contagion. Fourth, the importance of voluntary negotiations in good faith and creditor committees should not be understated.

Like the Treaty Team, the Contractual Team has a dual task: first, develop the existing contractual tools (collective action clauses, *pari passu* clauses, bondholder committees, etc.) to improve the process of sovereign debt restructurings and deliver a speedy and litigation free or at least 'litigation light' restructuring. Second, the team must refute the arguments being made for the necessity of a treaty-based approach.

On the first point, the Contractual Team will point out that, with a few notable exceptions, the system has worked reasonably well to date. The contractual approach balances the bargaining power of the parties, since unlike the position in corporate insolvencies under domestic law, creditors cannot force the sale of the debtor's assets, control the debtor's financial affairs, enforce full disclosure, or sanction misfeasance. The current regime allows creditors and debtors to develop a solution through an ad hoc regime that recognizes the insolvency's unique features. Market associations can adopt practices that are designed to achieve an orderly resolution (e.g. New York bonds have adopted the collective action clauses). In the end, the bond is the product of negotiations between the debtor and creditor, thus, it should reflect what both parties considered to be a fair arrangement at the time.

In building this argument, the Contractual Team expects to clarify several issues. To highlight a few:

Degree of Compulsion versus Voluntarism The Contractual Team may need to decide whether they will advocate for a purely contractual approach or whether their argument will support a contractual approach with statutory mandates in the contracts. In essence, the Contractual Team will have to decide between either supporting the introduction of an element of compulsion, or strictly advocating for proposals that are 'voluntary' (e.g. the Euro-zone Collective Action Clause being an example of a contractual solution that is backed by legislative requirements).

Scope of the Report The Contractual Team may need to decide whether to consider only foreign law governed bonds or also domestic law governed bonds, and whether to deal only with bonds or look at all forms of sovereign debt, such as loans and also debts owed by sovereigns to other sovereigns. The Greek PSI raised some important inter-creditor issues, insofar as debt owed to sovereign creditors was excluded from the restructuring.

Provisions on Creditor Committees and Good Faith The Contractual Team may discuss whether bond terms and conditions should include provisions on creditor committees and good faith engagement. To date, there has been some reluctance to include these provisions because creditors can work together anyway. The team recognizes that a demand may exist and that such an essential issue should be addressed.

Model Provisions The Contract Team may consider proposing model provisions, which are not mandatory but recommended (e.g. model *pari passu* clause, model collective action clauses, etc.).

A much wider range of topics may be discussed for possible inclusion: provisions in respect of the enforcement of creditor committees; standstills (a very difficult topic for both the 'treaty' approach and the 'market' approach); implications of sovereign rating downgrade; credit default swap triggers; and accounting asset impairment issues, which framed the first round of Greek PSI to a great extent and *pari passu* clauses.

As part of its dual role, the Contractual Team will argue that the statutory route is not preferable. As highlighted by the Hague Conference Report, central concerns with the statutory route are the dual role of the IMF as a creditor and decision-maker, the impact on the cost of sovereign financing, the intervention in contractual rights, the move toward rules even though it may be said that the individual nature of each sovereign insolvency calls for ad hoc solutions, and the desire to maintain room for governments to influence the terms of restructurings.

These arguments and others are being refined and sharpened for the debate in Washington.

4. Conclusion

The arguments of the Contractual Team and Treaty Team in Washington can be expected to produce a lively, thoughtful, and insightful debate on necessary reforms for sovereign bankruptcy restructuring. On one side, the contractual approach will advocate a voluntary regime that is forward looking and independent of statutory development; on the other side, the Treaty Team will seek to demonstrate the inadequacies of the purely contractual approach and the need for a minimal treaty or statutory framework to avoid those pitfalls. Lee Buchheit has been a major contributor to advancing the contractual framework to its present position, and his advocacy of a realistic and minimal treaty approach reflects that long experience and provides a stimulus and a guide to the Teams' efforts.

Mark Jewett
Ottawa
3 November 2013

CONTENTS

Table of Cases xxxv
Table of Legislation xxxix
List of Contributors xlvii
List of Abbreviations li

I SOVEREIGN DEBT RESTRUCTURING

1. Minimizing Holdout Creditors: Carrots
Lee C. Buchheit and Elena L. Daly
1. Introduction 1.01
2. The Context 1.02
3. Techniques to Encourage Creditor Participation 1.11
4. Implications 1.35

2. Minimizing Holdout Creditors: Sticks
Lee C. Buchheit and Elena L. Daly
1. Introduction 2.01
2. The Context 2.02
3. Techniques to Discourage Holdouts 2.10
4. Conclusion 2.35

3. Managing Holdouts: The Case of the 2012 Greek Exchange
Jeromin Zettelmeyer, Christoph Trebesch, and G. Mitu Gulati
1. Introduction: Argentina versus Greece 3.01
2. The Basics 3.04
3. Why Did the Restructuring Succeed? Creditor Incentives 3.24
4. Conclusions 3.54

4. Revisiting the *Pari Passu* Clause
Georges Affaki
1. Introduction 4.01
2. Equal Ranking 4.02
3. Earmarking of Assets 4.10
4. Equal Payment 4.15
5. The Elliott–Peru Saga 4.17
6. Targeting Third Parties 4.27
7. The Quest for the Origins of the *Pari Passu* 4.32

8. Chaos in the Market 4.46
9. Conclusion 4.50

5. The Role of the International Monetary Fund
Rosa M. Lastra
1. Introduction 5.01
2. The History 5.03
3. The Tools 5.14
4. Sovereign Debt and the IMF 5.23
5. Conclusions 5.64

6. Debt Relief for Low-Income Countries
Thomas A. Duvall, III
1. Introduction 6.01
2. The Initial HIPC Debt Initiative 6.03
3. The Enhanced HIPC Debt Initiative 6.12
4. The Multilateral Debt Relief Initiative 6.25
5. Conclusions 6.29

7. The Longer-Term Consequences of Sovereign Debt Restructuring
Odette Lienau
1. Introduction 7.01
2. Avoiding Conflation in Key Terms 7.04
3. The Possible Consequences of Selective Emphasis 7.08
4. A Focus on the Longer-Run Ramifications of Debt Restructuring 7.15
5. Conclusion 7.29

II ENFORCEMENT OF SOVEREIGN DEBT

8. Defences
Carmine D. Boccuzzi, Jr, Michael M. Brennan, and Jacob H. Johnston
1. Introduction 8.01
2. Sovereign Debt Litigation Defences 8.04
3. Conclusion 8.46

9. Special Immunities: Central Bank Immunity
Thomas C. Baxter, Jr, and David Gross
1. Introduction 9.01
2. Argentina I 9.08
3. Argentina II 9.19
4. Conclusion 9.33

10. **Special Immunities: Bank for International Settlements**
Diego Devos
1. Introduction 10.01
2. The Bank for International Settlements and its Immunities 10.03
3. BIS Immunities Challenged by Holdout Bondholders Creditors of Argentina 10.12
4. Conclusions 10.28

11. **Creditors' Remedies**
W. Mark C. Weidemaier and Ryan McCarl
1. Introduction 11.01
2. The Implications of *NML v. Argentina*: A Pessimist's View 11.09
3. An Alternative Story: *NML Capital* as an Outlier 11.27
4. Conclusion 11.43

12. **Sovereign Arbitration**
Karen Halverson Cross
1. Introduction 12.01
2. Arbitration Clauses in Sovereign Debt Contracts 12.02
3. Investor–State Arbitration of Sovereign Debt Disputes 12.08
4. Conclusion 12.52

III COMPLICATING FACTORS

13. **Restructuring in a Monetary Union: Legal Aspects**
Antonio Sáinz de Vicuña
1. Introduction 13.01
2. Sovereign Debt Restructuring in the Case of a State Participating in the European Monetary Union: Elements of Differentiation Vis-à-Vis other Sovereign Debt Restructurings 13.06
3. Analysis of Some Legal Issues Arising in the Restructuring of the Sovereign Debt of the Hellenic Republic in 2012 13.20
4. Legal Framework for Debt Issuance by States Participating in the European Monetary Union 13.34
5. Idea of Establishing a Statutory Framework for Debt Restructuring within a Regional Monetary Union 13.47
6. Conclusions 13.50

14. **Restructuring in a Monetary Union: Economic Aspects**
Daniel Gros
1. Introduction 14.01
2. Sovereign Debt in a Monetary Union 14.10
3. Who Holds Sovereign Debt in Europe? 14.21

4. Strengthening Financial Market Resilience 14.30
5. Concluding Remarks 14.52

15. **Sovereign Debt and Banking Crises: An 'Arial View'**
Anna Gelpern
1. Introduction: Font Matters 15.01
2. Far from Europe 15.05
3. Banks or Governments 15.09
4. Governments or Banks 15.24
5. Back to Europe (the Doom Loop) 15.39
6. Conclusions 15.43

16. **International Lender of Last Resort: A Floor of Support for Troubled Sovereign Debt**
Adam Lerrick
1. Introduction 16.01
2. A Third Party in a Two-Party Game 16.08
3. For an International Lender of Last Resort: Incentives, Discipline, and Control of Risk 16.15
4. A Floor of Support to Preserve the Flow of Private Sector Funds 16.21
5. A Floor of Support to Restore Private Sector Investment Flows 16.33
6. A Floor of Support to Underpin an Orderly Restructuring 16.42
7. Toward a Credible International Lender of Last Resort 16.49

17. **Odious Debt**
Sir William Blair
1. Introduction 17.01
2. The Position of an Assignee of the Debt 17.09
3. Turning Metal into Gold: A Case of Alchemy 17.20
4. The Lessons to Be Learned 17.34
5. The Debt Relief (Developing Countries) Act 2010 17.38
6. Postscript 17.42

18. **Sovereign Contingent Liabilities**
Lee C. Buchheit and G. Mitu Gulati
1. Introduction 18.01
2. Sovereign Comfort 18.03
3. Contingent Charms 18.09
4. The Explosion of 2008–12 18.12
5. Precedents 18.18

6. The Restructurer's Dilemma 18.24
7. Restructuring Sovereign Contingent Obligations 18.33
8. Conclusions 18.51

IV ECONOMICS OF SOVEREIGN BORROWING

19. **Why Governments Default**
Willem H. Buiter and Ebrahim Rahbari
1. Introduction 19.01
2. Enforcement of Private Debt Contracts 19.03
3. Sovereign Default 19.08
4. So Why Do Governments Default? 19.26
5. The Political Economy of When and How to Default as a Sovereign 19.71
6. Conclusions 19.80

20. **Sovereign Debt Markets**
Gene Frieda
1. Introduction 20.01
2. Sovereign Borrowing: The Last Thirty Years 20.11
3. Macro Drivers of Demand for Sovereign Debt 20.19
4. Emerging Market Self-Insurance and the Rise of China 20.24
5. Surfing the China Wave 20.29
6. The Apparent End of 'Original Sin' 20.35
7. Sovereign Debt Demand Dynamics 20.43
8. Financial Weapons of Mass Destruction 20.57
9. Europe: A Microcosm of Past, Present, and Future Crises 20.68
10. Lessons Learned, Ignored, and Forgotten 20.86
11. The Fallen Saints of Original Sin 20.88
12. The Limits of Conflict Resolution 20.100
13. Hostages to Benchmarks and Ratings 20.106
14. Conclusion 20.109

21. **Borrowing and Debt: How Do Sovereigns Get into Trouble?**
Arturo C. Porzecanski
1. Introduction 21.01
2. Budgetary Outcomes 21.07
3. Contingent Liabilities and Currency Mismatches 21.12
4. Maturity Mismatches and High Coupons 21.24
5. Access to Financing 21.35
6. Indicators of Debt Sustainability 21.44
7. Conclusions 21.55

V PROPOSALS TO REFORM SOVEREIGN DEBT SYSTEMS

22. Statutory Sovereign Debt Resolution Mechanisms
Rodrigo Olivares-Caminal

1. Introduction 22.01
2. The Sovereign Debt Restructuring Mechanism (SDRM) 22.04
3. The European Stability Mechanism: An Institution Designed to Avert Financial Crises 22.36
4. Perfecting the Status Quo 22.69
5. Concluding Remarks 22.77
6. Corollary 22.81

23. Debt Restructuring and Economic Recovery
Sean Hagan

1. Introduction 23.01
2. Corporate Debt Restructuring in the Context of a Systemic Crisis 23.05
3. The Resolution of Financial Institutions in a Cross-Border Context 23.21
4. Household Debt and its Systemic Implications 23.44
5. Restructuring Sovereign Debt: An Unresolved Problem 23.53
6. Conclusion 23.77

24. Corporate Bankruptcy Law and State Insolvencies
Philip R. Wood QC (Hon)

1. Introduction 24.01
2. How Do Sovereign Bankruptcies Work? 24.05
3. What Rights Do Creditors Have? 24.12
4. Moratorium on Payments and Attachments 24.22
5. Bankruptcy Ladder of Priorities 24.27
6. Control of the Debtor's Financing 24.43
7. Reorganization Plans 24.54
8. Discharge of a Debtor 24.65
9. Other Differences between Corporate and Sovereign Insolvencies 24.67
10. International Bankruptcy Court 24.68
11. General Differences in Status 24.72
12. Conclusion 24.73

25. European Collective Action Clauses
David Billington

1. What is a Collective Action Clause? 25.01
2. The Holdout Creditor Problem 25.03
3. Are CACs the Only Way? 25.07

4. Collective Action Clauses in Sovereign Debt 25.10
5. The Move towards Standardization: Model CACs pre-2013 25.17
6. The European Sovereign Crisis and Response 25.21
7. The Model Clause in Detail 25.25
8. Conclusion 25.73

26. Eurozone Financial Rescue and Stabilization Measures, and their Legal Foundations
Andrew Yianni and Nikita Aggarwal
1. Introduction 26.01
2. Background to the Crisis 26.04
3. EU Financial Rescue and Stabilization Measures, and Legal Foundations 26.20
4. Future Financing Measures: Longer-Term Solutions 26.69
5. Concluding Observations 26.76

27. UNCTAD Principles on Responsible Sovereign Financing
Juan Pablo Bohoslavsky and Yuefen Li
1. Introduction 27.01
2. The Need for Global Principles to Promote Responsible Sovereign Financing 27.06
3. The PRSLB Tackle Global Debt Problems with Well-Rooted and Tested Principles 27.19
4. Injecting Legitimacy into the PRSLB through its Decision-Making Process: Representation, Consultation, and Deliberation 27.32
5. Soft Law Facilitates Endorsement and Implementation 27.37
6. The Role of the United Nations in the Global Economic Agenda and the PRSLB 27.47
7. Concluding Remarks. The PRSLB in the Progression of International Law 27.57

28. Sovereign Debt in the Light of Eternity
Lee C. Buchheit
1. Introduction 28.01
2. The Moral Element 28.03
3. The Legal Element 28.10
4. The Financial Element 28.15
5. The Political Element 28.20

Appendix 471

Index 473

TABLE OF CASES

Abaclat and ors (Case formerly known as Giovanna a Beccara and ors) v Argentine Republic, Decision on Jurisdiction and Admissibility, ICSID Case No ARB/07/5 (4 August 2011) 12.01, 12.09, 12.11–12.12, 12.15, 12.17–12.18, 12.20–12.23, 12.25, 12.27–12.32, 12.34, 12.44–12.45, 12.51
Abaclat and ors (Case formerly known as Giovanna a Beccara and ors) v Argentine Republic, Decision on Jurisdiction and Admissibility, ICSID Case No ARB/07/5, Dissenting Opinion of Professor Georges Abi-Saab (28 October 2011). 12.24, 12.26,12.30
Accorinti and ors v ECB (Case T-224/12) (OJ C 243/37, 11 August 2012) 26.62
Allied Bank Int'l v Banco Credito Agricola de Cartago. 8.15
Allied Bank Int'l v Banco Credito Agricola de Cartago, 566 F Supp 1440, 1442 (SDNY 1983) 8.16
Allied Bank Int'l v Banco Credito Agricola de Cartago, 1984 US App. Lexis 23237 (2d Cir. 1984) 8.16–8.17, 8.19
Allied Bank Int'l v Banco Credito Agricola de Cartago, 757 F.2d 516, 519–20 (2d Cir. 1985) (No. 83-7714) 1.07, 8.17–8.18, 8.32, 8.37–8.38
Allied Bank v Banco Credito Agricola de Cartago, 757 F.2d 516 (2d Cir. 1985) (en banc); *cert. dismissed*, 473 US 934 (1985) 23.65
Ambiente Ufficio SpA and ors (Case formerly known as Giordano Alpi and ors) v Argentine Republic, Decision on Jurisdiction and Admissibility, ICSID Case No ARB/08/9 (8 February 2013). 12.28
Ambiente Ufficio SpA and ors (Case formerly known as Giordano Alpi and ors) v Argentine Republic, Decision on Jurisdiction and Admissibility, ICSID Case No ARB/08/9, Dissenting Opinion of Santiago Torres Bernárdez (2 May 2013) 12.28
ARA Libertad Case (Argentina v Ghana), Order, ITLOS Case No 20 (15 December 2012) 12.19
Argentine Republic v Amerada Hess Shipping Co, 488 US 428, 434 (1989) 8.09
Argentine Republic v Amerada Hess Shipping Corp, 488 US 428, 443 (1989) 9.01
Assenagon Asset Management SA v Irish Bank Resolution Corporation Ltd [2012] EWHC 2090 (Ch) 25.08

Banco Nacional de Cuba (BNC) v Sabbatino, 376 US 398, 401 (1964). 8.12–8.15
Blad v Bamfield (1674) 36 Eng Rep 992 . . . . 8.12
Bluebird Ptnrs, LP v First Fiduciary Bank, NA, 94 NY.2d 726, 733–4 (2000) 8.21
Borri v Argentine Republic, Request for a Ruling on Jurisdiction, No 6532, 27 May 2005. . . . . . 12.19
Bosphorus v Minister for Transport (Case C-85/95) [1996] ECR I–3953, I–3982. . . . . 26.23
BVerfG (German Federal Constitutional Court) 2011 Judgment, 2 BvR 987/10, n. 24 . . . 26.27, 26.39
BVerfG (German Federal Constitutional Court) 2012 Judgment, 2 BvR 1390/2012. . . . .26.27, 26.50

Ceskoslovenska Obchodni Banka, AS v The Slovak Republic (CSOB), Decision of the Tribunal on Objections to Jurisdiction, ICSID Case No ARB/97/4 (24 May 1999) 12.09, 12.17
CIBC Bank and Trust Co (Cayman) Ltd v Banco Central do Brasil, 886 F.Supp. 1105 (SDNY 1994) (No 94 Civ. 4733) 8.04, 8.30, 8.32–8.33
CIBC Bank and Trust Co (Cayman) Ltd v Banco Central do Brasil, 886 F.Supp 1105 (SDNY 1995). 8.30–8.33
Citibank NA v Export-Import Bank of the United States (SDNY filed 9 August 1976) (No 76 Civ. 3514 (CBM)) 4.12
Citizens Bank of Maryland v Strumpf, 516 US 16, 21 (1995) 9.25
Connecticut Bank v Congo, 309 F.3d 240, 252 (5th Cir. 2002). 8.08

Daimler Financial Services AG v Argentine Republic, Dissenting Opinion of Judge Charles N. Brower, ICSID Case No ARB/05/1 (15 August 2012) 12.49

Daimler Financial Services AG v Argentine Republic, Award, ICSID Case No ARB/05/1 (22 August 2012) 12.41, 12.49
Democratic Republic of the Congo & ors v FG Hemisphere Associates LLC, Judgment [2011] HKCU 1049, 8 June 2011 (Hong Kong Court of Final Appeal) 12.19
Diggs v Richardson, 555 F.2d 848 (DC Cir. 1976) 22.71
Donegal International Ltd v Republic of Zambia [2007] 1 Lloyds Rep 397 (UK Commercial Ct) 17.20, 17.29, 17.31, 17.34, 17.38–17.39

EFTA Case E-16/11, Surveillance Authority v Iceland, 2013 WestlawNext 178 (28 January 2013) 15.20
Elliott Assoc., No 2000/QR/92 (Case No 2000/QR/92, Court of Appeals of Brussels, 8th Chamber, 26 September 2000) 4.25–4.26, 10.13, 11.03, 23.68
Elliott Associates LP v Banco de la Nacion, 194 F.3d 363 (2d Cir. 1999) 8.22, 8.25–8.27, 8.29, 8.39
Elliott Associates LP v Banco de la Nacion, 200 WL 1449862 (SDNY 29 September 2000) 4.19
Elliott Assocs LP v Republic of Peru, 12 F.Supp.2d 328, 335 (SDNY 1998), *rev'd* 194 F.3d 363 (2d Cir. 1999) 8.23–8.24, 8.29
EM Ltd v Republic of Argentina, 2003 WL 22120745 (SDNY 12 September 2003) 9.10
EM Ltd v Republic of Argentina, 2003 WL 22454934 (SDNY 27 October 2003) 9.10
EM Ltd v Republic of Argentina, 382 F.3d 291, 292–94 (2d Cir. 2004) 9.10
EM Ltd v Republic of Argentina, 131 F.App'x 745, 747 (2d Cir. 2005) 8.46
EM Ltd v Republic of Argentina, 473 F.3d 463 (2d Cir. 2007) 9.08–9.09, 9.11–9.12, 9.14–9.15, 9.17, 9.31
EM Ltd v Republic of Argentina, 720 F.Supp. 2d 273 (SDNY 2010) 10.14
EM Ltd v Republic of Argentina, 133 S.Ct. 23 (2012) 9.34
Enron Creditors Recovery Corp v Argentine Republic, Annulment Decision, ICSID Case No ARB/01/3 (30 July 2010) 12.32
Eureko BV v Slovak Republic, Award on Jurisdiction, Arbitrability and Suspension, PCA Case No 2008-13, 26 October 2010, *upheld on appeal by the Frankfurt Court of Appeals* 12.35
Exp.-Imp. Bank of the Republic of China v Grenada, No 13 Civ. 1450 (SDNY 13 March 2013) 11.43

Fedax NV v Republic of Venezuela, Award, ICSID Case No ARB/96/3 (9 March 1998) 12.09–12.10, 12.17
Federal Administrative Tribunal [Switzerland], Judgment C-719/2011 of 16 August 2011 . . . . 10.24
Federal Tribunal [Switzerland], BGE 118 Ib 562 . . . . 10.21
Federal Tribunal [Switzerland], Judgment 5A-360/2010 of 12 July 2010, BGE 136 III 379 . . . . 10.19, 10.21
Federal Tribunal [Switzerland], Judgment 2C-764/2011 of 22 November 2011, BGE 137 I 371 . . . . 10.24
First National City Bank v Banco Para El Comercio Exterior de Cuba (Bancec), 462 US 611 (1983) 9.20, 9.35

Giovanni Alemanni and ors v Argentine Republic, ICSID Case No ARB/07/8 (claim registered 27 March 2007) 12.28, 12.32

Hague Arbitral Tribunal, Awards, 22 November 2002 and 19 September 2003 . . . . 10.25

Jackson v People's Republic of China (1982) 550 F Supp 869 (11th Cr) 27.44
JMD Holding Corp v Congress Fin. Corp, 795 NYS.2d 502, 507 (2005) 8.36

Karaha Bodas Co LLC v Perusahaan Pertambangan Minyak Dan Gas Bumi Negara, 313 F.3d 70, 82 (2d Cir. 2002) 9.12
Kensington Int'l Ltd v Republic of Congo [2003] EWCA Civ 709 . . . . 4.28

Lehman Bros. Holdings Inc, In re, 439 BR 811 (SDNY 2010) (No 08-13555(JMP)) 15.23
LG&E Energy Corp v Argentine Republic, Decision on Liability, ICSID Case No ARB/02/1 (3 October 2006) 12.12
Lightwater Corp. v Republic of Argentina, 2003 US Dist. Lexis 6156 (SDNY 2003) 9.08

Merck v Hauptzollamt Hamburg-Jonas (Case 292/82) [1983] ECR I-3781, 3792 . . . . 26.23
Moses v McDivitt, 88 NY 62, 65 (1882) 8.26

Nacional Financiera, SNC v Chase Manhattan Bank, 2003 WL 1878415 (SDNY 14 April 2003) 4.28
National City Bank of New York v Republic of China, 348 US 356, 362 (1955) 8.07
Nicaragua case, Court of Appeals of Brussels, 9th Chamber, 19 March 2004, unpublished; Court register Nr 2004/1831–2003/KR/334 . . . . 10.13
NML Capital Ltd v Banco Central de la Republica Argentina, 652 F.3d 172 (2d Cir. 2011) 9.19–9.21, 9.23, 9.26–9.27, 9.29, 9.31, 9.33, 9.35
NML Capital Ltd v Republic of Argentina 11.09, 11.20–11.22, 11.27–11.29, 11.43–11.44
NML Capital Ltd v Republic of Argentina, (Federal Ct in New York) 4.01
NML Capital Ltd v Republic of Argentina, Second Circuit decision 12.56
NML Capital Ltd v Republic of Argentina, 621 F.3d 230 (2d Cir. 2010) 8.33–8.34, 8.36
NML Capital Ltd v Republic of Argentina, 652 F.3d 172 (2d Cir. 2011) 10.14, 12.19
NML Capital Ltd v Republic of Argentina, 2011 US Dist. Lexis 99502 (SDNY 2 September 2011) 10.27
NML Capital Ltd v Republic of Argentina, (SDNY 7 December 2011) (No 1:08-cv-06978-TPG), ECFNo 353 . . . . 4.42–4.43, 11.04, 23.68
NML Capital Ltd v Republic of Argentina, 680 F.3d 254 (2d Cir. 2012) 12.19
NML Capital Ltd v Republic of Argentina, 699 F.3d 246 (2d Cir. 2012) 12.19, 13.48, 23.69, 23.71
NML Capital Ltd v Republic of Argentina, 699 F.Supp. 246 (2d Cir. 2012) 2.20
NML Capital Ltd v Republic of Argentina, (2d Cir. 26 October 2012) (Nos 12-105(L) etc.) (NML Second Circuit Opinion) 1.07, 4.16, 4.42, 11.04, 11.06, 11.13, 11.39
NML Capital Ltd v Republic of Argentina, (SDNY 21 November 2012) (No 1:08-cv-06978-TPG) 11.07
NML Capital Ltd v Republic of Argentina, No 12-105 et al, 2013 US App. LEXIS 17645 (2d Cir. NY 23 August 2013) 22.19, 23.69
NML v Argentina, Oral Argument Transcript of 27 February 2013 . . . . 11.36–11.38, 11.41

Oetjen v Central Leather Co, 246 US 297, 303–04 (1918) 8.13

Phosphates in Morocco (Italy v France) 1938 PCIJ (Ser. A/B) no 74 (14 June), 10–48 . . . . 22.25
Pravin Banker Assocs Ltd v Banco Popular del Peru, 109 F.3d 850 (2d Cir. 1997) 8.04, 8.38–8.45
Primus, In Re, 436 US 412, 424 n.15 (1978) 8.20

Red Mountain Fin. Inc v Democratic Republic of Congo et al. 2000 US Dist. LEXIS 22324 (CD Cal. 29 May 2001) (CV 00-0164 R) 4.28
Redwood Master Fund v TD Bank Europe Ltd and ors [2002] All ER (D) 141 . . . . 25.08
Republic of Argentina v Weltover Inc, 504 US 607, 614 (1992) 9.16, 12.19
Republic of Nicaragua v LNC Investments et al, Commercial Court of Brussels, September 2003 . . . . 4.28
Ricaud v American Metal Co, 246 US 304, 309 (1918) 8.13
Rogers v Petroleo Brasiliero SA, 673 F.3d 131, 140–41 (2d Cir. 2012) 8.10–8.11
Rosinvestco UK Ltd v Russian Federation, Final Award, SCC Arbitration V (079/2005) (12 September 2010) 12.43

Saluka Investments BV (The Netherlands) v Czech Republic, Partial Award (17 March 2006) 240–241 . . . . 12.40
Schooner Exchange v M'Fadden, 7 Cranch 116 (1812) 8.07
Sempra Energy Int'l v Argentine Republic, Annulment Decision, ICSID Case No ARB/02/16 (29 June 2010) 12.32
Stolt-Nielsen, 130 S Ct 1758, 1776 (2010) 12.26

Terrorist Attacks on September 11 2001, In re, 538 F.3d 71, 82 (2d Cir. 2008) 8.08
Thomas Pringle v Government of Ireland (Case C-370/12) [2012] ECR I-000, Judgment dated 27 November 2012 . . . . 13.15–13.16, 26.27, 26.33, 26.39, 26.45, 26.50–26.51

TSA Spectrum de Argentina, SA v Argentine Republic, Award, ICSID Case No ARB 05/5 (19 December 2008) 12.40
Twycross v Dreyfus [1876] T177. . . . . 28.10

Underhill v Hernandez, 168 US 250, 252 (1897) 8.12–8.13
United States v Wilson, 503 US 329, 342 (1992) 9.20

Van Gend en Loos v Nederlandse Administratie der Belastingen (Case 26/62) [1963] ECR 1 (ECJ) 26.23
Verlinden BV v Central Bank of Nigeria, 461 US 480, 486 (1983) 8.07, 8.09

TABLE OF LEGISLATION

INTERNATIONAL LEGISLATION

Convention on the Recognition and Enforcement of Foreign Arbitral Awards (New York, 10 June 1958, 330 UNTS 38) (New York Convention) 12.05, 12.16
Convention on the Settlement of Investment Disputes between States and Nationals of Other States (Washington DC, 18 March 1965, 575 UNTS 159) (ICSID Convention) 12.05, 12.15, 12.17, 12.23, 12.28–12.30, 12.35, 12.54
Art 25
(1) 12.23
(2)(b) 12.40
Art 52(1) 12.32
Arts 54–55 . . . . 12.16
European Convention on Human Rights (ECHR) 3.13, 10.19
Art 6(1) 10.19
Hague Agreements 1930 . . . . 10.05
Hague Agreement with Germany, 20 January 1930, Art X 10.08
Hague Convention respecting the Bank for International Settlements (BIS), 20 January 1930 . . . . 10.08
Headquarters Agreement between the BIS and Switzerland, 10 February 1987 (HQA) 10.08, 10.15, 10.19, 10.25
Art 4.1 . . . . 10.08, 10.10
Art 4.2 . . . . 10.25
Arts 4.3–4.4 . . . . 10.10
Art 22 . . . . 10.15, 10.22
Art 23 . . . . 10.25
ICSID Convention *see* Convention on the Settlement of Investment Disputes between States and Nationals of Other States
International Monetary Fund (IMF) Articles of Agreement 5.03, 5.06–5.07, 5.09, 5.11, 5.33, 5.35, 5.39, 5.64, 12.53, 22.24, 22.32, 22.69, 23.49, 23.56, 23.74–23.75
Art I 5.14
(v) 5.20, 5.39
Art IV 5.12, 5.14–5.15, 5.47, 5.60
(1) 23.49
(a) 5.06
(ii) 23.49
(5)(a) 5.07
Art V
(2)(b) 5.14
(3) 5.14
(a) 5.56, 23.56
Art VI(3) 13.09
Art VIII
(2) 5.14, 13.09
(a) 5.36
(b) 5.36, 22.32, 24.20
Art XXVIII(a) 22.24
Art XXIX 22.32
Second Amendment, adopted 30 April 1976, effective 1 April 1978 . . . . 5.09
London Debt Agreement 1953, settling Germany's external debts from the interwar period 19.21
Peace of Amiens 1802 . . . . 19.39
UN Charter
Art 1(3) 27.55
Art 25 . . . . 27.44
Art 55(2) 27.55
UN Convention against Corruption
Art 9 . . . . 27.44
Art 15*ff.* 27.44
Art 34 . . . . 27.44
UN Convention on Jurisdictional Immunities of States and their Property 2004
Art 10(1) 10.06
Art 19(c) 10.06
Art 21.1(c) 10.06
Vienna Convention on the Law of Treaties 1969
Art 26 . . . . 27.44
Art 28 . . . . 22.25
Art 53 . . . . 27.44
Art 71(1) 27.44
Vienna Convention on Succession of States in Respect of State Property, Archives and Debt 7.05
Art 33 . . . . 7.05

Free Trade Agreements

Australia–Chile FTA 2008, Art 10.1(j)(iii) 12.50
Canada–Chile FTA 1996, Art G-40 . . . . . . 12.50
Chile–US FTA 2003 . . . . 12.48
Annex 10-B 12.48

Colombia–Canada FTA 2008, Art 838, n.11 . . . 12.50
Colombia–US FTA 2006 . . . 12.48–12.49
Art 10.28, n.13 . . . 12.50
Annex 10-F . . . 12.48, 12.50
Dominican Republic–Central America Free Trade Agreement 2004
Annex 10-A . . . 12.50
Annex 10-E(3) . . . 12.50
Honduras–El Salvador FTA 2007, Art 10.01 . . . 12.50
Mexico–Chile FTA 1998, Art 9-01 . . . 12.50
Mexico–Colombia–Venezuela FTA 1994, Art 17-01 . . . 12.50
Mexico–Costa Rica FTA 1994, Art 13-01 . . . 12.50
Mexico–El Salvador–Guatemala–Honduras FTA 2000, Art 14-01 . . . 12.50
Mexico–Nicaragua FTA 1997, Art 16-01 . . . 12.50
North American Free Trade Agreement (Canada, US, Mexico) 1992 . . . 12.46–12.47
Art 1113(2) . . . 12.40
Art 1139 . . . 12.46, 12.50
Panama–Costa Rica FTA 2007, Art 10.40 . . . 12.50
Peru–China FTA 2009
Art 126, n.11 . . . 12.50
Annex 8 . . . 12.50
Peru–Mexico FTA 2011, Art 11.1 . . . 12.50
Peru–Singapore FTA 2008
Art 10.1, n.10-3 . . . 12.50
Art 10.18 . . . 12.50
Peru–US FTA 2006
Art 10-28, n.13 . . . 12.50
Annex 10-F . . . 12.50

Bilateral Investment Treaties

Azerbaijan–Croatia BIT 2007, Art 1.1 . . . 12.50
Canada–Czech BIT, Art I(d) . . . 12.47
Canada–Romania BIT, Art I(g) . . . 12.47
Colombia–Belgium BIT 2009, Art 1(2.1(a)) . . . 12.50
Colombia–China BIT 2008, Art 1(1.1) . . . 12.50
Colombia–India BIT 2009
Art 1(2.1) . . . 12.50
Annex 8 . . . 12.50
Colombia–Japan BIT 2011, Art 1 . . . 12.50
Colombia–Peru BIT 2007, Art 42 . . . 12.50
Colombia–Switzerland BIT 2006, Ad.Art 1(1)(c) . . . 12.50
Colombia–UK BIT 2010, Art 1(2)(b)(i) . . . 12.50
Cuba–Bolivia BIT 1995, Art 1.1 . . . 12.50
Cyprus–Greece BIT . . . 12.36
El Salvador–Nicaragua BIT 1999, Art 1 . . . 12.50
Germany–Greece BIT . . . 12.36–12.37
Art 1(2) . . . 12.37
Art 2 . . . 12.37
Art 3(1)–(2) . . . 12.37
Art 4 . . . 12.37
Art 11 . . . 12.37
India–Greece BIT, Art 1(3)(b) . . . 12.40
Italy–Argentina BIT . . . 12.09–12.10, 12.12, 12.23, 12.25–12.26, 12.28–12.29, 12.45
Preamble . . . 12.24
Art 6(3) . . . 12.10
Art 8 . . . 12.15
(3) . . . 12.15, 12.21
Mexico–Argentina BIT 1996, Art 1(a)(x) . . . 12.50
Mexico–Australia BIT 2005, Art 1(a)(x) . . . 12.50
Mexico–Austria BIT 1998, Art 1(2) . . . 12.47, 12.50
Mexico–Belarus BIT 2008, Art 1.5(c) . . . 12.50
Mexico–China BIT 2008, Art 1 . . . 12.50
Mexico–Cuba BIT 2001, Protocolo Ad: Art.1 . . . 12.50
Mexico–Czech Republic BIT 2002, Art 1.2 . . . 12.50
Mexico–Denmark BIT 2000, Art 1(1) . . . 12.50
Mexico–France BIT 1994, Art 1(1) . . . 12.50
Mexico–Germany BIT 1998, Art 1(1) . . . 12.50
Mexico–Greece BIT 2000, Art 1(1) . . . 12.50
Mexico–Iceland BIT 2005, Art 1(2)(d) . . . 12.50
Mexico–India BIT 2007, Art 1.7(c)–(d) . . . 12.50
Mexico–Italy BIT 1999, Art 1.1(c) . . . 12.50
Mexico–Korea BIT 2000, Art 1(1) . . . 12.50
Mexico–Netherlands BIT 1998, Art 1(2) . . . 12.50
Mexico–Panama BIT 2006, Art 1.6 . . . 12.50
Mexico–Portugal BIT 1999, Art 1(1) . . . 12.50
Mexico–Slovakia BIT 2007, Art 1.10(c)–(d) . . . 12.50
Mexico–Spain BIT 2006, Art 1.4 . . . 12.50
Mexico–Sweden BIT 2000, Art 1(3) . . . 12.50
Mexico–Switzerland BIT 1995, Art 1(3) . . . 12.50
Mexico–Trinidad BIT 2006, Art 1.5(j)–(k) . . . 12.50
Mexico–UK BIT 2006, Art 1 . . . 12.50
Mexico–Uruguay BIT 1999, Art 1(1) . . . 12.50
Peru–Belgium BIT 2005, Art 1.2 . . . 12.50
Peru–Canada BIT 2006, Art 1 . . . 12.50
Peru–Cuba BIT 2000, Art 1.1 . . . 12.50
Spain–Czech BIT . . . 12.38–12.39, 12.42
Art 1(2)(b) . . . 12.41
UK–Argentina BIT, Art 6(3) . . . 12.10
UK–Chile BIT, Art 4 . . . 12.48
UK–Soviet BIT . . . 12.43
Uruguay–US BIT 2005, Annex G . . . 12.50
US–Argentina BIT . . . 12.32
Art XI . . . 12.12

EU LEGISLATION

Council Decision 2011/199/EU of 25 March 2011 amending Article 136 of the Treaty on the Functioning of the European Union with regard to a stability mechanism for Member States whose currency is the euro, 6 April 2011 (OJ L 91/1) 22.43, 26.24, 26.27
Art 1 . . . . 26.27
Council Decision on the basis of Articles 126(9) (EU Council Recommendations in re Budget Deficits) and 136 (Specific Provisions for Member States whose Currency is the Euro) TFEU and the MOU 22.41
Directive 88/361/EEC (Exchange controls) 13.09
Directive 98/26/EC (Finality of payments) 4.29
Directive 2006/48/EC (Taking up and pursuit of the business of credit institutions) 14.34
Annex VI 14.34
Directive (Capital adequacy), Art 113 . . . . . 14.47
Directive (Large exposure) 14.50
Directive (Settlement finality) 10.13
ECB Decision 2009/16 of the ECB Governing Council of 2 July 2009 on the implementation of the covered bond purchase programme 26.63
ECB Decision 2010/5 of 14 May 2010 establishing a securities markets programme (OJ L 124/8, 20 May 2010) 26.65
Recital 2 . . . . 26.56, 26.67
Recital 4 . . . . 26.67
ECB Decision 2011/17 of the ECB Governing Council of 3 November 2011 on the implementation of the second covered bond purchase programme 26.63
ECB Decision 2012/32 of 19 December 2012 on temporary measures relating to the eligibility of marketable debt instruments issued or fully guaranteed by the Hellenic Republic (OJ L 359/74, 29 December 2012) 26.60, 26.62
ECB Rules of Procedure, setting out the legal instruments of the ECB, Art 17 . . . . . 26.53
EFSF Framework Agreement dated 7 June 2010, as amended with effect from 18 October 2011 . . . . 26.40
Art 2(3) 26.41
Art 7 . . . . 26.41
Art 8(2) 26.41
Annex 1 . . . . 26.41
European Bank Co-ordination Initiative ('Vienna Initiative') 23.27
European Union Economic and Financial Committee (EFC), Euro Area Model CAC 2012 (November 2011) 25.24, 25.30, 25.33–25.34, 25.37–25.38, 25.42–25.43, 25.47–25.49, 25.53, 25.59–25.60, 25.62, 25.65–25.66, 25.68–25.73
Greek Loan Facility Agreement, entered into on 8 May 2010 by the Kingdom of Belgium, Ireland, Kingdom of Spain, French Republic, Italian Republic, Republic of Cyprus, Grand Duchy of Luxembourg, Republic of Malta, Kingdom of the Netherlands, Republic of Austria, Portuguese Republic, Republic of Slovenia, Slovak Republic, Republic of Finland and the bank KfW (acting on behalf of the Federal Republic of Germany), as lenders, and the Hellenic Republic as borrower (and the bank of Greece as the agent of the borrower) 22.41, 26.29
Intercreditor Agreement entered into on 8 May 2010 between the Kingdom of Belgium, Federal Republic of Germany, Ireland, Kingdom of Spain, French Republic, Italian Republic, Republic of Cyprus, Grand Duchy of Luxembourg, Republic of Malta, Kingdom of the Netherlands, Republic of Austria, Portuguese Republic, Republic of Slovenia, Slovak Republic, and Republic of Finland (unpublished) 22.41, 26.29
Maastricht Treaty *see* Treaty on European Union 1992
Master Financial Assistance Facility Agreement between EFSF and Greece . . . 26.41
Regulation (EC) 3603/93 of 13 December 1993 specifying definitions for the application of the prohibitions referred to in Articles 104 and 104b(1) of the Treaty (OJ L 332/1, 31 December 1993) 13.10
Preamble 26.54
Regulation (EC) 1466/97 on the strengthening of the surveillance of budgetary positions and the surveillance and coordination of economic policies 26.24
Regulation (EC) 1467/97 on speeding up and clarifying the implementation of the Excessive Deficit Procedure 26.24
Regulation (EC)No 44/2001 on jurisdiction and the recognition of judgments in civil and commercial matters [2001] OJ L012/1 . . . . 12.06

Regulation (EC) 1055/2005 amending Regulation 1466/97 . . . . .26.24
Regulation (EC) 1056/2005 amending Regulation 1467/97 . . . . .26.24
Regulation (EU) 407/2010 of 11 May 2010 establishing a European financial stabilisation mechanism (OJ L 118/1) 22.42, 26.34, 26.38
Preambles 1–5 .26.35
Preamble 8 . . . . .26.36
Art 2(2) 26.34
Regulation 1175/2011 amending Regulation 1466/97 . . . . .26.24
Regulation 1177/2011 amending Regulation 1467/97 . . . . .26.24
Stability and Growth Pact (SGP), setting out fiscal and debt criteria to which countries pledged adherence . . . 20.69–20.71, 21.57–21.58, 22.46, 26.14, 26.24, 26.71
Statute of the European System of Central Banks (ESCB) and of the ECB 26.55
Art 2. . . . . .26.55
Art 7. . . . . 25.50, 26.75
Art 18
(1) 26.57
(2) 26.53, 26.59, 26.61
Art 20. . . . . .26.53
Art 21(1) 26.54, 26.59
Art 25(2) 26.75
Treaty of Amsterdam 1997 . . . . .26.04
Treaty Establishing the European Stability Mechanism (ESM) 2012 . . . . . .2.25, 5.38, 5.42, 5.63, 13.39–13.40, 13.45–13.46, 13.48, 22.44, 22.46–22.47, 22.51, 22.64, 22.67, 22.75, 22.79, 22.81, 26.27, 26.46, 26.69
Recital 9 . . . . .22.58
Recital 10 . . . . .22.60
Recital 12 . . . . .22.62
Recital 13 . . . . .5.42, 22.37, 22.47
Recital 14 . . . . 22.37, 22.58
Recital 17 . . . . .22.60
Art 1(1) 22.45
Art 2(1)–(3) 22.57
Art 3. . . . . 22.45, 22.48
Art 4
(2)–(5) 22.51
(8) 22.52
Art 5
(1) 22.51
(4) 22.59
(7)(c) 22.51
Art 6
(1) 22.51
(3) 22.59
Art 7. . . . . .22.53
Art 8
(1)–(2) 22.49
(4) 22.49, 22.56
(5) 22.56, 22.60
Art 9. . . . . .22.49
(2) 26.50
(3) 22.56, 26.50
Art 10. . . . . .22.66
Art 12. . . . . .22.45
(1) 22.55
(2) 14.40
(3) 13.39, 22.63
Art 13. . . . . .22.62
(1)(a)–(c) 22.62
(2) 22.62
(3) 22.55, 22.62
(4)–(7) 22.62
Art 14. . . . . .22.55
Art 15. . . . . .22.55
(5) 22.62
Art 16. . . . . .22.55
(5) 22.62
Arts 17–18 . . . . .22.55
Art 21(3) 22.48
Art 24(1) 22.56
Art 25
(1) 22.56
(2) 22.49, 26.50
Art 29. . . . . .22.54
Art 30(1)–(2) .22.54
Art 31(1) 22.45
Art 37. . . . . .13.45
(2)–(3) 22.61
Art 38. . . . . .22.59
Arts 39–40 . . . . .22.50
Art 44. . . . . .22.57
Art 48. . . . . .22.44
Treaty on the European Community (TEC) 26.04
Treaty on European Union 1992 (TEU) (Maastricht Treaty) 13.09, 21.58, 26.04–26.05, 26.24, 26.53, 26.76
Pt 3 . . . . .26.22
Art 1. . . . . .26.21
Art 3. . . . . .26.53
Art 4(3) 26.43
Art 5(3) 26.05
Art 48. . . . . .26.22
Arts 109h–109i (later renumbered Arts 119–120) 13.09
Protocol 19 . . . . .26.23
Treaty on the Functioning of the European Union (TFEU). 5.63, 13.15, 13.18, 13.21, 13.27, 26.04, 26.53
Arts 3–4 . . . . .26.05

Art 50 .... 13.18
Arts 63–64 .... 13.09
Art 65 .... 13.09
(1)(b) 13.09
Art 66 .... 13.09
Art 119 .... 26.53
(2) 26.24
Art 121 .... 22.60, 26.24
Art 122(2) 13.27, 22.42, 26.23, 26.25, 26.28, 26.31, 26.35, 26.37
Art 123 .... 5.63, 13.10, 13.27, 15.44, 26.23–26.24, 26.28, 26.53, 26.62
(1) 26.28, 26.54, 26.56, 26.59, 26.64, 26.67–26.68
(2)–(3) 26.28, 26.54
Art 124 .... 26.23, 26.28
Art 125 .... 5.63, 13.15–13.16, 15.44, 22.43, 26.23–26.25, 26.27, 26.31–26.33, 26.37, 26.39, 26.44, 26.50–26.51, 26.72
(1)–(2) 26.28
Art 126 .... 26.24
Art 127 .... 26.24, 26.62
(1) 26.53, 26.55–26.56
(2) 26.53
(5) 26.53, 26.55
(6) 26.75
Art 127(1) 13.08
Art 130 .... 25.50, 26.53
Art 136 .... 22.43, 22.60, 26.27
(3) 26.23, 26.27–26.28
Art 140 .... 26.24
(2) 22.57
Art 143 .... 26.34
Art 219 .... 26.53
Art 267 .... 26.23
Art 273 .... 22.61
Art 282(2) 26.53
Protocol 4 on the Statute of the European System of Central Banks (ESCB) and the ECB, OJ C 115, 9 May 2008, 230 .... 26.53
Art 2 .... 26.53
Art 3 .... 26.53
Art 3.1 .... 26.53
Art 3.3 .... 26.53
Art 7 .... 26.53
Arts 18.1–18.2 .... 26.53
Art 20 .... 26.53
Arts 21.1–21.3 .... 26.53
Art 29 .... 22.50
Protocol 12 .... 26.24
Protocol 15 (Certain Provisions Relating to the United Kingdom), s 10 .... 13.10
Protocol 19 .... 26.23
Treaty of Lisbon 2007 .... 12.35, 26.04
Arts 123–124 .... 15.44
Art 125 .... 15.44, 19.62
Treaty of Nice 2001 .... 26.04
Treaty on Stability, Coordination and Governance (TSCG) 22.46, 26.24

NATIONAL LEGISLATION

Argentina

Anales de Legislacion Argentina 1972, Tit. I, Ley No 19,551, Art 4 .... 4.07
Law 26,017 2005 ('Lock Law'), Boletin Oficial de la Republica Argentina, CXIII, no 30.590, 2005 .... 4.40, 11.11–11.12, 11.39, 11.44, 12.11, 23.68

Belgium

Law of 19 November 2004 .... 10.13
Law of 28 April 1999, Art 9 .... 4.29, 10.13

Canada

Foreign Investment Protection Agreement 2004, Art 1 .... 12.47

France

Civil Code, Art 2093 .... 4.05

Germany

Act on the Joint Rights of Bondholders 1899 .... 25.11
Civil Code 25.11
Constitution 26.39, 26.50, 26.72

Greece

Bondholder Act 2012 .... 3.14, 3.16, 3.19, 3.43
Constitution 3.13
Law 4050/2012 on Amendment of Securities Issued or Guaranteed by the Greek Government by Consent of the Bondholders 13.43

Phillipines

Civil Code, Art 2244, s 14 .... 4.06

Spain

Bankruptcy Act of 9 July 2003 (Ley Concursal 22/2003) 4.06
Civil Code
Art 1924 .... 4.06
(3) 4.06
Commercial Code, Art 913 .... 4.06

Switzerland

Act regarding the Federal Administrative Tribunal, Art 32, (1)(a) 10.24

Decision of the Swiss Federal Council of 30 October 1996 (1997) 7 RSDIE 668 . . . . .10.21
Federal Act of 11 April 1989 on Debt Prosecution and Bankruptcy (SR 281.1)
Art 22(1) 10.16
Art 30a. 10.16
Federal Act of 22 June 2007 on the Privileges Immunities and Facilities and the Financial Subsidies granted by Switzerland as a host state (SR 192.12) 10.08, 10.20

United Kingdom

Bills of Exchange Act 1882 . . . . .17.16
Debt Relief (Developing Countries) Act 2010 . . . . .10.13, 17.02, 17.07–17.08, 17.38–17.40

United States of America

12 USC, § 1828(s)(5). 15.25
Bankruptcy Code 4.05, 23.51
Chapter 11 . . . . 2.26–2.27, 5.35, 12.46, 19.18, 22.20, 22.27
Chapter 13 . . . . 23.50, 23.52
§ 502(c)(1). 18.32
§ 1322(b)(2). .23.50
Constitution. 8.07
16th Amendment. 19.40
Dodd-Frank Wall Street Reform and Consumer Protection Act 2009 (12 USC) 15.44, 23.34
§ 5394(c) 15.44
§ 210(a)(1)(N) .23.31
Executive Order 13,303 Protecting the Development Fund for Iraq and Certain other Property in which Iraq has an Interest, 68 Fed Reg 31931 (28 May 2003) 22.71
Executive Order 13,315, 28 August 2003 . . . . .22.71
Executive Order 13,350, 29 July 2004 . . . .22.71
Executive Order 13,364 Modifying the Protection Granted to the Development Fund for Iraq and Certain Property in which Iraq Has an Interest and Protecting the Central Bank of Iraq, 69 Fed Reg 70177 (29 November 2004). 22.71
Federal Reserve Act 1913 . . . . .9.03
Federal Rules of Civil Procedure 2.33–2.34, 10.27
r 23(b)(1)(B) 2.33
r 65 . . . . .11.08
(d)(2) 11.22
Financial Institutions Reform, Recovery, and Enforcement Act (FIRREA) 1989, § 1404(e)(1)(A), Pub. L. No 101–73, 103 Stat. 183 . . . . .15.25
Foreign Sovereign Immunities Act 1976 (FSIA) (28 USC) 1.07, 8.09–8.12, 8.24, 8.48, 9.01–9.02, 9.05–9.06, 9.10–9.11, 9.16, 9.18, 9.20, 9.35, 23.67
§ 1602 . . . . .9.02
§§ 1602 *et seq*. 9.01
§ 1603(d). 9.16
§§ 1604–1605 . . . . 8.09, 9.02
§§ 1606–1607 . . . . .9.02
§ 1609 . . . . 8.09, 9.12
§ 1610 . . . . 8.09, 9.12, 9.17–9.18
(a) 9.13
(1) 9.13
(2) (exception to immunity from attachment for property used for the commercial activity on which the claim is based) 9.13, 12.05
(6) (exception to immunity from attachment for enforcing foreign arbitral awards) 12.05
(d) 9.13
§ 1611 . . . . .9.12
(b) 9.18
(1) 9.18–9.20, 9.22–9.23, 9.29, 9.31–9.32, 9.35, 10.14, 12.19
Glass–Steagall Act 1933 . . . . .27.09
Gramm–Leach–Bliley Act. 27.09
Model Bilateral Investment Treaty 2004, Art 1. . . . . .12.47
Model Bilateral Investment Treaty 2012, Art 1. . . . . .12.47
National Emergencies Act (50 USC), § 202(d). 22.71
Negotiable Instruments Law, Section 3–104, para (1)(b) 25.10
New York Judiciary Law, section 489. . . . . 8.21–8.22, 8.27–8.29
NY Uniform Commercial Code
Art 4-A. 4.49
Art 4-A-503 . . . . .4.49
Restatement (Revised) of Foreign Relations Law, § 428 cmt c (1983) 8.12
Trust Indenture Act 1939 . . .24.56, 25.10–25.11
Section 316 . . . . .24.56

RULES, STATUTES, DECISIONS AND RESOLUTIONS OF INTERNATIONAL ORGANIZATIONS AND OTHER INTERNATIONAL FORA

Basel 'Concordats' .13.27
Basel III Accord 13.01, 19.14
Brussels Protocol regarding immunities of BIS 1936 .10.08
Chiang-Mai Initiative, which pools the reserves of thirteen Asian central banks, or agencies yet to be formed 16.19
Financial Stability Board (FSB) proposed framework 'Key Attributes of Effective Resolution Regimes for Financial Institutions' (October 2011) 23.28–23.30, 23.33, 23.35–23.40, 23.78
Geneva Supervisory Authority of Debt Enforcement and Bankruptcy Matters, Decision of 9 April 1997 (1998) 62 Bulletin des Poursuites et Faillites 220 .10.21
IMF and World Bank Heavily Indebted Poor Countries (HIPC) Initiative 2005. . . . . .6.01–6.18, 6.20–6.31, 6.33–6.35, 7.07, 13.12, 17.07, 17.39–17.40, 19.27, 22.21
International Swaps and Derivatives Association (ISDA) standard agreement. 13.03
Multilateral Debt Relief Initiative (MDRI) 6.25, 6.27–6.30, 6.32, 6.35, 22.21
Statute of the International Court of Justice, Art 38. . . . . .27.45
Statutes of the BIS of 20 January 1930
Art 3. . . . . 10.09, 10.19
Art 21. . . . . .10.15
(lit.j). 10.19
Art 24. . . . . .10.15
Art 54. . . . . .10.25
Art 55(1)–(3) 10.10
UN General Assembly Resolution 65/144 on external debt sustainability and development, 20 December 2010. . . . . .27.50
UN Security Council Resolution No 1483/03, 22 May 2003. . . . .2.23–2.25, 22.70–22.72
UN Security Council Resolution No 1546/04, 8 June 2004. . . . 22.70–22.71
UN Security Council Resolution 1956. . . . . .2.24
UNCTAD Principles on Responsible Sovereign Lending and Borrowing (PRSLB) 2009 . . . . . . 5.37, 27.01–27.72
Preamble 27.37
Principle 1 . . . . .27.25
Principles 3–4. . . . . .27.22
Principle 5 . . . . 27.22–27.23
Principle 6 . . . . .27.27
Principle 7 . . . . 27.29–27.30
Principle 8 . . . . .27.25
Principle 9 . . . . .27.28
Principle 10 . . . . 27.22–27.24
Principle 11 . . . . 27.23–27.24
Principle 12 .27.23
Principle 13 . . . . 27.24, 27.38
Principle 14 .27.22
Principle 15 . . . . 27.29–27.30
United Nations Commission on International Trade Law (UNCITRAL) Rules. 12.15

LIST OF CONTRIBUTORS

Dr Georges Affaki is managing director, member of the Executive Committee, and global coordinator for corporate banking at BNP Paribas CIB Legal. He is Chairman of the International Chamber of Commerce (ICC) Legal Committee of the Banking Commission and associate professor of law at Université Panthéon-Assas (Paris II). He is a Council member of the Institute of World Business Law and a Governing Council member of the International Institute for the Unification of Private Law (UNIDROIT) Foundation. Dr Affaki has written extensively on international banking and international arbitration.

Nikita Aggarwal is a former associate at Clifford Chance. During her time at the firm she specialized in financial regulation and sovereign debt restructuring. She graduated in law from the London School of Economics and Political Science.

Thomas C. Baxter, Jr is general counsel and executive vice president at the Federal Reserve Bank of New York. He is a vice-chairman of the Committee on International Monetary Law of the International Law Association (MOCOMILA).

David Billington is a partner based in the London office of Cleary Gottlieb Steen & Hamilton LLP. His practice focuses on international financial and restructuring transactions. He has experience in syndicated bank lending, high yield bonds, structured and real estate finance, and securitization. He is recognized as a leading banking and finance lawyer by Chambers UK, and, in 2013, *Finance News* named David one of its 'Top 40 under-40 Rising Stars of Legal Service'.

Sir William Blair is a High Court judge in England and Wales, being one of the nominated judges who sit in the Commercial Court. He chairs the Committee on International Monetary Law of the International Law Association (MOCOMILA).

Carmine D. Boccuzzi, Jr is a partner at Cleary Gottlieb Steen & Hamilton LLP, which firm represents Argentina in its sovereign debt litigation.

Juan Pablo Bohoslavsky is currently sovereign debt expert for the United Nations Conference on Trade and Development (UNCTAD) in Geneva. He studied law in Argentina, Europe, and the United States, having obtained a doctoral degree. He has been a legal consultant to corporations, the United Nations Economic Commission for Latin America and the Caribbean (UNECLAC), and the Argentinian government. He has published books and articles on sovereign financing, foreign investment, and human rights.

Michael M. Brennan is an associate at Cleary Gottlieb Steen & Hamilton LLP, which firm represents Argentina in its sovereign debt litigation.

Lee C. Buchheit is a senior partner in the Sovereign Practice Group of Cleary Gottlieb Steen & Hamilton LLP, based in that firm's New York office. Mr Buchheit has advised many sovereign borrowers over the last thirty years on liability management issues.

Willem H. Buiter, CBE, FBA, is global chief economist of Citigroup since 2010. He has taught at the London School of Economics and at the universities of Princeton, Bristol, Yale and

Cambridge. He has a BA from the University of Cambridge and a PhD from Yale University. He was an external member of the Monetary Policy Committee of the Bank of England from 1997 to 2000, and chief economist and special counsellor to the President at the European Bank for Reconstruction and Development (EBRD) from 2000 to 2005. He has been an adviser to multilateral organizations, national governments, central banks, and private sector clients.

Sir Ross Cranston FBA is a High Court judge in England and Wales and a visiting professor at the London School of Economics and Political Science.

Elena L. Daly is an international lawyer in private practice, currently based in Paris. She has previously served as the general counsel of a major hedge fund. Ms Daly received her legal training at Cleary Gottlieb Steen and Hamilton LLP and has been involved in sovereign debt management matters for the last twenty years.

Diego Devos is general counsel of the Bank for International Settlements (BIS) and a member of the Bank's Executive Committee. He has published various articles and reports on contract law, banking, and financial law.

Thomas A. Duvall is a former chief counsel in the Legal Department of the World Bank, where he was responsible for providing legal support for the Bank's participation in the Heavily Indebted Poor Countries (HIPC) Debt Initiative. He also provided legal counsel for the Bank's support for debt and debt service reduction operations for middle-income countries under the Brady plan. He is a graduate of the University of Virginia School of Law, where he was Managing Editor of the *Virginia Law Review*. Prior to joining the Bank, he was an associate at Cleary, Gottlieb, Steen and Hamilton.

Gene Frieda has served as a senior global strategist for Moore Capital since 2007, focusing on global macro policy issues. Mr Frieda earned his MSc in Economics from the London School of Economics, and holds BA degrees in Political Science and Economics from the University of Oklahoma. He is a member of the World Economic Forum's Global Agenda Council on New Economic Thinking and the Political Economy of Financial Markets project at Oxford University.

Anna Gelpern is a law professor at Georgetown. She writes about international finance, sovereign debt, and regulation.

Daniel Gros is director of the Centre for European Policy Studies (CEPS). He holds a PhD in economics from the University of Chicago. He has taught at a number of universities and has published widely on European monetary affairs.

David Gross is counsel and vice president at the Federal Reserve Bank of New York. He is the secretary of the Committee on International Monetary Law of the International Law Association (MOCOMILA).

Mitu Gulati teaches law at Duke University. His research focuses on sovereign debt contracts and debt restructurings, a topic on which he frequently collaborates with other scholars.

Sean Hagan is General Counsel and Director of the Legal Department at the International Monetary Fund. In this capacity, Mr Hagan advises the Fund's management, Executive Board and membership on all legal aspects of the Fund's operations, including its regulatory, advisory, and lending functions. Mr Hagan has published extensively on both the law of the Fund and a broad range of legal issues relating to the prevention and resolution of financial crisis, with a particular emphasis on insolvency and the restructuring of debt, including sovereign debt. Prior to beginning work at the IMF, Mr Hagan was in private practice, first in New York and subsequently in Tokyo. Mr Hagan received his Juris Doctor from the Georgetown University Law Center and also received a Masters of Science in International Political Economy from the London School of Economics and Political Science.

Karen Halverson Cross received her JD degree from Harvard Law School. She joined the faculty of John Marshall Law School in Chicago after a Fulbright scholarship and several years as an associate at Cleary, Gottlieb, Steen & Hamilton in New York. She teaches contract law, international commercial arbitration, and international business transactions at John Marshall and at universities abroad, including most recently at the Universidade Católica Portuguesa in Lisbon and the Central European University in Budapest.

Jacob H. Johnston is an associate at Cleary Gottlieb Steen & Hamilton LLP, which firm represents Argentina in its sovereign debt litigation.

Rosa María Lastra is professor in International Financial and Monetary Law at the Centre for Commercial Law Studies (CCLS), Queen Mary University of London. She has served as a consultant to the International Monetary Fund, the European Central Bank, the World Bank, the Asian Development Bank, the Federal Reserve Bank of New York, and the House of Lords. She studied at Valladolid University, Madrid University, London School of Economics and Political Sciences, and Harvard Law School. Her research and writings focus on international finance, EU law, central banking, monetary law, financial regulation, and cross-border resolution of banking crises.

Adam Lerrick is a scholar at the American Enterprise Institute. From 2001 to 2010, he was the Friends of Allan H. Meltzer Professor of Economics at Carnegie Mellon University. Mr Lerrick led the Argentine Bond Restructuring Agency, the largest foreign creditor in the US$100 billion Argentina debt restructuring. Mr Lerrick served as adviser on international economic policy to the Joint Economic Committee of the US Congress. As an investment banker, he was head of product development at Salomon Brothers and then at Credit Suisse First Boston. Awarded a PhD in economics from the Massachusetts Institute of Technology, Mr Lerrick was named Institute Scholar.

Yuefen Li is head of the Debt and Development Finance Branch of the United Nations Conference on Trade and Development (UNCTAD) and manager of the UNCTAD Project on Promoting Responsible Sovereign Lending and Borrowing. She has published books, papers, and articles in professional journals and newspapers, and contributed extensively to UNCTAD publications and documents.

Odette Lienau is an associate professor of law at Cornell University Law School and the author of *Rethinking Sovereign Debt: Politics, Reputation, and Legitimacy in Modern Finance*. She received her JD from New York University School of Law and her PhD in government from Harvard University, and previously practised in the Bankruptcy & Restructuring Group of Shearman & Sterling LLP in New York City.

Ryan McCarl is a student at the University of Chicago Law School.

Rodrigo Olivares-Caminal is a professor in Banking and Finance Law at the Centre for Commercial Law Studies (CCLS), Queen Mary University of London. He has acted as a Sovereign Debt Expert for the United Nations Conference on Trade and Development

(UNCTAD) and served as a consultant to the World Bank, the African Development Bank, the European Central Bank, the Organisation for Economic Cooperation and Development (OECD), and the Inter-American Development Bank.

Professor Arturo Porzecanski is distinguished economist in residence and director of the International Economic Relations Program at the School of International Service, American University in Washington DC. Prior to starting his academic career in 2005, he worked on Wall Street as an international economist for nearly three decades, starting as a junior economist at JP Morgan in 1977 and ending as chief economist for emerging markets at ABN AMRO Bank (2000–05). He is the author of numerous articles and book chapters on sovereign debt issues, and holds a PhD in international economics from the University of Pittsburgh.

Ebrahim Rahbari is a director in the Global and European Economics Team at Citi Research in London and Citi's lead economist for Germany. Ebrahim has written widely on all aspects of the European sovereign debt and banking crisis and its policy responses, as well as global economic trends. Ebrahim holds a Master's degree and PhD in economics from London Business School and a BA (Hons) in economics and management from Oxford University (Balliol College).

Antonio Sáinz de Vicuña has been general counsel of the European Central Bank since 1998. He is a graduate in law and economic sciences of the Universidad Complutense de Madrid, and has a Master's degree in international law from Cambridge University. He has been Chief Legal Adviser in the Spanish Ministry of Foreign Affairs. He is vice-president of the Committee on International Monetary Law of the International Law Association (MOCOMILA).

Christoph Trebesch is an assistant professor at the University of Munich, Department of Economics. His research interests include international finance and international macroeconomics—in particular, sovereign debt and default.

Mark Weidemaier is Ralph M. Stockton, Jr Associate Professor of Law at the University of North Carolina at Chapel Hill.

Philip Wood QC (Hon) holds a BA (Cape Town), MA (Oxon), and LLD (Lund, Hon). He is head of Allen & Overy Global Law Intelligence Unit and special global counsel, Allen & Overy LLP. In addition, Philip is a visiting professor in international financial law, University of Oxford, Yorke Distinguished Visiting Fellow, University of Cambridge, visiting professor, Queen Mary, University of London, and visiting professor, London School of Economics and Political Science. He is also chairman of the Sovereign Bankruptcy Group of the International Law Association.

Andrew Yianni is a partner at Clifford Chance based in London. He heads the firm's Sovereign Advisory Group and has worked on sovereign debt restructuring arrangements for close to 30 years. Clients include sovereigns, central banks, international commercial and investments banks and international financial institutions. He has an honours degree and a masters degree in Economics and has published widely in the sovereign debt field. As part of the Clifford Chance team advising ESM and EFSF he has been extensively involved in all aspects of the Eurozone debt crisis.

Jeromin Zettelmeyer is deputy chief economist of the European Bank for Reconstruction and Development (EBRD) and non-resident senior fellow of the Peterson Institute for International Economics. He is co-author of *Debt Defaults and Lessons from a Decade of Crises* (with F. Sturzenegger, MIT Press, 2007) and (with C. Trebesch and M. Gulati) 'The Greek Debt Restructuring: An Autopsy' ((2013) 28 *Economic Policy* 75).

LIST OF ABBREVIATIONS

ABSs	asset-backed securities
AERPP	*American Economic Review Papers and Proceedings*
AfDB	African Development Bank
AfDF	African Development Fund
AJIL	*American Journal of International Law*
Am Econ Rev	*American Economic Review*
Am J Comp L	*American Journal of Comparative Law*
Am J Int'l Arb	*American Journal of International Arbitration*
Am J Int'l L	*American Journal of International Law*
Aus Econ Rev	*Australian Economic Review*
BDF FS Rev	*Banque de France Financial Stability Review*
BCBS	Basel Committee on Banking Supervision
BCRA	Banco Central de la República Argentina
Benelux	Belgium, Netherlands, and Luxembourg
BIS	Bank for International Settlements
BIT	bilateral investment treaty
BPEA	*Brookings Papers on Economic Activity*
bps	basis points
Brook J Int'l L	*Brooklyn Journal of International Law*
Bus L	*Business Law*
BVerfG	*Bundesverfassungsgericht* [German Federal Constitutional Court]
BVI	British Virgin Islands
CAC	collective action clause
Cal L Rev	*California Law Review*
Canada–US LJ	*Canada–United States Law Journal*
CBPP	covered bond purchase programme
CCL	Contingent Credit Line (IMF)
CDO	collateralized debt obligation
CDS	credit default swap
CFB	Corporation of Foreign Bondholders (UK)
CHF	Swiss franc
Chi J Int'l L	*Chicago Journal of International Law*
CID	Center for International Development at Harvard University
CIF	co-investment fund
CJEU	Court of Justice of the European Union
CMG	crisis management group
CMLJ	*Capital Markets Law Journal*
COFER	Currency Composition of Official Foreign Exchange Reserves (IMF)
Colum J Transnat'l L	*Columbia Journal of Transnational Law*
Conn J Int'l L	*Connecticut Journal of International Law*
Contemp Econ Pol'y	*Contemporary Economic Policy*
Cornell L Rev	*Cornell Law Review*

DIP	debtor-in-possession
DMO	Debt Management Office
DRF	Debt Reduction Facility (IDA); Dispute Resolution Forum
DSA	debt sustainability analysis
DSF	Debt Sustainability Framework (World Bank/IMF)
Duke L & Contemp Probs	*Duke Law and Contemporary Problems*
Duke LJ	*Duke Law Journal*
EAFRD	European Agricultural Fund for Rural Development
EAGF	European Agricultural Guarantee Fund
EAMS	euro area member state
EBRD	European Bank for Reconstruction and Development
ECA	European Court of Auditors
ECB	European Central Bank
ECCL	enhanced conditioned credit line
ECCL+	enhanced conditioned credit line with sovereign partial risk protection
ECHR	European Convention on Human Rights
ECJ	European Court of Justice
Ecofin	Economic and Financial Affairs Council (EU)
Econ Pol'y	*Economic Policy*
EDA	European Debt Agency
EDP	Excessive Deficit Procedure
EDRF	European Debt Redemption Fund
EEA	European Economic Area
EFC	Economic and Financial Committee (EU)
EFF	European Fisheries Fund
EFSF	European Financial Stability Facility
EFSM	European Financial Stabilization Mechanism
EFTA	European Free Trade Area
EIB	European Investment Bank
EJB	European junior bond
ELA	emergency liquidity assistance (ECB)
Emory LJ	*Emory Law Journal*
EMR	*Emerging Markets Review*
EMS	European Monetary System
ERM	Exchange Rate Mechanism
ESAF	Enhanced Structural Adjustment Facility (IMF)
ESBie	European safe bond
ESCB	European System of Central Banks
ESF	European Social Fund; Exogenous Shocks Facility (IMF)
ESM	European Stability Mechanism
Eur J Int'l L	*European Journal of International Law*
Eur J Pol Econ	*European Journal of Political Economy*
Eurofima	European Company for the Financing of Railroad Rolling Stock
FAT	Federal Administrative Tribunal (Switzerland)
FBPC	Foreign Bondholders Protective Council (US)
FC	foreign currency
FCL	Flexible Credit Line (IMF)
FDFA	Federal Department of Foreign Affairs (Switzerland)

FDI	foreign direct investment
FDIC	Federal Deposit Insurance Corporation
FEDER	European Regional Development Fund
FET	fair and equitable treatment
FIRREA	Financial Institutions Reform, Recovery, and Enforcement Act of 1989 (US)
Fordham Int'l LJ	*Fordham International Law Journal*
FPA	Foreign Policy Association
FRAN	floating rate accrual note
FRBNY	Federal Reserve Bank of New York
FRCP	US Federal Rules of Civil Procedure
FSAP	Financial Sector Assessment Programme; Financial Services Action Plan
FSB	Financial Stability Board
FSIA	Foreign Sovereign Immunities Act of 1976 (US)
FTA	free trade agreement
G-7	Group of Seven
G-8	Group of Eight
G-10	Group of Ten
GDP	gross domestic product
Geo LJ	*George Washington Law Journal*
Georgetown J Int'l Law	*Georgetown Journal of International Law*
Geo Wash Int'l L Rev	*George Washington International Law Review*
Ger LJ	*German Law Journal*
GGB	Greek government bond
GKO	*Gosudarstvennoye Kratkosrochnoye Obyazatyelstvo* ('government short-term commitment')
GLF	Greek Loan Facility (EU/IMF)
Goettingen J Int'l L	*Goettingen Journal of International Law*
GRA	General Resource Account (IMF)
GSE	government-sponsored enterprise
G-SIFI	global systemically international financial institution
GYBIL	*German Yearbook of International Law*
Harvard Int'l LJ	*Harvard International Law Journal*
HIPCs	heavily indebted poor countries
Hofstra L Rev	*Hofstra Law Review*
HQA	Headquarters Agreement (BIS)
IADB	Inter-American Development Bank
IAN	interest arrears note
IAS	International Accounting Standard
IASB	International Accounting Standards Board
IBRD	International Bank for Reconstruction and Development
ICJ	International Court of Justice
ICLQ	*International and Comparative Law Quarterly*
ICMA	International Capital Markets Association
ICSID	International Centre for Settlement of Investment Disputes (World Bank)
ICSID Rev	*ISCID Review*
IDA	International Development Association
IDGs	International Development Goals

IFC	International Finance Corporation
IFI	international financial institution
IIA	international investment agreement
IIF	Institute of International Finance
IISD	International Institute for Sustainable Development
ILA	International Law Association
ILOLR	international lender of last resort
IMF	International Monetary Fund
IMFC	International Monetary and Financial Committee
IMF Econ Rev	*IMF Economic Review*
INSOL International	International Federation of Insolvency Professionals
Int'l Com L Quarterly	*International and Comparative Law Quarterly*
Int'l Fin L Rev	*International Financial Law Review*
Int'l Fin Rev	*International Finance Review*
Int'l Tax & Bus Lawyer	*International Tax and Business Lawyer*
ISDA	International Swaps and Derivatives Association
ISIN	International Securities Identification Number
ITLOS	International Tribunal for the Law of the Sea (UN)
J Bank Fin	*Journal of Banking and Finance*
J Dev Econ	*Journal of Development Economics*
J Econ Lit	*Journal of Economic Literature*
J Econ Persp	*Journal of Economic Perspectives*
JIBFL	*Journal of International Banking and Financial Law*
JIBL	*Journal of International Business and Law*
JIBLR	*Journal of International Banking Law and Regulation*
J Int'l Arb	*Journal of International Arbitration*
J Int'l Banking L & Reg	*Journal of International Banking Law and Regulation*
J Int'l Banking Reg	*Journal of International Banking Regulation*
J Int'l Econ	*Journal of International Economics*
J Int'l Econ L	*Journal of International Economics Law*
J Int'l Money & Fin	*Journal of International Money and Finance*
JLA	*Journal of Legal Analysis*
JME	*Journal of Monetary Economics*
JRF	*Journal of Restructuring Finance*
J Theor Biol	*Journal of Theoretical Biology*
Law & Bus Rev Am	*Law and Business Review of the Americas*
Law & Contemp Probs	*Law and Contemporary Problems*
Law & Soc Inq	*Law and Social Inquiry*
LC	local currency
LDCs	least-developed countries
LGD	loss given default
LIA	lending into arrears
LMU	Latin Monetary Union
LOLR	lender of last resort
LTRO	longer-term refinancing operation
MDGs	Millennium Declaration Goals
MDRI	Multilateral Debt Relief Initiative (IMF)

MFN	most-favoured nation
Mich L Rev	*Michigan Law Review*
MONA	Monitoring of Fund Arrangements database (IMF)
MOU	memorandum of understanding
MRO	main refinancing operation
MTO	medium-term fiscal objective
NAFTA	North American Free Trade Agreement
NBC	National Bankruptcy Conference
NBER	National Bureau of Economic Research
NGO	non-governmental organization
NPC	negative pledge clause
NPV	net present value
ODA	official development assistance
OECD	Organisation for Economic Co-operation and Development
OFZ	*Obligatsyi Federal'novo Zaima* ('federal loan obligation')
OID	original issue discount
OMT	outright market transaction
Open Econ Rev	*Open Economies Review*
OSI	official sector involvement
PCA	Permanent Court of Arbitration
PCCL	precautionary credit line
PCIJ	Permanent Court of International Justice
PCL	Precautionary Credit Line (IMF)
PCS	preferred creditor status
PEM	public expenditure management
PIN	Public Information Notice (IMF)
PLL	Precautionary and Liquidity Line (IMF)
PRGF	Poverty Reduction and Growth Facility (IMF)
PRIN	principle note
Proc R Soc B	*Proceedings of the Royal Society of Biological Sciences*
PRS	poverty reduction strategy
PRSLB	Principles on Responsible Sovereign Lending and Borrowing (UNCTAD)
PRSP	poverty reduction strategy paper
PSI	private sector involvement
RCF	Rapid Credit Facility (IMF)
Rev Econ & Inst	*Review of Economics and Institutions*
RFI	Rapid Financing Instrument (IMF)
RSDIE	*Revue Suisse de Droit International et Européen* [*Swiss Review of International and European Law*]
S&P	Standard & Poor's
SBA	Stand-By Arrangement (IMF)
SDRs	special drawing rights
SDRM	sovereign debt restructuring mechanism
SGP	Stability and Growth Pact
SMP	Securities Market Programme (ECB)
SPV	special purpose vehicle

SRF	Supplemental Reserve Facility (IMF)
SSRN	Social Science Research Network
Stanford J Int'l L	*Stanford Journal of International Law*
TDM	*Transnational Dispute Management*
Temple L Rev	*Temple Law Review*
TEU	Treaty on the European Union
TFA	Task Force Argentina
TFEU	Treaty on the Functioning of the European Union
Theor Popul Biol	*Theoretical Population Biology*
U Chicago L Rev	*University of Chicago Law Review*
UCLA J Int'l L & Foreign Aff	*University of California, Los Angeles, Journal of International Law and Foreign Affairs*
UCLA L Rev	*University of California, Los Angeles, Law Review*
U Ill L Rev	*University of Illinois Law Review*
UNCITRAL	United Nations Commission on International Trade Law
UNCTAD	United Nations Conference on Trade and Development
UNHCR	United Nation High Commissioner for Refugees
UNJY	*United Nations Juridical Yearbook*
UNSC	United Nations Security Council
VAT	value added tax
Virginia L Rev	*Virginia Law Review*
VRRs	value recovering rights
Yale J Int'l L	*Yale Journal of International Law*
YB Int'l Arb	*Yearbook on International Arbitration*
World Bank Econ Rev	*World Bank Economic Review*
WIPO	World Intellectual Property Organization
WTO	World Trade Organization

Part I

SOVEREIGN DEBT RESTRUCTURING

1. Minimizing Holdout Creditors: Carrots 3
Lee C. Buchheit and Elena L. Daly

2. Minimizing Holdout Creditors: Sticks 15
Lee C. Buchheit and Elena L. Daly

3. Managing Holdouts: The Case of the 2012 Greek Exchange 25
Jeromin Zettelmeyer, Christoph Trebesch, and G. Mitu Gulati

4. Revisiting the *Pari Passu* Clause 39
Georges Affaki

5. The Role of the International Monetary Fund 49
Rosa M. Lastra

6. Debt Relief for Low-Income Countries 69
Thomas A. Duvall, III

7. The Longer-Term Consequences of Sovereign Debt Restructuring 85
Odette Lienau

1

MINIMIZING HOLDOUT CREDITORS

Carrots

Lee C. Buchheit and Elena L. Daly

1. Introduction

This chapter discusses the methods by which voluntary private sector creditor participation in a sovereign debt restructuring can be encouraged through techniques that reward such participation, structurally or monetarily—the 'carrots'. The next chapter (Chapter 2) addresses the techniques that actively *dis*courage non-participation in these affairs—the 'sticks'. **1.01**

2. The Context

In comparison with their corporate and individual debtor counterparts, sovereign borrowers are both uniquely vulnerable to, and uniquely protected against, creditor legal remedies. **1.02**

A. Sovereign debtors are uniquely vulnerable

Sovereigns are uniquely vulnerable in the sense that a bankruptcy code will not shield an overextended sovereign borrower from hostile creditor actions, nor will it permit such a sovereign to engage in an orderly, court-supervised, reorganization of its financial affairs.[1] Sovereigns are not subject to national bankruptcy codes, their own or anyone else's. Thus, when a sovereign signs a foreign law-governed debt instrument in favour of a private sector creditor, there are only two alternatives: pay the debt according to its terms; or face a potential legal action for enforcement of the instrument. For the sovereign borrower—and for only the sovereign borrower—'seeking the protection of the bankruptcy courts' is not an option. **1.03**

[1] An IMF-led effort to create a form of transnational bankruptcy code for sovereigns in 2002—the Sovereign Debt Restructuring Mechanism (SDRM)—did not garner the necessary political support: *see* Anne Krueger, 'International Financial Architecture for 2002: New Approach to Sovereign Debt Restructuring', Speech at the National Economists' Club Annual Members' Dinner, 26 November 2001, available online at <http://www.imf.org/external/np/speeches/2001/112601.htm>. *See* generally Sean Hagan, 'Designing a Legal Framework to Restructure Sovereign Debt' (2005) 36 Georgetown J Int'l Law 299.

B. Sovereigns are uniquely shielded

1.04 Very little may therefore stand in the way of a creditor intent on obtaining a court judgment against a defaulting sovereign borrower. It is when that creditor seeks to enforce the judgment that the sovereign's unique protections will manifest themselves.

1.05 Although the laws of most countries now embrace the 'restrictive' theory of sovereign immunity (sovereigns can be held legally accountable when they engage in commercial activities outside of their borders), foreign state property is still generally accorded a special immunity status under many legal regimes.[2] Sovereigns typically do not own many assets in their own name outside of their borders. Entities such as a central bank or a state-owned enterprise may hold such assets abroad, but these entities are likely to be treated as having a legal personality distinct from the sovereign, and their property will not normally be available to satisfy claims against the sovereign itself.[3] In addition, the few assets that are frequently held abroad in the name of sovereigns, such as embassies and consulates, will typically be clothed with special immunity from creditor seizure either by statute or pursuant to customary international law.[4]

1.06 A creditor that obtains a court judgment against a sovereign debtor will therefore experience a moment of emotional satisfaction; obtaining financial satisfaction may be a more tedious, not to say exasperating, process.[5]

C. The chemistry of sovereign debt workouts

1.07 Mixing this unique vulnerability to creditor lawsuits with this unique degree of protection against creditor remedies produces the essential chemistry of a negotiated sovereign debt workout. Each side, debtor and creditor, comes to the negotiating table boasting a special advantage and nursing a special weakness. Each side should therefore see merit in pursuing a consensual resolution of the problem.[6]

---

[2] Joseph W. Dellapenna, *Suing Foreign Governments and Their Corporations*, 2nd edn (Boston, MA: Brill Academic Publishers, 2003), §§12.1 *et seq.*

[3] Dellapenna (n. 2), §§2.5, 2.6.

[4] Dellapenna (n. 2), §11.7.

[5] *See* Alison Frankel, 'How Argentina Lost Game of Chicken with Renegade Bondholders', *Reuters.com*, 26 November 2012, available online at <http://blogs.reuters.com/alison-frankel/2012/11/26/how-argentina-lost-game-of-chicken-with-renegade-bondholders/>.

[6] The policy of the US government has been to encourage negotiated solutions to sovereign debt problems. The United States has not wanted to see either side—debtors or creditors—obtain a decisive legal advantage that might erode their willingness to negotiate. This first became apparent in 1985 when the US government intervened on behalf of creditors in a federal court case, arguing that sovereign debtors could not pass laws or decrees that effectively unseated creditors from pursuing their legal remedies in US or other foreign courts. *See* Brief for the United States as *Amicus Curiae*, July 1984, at 6–7, 18, *Allied Bank Int'l v. Banco Credito Agricola de Cartago*, 757 F.2d 516 (2d Cir. 1985) (No. 83-7714). The US government's most recent intervention (28 December 2012), this time on behalf of a sovereign debtor, contained the most explicit statement to date of its desire to preserve what would, in nineteenth-century diplomatic parlance, have been termed strategic balance:

> A sovereign's potential resistance to paying non-exchanged debt is a critical tool in its efforts to negotiate broad creditor support for restructuring. This leverage will be lost if creditors believe that a holdout strategy will eventually result in substantial or full payment. If enough creditors adopt this strategy, foreign sovereign debt restructuring will become impossible. While holdouts retain the right to assert legal claims in court and enforce resultant judgments in appropriate circumstances and in a manner consistent with the FSIA [US Foreign Sovereign Immunities Act of 1976], the creation of new rights and new vehicles for enforcement alters and destabilizes the landscape of sovereign debt restructuring.
>
> (Brief for the United States as *Amicus Curiae* in Support of the Republic of Argentina's Petition for Panel Rehearing and Rehearing *En Banc*, December 2012 at 4, *NML Capital, Ltd et al. v. Republic of Argentina* (12-105-cv(L), 2d Cir. 2012))

The logic of a negotiated workout, as it applies to a class of creditors, is invincible. If any significant percentage of a sovereign's lenders resort to their legal remedies, the paucity of attachable assets outside the sovereign's jurisdiction will surely result in most of them going without a recovery. But that logic is less compelling when applied to an individual creditor. When most of a sovereign's other lenders have agreed voluntarily to restructure their claims, this may leave an opening for a small group of determined creditors to extract a preferential settlement by threatening legal action. And if threats alone are not enough to open the sovereign purse strings, perhaps some stray attachable assets can be found to satisfy a small number of judgments. At the very least, the holdouts may reason, the negative publicity occasioned by lawsuits, attachments, injunctions, and other unpleasantries should put pressure on the sovereign to settle on terms advantageous to the holdouts.[7] In short, what is inescapable for the many (a negotiated settlement) may provide a lucrative business opportunity for the few. 1.08

Apart from creditors who may approach a sovereign debt restructuring with malice aforethought, other debtholders may simply be unpersuaded that the sovereign requires debt relief of the kind or to the degree that it is seeking in the restructuring. This problem will be particularly acute if the debt had originally been placed with retail (individual) investors. The proverbial 'mom and pop' investors are likely to argue that they were beguiled into giving the Republic of Ruritania their retirement nest egg by the presence of sonorous phrases such as 'the full faith and credit of Ruritania is pledged for the repayment of this debt' in the offering documents. Unpersuaded (but not necessarily litigious) and unsophisticated creditors may decline to participate in a sovereign debt workout and find themselves tagged with the epithet 'holdout'. 1.09

As a class, holdouts may thus include both the opportunistic and the befuddled, the blade runners and the sheep, those trying cynically to score a windfall by exploiting a sovereign's unique legal vulnerability and those just trying to recover their meagre life savings. But one thing will always be true: if the holdout population in a sovereign debt restructuring is too large, the restructuring will fail and years, perhaps decades, of litigation will ensue.[8] Minimizing the size of the holdout population is therefore one of the highest priorities for a sovereign debt restructurer. 1.10

3. Techniques to Encourage Creditor Participation

A sovereign debtor can dangle a number of inducements in an effort to increase voluntary creditor participation (and proportionally decrease the size of the holdout population) in a sovereign debt restructuring. Unfortunately, the most obvious measure that the sovereign debtor can take—to offer more creditor-friendly restructuring terms—is generally not possible. The sovereign debtor would not have commenced a wrenching operation such as a generalized debt 1.11

[7] Argentina's flagship navy vessel, the *Libertad*, was detained in Ghana on 2 October 2012 after Elliott, a US fund, secured an attachment order to collect on its Argentine-defaulted bonds. The vessel was ultimately freed, but not until the UN's International Tribunal for the Law of the Sea issued an order on 15 December 2015. *See The Economist*, 'Caught Napping', 13 October 2012, available online at <http://www.economist.com/node/21564542>; Jude Webber, 'Argentina to Call on UN over Seized Ship', *Financial Times*, 12 November 2012, available online at <http://www.ft.com/cms/s/0/f51d20ee-2ce6-11e2-9211-00144feabdc0.html#axzz2cECPVVKX>.

[8] The most prominent sovereign debt litigation involves Argentina's decade-long fight with holders of Argentine bonds that went into default in 2001. *See The Economist*, 'Argy-Bargy', 1 December 2012, available online at <http://www.economist.com/news/finance-and-economics/21567386-argy-bargy>.

restructuring had its existing debt burden been supportable. The entire point of the exercise is to return the country to a sustainable, manageable debt position and that will inevitably require a degree of creditor discomfort. Offering generous financial terms in the restructuring that are the product of a yeasty optimism about the country's economic prospects will no doubt plough the road for this restructuring, but that road will quickly lead to the *next* restructuring.

1.12 The techniques for encouraging voluntary creditor participation (as opposed to *dis*couraging non-participation, the subject of Chapter 2) break down into the following broad categories:

(a) a menu of options;
(b) structural and documentation improvements to the debt instruments;
(c) financial sweeteners;
(d) loss reinstatement features;
(e) parity of treatment assurances; and
(f) value recovery instruments.

A. Menu of options

1.13 The sovereign can offer creditors the ability to choose from a menu of restructuring options, all of which can be calibrated so as to have an equivalent net present value at the time the restructuring closes. This caters to the differing preferences of creditors, the idiosyncrasies of the regulatory and accounting regimes in the jurisdictions where the creditors operate, and conflicting assessments of future interest rate movements. Some lenders, for example, will abhor taking a discount to the principal amount of their claim; they will trade a lower coupon and a longer maturity in a par exchange instrument to avoid such a 'haircut' to principal. Others will be prepared to give up a portion of principal in return for a higher coupon and shorter maturity. Others may want an instrument benefitting from collateral security, even if this means a lower rate of interest. Some lenders will be prepared to capitalize a portion of the interest payable on the new instrument; some will not. Some prefer a floating rate of interest; others, a fixed rate.

1.14 Menus of this kind were a hallmark of the Brady bond debt exchanges of the early 1990s.[9] They are not, however, without cost. Multiplying the number of new instruments issued in a sovereign debt exchange, wholly apart from the additional transaction cost and complexity, may limit the size and thus the liquidity of each instrument. Also, some sovereigns may, for political or optical reasons, need to show a debt stock reduction resulting from the transaction. A heavily subscribed par exchange option will obviously thwart this objective. Each menu option may be equivalent in a net present value sense, but this does not translate into equal cash flow consequences for the debtor. In some of the Brady bond exchanges—Brazil in 1995 is the best example—the sovereign started off by telling creditors that they were perfectly free to choose among a menu of options on offer, only later to command a mandatory 'rebalancing' that forced creditors to take an allotment of one of those options, the discount bond.[10]

B. Structural/documentation improvements

1.15 As an inducement to joining a restructuring, the sovereign can offer an improvement in the structure or in the documentation of the new (restructured) instruments in comparison with the paper that the creditor may currently be holding. Perhaps the classic example of

[9] *See* John Clark, 'Debt Reduction and Market Reentry under the Brady Plan' (1993–94) 18(4) FRBNY Quarterly Rev 41.
[10] Clark (n. 9), 45.

a structural enhancement was the full collateralization of the principal due at maturity of Brady bonds issued in the 1990s.[11] Other possible structural improvements include a co-financing feature (see paragraphs 1.16–1.17) or a partial guarantee from a multilateral financial institution (see paragraph 1.18). Examples of documentary improvements may include a listing of the new instrument on a securities exchange, a shift of the specified governing law from that of the sovereign's own jurisdiction to a foreign governing law, tighter financial covenants, a broader waiver of sovereign immunity, eligibility to use the new instruments in a debt-for-equity or debt-for-privatization programme, and so forth.

A good example of a structural enhancement for a new instrument being offered in a sovereign debt exchange is a co-financing feature. The creditors' perspective on this technique is simple enough: sovereign borrowers have (almost invariably) continued to pay certain types of lender, such as the World Bank and other multilateral financial institutions, even while the sovereign may have been busily restructuring its commercial bank creditors, bondholders, and bilateral (government-to-government) creditors. If the payments due under a new instrument being issued in a debt restructuring can be linked to loans from one of these 'preferred' creditors, the argument goes, the new instrument will benefit from the aura of that preferred status. The trick, of course, is to ensure that the linkage cannot be broken or circumvented. A failure by the borrower to make a full payment under the private sector instrument *must* trigger a proportional default on the loan by the traditional preferred creditor; otherwise, the arrangement misfires. Only in this way can the sovereign borrower be forced into the position of having to alienate the affections of one of its multilateral lenders if ever it seeks to default or restructure the new instrument being issued to private sector creditors. **1.16**

Co-financing techniques of this kind became popular in the late 1980s as sovereign debtors caught up in the debt crisis of that era found it increasingly difficult to borrow the money they needed to remain current on the interest payments due under their commercial bank indebtedness.[12] The technique then seemed to pass out of mind and memory until the massive Greek restructuring of early 2012. As an inducement for creditors to participate in that restructuring—a particularly savage one that imposed a 53.5 per cent principal haircut—the new Greek bonds were linked by a co-financing agreement to Greece's payments under a €30 billion credit facility granted by the European Union's bailout mechanism, the European Financial Stability Facility (EFSF).[13] The theory was that Greece would never wish to anger its European partners by defaulting on an EFSF loan. The co-financing feature was thus intended to bring the new private sector bonds under this protective umbrella. **1.17**

Another possible structural enhancement is a partial guarantee of the new debt instruments by a multilateral financial institution. The Republic of the Seychelles, in 2010, obtained a partial guarantee from the African Development Bank for the new notes issued in connection with the Seychelles' debt restructuring. The Federation of St Kitts and Nevis used a similar enhancement—a partial guarantee from the Caribbean Development Bank—in its debt restructuring in 2012. **1.18**

[11] *See* generally Charles Collyns and Mohamed El-Erian, *Restructuring of Commercial Bank Debt by Developing Countries: Lessons from Recent Experience*, IMF Paper on Policy Analysis and Assessment (June 1993).

[12] *See* Lee C. Buchheit, 'Alternative Techniques in Sovereign Debt Restructuring' [1988] U Ill L Rev 371, 384–5.

[13] Allen & Overy, *How the Greek Debt Reorganisation of 2012 Changed the Rules of Sovereign Insolvency* (September 2012), available online at <http://www.allenovery.com/SiteCollectionDocuments/AO%20-%20 Greek%20debt%20reorganisation%20of%202012.pdf>, 28.

1.19 Documentation improvements will have no immediate basis point cost to the sovereign at the time of the restructuring; that is their charm. Their significance (and cost) may become apparent down the road only if some further treatment of the new instruments is required. Any feature that makes those instruments more difficult to restructure in the future, such as a shift to a foreign governing law in lieu of local law, may then be regretted, but for politicians facing the need to conclude a debt restructuring successfully this year, the operative words in this description are 'down the road' and 'in the future'.

C. Financial sweeteners

1.20 Sovereigns are sometimes advised to blend a drop or two of honey into the restructuring medicine in order to make the mixture go down the lenders' throat more easily. Such *douceurs* come in several varieties. For example, up-front cash payments can be made to those creditors joining the debt restructuring, sometimes labelled 'participation fees', 'consent fees', or 'goodwill payments'. A bit of camouflage can be added by styling the sweetener an 'early bird fee' available only to those who commit by a specified date (a very popular technique in the restructurings of commercial bank loans in the 1980s). In situations in which the sovereign has suspended interest payments on its existing instruments in the lead-up to a restructuring, the sweetener may involve nothing more than an undertaking to pay all accrued interest in cash on the closing date of the restructuring rather than to capitalize those amounts.

1.21 The problem, as always in these affairs, will be money. The sovereign must either raise the funds required for the sweetener by suspending payments on its existing loans from the very same creditors who will be receiving the sweetener when they join the restructuring, or else borrow the money from an official sector source. The former smacks of pilfering someone's car keys and then offering to give them back to the owner in return for a ride to town. The latter requires a broad-minded and indulgent official sector lender prepared to use its taxpayers' money to raise the saccharine content of a settlement with private sector lenders.

D. Loss reinstatement features

1.22 At base, a sovereign debt restructuring is as much an implicit bargain between the debtor and its creditors as it is an explicit contract. The creditors are asked to provide debt relief in the form of lower interest rates, a reduction of principal, and/or a stretch-out of maturities. In return for these concessions, the borrower promises to service the new (restructured) instruments on their amended terms. But what happens if the borrower cannot, or will not, continue normal debt servicing of the new instruments and another restructuring—a 're-restructuring'—is proposed? The creditors come to that next restructuring permanently impaired; they are clutching instruments with a lower face amount, a reduced interest rate, and/or a delayed maturity in comparison with the paper they held at the time of the first restructuring. The implicit bargain of 'debt relief now for full performance later' will have been shattered, with lasting prejudice to the creditor side of the table.

1.23 A technique to redress this balance was first used by Ecuador in its debt restructuring of 2000 and dubbed 'principal reinstatement'.[14] Ecuador had inflicted a 45 per cent loss on it bank creditors as part of its Brady bond restructuring in 1995—the most generous terms that had

[14] *See* Lee C. Buchheit, 'How Ecuador Beat the Brady Bond Trap' (2000) 19 Int'l Fin L Rev 17, 19. A very similar clause was employed in Belize's debt restructuring of 2013. *See* Belize, *Offer to Exchange*, Offering Memorandum, 15 February 2013, 127–8.

been given to a Latin American sovereign borrower up to that point. Exactly five years later, however, Ecuador defaulted on its recently issued Brady bonds and requested yet another round of restructuring. To assuage creditor concerns that such serial restructurings would relentlessly erode the face amount of their claims, Ecuador promised that if it were to default again within the first ten years after issuance of its new bonds in 2000, a portion of the previously forgiven principal would automatically balloon back, returning creditors (more or less) to the status quo ante of the prior debt restructuring. Naturally, another default within that period would most likely entail yet another round of restructuring, but the theory was that the creditors would come to that future negotiating table with the principal amount of their claims reinstated.

A loss reinstatement feature modelled on the Ecuador clause was also included in the Seychelles restructuring of 2010 and the St Kitts and Nevis restructuring of 2012, although in both of these cases the trigger for the principal reinstatement was a failure by the debtor country to implement its International Monetary Fund (IMF) programme. The St Kitts and Nevis Principal Reinstatement Clause reads as follows: **1.24**

> If the Relevant Event has not occurred by 31 March 2014, the Issuer shall deliver Par Bonds to the holders thereof on the next Payment Date. Such Par Bonds shall be in an amount equal to 40 per cent of the face amount of the Bonds issued on the Issue Date . . . having the same terms and conditions as the Par Bonds in all respects except that interest shall only accrue from the date of such further issuance and no scheduled payments (including the Goodwill Payment thereunder) under the Par Bonds falling on or prior to the date of such further issuance will be made. . . . '**Relevant Event**' means that a press release has been issued by the International Monetary Fund (the '**IMF**') confirming that the IMF Executive Board has approved the sixth review under the IMF Stand-By Arrangement with the Issuer existing at the time of the issue of the Bonds.

E. Assurances of parity of treatment

Creditors caught up in a sovereign debt workout fear two things. First, they detest being made to look like incompetent debt negotiators—something that would obviously happen if another group of creditors were to secure a better deal for themselves after the first bunch had signed on to more severe restructuring terms. Second, they do not want to see the cash savings that accrue to the sovereign borrower as a result of their own generosity being diverted into the pockets of other lenders who refused to join the restructuring. **1.25**

These sentiments can prompt a call for inclusion of contractual provisions in the new debt instruments that assure a parity of treatment with other creditors.[15] The clauses come in two varieties. The first, best illustrated by the so-called 'comparable treatment' provision included in all agreed minutes signed with Paris Club creditor countries, explicitly forbids the sovereign debtor from granting more favourable restructuring terms (expressed in a net present value sense) to any other group of creditors, including private sector creditors. A Paris Club Comparable Treatment Clause reads as follows: **1.26**

> In order to secure comparable treatment of its debt due to all its external public or private creditors, the Government of the Republic of Ruritania commits to seek promptly from all its external creditors debt reduction and reorganization arrangements on terms comparable in net present value to those set forth in the present Agreed Minutes for credits of comparable maturity. Comparability of treatment for debt reduction in net present value is assessed not only on the basis of the reduction in the face value of the debt but also on the terms of repayment of the debts not cancelled. Consequently, the Government of the Republic of Ruritania

[15] *See* Lee C. Buchheit, 'The Search for Intercreditor Parity' (2002) 8 Law & Bus Rev Am 73.

commits to accord all categories of creditors—and in particular creditor countries not participating in the present Agreed Minutes, commercial banks and suppliers—a treatment not more favorable than that accorded to the Participating Creditor Countries.

1.27 The second, sometimes called 'most favoured creditor' provisions, mandate that if ever the sovereign gives a better deal to any other similarly situated lender, it will make the same offer to all those who accepted the original debt restructuring. Most favoured creditor provisions are designed to assure participating creditors simultaneously that they will not be embarrassed by a future settlement with other creditors on more favourable terms and to dispel any hope on the part of non-participating creditors that a better offer may follow this one. In this way, they serve an *in terrorem* function vis-à-vis the holdouts.[16] It should be obvious that the sovereign lacks the resources to offer a much improved deal to *all* of its creditors. The prospective holdouts are therefore expected to absorb the message that a preferential payout to them will effectively be blocked by the operation of the most favoured creditor clause, because that clause would require any improved terms to be offered to all other creditors as well. Belize's Most Favored Creditor Clause, for example, reads as follows:

> Belize shall not enter into any arrangement to pay or to settle an Untendered Material Claim on terms more favorable to the holder thereof (in a net present value sense) than the terms offered in the Offering Memorandum to the holders of tendered Eligible Claims, without simultaneously making those more favorable terms available to each holder of a tendered Eligible Claim.

F. Value recovery rights

1.28 One of the most popular techniques for encouraging private sector participation in a sovereign debt restructuring has been to offer participating creditors a value recovering right (VRR) as part of the restructuring package. Value recovering rights were originally intended to mimic the 'equity kickers' frequently used in corporate debt workouts. In those situations, creditors are asked to grant debt relief to a corporate borrower, but have no way of recouping their losses if the reorganization succeeds in returning the debtor company to financial health. The solution is to give creditors an equity stake in the company as part of the restructuring. If the company prospers in the future, the value of that equity will rise and allow creditors to recover some of the forgone principal or interest on their loans.

1.29 The obvious problem in transposing this technique to a sovereign debt setting is that sovereigns do not have shareholder's equity that can be distributed to indulgent creditors. When commercial banks were asked to take outright losses on their sovereign loan portfolios starting in 1990 with the Mexico Brady exchange, they argued that the price of oil—Mexico's main primary commodity export—would be a reasonable indicator for predicting Mexico's future economic prosperity. If the price of oil were to increase beyond a specified benchmark, the creditors argued, this would be a sure sign that the country could afford to recompense them for a portion of the sacrifices that the Brady initiative had inflicted on Mexico's creditors.

1.30 Mexico was thereby persuaded to issue oil recovery warrants as part of its Brady bond exchange. The warrants were free-standing instruments that entitled the holder to receive a

[16] Anna Gelpern, *After Argentina*, Rutgers School of Law Newark Research Paper No. 011/Institute for International Economics Working Paper No. 2005-PB05-2 (September 2005), available online at <http://ssrn.com/abstract=880794> or <http://dx.doi.org/10.2139/ssrn.880794>, 5 and 6.

cash payment in respect of any period (starting in 1996, five years after the Mexican Brady exchange closed) in which the inflation-adjusted price of a barrel of Mexican crude oil exceeded US$14.[17] Virtually all other oil-exporting countries that implemented a Brady exchange in the 1990s, such as Venezuela and Nigeria, were obliged to issue oil warrants of a similar nature. Ecuador in 1995 was the visible exception.

For Brady countries that lacked a principal export like oil, the creditors had to look for other benchmarks that could reliably signal whether the country had returned to financial health. The most popular benchmark was gross domestic product (GDP). A GDP warrant will call for a cash payment if the debtor country's GDP in a future year exceeds a baseline projection for that year. There were other variations as well. Uruguay, for example, opted to issue a warrant whose payments were linked to the price of a basket of traditional Uruguayan exports. **1.31**

Value recovery rights have had a chequered career in sovereign debt restructurings. They are typically designed to be well 'out of the money' (that is, below the point at which the benchmark would require cash payments to be made on the instrument) at the time of issuance, but for this reason they are utterly misprized by the market when first issued. The sovereign debtor consequently gets little or no credit, in the sense of more favourable restructuring terms, when the VRRs are included in a debt restructuring package. If the debtor were to ask its creditors 'What restructuring terms will you give me in a package *with* a VRR and what terms with*out* a VRR?', the answer from the lenders would likely be 'The same terms'. **1.32**

Many of the VRRs issued as part of the Brady bond restructurings of the 1990s have subsequently come into the money and the issuing countries have been making quarterly cash payments, even after the underlying Brady bonds have been retired (the VRRs are usually detachable from the underlying bonds and will continue to trade in the market). Rarely, however, are those payments made to the creditors who actually granted debt relief by accepting Brady bonds in the 1990s. Because VRRs are typically formatted as free-standing, freely tradable instruments, most have long since passed into the hands of investors who, if they recognized the phrase 'Brady era' at all, would assume that it was roughly coterminous with the Peloponnesian War. **1.33**

Value recovery rights have also featured in more recent sovereign debt restructurings. Argentina issued a GDP-linked warrant as part of its bond restructuring in 2005 and has been paying on it (heavily) ever since.[18] Greece included a GDP-linked warrant in its €206 billion bond restructuring in early 2012.[19] **1.34**

4. Implications

A. The 'floats all boats' argument

For obvious reasons, sovereign borrowers would prefer not to have to offer carrots to entice creditors to join a debt restructuring. All such features involve either cost or risk to the **1.35**

---

17 *See* Lee C. Buchheit, 'No Easy Route to Recovery Value' (1991) 10 Int'l Fin L Rev 7.

18 *See Euromoney*, 'Argentine GDP Warrants', 25 January 2006, available online at <http://www.euromoney.com/Article/1014876/Argentine-GDP-warrants.html>.

19 *See* Ministry of Finance of Hellenic Republic, 'PSI [private sector involvement] Launch Press Release', 21 February 2012, available online at <http://www.minfin.gr/portal/en/resource/contentObject/id/7ad6442f-1777-4d02-80fb-91191c606664>; *see* also Allen & Overy (n. 13), 35.

sovereign. Sweeteners such as consent fees require an immediate diversion of scarce cash; VRRs may require such a diversion in the future. Structural/documentation inducements, such as tougher legal terms in the new debt instruments or co-financing links to official sector loans, will make it more difficult to seek additional debt relief from those instruments if this becomes necessary in the future.

1.36 The sovereign borrower's strongest argument to resist calls for the inclusion of such enticements in a debt restructuring is straightforward: if the restructuring (coupled with the sovereign's economic adjustment measures) succeeds in returning the country to a sound financial footing, then everyone wins. Most holders of sovereign bonds are institutional investors that mark their positions to market each day. The mark-to-market value of those positions will decline as the sovereign enters its debt restructuring, but will, everyone hopes, be restored to robust value once a successful debt restructuring closes. It is in this way, the sovereign will argue, that palpable value can be returned to participating creditors, at least in comparison with the depressed levels at which the debt was trading before the restructuring closed. Ancillary inducements to participation of the kind discussed in this chapter will, if the debt restructuring is successful in restoring the borrower to economic health, be viewed in hindsight as trivial or even silly. But if the sovereign does *not* recover its financial footing for some reason, such features are unlikely to be of much comfort to the afflicted creditors. In short, the sovereign's argument is that restored prosperity is the rising tide that will float all boats.

B. Utility

1.37 Hanging over all discussions about adding carrots to a sovereign debt restructuring package is the question 'Do they really matter?'; in other words, will the decision of even a single creditor about whether to participate in the restructuring turn on the presence or absence of these features? Or, as the sovereign borrower might suspect, are these features being proposed by creditors merely as a way of squeezing some extra value out of a deal that they know they will accept with or without the carrots? No one can prove the counterfactual, so these concerns are likely to remain in the realm of suspicions.

C. Futility

1.38 All vendors of Christmas trees will attest to the truth of the following proposition: no matter how many ornaments you hang on the tree, if the customer is not in the Christmas spirit, you are unlikely to make a sale. Or, if you prefer a mammalian to an arboreal analogy, no matter how large the dangling carrot, a donkey without an appetite is unlikely to move forward.

1.39 As applied to a sovereign debt restructuring, the lesson of these truisms is that no matter how succulent or how numerous the ancillary enticements that may be added to a debt restructuring package, a creditor who acquired the underlying paper with the express intention of staying out of the deal and pursuing a preferential recovery at the sharp end of a litigation is unlikely to be dissuaded from this path by the presence of those inducements. The addition of sweeteners such as those discussed in this chapter may—repeat, *may*—operate at the margin to bring into a debt restructuring creditors who are otherwise predisposed to being seduced (and to that extent the holdout population may be reduced), but they will not melt the flinty heart of the deeply dyed holdout.

1.40 The sovereign debtor may therefore reasonably ask whether the inclusion of such carrots in a restructuring package is an exercise in futility—and a damnably expensive exercise at that. The answer to this question turns on the significance of the relative size of a holdout population. The goal, express or implied, in most sovereign debt restructurings is to achieve a creditor participation rate at a level (usually higher than 90 or 95 per cent) that renders the holdouts no more than an irksome nuisance.

A negligible holdout population, even if one assumes that they will all eventually succeed in obtaining a full recovery, will not threaten the sovereign's future debt service capacity. On the other hand, leaving behind a sizable holdout community may undermine the financial predicates of the entire restructuring, possibly presaging another debt crisis in the near future. **1.41**

So it boils down to this: how many marginal creditors will join a deal that includes one or more inducements of the kind discussed in this chapter when they would reject a deal bereft of those enticements? This is always a judgement call. For the advisers/arrangers in a sovereign debt restructuring, this judgement will require close and accurate market soundings. For the sovereign borrower, it is usually a straight cost–benefit analysis: are the marginal, seducible creditors numerous enough to justify the cost and risks of giving the inducements to *all* participating lenders? **1.42**

D. The political dimension

Finally, there is the political dimension. Before a sovereign ever gets to the point of proposing a debt restructuring, its citizens will have borne the pain of an economic collapse accompanied by a heavy dose of fiscal adjustment and austerity. The debt restructuring, when it eventually comes, is therefore likely to be perceived by those citizens as an equitable sharing of the burden with the country's other stakeholders—that is, its creditors. No one will begrudge seeing the mark-to-market value of the portfolios of the participating creditors inflate if and when prosperity returns to the country. But why, domestic critics of the debt restructuring package may ask, should these other stakeholders need to be induced, coaxed, and sweet-talked into bearing their fair share of the misery? **1.43**

2

MINIMIZING HOLDOUT CREDITORS

Sticks

Lee C. Buchheit and Elena L. Daly

Praise the Lord and pass the ammunition.
(Howell Forgy, US Navy lieutenant, Pearl Harbor, 7 December 1941[1])

1. Introduction

This chapter discusses the techniques that have developed over the last thirty years to discourage holdout creditor behaviour in a sovereign debt workout—the proverbial 'sticks'. For the engineer of sovereign debt workouts, the question is not usually one of carrots *or* sticks; rather, it is sometimes a matter of blending enough carrot juice into the recipe so that the required creditor voting threshold to approve a more coercive measure can be reached. **2.01**

2. The Context

Corporate bankruptcies are not normally troubled by holdout creditors. Most bankruptcy codes that permit a reorganization of a corporate debtor's affairs (as opposed to an outright liquidation of the company) will have some method for imposing the will of the majority of similarly situated creditors on any naysaying minority. In the absence of any form of cram-down mechanism in a bankruptcy code, however, all sovereign debt workouts face the prospect of non-participating (holdout) creditors. **2.02**

A. The holdout creditor problem

Holdout creditors in a sovereign debt restructuring pose the following difficulties. **2.03**

i. Money

The debt sustainability analysis that precedes most sovereign debt workouts will assume that all, or nearly all, of the debt instruments targeted for restructuring will participate in the transaction. Any significant holdout population may therefore render obsolete the financial predicates underlying the entire operation. This leaves only two options: begin the whole process again (a tedious, embarrassing, and probably expensive option); or press ahead despite the holdouts and face the likelihood of messy, post-closing litigation. **2.04**

[1] *Oxford Dictionary of Quotations*, 3rd edn (Oxford: Oxford University Press, 1979), 216.

ii. Emotions

2.05 Holdouts stir strong emotions. Holdouts who bought their claims in the secondary market at a small fraction of their face value—'vulture creditors', to use the pejorative label—stir particularly strong emotions. The sovereign debtor, with its citizens groaning under a multi-year austerity programme, will tend to see vultures as attempting to pry the gold teeth out of the corpse. For their part, fellow creditors who elect to provide debt relief to the sovereign borrower may view the holdouts as seeking to benefit from their generosity. The holdout, after all, is demanding a preferential recovery made possible only by the willingness of the sovereign's other creditors to reduce or extend their own claims. Imagine denying yourself a long-awaited family vacation in order to make a sizable donation to a charity for starving orphans. Now imagine opening your morning newspaper to read that the operators of that charity have absconded with all of the money and treated themselves to what sounds like a remarkably enjoyable weekend in Las Vegas. That is how many participating creditors feel about the holdouts in a sovereign debt restructuring and it explains creditor demands for contractual protections against preferential payouts of other lenders.[2]

iii. Intercreditor equity

2.06 Then there is the matter of basic fairness. The phrase 'voluntary sovereign debt restructuring' is oxymoronic. No creditor willingly abandons the value of its claim; it will do so only, as the French say, for want of better and for fear of worse. Paying holdouts in full while visiting losses on other similarly situated lenders therefore raises a stark issue of intercreditor equity.

iv. Publicity

2.07 *Not* paying holdouts, however, invites its own set of problems. An unpaid creditor can be a festering sore. For so long as the payment default persists, it will remind new investors in the debtor country of the unfortunate fate of their predecessors. The stench of the corpse of a prior creditor rarely stimulates the investment appetite of a new lender.

v. Litigation

2.08 Modern sovereign debt instruments are enforceable in domestic courts, often outside of the debtor's own jurisdiction. Quite apart from the expense and nuisance of lawsuits and arbitrations, litigation—and the enforcement process that follows litigation—can interfere with the borrower's new fundraising efforts. Argentina has been litigating with holdout creditors for well over a decade,[3] during which period the country has been unable to return to normal market borrowing practices.

B. The spectre of holdouts

2.09 Far more damage, however, has been done by the *prospect* of holdout creditors in a sovereign debt workout than has ever been inflicted by the holdouts themselves. A jittery sovereign debtor (and perhaps its official sector sponsors) may conjure up images of ghastly headlines in the *Financial Times*, multi-decade lawsuits, allegedly indelible stains on the country's reputation, and higher future borrowing costs. The spectre of holdouts can therefore fuel a well-recognized tendency of sovereign debtors toward pathological procrastination in

---

[2] *See* Chapter 1, paragraphs 1.25–1.27.

[3] *See* Robin Wigglesworth and Jude Webber, 'An Unforgiven Debt', *Financial Times*, 28 November 2012.

implementing a needed sovereign debt restructuring.[4] These delays inevitably make things worse for both the sovereign and its creditors. In the frantic scramble to avoid an unavoidable debt management transaction, the sovereign may enter into new borrowings on ruinous terms, run its reserves down to a dangerous level, and stumble into a situation in which the only option left is the worst one—a chaotic payment default.

3. Techniques to Discourage Holdouts

The following techniques have been tried over the last thirty years in an effort to discourage holdouts in a sovereign debt restructuring. **2.10**

A. Frighten them

By far the most popular—one is almost tempted to say 'ubiquitous'—technique for discouraging holdouts is to threaten them with a prolonged payment default unless they join the restructuring. The strategy is simple enough: crush the holders' expectation of being paid on the instruments they now own as essential psychological preparation for an offer to exchange those instruments for new credits with a lower face amount, a reduced coupon, and/or a longer maturity date. Even if this threat is not made explicit in the offering documents for the restructuring, it will always be implicit. No debt restructuring will prosper if the borrower begins by assuring its lenders of full and timely payment should they decline to participate. **2.11**

Louis XIV embossed his cannon with the Latin legend, *Ultima ratio regis*—'The king's last argument'. In a sovereign debt context, payment default is the king's last argument. Expressing that argument in the offering documents for a debt restructuring, however, has become something of an art form. In its 2005 exchange offer, for example, the Republic of Argentina adopted an 'abandon hope, all ye who do *not* enter here' tone. Under 'Risk Factors' in the offering document came the following minatory text: **2.12**

> **Risks of Not Participating in the Offer**
>
> Eligible Securities that are not tendered may remain in default indefinitely.
>
> Eligible Securities not exchanged pursuant to the Offer will remain outstanding. Argentina has announced that it has no intention of resuming payments on any Eligible Securities that remain outstanding following the expiration of the Offer. Consequently, if you elect not to tender your Eligible Securities pursuant to the Offer there can be no assurance that you will receive any future payments in respect of your Eligible Securities.[5]

St Kitts and Nevis is even blunter in its debt restructuring of 2012: **2.13**

> **Risks of Not Participating in the Offer**
>
> *Treatment of Eligible Claims not tendered*
>
> The Eligible Claims that are not tendered may remain outstanding indefinitely. The Federation does not intend to resume payments on instruments that are not exchanged pursuant to the

[4] *See* Ugo Panizza, *Do We Need a Mechanism for Solving Sovereign Debt Crises? A Rule-Based Discussion*, Geneva Graduate Institute of International and Development Studies Working Paper No. 03/2013, Preliminary Draft (February 2013), available online at <http://repec.graduateinstitute.ch/pdfs/Working_papers/HEIDWP03-2013.pdf>. For a light-hearted treatment of the problem, *see* Lee C. Buchheit, 'An Open Letter to the Minister of Finance of Ruritania', *The Banker*, September 2011, 8.

[5] Republic of Argentina, *Prospectus Supplement*, 10 January 2005, S-29.

> Exchange Offer. Consequently, if a Holder elects not to tender its Eligible Claims, it is unlikely that it will receive any future payments in respect of such instruments.[6]

2.14 Belize, in 2006, opted for a milder approach, but the underlying message was the same:

> **Risks of Not Participating in the Offer**
>
> *Treatment of Eligible Claims not tendered*
>
> Belize does not foresee that it will have the resources to pay any non-tendered Eligible Claims according to their existing terms. Moreover, Belize shall not pay any amount in respect of a non-tendered Eligible Claim if, at the time such payment is due, a payment default then exists under any New Bond.[7]

2.15 The obvious risk of announcing in advance that any holdout creditors will be consigned to the outer darkness is that the sovereign may have to make good on that promise once the debt restructuring closes. Bereft of any hope that payments will resume voluntarily, the creditors are left with only their legal remedies, and while that option may not be pleasant for the creditors, it is equally distasteful for the debtor. The less adamant versions of the warning to prospective holdouts, such as the language used by Belize, are designed to give the sovereign some manoeuvring room should the holdout population turn out to be sufficiently small that it becomes cost-effective for the borrower to pay rather than to litigate.

B. Deter them

2.16 All sovereign debt exchanges call for a relative, not an absolute, judgement on the part of the creditors. What is on offer (a debt instrument conveying a measure of debt relief to the borrower) may not be pretty, but its real attractiveness can be judged only in comparison with what the creditor already is holding. Sovereigns sometimes attempt to influence this relative judgement by spiffing up the new instruments they are proffering in exchange,[8] but the same objective can also be achieved by making the old instruments uglier. Threatening a prolonged (for which, read 'eternal') payment default on those old instruments (the technique described in the last section) is one way in which to do this, but there are others.

i. Exit consents

2.17 Even in debt instruments that require the unanimous consent of the holders to effect a change to the payment terms of the instrument (the dates and amounts of payment), the other provisions of the instrument can usually be amended with only a majority, or sometimes two-thirds, vote of the holders. Starting with Ecuador's debt restructuring in 2000, sovereigns have taken advantage of this feature of their debt contracts to employ a technique known as an 'exit consent'. The tactical objective of an exit consent is to amend the instruments that will be left in the hands of holdout creditors after the restructuring closes in a manner that will make those instruments less valuable or more difficult to enforce. Confronted with the prospect of continuing to hold such a defaced instrument (the theory goes), the prospective holdout will reconsider the wisdom of holding out.

2.18 It works like this: the sovereign debtor embeds in its exchange offer a provision by which each participating creditor agrees to one or more amendments to the bonds that it is tendering

---

[6] Federation of Saint Christopher (St Kitts) and Nevis, *Offer to Exchange*, Offering Memorandum, 27 February 2012, 44.

[7] Belize, *Offer to Exchange*, Offering Memorandum, 18 December 2006, 14.

[8] *See* Chapter 1, titled 'Minimizing Holdout Creditors: Carrots'.

in the exchange. These amendments cannot affect *payment* terms if the instrument in question calls for unanimous creditor consent to changes to payment provisions, but they could, for example, change the governing law of the old bonds, strip out or amend the waiver of sovereign immunity, remove the acceleration remedy, delete events of default, and so forth—matters that require approval by only a majority of holders. The intended effect of these amendments is to render these old bonds less valuable in the hands of holdouts, thus altering the balance of the relative judgement described at paragraph 2.16.

The theory of exit consents is that tendering bondholders will not care about defacing their existing bonds; after all, by tendering in the exchange, they have already evidenced their intention to shed those old bonds (the 'exit' part of an exit consent). But between the time that they submit their tenders and the point at which their old bonds are accepted in the exchange and cancelled, the participating bondholders remain the legal owners of the old bonds and are entitled to give their consent to proposed amendments (the 'consent' part). **2.19**

Why amend a debt instrument that one is about to jettison? The simple answer is that participating lenders have a direct and legitimate interest in encouraging all of their fellow creditors to join the party.[9] Holdout creditors represent a litigation and attachment threat to the debtor's assets, the very assets from which participating creditors hope to be repaid in the future. Moreover, as the Argentine holdout litigation has now graphically demonstrated, holdouts may seek to gain leverage over the borrower by attempting to interfere with the borrower's payments to the lenders participating in the debt restructuring.[10] Suppressing and de-fanging holdouts should therefore be a matter of considerable importance to those lenders that have decided to accept the sovereign's exchange offer. **2.20**

Ecuador was the first country to use exit consents in a sovereign bond exchange in 2000.[11] Since then, the technique has become a conventional part of the sovereign debtor's arsenal in debt restructurings that involve exchange offers. Interestingly, before the Argentine litigation demonstrated that holdouts represent a clear and present danger to their fellow creditors, some contract drafters actually felt it appropriate to narrow the scope for future exit consents by adding items such as changes to governing law or sovereign immunity to the list of amendments requiring the unanimous consent of holders. **2.21**

One exit consent used by Uruguay in its 2003 restructuring addressed directly the problem of holdout creditors attempting to interfere with a sovereign borrower's payments on the new bonds that it issues in a debt exchange. US law gives foreign state property in the United States a complete immunity from pre-judgment attachment unless the foreign state has expressly waived that immunity. In addition, absent an express or implied waiver, a creditor can attach such property after receiving a judgment only if it is the very property upon which the judgment creditor's claim is based. Uruguay had given such express waivers in each of the bonds covered by its 2003 debt restructuring. Uruguay therefore sought and received in its exchange offer an exit consent that revoked its prior express waiver of immunity to the extent—but *only* to the extent—that it applied to the payments under Uruguay's new bonds. **2.22**

---

[9] *See* Lee C. Buchheit and G. Mitu Gulati, 'Exit Consents in Sovereign Bond Exchanges' (2000) 48 UCLA L Rev 59, 82–3.

[10] *See NML Capital Ltd v. Republic of Argentina*, 699 F. Supp. 246 (2d Cir. 2012).

[11] *See* Lee C. Buchheit, 'How Ecuador Beat the Brady Bond Trap' (2000) 19 Int'l Fin L Rev 17.

The effect of this amendment was to re-immunize those payment streams (to the extent that they take place in the United States) from attachment by holdout creditors.[12]

ii. Immunize debtor assets

2.23 The exit consent that re-immunized Uruguayan assets from attachment by holdout creditors in 2003 prefigured a much more sweeping action by the United Nations Security Council (UNSC) following the ousting of Saddam Hussein in that same year. By the time he was asked to leave office, Saddam had accumulated a debt stock, most of it in default, equal to about US$140 billion. Iraq's economic recovery following the removal of the Saddam regime depended critically upon a satisfactory resolution of that gargantuan debt stock. UNSC Resolution 1483 (22 May 2003) was the instrument by which the international community sought to facilitate this debt restructuring.[13]

2.24 Among other things, Resolution 1483 strongly encouraged both Iraq and its Saddam-era creditors (official and private) to set about a comprehensive restructuring of those debts. Recognizing that holdouts in such a restructuring could significantly undermine its effectiveness, however, the Security Council immunized all petroleum assets of Iraq against 'any form of attachment, garnishment, or execution', and clothed the proceeds of Iraqi oil sales (as well as the bank account into which the proceeds of all such oil sales were to be directed) with privileges and immunities identical to those enjoyed by the United Nations itself.[14] The obvious and intended effect of immunizing Iraqi assets in this way was to deflate any expectation on the part of prospective holdout creditors that a better recovery might follow litigation and enforcement of a judgment. The UNSC-mandated immunities for Iraq remained in place through the middle of 2011[15]—long enough for Iraq to complete a successful restructuring of its Saddam-era debt stock that imposed an 89.75 per cent net present value loss on the affected creditors. Resolution 1483 was later described by the US Congressional Research Service as 'a stay on the enforcement' of debt claims.[16]

2.25 It has been proposed elsewhere[17] that the 2012 Treaty Establishing the European Stability Mechanism might be amended to immunize, within the eurozone, the assets of a debtor country receiving financial support from the European Stability Mechanism (ESM—the European bailout fund) against attachment by a creditor who was invited to participate in

---

[12] *See* Lee C. Buchheit and Jeremiah S. Pam, 'Uruguay's Innovations' (2004) 19 J Int'l Banking L & Reg 28.

[13] Available online at <http://www.un.org/ga/search/view_doc.asp?symbol=S/RES/1483%282003%29>.

[14] UNSC Resolution 1483 (n. 13), para. 22.

[15] *See* UNSC Resolution 1956, available online at <http://www.un.org/ga/search/view_doc.asp?symbol=S/RES/1956%282010%29>.

[16] Congressional Research Service, *Iraq's Debt Relief: Procedure and Potential Implications for International Debt Relief*, 6 December 2006, at CRS-11. Note, too, at CRS-13:

> The Iraq case thus illustrates that the United States and the international community are willing to shield a debtor from its creditors bankruptcy regime. This can be accomplished multilaterally through U.N. Security Council Resolutions or bilaterally, on a case-by-case basis, through executive orders. Since these measures were not taken in other recent financial crisis-afflicted countries, such as Argentina or Brazil, it appears that policymakers are only willing to use such measures selectively, and for countries that exhibit a perceived threat to U.S. and international security. This understanding is made more explicit by implementing the stay through the United Nations, a political institution seen principally as focused on international security, rather than the International Monetary Fund, which is primarily a financial institution.

[17] *See* Lee C. Buchheit, Mitu Gulati, and Ignacio Tirado, 'The Problem of Holdout Creditors in Eurozone Sovereign Debt Restructurings' [2013] 4 JIBFL 191.

an ESM-approved debt restructuring, but declined to do so. The objective of such a measure would be similar to UNSC Resolution 1483 for Iraq: to encourage creditor participation in debt restructurings by dimming the outlook for a successful alternative litigation strategy.

C. Bind them

Concerns about the disruptive effect of holdout creditors contributed to the movement to find a method for binding dissenting minorities in sovereign debt workouts. Three ideas were put forward at roughly the same time (2001–03): a formal sovereign debt restructuring mechanism (SDRM), modelled on Chapter 11 of the US Bankruptcy Code; wider use of collective action clauses (CACs) in sovereign bonds; and, for certain types of debt restructuring, use of the US federal class action mechanism to bind all holders to a debt settlement acceptable to a supermajority of creditors. To date, only one idea—CACs—has prospered. **2.26**

i. Sovereign debt restructuring mechanism (SDRM)

The absence of a formal bankruptcy mechanism for sovereigns has long attracted academic comment.[18] In late 2001, one month before Argentina's default on approximately US$100 billion of bond indebtedness, the deputy managing director of the International Monetary Fund (IMF), Anne Krueger, made a specific proposal to fill that gap.[19] The SDRM, as Krueger proposed it, was intended to replicate the main features of a Chapter 11 corporate bankruptcy reorganization: an automatic stay on creditor enforcement actions; supermajority creditor control of the process; and a quasijudicial oversight body.[20] **2.27**

After considerable work on the design of the SDRM, the idea was eventually dropped in the face of political opposition from certain large shareholders of the IMF—particularly the United States.[21] The eurozone debt crisis, coupled with some recent judicial successes by holdouts in the Argentine restructuring, has prompted a renewed interest in an SDRM-like solution. **2.28**

ii. Collective action clauses (CACs)

The SDRM found itself in an unexpected foot race in 2002; its competitor, strongly backed by the US Treasury, was a proposal to expand the use of CACs in sovereign bonds as a means of facilitating a restructuring of those instruments should that become necessary. The CAC is a contractual provision in multi-creditor debt instruments that permits a specified supermajority of holders to agree to a modification of the instrument—even a modification affecting payment terms—with the consequence that this decision will bind any dissenting minority holders. **2.29**

From its inception (in England in 1879), the CAC approach has had only one purpose: to eliminate the problem of holdout creditors in a bond restructuring. The author of that first CAC described its objective as follows: **2.30**

> The object of conferring this power on the majority is to protect it against unreasonable conduct on the part of the minority, and to prevent a deadlock happening when unanimity cannot

---

[18] Kenneth Rogoff and Jeromin Zettelmeyer, *Bankruptcy Procedures for Sovereigns: A History of Ideas, 1976–2001*, IMF Working Paper No. 02/133 (August 2002), available online at <http://www.imf.org/external/pubs/ft/wp/2002/wp02133.pdf>.

[19] Anne Krueger, 'International Financial Architecture for 2002: New Approach to Sovereign Debt Restructuring', Speech at the National Economists' Club Annual Members' Dinner, 26 November 2001, available online at <http://www.imf.org/external/np/speeches/2001/112601.htm>.

[20] *See* Sean Hagan, 'Designing a Legal Framework to Restructure Sovereign Debt' (2005) 36 Georgetown J Int'l Law 299, 341–4.

[21] Hagan (n. 20), 390–4.

> be obtained. Unless the majority is thus enabled, in special circumstances, to determine what is to be done on behalf of the whole body, the minority is placed in a position to dictate to the majority, and the whole of the majority, however large, may be placed in peril by the stupidity, fraud or greed of an insignificant minority, or by the delay which would result if it were necessary to obtain the consent of every debenture or stock holder.[22]

2.31 Although commonplace in both corporate and sovereign bonds governed by English law since the late nineteenth century, CACs had made only limited inroads into US law-governed bonds in the early twentieth century.[23] There was, however, no public policy objection to the use of CACs in sovereign bonds issued in the United States and a G-10 working group recommended in 2002 that these provisions become a standard feature in the sovereign bonds of emerging market issuers.[24]

2.32 Collective action clauses began to appear in New York law-governed sovereign bonds starting in early 2003. Ten years later, they have become a nearly invariable feature of sovereign bond documentation. At the time of writing, however, only one country has used a CAC in its New York law-governed bonds to restructure those instruments: Belize did so in its debt restructuring of 2007,[25] and again in its restructuring of 2013.[26]

iii. Class action mechanisms

2.33 A third idea for addressing the problem of holdout creditors in a sovereign debt restructuring was floated in 2002.[27] It suggested that the class action mechanism contained in the US Federal Rules of Civil Procedure (FRCP) might provide a procedural framework for ensuring that a sovereign debt restructuring (at least one covering bonds governed by the law of a US jurisdiction) acceptable to the broad majority of holders could become binding on all similarly situated creditors. The device would involve a mandatory class action under FRCP 23(b)(1)(B).

2.34 Under that Rule, a mandatory class action is suitable where:

> . . . adjudications with respect to individual members of the class . . . would as a practical matter be dispositive of the interests of the other members not parties to the adjudications or substantially impair or impede their ability to protect their interests . . . [28]

In a sovereign debt context, the theory is that the sovereign has only a limited amount of resources that it can devote to future debt service. Allowing the more aggressive or litigious creditors to deplete that limited fund of assets would result only in the vast majority of similarly situated creditors having to settle for the dregs. The FRCP mandatory class action mechanism is the only existing procedural device in the United States by which the majority of creditors can ensure a rateable allocation of the sovereign's debt servicing capacity in the future.

---

[22] Francis Beaufort Palmer, *Company Precedents*, 6th edn (1895), 651.

[23] The reasons for the limited use of CACs in the United States during this period are of only historical interest. *See* Lee C. Buchheit and G. Mitu Gulati, 'Sovereign Bonds and the Collective Will' (2002) 51 Emory LJ 1317, 1326.

[24] *See* Group of Ten (G-10), *Report of the G-10 Working Group on Contractual Clauses* (26 September 2002), available online at <http://www.bis.org/publ/gten08.htm>.

[25] *See* Lee C. Buchheit and Elizabeth Karpinski, 'Belize's Innovations' (2007) 22 JIBFL 278.

[26] *See* Government of Belize, 'Belize Debt Exchange Offer Successful', Press release, 8 March 2013, available online at <https://www.centralbank.org.bz/docs/rsh-1.7-information-for-creditors/press-release---belize-debt-exchange-offer-successful-march-08-2013.pdf?sfvrsn=2>.

[27] *See* Buchheit and Gulati (n. 23), 1352–7.

[28] Quoted in Buchheit and Gulati (n. 23), 1353.

4. Conclusion

In the end, the question comes down to this: are the problems posed by holdout creditors in a sovereign debt restructuring sufficiently serious to warrant remedies such as a full-blown SDRM-type mechanism, or even a more limited measure, such as expanding the category of state assets that will be immunized from attachment by litigious holdouts? Some recent analyses suggest that holdouts are not the lethal threat to sovereign debt restructurings that the newspaper headlines might lead one to believe.[29] In truth, given the aggregate size of the sovereign debts that have been restructured over the last thirty years, the number of successful holdout legal actions has been surprisingly small. **2.35**

That said, holdout behaviour is infectious. The limited nature of the holdout problem to date may be explained by the fact that most holdouts have not been able to realize preferential recoveries in comparison with their colleagues who joined sovereign debt restructurings. But this could change very quickly if holdouts were to begin to prosper. Greece, for example, elected to pay the limited number of holdouts from its 2012 debt restructuring (approximately 3 per cent of the total eligible debt stock) in full. A well-publicized litigation success of a creditor that spurned a sovereign's debt restructuring will also spark copycat behaviour in the next debt workout for the next country. **2.36**

History tells us that creditor majorities will eventually find ways in which to protect themselves against exploitative minorities, just as minorities eventually safeguard themselves against oppressive or abusive behaviour by creditor majorities. In the late nineteenth century, the solution devised to the holdout creditor problem in corporate bonds was the collective action clause—precisely the same solution that has been resurrected in the early twenty-first century for sovereign bonds. A fundamental principle of all corporate insolvency regimes is the rateable treatment of similarly situated creditors. That is the principle that would have guided—and may still guide—an SDRM-type solution for sovereign workouts. Creditor majorities are suspicious of uncooperative minorities; the sentiment is usually requited by the minorities. But both are suspicious of debtors who may perceive, in the internecine feuds of its creditor group, an opportunity to secure unjustifiable concessions. **2.37**

[29] *See* Moody's Investors Service, 'The Role of Holdout Creditors and CACs in Sovereign Debt Restructurings', 19 March 2013, available to subscribers online at <http://www.moodys.com/research/Sovereign-Defaults-Series-The-Role-of-Holdout-Creditors-and-CACs--PBC_150162> ('Concerns about free rider problems have proven exaggerated as well').

3

MANAGING HOLDOUTS

The Case of the 2012 Greek Exchange

Jeromin Zettelmeyer, Christoph Trebesch, and G. Mitu Gulati

1. Introduction: Argentina versus Greece

Perhaps the most discussed issue in the modern literature on sovereign debt restructurings is how to manage holdout creditors. Argentina's long battle with holdouts provides an illustration. More than eleven years after its default in 2001, Argentina is still mired in litigation against hundreds of creditors in multiple fora. It is so fearful of creditors being able to attach its assets that it spends considerable resources every year in hiding them. For those same reasons, we suspect, it has also avoided re-entering the international bond markets. By contrast, in March 2012, Greece conducted what is arguably the largest sovereign debt restructuring in history, imposing haircuts on creditors larger than those that Argentina did in its 2005 and 2010 exchanges, and yet Greece has largely escaped creditor litigation. This chapter sets out the facts of the Greek exchange that explain why it was able to sidestep the problem of holdout creditors.[1] **3.01**

It is fitting that we are telling this story in a volume in honour of Lee Buchheit. Few will dispute that Lee's skill and brilliance as a debt restructurer enabled the Greek restructuring to occur in the way that it did. His illustrious career has seen him introduce numerous innovative techniques to engineer restructurings and obtain large volumes of debt relief for a multitude of sovereigns over the years. The Greek deal, though, may well be his most spectacular achievement. **3.02**

We cannot begin to do justice to the struggles that engineering this deal took. Suffice it to say that there was enormous drama. That story will hopefully get told by one of the many journalists who followed the Greek debt drama. Our story is going to be drier—more about numbers and legal concepts—but no less important (we think). We begin with a description of the exchange and then move on to the techniques used by Greece to induce creditors to enter the exchange. **3.03**

[1] For a fuller treatment of the Greek 2012 exchange, *see* Jeromin Zettelmeyer, Christoph Trebesch, and Mitu Gulati, 'The Greek Debt Restructuring: An Autopsy', *Economic Policy* (forthcoming).

2. The Basics

3.04 The Greek restructuring process was as a hybrid between a negotiation led by a steering committee of creditors—along the lines of the 'London Club' restructuring of bank loans in the 1980s and early 1990s—and a take-it-or-leave-it debt exchange offer, which was typical of most bond restructurings since the late 1990s. The latter took place after the negotiations had been completed. Between November 2011 and late February 2012, Greece engaged in formal negotiations with a group of creditors led by a steering group of twelve banks, insurers, and asset managers on behalf of a larger group of thirty-two creditors. On 21 February 2012, Greece and the steering committee announced, in parallel press releases, that the terms of the offer had been agreed.

3.05 The rebirth of the creditor committee was likely the result of the fact that much of Greece's outstanding debt was held by large banks. The last time commercial banks played such a dominant role in a debt exchange operation was during the 1980s debt crisis, when large US and European banks held most of the defaulted debt of Latin American or African sovereigns. In contrast, recent bond exchanges in emerging markets have typically had a more dispersed creditor structure, with institutional investors holding most of the debt.[2]

3.06 Table 3.1 provides an overview of the Greek creditor committee. The thirty-two committee members held between 30 and 40 per cent of Greece's debt to private creditors. The largest single bondholder, however, was the European Central Bank (ECB), with €42.7 billion (16.3 per cent) of total bonds outstanding. The majority of those bonds were purchased during 2010 through the ECB's Securities Market Programme (SMP) at a time when the official sector assumed that no restructuring of the Greek debt would become necessary. In addition, national central banks, such as the Banque du France or the Bank of Italy, held €13.5 billion of Greek bonds—about 5 per cent of the total.

3.07 In addition to serving as a coordination device among Greece's largest private sector bondholders, the committee served as a point of contact for Greece's official creditors, in particular the International Monetary Fund (IMF), the European Union (EU), and the ECB, which were indirectly involved throughout the negotiation process. This likely helped in designing some features of the deal, such as the co-financing agreement between Greece and the European Financial Stability Fund (EFSF), which might have been more difficult without some form of formal creditor representation.

A. Terms and conditions

3.08 Greece's debt restructuring proposal, published on 24 February 2012, was directed at the holders of all its sovereign bonds issued prior to 2012,[3] with a total face value of €195.7 billion, as well as thirty-six sovereign-guaranteed bonds issued by public enterprises (railways, defence systems, and Athens public transport) with face value of just under €10 billion. The

[2] *See* Udaibir Das, Michael G. Papaioannou, and Christoph Trebesch, *Sovereign Debt Restructurings 1950–2010: Literature Survey, Data, and Stylized Facts*, IMF Working Paper 12/203 (August 2012), available online at <http://www.un.org/esa/ffd/ecosoc/debt/2013/IMF_wp12_203.pdf>, Table 4. The 1990s debt crisis in Russia is a further exception, because Western banks played an important role in the restructuring of Soviet-era debt in 1997 and again in 2000.

[3] Depending on how one counts them, eight-one or ninety-nine issues. Eighteen Greek-law titles were listed using two different bond International Securities Identification Numbers (ISINs).

Table 3.1 Composition and estimated Greek bond holdings of creditor committee

Steering Commitee (12 members)		Further members of the Creditor Committee			
	Holdings (€ bn)		Holdings (€ bn)		Holdings (€ bn)
Allianz (Germany)	1.3	Ageas (Belgium)	1.2	MACSF (France)	n/a
Alpha Eurobank (Greece)	3.7	Bank of Cyprus	1.8	Marathon (US)	n/a
Axa (France)	1.9	Bayern LB (Germany)	n/a	Marfin (Greece)	2.3
BNP Paribas (France)	5.0	BBVA (Spain)	n/a	Metlife (US)	n/a
CNP Assurances (France)	2.0	BPCE (France)	1.2	Piraeus Bank (Greece)	9.4
Commerzbank (Germany)	2.9	Credit Agricole (France)	0.6	RBS (UK)	1.1
Deutsche Bank (Germany)	1.6	DekaBank (Germany)	n/a	Société Gén. (France)	2.9
Greylock Capital (US)	n/a	Dexia (Belg/Lux/Fra)	3.5	Unicredit (Italy)	0.9
Intesa San Paolo (Italy)	0.8	Emporiki (Greece/France)	n/a		
Landesbank BW (Germany)	1.4	Generali (Italy)	3.0		
ING (France)	1.4	Groupama (France)	2.0		
National Bank of Greece	13.7	HSBC (UK)	0.8		

Sources: See Jeromin Zettelmeyer, Christoph Trebesch, and Mitu Gulati, 'The Greek Debt Restructuring: An Autopsy', *Economic Policy* (forthcoming).

large majority of the sovereign bonds—€177.3 billion of €195.7 billion in face value, almost 91 per cent—had been issued under Greek law, while the guaranteed bonds were fairly evenly divided between foreign and domestic law issues. Importantly, the proposal excluded the bond holdings of the ECB and other central banks: just ahead of the publication of the offer, these had been swapped into a new series with identical payment terms and maturity dates.[4] It has also been suggested that a large number of sovereign guaranteed loans and bonds—perhaps as many as 600 such instruments—may have been left out of the exchange.

For the large majority of bondholders—all holders of Greek-law sovereign bonds, plus all holders of English-law bonds, both sovereign and guaranteed, amounting to about €197 billion—Greece's 'invitation' comprised two components:[5] **3.09**

- an offer to exchange the bonds against a package of new securities, referred to as the 'private sector involvement (PSI) consideration' in Greece's official communications, which package comprised:
  (i) one- and two-year notes issued by the EFSF, amounting to 15 per cent of the old debt's face value;

[4] As part of this swap arrangement, the ECB committed to return any profits made through its Greek government bond holdings to its shareholders.

[5] There were also a small number of bonds under other laws (Swiss, Japanese, and Italian).

(ii) twenty new government bonds maturing between 2023 and 2042, amounting to 31.5 per cent of the old debt's face value, with annual coupons of between 2 and 4.3 per cent, which bonds were issued under English law and governed by a 'co-financing agreement' with the EFSF, which instituted a sharing provision for the private bondholders vis-à-vis the EFSF; and

(iii) a security linked to gross domestic product (GDP), which could provide an extra payment stream of up to one percentage point of the face value of the outstanding new bonds if GDP were to exceed a specified target path; and

- a 'consent solicitation', in which bondholders were asked to vote for an amendment of the bonds that permitted Greece to exchange the bonds for the new package of securities.

3.10 Bondholders that accepted the offer (or those that held bonds which were successfully amended) would also be compensated for any accrued interest still owed by the old bonds, in the form of six-month EFSF notes.

3.11 The two components of the invitation were linked: by accepting the exchange offer, bondholders would be simultaneously voting in favour of the amendment. Alternatively, they could choose to ignore or reject the exchange offer, but in this case they were deemed to have voted against the amendment only if they submitted a specific instruction to that effect.

3.12 The rules for accepting the amendment differed according to their governing law and the bond contract. In the case of the English-law bonds, the amendment rules were laid out in 'collective action clauses' (CACs) contained in the original bond contracts. Typically, these envisaged a quorum requirement (that is, a minimum threshold of voter participation to declare a vote valid) of between two-thirds and 75 per cent in a first attempt, followed by a lower quorum of between one third and 50 per cent in a second ('adjourned') meeting if the initial quorum requirement was not met. Assuming that the quorum was met, the threshold for passing the amendment was usually between two-thirds and 75 per cent of face-value-weighted votes in the first meeting, and might be as low as 33.33 per cent at the second meeting. If the second meeting failed to produce a result, the amendment attempt failed.

3.13 The Greek-law sovereign bonds contained no such CACs, which, in theory, meant that these bonds could be restructured only with the unanimous consent of all bondholders. In other words, they would have been near impossible to restructure. This is where Lee comes in. Early in 2010, well before the idea of restructuring the Greek debt was being taken seriously, he had noticed the fact that the overwhelming majority (more than 90 per cent) of the outstanding Greek bonds had been issued under local Greek law. That meant that the bond contracts could be changed by Greece simply by passing a new law. In theory, Greece could have used this instrument to legislate different payment terms, or to give itself the power to exchange the bonds for the new securities. But Lee recognized that this may have been viewed as an expropriation of bondholders by legislative fiat, and could have been challenged under the Greek Constitution, the European Convention on Human Rights, and principles of customary international law. Instead, Lee advocated that Greece use its control of the local law to superimpose a form of creditor democracy onto the bonds—a mechanism by which the creditors themselves could vote on whether they wanted the proposed restructuring or not.

3.14 Following Lee's counsel, the Greek legislature passed a law on 23 February 2012 (the Greek Bondholder Act 2012) that imposed CACs on all of Greece's local law bonds. These CACs allowed the restructuring of the Greek law bonds with the consent of a qualified majority, based on a quorum of votes representing 50 per cent of face value and a consent threshold of two-thirds of the face value voters taking part in the vote. Importantly, this quorum and threshold applied across the totality of all €177.3 billion Greek law sovereign bonds outstanding, rather than bond by bond. While this 'retrofit CAC' gave bondholders collectively a say over the restructuring that was roughly analogous to that afforded to English-law bondholders, the sheer size of purchase that would have been necessary for bondholders to establish a blocking position made it near impossible for individual bondholders (or coalitions of bondholders) to block the restructuring.

The offer was subject to conditions: a 'financing condition' that made the offer contingent on Greece obtaining the EFSF notes that were to be delivered to creditors in the exchange (this in turn depended on the completion of some prior actions under Greece's IMF- and EU-supported programme); and a 'minimum participation condition', according to which the proposed exchange and amendments would *not* go forward if this were to result in a restructuring of less than 75 per cent of face value. Conditions of the type had been used in most debt exchange offers since the mid-1990s to reassure tendering bondholders that they would not be left out in the cold (that is, holding a smaller, and potentially illiquid, claim) in the event that most other bondholders chose not to accept the offer. **3.15**

At the same time, the threshold for unequivocally going forward with the exchange and amendments was set at 90 per cent of total participation (including via amended bonds). This implied, in particular, that if Greece were to succeed with its attempt to amend its domestic law sovereign bonds within the framework set out by the 2012 Act, the exchange would likely go forward, since the Greek-law sovereign bonds alone amounted to about 86 per cent of the total eligible debt. Between the two thresholds, Greece would allow itself discretion 'in consultation with its official sector creditors' on whether or not to proceed with the exchange and amendments. **3.16**

Greece gave its creditors two weeks in which to accept or reject the offer. This tight deadline was the result of the pressure to complete at least the domestic-law component of the exchange before 20 March, when a large Greek-law bond issue was coming due for repayment. Specifically, bond tenders and/or votes on the proposed amendments had to be registered by 8 March, with bondholder meetings for the foreign-law bonds scheduled to take place later that month. **3.17**

B. Outcome of the restructuring

On 9 March, the Greek ministry of finance announced that, out of the €177.3 billion in sovereign bonds issued under domestic law, €146.2 billion had accepted the exchange offer and consent solicitation, €5.9 billion had consented to the amendment without tendering their bonds, and €9.3 billion had voted against. Hence the quorum and voting thresholds for amending the Greek sovereign bonds were easily met. In addition, €6.4 billion out of €6.7 billion in Greek-law guaranteed debt was tendered for exchange. Participation among the foreign-law bondholders was lower: out of a total of €21.6 billion foreign-law bonds (both sovereign and sovereign-guaranteed), exchange tenders and amendment consents were received for only €13.1 billion. **3.18**

In sum, the government's minimum participation condition was met by a wide margin: following the application of the new Act, the sum of amended domestic law sovereign bonds (€177.3 billion) and tendered guaranteed and foreign bonds would amount to at least **3.19**

€196.8 billion (95.7 per cent). Since EFSF financing had also been made available in the meantime, the government announced that it would proceed with the exchange, invoking the 2012 Act and exchanging all Greek-law sovereign bonds. At the same time, the participation deadline for all foreign-law bondholders was extended—initially to 23 March and subsequently to 4 April.

3.20 On 12 March 2012, all Greek-law sovereign bonds were exchanged for the new 'package' of English-law sovereign bonds, EFSF notes, and accrued interest notes. Greece's twenty new bonds started trading, at yields in the range of just under 14 per cent (longer bonds) to about 17.5 per cent (shorter bonds). Weighted by principal, the average 'exit yield' was 15.3 per cent. While not unusually high compared to emerging market debt restructurings of the past, this was higher than the sovereign yield of any other euro area country at the time.

3.21 Greece's exchanged or amended foreign-law or guaranteed instruments settled in two batches, on 11 and 25 April. The latter became necessary to accommodate some of the adjourned bondholder meetings—that is, when a second meeting had become necessary because the initial meetings, held in late March, had not obtained a quorum.

3.22 By the end of the process, Greece had achieved total participation of €199.2 billion, or 96.9 per cent. Holders of €6.4 billion of eligible debt (3.1 per cent of the total) held out. The holdouts were scattered across twenty-five sovereign or sovereign-guaranteed bonds, of which twenty-four were foreign-law titles: seven bonds for which no amendment was attempted; one inquorate bond; and sixteen bonds for which the amendment was rejected by the bondholders. In addition, there were holdouts for one Greek-law guaranteed bond (an Athens Urban Transport bond maturing in 2013). All other Greek-law sovereign and sovereign-guaranteed bonds were amended and exchanged in full.

3.23 The question of whether Greece should default on the holdouts has reportedly been a subject of debate within the Greek government. At time of writing in September 2013, the opponents of default have prevailed. The first bond involving holdouts—an English-law title with an outstanding face value of €435 million owned almost entirely by Dart Management, a distressed debt fund—was repaid on 15 May 2012.

3. Why Did the Restructuring Succeed? Creditor Incentives

3.24 Each holder of Greek bonds, even members of the steering committee that negotiated the terms of the exchange offer with Greece, was in principle free to accept or reject Greece's exchange offer. This leads to the question of what ultimately induced the high creditor participation of almost 97 per cent, notwithstanding a present value haircut of more than 50 per cent for all but the most long-term creditors and over 75 per cent for bonds with short residual maturities.

3.25 For the large creditors—and in particular, the large European banks—there is an answer: without their participation, the restructuring would have fallen apart, leading almost inevitably to a disorderly default. Further, any attempt to freeride was, or would have been, squashed by their home country authorities, who were also Greece's official creditors. Hence it is not surprising that, on 6 March, just prior to the exchange deadline, the major members of the creditor committee that had negotiated with Greece released press statements that they were committed to participate in the offer.

However, based on estimates by markets analysts, by early 2012, institutions that were either large enough to internalize their impact on the deal or susceptible to official pressure held at most €120 billion out of the almost €200 billion that were eventually exchanged. The question is how the exchange dealt with the remaining €80 billion (at least) of potential freeriders. To answer this, it is useful to step back in history. **3.26**

The freerider problem is inherent in all take-it-or-leave-it exchange offers. Conditional on acceptance of the offer by the remaining creditors, all but very large creditors—whose failure to participate would by itself trigger a disorderly default—should have an incentive to 'hold out' for full repayment or better terms. Indeed, as a matter of historic fact, holdouts *do* tend to be repaid in full, or settle on better terms than the majority that accepts an exchange offer. Anticipating this, all small creditors should want to be holdouts. And yet this is not the case: almost all debt exchange offers, starting with the Brady deals of the 1990s, have been successes in the sense that creditor participation has been very high. It follows that debtors (and/or creditors collectively) must have found some way of dissuading potential holdouts. **3.27**

To a first approximation, one can distinguish between three mechanisms. First, countries can deter freeriding by creating the expectation that holdouts may well receive a worse deal than participating creditors (including nothing). This sometimes happens implicitly—by creating ambiguity about how holdouts will be treated—but more often through explicit threats. In some cases, such as Argentina's 2005 restructuring, these threats have been backed up by action. Threatening not to repay holdouts is particularly credible when a country has already defaulted—that is, the exchange constitutes an attempt to reach a settlement with a majority of creditors. **3.28**

Second, freeriding can be legally suppressed if the bond to be restructured is equipped with a CAC that allows a qualified majority of creditors to change the payment terms of the bonds against the opposition of a group of holdouts. However, notwithstanding a steady stream of advocacy from lawyers and economists since the mid-1990s, the actual use of such clauses in sovereign debt restructurings had remained limited. The reason for this was in part that there was a strong norm in the New York market of requiring unanimous approval from the bondholders before any change in payment terms could be binding on all. This norm changed only in 2003. Further, even when there were CACs, these were of limited utility in big restructurings involving dozens, if not hundreds, of bond issues, because these clauses had to be voted on bond by bond, and holdouts could acquire blocking positions in individual bond issues. **3.29**

Finally, countries can give potential freeriders an incentive to tender by offering instruments that are perceived to afford better protection from a *future* sovereign default. This can be achieved in several ways, by offering investors either collateralized securities, cash, securities issued by a more creditworthy borrower, or securities that would be harder to restructure in a future default and hence de facto senior. The best-known examples in this category are the 'Brady bonds'—the international bonds offered to bank creditors that had suffered default in the 1980s. Having survived unscathed throughout the default period, international bonds were perceived as safer (and potentially more liquid) than bank debt; furthermore, the principal of the new bonds was collateralized using US Treasury bonds. Another example was the Russian 2000 debt exchange, which replaced restructured Soviet-era debt that was technically owed by a state-owned bank with Eurobonds owed directly by the Russian sovereign, and issued under foreign law, which had not defaulted on its international debt. The signal was that Russia would be less likely to default on these bonds in the future. **3.30**

3.31 Greece's evolving debt exchange plan started out as an attempt to deal with freeriding only through the last mechanism—as a purely voluntary offer involving an upgrade from Greek law to English law, combined with either collateralized principal or a payout in the form of cash or very safe short-term bills—but eventually added the second mechanism—CACs, 'retrofitted' through an Act of Parliament—and finally, at the last minute, the first—an explicit threat that holdouts might do worse than non-participating creditors. Hence, in the end, Greece relied on all three classes of mechanism to dissuade freeriders. However, there were differences compared to previous debt restructuring in *how* it used these instruments, which included several legal and institutional innovations.

A. Carrots: EFSF bills and a de facto seniority upgrade

3.32 The notion that the Greek exchange would be strictly voluntary—in the sense that no creditor would be forced to participate—was a constant mantra of both Greece and most of its official creditors from the moment at which the inevitability of a debt restructuring was finally, in mid-2011, accepted by the official sector. This continued even after it became clear, following the 26 October Brussels Eurogroup summit, that Greece would have no choice but to seek a much deeper debt relief than the one originally envisaged in July, and changed only in late January 2012, when Greek policymakers began to contemplate openly the possibility of 'retrofitting' CACs to Greek law bonds in order to bind holdouts.

3.33 The question is whether the idea of a purely voluntary restructuring combined with a deep haircut ever made any sense, and if so, what would incentivize it. The notion of a purely voluntary exchange with high participation had some plausibility in the case of Greece—ironically, because many market participants did *not* believe that even a successful exchange would restore Greece's debt to a sustainable level. In such a situation, creditors (even small ones that can freeride) might be willing to trade their debt instrument for a new bundle at a loss, if the bundle includes some cash upfront and/or bonds that are perceived to be harder to restructure in a new crisis (for example because they are issued under foreign law). Offering such a debt instrument can act as a stick as well as carrot, since holdouts risk being left with an inferior debt instrument that may have little or no value in the event of a future default (namely, Greek-law bonds the terms of which can be unilaterally changed through an Act of Parliament).

3.34 The limitation of this argument was that it did not apply to short-term bondholders, for whom the risk of being caught by a new default following a (temporarily) successful voluntary debt exchange was low, nor, of course, to holders of foreign-law bonds. As a result, asking bondholders to accept a large reduction in promised payments in exchange for 15 cents on the euro in cash and somewhat safer (English-law) instruments was unlikely to persuade this subset of investors. Perhaps in recognition of this—and in light of a tough line by the official sector, whose financing package was predicated on almost full private sector participation—the Greek government decided to abandon the voluntary framework.

3.35 It did not, however, abandon the idea of offering cash and a de facto seniority upgrade as a way of incentivizing acceptance of the exchange offer. In the end, the offer had the flavour of offering a bird in the hand in exchange for two in the bush. Three factors contributed to this, as follows.

3.36 First, a large portion of the new securities bundle—15 per cent of original principal—took the form of highly rated EFSF bills that were almost as good as cash. While cash sweeteners had been used in past debt deals, the cash received by creditors—both as a share of original principal and particularly as a share of the total value received—was more modest. According to Cruces and Trebesch (2011),[6] average cash payments across some 180 debt restructurings since 1975 amounted to only 3.6 per cent. Importantly, these often compensated bondholders for arrears and past due or accrued interest rather than for forgoing *future* promised revenue, which was the exclusive purpose of the 15 cents on the euro in EFSF bills (there were no arrears in Greek restructuring and accrued interest was repaid separately). Moreover, in the case of Greece, the 15 cents on the euro in quasi-cash represented an outsized share of the value of the new bundle of securities—namely, almost two-thirds. Hence the Greece debt restructuring could be more accurately described as a fixed-price debt buyback with an added 'bond sweetener' rather than as a bond exchange with a cash sweetener.

Second, as already mentioned, the new bonds were issued under English law, and included standard creditor protections such as *pari passu*, negative pledge, and cross-default clauses. Greek-law sovereign bonds contained almost none of these standard protections. However, the contract provisions were arguably less important than the governing law. Greek-law bondholders who had just experienced the power of the local legislature to change contract provisions retroactively (see paragraph 3.43) would find some comfort in the fact that, in the event of a new restructuring, English law bonds would preclude a change of their contractual rights through the channel of legislative fiat. **3.37**

Finally, the new bonds were issued under a 'co-financing agreement' between Greece, the EFSF, a paying agent acting on behalf of Greece (initially, the Bank of Greece), and a trustee (Wilmington Trust Company) representing the interests of Greece's new bondholders and the EFSF.[7] The purpose was to create an exact symmetry between Greece's debt service to the new bondholders and its debt service to the EFSF related to the EFSF notes and bills that it had received for the purposes of the debt exchange (Greek debts to the EFSF unrelated to the debt restructuring were excluded from the co-financing agreement). In particular, Greece and the remaining signatories of the agreement committed to a payment schedule in which the EFSF and bondholders would be repaid pro rata and on the same day. In the event of a shortfall in payments by Greece, the common paying agent committed to allocating this shortfall pro rata between the EFSF and the bondholders. Hence the co-financing agreement made it difficult for Greece to default on its bondholders without also defaulting on the EFSF. **3.38**

The co-financing agreement also has features that give the creditors additional protection compared to a standard bond contract. In particular, the payment terms of the new bonds cannot be amended without the consent of the EFSF (and hence Greece's official creditor community). The consent of the EFSF is also required with respect to Greece issuing additional bonds beyond a specified ceiling known as the 'permitted aggregate principal amount', initially set at €70 billion, increased to a maximum of €90 billion. This gives Greece's official sector creditors a legal instrument to protect both themselves and Greece's new private bondholders against future dilution of their debts. It also effectively gives the European **3.39**

---

[6] *See* Juan J. Cruces and Christoph Trebesch, *Sovereign Defaults: The Price of Haircuts*, CESifo Working Paper 3604 (October 2011), available online at <http://papers.ssrn.com/sol3/papers.cfm?abstract_id=1943411>.

[7] Lee had contemplated using this idea as far back as 1988. *See* Lee C. Buchheit, 'Alternative Techniques of Sovereign Debt Restructuring' [1998] U Ill L Rev 371. However, in the 1980s, multilaterals had been reluctant to tie their fates to those of the private creditors.

countries that are EFSF shareholders control over an important aspect of Greece's public finances (its bond issuance to the private sector) over the thirty-year repayment period of the new bonds—that is, much beyond the horizon of the programme period. This commitment would remain if Greece were to abandon its EU–IMF-supported programme.

3.40 It is impossible to say exactly how much the upgrade in 'safety'—EFSF bonds plus enhanced creditor rights—contributed to the success of the exchange offer. However, the fact that over 82.5 per cent of Greek law bondholders exchanged their bonds and an additional 3.3 per cent voted in favour of the amendment suggests that it must have played some role. This participation level exceeded the holdings of the institutions that were either members of the steering committee or the Institute of International Finance (IIF), or otherwise susceptible to regulatory pressure from the official creditor countries by a wide margin—perhaps as much as 20 percentage points. Thus there must have been a contingent of potential freeriders that voluntarily opted in favour of the offer or amendment.

B. Collective action

3.41 Among the many records broken by the Greek debt restructuring is one relating to the extensive use of CACs as compared to previous debt restructurings. Among the foreign law bonds that had such clauses, Greece attempted to use them in all but the Japanese-law bonds (for which local securities laws would have made their activation too difficult within the short time frame envisaged). All in all, amendments based on CACs were tried in thirty-six cases and succeeded in seventeen of those.

3.42 The fact that only just under half of the amendments were successful illustrates the difficulties with using bond-by-bond CACs in comprehensive restructuring attempts, in which blocking minorities in one issue cannot be offset by pro-restructuring majorities elsewhere. Nonetheless, CACs in foreign-law bonds made a difference in the sense that final creditor participation among the foreign-law titles for which amendments were tried was about 78 per cent, as against just 31 per cent participation among the holders of foreign-law bonds that were only offered for exchange.

3.43 Unlike most foreign-law bonds, the Greek-law sovereign bonds had no possibility of amendment whatsoever. After it became clear that the freerider problem would likely preclude the desired high participation in the exchange unless Greece either threatened holdouts or introduced some form of collective action feature in the domestic-law bonds, Greece opted for the latter. An Act of Parliament passed on 23 February 2012 (one day before the formal exchange offer) allowed it to impose the new payment terms on holdouts with the agreement of two-thirds of face-value-weighted votes. Unlike the foreign-law bonds, this threshold applied across bonds rather than only bond by bond, subject only to a participation quorum of at least 50 per cent of face value. In the end, this aggregation feature turned out to be pivotal for the results of the debt exchange, allowing the restructuring of 100 per cent of the Greek-law sovereign bonds, which themselves made up over 86 per cent of the bonds covered by the restructuring.

3.44 The aggregation and voting rules defined by the new law walked a fine line between giving Greece a good chance to meet the required thresholds and avoiding drafting the 'retrofit collective action clause' in a way that would look too opportunistic or coercive, and therefore add legal risk. The broad aggregation feature, in which all outstanding Greek bonds were essentially treated as one, reflected the first objective. By dropping any bond-by-bond majority requirement, it went beyond previous sovereign bonds containing aggregation features (such as those issued as a result of the 2003 Uruguay and 2005 Argentina debt exchanges) that required both a supermajority across all of the bonds *and* supermajorities (albeit lower ones) for each individual series. However, in light of the constraints imposed by its official creditors, Greece arguably needed this feature to obtain high participation.

The two-thirds majority threshold and the 50 per cent quorum requirement, on the other hand, were easier to justify on the basis of standard practice. They represented a compromise between the thresholds and quorums required by Greece's English-law bonds for the purposes of passing an amendment in an initial bondholder meeting (typically, either a two-thirds or 75 per cent quorum and a 75 per cent voting threshold) and the rules for an adjourned meeting if the first one did not satisfy the quorum requirement (typically, just a one third or 50 per cent quorum). Given the lack of an adjournment possibility, the thresholds chosen for the Greek-law bonds were probably defensible in the event of bondholder litigation. The fact that the Greek bondholder law was defined narrowly to apply only to sovereign debt but not to sovereign-guaranteed debt issued by a different debtor reflected similar considerations. **3.45**

The fine line between wanting the exchange to succeed and not wanting to appear overly coercive was also reflected in the way in which the proposed amendment itself was defined. Greece could have chosen to define the 'bundle' of securities given to holdouts as a result of an amendment slightly differently from the bundle that was offered for exchange. For example, Greek law bondholders that did not tender their bonds could have been given (upon a successful amendment) a bundle consisting of the EFSF bills, the GDP warrants, and a set of *domestic* law bonds, *not* subject to the co-financing agreement with the EFSF, with identical payment terms to those of the new English-law bonds received by creditors tendering their bonds. This would have created an incentive to tender as long as bondholders believed that the amendment stood a reasonable chance of going through. Unless these investors had a strong preference for litigation, it would have made no sense to hold out, since they would have risked ending up with an instrument with identical payment terms, but inferior creditor rights. **3.46**

In the end, Greece decided not to take this approach, apparently because it was deemed too aggressive: the majority would have imposed *worse* (non-payment) conditions on holdouts than it received itself, rather than forced holdouts to accept the same conditions. However, there are legal precedents in sovereign debt for just that sort of strategy, including in exchanges that are viewed as not particularly coercive.[8] At the same time, forgoing the aggressive strategy created significant risks. Small investors, even those that wanted the exchange to succeed, may not have bothered to vote or accept the exchange offer on the assumption that they would receive the 'PSI consideration' anyway by way of an amendment. If too many investors had acted like this, the amendment would have failed. The fact that Greece was willing to take that risk suggests that it must have placed considerable importance on minimizing the confrontational character of its collective action strategy. **3.47**

[8] Namely, the use of 'exit consents' to strip bonds of creditors' rights, used in Ecuador (2000), but also in the Uruguay (2003) and Dominican Republic (2005) exchanges. The last two were widely viewed as creditor-friendly. *See* Das et al. (n. 2).

C. Threatening holdouts

3.48 Although the government abandoned the voluntary approach when it decided to enact an aggregate CAC to bind holdouts, Greece went out of its way to appear non-coercive in every other respect. In addition to the definition of the amendment sought—leading to the same bundle of securities for everyone, with identical rights, regardless of whether investors accepted the exchange offer or not—this manifested itself in Greece's public communication, which left the possibility open that Greece might honour its debt to foreign-law holdouts on the original payment terms.

3.49 In a 21 February press release announcing the main terms of its imminent debt exchange offer, as well as its intention to retrofit a CAC to Greek law bonds, the Greek government continued to describe the offer as 'voluntary'. Similarly, the formal 24 February invitation memorandum refers to the exchange as a 'voluntary liability management transaction by way of a voluntary bond exchange'. The same memorandum contains a section describing the 'risks of not participating in the invitation', which essentially states that unless the exchange goes through as envisaged, Greece might not have sufficient financing to continue to service its debt. This falls well short of a threat to default on holdouts; it is simply a factual description of the constraints faced by Greece.[9]

3.50 If Greece had stuck to this line, the exchange may have gone down in history as a rare example of an exchange in which a large haircut was achieved without threatening holdouts. On 5 March, however, three days before the expiry of the exchange deadline, Greece increased the pressure on creditors, in the form of a press release stating that:

> Greece's economic programme does not contemplate the availability of funds to make payments to private sector creditors that decline to participate in PSI.... If PSI is not successfully completed, the official sector will not finance Greece's economic programme and Greece will need to restructure its debt on different turns that will not include co-financing, the delivery of EFSF notes, GDP-linked securities, or the submission to English law.

On the same day, Greek finance minister Evangelos Venizelos was quoted as saying: 'Whoever thinks that they will hold out and be paid in full, is mistaken.'[10]

3.51 Considering this, how 'coercive' was the Greek exchange in historical perspective? Table 3.2 benchmarks the procedural approach in the Greek exchange against that of previous cases of the 1990s and 2000s, using an index of government coerciveness during sovereign debt crises developed by Enderlein et al. (2012), which captures nine dimensions of payment and negotiation behaviour vis-à-vis creditors. The index is additive, so that the maximum degree of debtor coerciveness is 10 (all criteria were fulfilled in the runup to a restructuring), while the lower bound is 1 (no criterion observed).[11]

---

[9] The key sentence reads (p. 81):

> If...the Republic does not complete [the transactions contemplated in the Invitation] or other transactions resulting in debt relief or if the Republic cannot secure access to private sector funding or additional official sector funding in amounts equivalent to the benefit to the Republic of completing the Invitation, the Republic may not be able to continue regular payments on all of its indebtedness. This would impair the value of the Designated Securities.

[10] Reuters, 5 March 2012.

[11] For details, *see* Henrik Enderlein, Christoph Trebesch, and Laura von Daniels, 'Sovereign Debt Disputes: A Database on Government Coerciveness in Debt Crises' (2012) 31 J Int'l Money & Fin 250.

Table 3.2 Debtor coerciveness in previous distressed debt exchanges, 1990–2010

	Date	Overall coerciveness (max. 10)	Post-default	Full moratorium?	Forced exchange	Explicit threats
Mexico (Brady deal)	4.2.90	3	Yes	No	No	Yes
Nigeria (Brady deal)	1.12.91	8	Yes	No	Yes	Yes
Venezuela (Brady deal)	5.12.90	5	Yes	No	No	Yes
Philippines (Brady deal)	1.12.92	3	No	No	No	Yes
Argentina (Brady deal)	7.4.93	6	Yes	Yes	No	Yes
Jordan (Brady deal)	23.12.93	7	Yes	Yes	Yes	Yes
Brazil (Brady deal)	15.4.94	7	Yes	Yes	No	Yes
Bulgaria (Brady deal)	29.6.94	6	Yes	Yes	No	Yes
Dominican Rep. (Brady deal)	1.8.94	7	Yes	Yes	No	Yes
Poland (Brady deal)	27.10.94	5	Yes	Yes	No	No
Ecuador (Brady deal)	1.2.95	7	Yes	Yes	No	Yes
Panama (Brady deal)	1.5.96	5	Yes	Yes	No	No
Peru (Brady deal)	1.3.97	9	Yes	Yes	No	Yes
Russia (Soviet-era debt)	1.12.97	5	Yes	Yes	No	No
Pakistan (Bond debt)	13.12.99	3	No	No	No	Yes
Ukraine (Global Exch.)	7.4.00	2	No	No	No	Yes
Ecuador	23.8.00	6	Yes	No	Yes	No
Russia (PRINs & IANs*)	25.8.00	6	Yes	Yes	No	No
Moldova (Bond debt)	1.10.02	2	No	No	No	Yes
Uruguay	29.5.03	1	No	No	No	No
Argentina (Ext. debt)	1.4.05	9	Yes	Yes	Yes	Yes
Dominican Rep. (Bond debt)	11.5.05	2	No	No	No	No
Grenada	15.11.05	2	Yes	No	No	No
Belize	20.2.07	2	Yes	No	No	No
AVERAGE		4.9				
Memorandum item:						
Greece	**9.3.12**	2	**No**	**No**	**No**	**Yes**

*PRIN = Principle note; IAN = Interest into arrears note

Note: The column on 'Overall coerciveness' shows the total index value from the agreement-based dataset in the source paper. The table also shows the binary coding results of four subindicators: 'Post-default' captures whether the country missed any payments prior to the exchange, or not; 'Full moratorium' captures whether the country fully suspends interest and principal payments, even refusing to make token payments; 'Forced exchanges' are cases without formal or informal negotiations between the government and its creditors (enforced or non-negotiated restructurings); the criterion on 'Explicit threats' is fulfilled whenever a key government actor publicly threatens to repudiate on debt, e.g. via an indefinite moratorium.

Source: Henrik Enderlein, Christoph Trebesch, and Laura von Daniels, 'Sovereign Debt Disputes: A Database on Government Coerciveness in Debt Crises' (2012) 31 J Int'l Money & Fin 250, except for coding of Greece.

3.52 As can be seen from Table 3.2, Greece ranks low in terms of coercive restructurings, because it fulfils only the criterion on 'explicit threats'. Among all distressed debt restructurings shown, only Uruguay 2003 was less coercive in procedural terms as far as debtor behaviour is concerned.

3.53 The fact that Greece repaid its first holdouts on 15 May 2012 in full and, as of July 2013, shows no signs of renewing its threats against the holdouts is consistent with this non-confrontational approach. However, it is also standard, even in more confrontational debt restructurings. As far as we are aware, all debt exchanges since the late 1990s that left a small group of holdouts resulted either in the full repayment of these holdouts or in a settlement at more favourable terms than those obtained by the creditors that accepted the exchange offer.

4. Conclusions

3.54 The Greek restructuring was remarkable in many ways. The retrofit CACs, the size of the deal, and the size of the haircut all received attention from the financial press. The Greek deal also hit firsts (or near-firsts) in terms of the use of aggregation provisions, co-financing with a multilateral, and the inclusion of guarantees within a restructuring.

3.55 For Greece, however, it was not legal and financial pyrotechnics that counted, but what relief the restructuring ultimately delivered to the Greek people. For Lee Buchheit, that has always been his own metric of success. If asked, we suspect that he would say that had politicians been willing to acknowledge Greece's problems earlier (when they should have been blindingly obvious), a lot more could have been done to give the Greek people relief. As things stand now, despite the obvious success of the Greek restructuring in terms of the amount of debt that got reduced, the Greek economy continues to stagger under a monumental debt load. The only difference is that the debt is now largely owed to the official sector. Perhaps Lee's next challenge will be to design the first large-scale restructuring of official sector sovereign debt.

4

REVISITING THE *PARI PASSU* CLAUSE

Georges Affaki

1. Introduction

4.01 The history of the use and misuse of the *pari passu* clause in financial agreements owes much to a distinguished jurist, Lee C. Buchheit. He offered the world research of an unprecedented depth into the origin of the clause, its evolution over the years, and the reasons underlying the unexpectedly broad interpretation promoted by some investors in distressed debt. That research is the best antidote to the misuse of the *pari passu* clause in the courtroom including, most recently, in *NML Capital Ltd v. Argentina* before the federal courts in New York.

2. Equal Ranking

4.02 Young lawyers joining banking practices consider *pari passu* clauses to be a matter of fact: they were systematically stipulated in all loans—bilateral and syndicated—and bond issues that lawyers came across.

4.03 *Pari passu* clauses usually appear in rather concise language—some suggest that 'opaque' would be a better adjective—rarely exceeding two lines, as the following standard model *pari passu* clause extracted from a syndicated loan agreement demonstrates:

> The Borrower represents that its payment obligations under this facility rank and will rank *pari passu* with all its other present and future unsecured and unsubordinated external indebtedness.

4.04 It is rare that such clauses attract the curiosity of students or that their study figures anywhere other than among the standard boilerplate provisions that banking law syllabuses reserve to the end of a course on loan documentation. While recent research traced the origin of the *pari passu* clause to the nineteenth century, it is difficult to point to any in-depth scholarly research dedicated to it, at least until it was drawn by vulture funds into adversarial court proceedings in the beginning of the twenty-first century.[1] And that was perfectly understandable: why should it be any different for a clause the contemporary Latin title of which

[1] Even the author of the most comprehensive research ever undertaken on the topic, Lee C. Buchheit, initially considered the *pari passu* clause to be unworthy of any meaningful academic study and dedicated to it no more than a single page (one-and-a-half with an advertisement) in his famous monthly column on standard clauses in international financial documentation, published in the *International Financial Law Review* between 1992 and 1994. *See* L. Buchheit, 'The *Pari Passu* Clause *Sub Specie Aeternitatis*' (1991) 10 Int'l Fin L Rev 11. Of course, he has since made amends by dedicating much more substantial publications to this topic. *See* in particular L. Buchheit and Jeremiah S. Pam, 'The *Pari Passu* Clause in Sovereign Debt Instruments' (2004) 53 Emory LJ 869.

translates literally as 'equally' and which merely provides that two or more debt instruments stand equally without preference or priority among themselves?

4.05 Of course, one could very legitimately question the very rationale of the clause: why is it necessary to ask a borrower to refrain from unilaterally changing such equal standing and subordinating a lender without that lender's explicit consent? In many laws, including the French Civil Code, the US Bankruptcy Code, and English equity law,[2] involuntary legal subordination of an existing creditor is simply not possible.

4.06 Recent research has demonstrated the connection between the rise of *pari passu* clauses to the status of boilerplate and a number of national laws that permit an involuntary subordination of categories of creditor.[3] Those laws are essentially found in jurisdictions of a Spanish legal tradition that have followed the precedents of article 913 of the Spanish Commercial Code and of article 1924 of the Spanish Civil Code. Both provisions rank creditors holding notarized debt titles (*escritura publica*) ahead of other unsecured creditors.[4] The rationale for this rule, which goes back to the nineteenth century, is evidentiary: notarized credits are considered to be more certain than non-notarized ones, because they avoid doubt regarding the authenticity of the debt. While Spain abolished this rule in its Bankruptcy Act of 9 July 2003 (Ley Concursal 22/2003), the Philippines kept a similar procedure. Article 2244 of the Philippines Civil Code, setting out the priorities of creditor claims over property of a debtor, gives priority to a credit that 'appears in a public instrument' (section 14).

4.07 Argentina offered another example of discriminatory provisions when enacting, in 1972, a law that, in the event of the bankruptcy of an Argentinian borrower, subordinated the claims of foreign creditors to those of local creditors.[5]

4.08 In cases such as these, a *pari passu* covenant is expected to prevent the borrower from breaking the equal ranking among its unsecured creditors. Hence the drafting of the clause in terms both of a representation and a covenant: 'rank and will rank...' Of course, nothing in this clause prevents the incurrence of secured debt, the limitation of which is the appanage of a different clause: the negative pledge clause.

4.09 But if the benefit of *pari passu* clauses is expected to be seen in the event of bankruptcy of the borrower, why are *pari passu* clauses appearing in sovereign lending, in which any formal bankruptcy regime for insolvent states is still inconceivable? Among the answers that have been proposed to explain the migration of the *pari passu* clause from private to sovereign debt instruments, that which attempts to present it as an accident that only later morphed into an indispensable fixture that no contract drafter dares question is supported by no corroborating evidence and should be set aside. A more convincing answer can be inferred from recent empirical research attributing the phenomenon to lenders seeking to prevent

---

[2] Article 2093 of the French Civil Code. *See* also J. Story, *Commentaries on Equity Jurisprudence, Vol. 1* (Boston, MA: Little, Brown and Co., 1873), 590; W. J. Gough, *Company Charges*, 2nd edn (London: Butterworths, 1995), 948.

[3] Buchheit and Pam (n. 1), 869.

[4] Article 1924(3) of the Spanish Civil Code: 'Con relación a los demás bienes muebles e inmuebles del deudor, gozan de preferencia: ... Los créditos que sin privilegio especial consten: En escritura pública ...'

[5] *Anales de Legislacion Argentina*, Tit. I, Ley no. 19,551, art. 4. *See* Buchheit and Pam (n. 1), 905, citing E. Cardenas, 'International Lending: Subordination of Foreign Claims under Argentine Bankruptcy Law', in D. Suratgar (ed.) *Default and Rescheduling: Corporate and Sovereign Borrowers* (Washington, DC: Euromoney Publication/International Law Institute, 1984), 63.

sovereign borrowers from discriminating between creditors by earmarking revenues—particularly foreign currency revenues—to a particular creditor.

3. Earmarking of Assets

Embarking on an odyssey that led back to the London market in the 1820s, researchers identified a practice whereby the then newly independent Latin American republics allocated assets or revenue streams as security for the funds that they were seeking to raise.[6] This earmarking of assets was not, strictly speaking, a security right over the assets of the borrower. The use in the offering circulars for such bonds of typical secured transaction phraseology ('pledge', 'mortgage', 'hypothecation') does not change this fact; rather, it is no more than an undertaking by the borrower to recognize a preferential right for one or more creditors over the earmarked funds. Yet this practice benefiting selected creditors was susceptible to causing concern to other creditors of that sovereign. Because traditional negative pledge clauses were ill-suited to restricting earmarking, which was not a security right, ranking the debt by means of the *pari passu* covenant was potentially the answer. **4.10**

It was tested in 1976 in the matter of a loan granted to Zaire by a group of commercial banks. The loan contained the typical *pari passu* and negative pledge clauses. Two other banks, Manufacturers Hanover and the US Eximbank, proposed that Zaire should enter into a new credit facility involving the earmarking of proceeds from the sale of Zaire's copper exports and their channelling towards an account held with Manufacturers Hanover. **4.11**

Understandably, the other original lenders considered the new arrangement to be unacceptable. While the earmarking of the proceeds from the sale of the copper was not a security right violating the negative pledge covenant, the other lenders considered that they had sufficient grounds to file a complaint with the federal courts, alleging, among other things, that Manufacturers Hanover and the US Eximbank had tortiously interfered with their contract right.[7] The case was settled and the proposed facility was not implemented. **4.12**

Following that incident, the drafting of the *pari passu* and negative pledge clauses changed to prohibit also preferential arrangements having the practical effect of constituting a security interest. **4.13**

For over a century, the daily negotiation and application of *pari passu* clauses generated a debate proportionate to the size of the clause itself: very limited. This peaceful existence came to an abrupt halt when a new 'rateable payment' interpretation, rather than the classical 'rateable ranking' that had been generally accepted so far in the market, entered briskly centre stage—a stage that was not a university lecture theatre, but a courtroom drama. **4.14**

4. Equal Payment

Today, two radically different interpretations of the *pari passu* clause are pitted against each other. The classical, narrow interpretation requires that the obligations within the scope of **4.15**

[6] Buchheit and Pam (n. 1), 907, and the historical references cited by the authors.
[7] *Citibank NA v. Export-Import Bank of the United States* (SDNY filed 9 August 1976) (No. 76 Civ. 3514 (CBM)).

the *pari passu* clause rank equally and rateably. This means that the debtor is not entitled to alter the legal ranking of the *pari passu* debt by subordinating it to other debts so that, in the event of insolvency, the *pari passu* bonds or debt rank equally with other unsecured debt. In the case of a sovereign borrower, the *pari passu* clause would preclude it from creating, by legislative or executive means, a discriminatory and mandatory order of priorities subordinating the *pari passu* debt to other unsecured debt. On the face of it, nothing in the *pari passu* clause offers grounds on which to argue that the debtor is not entitled to discriminate between its creditors by choosing whom to pay and when.

4.16 In contrast, the new, broad interpretation postulates that an insolvent debtor must pay all of its creditors rateably, regardless of any priority order that may be imposed by the bankruptcy laws. Under this interpretation, the imperative 'rank' becomes 'pay'. This broad interpretation clearly has dramatic consequences. It could throw into doubt the validity of customary, and essential, preferential payments to lenders of last resort, such as the International Monetary Fund (IMF)[8] or the European Central Bank (ECB). A sovereign borrower could be precluded from paying its foreign diplomatic missions and, if the *pari passu* clause is not limited to foreign currency debts, using local currency to pay its civil servants, the army, and the public health service. The whole economy would come to a halt and the security of the nation would be put in question.

5. The Elliott–Peru Saga

4.17 The first proponents of this new interpretation of the *pari passu* clause were New York-based vulture fund Elliott Associates, LP and its affiliates. A vulture fund is a hedge fund running a portfolio dedicated to investing in distressed debt, usually purchased on the secondary market for a fraction of its nominal value following the borrower's default—hence the evocative appellation 'vulture'. The vulture fund then resorts to extensive and aggressive litigation as the means of extracting costly settlements from the borrowers at the expense of other creditors who have chosen to participate in an orderly rescheduling of the debt.

4.18 In 2000, Elliott purchased Peruvian sovereign debt dating from 1983, governed by New York law, and containing a *pari passu* clause. Elliott knew that Peru was scheduled, in September 2000, to repay holders of external bonds that Peru had issued to restructure its old bonds.

4.19 The payment was to flow through Chase Manhattan as the fiscal agent for the Brady bonds to the accounts of the bondholders with the Euroclear System in Belgium and the Depository Trust Company in the United States. To intercept the bond payment, Elliott served restraining notices on Chase and on the operator of the Euroclear system, Morgan Guarantee Trust Company.[9]

4.20 Elliott also went to the courts in Brussels seeking an injunction against Euroclear to prevent it from processing any payment received from Peru in respect of its bonds.

4.21 In support of its motion, Elliott argued *ex parte* that Peru was attempting to make payments in violation of the equal treatment principle among foreign creditors indicated in the *pari passu* clause, under which Elliott was excluded.

[8] *NML Capital Ltd et al. v. Republic of Argentina*, 2nd US Court of Appeals, 12-105, Petition for Panel Rehearing of the Republic of Argentina, at 15.

[9] *Elliott Associates LP v. Banco de la Nacion*, 200 WL 1449862 (SDNY 29 September 2000).

Elliott produced an affidavit from a distinguished New York University academic, Andreas F. Lowenfeld, who stated: **4.22**

> I have no difficulty in understanding what the *pari passu* clause means: it means what it says—a given debt will rank equally with other debt of the borrower.
>
> A borrower from Tom, Dick, and Harry can't say 'I will pay Tom and Dick in full, and if there is anything left over I'll pay Harry'. If there is not enough money to go around, the borrower faced with a *pari passu* provision must pay all three of them on the same basis.

What Elliott argued that Professor Lowenfeld was saying is that 'equal ranking' means 'equal payment'; if there is not enough money to pay all equally ranking creditors in full, each creditor must receive a rateable share even though—and this is key—the debtor is not in bankruptcy. **4.23**

To appreciate fully the disruptive effect of the new 'equal payment' interpretation, it is important to note that Elliott was pursuing its enforcement not so much against the Republic of Peru, an immune sovereign, as against the third-party recipients of the purported non-rateable payments—that is, the new bondholders who had not invited Elliott to share the payment of their bonds. **4.24**

The Belgian Court of Appeal accepted Elliott's motion to enjoin the payment of Peru's Brady bonds.[10] The case settled shortly thereafter, with Peru paying Elliott everything that it was seeking. **4.25**

This *ex parte* decision by a Belgian court interpreting the law of the State of New York as it applied to a loan agreement, with no judicial precedent or authority but the affidavit of a single academic, was sufficient to unleash the 'rateable payment' interpretation of the *pari passu*.[11] **4.26**

6. Targeting Third Parties

Elliott and other vultures subsequently embarked on a litigation spree across the United States and Europe. The scenario was the same: the vulture fund would buy sovereign debt in default for a few cents on the dollar, then sue the defaulting state and third-party creditors, suppliers, and trade finance banks who had entered into new financing with that state and who were aware of, ought to have been aware of, or could not have ignored, the original debt instrument and the *pari passu* clause therein contained. Should any of those third-party creditors receive payment under goods or equipment that they supplied to the defaulting state, this was sufficient for them to become putative defendants in the alleged conspiracy to deprive the vulture fund of its purported right to rateable payment under the *pari passu* clause. **4.27**

While many courts, including those in England, the United States, and France,[12] have denied those claimants the benefit of the 'rateable payment' interpretation of *pari passu*, **4.28**

---

[10] Court of Appeal of Brussels, 26 September 2000, Case no. 2000/QR/92 (original ruling in French on file with the author).

[11] Thirteen years later, in a letter to the *Financial Times*, Professor Lowenfeld reiterated his interpretation of the *pari passu* clause (*Financial Times*, 8 April 2013, 'Letters'). However, he omitted from his account of the Elliott saga before the Brussels courts the fact that the petition for injunction was argued *ex parte* and that the court in Brussels was asked to rule under New York law.

[12] *Red Mountain Fin. Inc. v. Democratic Republic of Congo et al.* 2000 US Dist. LEXIS 22324 (CD Cal. 29 May 2001) (CV 00-0164 R); *Nacional Financiera, SNC v. Chase Manhattan Bank*, 2003 WL 1878415 (SDNY 14 April 2003); *Kensington Int'l Ltd v. Republic of Congo* [2003] EWCA Civ 709.

Belgian courts persisted in granting again an injunction against Euroclear, restraining it from processing the repayment of Nicaraguan debt to the benefit of another vulture, LNC.[13]

4.29 The market was in shock. States that had defaulted decades ago on their sovereign debts and negotiated a restructuring with the London or the Paris Clubs risked losing suppliers or purchase money financiers willing to cater for the elementary financing needs of the state or its people. Lawmakers were asked to step in and grant statutory immunity to clearing systems and their operators, and, by doing so, to protect creditors from liability under vulture attack.[14]

4.30 *Pari passu* clauses were, in effect, being turned into 'sharing clauses', which are another—totally distinct—type of standard syndicated loan clause designed to ensure that any disproportionate payment received by one member of the syndicate will be shared rateably with all of the rest. But the fact remains that sharing clauses are distinct from *pari passu* provisions. It has been pertinently remarked that if it were intended that a *pari passu* should mean that, 'Following a payment default, the borrower agrees that it will not pay any creditor unless, simultaneously with that payment, a rateable payment is made under this agreement', the clause would be drafted in those terms.[15] But *pari passu* clauses are *not* drafted that way; instead, they indicate that the borrower cannot change the ranking of the debt. And contracts mean what the parties intend them to mean.

4.31 However, rather than being the conclusion, that finding was the beginning of research of unprecedented depth into the origin of the *pari passu* clause, its migration over the years, and the purpose that its initial drafters were trying to achieve by stipulating it in their contracts.

7. The Quest for the Origins of the *Pari Passu*

4.32 A first-class research team undertook an unprecedented exercise in legal paleontology. Over several years, Professors Buchheit, Pam, Gulati, and others exhumed the archives of banks in the United States and Europe, examining hundreds of credit agreements and note issue documents. But the end justified the effort: they were able to offer the world a unique insight into *pari passu*. This chapter is thus a tribute to their outstanding contribution.

---

13 *Republic of Nicaragua v LNC Investments et al.*, Commercial Court of Brussels, September 2003.

14 In Belgium, article 9 of Law 28 April 1999, which transposed into Belgian law EU Directive 98/26/CE of 19 May 1998 concerning the Finality of Payments, was amended on 19 November 2004, entering into effect on 8 January 2005 (*Moniteur Belge*, 28 December 2004, 85855). The new amendment provides as follows, thus granting immunity to clearing systems against restraining orders:

> Tout compte de règlement sur espèces auprès d'un organisme gestionnaire ou d'un agent de règlement d'un système, *de même que tout transfert de sommes, via un établissement de crédit de droit belge ou étranger, à porter à un tel compte de règlement sur espèces*, ne peut être saisi, mis sous séquestre ou bloqué d'une manière quelconque par un participant (autre que l'organisme gestionnaire ou l'agent de règlement), une contrepartie ou un tiers règlement dans les systèmes de paiement et de règlement des opérations sur titres, tel qu'amendé par la loi du 19 novembre 2004.

In France, a draft law targeting a similar effect was considered by Parliament, but put to a halt before formal adoption as a result of supervening parliamentary elections. *See* G. Affaki, 'Du Sens des Mots et du Bon Sens: De la Bonne Interprétation de la Clause *Pari Passu*', in *Mélanges à Philippe Letourneau* (Paris: Dalloz, 2007), 2 *et seq.*

15 *See* Buchheit and Pam (n. 1).

The findings of this research are now part of the syllabuses of all serious international financial law courses. Briefly, the story falls into three acts, as follows, and includes a post-research development. **4.33**

A. Act 1

The *pari passu* clause was traced back to the nineteenth century, where it was found in secured debt instruments confirming the rateable ranking of the rights of secured creditors to the collateral. At that time, railway companies in England would issue multiple series of bonds, all secured by a common pool of collateral—typically, the railway's land and rolling stock. Absent agreement to the contrary, the conflicting claims of the bondholders against the collateral would have been ranked under English law in the chronological order in which the bonds were issued. In the United States, some courts adopted a similar first-to-be-issued test, while other courts differed, choosing instead the date of maturity of the debt. In both cases, *pari passu* clauses offered an assurance of a rateable ranking. **4.34**

B. Act 2

By the middle of the twentieth century, cross-border lending was mainly unsecured, essentially during the Depression era in the 1930s. This was essentially the result of borrowers defaulting on secured loans and the difficulty in enforcing security over worthy collateral. Rather than adopt a *pari passu* clause, the borrower employed a negative pledge clause to assure unsecured creditors that the borrower would not pledge its assets in favour of other lenders. **4.35**

C. Act 3

By the late twentieth century, international commercial banks took over part of the burden of multilateral development banks and became the main source of private capital flows to the emerging markets. These new lenders wanted, in addition to negative pledge clauses, *pari passu* clauses that would provide them with assurance against involuntary subordination of their claim. The combination of the *pari passu* and the negative pledge clauses in the loan document assured lenders that they could resort to the borrower's general assets by restricting its ability to incur secured debt and senior debt. **4.36**

The *pari passu* clause also offered a useful supplement to negative pledges, which restricted only the creation of *formal* security interests, but did not prevent borrowers from earmarking some of their assets in favour of a particular lender. An example is the case identified in Professor Buchheit's research in relation to the 1972 loan to Zaire discussed at paragraphs 4.11–4.12. **4.37**

D. Act 4

Not strictly a finding of the Buchheit et al. research, this 'fourth act' comprises a case the climax of which took place after its publication. **4.38**

The case arose in relation to the Argentinian foreign debt rescheduling. In 2005 and 2010, Argentina restructured most of the New-York-law-governed bonds that it had issued since 1994 (the old bonds) by making an exchange offer for new bonds that imposed a 75 per cent haircut on the old bondholders. About 91 per cent of the holders of the old bonds accepted the exchange, but a number of old bondholders refused and became holdouts. **4.39**

In 2005, Argentina passed a law (the Lock Law) prohibiting the payment of holdout bondholders. This law was considered to be a condition for the success of the exchange given that, **4.40** in its absence, the holdouts would receive 100 per cent of the nominal amount of their old bonds. The bulk of the holdouts were not original bondholders who purchased the original old bonds on nominal value; rather, they were vulture funds, which had paid much less for their bonds in the secondary market a short time before the exchange. The plaintiff, NML Capital Ltd, was one of these funds.

4.41 NML Capital claimed before the US Court for the Southern District of New York that Argentina's statutes and its persistence in denying payment to the holdouts while honouring the exchanged bonds violated the *pari passu* clause contained in the old bonds to the detriment of their holders. That clause stipulated:

> The securities will constitute... direct, unconditional, unsecured and unsubordinated obligations of the Republic and shall at all times rank *pari passu* without any preference among themselves. The payment obligations of the Republic under the securities shall at all times rank at least equally with all its other present and future unsecured and unsubordinated indebtedness...

4.42 Both the District Court[16] and, on appeal, the US Federal Court of Appeals for the Second Circuit accepted the claim.[17] The Circuit Court decision of 26 October 2012 is particularly devastating to Argentina. While it did not clearly indicate whether it upholds the narrow or the broad interpretation of the *pari passu* clause, the Court affirmed the lower court's ruling that Argentina's laws and non-payment of the holdouts violated the *pari passu* clause. Consequent to that finding, the Court granted injunctive relief, ordering Argentina specifically to perform its obligations under the *pari passu* clause. The order stipulated that whenever the Republic pays any amount due under the terms of the exchanged bonds, it must 'concurrently or in advance' pay the holdout plaintiffs the same fraction of the amount due to them. The Court labelled that payment obligation 'the rateable payment'. Although the appellate court remanded the case to the District Court to clarify how the payment formula should function and how the injunction should apply to third-party intermediary banks, it unreservedly affirmed the judgment.

4.43 Perhaps of greater concern to the topic dealt with in this chapter is the finding by the Court that Argentina's interpretation of the *pari passu* clause as referring only to legal subordination of debt is neither well settled nor uniformly acted upon. In a surprising divinatory interpretation exercise, the Court decided that any such interpretation fails to give effect to the differences between the two sentences of the *pari passu* clause cited at paragraph 4.41. In contrast, the Court ruled, pairing the two sentences shows that the bond issue agreement manifested an intention to protect bondholders from more than only formal subordination. The Court concluded:

> The first sentence 'The securities will constitute... direct, unconditional, unsecured and unsubordinated obligations...' prohibits Argentina, as bond *issuer*, from formally subordinating the bonds by issuing superior debt. The second sentence 'The payment obligations... shall at all times rank at least equally with all its other present and future unsecured and unsubordinated indebtedness' prohibits Argentina, as bond *payor*, from paying on other bonds without paying on the old, unexchanged bonds. Thus, the two sentences of the *pari passu* clause protect against

[16] *NML Capital Ltd et al. v. Republic of Argentina*, US District Court, Case 1:08-cv-06978-TPG (SDNY 7 December 2011).

[17] *NML Capital Ltd et al. v. Republic of Argentina*, 2nd US Court of Appeals, 12-105 (26 October 2012).

different forms of discrimination: the issuance of other superior debt (first sentence) and the giving of priority to other payment obligations (second sentence).[18]

However, while finding that Argentina had ranked its payment obligation to the holdout creditors below that of the exchange bondholders, the Court did not indicate whether any single non-payment on the old bonds while making timely payment on the new bonds would be enough, or whether a law ordering a stay on the payment of old bonds is required to uphold the claimed breach of the *pari passu* clause. **4.44**

Argentina has appealed the decision ordering it to make immediate rateable payment to the holdout vulture. The US government intervened in the appeal in support of Argentina and indicated that the decision goes 'counter to long standing US efforts to promote orderly restructuring of sovereign debt'.[19] At the time of writing, the Court had not yet issued its ruling. **4.45**

8. Chaos in the Market

In the meantime, contradictory interpretations of the decision are creating grave uncertainty in the financial market: is the decision limited to sovereign debt or does it also cover *pari passu* covenants in bank lending and corporate bonds? Could it apply outside the strict New York state law governing the bonds in dispute? **4.46**

In a noticeable disclosure, Belize added to new bonds issued on 31 March 2013 as part of its external debt restructuring a new type of *pari passu* clause that provides as follows: **4.47**

> The New Bonds will be general, direct, unconditional, unsubordinated and unsecured obligations of Belize and will rank at least equally among themselves and with all of Belize's existing and future unsecured and unsubordinated bond indebtedness (*it being understood that this equal ranking status shall not require Belize to pay all items of its bond indebtedness on a ratable basis*).[20]

While this stab at transparency should be lauded in principle, it is regrettable that what is expected to be standard boilerplate should go so far in explaining what it does *not* mean. **4.48**

Because the restraining order issued by the District Court did not stop at ordering Argentina to pay rateably all its bondholders, but also extended its imperium to all parties involved, directly or indirectly, in advising upon preparing, processing, or facilitating any payment on the exchange bonds, banks holding money in trust for the exchange bondholders are direct targets of the order. Those banks are pure intermediaries in the process of sending money from Argentina to the holders of the exchange bonds. As such, they do not have any obligation to Argentina.[21] Forcing them to stop payment in this case imposes significant costs on those banks and risks delays in payments unrelated to the targeted exchange bond payments. That argument, forcefully put forward to the District Court by the Federal Reserve Bank of New York, failed to convince.[22] It was, however, well identified by the Circuit Court, which remanded that part of the injunction to the District Court to address its application to third **4.49**

---

[18] *NML Capital Ltd et al. v. Republic of Argentina* (n. 16), at 18.

[19] Brief on file with the author.

[20] Emphasis added. Honduras adopted wording to the same effect in its bond-offering memorandum in March 2013.

[21] *See* article 4-A of the Uniform Commercial Code and article 4-A-503 NY UCC cmt.

[22] Letter of Thomas C. Baxter, Jr, General Counsel for the Federal Reserve Bank of New York, on file with the author.

parties and, in particular, to intermediary banks. At the time of writing, the District Court had not yet handed down its ruling—and the chaos that this limbo situation is creating in the market is indescribable.

9. Conclusion

4.50 Until common sense returns to sovereign lending, the use of collective action clauses (CACs) could provide a reasonable answer to the problem of holdout creditors. Where a debt provides such a clause, the minority creditors are bound by majority (generally, two-thirds) decision. This would also apply to an exchange of bonds in the case of a restructuring of debt. In the case of Argentina, for example, the holdout vulture funds would have been forced to accept the majority bondholders' decision to swap their old bonds for the new bonds. All of the exchanged bonds include CACs.

4.51 For as long as CACs do not become boilerplate, existing debt without such clauses will continue to provide holdout creditors with ammunition to perpetuate the all-out litigation of which their apocryphal interpretation of the *pari passu* clause is the linchpin.

4.52 The compelling research of Lee C. Buchheit and his legal ethnologue companions has demonstrated that at no time in its history did the *pari passu* clause carry any intention of its drafters to require a borrower to make, on a strictly lockstep basis, rateable payments to all of its equally ranking creditors. Nor was the clause ever meant to offer a legal basis for an unsecured creditor to enjoin non-rateable payments to another creditor or to expose the recipient of the differential payments, or the party through which such payments are processed, to claims for damages. When calm and common sense eventually return to the lending market, it will result in large part from Lee's efforts.

5

THE ROLE OF THE INTERNATIONAL MONETARY FUND

Rosa M. Lastra

1. Introduction

This chapter discusses the role of the International Monetary Fund (IMF) in sovereign debt restructuring and in the promotion of sound sovereign debt management. The chapter commences with a short history of the IMF.[1] It then presents a study of the main policy and legal tools that the Fund has in the pursuit of its objectives—notably, surveillance and conditional financial assistance—before it moves into the analysis of the role of the IMF in the resolution of sovereign debt problems. In the absence of an international bankruptcy regime for sovereigns (an institutional vacuum), there have been calls to grant the Fund a formal role in this process via the so-called sovereign debt restructuring mechanism (SDRM),[2] further discussed in Chapter 22. But with or without an SDRM, the Fund has a unique position as arbiter in negotiations between debtor and creditor countries, as gatekeeper of stability and creditworthiness (via conditionality and surveillance), and as international lender of last resort. **5.01**

A key theme in this chapter is the relationship between the IMF and private sector creditors. In the early days of the Fund, there was no direct involvement with adjustments of private sector debts. Starting in the summer of 1982, with the Mexican crisis, the Fund performed the 'master of ceremonies' role. Private creditors profoundly dislike the Fund when its debt sustainability analyses call for debt restructuring, but need the Fund to vouchsafe the accuracy of the debtor country's projections. In Europe, since 2010, the Fund has been drawn into an entirely new role, that of one-third participant in full bailout programmes, most of which go to pay private creditors at par. In response to these developments in the eurozone and the ongoing litigation against Argentina, the publication of a comprehensive paper in April 2013 charts a new path for the Fund in sovereign debt workouts.[3] The recent IMF **5.02**

---

[1] Throughout the chapter, the terms 'IMF' and 'Fund' are used interchangeably. 'Fund' is the preferred abbreviation in the institutional context; 'IMF' is the preferred abbreviation in the media and academia.

[2] *See* Anne Krueger, 'International Financial Architecture for 2002: New Approach to Sovereign Debt Restructuring', Speech at the National Economists' Club Annual Members' Dinner, 26 November 2001, available online at <http://www.imf.org/external/np/speeches/2001/112601.htm>; *see* generally Sean Hagan, 'Designing a Legal Framework to Restructure Sovereign Debt' (2005) 36 Georgetown J Int'l Law 299.

[3] *See* IMF, *Sovereign Debt Restructuring: Recent Developments and Implications for the Fund's Legal and Policy Frameworks* (26 April 2013), available online at <http://www.imf.org/external/np/pp/eng/2013/042613.pdf>.

report on Greece[4] amounts to a *mea culpa*, with the Fund acknowledging that it was a mistake ever to let itself be lured into lending to a debtor country with an unsustainable debt stock the money needed to repay existing creditors at par. One consequence of this mistake may be to put the Fund's de facto preferred creditor status in jeopardy.[5]

2. The History

5.03 The IMF was established following the conclusion of the International Monetary and Financial Conference of the United and Associated Nations, commonly referred to as the 'Bretton Woods conference', in 1944. The Articles of Agreement of the Fund were adopted on 22 July 1944 and came into force on 27 December 1945.[6] The IMF began operations in Washington DC in May 1946.[7]

5.04 The Fund was the brainchild of Harry Dexter White and John Maynard Keynes. They drafted their proposals in 1941 and 1942. White was concerned about the needs of creditor countries, while Keynes was concerned about the needs of debtor countries. White's proposal was greatly influenced by the experience of the Great Depression in the United States that followed the stock market crash of 1929. In the introduction to his plan,[8] he stated:

> No matter how long the war lasts nor how it is won, we shall be faced with three inescapable problems: to prevent the disruption of foreign exchanges and the collapse of monetary and credit systems; to assure the restoration of foreign trade; and to supply the huge volume of capital that will be needed virtually throughout the world for reconstruction, for relief, and for economic recovery. If we are to avoid drifting from the peace table into a period of chaotic competition, monetary disorders, depressions, political disruptions, and finally into new wars within as well as among nations, we must be equipped to grapple with these three problems and to make substantial progress toward their solution.

5.05 Keynes' proposal was inspired by the analysis of Britain's post-war prospects. Demand for imports would rise with the end of wartime austerity, while Britain's future capacity to export would be cut because of the wartime conversion of industries to military manufacturing and the difficulties of reconversion. Keynes proposed the establishment of an international clearing union, aimed at avoiding balance-of-payments imbalances through a set of rules

---

4 *See* IMF, *Greece:* Ex Post *Evaluation of Exceptional Access under the 2010 Stand-By Arrangement*, IMF Country Report No. 13/156 (June 2013), available online at <http://www.imf.org/external/pubs/ft/scr/2013/cr13156.pdf>. The report points out (at page 28, point 57) that 'the SBA [Stand-By Arrangement]-supported programme served as a holding operation' and that 'An upfront debt restructuring would have been better for Greece'; 'The delay provided a window for private creditors to reduce exposures and shift debt into official hands. This shift occurred on a significant scale and left the official sector on the hook' (page 33, point 68).

5 *See* Christopher Spink and John Geddie, 'IMF Set to be Dragged into Greek OSI [official sector involvement]', *International Financing Review*, 11 May 2013, available online to subscribers at <http://www.ifre.com/imf-set-to-be-dragged-into-greek-osi/21085086.article>.

6 'Bretton Woods constituted the first formal international agreement applicable for economic transactions among the countries that had subscribed to it': *see* Manuel Guitián, *The Unique Nature of the Responsibilities of the International Monetary Fund*, IMF Pamphlet Series No. 46 (Washington DC: IMF, 1992), 2.

7 For a history of the IMF, *see* generally Rosa Lastra, *Legal Foundations of International Monetary Stability* (Oxford: Oxford University Press, 2006), ch. 12.

8 His plan was entitled 'Preliminary Draft Proposal for a United Nations Stabilization Fund and a Bank for Reconstruction and Development of the United and Associated Nations' and dated April 1942. The proposal is reproduced in J. Keith Horsefield, *The International Monetary Fund 1945–1965, Volume III: Documents* (Washington DC: International Monetary Fund, 1969), 37–82. The final version of Mr White's plan was issued by the US Treasury in printed form on 10 July 1943 and is reproduced in Horsefield, at 83–96.

governing the overdrafts on the union accumulated by debtors (such as the United Kingdom) and the positive balances acquired by creditors (such as the United States).[9]

According to the original IMF Articles of Agreement, the IMF's mandate was to maintain the 'par value regime' by enforcing rules about adjustment in international monetary relations and by providing temporary resources to deal with short-term balance-of-payments problems. The par value regime was a two-tier system of convertibility, also known as the 'gold-dollar standard'. The value of the currency of each participating member was defined in terms of gold or, alternatively, in terms of the US dollar of 1 July 1944, which had a fixed gold value (an ounce of gold was equal to US$35).[10] The US monetary authorities guaranteed the convertibility of the dollar into gold at the fixed price of US$35 per ounce of gold. The monetary authorities of the participating countries committed themselves to converting their currency into dollars at a fixed price, which was called the 'official exchange rate' or the 'parity rate'. **5.06**

How fixed was fixed? This is an 'eternal' challenge whenever we talk about exchange rates, as evidenced by recent events in the eurozone. The original IMF Articles of Agreement foresaw the possibility of adjusting the rate of an individual currency if it fell into a 'fundamental disequilibrium'—a term that, despite its importance, was not defined.[11] **5.07**

The gold-dollar two-tier system of convertibility had an inherent flaw in that the United States was willing to convert gold balances of dollars held by the monetary authorities of other members, while private gold markets were permissible and were in operation. In the beginning of the 1960s, it became clear that the gold reserves were insufficient for the growing demands of the international monetary system. Indeed, although the IMF was founded in 1944, the 'proper' Bretton Woods regime did not start functioning until 1959, once European countries achieved convertibility for their currencies. And, since the Bretton Woods regime was abandoned at the beginning of the 1970s, the 'life' of the par value regime was short and problematic. **5.08**

---

[9] Keynes' plan was entitled 'Proposals for an International Currency (or Clearing) Union'. The fourth draft of his proposal (1942) is reproduced in Horsefield (n. 8), 3–18. The final draft, which the British government issued in April 1943 as a White Paper (Cmd 6437), is reproduced in Horsefield (n. 8), 19–36. The title of the final British draft dropped the word 'currency' and was simply entitled 'Proposals for an International Clearing Union'.

[10] Article IV, section 1(a), of the original Articles of Agreement clearly stated: 'The par value of the currency of each member shall be expressed in terms of gold as a common denominator or in terms of the United States dollar of the weight and fineness [*sic*] in effect on July 1, 1944.'

[11] Article IV, section 5(a), concerning 'changes in par values' stated: 'A member shall not propose a change in the par value of its currency except to correct a fundamental disequilibrium.' Harry Dexter White, in an unpublished memorandum of August 1946, reproduced in Joseph Gold, 'The Legal Structure of the Par Value System' (1973) 5 Law and Policy International Business 155, 161, explains why such a term was not defined:

> In the drafting of the Articles of Agreement, no attempt was made to define fundamental disequilibrium. This, as we know, was not oversight. It was generally agreed that a satisfactory definition would be difficult to formulate. A too rigid or narrow interpretation would be dangerous; one too loose or general would be useless in providing a criterion for changes in currency parities. It was felt that the matter was so important, and the necessity for crystallization of a harmonious view so essential that it was best left for discussion and formulation by the Fund. Because of the key position of the term and the importance attached to its precise meaning, it would be desirable, if possible, to reach agreement on a tentative formulation before any definitive position to be taken by any of the officials of the Fund.

5.09 The inevitable happened—first, de facto; then, *de jure*. The par value regime was de facto abandoned on 15 August 1971, with the announcement by President Nixon (during television prime time, while audiences were watching *Bonanza*) of the closing of the 'gold window'. *De jure*, the second amendment to the IMF's Articles of Agreement, which was adopted on 30 April 1976 and which came into effect on 1 April 1978, allowed members to choose their exchange arrangement and to determine the external value of their currency.

5.10 But the IMF has proven to be the master of reinvention; indeed, its influence remains undiminished. Like a phoenix rising out of its own ashes, following the abandonment of what had been its *raison d'être*—the par value regime—the IMF has been singularly adept at finding new roles. Why? The simple answer might be 'Because there is no other institution in town'. The IMF has survived because its role is indispensable when it comes to solving countries' external payments and debt problems, as the experiences in the 1980s, 1990s, and the twenty-first century so far have confirmed.

5.11 The challenges faced by the IMF have changed since the collapse of the Bretton Woods regime. The IMF played a leading role in the sovereign debt restructuring of the least-developed countries (LDCs) in the 1980s, in the transition to a market economy of formerly communist countries in the early 1990s, and in the resolution of financial crises in Mexico and Asia, Russia and Brazil in the mid-to-late 1990s, although its handling of such crises (via the so-called 'bailout packages') has been the subject of much controversy. And then there are the ongoing challenges following the international financial crisis of 2008 and the eurozone debt crisis since 2010 (which problems had commenced in 2009). With minimum amendments to the IMF Articles of Agreement, the IMF has been called to respond to all of these issues—financial reform, capital markets, financial crises, financial stability, and sovereign debt crisis—with its array of tools: surveillance; conditional financial assistance; and technical assistance.

5.12 Let us start with what the IMF can no longer do, and then assess what the IMF *can* do or *should* do. To begin, since the entry into force of the second amendment, the Fund has no substantive legal rights with respect to the choice of exchange rate arrangements of its members. In lieu of the par value regime, the second amendment places the functions of surveillance—Article IV of the IMF Articles of Agreement—at the centre of the Fund's activities. This is fundamental to understanding the changes in the role of the Fund: a seismic shift from a rules-based system to a discretionary system in which judgement is of the essence.[12]

5.13 But before we leave exchange rates (a subject that always divides the economics profession), let us consider the following: the reality of exchange markets is that exchange rates do fluctuate. Under a system of flexible exchange rates, such variations (appreciation or depreciation of the currency vis-à-vis other currencies) are triggered by market forces. Under a system of government-controlled exchange rates, such variations (devaluation or revaluation) are officially imposed decisions.

3. The Tools

5.14 The main functions performed by the IMF in relation to its members are surveillance (Article IV), financial assistance (Article V, section 3), and technical assistance (Article V,

[12] *See* Manuel Guitián, 'The IMF as a Monetary Institution: The Challenge Ahead', *Finance and Development*, September 1991, 38.

section 2(b)). These are the tools that the IMF uses when it deals with countries, whether debtor countries or creditor countries. Indeed, the Fund uses surveillance, financial assistance, and technical assistance as instruments to accomplish its objectives as defined in Article I of the Articles of Agreement. From the point of view of the member states, they constitute the main 'services' that the Fund provides to them.[13] The authority of the IMF to perform specific services for members that are not mentioned in the Articles, but which are sufficiently related to the purposes of the institution is made explicit by the second amendment, Article V, section 2(b).

By analogy with the tools that authorities have at the national level to deal with bank debt **5.15** problems—namely supervision, regulation, and crisis management, comprising lender of last resort, deposit insurance, resolution, and insolvency—we can look at the tools that the IMF has to deal with external debt problems of member countries. The IMF has surveillance (the equivalent of supervision), which is a 'stick' that allows it to demand changes in countries' policies when a country negotiates a programme of assistance on the basis of some conditions. The old adage 'If I am going to help you on a rainy day, I need to know what is going on on a sunny day' applies to the Fund operations. The Fund typically provides financial assistance on a conditional basis and the basis for accepting any given conditions rests upon the knowledge that the Fund has acquired of the country via surveillance (Article IV consultations and multilateral surveillance).

The Fund's regulatory, rule-making role is limited, because it shares it with a number of **5.16** international standard-setters, such as the Financial Stability Board (FSB) and the Basel Committee on Banking Supervision (BCBS), and because the 'rules' are soft law (that is, standards and codes without formal enforcement proceedings).

The IMF is the international lender of last resort, in that 'it goes in when everyone goes out'. **5.17** Effectively, countries seek IMF financial assistance when private financial assistance becomes unavailable or prohibitively expensive, as will be seen in paragraphs 5.55–5.63. Financial assistance from the IMF provides the 'carrots' for the country, while conditionality and surveillance constitute the 'sticks'.

A few more words about surveillance:[14] IMF surveillance has evolved significantly over the **5.18** last decades (thanks to the ample room of interpretation granted to the Fund in the exercise of surveillance), with increased attention to financial sector issues and policies being the most significant development. While surveillance historically has typically focused on jurisdiction over the exchange arrangements of members and macro-economic policies, surveillance nowadays also takes into account other issues, often involving the workings of the private sector, such as good governance (both political and corporate governance), legal and institutional reform, bank resolution, restructuring, financial reform, etc. Surveillance needs to be sufficiently robust to empower the Fund to detect incipient financial tensions and vulnerabilities in international capital markets.

---

[13] From the Fund's perspective, its powers can be broken down into three categories: (i) regulatory (jurisdiction, Article VIII, section 2, and Article IV); (ii) financial (Article V, section 3); and (iii) advisory (technical assistance, Article V, section 2(b)). For an extensive analysis of IMF surveillance, conditionality, and technical assistance, *see* Lastra (n.7), ch. 13.

[14] *See* generally IMF, 'IMF Surveillance', IMF Factsheet (30 March 2013), available online at <http://www.imf.org/external/np/exr/facts/surv.htm>.

5.19 And a few other words about conditionality:[15] 'conditionality' refers to the policies and procedures developed by the Fund to govern the access to and the use of its resources by member countries. Since these resources exist for the benefit of the entire membership and are finite, their use needs to be temporary and consistent with the purposes of the Fund.

5.20 Conditionality has served a variety of purposes over the years.[16]

(1) It is a filter through which to channel financial assistance. This filtering rationale is essential when considering the IMF's role as international lender of last resort: the provision of financial assistance to countries in need is not automatic, but conditional on the adoption and implementation of adjustment policies. The logic behind conditionality is simple: a country with external payments problems is spending more than it is taking in; unless economic reform takes place, it will continue to do so.[17]
(2) Conditionality represents the essence of the 'adequate safeguards' prescribed in Article 1(v) of the Articles of Agreement.[18] Conditionality is consistent with the nature of the IMF resources, which are finite and exist for the benefit of the entire membership. Conditionality protects the quality of the IMF asset portfolio.[19]
(3) Conditionality can help to promote 'good policies'. Countries seeking IMF financial assistance know that only good policies will 'earn' them a programme. This knowledge makes the 'ownership' issue all the more difficult.
(4) It signals policy credibility to the markets. The existence of an IMF programme encourages private investment into the country. This explains why countries are ready to tighten their own belt (and the belts of their citizens) in order to get and maintain an IMF programme. The eagerness to get or maintain a programme may also help to explain why, in some instances, specific measures in a programme have been proposed, without a full awareness or analysis of their potentially negative social implications. The importance attached by countries to IMF conditionality goes beyond the importance that they attach to the fulfilment of other obligations undertaken as members of international organizations.
(5) Finally, conditionality serves as a substitute for collateral. Banks require collateral in commercial lending. Conditionality operates as a substitute for collateral in lending to sovereign borrowers.

5.21 Countries in need of balance-of-payments support subject themselves to conditionality, surveillance, and technical assistance as the price that must be exacted to obtain financial support. Members are not always keen to tighten their own belts and the belts of their citizens to obtain the resources that they need to address balance-of-payments difficulties, but they are well aware that non-observance of their financial obligations under the Fund conditions will lead them into further trouble.

---

[15] *See* generally IMF, 'IMF Conditionality', IMF Factsheet (2 April 2013), available online at <http://www.imf.org/external/np/exr/facts/conditio.htm>.

[16] *See* generally Rosa Lastra, 'IMF Conditionality' (2002) 4(2) J Int'l Banking Reg 167.

[17] This is the rationale of the 'phasing out' technique of conditionality: successive tranches of financing are delivered only if key objectives remain attainable.

[18] Article 1(v) reads: '[T]o give confidence to members by making the general resources of the Fund temporarily available to them under adequate safeguards.'

[19] *See* Manuel Guitián, 'Conditionality: Past, Present, Future' (1995) 42 IMF Staff Papers 792, 796.

We have discussed the analogy between supervision and surveillance, and between national and international lender of last resort. In banking, crisis management ends with resolution and insolvency, but as Lee Buchheit explains (with Elena Daly) in Chapter 1 on 'Carrots', the situation is very different when it comes to sovereigns: 5.22

> Sovereigns are not subject to national bankruptcy codes, their own or anyone else's. Thus, when a sovereign signs a foreign law-governed debt instrument in favour of a private sector creditor, there are only two alternatives: pay the debt according to its terms; or face a potential legal action for enforcement of the instrument. For the sovereign borrower—and only for the sovereign borrower—'seeking the protection of the bankruptcy courts' is not an option.

4. Sovereign Debt and the IMF[20]

Over the years, the IMF has developed a number of policies to deal with debt crises and the problems of recalcitrant sovereign debtors. Debt crises are of two types: those arising in low-income (and heavily indebted) countries with no access to international private capital markets—that is, those countries that fall under the IMF's Heavily Indebted Poor Countries (HIPC) initiative; and those arising in middle-income countries with access to international private capital markets. Chapter 6 deals with the former; this chapter therefore considers only the role of the IMF in those countries in which official financial assistance coexists with private financing (borrowing in international capital markets). 5.23

In 2004, Lee Buchheit wrote that there had been three periods of intense intellectual activity in the field of sovereign debt management since Mexico's default on 22 August 1982.[21] The first period lasted from 1982 to 1985. During this time, the key issues in sovereign debt were the restructuring of billions of dollars of commercial bank loans in a way that would not threaten the stability of the domestic financial systems of the creditor countries. The IMF acted as an honest broker, as a 'master of ceremonies', as an arbiter in sovereign debt negotiations (and debt restructuring) between debtor countries and creditors and creditor countries.[22] The IMF gave or withheld its blessing to the member country's plan of reform. 5.24

The second period lasted from 1990 to 1993, following the adoption of the so-called 'Brady initiative'. Commercial bank loans were no longer 'rolled over', but instead were transformed 5.25

---

[20] *See* generally Lastra (n. 7), ch. 14.

[21] *See* Lee Buchheit, 'A Quarter Century of Sovereign Debt Management: An Overview' (2004) 35 Georgetown J Int'l Law 637.

[22] In the words of Walter Robicheck, adviser to the IMF Managing Director from 1982 to 1984:

> The role of the IMF as an honest broker between debtor countries and their creditor banks consists of serving as ultimate judge of the appropriate mix between the magnitude of a heavily indebted developing country's adjustment effort and the commitment to it of new external finance for its remaining balance of payments deficit. This judgment calls for the performance of three major tasks. The first is to help a country frame an adjustment program that would qualify for a standby or extended arrangement with the IMF. This task involves the prudent exercise of conditionality. The second is to commit IMF resources in support of such an adjustment program, which involves setting the IMF's own contribution toward financing a country's balance of payments deficit. In setting its own contribution, the IMF takes into account the enhanced leverage which this commitment of its own resources affords the country with other foreign lenders and, more particularly, with the banks with exposures in the country. Third, the IMF intercedes directly in support of the country's efforts for raising external finance from third parties. This task is commonly referred to as its catalytic role.

See E. Walter Robicheck, 'The International Monetary Fund: An Arbiter in the Debt Restructuring Process' (1984) 23 Colum J Transnat'l L 143, 146.

into freely tradeable securities ('Brady bonds') at a discount (that is, debt reduction): 'A new species of investor—the bond investor—was introduced to the rewards and to the risks of lending to sovereign borrowers.'[23] Since countries had defaulted on their bank loans, but continued to service their bonds (although the outstanding amount of bonds was very small in the 1970s and 1980s), the bonds acquired an aura of de facto seniority that was a contributing factor to the growth of bond issues in the 1990s.[24] The myths perpetuated by these investors with regard to the alleged 'inviolability' of bonds were not disabused by the so-called 'official bailouts' given to Mexico, Thailand, Indonesia, South Korea, and Brazil. After Russia, however, it became clear that sovereign bonds were not 'inviolable' and that therefore restructuring was indeed possible.

5.26 This brought us into the third period of intellectual activity, which commenced in 2000. The question at the beginning of the twenty-first century was how to restructure sovereign bonds in an orderly fashion. While bank creditors are easily identifiable, bond creditors are numerous, anonymous (in the case of bearer bonds), and more difficult to coordinate. In addition, many investors who hold these bonds have no close links with the debtor countries and no commitment to repeat or further investments. The variety of bond instruments and the range of jurisdictions in which debt is issued further complicate the restructuring. Finally, the problems are exacerbated by the incentives that some private creditors have to 'hold out' from the restructuring in the hope of obtaining more favourable terms, or to sue in order to get better terms. If holdouts succeed (as they have done at times, as surveyed elsewhere in this book), the success of this litigation hinders creditor coordination and exacerbates the freerider incentives, the problems of the dissenting minority. This third period of intellectual activity has led to a reliance on market-based, contractual techniques—in particular, collective action clauses (CACs) in bond agreements, examined in Chapter 1—to confront the problems of sovereign debt workouts and in particular the holdout problem.[25] One of the most significant innovations—first used in Uruguay—has been the 'aggregation mechanism',[26] also advocated in the recent IMF document on sovereign debt restructuring.[27]

5.27 The problems posed by the so-called 'holdout' creditors in a sovereign debt restructuring are also at the root of the SDRM proposed by the IMF.[28] Indeed, they are at the root of some of

[23] Robicheck (n. 22).

[24] Robicheck (n. 22).

[25] *See* Lee Buchheit and G Mitu Gulati, 'Sovereign Bonds and the Collective Will' (2002) 51 Emory LJ 1317, 1324.

[26] *See* Lee Buchheit and Jeremiah Pam, 'Uruguay's Innovations' (2004) 19 J Int'l Banking L & Reg 28. A major innovation of Uruguay's version of the CAC was the 'aggregation mechanism', by which a proposed amendment to the payment terms of two or more series of bonds could be incorporated through aggregated voting to other series of bonds simultaneously by the approval of a double majority (of 85 per cent of the aggregate principal amount of all affected series and by 662, or 3 per cent, of each specific series). The Uruguay transaction challenged the widely held view that investors would refuse to take seriously a proposal to restructure sovereign bonds unless forced to confront an open payment default. The way in which the transaction was structured increased the participation of bondholders. It also challenged the view that CACs were of marginal importance for small issues of bonds. The aggregation voting mechanism à la Uruguay also facilitates a more comprehensive approach to sovereign debt workouts than a single-series CAC, since it affects multiple series of bonds, rather than an individual bond issue. In this respect, the aggregation mechanism bridges the gap between the SDRM proposals (dealing with the whole existing stock of debt, thus including different classes of creditors) and the single-series CAC.

[27] *See* IMF (n. 3).

[28] *See* Anne O. Krueger and Sean Hagan, 'Sovereign Workouts: An IMF Perspective' (2005) 6 Chi J Int'l L 203.

the key challenges in any restructuring, as the recent litigation on *pari passu* (see Chapter 4) has shown.

Creditor litigation against sovereign debtors has increased in recent years. The restrictive theory of sovereign immunity[29] now prevails in most jurisdictions, so that a sovereign state can be subject to civil proceedings in a foreign court with respect to its commercial activities. Sovereign immunity is now largely confined to *acta jure imperii* as opposed to *acta jure gestionis*.[30] Sovereign debt documentation typically provides—by means of a waiver of sovereign immunity—for the sovereign's consent to a foreign jurisdiction and judgment enforcement proceedings.[31] **5.28**

The problem with sovereign debt crises is threefold. **5.29**

(1) They are not isolated events, but a recurrent feature in the history of international finance. The history of sovereign debt is also the history of sovereign debt crises.
(2) They seldom arise alone: they typically come together with banking crises, economic crises, social crises, and also political crises.
(3) They exacerbate the intertemporal problems of debt repayment.

Economists typically differentiate between illiquidity and insolvency, but an insolvent country is more difficult to identify conceptually than an insolvent company (or bank):

> An insolvent country is one that cannot pay its debts, not because it has insufficient assets but because it cannot mobilize the revenues required to service its debt without imposing great pain on its citizens, jeopardizing the survival of its government and impairing the social and political stability of the country itself.[32]

A lot has changed in the last few years in particular in the context of the aftermath of the global financial crisis, which mutated into a sovereign debt crisis in some eurozone member states in 2010. Indeed, since May 2010 (when the sovereign debt problems of Greece turned into a crisis that threatened to compromise the very existence of the euro), we have entered into a *fourth* period of feverish intellectual activity, focusing on how to restructure sovereign debt in a monetary union (see Chapters 13 and 14).[33] **5.30**

---

[29] As acknowledged, the doctrine of sovereign immunity (precluding bringing suits against the government without its consent) is founded in the ancient principle that 'the King can do no wrong'. *See* Hal Scott, 'A Bankruptcy Procedure for Sovereign Debtors?' (2003) 37 The International Lawyer 103: 'Bond debt obligations are not normally protected in foreign courts by sovereign immunity as the issuance of such debt is regarded as a commercial activity, and commercial activities are outside the protection of sovereign immunity.'

[30] *See* Roy Goode, *Commercial Law*, 2nd edn (London: Penguin Books, 1995), 21:

> When in 1981 the House of Lords decided to abandon the old rule and bring English law into line with that of other jurisdictions by removing sovereign immunity in relation to the trading activities of the state, it thereby received into English law a restrictive doctrine of sovereign immunity which had by that time become adopted by almost all influential trading nations.

[31] *See* International Law Association (ILA), *Berlin Conference (2004): Report of the International Monetary Law Committee* (1 June 2004), available online at <http://www.ila-hq.org/en/committees/index.cfm/cid/22>, 6. Under US law, foreign state property enjoys immunity from pre-judgment attachment unless the state has expressly waived that immunity, and from post-judgment attachment unless the sovereign has explicitly or implicitly waived that immunity or the property seized is the very property upon which the plaintiff's claim is based.

[32] *See* Peter Kenen, 'The International Financial Architecture: Old Issues and New Initiatives' (2002) 5 International Finance 23, 31.

[33] Lee Buchheit has played a fundamental role in events in the eurozone. *See*, e.g., Robin Wigglesworth, 'Lee Buchheit: Crusader for Financially Stricken Countries', *Financial Times*, 28 May 2013, available online at <http://www.ft.com/cms/s/0/f0c2519c-c79e-11e2-9c52-00144feab7de.html#axzz2cPXzWlC6>.

5.31 In response to these developments (as well as the ongoing litigation against Argentina), the April 2013 IMF paper on sovereign debt restructuring[34] plots a new path for the Fund's involvement in sovereign debt workouts in relation to four issues.

(1) Acknowledging that debt restructurings have been often 'too little and too late', the Fund will require increased rigour and transparency of debt sustainability and market access assessments, and will explore ways in which to prevent the use of Fund resources to bail out private creditors.
(2) Acknowledging the limitations of the current contractual, market-based approach to restructuring in addressing collective action problems, the Fund will respond by introducing more robust aggregation clauses and by considering ways in which to condition the use of its financing to the resolution of such collective action problems.
(3) The growing role of official lending calls for a clearer framework for official sector involvement (OSI), especially with regard to non-Paris Club creditors.
(4) Finally, a review of the IMF Policy on Lending into Arrears (LIA) (private arrears) is needed in light of the increased complexity of the creditor base. Consideration could also be given to extending the LIA policy to include official arrears.

5.32 The recent country report on Greece,[35] in which the Fund acknowledges mistakes in its debt sustainability analysis, calls for a reassessment of the Fund's lending policies in the case of monetary union and for 'spreading the burden of adjustment across different strata of society'. Additionally, the report emphasizes the need to streamline the Troika process and 'for Fund staff to be more sceptical about official data during regular surveillance'. Clearly, the way forward is going to include a stricter assessment of a country's debt sustainability before the Fund provides financial support.

A. Statutory and contractual solutions

5.33 Sovereign debtors are unique, as has already been pointed out. Unlike corporate or household borrowers, there is no institutional framework (no international bankruptcy court, nor a transnational sovereign bankruptcy regime or code) that will permit sovereign borrowers to obtain debt relief when their financial obligations outstrip their ability to pay without worrying about hostile creditor actions. In order to solve this problem, four policy options have been put forward:[36]

(1) a voluntary contractual regime based on CACs;
(2) a limited statutory regime based on a model law/statute, a treaty, or an amendment to the IMF Articles of Agreement;[37]
(3) a wider statutory regime, akin to the SDRM proposals, possibly giving a role to the IMF; and
(4) a less protective regime strengthening creditors' positions and diluting protections for insolvent states.

---

34 *See* IMF (n. 3).

35 *See* IMF (n. 4).

36 *See* generally ILA, *The Hague Conference (2010): Sovereign Insolvency Study Group—State Insolvency: Options for the Way Forward* (August 2010), available online at <http://www.ila-hq.org/download.cfm/docid/0A7ACEAC-94A3-4B47-B9E642CF4BEA5D81>.

37 An amendment to the IMF Articles of Agreement requires the approval by three-fifths of the members, holding 85 per cent of the total voting power (the United States—with close to 17 per cent of the voting power—has an effective veto).

The ad hoc resolution of international debt crises and the involvement of a variety of actors, including international organizations (notably the IMF), informal clubs (the Paris Club for official debt, the London Club for commercial bank debt), national authorities, and private financial institutions have sometimes been criticized as inefficient. A centralized, statutory solution has been hailed in some official and academic circles as an improvement over the current piecemeal approach. Others have suggested resorting to arbitration or to a dispute resolution mechanism akin to the World Trade Organization (WTO) dispute settlement system.[38] **5.34**

The possible adoption of an SDRM would entail the creation at an international level of a bankruptcy procedure for countries, akin to Chapter 11 of the US Bankruptcy Code and of an independent dispute resolution forum to verify claims.[39] The IMF could be the locus of such an SDRM. The IMF started considering the SDRM in 2001[40] and the idea of an international bankruptcy procedure was also discussed in the 1980s.[41] In 2002, the International Monetary and Financial Committee (IMFC) endorsed the Fund's work and encouraged the IMF to continue to examine the legal, institutional, and procedural aspects of two approaches, which could be complementary and self-reinforcing: a statutory approach, which would enable a sovereign debtor and a supermajority of its creditors to reach an agreement binding all creditors; and an approach, based on contract, which would incorporate comprehensive restructuring clauses in debt instruments.[42] The adoption of such an SDRM would in principle imply an amendment to the IMF's Articles of Agreement. Enthusiasm for some form of SDRM has been reignited in the light of the Argentine litigation[43] (discussed in other chapters) and the eurozone woes. **5.35**

An alternative and more modest proposal would be either an amendment to or a creative interpretation of Article VIII, section 2(a), of the IMF Articles of Agreement. The section reads as follows: 'Subject to [conditions not relevant here], no member shall, without the approval of the Fund, impose restrictions on the payment of payments and transfers for current international transactions.' It could be amended either to affect creditor rights (rendering unenforceable in the territories of any IMF member country a debt instrument that was invited to participate in a sovereign debt adjustment programme, but which declined to do so[44]) or creditor remedies (immunizing in all IMF member countries the assets and revenue streams of the debtor country against which attachment by the holder of a debt instrument **5.36**

---

[38] The author is grateful to the members of the Sovereign Bankruptcy Group of the ILA for the discussions held in the last few months in order to improve the status quo with regard to sovereign debt workouts. While some members support a statutory/treaty solution, others prefer to continue with a market-based approach, albeit subject to revisions/improvements.

[39] A dispute resolution forum would be established to resolve disputes that may arise during the voting process or when claims are being verified. *See* IMF, 'Proposals for a Sovereign Debt Restructuring Mechanism (SDRM)', IMF Factsheet (January 2003), available online at <http://www.imf.org/external/np/exr/facts/sdrm.htm>.

[40] *See* Krueger (n. 2).

[41] *See*, e.g., Benjamin Cohen, 'A Global Chapter 11' (1989) 75 Foreign Policy 109.

[42] *See* IMF, *Communiqué of the International Monetary and Financial Committee of the Board of Governors of the International Monetary Fund*, 20 April 2002, available online at <http://www.imf.org/external/np/sec/pr/2002/pr0222.htm>.

[43] *See* Alison Frankel, 'How Argentina Lost Game of Chicken with Renegade Bondholders', *News and Insights: Thomson Reuters* (26 November 2012), available online at <http://newsandinsight.thomsonreuters.com/Legal/News/2012/11_-_November/How_Argentina_lost_game_of_chicken_with_renegade_bondholders/>.

[44] As acknowledged, IMF Articles of Agreement Article VIII, section 2(b), declares 'unenforceable in the territories of any member' certain types of contract that are inconsistent with Fund-approved exchange control regulations.

that was invited to participate in a Fund-approved sovereign debt adjustment programme, but declined to do so).[45]

5.37 The adoption of a voluntary 'code of conduct' with principles that could guide the negotiations of sovereign debtors and their creditors has been discussed in several fora.[46] The United Nations Conference on Trade and Development (UNCTAD) released its Draft Principles on Promoting Responsible Sovereign Lending and Borrowing—further discussed in Chapter 27—in April 2011.[47] A code of conduct accepted by market participants should also be helpful to guide judges dealing with the problems of litigious dissenting minorities.

5.38 It might be argued, however, that the various solutions—statutory, contractual, or soft law/code of conduct—might be pursued in tandem, as evidenced by the 'standardization' of CACs in sovereign bonds in recent years, or by the inclusion of CACs in the Treaty establishing the European Stability Mechanism (ESM),[48] as discussed in Chapter 26.

5.39 The approach favoured by the IMF in the resolution of sovereign debt crises has changed over time. However, two principles remain constant. First, the IMF provides financial assistance to remedy temporary balance-of-payments problems (whether they are general or special balance-of-payments problems) and is not designed to provide long-term financial assistance to countries with unsustainable debt burdens—although the *mea culpa* in the case of the assistance to Greece is a departure from this principle[49]—nor to finance long-term development projects (the domain of the World Bank). This means that the IMF will, in principle, provide financial support only when the problems are of 'liquidity', not when the problems are of 'prolonged and unsustainable debts' (insolvency). The central criterion to determine whether or not to provide such support is the debt sustainability analysis (DSA)[50]—in itself a judgement call—of whether a country has the capacity to grow out of its debt, as Sean Hagan points out in his chapter in this volume (Chapter 23). Second, any financial assistance provided by the Fund must be consistent with its Articles of Agreement. This second principle, which is at the root of conditionality, is also at the root of the other policies and procedures adopted by the Fund over the years to safeguard the quality of the

---

[45] The author is grateful to Lee Buchheit for observations and guidance on these points, and to the Sovereign Bankruptcy Group of the International Law Association (chaired by Philip Wood and to which the author contributes as an observer) for enlightening discussions on these issues.

[46] International Federation of Insolvency Professionals (INSOL International), *Statement of Principles for a Global Approach to Multi-Creditor Workouts*, available online at <http://www.ifecom.cjf.gob.mx/PDF%5Carticulo%5C4.pdf>.

[47] Available online at <http://unctad.org/en/docs/gdsddf2011misc1_en.pdf>.

[48] Available online at <http://www.european-council.europa.eu/media/582311/05-tesm2.en12.pdf>. From 1 January 2013, all eurozone member states are required to include the Model CAC in both international and domestic government securities.

[49] *See* IMF (n. 4).

[50] In a DSA, a judgement is made about a member's ratio of debt to gross domestic product (GDP). It is deemed unsustainable if the debt-to-GDP ratio is likely to continue to rise in the medium term, no matter what adjustment measures are introduced and no matter how much financing is provided by the Fund. The Fund's approach to debt sustainability analysis differentiates between market-access countries, which typically have significant access to international capital markets, and low-income countries, which meet their external financings needs mostly through concessional resources. The assessments of public and external debt sustainability are conducted in the context of both IMF programme design and reviews, and Article IV surveillance. The framework for public debt sustainability analysis was reformed in 2011 and guidance to staff on the implementation of the new framework was introduced in May 2013. *See* IMF, *Staff Guidance Note for Public Debt Sustainability Analysis in Market-Access Countries* (9 May 2013), available online at <http://www.imf.org/external/np/pp/eng/2013/050913.pdf>.

IMF asset portfolio (the 'adequate safeguards' of Article 1(v) of the Articles of Agreement) and therefore to safeguard repayment.

When the IMF provides financial support to troubled countries, the IMF often has a vested interest, since it is a creditor in its own right.[51] **5.40**

B. The IMF's preferred creditor status

The Fund's influential role in sovereign debt workouts has been a characteristic feature of the international financial system since 1982 and one that has had a profound influence on private creditors' incentives, on the one hand, and on the design of certain IMF policies, on the other.[52] It is in this context that the Fund's LIA policy, the concept of 'burden sharing', and the defence of its de facto 'preferred creditor' status must be understood. The latter practice has been recognized in the Paris Club and in other fora for sovereign debt restructuring, but creditors have not legally subordinated their claims to those of the Fund. **5.41**

Interestingly, the IMF preferred creditor status has found its way into a legislative text via the adoption of the ESM Treaty[53] (signed in February 2012 and ratified in September 2012). Recital 13 of the ESM Treaty reads as follows: **5.42**

> Like the IMF, the ESM will provide stability support to an ESM Member when its regular access to market financing is impaired or is at risk of being impaired. Reflecting this, Heads of State or Government have stated that the ESM loans will enjoy preferred creditor status in a similar fashion to those of the IMF, while accepting preferred creditor status of the IMF over the ESM. This status will be effective as of the date of entry into force of this Treaty. In the event of ESM financial assistance in the form of ESM loans following a European financial assistance programme existing at the time of the signature of this Treaty, the ESM will enjoy the same seniority as all other loans and obligations of the beneficiary ESM Member, with the exception of the IMF loans.[54]

The Fund justifies this priority ranking on the grounds that the IMF is not a commercial organization seeking profitable lending opportunities. In fact, the Fund likes to remind its members that it often lends precisely at the point at which other creditors are reluctant to do so, and at interest rates that are below those that would be charged at that juncture by **5.43**

[51] In the relations between the IMF and commercial bank creditors in the 1970s, the commercial banks were often 'third-party beneficiaries of the Fund's stabilization programmes'. The de facto (unofficial) coordination of banks' private loans with IMF financing explains the influential role of the IMF in the debt restructuring proceedings and negotiations in the 1980s. The banks typically required that countries reach an arrangement with the Fund as a precondition for rescheduling, as an assurance that the policies pursued by the debtor in question would help to restore external viability and would be subject to enhanced Fund surveillance. *See* Lee Buchheit and Mark Walker, 'Legal Issues in the Restructuring of Commercial Bank Loans to Sovereign Borrowers', in Michael Gruson and Ralph Eisner (eds) *Sovereign Lending: Managing Legal Risk* (London: Euromoney Publications, 1984).

[52] *See* Lee Buchheit, 'The Role of the Official Sector in Sovereign Debt Workouts' (2005) 6 Chi J Int'l L Symposium 333, 341.

[53] *See* n. 48.

[54] In the Statement by the Eurogroup of 28 November 2010, available online at <http://www.consilium.europa.eu/uedocs/cms_data/docs/pressdata/en/ecofin/118050.pdf>, it was clearly stated:

> In all cases, in order to protect taxpayers money, and to send a clear signal to private creditors that their claims are subordinated to those of the official sector, an ESM loan will enjoy preferred creditor status, junior only to the IMF loan.

Unlike the IMF, the EFSF has the same standing as any other sovereign claim on the country (*pari passu*): *see* EFSF, *European Financial Stability Facility (EFSF)*, available online at <http://www.efsf.europa.eu/attachments/faq_en.pdf>.

the private sector. In so doing, the IMF helps countries to catalyse private financing, and to avoid disorderly adjustment and policies that would harm themselves, private creditors, and other countries. Putting IMF claims together with commercial claims in a workout would fundamentally undermine the Fund's capacity to play that vital role in future.

5.44 From the IMF's own perspective, its preferred creditor status has been fundamental to the Fund's financial responsibilities:

> If the Fund were no longer a preferred creditor, the risk on its lending would increase and the funds made available by creditor members could no longer be regarded as risk free. If reserve positions in the Fund are not regarded as fully liquid and of the highest quality, members cannot treat them as part of their international reserves, which is crucial for the Fund's financing mechanism to operate.[55]

5.45 From the members' perspective, remaining current (that is, not being in arrears) with the Fund is considered essential to accessing additional financing or debt relief from other official creditors. Members thus give priority to repayment of their obligations to the Fund over their obligations to other creditors.

5.46 The concept of 'burden sharing' (that is, dividing the burden of financing or restructuring between the IMF and other creditors) has been an important component of the IMF strategy toward the resolution of debt crises. The concept of sharing is a very difficult one to enforce and implement:

> My three year old daughter often tells her brothers: 'Share, you have to share'. Her concept of sharing, though, is 'unilateral'. If she has something, she does not expect to share it. If the others have something, they should share it with her. In international finance, this 'selfish' behaviour of small children often gets replicated.[56]

In the words of Lee Buchheit: 'Creditors to the same borrower exist in a Hobbesian state of nature.'[57] While in corporate lending these Hobbesian tensions have a logical stopping point, which is bankruptcy, in the sovereign context, there is no neutral referee such as a bankruptcy judge, which means that every class of creditor, and every creditor within every class, must look out for itself.

5.47 Contractual provisions in loan and bond agreements have limitations, and sometimes fail to achieve parity of treatment. This is where the IMF can step in and play a useful role: the role of a referee, someone 'above' the creditor and creditor groups, who can decide who should contribute and how much. The IMF has inside information about the debtor countries through its surveillance function (Article IV consultation), and can help debtors to sort out their problems through balance-of-payments assistance, and technical assistance. This unique set of IMF responsibilities helps countries to restore their creditworthiness through economic reform (remembering here the 'logic' of conditionality: that a country that overspends—that is, spends more than it takes in—will continue to overspend unless economic reform takes place).

---

55 *See* IMF, *Financial Risk in the Fund and the Level of Precautionary Balances* (3 February 2004), available online at <http://www.imf.org/external/np/tre/risk/2004/020304.pdf>, Box 1.

56 Rosa M. Lastra, *Legal Foundations of International Monetary Stability* (Oxford University Press, 2006), 487–8.

57 Lee Buchheit, 'The Search for Intercreditor Parity' (2002) 8 Law & Bus Rev Am 73.

Recent developments in the eurozone may challenge the IMF's cherished preferred creditor status if Greece chooses to restructure debt owed to the IMF and other official sector lenders.[58] 5.48

C. The IMF's Lending into Arrears policy

A few words about the Fund's LIA policy:[59] the Fund's policy regarding sovereign arrears 5.49 to private creditors (including both commercial banks and bondholders) has undergone a number of developments in response to the evolution of international capital markets over the last decades.[60] The Fund's arrears policy was first articulated in a decision adopted by the Fund's Executive Board in 1970.[61] From 1970 to 1980, the policy of the Fund was 'not to lend into arrears'. This policy of non-toleration of arrears to private creditors implied that no financing was provided until the debtor country had reached agreement with its official and private creditors. In 1980, the Fund's Board signalled that it was prepared to show even greater tolerance towards arrears in the context of Fund-supported stabilization programmes.[62]

However, by the late 1980s, there was a growing recognition that the problems faced by 5.50 many debtors were of sustainability rather than liquidity. In May 1989, the IMF Executive Board concluded that its policy of non-toleration of arrears provided creditors with excessive leverage over the sovereign debtors caught up in the debt crisis. As a result, the Fund again modified its arrears policy to tolerate temporary arrears to commercial banks, enabling

58 *See* Spink and Geddie (n. 5):

> It is increasingly likely—they claim—that Greece will become the first sovereign ever to choose to restructure debt owed to the IMF—putting in question for the first time the IMF's status as an unchallengeable preferred creditor when it comes to sovereign debt.... A restructuring... is all but inevitable as part of the so-called Official Sector Involvement (OSI) that would also see Greece restructure debt owed to fellow Eurozone member and the ESFS.... The Fund has thus far remained resolute that its loans to Greece's bailout cannot be revised.... 'A return to genuine market access will require these countries to make themselves presentable to the market' said Buchheit. 'With huge debt stocks, now owed mainly to official sector lenders, hanging over their heads, it may be difficult to make that case. The options for the debtor countries? Reduce or stretch the official sector debts—or remain wards of the official sector for an indefinite period'. It is against this background that Greece's financial minister Yannis Stournaras told Greek television... that the country plans to return to the capital markets by the end of next year.

59 *See* generally Lee Buchheit and Rosa Lastra, 'Lending into Arrears: A Policy Adrift' (2007) 41(3) The International Lawyer 939–55:

> The International Monetary Fund's lending into arrears policy ('*LIA*'), as it is being implemented in 2007 (some 18 years after its debut), may be a perfectly sensible measure to protect the Fund's own lending into a distressed situation. Or it may be a pretext for the Fund to assert a degree of supervision over the methods by which sovereign debtors reach settlements with their private sector creditors. Or it may be both. Therein lies the problem. No one—the IMF least of all—seems prepared to articulate the definitive rationale and objective of the LIA policy. This makes a critical analysis of the policy, whether attempted by the IMF Executive Board, sovereign debtors or private lenders, very difficult.

60 IMF, *Fund Policy on Lending into Arrears to Private Creditors: Further Consideration of the Good Faith Criterion* (30 July 2002), available online at <http://www.imf.org/external/pubs/ft/privcred/073002.pdf>, 3.

61 Decision No. 3153-(70-95), adopted 26 October 1970, available in IMF, *Selected Decisions, Seventeenth Issue* (Washington DC: IMF, 1992). *See* also IMF, *Selected Decisions and Selected Documents of the IMF, Thirty-Sixth Issue: Payments Arrears* (31 December 2011), available online at <http://www.imf.org/external/pubs/ft/sd/index.asp?decision=3153-(70/95)_2>.

62 *See* IMF, *Selected Decisions and Selected Documents of the IMF, Thirty-Sixth Issue: Review of Fund Policies and Procedure on Payments Arrears, 17 October 1980* (31 December 2011), available online at <http://www.imf.org/external/pubs/ft/sd/index.asp?decision=EBM/80/154>.

the Fund to support adjustment programmes even if no agreement had yet been reached between the debtor country and its bank creditors.[63]

5.51 As discussed earlier, since 1989, with the adoption of the Brady Plan, dramatic changes in the composition of capital flows to emerging market economies have taken place, with bonds replacing syndicated bank loans as the primary vehicle for financing emerging market sovereigns. All of this prompted yet another rethink of the LIA policy. In 1998, the Fund's directors agreed that Fund support following a default on sovereign bonds (an extension of the LIA policy) would be considered on a case-by-case basis, but only where: (i) prompt Fund support was considered essential for the successful implementation of the member's adjustment programme, (ii) negotiations between the member and its private creditors had begun; and (iii) there were firm indications that the sovereign borrower and its private creditors would *negotiate in good faith* on a debt restructuring plan.[64] The first two criteria replicated those in the 1989 Summing Up, while the third criterion (good faith negotiations) was intended to address specific concerns relating to bond restructuring.[65]

5.52 Further Executive Board discussions about the LIA policy took place in 1999, after the Asian debt crisis.[66] The Board concluded that bondholders, by simply refusing to negotiate with a sovereign debtor, could effectively prevent the Fund from assisting a member country. This prompted a 1999 revision of the policy.[67] The simple 'good faith negotiation' criterion of the 1998 iteration of the policy was replaced by the following formulation: '[T]he member is . . . making a good faith effort to reach a collaborative agreement with its creditors.' As stated elsewhere:

> The shift in emphasis between the 1998 and 1999 versions is obvious. The focus in 1999 was on the nature of the resulting agreement with creditors ('collaborative'), not on the willingness of the sovereign to enter into genuine (good faith) negotiations. And in this shift of emphasis, the Fund for the first time introduces a motivation for the LIA policy that goes beyond the traditional 'protect Fund resources' explanation. In other words, by 1999, the Executive Board had decided that it had a legitimate interest in seeing that member countries dealt with their private creditors, and *vice versa*, according to someone's notion of fair play.[68]

5.53 On 4 September 2002, the Executive Board considered once again the good faith criterion in the Fund's LIA policy,[69] based on a paper prepared by IMF staff in light of the bond restructurings concluded by Ecuador, Pakistan, and Ukraine.[70] This time around, the good

---

[63] Chairman's Summing-Up Following the Executive Board Meeting of 23 May 1989. *See* EBM/89/61, 24 May 1989.

[64] Concluding Remarks by the Chairman on Involving the Private Sector in Forestalling and Resolving Financial Crises, Buff/98/85 (9/14/98), 5.

[65] *See* Buchheit and Lastra (n. 59).

[66] *See* EBS/99/67, 30 April 1999, 9.

[67] The staff paper prepared by the Policy Department and Review and Legal Departments and approved by Jack Boorman and François Gianviti *Fund Policy on Arrears to Private Creditors: Further Considerations* (29 April 1999) was discussed by the Executive Board on 14 June 1999. *See* 'Summing-Up by the Acting Chairman, Executive Board Meeting, 14 June 1999', in IMF, *IMF Policy on Lending into Arrears to Private Creditors* (Washington, DC: IMF, 1999), available online at <http://www.imf.org/external/pubs/ft/privcred/lending.pdf>, vii.

[68] *See* Buchheit and Lastra (n. 59) 946.

[69] *See* IMF, 'IMF Board Discusses the Good-Faith Criterion under the Fund Policy on Lending into Arrears to Private Creditors', Public Information Notice (PIN) No. 02/107, 24 September 2002, available online at <http://www.imf.org/external/np/sec/pn/2002/pn02107.htm#P40_2845>.

[70] *See* IMF, *Fund Policy on Lending into Arrears to Private Creditors: Further Consideration of the Good Faith Criterion*, Prepared by the International Capital Markets, Policy Development and Review and Legal Departments (in consultation with the other departments), approved by Gerd Häusler, Timothy Geithner, and François Gianviti, SM/02/248 (30 July 2002), available online at <http://www.imf.org/external/pubs/ft/privcred/073002.htm>.

faith criterion was elaborated into a full-blown set of prescriptions and procedural rules for conducting negotiations with creditors. The problem with these detailed prescriptions is that it changes the basic motivation of the IMF from that of safeguarding its own resources to that of acting as a referee, with the conclusion that:

> [I]n its role as a self-appointed referee in negotiations between sovereign debtors and their bondholders, the IMF suffers from these disabilities: This referee never actually enters the arena; it relies for information on how the game is going based on verbal reports by the two contestants. This referee can sanction only one of the teams. Finally, this referee has, well before the game has begun, already decided the final score.[71]

In the recent IMF paper on sovereign debt restructuring,[72] the Fund acknowledges that 'the application of the LIA policy appears to have been uneven' and that therefore a review of the LIA policy is again needed. While in the Dominican Republic, Seychelles, and St Kitts and Nevis IMF staff judged that the 'authorities were engaged in good faith efforts to reach a collaborative agreement with creditors', the assessment of this 'good faith efforts' criterion was inconsistent. In the case of Argentina, 'no constructive dialogue was observed'. The paper points out that 'it may be difficult for any creditor committees to be deemed representative of such a wide diversity of interests'. **5.54**

D. International lender of last resort

The debate about the need for an international lender of last resort (ILOLR) is a consequence of the globalization and interdependency of financial markets across the world. The fear that a domestic conflict can expand—by contagion—to other countries has led to the emergence of the IMF as a de facto ILOLR. Proposals to entrust the IMF with such a role were first debated in 1995 following the Mexican crisis. The crises in Thailand, Indonesia and South Korea reignited the debate in 1997, as the Fund provided—through standby arrangements—a rescue package to these countries. **5.55**

What became known in the jargon as a 'bailout package' was deemed necessary at the time to restore confidence and to renew access to funding in the international capital markets. The creation of the Supplemental Reserve Facility (SRF) in 1997 was a step forward in the 'formalization' of the role of the Fund as ILOLR—a 'special' policy, according to Article V, section 3(a). The Fund also created another facility to deal with the contagion effects of a crisis, the Contingent Credit Line (CCL), in 1999. However, the CCL was never used and was allowed to expire in 2003. **5.56**

In the aftermath of the global financial crisis, the IMF adopted the so-called Flexible Credit Line (FCL) in 2009 to reduce the stigma effect of applying for assistance, a key challenge in the design of a lender of last resort.[73] Access to the FCL is restricted to countries that meet strict qualification criteria, and provides countries with large and up-front access to IMF resources. But once a credit line has been approved, a country can draw on it with no ongoing conditions. The FCL works as a renewable credit line at low cost to help in tough times. In situations in which a fully fledged economic programme is either not necessary or not **5.57**

---

[71] *See* Buchheit and Lastra (n. 59) 952.

[72] *See* IMF (n. 3), paras 50–52.

[73] See IMF, *The IMF's Flexible Credit Line (FCL)*, IMF Factsheet (3 April 2012), available online at <http://www.imf.org/external/np/exr/facts/fcl.htm>.

feasible, the Fund can provide financial support to meet urgent balance-of-payments needs under the Rapid Financing Instrument (RFI) and Rapid Credit Facility (RCF).

5.58 In 2010 the IMF introduced the Precautionary Credit Line (PCL), which was replaced by the Precautionary and Liquidity Line (PLL) in 2011.[74] The PLL combines a qualification process (similar to that of the FCL, *ex ante* conditionality) with focused *ex post* conditionality aimed at addressing the remaining vulnerabilities identified during qualification. Countries eligible for the PLL may face moderate vulnerabilities and may not meet the FCL qualification standards, but they do not require the same large-scale policy adjustments normally associated with regular standby arrangements.

5.59 A distinctive feature of the crises at the end of the twentieth century and beginning of the twenty-first century is that the acute balance-of-payments problems that these countries suffered stem from the capital account instead of the current account. A few considerations ought to be made when comparing the lender of last resort role of the central bank at the national level and the role of the IMF as ILOLR.[75]

5.60 First, the IMF cannot create money, which limits its lending capacity.[76] Goodhart contends that the key factor determining the scope and scale of a domestic lender of last resort is its ability to absorb losses, an ability that rests ultimately with the government. Since governments are constrained by the domain of their domestic jurisdiction, they cannot create foreign currency. So, just as commercial banks will turn to their central bank when they cannot borrow at acceptable terms in the money markets, these national governments and central banks will turn to an ILOLR when they cannot borrow foreign currency on acceptable terms in the international money market.[77] Second, the lender of last resort should generally address problems of illiquidity, not of insolvency. Problems of insolvency are best dealt with—nationally and internationally—by other legal and policy mechanisms of crisis management. Third, the risk of contagion is the key factor affecting the discretionary decision to provide (or not to provide) lender of last resort assistance.[78] Fourth, any degree of protection

[74] *See* IMF, *The IMF's Precautionary and Liquidity Line (PLL)*, IMF Factsheet (3 April 2013), available online at <http://www.imf.org/external/np/exr/facts/pll.htm>. The duration of PLL arrangements can be either six months or one to two years. Access under the six-month PLL is limited to 250 per cent of quota in normal times, but this limit can be raised to 500 per cent of quota in exceptional circumstances resulting from exogenous shocks, including heightened regional or global stress. One- to two-year PLL arrangements are subject to an annual access limit of 500 per cent of quota and a cumulative limit of 1,000 per cent of quota. The repayment term of the PLL is the same as for the Stand-by Arrangements (SBA).

[75] Stanley Fischer has argued that although the IMF is not an international central bank, it acts in important respects as an ILOLR—a role that, in his opinion, is needed in the international monetary system. *See* generally Stanley Fischer, *On the Need for an International Lender of Last Resort*, Princeton University Essays in International Economics No. 220 (November 2000), available online at <http://www.princeton.edu/~ies/IES_Essays/E220.pdf>. According to Olivier Jeanne, the need for a lender of last resort can be rationalized by the fact that emerging countries' external debt is mostly denominated in foreign currency, which national lenders of last resort hold in insufficient quantity to repay all creditors at short notice: *see* Olivier Jeanne, 'The IMF: An International Lender of Last Resort', IMF Research Bulletin (September 2000), available online at <http://www.imf.org/external/pubs/ft/irb/2000/eng/02/index.htm>.

[76] According to Forrest Capie and Geoffrey Wood, 'Unless the IMF…can issue any currency it wishes on demand and without limit, there can be no ILOLR': *see* Forrest Capie and Geoffrey Wood, 'The IMF in a Changing World', Paper prepared for *Essays in Honour of Sir Joseph Gold*, mimeo, 7 November 2001.

[77] *See* Charles Goodhart, 'Myths about the Lender of Last Resort' (1999) 2 International Finance 339, 348–52.

[78] *See* Charles Goodhart and Haizhou Huang, *A Model of Lender of Last Resort*, LSE Financial Markets Group Discussion Paper No. 313 (January 1999), available online at <http://www.lse.ac.uk/fmg/workingPapers/discussionPapers/fmgdps/dp313.pdf>. Goodhart and Huang's model suggests that contagion (and not moral hazard) is the main concern in providing a lender of last resort.

justifies regulation and supervision, nationally and internationally: the greater the expected protection, the more justifiable regulation and supervision becomes. It then follows that any degree of international protection justifies strengthening international banking rules and enhancing surveillance of domestic bank supervisory and regulatory policies. Greater and closer surveillance over financial systems, and their supervision and regulation, has become an important component of an Article IV consultation, in particular under the Financial Services Action Plan (FSAP).

Notwithstanding the need for an ILOLR, there are serious drawbacks to official sector bailout packages, given the finite nature of IMF resources and the magnitude of private capital flows nowadays.[79] **5.61**

(1) They give rise to moral hazard incentives, such as investors' folly, reckless bank lending, irresponsible policies, delays in policy change, etc.
(2) Other techniques to deal with crises may prove more efficient and less costly than bailouts.
(3) Unlike domestic central banks, the IMF cannot print money and thus cannot lend freely. In neither the Mexican nor the Asian bailout packages, nor in the packages for Greece or Portugal, did the IMF provide the funds alone; instead, the IMF acted as a leader or coordinator in the design of the packages (akin to the role of the lead bank in a syndicated loan).
(4) Bailouts may be inequitable if they allow investors to 'escape' when they should take a hit for their bad decisions.
(5) Crises are often a good stimulus for reform; the moral hazard of bailout packages may allow bad policies to remain in effect much longer. At the end of the day, the final response must be at the domestic level: reforming the domestic financial sector and strengthening the institutional framework.
(6) Standby arrangements of the magnitude of Mexico or Korea stretch IMF resources, which exist for the benefit of the entire membership, impeding the alternative use of those resources for other purposes. The IMF—and, for that matter, the ESM—can engage at any given time in only a limited number (very few) of bailout packages, thus raising questions of possible asymmetrical treatment of members.
(7) Finally, given the recurrent nature of crises, and the difficulties of predicting and preventing the next one, one might wonder if today's solution (that is, a bailout package) might be a good response for tomorrow's crisis.

The key to determining the success (or failure) of bailout packages—indeed, of any crisis resolution mechanism—is the ability to renew access to funding in the international capital markets and thereby help to restore confidence in the country. Like in a fair, the merry-go-round keeps on going until it comes to a halt. After the relative success stories of Mexico, Thailand, Indonesia, and South Korea came the defaults of Russia (a 'managed' default) and Argentina (a 'chaotic' default—a failure). And more recently in Europe, it may have been relatively easy to 'bail out' Greece, Portugal, or Ireland, but Spain and Italy are quite another story. **5.62**

[79] For further discussion of the role of the IMF as ILOLR, *see* Rosa Lastra, 'Lender of Last Resort: An International Perspective' (1999) 48 ICLQ 339.

5.63 The IMF is now firmly inserted in the European Union process. Given the 'no bailout' clauses of the Treaty on the Functioning of the European Union (TFEU)—Article 125 TFEU prohibits the bailout of governments, while Article 123 TFEU prohibits the monetization of government debt—and the concerns of creditors countries (notably Germany) to effectively bail out debtor countries (notably Greece, but others followed), the eurozone turned to the IMF in its capacity as ILOLR. The wavering and changing policies of the European Union—further discussed in Chapters 25 and 26—have left the Fund befuddled at times. The IMF, of course, possesses the know-how and the credibility when it comes to assisting countries in financial need. And the European Union/eurozone has been in a learning process when it comes to sovereign debt problems. The 'troika'—the IMF, the European Central Bank (ECB), and the European Commission—has become the foundation that supports the programmes under the architecture evolving to deal with sovereign debt problems that has culminated with the adoption of the ESM Treaty. The ESM, lest we forget, is modelled upon the IMF (although the ESM can also recapitalize banks), while the ECB does have the limitless capacity to act as supranational lender of last resort (both the ESM and IMF have finite resources). The new role that the IMF has adopted since 2010 as one-third participant in full bailout programmes, most of which go to pay private creditors at par, may damage the credibility of its debt sustainability analyses and may potentially jeopardize its preferred creditor status.[80] The *ex post* evaluation of Greece[81] is an acknowledgement that things need to change.

5. Conclusions

5.64 The IMF's singular set of responsibilities (in particular, surveillance and conditional financial assistance) and its role in sovereign debt negotiations explain its central position in the 'international financial architecture'. In the absence of an international bankruptcy regime for sovereigns, there have been calls to grant the Fund a formal role in this process via the so-called SDRM or—following a more minimalist approach—via an amendment to the IMF Articles of Agreement to provide greater predictability and consistency in sovereign debt workouts. The role of the Fund in this regard will continue to evolve: to its unique position as arbiter in negotiations between sovereign debtors and their creditors, as gatekeeper of stability and creditworthiness (via conditionality and surveillance), and as ILOLR may, in the near future, be added a more formal institutional role in sovereign debt restructurings.

[80] *See* Spink and Geddie (n. 5).
[81] *See* IMF (n. 4).

6

DEBT RELIEF FOR LOW-INCOME COUNTRIES

Thomas A. Duvall, III

1. Introduction

In the mid-1990s, it became apparent to the international community that the existing mechanisms for providing debt relief to low-income countries were inadequate to address their debt situation. In 1996, the President of the World Bank and the Managing Director of the International Monetary Fund (IMF) proposed a framework for resolving the debt problems of the heavily indebted poor countries (HIPCs) in cases in which existing debt relief mechanisms were inadequate. The HIPC Debt Initiative framework was exceptional in that it was, for the first time, an initiative seeking to address the debt problems of low-income countries in a comprehensive manner, involving all creditors, including the IMF, the World Bank, and other multilateral creditors. The aim of the framework was to reduce the overall debt[1] of eligible countries to a sustainable level once they completed an extended period of strong policy performance, including the sustained implementation of macroeconomic policies, together with structural and social policy reforms. Changes were made in the framework in 1999 with the introduction of the Enhanced HIPC Initiative in order to provide faster, deeper, and broader debt relief to HIPCs. In 2005, debt relief provided under the HIPC Initiative was supplemented with the introduction of the Multilateral Debt Relief Initiative (MDRI), which provided for the cancellation of debts owed to certain multilateral creditors in addition to the debt relief provided by them under the HIPC Initiative. To date, thirty-six low-income countries, mostly in Africa, have received debt relief under the HIPC Initiative and MDRI of some US$128 billion in nominal terms. The initiatives have largely been successful in reducing the debt of HIPCs to a sustainable level. Care will be needed going forward, however, to reduce the risk that such countries do not undertake new financing that may lead to a build-up of future unsustainable debt. **6.01**

The HIPC Debt Initiative framework was based on six guiding principles: debt sustainability should be determined on a case-by-case basis; relief should be provided only when the country has shown, through a track record of reform and sound policies, the ability to put to **6.02**

[1] Debt covered under the HIPC Debt Initiative is limited to medium and long-term public and publicly guaranteed external debt, with the following exceptions: short-term debt in arrears for more than one year; private sector debt previously covered by Paris Club creditors; debt of public enterprises (defined as at least 50 per cent owned by the government) regardless of whether the debt is formally publicly guaranteed; and debt of public enterprises being privatized if that debt remains a liability of the government.

good use the support provided; the HIPC debt relief measures should build on existing debt relief mechanisms; the additional action provided under the HIPC Debt Initiative should be coordinated among all creditors involved, with broad and equitable participation; action provided by multilateral creditors should preserve their financial integrity and preferred creditor status; and any new external finance for countries receiving debt relief should be on appropriately concessional terms.[2]

2. The Initial HIPC Debt Initiative

6.03 Initially, the HIPC Debt Initiative included a two-stage process for HIPCs to receive debt relief. During the first stage, a country would establish the three-year track record needed to qualify for debt stock reduction from Paris Club creditors under Naples terms.[3] Toward the end of the first stage, the IMF and the World Bank, together with the country, would prepare a debt sustainability analysis (DSA) to determine whether the debt relief provided by the Paris Club creditors under Naples terms (together with comparable treatment by the country's other bilateral and commercial creditors) would be sufficient for the country to achieve debt sustainability in a further three years. The preparation of the DSA is referred to in the HIPC Debt Initiative as the 'decision point'. If the DSA were to show that the debt relief provided by the Paris Club creditors under Naples terms, along with comparable relief from the country's other bilateral and commercial creditors, would result in a sustainable debt situation, the country would not be eligible for support under the HIPC Debt Initiative. If the DSA were to show that the country's debt would *not* be sustainable, the country would enter the second stage of the process.[4] During this second stage, the country would undertake a second three-year adjustment programme supported by the IMF and the World Bank, and during which the international financial community would provide extraordinary support to help to ease the country's debt burden and undertake to provide debt relief at the end of that three-year period to bring the country's debt to a sustainable level, provided that the country achieved a satisfactory track-record of adjustment and reform. The end of the second stage is referred to in the HIPC Debt Initiative as the 'completion point'.

[2] IMF and World Bank, *A Framework for Action to Resolve the Debt Problems of the Heavily Indebted Countries: Report of the Managing Director of the IMF and the President of the World Bank*, 12 April (Washington DC: IMF/World Bank, 1996).

[3] Under Naples terms, Paris Club creditors provided debt stock relief involving a 67 per cent net present value (NPV) reduction in eligible debt to low-income countries that successfully completed a three-year IMF-supported adjustment programme and had a good payments record. The Paris Club is an informal grouping of nineteen official bilateral creditors (Australia, Austria, Belgium, Canada, Denmark, Finland, France, Germany, Ireland, Italy, Japan, the Netherlands, Norway, Russian Federation, Spain, Sweden, Switzerland, the United Kingdom, and the United States). The role of the Paris Club is to provide a means for providing debt relief on debts owed to the creditors by developing and emerging economies in a coordinated manner. Paris Club debt relief is premised on comparability of treatment by non-multilateral creditors. Under this principle, a country receiving debt relief from Paris Club creditors agrees to solicit comparable debt relief from its private creditors and non-Paris Club bilateral creditors.

[4] For borderline cases, in which there was doubt that debt sustainability would be achieved by the completion point based on a Naples-terms debt stock reduction operation, the HIPC Debt Initiative envisioned that a country would defer that debt stock reduction operation until the completion point, and receive a further debt flow rescheduling under Naples terms in the period between the decision and completion points. If the outcomes at the completion point were worse than projected, the country would receive debt relief under the HIPC Debt Initiative.

During the three-year period between the decision and completion points, the country would undertake an adjustment programme supported by the IMF and the World Bank. Paris Club creditors would provide debt flow rescheduling involving net present value (NPV) concessionality of up to 80 per cent as needed on a case-by-case basis. Paris Club creditors would also undertake to provide debt stock reduction with NPV concessionality of up to 80 per cent at the end of the period if the country successfully implemented the adjustment programme.[5] Other official bilateral and commercial creditors would offer similar terms. Donors and multilateral institutions would provide enhanced assistance to the country during the period in the form of grants and concessional loans, and would undertake to reduce the present value of the debt owed to them by the country to a level that would result in overall debt sustainability, provided that the country successfully implemented the adjustment programme.[6] **6.04**

The six-year performance period under the HIPC Debt Initiative (the three-year period prior to the decision point plus the three-year period between the decision and completion points) would be implemented flexibly on a case-by-case basis, with countries receiving credit toward the decision point for programmes that were already under way. The second stage could also be shortened, on an exceptional basis, for countries that already had sustained records of strong performance. If the country did not achieve a satisfactory track record of adjustment and reform during the second stage after the decision point, the completion point could be delayed. If there were significant delays, assistance under the HIPC Debt Initiative could be ended, and the country would need to return to the first stage and restart the decision point process. **6.05**

The HIPC Initiative was envisioned to be available only for a short period. Potentially eligible countries would have two years in which to enter the first stage.[7] The inclusion of this 'sunset clause' was intended to signal that the time frame for qualifying for eligibility under the HIPC Initiative was not unlimited, and thereby provide an incentive to countries to adopt IMF and World Bank-supported programmes early. The sunset clause was also intended to limit the build-up of more debt before the application of HIPC Initiative debt relief and thus to mitigate moral hazard. **6.06**

The process established for the original HIPC Debt Initiative is summarized in Figure 6.1.[8] **6.07**

---

[5] In November 1996, the Paris Club creditors agreed, under the so-called 'Lyon terms', to provide up to 80 per cent debt relief to eligible countries under the framework of the HIPC Debt Initiative.

[6] Multilateral creditors could decide to take some of the action required of them at the completion point during the second stage between the decision and completion points, with such interim measures counting toward the action required at the completion point.

[7] The 1996 programme for action stipulated that:

> ...the Initiative would be open to all HIPCs that pursue or adopt programs of adjustment and reform supported by the IMF and World Bank in the next two years, after which the Initiative would be reviewed and a decision made whether it should be continued.
>
> (IMF and World Bank, *The Heavily Indebted Poor Countries (HIPC) Debt Initiative: A Program of Action—Report of the President of the World Bank and the Managing Director of the IMF*, 20 September, Washington DC: IMF/World Bank, 1996)

[8] IMF and World Bank, *The HIPC Debt Initiative: Elaboration of Key Features and Proposed Procedures*, 26 August (Washington DC: IMF/World Bank, 1996).

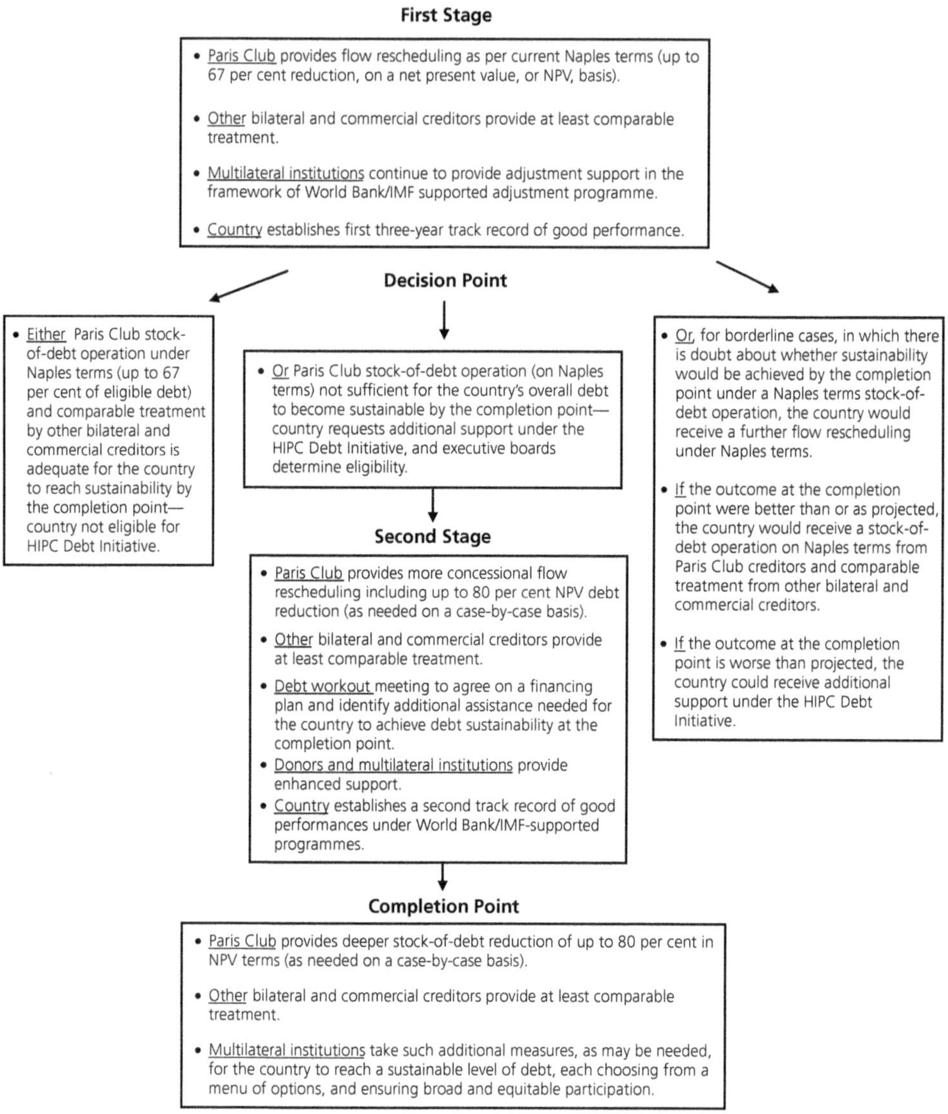

Figure 6.1 Summary of the HIPC Debt Initiative

6.08 Under the original HIPC Debt Initiative, eligibility was limited to those countries that were eligible to receive financing from the International Development Association (IDA)[9] and the IMF's Enhanced Structural Adjustment Facility (ESAF) that were not expected to achieve a sustainable external debt situation at the completion point after receiving debt relief to the full

[9] The IDA is the part of the World Bank that provides financing to the world's poorest countries. Established in 1960, the IDA provides concessional loans and grants for projects and programmes in eighty-one countries. The IDA's concessional loans (referred to as 'IDA credits') bear little or no interest and are repayable over a period ranging between twenty-five and forty years, including a five- to ten-year grace period. The IDA is funded largely by contributions from its richer member countries. Additional funds come from contributions from the net income of the International Bank for Reconstruction and Development (IBRD) and the International Finance Corporation (IFC), and from repayments of IDA credits.

extent possible under existing mechanisms.[10] External debt sustainability would be assessed by the IMF and the World Bank on a case-by-case basis, based on the following ranges: a ratio of the NPV of debt to exports (the NPV debt–exports ratio)[11] of between 200 and 250 per cent, or below, at the completion point; and a ratio of debt service to exports of between 20 and 25 per cent, or below, by the completion point.[12] Within those ranges, debt sustainability was determined on a case-by-case basis in conjunction with various measures of vulnerability, including the external debt service burden on the government budget, the diversity of the country's export base, its reserve coverage and resource balance, and other relevant factors, and the IMF and the World Bank would establish targets for the NPV debt–export ratio and debt service ratio for the country at the completion point. The IMF and the World Bank estimated the amount of the NPV reduction required by multilateral creditors at the completion point, taking into account the debt relief assumed to be provided by bilateral and commercial creditors. If the action committed by creditors at the decision point would bring the actual NPV debt–exports ratio and the debt service to exports ratio at the completion point to the agreed debt sustainability target, creditors would deliver the debt relief determined at the decision point. If the actual ratios at the completion point were higher than the targets primarily as a result of exogenous factors, debt relief assistance would be increased to achieve debt sustainability.

As noted, the HIPC Initiative was premised on the principle that all creditors would participate in providing assistance beyond existing mechanisms as needed for eligible countries to reach debt sustainability. The amount of assistance to be provided by each group of creditors would be determined on a case-by-case basis with the goal of delivering debt sustainability and equitable burden-sharing of the additional relief, and of preserving the preferred creditor status of the multilateral financial institutions. Paris Club creditors were expected to provide 80 per cent NPV reduction of eligible debt. Consistent with Paris Club requirements, countries receiving assistance under the HIPC Initiative would be required to seek treatment on debt owed to other bilateral and commercial creditors on terms at least comparable to those agreed with the Paris Club. Multilateral creditors would take action to reduce the NPV of their claims sufficiently to achieve debt sustainability, after taking into account the amount of NPV reduction provided by Paris Club creditors and at least comparable action by other bilateral and commercial creditors. The action by multilateral creditors would involve broad and equitable participation by all creditors, and preserve the financial integrity of the institutions and their preferred creditor status. It is important to note that participation in the HIPC Debt Initiative by creditors was voluntary. There was no mechanism for forcing creditors to participate. While those multilateral and bilateral creditors holding most the debt of eligible countries committed to participate, some multilateral and bilateral creditors did not. 6.09

[10] Based on this criterion, forty-one developing countries, mostly in Africa, were potentially eligible for assistance under the HIPC Initiative.

[11] The ratio was calculated on the basis of the present value of all future debt service payments on disbursed and outstanding public and publicly guaranteed debt, and the three-year average of actual exports in the years prior and up to the completion point.

[12] While in most cases, the range of 200–250 per cent for the NPV of debt to exports ratio was believed to provide sufficient assurance of debt sustainability, it was determined that the range would not be sufficient in a limited number of cases in which the country had a large export base compared to other measures of debt-servicing capacity, such as fiscal revenues and gross domestic product (GDP). In such cases, it was agreed in 1997 that countries would be eligible for assistance under the HIPC Initiative even if the NPV of debt-to-exports target at the completion point was below 200 per cent. In those cases, the NPV of debt-to-exports target and the amount of assistance to be provided under the HIPC Initiative would be determined in order to achieve an NPV of debt-to-fiscal revenue target of 280 per cent at the completion point.

Similarly, there was no mechanism for commercial creditors to agree to participate generally in the HIPC Debt Initiative. The provision of debt relief to a country by those creditors that did commit to participate was, however, normally conditioned upon participation of a critical mass of the country's creditors.

6.10 The IMF's assistance was provided at the completion point through special ESAF[13] operations—either through grants or loans—to be paid into an escrow account and used only to cover debt service payments to the IMF. Such operations were financed as part of the funding for a continuation of the ESAF. The World Bank's assistance was provided through debt relief on credits provided by the IDA. Such debt relief was financed by transfers from International Bank for Reconstruction and Development (IBRD) net income or surplus. Such transfers were made to a multilateral HIPC trust fund, administered by the IDA. When a country reached its completion point, funds from the trust fund were transferred to the IDA. Two different approaches were followed: either the credits were sold to the trust fund for the NPV amount and then cancelled, or the trust fund resources were used to pay the debt service of the credits as they fell due. In addition, the World Bank provided assistance during the interim period between the decision and completion points. Countries received IDA grants instead of IDA credits during this period to prevent the further accumulation of debt. In the case of those countries with loans outstanding from the IBRD, supplemental IDA allocations were provided to the extent needed to service the IBRD loans. Contributions to the multilateral HIPC trust fund from other donors were provided to other multilateral creditors to finance their costs of debt relief under the HIPC Initiative.[14]

6.11 From the inception of the HIPC Initiative until September 1999, the boards of executive directors of the IMF and the World Bank considered fourteen countries for eligibility under the HIPC Initiative and agreed to extend assistance to seven of them, four of which reached their completion points.[15] The total debt relief expected for all seven countries under the initial HIPC Debt Initiative amounted to more than US$6 billion in nominal terms and was expected to reduce the NPV of the countries' debt by more than US$3 billion.

3. The Enhanced HIPC Debt Initiative

6.12 As experience was gained in implementing the HIPC Debt Initiative, it became evident that certain changes were warranted in order to enhance the prospects that countries would receive enough assistance to achieve a lasting exit from recurrent debt problems and to seek to ensure that the savings provided by debt relief were used for poverty alleviation. At the G-7 Summit in Cologne, Germany, in June 1999, government leaders endorsed a number of proposals of their finance ministers to provide 'faster, deeper and broader debt relief for the poorest countries that demonstrate a commitment to reform and poverty alleviation'.[16] The proposals included the following.

[13] The ESAF was the concessional lending window of the IMF, available for lending to low-income countries.

[14] The HIPC trust fund was amended in 2007 to allow it to receive contributions for arrears clearance and contributions to close the structural gap of the MDRI financing framework in addition to contributions to finance debt relief by the IDA and other multilateral creditors under the HIPC Debt Initiative.

[15] The seven countries, listed in the order in which they reached the decision point, were Uganda, Bolivia, Burkina Faso, Guyana, Cote d'Ivoire, Mozambique, and Mali. Of the seven, Uganda, Bolivia, Guyana, and Mozambique had reached the completion point under the initial HIPC Debt Initiative on or before September 1999.

[16] *Report of Group of Seven Finance Ministers on the Köln Debt Initiative to the Köln Economic Summit*, Cologne, 18–20 June 1999, available online at <http://www.g8.utoronto.ca/finance/fm061899.htm>.

- The savings from debt relief for countries receiving assistance should be targeted to poverty reduction in accordance with poverty reduction plans prepared by the countries with the assistance of the IMF and World Bank.
- The NPV debt–exports ratio should be lowered from a range of 200–250 per cent to a single target of 150 per cent in order to provide deeper debt relief and to broaden the number of countries that would be eligible for assistance. The NPV debt-to-fiscal revenue ratio should be lowered from 280 per cent to 250 per cent. The openness criterion from exports of 40 per cent of gross domestic product (GDP) was lowered to 30 per cent. And the revenue threshold was lowered from 20 per cent to 15 per cent.
- The amount of debt relief to be provided at the completion point would be calculated based on actual data at the decision point instead of projected data for the completion point in order to make the process more predictable and to provide greater certainty about the level of debt relief.
- The completion point should be a floating point tied to the implementation by the country of key structural reforms instead of a fixed date, thereby allowing countries to reach the completion point earlier through improved performance.
- Paris Club creditors should forgive up to 90 per cent, and more if needed, of eligible debt for countries qualifying for assistance under the HIPC Debt Initiative.
- For those countries not qualifying for assistance under the HIPC Debt Initiative, Paris Club creditors should provide a unified 67 per cent NPV reduction under Naples terms.
- Bilateral creditors should forgive official development assistance (ODA) debt for countries qualifying for assistance under the HIPC Debt Initiative on top of amounts needed for countries to achieve debt sustainability and extend new ODA, preferably in the form of grants.
- Countries should receive earlier delivery of assistance from the IMF, World Bank, and other international financial institutions (IFIs) under the HIPC Debt Initiative. The IFIs should advance assistance by providing interim debt relief prior to the completion point and by frontloading debt stock relief after the completion point in such a way as to reduce debt service payments more strongly in the early years.

Subsequently, in August and September 1999, the IMF and the World Bank approved modifications to the HIPC Debt Initiative consistent with the proposals endorsed at the G-7 Summit,[17] and the Paris Club adopted the Cologne terms for the debt relief to be provided on debt owed to Paris Club creditors.[18] The HIPC Debt Initiative, as modified, is referred to as the Enhanced HIPC Debt Initiative. It was expected to increase the likely eligibility for HIPC debt relief from twenty-nine to thirty-six countries and more than double the amount of debt relief provided by the HIPC Debt Initiative relative to the initial framework. **6.13**

[17] IMF and IDA, *Modifications to the Heavily Indebted Poor Countries (HIPC) Initiative*, 23 July (Washington DC: IMF/IDA, 1999).

[18] To qualify for Cologne terms, a country needed to be eligible for Naples terms and: (i) have a sound track record with the Paris Club and continuing strong economic adjustment; and (ii) have been declared eligible under the Enhanced HIPC Initiative by the IMF and World Bank. Under the Cologne terms, Paris Club creditors could provide interim relief between the decision and completion points through a 90 per cent debt service reduction of commercial claims and a long-term rescheduling of the remaining 10 per cent and 100 per cent of official development assistance (ODA) claims. At the completion point, up to 90 per cent or more, if necessary, of the commercial claims would be cancelled, with the remaining amount being rescheduled.

6.14 With the introduction of floating completion points under the Enhanced HIPC Initiative, the focus of the assessment by the IMF and the World Bank of the performance required by a country to reach the completion point shifted from the length of the country's track record to the accomplishment by the country of particular achievements and outcomes, with more weight given to social- and poverty-related reforms, along with macroeconomic stability. To reach the completion point, a country would need to have a minimum track record of three years' solid economic performance under IMF and World Bank-supported programmes (which could include periods prior to the decision point). The country would also need to have appropriate macroeconomic policies in place at the completion point, which would require that the IMF-supported programmes be on track at that point. The country would also need to have reached a macroeconomic position conducive to underpinning sustainable growth and poverty reduction, determined based on low inflation, having a fiscal policy consistent with a low and sustainable level of bank financing of budget deficits, and an adequate reserve cushion. The IMF and the World Bank would also agree with the country on the key structural and social development actions on reforms that would need to be achieved in order to reach the floating completion point. While the agreed measures would be those that could be expected to take up to three years to implement, the country could reach the completion point earlier if it were able to implement them earlier. For those countries that had a recognized track record of good performance prior to the decision point and which had adopted effective poverty action plans, the floating completion point was tied to measures that the country could be expected to complete in two years (or even one year for exceptionally strong performers of agreed social sector targets, which would also be a requirement for reaching the floating completion point).

6.15 One of the objectives of the Enhanced HIPC Initiative was to strengthen the linkage between debt relief and poverty reduction. Specifically, debt relief provided under the Enhanced HIPC Debt Initiative was expected to be part of a broader effort of the recipient country to implement a poverty reduction strategy using all available resources under an enhanced framework for poverty reduction. Countries were expected, with the assistance of the IMF and World Bank, to develop a country-driven poverty reduction strategy, with the broad participation of civil society, elected institutions, key donors, and relevant IFIs, oriented to achieve outcome-related goals for poverty reduction. The country-led strategy would be presented in a poverty reduction strategy paper (PRSP), intended to be the key instrument for the country's relations with the donor community.[19] The PRSP would be endorsed by the boards of executive directors of the IMF and the World Bank as the basis for their concessional

[19] The PRSP represented a new approach to strengthening the link between debt relief and poverty reduction, and to enhancing the poverty-reduction focus of all IMF and World Bank concessional lending. The underlying goal of the approach was to support a comprehensive, country-led effort to help to sharpen the poverty focus and effectiveness of development strategies in low-income countries, and of support for those strategies. The resulting strategies were intended to focus on policy actions to increase growth and reduce poverty, within a coherent macroeconomic framework. Such strategies were to be country-owned and designed in a participatory fashion (taking into account the views of parliaments and other democratic bodies including, where they exist, the donor community, civil society and the poor themselves), comprehensive in approach, and based on a medium- and long-term perspective, including appropriate monitoring indicators against which progress was to be measured. Such strategies were also expected to be linked clearly with the agreed International Development Goals (IDGs) for poverty reduction, education, health, and gender equality. The IDGs organized various United Nations declarations into a number of internationally agreed targets for the year 2015 (relative to 1990). They included: reducing the incidence of extreme poverty by half; reducing infant and child mortality by two-thirds; achieving universal enrolment in primary education; and eliminating gender disparity in education (by 2005). A PRSP was expected to be prepared every three years, with annual progress reports in intervening years.

lending to support the country, as well as for debt relief under the Enhanced HIPC Initiative. In general, countries should have a PRSP in place at the decision point under the Enhanced HIPC Initiative. It was recognized that such a requirement could unduly delay the decision point for some countries. Such countries were allowed to reach the decision point provided that they had an interim PRSP in place. All countries would be required to have made progress in implementing their poverty reduction strategy by the completion point.

Countries that had reached their decision and/or completion points under the initial HIPC Initiative were eligible to receive additional assistance under the Enhanced HIPC Initiative. To receive such assistance, those countries would need to accomplish agreed social sector policy and poverty reduction actions, with the amount of additional assistance being determined through an updated DSA based on the country's current debt, exports, and revenue data, and current discount rates for calculating NPV. 6.16

Although the Enhanced HIPC Initiative provided for making a determination at the decision point of the amount of debt relief to be provided to a country at the completion point, provision was made for 'topping up' debt relief at the completion point in exceptional circumstances if there were a fundamental change in the country's economic circumstances at that time resulting from an exogenous development. The DSA prepared by the IMF and World Bank for a country reaching the completion point would assess the extent to which the debt relief provided to the country would achieve long-term debt sustainability. The DSA would provide the basis for assessing whether the country had experienced a fundamental change in economic circumstances since the decision point and, if so, whether this change was attributable to domestic or external exogenous developments that had taken place after the country reached its decision point. 6.17

For countries that were determined to require the topping up of HIPC Initiative assistance, the amount of additional debt relief to be provided would be that amount calculated to reduce the country's outstanding debt at the completion point to the debt sustainability targets used at the decision point (that is, NPV of debt equivalent to 150 per cent of exports or, in fiscal window cases, 250 per cent of government revenues). The calculation would be based on actual data available at the completion point, taking into account any new debt accumulated by the country after the decision point and all debt relief previously committed to the country, including any additional bilateral debt forgiveness beyond the amount required under the HIPC Initiative. 6.18

The topping-up assistance to be provided by the IMF and World Bank would be contingent upon other creditors providing satisfactory assurances that they would provide their share of the additional assistance. 6.19

As noted, the initial HIPC Debt Initiative was not expected to be open-ended; it was expected to remain available to potentially eligible countries for only two years. Owing to slower-than-expected progress, the sunset clause was extended four times to allow more time for countries to start qualifying programmes so as to be able to benefit subsequently from HIPC Initiative debt relief. Finally, the boards of executive directors of the IMF and the World Bank decided to let the sunset clause take effect at the end of 2006. They also agreed to limit the list of potentially eligible countries to those countries meeting the HIPC Initiative's income and indebtedness criteria based on end-of-2004 data and to grandfather them for eligibility. With those decisions, all of the countries on that list remain potentially eligible for 6.20

debt relief under the HIPC Initiative.[20] This approach was taken to provide comprehensive coverage for countries and their debt, and to treat countries equally. The purpose was to ensure that all potentially eligible HIPCs would continue to have the possibility of receiving maximum debt relief under existing debt relief mechanism, rather than leaving a few with unsustainable debt burdens that would need to be addressed either case by case or through some other debt relief framework. The approach also allowed them to go through the HIPC process at their own pace, without creating undue pressure.

6.21 With the increase in debt relief provided under the Enhanced HIPC Debt Initiative, the modalities for providing debt relief by the multilateral creditors changed from those employed under the original initiative. With respect to debt relief from the World Bank, for the first time the IDA itself assumed responsibility for providing debt relief to eligible countries. It was recognized that the World Bank contributions to the HIPC trust fund would not be sufficient to finance the debt relief commitments required of the IDA under the Enhanced HIPC Initiative. Therefore, at the decision point, the IDA agreed to assume responsibility for providing the debt relief to the country, with the IDA being reimbursed on a pay-as-you-go basis by amounts contributed to the HIPC trust fund by the World Bank to the extent that amounts so contributed were available.[21] Provided that there were sufficient resources in the World Bank component of the HIPC trust fund to do so, the HIPC trust fund would provide annual transfers to the IDA that matched the amount of debt relief that it had provided during the same period. Under the Enhanced HIPC Initiative, the IDA agreed that it would deliver, to the extent feasible, its full share of debt relief to the country within twenty years after the decision point, providing annual relief of not less than 50 per cent of IDA debt service due on the amount of IDA credits disbursed and outstanding at the decision point. The IDA also agreed to provide debt relief during the interim period between the decision and completion points in an amount up to one third of the total NPV debt relief that it was to provide to the country.[22]

---

[20] The list included fourteen countries assessed as meeting the two criteria based on the end-2004 date. Of those, three countries indicated that they did not wish to be considered for HIPC Initiative debt relief, leaving eleven countries that might potentially benefit from relief. The boards of executive directors of the IMF and World Bank also decided that the list of potentially eligible countries could be amended to include other countries for which end-of-2004 data subsequently became available and which were assessed to meet the criteria. The eleven 'grandfathered' countries included Central African Republic, Comoros, Cote d'Ivoire, Eritrea, Haiti, Krygyz Republic, Liberia, Nepal, Somalia, Sudan, and Togo. Bhutan, Lao PDR, and Sri Lanka were the three countries assessed as meeting the criteria, but which indicated that they did not wish to be considered for HIPC Initiative debt relief. Data was insufficient to assess the potential eligibility of Afghanistan and Myanmar. Afghanistan was subsequently included in the list. In 2011, the boards of executive directors of the IMF and the World Bank agreed to add an end-of-2010 indebtedness criterion for eligibility under the HIPC Initiative and to ring-fence further the list of potentially eligible countries based on that criterion. This change resulted in the exclusion from eligibility of two of the countries that had previously indicated that they did not wish to avail themselves of assistance under the HIPC Initiative, as well as one country the debt of which was below the indebtedness criterion based on end-of-2010 data. As a result of this change and taking into account that some of the fourteen countries had qualified for assistance under the HIPC Initiative since 2006, only three countries (Eritrea, Somalia, and Sudan) currently remain potentially eligible for assistance under the HIPC Initiative.

[21] Contributions from the World Bank to the HIPC trust fund were made on an annual basis from the IBRD's net income or surplus. The amount of the annual contributions was therefore subject to the amount of the IBRD's net income for the prior year that could be allocated to the HIPC trust fund, taking into account other demands for the use of such income. It was expected that donors to the IDA would fund the costs of IDA debt relief that could not be financed from the HIPC trust fund as part of the replenishments of IDA resources.

[22] The World Bank raised this limit to 50 per cent for some countries. For those HIPCs with significant outstanding IBRD debt (Cameroon, Cote d'Ivoire, and Honduras), debt relief on such debt was provided by the IDA. During the interim period, the IDA provided supplemental HIPC debt relief grants annually to cover the debt relief to be provided on the IBRD loans. At the completion point, the IDA provided a single supplemental

The IMF HIPC debt relief was provided through special operations of the Poverty Reduction and Growth Facility (PRGF)–HIPC trust.[23] At the decision point, the IMF committed to deliver its HIPC assistance in the form of grants paid to the country's account in the PRGF–HIPC trust, administered by the IMF as trustee, which were used to help to meet the country's debt service payments to the IMF. During the interim period between the decision and completion points, the country could receive up to 20 per cent of total IMF assistance annually—up to a maximum of 60 per cent of overall IMF assistance during the interim period.[24] The remainder of the IMF assistance was delivered following the completion point in the same manner, with the schedule for the grants being set to reflect country-specific considerations, including the profile of the country's total debt service obligations and the degree of front-loading desired given the state of preparation of the country's PRSP, poverty spending needs, and absorption capacity. The cost to the IMF of its debt relief under the HIPC Initiative was financed largely by bilateral contributions and from investment income on the profits from the IMF'S gold sales. 6.22

The African Development Bank (AfDB) provided its debt relief under the Enhanced HIPC Initiative by releasing eligible countries from 80 per cent of their annual debt service obligations until the total debt relief was delivered. Debt service delivery would commence at the decision point, with no more than 40 per cent of HIPC assistance being provided between the decision and completion points. Whenever possible, total debt relief would be provided within fifteen years. The costs to the AfDB of its participation in the HIPC Initiative are funded through internally generated resources, as well as donor contributions to the HIPC trust fund, and administered by IDA. The contribution from AfDB's internal resources typically finances 15–20 per cent of the estimated cost of each beneficiary country, while 80–85 per cent of the cost is financed through donor contributions. 6.23

The Inter-American Development Bank (IADB) provided debt relief under the Enhanced HIPC Initiative generally by providing relief of 50 per cent of its concessional loans and, after 2008, selective cancellation of such loans. Such debt relief was financed from internal resources and contributions to the HIPC trust fund. 6.24

4. The Multilateral Debt Relief Initiative

In 2005, the G-8 put forth a proposal to complete the process of debt relief for the HIPCs through additional development resources to provide significant support for countries' efforts to reach the Millennium Declaration Goals (MDGs), while ensuring that the financing capacity of the IFIs was not reduced. The proposal called for 100 per cent cancellation of the 6.25

HIPC debt relief credit to prepay the amount of IBRD debt outstanding required to achieve the remaining NPV relief to be provided on the country's IBRD debt.

[23] The PRGF–HIPC trust is a trust fund of the IMF, established to provide debt relief under the HIPC Initiative and to subsidize PRGF lending. The resources available to the trust consist of grants and deposits pledged from ninety-three member countries and contributions from the IMF itself. The bulk of the IMF's contribution comes from off-market gold transactions made during 1999–2000.

[24] The IMF increased the limits to 25 per cent and 75 per cent, respectively, for certain countries in order to align the provision of HIPC assistance with the profile of the country's debt service obligations to the IMF.

outstanding debt obligations of HIPCs to the IMF, the IDA, and the African Development Fund (AfDF).[25]

6.26 Under the proposal, HIPCs would have 100 per cent of their debts to the IDA and AfDF cancelled when they reached the completion points under the Enhanced HIPC Initiative, subject to an agreed cut-off date,[26] after which new disbursements from the IDA and AfDF would not be eligible for relief. To ensure that their financing capacity was not reduced and that the proposal would not reduce the resources available from them for poverty reduction activities, the proposal provided that contributors to the IDA and AfDF would provide additional contributions, based on agreed burden shares, to match dollar for dollar the forgone principal and service charge repayments of the cancelled debt.[27]

6.27 The proposal also provided for 100 per cent debt stock relief on debts owed by HIPCs to the IMF when they reached the completion points[28] under the Enhanced HIPC Debt Initiative, subject to a cut-off date of 1 January 2005, after which new disbursements would not be eligible for relief. The proposal called for the IMF to meet the costs of providing such relief through existing IMF resources. For those countries for which the IMF's debt relief could not be met from existing IMF resources,[29] donors would commit to provide the extra resources needed.

6.28 Eighteen countries had reached their completion points under the Enhanced HIPC Initiative at the time that the MDRI came into effect. In order to qualify for debt cancellation under the MDRI, those countries needed to meet the following criteria:

(a) satisfactory macroeconomic performance under an IMF PRGF programme or equivalent;
(b) satisfactory progress in implementing a poverty reduction strategy (PRS); and
(c) implementation of a public expenditure management (PEM) system that meets minimum standards for governance and transparency in the use of public resources.

5. Conclusions

6.29 Although some challenges remain, the HIPC Initiative has largely been completed. Of the thirty-nine countries potentially eligible under the HIPC Initiative, as of December 2012,

[25] The IDA is the concessional financing arm of the World Bank and the AfDF is the concessional financing arm of the AfDB. The IMF has also provided assistance under MRDI to two non-HIPCs (Cambodia and Tajikistan). In 2007, the IADB agreed to provide MDRI debt relief to post-completion-point HIPCs in Latin America and the Caribbean by means of 100 per cent debt relief on credits disbursed to HIPCs before the end of 2004 under the IADB's concessional lending window and still outstanding on 1 January 2007 or the date of the completion point.

[26] The cut-off date for the IDA was set at 31 December 2003. Amounts of existing IDA credits that were undisbursed as of that date, as well as any new credits approved after that date, would not qualify for cancellation under the MDRI.

[27] The additional resources provided by contributors would be allocated through the existing mechanisms of the IDA and AfDF on the basis of governance, need, and ability to use the resources effectively for poverty reduction and growth, so that all low-income countries would receive an increase in net assistance flows commensurate with performance, thereby reinforcing existing incentives for countries to pursue responsible, pro-growth policies, maintaining equity between HIPCs and other low-income countries, and addressing moral hazard problems, since new development assistance would be allocated based on current performance and not current debt payment obligations.

[28] For those countries that had already reached their completion points prior to the establishment of the MDRI, debt cancellation under the MDRI commenced on 1 July 2006.

[29] Somalia, Liberia, and Sudan.

thirty-six had reached their decision points, while thirty-five had reached their completion points and also received additional debt cancellation under MDRI (see Table 6.1).[30]

Debt relief committed to the post-decision-point countries amounts to around US$126 billion in nominal terms, of which about US$50 billion is under the MDRI (including projected assistance under the MDRI to HIPCs between the decision and completion points). Debt relief under the HIPC Initiative and MDRI to the thirty-six post-decision-point countries represents around a third of those countries' 2011 GDP. Together with debt relief under traditional mechanisms and additional (that is, beyond HIPC) relief from Paris Club creditors, this assistance is estimated to reduce the debt burden for those countries by 90 per cent relative to pre-decision-point levels.[31] **6.30**

Table 6.1 Countries that have qualified, are eligible, or potentially eligible for, and which may wish to receive, HIPC Initiative assistance (at December 2012)

Post-completion-point countries (35)		
Afghanistan	The Gambia	Mozambique
Benin	Ghana	Nicaragua
Bolivia	Guinea	Niger
Burkina Faso	Guinea-Bissau	Rwanda
Burundi	Guyana	São Tomé & Principe
Cameroon	Haiti	Senegal
Central African Republic	Honduras	Sierra Leone
Comoros	Liberia	Tanzania
Republic of Congo	Madagascar	Togo
Democratic Republic of Congo	Malawi	Uganda
Côte d'Ivoire	Mali	Zambia
Ethiopia	Mauritania	
Interim countries (between decision and completion point) (1)		
Chad		
Pre-decision-point countries (3)		
Eritrea	Somalia	Sudan

[30] *See* IDA and IMF, *Heavily Indebted Poor Countries (HIPC) Initiative and Multilateral Debt Relief Initiative (MDRI): Statistical Update* (April 2013), available online at <http://www.imf.org/external/pp/longres.aspx?id=4755>.

[31] Paris Club creditors have provided debt relief beyond that required under the HIPC Initiative amounting to almost US$12 billion in end-of-2010 NPV terms. In addition to debt relief under the HIPC Initiative, the European Union has provided debt relief under the Least Developed Countries (LDC) Initiative by cancelling debt outstanding on special loans after the application of HIPC Debt Initiative relief. Through the end of July 2011, such relief amounted to €77 million. Most multilateral and bilateral creditors also cancelled the remaining debt of Haiti after application of HIPC and MDRI relief to help the country to recover from the January 2010 earthquake.

While the two initiatives have been successful in reducing the debt burden of the post-decision-point countries, the progress of those countries in achieving the MIDGs has been uneven: poverty-reducing spending in those countries increased by more than three percentage points of GDP, on average, between 2001 and 2010. For most of the thirty-five completion-point countries, universal primary education is within reach, but half

6.31 The total cost of HIPC Initiative debt relief to creditors was estimated at US$76 billion in end-2011 NPV terms. Paris Club and other bilateral creditors account for over 55 per cent of the total, with multilateral creditors accounting for the remainder.[32] Among the multilateral creditors, the IDA accounts for 20 per cent of the total cost, the IMF for 9 per cent, and the AfDB Group for 7 per cent. Most of the cost for bilateral creditors was borne by Paris Club creditors (36 per cent of the total cost), with non-Paris Club creditors and commercial creditors accounting for 13 per cent and 6 per cent, respectively, of the total costs.

6.32 In addition, the total cost of debt cancellation under the MDRI for the four participating multilateral creditors is estimated at US$36.9 billion in end-2011 NPV terms. About 65 per cent of the total estimated MDRI costs will be borne by the IDA, with the share of the IMF and AfDF amounting to 12 per cent and 15 per cent, respectively, and that of the IADB amounting to 8 per cent.[33]

6.33 Notwithstanding the substantial success in largely completing the implementation of the HIPC Initiative, some ongoing challenges remain. One of the underlying principles of the HIPC Initiative is the broad and equitable participation of all of the country's creditors. To ensure that the country's debt burden indicators are reduced to the HIPC Initiative thresholds, it is critical that all creditors deliver their share of debt relief. The Paris Club creditors and large multilateral creditors have provided their full share of debt relief under the HIPC Initiative. However, there are some smaller multilateral creditors,[34] non-Paris Club bilateral creditors, and commercial creditors that have not done so. Together, such creditors account for about 25 per cent of the total costs of debt relief under the HIPC Initiative. Non-Paris Club bilateral creditors as a whole have delivered around 50 per cent of their share of HIPC Initiative debt relief, while about a third of such creditors have not delivered any debt relief. The delivery of debt relief by commercial creditors has increased in recent years,[35] largely owing to a few large-debt buy-back operations supported by the IDA's Debt Reduction Facility (DRF).[36] Litigation by holdout creditors remains a potential concern, however.

---

still need to implement additional reforms to achieve that target. More than half of them are expected to meet their targets for gender equality and preventing the spread of HIV/AIDS, tuberculosis, and malaria, and about half are on track to reduce childhood mortality rates and to ensure environmental sustainability. Only a quarter are on track to meet the goal of eradicating extreme poverty and progress is less certain on meeting the goal of improving maternal health.

[32] As of December 2012, bilateral donors have contributed almost US$4.3 billion to the HIPC trust fund to support the costs of debt relief provided by the AfDB, the IADB, and nine other regional and subregional creditors.

[33] To date, the cost to the IDA of providing debt relief under the HIPC Debt Initiative and MDRI has been fully funded by contributions from bilateral donors and from the IBRD's net income and surplus.

[34] In addition to the IMF, IDA, AfDB, and IADB, another twenty multilateral creditors, accounting for 13 per cent of total HIPC Debt Initiative costs, have committed to deliver HIPC debt relief. Another eight have not yet done so. Those eight represent less than 0.6 per cent of the total HIPC Debt Initiative costs.

[35] Commercial creditors account for about 6 per cent of the total cost of debt relief under the HIPC Debt Initiative.

[36] The IDA DRF was established in 1989. The Facility is a trust fund, administered by the IDA. The Facility is funded by contributions to the trust fund from bilateral donors and from the IBRD's net income and surplus. The DRF provides grant funding to low-income countries to enable them to buy back, at a deep discount, debts owed to external, commercial creditors. The Facility has supported twenty-five completed buyback operations in twenty-two IDA-only countries, extinguishing about US$10.3 billion of principal and associated interest arrears and penalties. The Facility has supported buyback operations in twenty-one HIPCs and thereby played an important role in facilitating debt relief on commercial debt under the HIPC Initiative.

The situation of the four countries that have not yet completed the requirements for full debt relief under the HIPC Initiative is also challenging. **6.34**

While the HIPC Initiative and MDRI have largely been successful in reducing the debts of low-income countries to a sustainable level, it is also important that new financing for such countries is undertaken in a manner that reduces the chances of an excessive build-up of future debt. To help to guide the borrowing decisions of low-income countries in a way that matches their financing needs with their payment ability, the World Bank and the IMF introduced in 2005 the joint World Bank–IMF Debt Sustainability Framework (DSF). The World Bank and the IMF conduct regular DSAs for low-income countries, focusing on the country's projected debt burden over the next twenty years and it vulnerability to external and policy shocks, an assessment of the risk of debt distress over that period, based on indicative debt burden thresholds that depend on the quality of the country's policies and institutions, and recommendations for a borrowing strategy that limits the risk of debt distress. To assess debt sustainability, the country's debt burden indicators are compared to indicate thresholds over the twenty-year projection period. A debt-burden indicator that exceeds its indicated threshold suggests a risk of experiencing some form of debt distress. There are four ratings: (i) low risk, when all indicators are below the thresholds; (ii) moderate risk, when indicators are below the thresholds in the baseline scenario, but stress tests indicate that thresholds could be breached if there were external shocks of abrupt changes in macroeconomic policies; (iii) high risk, when the baseline scenario and stress text indicate a protracted breach of the thresholds, but the country does not currently face repayment difficulties; and (iv) in debt distress, when the country is experiencing repayment difficulties. The DSF classifies countries into one of three categories based on the strength of their policy performance (strong, medium, and poor) and uses different indicative thresholds for each category, recognizing that debt accumulation by countries with strong policy performance is less risky than that of countries with poor performance (see Table 6.2). **6.35**

Debt sustainability analyses are taken into account to determine access to IMF financing, as well as for the design of debt limits in IMF-supported programmes. The World Bank uses DSAs to determine the mix of grants and loans to be provided by the IDA to low-income countries. The IMF and the World Bank encourage low-income countries to use DSAs to develop their medium-term debt strategies, and encourage other creditors to take account of the DSAs in their lending decisions. **6.36**

As of August 2013, based on the latest available DSAs, one pre-decision-point HIPC was rated as being in debt distress and six post-completion-point HIPCs were rated as being at high rate of debt distress. The IMF and World Bank are closely monitoring the debt situation **6.37**

Table 6.2 Debt burden thresholds under the Debt Sustainability Framework

	Present value of debt			Debt service	
	% of exports	% of GDP	% of revenue	% of exports	% of revenue
Weak policy	100	30	200	15	18
Medium policy	150	40	250	20	20
Strong policy	200	50	300	25	22

of those countries. In addition, as a result of the limited availability of concessional finance, a number of low-income countries—mainly those at low or moderate risk of debt distress—are relying on non-concessional external borrowing to finance infrastructure investment. Increased recourse to non-concessional financing by HIPC and other low-income countries warrants close monitoring of their debt vulnerabilities.

7

THE LONGER-TERM CONSEQUENCES OF SOVEREIGN DEBT RESTRUCTURING

Odette Lienau

1. Introduction

7.01 Sovereign borrowers contemplating a debt restructuring often do so in the context of a current or impending financial crisis or a broader economic upheaval. Government officials feel that they have no choice but to act quickly, and the subsequent discussion with advisers, other domestic actors, and creditors focuses on which calculations and techniques to use. When officials do take a moment to prepare for the long-run effects of their decisions—as they certainly should—they may well come across alarming headlines, such as this example from the web journal centralbanking.com: 'IMF working paper warns of dangers in sovereign debt restructuring... Researchers find debt restructurings have adverse impact on economic growth; say debt sustainability is a crucial consideration.'[1] Such headlines echo a common refrain, not only among creditors, but also among analysts working independently and with international financial institutions (IFIs), which portrays the consequences of restructuring as almost entirely negative—as 'costs' to be avoided if at all possible.[2]

7.02 What is the potential effect of such language? And to what degree does it present the complete picture? To begin with, such dire wording could dissuade state decision-makers from embarking upon a restructuring well past the point at which debt levels have become unsustainable. Indeed, countries by and large make significant efforts to avoid a default, even when external observers and advisers consider restructuring all but inevitable. Even in the infamous Argentinian case, government officials continued payments on their external debt after being advised to restructure by none other than Wall Street bankers and the US Treasury.[3]

---

[1] Central Banking Newsdesk, 'IMF Working Paper Warns of Dangers in Sovereign Debt Restructuring', *CentralBanking.com*, 15 August 2012, available online at <http://www.centralbanking.com/central-banking/research/2198945/imf-working-paper-warns-of-dangers-in-sovereign-debt-restructuring>.

[2] Indeed, the IMF working paper to which the headline refers begins its concluding points with the line 'Debt restructurings can have drastic adverse consequences for economic growth, trade, capital flows, banks and other financial institutions': Udaibir S. Das, Michael G. Papaioannou, and Christoph Trebesch, *Sovereign Debt Restructurings 1950–2010: Literature Survey, Data, and Stylized Facts*, IMF Working Paper No. 12/203 (August 2012) available online at <http://www.un.org/esa/ffd/ecosoc/debt/2013/IMF_wp12_203.pdf>, p. 95. While this is a fair characterization, the literature and evidence actually presented by the authors is somewhat less alarming, particularly in considering long-run consequences.

[3] For an extensive account, *see* Paul Blustein, *And the Money Kept Rolling In (and Out): Wall Street, the IMF, and the Bankrupting of Argentina* (New York: Public Affairs, 2005). For a brief overview by Argentina's former finance minister, in light of recent Greece–Argentina analogies, *see* Domingo Cavallo, 'Looking at

Furthermore, the literature on the costs of sovereign debt default and restructuring offers more nuance than is sometimes presented in synopses meant for a wider readership. These studies, primarily from economics and political economy, take care to distinguish between the consequences of initial default and crisis episodes as opposed to those of completed restructurings, and note when costs become less severe over time. This subtlety and temporal dimension, however, tends to recede in overviews for the broader public.

7.03 This chapter focuses on both of these elements of the sovereign debt restructuring discussion: the potentially independent effect of how restructuring costs are framed, as well as the ways in which the actual consequences detailed by the empirical literature differ somewhat from the popular presentation. It begins with an overview of key terms that might be conflated in considering the effects of debt crises, and then highlights the possible consequences of overemphasizing undifferentiated costs, in particular for distributing the burden of adjustment when a country runs into debt difficulties. The third section takes a closer look at the recent empirical literature on how a restructuring may impact a country's major transnational economic links. Studies suggest that, in key areas (future capital market access and cost of credit, trade, effect on private capital flows), the negative ramifications tend to decline over time and also can be impacted by the nature of the restructuring itself. The conclusion contends that both researchers and readers need to remain aware of how the costs of debt restructuring are characterized, keeping in mind that the presentations themselves can have second-order ramifications for how debt crises unfold. It also suggests that, given the concentration of a restructuring's most severe consequences in the actual default period, mechanisms that streamline the process deserve even more support than they have received thus far. Throughout this discussion, the chapter emphasizes that restructuring almost always constitutes only one part of a larger domestic and international political and economic process. It is a crucial tool for dealing with unsustainable debt burdens and potentially for putting states on a stable economic footing going forward. However, it can hardly be considered sufficient in and of itself for such a major undertaking. Ultimately, a broader array of domestic policy choices—along with external factors, such as export commodity prices, interest rates, and variations in the regional and global economy—necessarily influence the final outcome.

2. Avoiding Conflation in Key Terms

7.04 Although the basic contours of debt restructuring are discussed more thoroughly elsewhere in this volume, it is helpful to begin here with some key terms. This is particularly true because colloquial discussion tends to conflate completed restructurings, which can be understood as negotiated partial defaults,[4] with initial default episodes or unsettled debt crises. Such ambiguity supports the alarmism surrounding conversations about the ramifications of debt restructuring, in particular by merging the almost inevitably messy default and restructuring period itself with its longer-run consequences.

Greece in the Argentinean Mirror,' *Vox*, 15 July 2011, available online at <http://www.voxeu.org/article/looking-greece-argentinean-mirror>.

[4] Carmen M. Reinhart and Kenneth S. Rogoff briefly outline this perspective in *This Time is Different: Eight Centuries of Financial Folly* (Princeton, NJ: Princeton University Press, 2009), 62.

Sovereign debt can be understood as debt owed by the central government of a sovereign state to public or private creditors, although it may also include debt owed by state-owned enterprises or other quasi-sovereign entities, or debt guaranteed by the government.[5] This debt can be issued to domestic creditors or external (international) creditors, and it can be issued in local or foreign currency and subject to local regulations or to the regulatory framework of another state.[6] The debt may be intermediated—that is, owed to banks or other financial houses, which in turn have private depositors—or it may be disintermediated—that is, issued through bonds and held directly by institutional or private investors. And creditors themselves often include private institutions, individuals, IFIs, and other governments. This panoply of relations, each of which may be implicated in a particular debt instrument, makes any given sovereign debt restructuring a complex affair. The process itself can involve many or all of a state's outstanding debt instruments and so bring in a large range of creditors, or it may focus on one instrument or a series of related instruments. Furthermore, larger economic crises frequently accompany debt restructurings, with implications for the broader domestic, regional, or international economic system. Indeed, sovereign debt crises have tended to arrive in cycles affecting multiple countries at once.[7] As such, it is difficult to provide a generalized overview of the many processes that have emerged historically. **7.05**

The basic mechanisms of a restructuring, however, tend to translate across very different cases and, at their core, involve alterations to the original payment terms of a debt instrument.[8] The target instruments—be they bank loans or bonds—are exchanged either for new debt instruments (in a debt exchange) or for cash (in a buyback). As part of this process, the restructuring involves one or both of two changes to the original instrument: in a debt reduction, the face (or nominal) amount of the debt owed may be reduced as part of the exchange or buyback; in a debt rescheduling, the original debt instruments may be exchanged for new instruments that have longer maturities (pushing a larger portion of the payments into the future), and possibly those that have lower interest rates. In either of these situations, the ultimate payout to creditors will differ from that which they originally anticipated. It can therefore be distinguished from simply curing a default—catching up on missed payments to return to and continue upon the original payment schedule. **7.06**

Discussions elsewhere in this volume detail the particular organizations and institutional frameworks—such as the Paris and London Clubs, the International Monetary Fund (IMF), and its Heavily Indebted Poor Countries (HIPC) Initiative—and legal mechanisms—such as **7.07**

[5] This definition is broader than that provided in, e.g., Article 33 of the Vienna Convention on Succession of States in Respect of State Property, Archives and Debt, which defines state debts as 'any financial obligation of a predecessor State arising in conformity with international law towards another State, an international organization or any other subject of international law'. The Convention has not entered into force, and the definition itself has been criticized as overly narrow, for example because it excludes the significant debts owed to private creditors.

[6] Sovereigns generally issue debt domestically to target local capital markets and issue debt externally to attract foreign investors. However, in some instances, domestically based creditors may hold foreign-issued debt and vice versa.

[7] *See*, among others, Peter H. Lindert and Peter J. Morton, 'How Sovereign Debt Has Worked,' in Jeffrey Sachs (ed.) *Developing Country Debt and Economic Performance, Vol. I: The International Financial System* (Chicago, IL, and London: University of Chicago Press, 1989), 39–106; Reinhart and Rogoff (n. 4); Federico Sturzenegger and Jeromin Zettelmeyer, *Debt Defaults and Lessons from a Decade of Crises* (Cambridge, MA: MIT Press, 2006), 3–10.

[8] Sturzenegger and Zettelmeyer define debt restructurings as 'changes in the originally envisaged payments either after a default or under the threat of default': Sturzenegger and Zettelmeyer (n. 7), 3.

collective action clauses (CACs) and exit consents—by which sovereigns and their creditors restructure debt. Each restructuring, however, does involve achieving agreement with creditors through a more-or-less consensual and ultimately legally binding process. It is therefore distinct from a simple default or non-payment of principal or interest when due (which may involve all or only part of a sovereign's outstanding obligations), a moratorium involving the non-payment of given debts for a certain time, or a full repudiation, in which the sovereign government declares that it will no longer make additional payments to creditors. Although these terms are sometimes used interchangeably, the differences are important. In particular, many restructurings begin with a period of default, in which no payments are made on the relevant debt, while the sovereign consults with advisers and possibly creditor representatives to determine possible avenues forward. The ramifications of a restructuring differ according to whether the focus of study is the initial default and crisis episode, the period immediately following a settlement, or the longer-run outcome.

3. The Possible Consequences of Selective Emphasis

7.08 How do these distinctions relate to general characterizations of sovereign debt restructuring as entailing 'danger' and 'adverse impacts'? Certainly, there are significant risks, but what are the likely effects of emphasizing costs without attendant clarifications about their severity or longevity? Significant research on the effects of framing—understood as the necessarily social and selective presentation of information—has emerged in multiple disciplines over the last three decades.[9] Particularly relevant here are 'emphasis framing effects', in which 'preferences change due to different weights given to subsets of relevant information'.[10] Any research summary, historical study, or other presentation of data inevitably involves a focus on some subset of the abundant information available. An analyst's choice of which focus to adopt and which data to emphasize may in turn shape the policy preferences of readers and the ultimate policy choices made.

7.09 Moving into the sovereign debt arena, the clearest probable outcome of a generalized emphasis on cost is that decision-makers will be more likely to avoid or delay restructuring than they would have been with an alternative framing. There is disagreement about the ideal point at which a particular country should restructure debt, and certainly decisions evaluated after the fact may appear less rational than they were at the time of the decision. For example, the Argentinian choice in mid-2001 to delay serious restructuring by swapping shorter-term debt for longer-term instruments with higher eventual costs seems imprudent in retrospect.[11] However, commentators point out that Argentina's actions were in fact 'part of a plausible crisis aversion strategy' and note that '[t]he fact that these strategies failed ex post does not imply that the probability that they would succeed was zero ex ante'.[12]

[9] This line of research is indebted to a series of articles by Daniel Kahneman and Amos Tversky in the late 1970s and early 1980s. *See*, e.g., Amos Tversky and Daniel Kahneman, 'The Framing of Decisions and the Psychology of Choice' (1981) 211 Science 453.

[10] Monika Butler and Michel André Maréchal, *Framing Effects in Political Decision Making: Evidence from a Natural Voting Experiment*, CEPR Discussion Paper No. DP6200 (March 2007), available online at <http://www.cesifo-group.de/portal/pls/portal/docs/1/1187740.PDF>, 5.

[11] Indeed, the chief architects of the deal were even indicted for their participation in the bond swap. *See Mercopress*, 'Former Argentine Leader Indicted for 2001 Bond Swap', 29 September 2006, available online at <http://en.mercopress.com/2006/09/29/former-argentine-leader-indicted-for-2001-bond-swap>.

[12] Sturzenegger and Zettelmeyer (n. 7), 247. The authors present a model of the likely analysis at 242–7.

Notwithstanding the different possible interpretations of such cases, the historical evidence suggests that countries tend to postpone a restructuring decision for too long, rather than rush into an admission of unsustainability too early.[13] Emphasizing the danger of restructuring without any accompanying caveats only exacerbates this tendency.

If, indeed, high (and undifferentiated) costs are emphasized, increasing the likelihood of avoiding or delaying restructuring, what are the second-order effects of this framing? In the absence of restructuring, the key alternative approach is to engage in austerity measures (or 'planned fiscal consolidation'), cutting government programmes and investment in an effort to return to sustainable debt levels.[14] Laying aside for now the frequent unpopularity of such programmes, these measures can eventually become counterproductive. One concern with a debt restructuring is that the negative consequences—for example for future capital access, trade, or economic output—are so severe and long-lasting that the decision cripples the economy and ultimately does more harm than good. But parallel concerns exist for austerity measures, which may so depress domestic spending, local demand, and national output that the economy is unable to recover and to repay the (still outstanding) debt or to attract additional investment. The continued floundering of the Greek economy in the context of broader European policy offers but one example.[15] Indeed, in the first days of 2013, IMF chief economist Olivier Blanchard co-published a working paper suggesting that the organization had misjudged and underestimated the negative effect of austerity measures on growth in European countries during the crisis.[16] This has been interpreted as something of a *mea culpa* for Fund-backed policies in countries such as Greece, whose population has continued to suffer the effects of an economic depression.[17] 7.10

Aside from the potential consequences for the country as a whole, a decision to avoid or delay restructuring can have domestic distributional effects as well. One clear example is the way in which government austerity measures harm those individuals who depend on public 7.11

---

[13] This is the assumption of, for example, the United Nations Conference on Trade and Development (UNCTAD) in its work on debt restructuring. *See* UNCTAD Secretariat, *Sovereign Debt Crises and Restructurings: Lessons Learnt and Proposals for Debt Resolution Mechanisms*, Concept Note Presented at the Special Event of the Second Committee of the General Assembly (25 October 2012), available online at <http://www.un.org/en/ga/second/67/debtnote.pdf>, 4. For a wonderful 'open letter' advising against 'pathological procrastination' in debt restructuring by this volume's co-editor, Lee Buchheit, addressed to the Minister of Finance of the Republic of Ruritania (an imaginary country frequently featured in student exams), *see Six Lessons from Prior Sovereign Debt Restructurings*, Working Paper Prepared for a Conference on Resolving the European Debt Crisis (September 2011), available online at <http://www.piie.com/publications/papers/buchheit20110913.pdf>, 4–5. Viral Acharya and Raghuram Rajan have recently developed a model of why governments with short time horizons might delay restructurings past the point that would most benefit long-term growth: Viral V. Acharya and Raghuram G. Rajan, *Sovereign Debt, Government Myopia, and the Financial Sector*, Working Paper (April 2012), available online at <http://www.econ.nyu.edu/user/galed/fewpapers/FEW%20F12/Acharya-Rajan.pdf>.

[14] Set aside here is the possibility that the government might inflate away its debt denominated in local currency, particularly given that many of the major recent debt crises—in Asia, Europe, and Latin America—have implicated a significant stock of foreign-denominated debt in externally controlled currencies.

[15] For an important overview of both the practical problems with austerity measures and their intellectual history, *see* Mark Blyth, *Austerity: The History of a Dangerous Idea* (Oxford and New York: Oxford University Press, 2013).

[16] Olivier Blanchard and Daniel Leigh, *Growth Forecast Errors and Fiscal Multipliers*, IMF Working Paper No. 13/1 (3 January 2013), available online at <http://www.imf.org/external/pubs/ft/wp/2013/wp1301.pdf>.

[17] *See*, e.g., Howard Schneider, 'An Amazing *Mea Culpa* from the IMF's Chief Economist on Austerity,' *Washington Post online*, 3 January 2013, available online at <http://www.washingtonpost.com/blogs/wonkblog/wp/2013/01/03/an-amazing-mea-culpa-from-the-imfs-chief-economist-on-austerity/>.

programmes or who work in the public sector, including those living below the poverty line and government employees providing public services.[18] To the extent that a government subsidizes staple foods or utilities, the pain may be more broadly shared, but people with a lower capacity to absorb the additional costs will still disproportionately bear the burden. Conversely, groups with a greater stake in maintaining international ties in the short and long terms may disfavour significant restructuring, and may press instead for public cuts, debt swaps providing temporary liquidity, and similar policies. Of course, governments are certainly able to engage in a mix of policies that anger everyone, as the Argentinian events of 2001–02 amply demonstrate. Still, these distributional predictions seem to hold up anecdotally and seem to be supported by the available empirical literature. For example, Michael Tomz's analysis of public opinion surveys administered during the Argentinian crisis found that private sector workers and wealthier citizens were, on average, more inclined to support foreign debt payment than public sector workers or the poor and unemployed. He also found that those who valued future capital flows into the country much preferred to repay foreign debts.[19] Looking at the Latin American debt crisis of the 1980s, Jeff Frieden highlighted the ways in which continued debt repayment had significant internal distributional effects, with key losers including public sector employees and those in more precarious economic circumstances.[20] More recently, Icelandic voters in the 2011 debt repayment referendum seemed to follow this pattern, with the unemployed more in favour of default than those with considerable investment assets or with an interest in future borrowing costs.[21]

7.12 These distributional effects have a correlate in the international arena as well, particularly given the degree to which many countries are now embedded in regional and international economic relations. If sovereign debt is largely domestically held, then the effects of either an austerity package or a restructuring approach will cross borders only indirectly, through possible ramifications for trade, investment, or other economic relationships. However, to the extent that foreign-held sovereign debt is implicated, the consequences of a choice to restructure or retrench will be broader. Most directly, creditors to the sovereign debtor will almost certainly prefer that the country's population bear any necessary adjustment costs, including through steeper public spending cuts and tax increases. Indeed, creditors are likely to go to considerable lengths to avoid admitting that their investments have been excessively risky and taking a corresponding loss on their books. Just as government officials may prefer to gamble that obtaining short-term liquidity at the expense of higher long-term debt burdens will carry them through a (hopefully) temporary financing difficulty, or that exogenous factors such as export markets will soon change for the better, already-implicated creditors may pressure governments not to

[18] Ample anecdotal evidence is provided by the still-unfolding European debt crisis and past crises elsewhere. This tendency has been well known for decades, as suggested by IMF economists acknowledging at the end of the 1970s that public sector workers often bear the brunt of budget cuts: Omotunde Johnson and Joanne Salop, 'Distributional Aspects of Stabilization Programs in Developing Countries' (1980) 27 IMF Staff Papers 1, 12.

[19] Michael Tomz, *Interests, Information, and the Domestic Politics of International Agreements*, Stanford University Working Paper (July 2004), available online at <http://www.stanford.edu/~tomz/working/Tomz2004a.pdf>. Tomz also highlighted that these findings tended to be conditional, with the correlation between policy preferences and economic self-interest strongest among those with higher education levels and presumably more economic awareness.

[20] Jeffry A. Frieden, 'Winners and Losers in the Latin America Debt Crisis,' in Barbara Stallings and Robert Kaufman (eds) *Debt and Democracy in Latin America* (Boulder, CO: Westview, 1989), 23–37.

[21] K. Amber Curtis, Joseph Jupille, and David A. Leblang, *I Save for IceSave: Self-Interest and Sovereign Debt Resettlement*, Working Paper (21 May 2012), available online at <http://ssrn.com/abstract=2063955> or <http://dx.doi.org/10.2139/ssrn.2063955>.

restructure. To the extent that the findings of third parties are framed to support an argument that restructuring is prohibitively costly and leads to long-lasting negative outcomes, the tendency to avoid or delay restructuring will bolster this transnational distributional effect.

A related, but less direct, consequence of framing involves the broader financial systems in which creditors are embedded. Certain creditors that have a high degree of exposure to sovereign debt may in turn be important financial institutions. To the extent that affected creditors are domestic, the resulting loss of confidence in national banks and financial institutions can further undermine the sovereign borrower's economic recovery.[22] Such outcomes can be managed, but have to be dealt with carefully if they are not to become additional sources of instability, as initially happened with the Russian default and restructuring of 1998.[23] If affected creditors are foreign, as historically has been the case in many emerging market states, these systemic ramifications will be felt most keenly in the foreign creditors' own countries and regions. This transnational dynamic was central in the 1980s Latin American debt crisis, in which American, and to a lesser extent European, bank exposure to Latin American sovereign debt rendered any settlement a matter of international concern. The fact that every systemically important bank was implicated in this lending meant that borrowers faced huge resistance to any effort to write down the face value of the debt.[24] The resulting series of ultimately unsuccessful reschedulings through the 1980s, leading eventually to Brady Plan restructurings in the early 1990s, offers one of the best-known instances of unfruitful delay in dealing with unsustainable debt burdens. The European debt crisis has displayed a similar dynamic, with nationally important banks exposed to sovereign debt and disagreement about which financial systems (and which populations) should bear the principal burden of adjustment. Public writing with too blunt an emphasis on restructuring costs can again support avoidance of and delays in restructuring, and bolster a policy preference for austerity and other related measures, and so deepen this transnational and systemic distributional effect. **7.13**

Given the particularity and uncertainty involved in policy choices about sovereign debt, it is hard to identify any independent framing effect generated by the tendency to emphasize adverse restructuring consequences with insufficient nuance. But despite these measurement difficulties, there is good reason to assume that such effects exist in light of their demonstrable presence in other arenas of human decision-making. This raises questions for researchers about when and how particular presentations of data tip the scales in favour of one or another policy approach. It also encourages a closer look at the subtleties of the underlying evidence for claims about the consequences of debt restructuring. **7.14**

4. A Focus on the Longer-Run Ramifications of Debt Restructuring

Given the tendency to focus on the high costs of debt default and restructuring, to what degree are such presentations complete? Certainly, there is an externally imposed economic **7.15**

[22] The interaction of sovereign debt crises and banking crises is discussed more thoroughly elsewhere in this volume.

[23] For a discussion of the Russian case, *see*, among others, Sturzenegger and Zettelmeyer (n. 7), 91–114; Sergei Gorbunov, 'From Financial Pariah to Star Reformer,' in Barry Herman, Jose Antonio Ocampo, and Shari Spiegel (eds) *Overcoming Developing Country Debt Crises* (Oxford: Oxford University Press, 2010), 161–78.

[24] For more on this dynamic and its affect on creditor resistance to debtor arguments, including those about principled debt cancellation, *see* the discussion in Odette Lienau, *Rethinking Sovereign Debt: Politics, Reputation, and Legitimacy in Modern Finance* (Cambridge, MA: Harvard University Press, forthcoming), ch. 6.

cost for the payment interruption or alteration itself. This exacerbates the pain associated with internal problems that often accompany (and may have necessitated) a serious restructuring. As Federico Sturzenegger and Jeromin Zettelmeyer point out:

> Even though it is often difficult to disentangle the costs of defaults from the costs of the shocks of economic crisis that trigger a default, there is no serious disagreement... that defaults and debt restructuring result in a cost to the debtor over and above that of the underlying shock.[25]

In light of the discomfort that accompanies any path that a sovereign debtor might take, the key questions then involve the nature, severity, and duration of such costs.

7.16 This section provides an overview of the empirical literature in economics and political economy to highlight that the evidence on the costs of sovereign debt default and restructuring is fairly nuanced. This literature generally separates out the ramifications of initial default and crisis episodes from the longer-run consequences of completed restructurings. The studies find that although the initial costs are high, the negative ramifications in areas such as capital market access, borrowing rates, trade, and private capital flows can drop significantly over time. Thus the popular tendency to emphasize high restructuring costs curtails the story in important ways. This framing may consequently shift policy preferences more than is fully justified by the evidence, resulting in distributional consequences both within debtor countries and across borders.

A. Future capital market borrowing

7.17 The first and most frequently discussed ramification of a debt restructuring is the possibility that it will affect a borrower's ability to access capital markets at reasonable rates in the future. While sovereign states contemplating a restructuring should bear in mind the risk of such an outcome, there is disagreement in the literature on the extent of this effect. Particularly in the long run, the likelihood of permanent exclusion or prohibitively high rates is lower than one might expect. However, the magnitude of creditor losses in a restructuring factors into this finding, with greater losses relating to longer exclusion periods and higher subsequent borrowing costs.

7.18 The theoretical foundations for this set of expectations around future borrowing lie in understandings of reputation or creditworthiness. In considering whether or not to lend to a sovereign state, potential creditors will assess the borrower's capacity and willingness to repay within the time frame specified. In addition to studying the underlying economic prospects and political characteristics of the state, creditors review the sovereign's repayment record on outstanding and former loans. This allows investors to make a reputational judgement of the borrower, determining whether and under what circumstances they believe a sovereign borrower will repay.[26] Potential creditors may conclude that a sovereign borrower that has

[25] Sturzenegger and Zettelmeyer (n. 7), 49. They continue: 'The fact that countries often desperately attempt to avoid debt restructurings even in situations where full repayment seems hopeless further suggests that there are costs of default, regardless of their origin.'

[26] Michael Tomz reviews data across three centuries to argue that creditors consider both payment record and the situational context of repayment to develop beliefs about a borrower's type—i.e. whether it is a 'lemon' that will default without justification, a 'fair weather' that will repay only when times are good, or a 'stalwart' that repays in good times and bad. This belief on the part of international investors as to which category a borrower falls into in turn constitutes the borrower's reputation, which guides investor risk assessments and lending decisions. *See* Michael Tomz, *Reputation and International Cooperation: Sovereign Debt across Three Centuries* (Princeton, NJ: Princeton University Press, 2007), 17, 23.

restructured debts in the past—with changes to the face value, interest rates, or maturities of the original debt instruments—will be more likely to default upon and restructure debts in the future. According to one analyst writing in the 1920s:

> Bankers almost universally recognize an unimpeachable record for financial uprightness as one of the most important considerations [in lending to foreign sovereigns]... past performances throw a flood of light on the probable future of a security issue.[27]

In a significant restructuring, the lender's actual return (the repaid principal amount plus interest) will be lower than that anticipated by the initial lending agreement. The existence of past restructurings by a borrower could therefore make investors less likely to lend, or at least more likely to charge a higher interest rate—the risk premium above what would otherwise be charged—to offset the possibility of a lower return down the road.

Notwithstanding this theoretical model, there is disagreement in the literature about the existence and degree of impact that a restructuring has on subsequent credit market interactions. The possibility of such an effect was first systematically studied in the 1980s, inspired at least in part by the Latin American debt crisis. There is general agreement that for the duration of an actual default crisis—before any settlement with creditors has been reached—most sovereign states will lose their access to credit markets.[28] And even after a settlement has been concluded, sovereign borrowers rarely attract new lending immediately. However, this is not necessarily the result of recalcitrance on the part of creditors. To begin with, it is unclear whether borrowers actually seek new lending so soon after debt negotiations.[29] Presumably, they would have attempted to meet their needs for increased liquidity as part of the settlement itself. Furthermore, particular debtors' episodes of default and restructuring have often been embedded in larger cycles of enthusiasm for and then distrust of international lending on the part of creditors. Therefore the exclusion of a debtor from credit markets may reflect broader international or regional trends as much as an assessment of a particular debtor's own actions.[30] **7.19**

Regardless of the reasons for immediate exclusion—and provided that foreign investors are generally engaged in international lending—several studies suggest that otherwise creditworthy sovereign states that restructure their debt have, in recent years, accessed international capital relatively quickly: within three years after the resolution of a crisis.[31] In previous eras, **7.20**

---

27 John Emmett Kirshman, *Principles of Investment* (Chicago, IL: A. W. Shaw, 1924), 286–7, as quoted in Tomz (n. 26), 76.

28 *See*, e.g., Ugo Panizza, Federico Sturzenegger, and Jeromin Zettelmeyer, 'The Economics and Law of Sovereign Debt and Default' (2009) 47(3) J Econ Lit 1, 25; Sturzenegger and Zettelmeyer (n. 7), 50.

29 As Michael Tomz and Mark Wright point out, 'realized borrowing is affected by the country's demand for credit, and so different equilibrium outcomes need not reflect a reduced supply of credit': Michael Tomz and Mark L. Wright, *Empirical Studies of Sovereign Default and Restructuring*, Federal Reserve Bank of Chicago Working Paper Series No. WP 2012-06 (28 November 2012), available online at <http://ideas.repec.org/p/fip/fedhwp/wp-2012-06.html>, 12.

30 Several studies suggest that an exclusion of sovereign borrowers that restructured their debts was unlikely to be related to the actual default itself, at least assuming a subsequent settlement with creditors. *See*, e.g., Lindert and Morton (n. 7); Erika Jorgensen and Jeffrey Sachs, 'Default and Renegotiation of Latin American Foreign Bonds in the Interwar Period', in Barry Eichengreen and Peter H. Lindert (eds) *The International Debt Crisis in Historical Perspective* (Cambridge, MA, and London: MIT Press, 1989), 48–85; William B. English, 'Understanding the Costs of Sovereign Default: American State Debts in the 1840s' (1996) 86(1) Am Econ Rev 259.

31 Gelos, Sahay, and Sandleris find that when older episodes are included, the average extended to 4.7 years after exiting a default, excluding countries (such as Argentina) with entirely unresolved defaults: Gaston Gelos, Ratna Sahay, and Guido Sandleris, 'Sovereign Borrowing by Developing Countries: What Determines Market

such as during the 1980s debt restructurings, the exclusion periods lasted longer,[32] although again exogenous, system-wide factors may have played a role. Furthermore, commentators point out that, even during these restructuring periods, most countries have been able to access official sector credit and in some cases have issued debt domestically.[33] That said, investors have tended to be more hesitant to return to lending where creditors had previously suffered a significant loss—that is, a loss of 50 per cent or more.[34]

7.21 There is also support from both theoretical modelling and empirical studies for the idea of excusable default, or the understanding that sovereign debt involves implicitly accepted contingencies that might excuse non-payment. If a country defaults as a result of one of these contingencies, creditors under this model will differentiate this excusable default from an unjustifiable repudiation, and the sovereign debtor should not suffer as high a degree of reputational harm.[35] There is some empirical support for this idea, in particular in findings that countries return to capital markets faster than the expected baseline if a default is precipitated by unexpected and uncontrollable factors such as a natural disaster.[36] While natural disasters constitute the archetypical *force majeure*, it is possible that the category of excusable default may include certain types of politically motivated action, including default or even repudiation justified along odious debt ideas—for example following a major regime change, overthrowing an oppressive and unrepresentative ruler. The expectation of debt continuity—that is, the rule that nations should repay loans even after a major regime change or expect reputational consequences—is fairly well established in contemporary financial practice. However, a careful reading of key historical cases, including Soviet Russia's 1918 repudiation of Tsarist debt, suggests that creditors in some contexts may accept political repudiation as a species of excusable default and be willing to extend credit even following such an action.[37] To an important degree, then, the consequences of sovereign default or restructuring cannot be understood as entirely independent of ideas of sovereign legitimacy,

Access?' (2011) 83(2) J Int'l Econ 243. If a more restrictive definition of market access as 'net resource transfers' is adopted, then delays may also be longer: Daniel A. Dias, Christine Richmond, and Taeree Wang, *Duration of Capital Market Exclusion: An Empirical Investigation*, UIUC Working Paper (2012). *See* Tomz and Wright (n. 29) for a discussion of these findings. Eduardo Levy-Yeyati also looks at net transfers and finds a negative, but fairly small (0.1–1 per cent of GDP), effect: Eduardo Levy-Yeyati, 'Optimal Debt? On the Insurance Value of International Debt Flows to Developing Countries' (2009) 20 Open Econ Rev 489.

[32] Gelos et al. (n. 31) find an exclusion period of four years during the 1980s, while Dias et al. (n. 31) suggest a longer period of five-and-a-half years during that time.

[33] Panizza et al. (n. 28), 25, fn. 39; Tomz and Wright (n. 29), 14.

[34] Juan Cruces and Christoph Trebesch, *Sovereign Defaults: The Price of Haircuts*, CESifo Working Paper Series No. 3604 (13 October 2011), available online at <http://papers.ssrn.com/sol3/papers.cfm?abstract_id=1943411>.

[35] Excusable default is modelled in Herschel I. Grossman and John B. Van Huyck, 'Sovereign Debt as a Contingent Claim: Excusable Default, Repudiation, and Reputation' (1988) 78(5) Am Econ Rev 1088. Under the assumptions of Grossman and Van Huyck's model, although countries may sometimes excusably default, they never repudiate their debts, because a trustworthy reputation is too valuable.

[36] Dias et al. (n. 31), even with their more restrictive 'net resource transfers' definition, find renewed capital market access at three years on average.

[37] In the Soviet case, although European and American creditors to the Tsarist regime were vehemently opposed to recognizing or lending to the Soviet regime, newer and unaffected American banks—including the precursors to Chase and Bank of America—extended trade financing after the repudiation and, finding the new regime reliable in repayment, attempted to facilitate the issuance of longer-term bonds. The post-repudiation failure to issue bonds was thus not the result of a uniform reputational assessment by creditors, but rather of the opposition of the US government to these efforts. For an in-depth discussion of this case, *see* Lienau (n. 24), ch. 3.

which have varied considerably over time and could affect reputational assessments in the future.

Assuming that a sovereign borrower has successfully restructured its debt, the key ramification becomes not complete exclusion, but rather the potentially higher cost of accessing external capital. Again, however, there is nuance in the extent and duration of this effect. In the period immediately following a successful restructuring, borrowing costs tend to be significantly higher for those countries that do return to the international capital markets. For example, Eduardo Borensztein and Ugo Panizza find that, for thirty-one emerging market countries in 1997–2004, borrowing costs the year after a restructuring has been concluded were 400 basis points (4 per cent) higher than during calmer times. However, this falls to 250 basis points the subsequent year, and then declines even further.[38] In their review of empirical studies, Udaibir Das, Michael Papaioannou, and Christoph Trebesch suggest an even steeper decline, to a premium of 50 basis points (or an increase of 0.5 per cent over the baseline) within a year or two after the end of a restructuring.[39] As with the speed of capital market access, however, there appears to be variation according to the circumstances and terms of previous restructurings. Juan Cruces and Christoph Trebesch find in a study of creditor restructuring losses since 1978 that debtors who negotiate for greater creditor losses are more likely to pay higher borrowing costs for a longer period of time, controlling for economic fundamentals. In particular, they find that a 22 per cent increase in the haircut is associated with a 150 basis point (1.5 per cent) increase in bond spreads over the baseline, dropping to a 70 basis point increase in the fourth and fifth years after a restructuring.[40] They clarify that the data does not indicate a direct mechanism by which haircuts affect sovereign borrowing, nor do they recommend attempting to minimize debt relief efforts. However, the study suggests that there may still be a trade-off between more significant relief and higher borrowing costs in the medium term; smaller (but perhaps insufficient) haircuts have had a relatively brief and minor effect on future borrowing costs. 7.22

In short, any blanket statement that debt restructuring will lead to either future capital market exclusion or to inordinately high borrowing costs is oversimplified, particularly in the long run. The negative impact tends to be concentrated in the period during and immediately after the default and restructuring itself, although very steep creditor losses may have longer-lasting effects. These findings offer debtors significant incentive, if any more is needed, to complete restructurings rarely and swiftly.[41] Furthermore, successful restructurings that help to put debtors on a sustainable economic path can make future lending more attractive in the international capital markets. For example, the significant and well-priced lending to sovereigns in the 1990s would be difficult to imagine in the absence of Brady 7.23

[38] Furthermore, the results in the second year are not statistically significant: Eduardo Borensztein and Ugo Panizza, 'The Costs of Sovereign Default' (2009) 56(4) IMF Staff Papers 683.

[39] They note that such findings confirm earlier historical data, leading 'many to conclude that banks and bondholders have very short memories': Das et al. (n. 2), 61. *See* also the discussion in Panizza et al. (n. 28), 26–7. Michael Tomz, on the other hand, has found in a historical study of thirty borrowers in 1872 a significant difference in the bond yields of recent defaulters, previous defaulters, and those with consistent repayment records: Tomz (n. 26), 57–60.

[40] Cruces and Trebesch (n. 34).

[41] Although there is significant variation in the time taken for restructurings, they have become more rapid as borrowers, creditors, official actors, and their advisers have developed standard procedures and approaches. The period of capital market exclusion has dropped as well, with longer average periods from default to new borrowing in the 1980s than in the 1990s: *see* Gelos et al. (n. 31).

Plan restructurings. This accords with the theoretical expectation that the determination of a borrower's creditworthiness involves evaluating not only willingness to pay, but also capacity to pay. Even if a debt restructuring raises doubts about a country's willingness to pay in the short run, it can in the long run improve a borrower's debt profile—both directly through the initial haircut and indirectly through the judicious use of funds otherwise earmarked for debt payment—and thus impact appraisals of a country's long-term prospects. Of course, a 'judicious use of funds' is far more difficult to define, operationalize, and analyse empirically than data on debt write-downs, capital market access, and borrowing costs. Thus the potential long-term *benefits* of restructuring are far more contingent and case-specific, and are less appropriate for the large-scale empirical research that has dominated discussion of the consequences of debt restructuring. In short, the literature on future capital market access and borrowing costs should offer food for thought, but framing the consequences of restructuring as dangerous or otherwise entirely negative is overly simplistic and likely incomplete.

B. Trade and capital flows to the private sector

7.24 Creditors and international advisers engaged in a sovereign debt restructuring will focus much of their energy on the government officials in charge of the negotiations. As such, discussions about possible consequences will likely put the state's future capital market access front and centre. But the effects of a debt restructuring are not limited to the flow of capital directly into state coffers. Countries are embedded in a broad array of transnational economic links—including trade, foreign direct investment (FDI), and aid among others—each of which might be impacted by the outcome of debt negotiations. The theoretical and empirical literature highlights trade relations and private sector capital access in particular as especially susceptible. However, in these areas as well there remains a fair amount of disagreement on the nature and extent of any negative effect. Particularly when the longer-run ramifications of a completed restructuring are separated out from the immediate effects of an ongoing default and crisis, the evidence for a high cost of restructuring is ambiguous.

7.25 Access to capital, and particularly to foreign exchange, is often intricately related to a country's import needs and export capacity. Especially given many economies' increased reliance on international trade, understanding the long-term impact of a sovereign debt restructuring on trade is crucial. One potential concern is that creditor country governments could impose explicit sanctions, such as embargos, tariffs, or non-tariff barriers, on the defaulting sovereign state in order to compel repayment. While this remains theoretically possible, there is scant evidence of such actions in the post-Second World War era, and the empirical support for such outcomes is contested even in earlier periods.[42] A second and more plausible consequence today is that debt

[42] Kris Michener and Marc Weidenmier suggest that trade might have been part of 'super-sanctions' in the gold standard era, Phillip Lane contends that trade sanctions were a classic punishment for default, and Carlos Diáz-Alejandro argues that Argentina avoided default in the 1930s in order to maintain trade relations with the United Kingdom: Kris James Michener and Marc D. Weidenmeier, *Super-Sanctions and Sovereign Debt Repayment*, National Bureau of Economic Research Working Paper 11472 (July 2005), available online at <http://www.nber.org/papers/w11472>; Philip R. Lane, 'Empirical Perspectives on Long-Term External Debt' (2004) 4(1) Topics in Macroeconomics 1; Carlos F. Diáz-Alejandro, 'Stories of the 1930s for the 1980s,' in Pedro Aspe Armella, Rudiger Dornbusch, and Maurice Obstfield (eds) *Financial Policies and the World Capital Market: The Problem of Latin American Countries* (Chicago, IL, and London: University of Chicago Press, 1983), 5–40. Michael Tomz, however, disagrees with the centrality of trade even in these periods, suggesting that capital market reputational concerns were more central: Tomz (n. 26), 158–95.

restructuring would impact the credits essential for facilitating international trade.[43] Indeed, some studies of trade shifts during debt crises demonstrate a suggestive correlation, although it is difficult to identify the causal mechanisms underlying any correlation between restructuring episodes and lower trade volumes.[44] It may well be that both a debt crisis and lower trade volumes are symptomatic of deeper economic problems.

Even within this correlation, it is again important to tease out the distinctions between possible effects during a crisis, immediately following a restructuring, and in the longer term. Andrew Rose considered the relationship of official sector (Paris Club) debt negotiations to trade, finding a decline of 8 per cent per year relative to expected levels, with long-lasting effects (of up to fifteen years) even after a restructuring.[45] However, the potential causal channel for this relationship remains unclear. When Jose Vicente Martinez and Guido Sandleris studied more closely the potential effect on the specific bilateral trade relationship with creditors affected by the default, they found a general trade decline lasting several years after a restructuring. Puzzlingly, however, an even more significant decline existed among non-creditor countries.[46] Furthermore, Alexander Agronovsky and Christoph Trebesch look at newly collected data to suggest that, after the conclusion of negotiated debt restructuring agreements between debtor and creditor countries during 1980–1997, debtor exports to creditor countries actually increased. While they find no similar effect for imports or for restructurings after 1997, they propose that coordinated policy intervention can help to sustain trade financing during and after crises.[47] Focusing on industry-level data, Eduardo Borensztein and Ugo Panizza suggest that the actual default period is costly for more export-oriented industries, which see lowered growth for each year of a default episode. However, they find that these effects are short-lived, fading quickly after a restructuring has been completed and the borrower emerges from a debt crisis.[48] This trade effect can have a distributional dimension as well, as domestic industries that compete with foreign imports may receive a boost during debt defaults.[49] In short, although declining trade seems to correlate with the actual restructuring period, the mechanisms and empirical evidence for a long-run negative effect on trade are underspecified or mixed. **7.26**

Another key transnational economic link that could be affected by a sovereign debt restructuring is the flow of capital to private enterprise. There is less empirical literature on this potential outcome, but in the last decade any such effect appears to be relatively brief and also may be offset by broadening the range of investment partners. Miguel Fuentes and **7.27**

[43] Emanuel Kohlscheen and Stephen A. O'Connell, *A Sovereign Debt Model with Trade Credit and Reserves*, Warwick Economic Research Papers No. 743 (2006), available online at <http://www2.warwick.ac.uk/fac/soc/economics/research/workingpapers/2006/twerp_743.pdf>.

[44] In their reviews of empirical findings on trade and debt default, both Tomz and Wright (n. 29), 15, and Panizza et al. (n. 28), 29, note the uncertainty as to which mechanisms link trade to default. Such ambiguity makes it difficult to recommend particular policy positions on the basis of any supposed link.

[45] Andrew Rose, 'One Reason Countries Pay Their Debts: Renegotiation and International Trade' (2005) 77 J Dev Econ 189. In concluding, Rose highlights the cases of Togo, Senegal, and Peru, which witnessed considerable declines in trade with creditor countries in the years following a rescheduling. He notes, however, that the causal mechanism for this decline is unclear.

[46] Jose Vicente Martinez and Guido Sandleris, 'Is it Punishment? Sovereign Defaults and the Decline in Trade' (2011) 30 J Int'l Money & Fin 909.

[47] Alexander Agronovsky and Christoph Trebesch, 'Trade Credit during Financial Crises: Do Negotiated Agreements Work?' (2009) 10 Int'l Fin Rev 439.

[48] Eduardo Borensztein and Ugo Panizza, 'Do Sovereign Defaults Hurt Exporters?' (2010) 21 Open Econ Rev 393.

[49] Sergi Lanau, 'Essays on Sovereign Debt Markets,' Unpublished (2008), cited in Panizza et al. (n. 28), 28.

Diego Saravia find that default episodes do tend to lead to lower FDI in a borrowing country by up to 2 per cent of gross domestic product (GDP) per year, but also that the negative effect is limited to those creditor countries directly affected by a default.[50] Ecuador's ability to attract significant direct investment from China after its 2008 selective debt default appears to be part of this dynamic.[51] Carlos Arteta and Galina Hale look more closely at external borrowing by domestic firms, finding a more significant drop of 20 per cent below the country-specific average during a sovereign debt crisis and up to two years after reaching a restructuring agreement. They determine that this decline is lower following agreements with commercial rather than official creditors, and also following agreements that include new lending.[52] Other work has found an even steeper drop, of up to 40 per cent, from the baseline of expected external private sector borrowing.[53] However, in considering an admittedly small, but diverse, sample of restructurings from 1998 to 2005, Panizza, Sturzenegger, and Zettelmeyer find that private capital flows dipped during the default year, but recovered soon after, and were higher than the pre-default trend only three years after the completed restructuring. They highlight Argentina as a particularly interesting case, in which the government chose to impose capital controls on private inflows that seemed excessive, despite the heavy losses to creditors in the restructuring.[54] They also note that two countries opting for an orderly pre-emptive restructuring, the Dominican Republic and Uruguay, witnessed a return of private inflows even before the restructuring had been completed.[55] Depending on the sovereign state in question, then, it is possible that other economic factors, which may improve in part as a result of changes made during the restructuring period, could help to counteract the negative consequences of a debt crisis on private capital access.

C. A note on broader domestic effects

7.28 This chapter has focused largely on the ramifications of a sovereign debt restructuring for the state's major transnational economic links. It is worth briefly noting, however, the potential effects of debt restructurings on national growth. From the perspective of government decision-makers, times of low national output make debt payment difficult and thus can render a debt restructuring more desirable.[56] But it is also possible that the reverse effect

[50] Miguel Fuentes and Diego Saravia, 'Sovereign Defaulters: Do International Capital Markets Punish Them?' (2010) 91 J Dev Econ 336.

[51] By 2010, less than two years after the default, China–Ecuador bilateral investment deals totalled more than US$5 billion, even as other investors were slower to return. *See*, e.g., 'Ecuador Sees $5 bln Investment from China This Yr—Minister' *Reuters*, 7 September 2010, available online at <http://uk.reuters.com/article/2010/09/07/ecuador-china-investment-idUKTOE68605320100907>.

[52] Carlos Arteta and Galina Hale, 'Sovereign Debt Crises and Credit to the Private Sector' (2008) 74 J Int'l Econ 53.

[53] Das, Papaioannou, and Trebesch identify drops of up to 40 per cent, with defaults to private creditors having the most significant ramifications in their analysis. They also find that, even in the absence of any default or restructuring, other sovereign risk measures (including bond spreads and lower credit ratings) negatively impact private sector borrowing. Thus it may be difficult to fully separate out the effect of the restructuring itself from the general negative outlook on the sovereign debt situation: Udaibir S. Das, Michael G. Papaioannou, and Christoph Trebesch, 'Spillovers of Sovereign Default Risk: How Much is the Private Sector Affected?', in Robert W. Kolb (ed.) *Sovereign Debt: From Safety to Default* (New York: Wiley, 2011), 33–42.

[54] Panizza et al. (n. 28), 34.

[55] Panizza et al. (n. 28), 34.

[56] Researchers have thrown into question whether in fact sovereigns default during 'bad times' of lower-than-expected GDP. Although negative economic factors would seem to make default more likely, sovereign states also default when GDP meets expectations. *See*, e.g., the discussions in Panizza et al. (n. 28), 17–20, and in Tomz and Wright (n. 29), 15–16.

holds true—that is, that restructuring could aggravate already-low GDP levels—although it is difficult to separate out a completely independent effect.[57] Initial studies suggest that output declines are likely during and perhaps also in anticipation of a default and restructuring episode. Although a small sample of recent restructuring cases displayed a fairly quick output recovery, it is difficult to determine whether long-run losses were entirely offset by higher post-restructuring growth rates.[58] The empirical literature does clearly indicate, however, that both the costs associated with sovereign debt restructuring and any output losses are exacerbated by an accompanying domestic banking crisis. And to the extent that sovereign debt is held domestically or has domestic ramifications through credit default swaps or other transmission mechanisms, any sovereign debt restructuring may significantly impact the local financial system.[59] The relationship between debt crises and banking crises is addressed elsewhere in this volume, so there is no need for a fuller overview here. However, this vulnerability should be considered and minimized well in advance of any restructuring.[60]

5. Conclusion

A state decision-maker faced with the choice of whether or not to restructure sovereign debt will likely be warned about the alienating effect that restructuring can have on the country's global partners. Any explicit warnings or threats will be bolstered by a general tendency, particularly in popular writing, to focus on the negative ramifications of a decision to propose new payment terms. While such costs certainly exist, what is the effect of emphasizing them over potential benefits? In a deeply interconnected world, an inordinate fear of limited capital market access, serious trade disruptions, or lowered foreign investment might deter a beneficial restructuring. Emphasizing the high costs or 'dangers' of restructuring, without further clarification of the severity or duration of such costs, will likely shift preferences away from restructuring and toward more intensive austerity measures. Apart from questions about the actual efficacy of such measures in promoting economic recovery, they also have important distributional effects, with greater adjustment burdens imposed on the debtor country rather than on external creditors and financial systems, and in particular imposed on those supported by or working for the public sector. In light of these second-order consequences, scholars and readers alike should take care to understand the potential ramifications of how findings are framed. **7.29**

Furthermore, emphasizing that restructuring has drastic negative effects is overly simplistic in light of the evidence. The empirical literature agrees on the existence of some costs, but hardly speaks with a single voice on whether those costs are especially severe or long-lasting. Particularly in the longer term, the negative ramifications of debt restructuring for key transnational economic relations, including capital market access, trade, and domestic investment, are fairly nuanced. In particular, costs tend to be concentrated in the actual default and **7.30**

---

[57] Again, the restructuring and any associated policies are likely to affect a range of other variables that in turn shape GDP, such as domestic banking, private sector capital access, and capital flight.

[58] Panizza et al. (n. 28), 37–8, citing Valerie Cerra and Sweta Chaman Saxena, 'Growth Dynamics: The Myth of Economic Recovery' (2008) 98(1) Am Econ Rev 439.

[59] *See*, e.g., the discussions in Panizza et al. (n. 28); Tomz and Wright (n. 29); Das et al. (n. 2).

[60] Measures can be taken to assess any such effect and attempt to contain it, as was the case with Jamaica in 2010. However, this relatively minor case likely shares little in common with larger systemic banking crises, such as that in Europe or the banking crisis associated with the 1980s Latin American debt crisis.

restructuring period. In light of the temporal dimension of the consequences that do appear to be common across different country cases, even greater effort should be made to streamline the restructuring process further. In the meantime, framing the ramifications of a debt restructuring too bluntly may well lead to greater avoidance and delay than is warranted.

7.31 Given the specificity of any given country case, sovereign debt restructuring is inevitably more art than science. In deciding whether or not to launch a restructuring effort, decision-makers generally have in mind a series of goals: increased liquidity and debt sustainability in the short and medium run; and an improvement of a country's economic fundamentals in the long run. While a restructuring may succeed in furthering one or all of these objectives, it plays only one role (and sometimes merely a supporting role) in a larger political and economic drama. Keeping in mind the important caveats offered by the literature, a restructuring may help to stabilize a given country and provide a foundation for future growth, but can hardly be considered financial salvation.

Part II

ENFORCEMENT OF SOVEREIGN DEBT

8. **Defences** 103
Carmine D. Boccuzzi, Jr, Michael M. Brennan, and Jacob H. Johnston

9. **Special Immunities: Central Bank Immunity** 117
Thomas C. Baxter, Jr, and David Gross

10. **Special Immunities: Bank for International Settlements** 127
Diego Devos

11. **Creditors' Remedies** 139
W. Mark C. Weidemaier and Ryan McCarl

12. **Sovereign Arbitration** 151
Karen Halverson Cross

8

DEFENCES

Carmine D. Boccuzzi, Jr, Michael M. Brennan, and Jacob H. Johnston[1]

> The payment of debts is necessary for social order. The non-payment is quite equally necessary for social order. For centuries humanity has oscillated, serenely unaware, between these two contradictory necessities.
>
> (Simone Weil)

1. Introduction

Debt crises 'have always been with us and always will be'.[2] From the beginning of recorded history, there have been states that have found themselves unable to pay their debts, and the resulting defaults have occurred in every region of the world,[3] with greater frequency among developing countries, for which 'serial default' has been described as 'a universal rite of passage'.[4] In such situations, some measure of debt forgiveness by creditors is necessary for a state to continue to deliver essential services to its populace, and indeed to continue its existence. **8.01**

On the other hand, the right to collect a debt and to rely on the provisions of a contract is implicit in a society governed by the rule of law. This is as true internationally as it is within a sovereign's borders.[5] If creditors do not expect repayment, they will not lend, and citizens of both rich and poor countries will be less prosperous.[6] Economic growth thus depends on some degree of 'respect for the rule of law and an independent judicial system that recognizes property rights, enforces contracts and protects basic citizens' rights'.[7] **8.02**

---

1 The authors would like to thank Sarah Heim and Daniel Northrop for their feedback on this chapter.

2 Barry Eichengreen, *Financial Crises and What to Do about Them* (New York: Oxford University Press, 2002), 4.

3 Carmen M. Reinhart and Kenneth S. Rogoff, *This Time is Different: A Panoramic View of Eight Centuries of Financial Crises* (Princeton, NJ: Princeton University Press, 2009), 5.

4 Reinhart and Rogoff (n. 3), 2.

5 Secretary General Kofi Annan, Address before the US Chamber of Commerce (10 June 1999):

> Without rules governing contracts and property rights; without confidence based on the rule of law; without trust and transparency—there could be no well-functioning markets. We know this when it comes to national economies, but we have yet to apply it fully to global markets.

6 Douglass C. North, *Institutions, Institutional Change and Economic Performance* (Cambridge: Cambridge University Press, 1990), 54: 'The inability of societies to develop effective, low-cost enforcement of contracts is the most important source of both historical stagnation and contemporary underdevelopment in the Third World.'

7 Michel Camdessus, Managing Director of the IMF, Address to the Board of Governors of the International Monetary Fund (29 September 1999).

8.03 Sovereign debt litigation pits these two seemingly irreconcilable interests against each other. In the corporate context, these competing forces are addressed through bankruptcy law, which aims to give debtors with unsustainable debt burdens a fresh start, while ensuring that creditors receive a fair share of the debtor's assets. In the sovereign debt context, in which bankruptcy protection does not exist, courts—with input from the United States' executive branch—must instead grapple with the two prongs outlined in Weil's epigraph and try to reach some sort of middle ground. The results of that attempt follow.

2. Sovereign Debt Litigation Defences

8.04 Creditor enforcement actions pose unique difficulties for foreign states in financial crisis, which, unlike private parties, must seek to restructure their debt voluntarily because they cannot discharge unsustainable debt by invoking bankruptcy protections.[8] Such actions, which generally result in attempts to seize sovereign property, can endanger a foreign state's economic recovery by interfering with the sovereign's essential public acts or the restructuring itself. This threat of interference has increased in recent years, in line with the rise of professional plaintiffs, generally hedge funds, which purchase distressed sovereign debt on the secondary market for pennies on the dollar, then seek to profit by rejecting the restructuring process and aggressively pursuing litigation for the debt's full face value.[9] Although, as the United States has recognized, this 'new class of holders of sovereign debt . . . plays an important and useful role in on-going efforts to deal with sovereign debt by providing added market liquidity',[10] their pursuit of profits often comes at the expense of the majority of creditors who agree to restructure their debt through cooperative negotiations.

8.05 In light of the risks posed by creditor litigation, foreign sovereigns have sought to avoid such actions by invoking various legal defences. First and foremost, foreign states have relied on principles of sovereign immunity, which renders all foreign states immune from the jurisdiction of US courts, and then provides several limited exceptions to that broad immunity. In circumstances in which an exception to sovereign immunity applies, foreign states have invoked as defences to creditor claims:

(1) principles of comity and the act-of-state doctrine, which precludes courts from considering in civil actions the validity of certain acts of a foreign state committed in its own territory;
(2) the principle of champerty, which bars suits seeking to collect on debt purchased with the intent to litigate; and
(3) contract-based arguments that draw from other areas of law or public policy, rather than the plain terms of the underlying agreement.

---

[8] *See Pravin Banker Assocs Ltd v. Banco Popular del Peru*, 109 F.3d 850 (2d Cir. 1997); Brief for the US as Amici Curiae, *CIBC Bank and Trust Co. (Cayman) Ltd v. Banco Central do Brasil*, 886 F.Supp. 1105 (SDNY 1994) (No. 94 Civ. 4733) (hereinafter *CIBC* Brief).

[9] Anne Krueger, 'International Financial Architecture for 2002: New Approach to Sovereign Debt Restructuring', Speech at the National Economists' Club Annual Members' Dinner, 26 November 2001, available online at <http://www.imf.org/external/np/speeches/2001/112601.htm>: 'The threat of disruption [caused by holdout creditors speculating on a state's debt] remains likely to deter countries from seeking a necessary restructuring for longer than is desirable either for the country itself or for the international community.'

[10] *CIBC* Brief (n. 8), 8.

As will be examined further in the following paragraphs, US courts have, for the most part, rejected these defences in the context of sovereign debt litigation. As a result, absent the ability to invoke sovereign immunity, creditors are generally able to bring claims for money judgments on debt obligations against foreign sovereigns in the United States. However, a sovereign debtor seeking to stabilize its economy or to restructure its debt may be able to defer the enforceability of its debt by obtaining a stay of litigation until it is able to get back on its feet. **8.06**

A. Foreign sovereign immunity

For much of the United States' history, foreign states had virtually absolute immunity from suit in US courts and creditors holding sovereign debt thus had little recourse against a defaulting sovereign.[11] This principle of sovereign immunity, unlike that afforded to states and the federal government, derived not from the Constitution, but from concerns of grace and comity between nations—that is, the reciprocal self-interest and respect for the power and dignity of sovereigns.[12] Thus, in instances in which creditors tried to enforce their defaulted debt against foreign states, courts deferred to the executive branch's determination of whether granting immunity was appropriate. The State Department, acting for the executive, almost universally recommended immunity for friendly foreign states by filing a formal suggestion of immunity with the court on the state's behalf. **8.07**

In 1952, the State Department issued the 'Tate Letter', in which it adopted, consistent with prevailing international norms, the view that foreign countries could be sued in US courts for their commercial acts, but not for public, sovereign acts.[13] This approach to sovereign immunity, known as the 'restrictive theory,' mirrored the legal distinction between *jure gestionis* and *jure imperii*, or commercial and public acts, widely accepted under international law.[14] The Tate Letter, however, left intact the absolute immunity from attachment and execution afforded to foreign state property, leaving creditors without the ability to enforce any judgments that they might obtain against a defaulting foreign sovereign.[15] If the state chose to pay a plaintiff, it generally did so voluntarily. Although the Tate Letter limited jurisdictional sovereign immunity, it did not have a dramatic impact on the number of foreign states sued in American courts, which continued to defer to the State Department in determining whether jurisdictional immunity applied. **8.08**

In 1976, Congress passed the Foreign Sovereign Immunities Act (FSIA) in order to free the US government from the case-by-case diplomatic pressures it faced in actions involving foreign states, to clarify and conform to the standards governing sovereign immunity, **8.09**

---

[11] *See Verlinden BV v. Central Bank of Nigeria*, 461 US 480, 486 (1983) ('From the Nation's founding until 1952, foreign states were "generally granted . . . complete immunity from suit," and the Judicial Branch deferred to the decisions of the Executive Branch on such questions'). In *Schooner Exchange v. M'Fadden*, 7 Cranch 116, 126 (1812) Chief Justice Marshall concluded that, while the jurisdiction of a nation within its own territory 'is susceptible of no limitation not imposed by itself', the United States had impliedly waived jurisdiction over certain activities of foreign sovereigns. That opinion came to be regarded as extending 'virtually absolute' immunity to foreign sovereigns: *Verlinden*, at 486.

[12] *Nat'l City Bank of New York v. Republic of China*, 348 US 356, 362 (1955); *see* also *Schooner Exchange* (n. 11), at 137 (sovereign immunity stems from the principle of 'perfect equality and absolute independence of sovereigns, and th[e] common interest impelling them to mutual intercourse').

[13] *See* Letter from Jack B. Tate, Acting Legal Adviser, Department of State, to Acting Attorney General Philip B. Perlman (19 May 1952), reprinted in (1952) 26 Department of State Bulletin 9840985.

[14] *In re Terrorist Attacks on September 11, 2001*, 538 F.3d 71, 82 (2d Cir. 2008).

[15] 'The Tate Letter did nothing to modify the complete immunity enjoyed by foreign sovereigns from execution against their property': *Connecticut Bank v. Congo*, 309 F.3d 240, 252 (5th Cir. 2002).

and to assure litigants that immunity decisions would be made on purely legal grounds.[16] As the Supreme Court has explained, the FSIA, which sets forth the sole basis for obtaining subject matter jurisdiction over a foreign state in US courts,[17] codified the restrictive theory of foreign sovereign immunity and, for the first time in the United States, partially lowered the immunity afforded sovereign property[18] to 'conform more closely with the provisions on jurisdictional immunity'.[19]

8.10 The FSIA thus represents the first hurdle that a creditor must overcome in enforcing debt against a foreign state in the United States. Unless the creditor can demonstrate that one of the FSIA's exceptions to jurisdictional immunity applies, it is barred from bringing suit against a sovereign. In the context of sovereign debt, however, sovereign immunity may not present much of an obstacle. Sovereign debt instruments now commonly include a waiver of jurisdictional immunity, and even when they do not, a sovereign will still be subject to jurisdiction in the United States under the 'commercial activity' exception to immunity where the instrument provides for performance—that is, payment—in the United States, or otherwise allows creditors to demand payment there.[20]

B. Comity and act-of-state doctrine

8.11 One of the first defences raised by a foreign state after the enactment of the FSIA was that principles of comity and the act-of-state doctrine rendered unenforceable in US courts debt that a foreign state was forbidden by its own regulations from paying. International comity is 'the recognition which one nation allows within its territory to the legislative, executive or judicial acts of another nation'.[21] Applying international comity, US courts will decline to rule on sovereign acts of other countries that have consequences within US territory. However, courts 'will not extend international comity to foreign proceedings when doing so would be contrary to the policies or prejudicial to the interests of the United States'.[22]

8.12 Under the act-of-state doctrine, suits that challenge the validity of a public act committed by a foreign sovereign within its own territory are rendered non-justiciable in US courts. In the context of a sovereign debt dispute, the doctrine would render the debt at issue unenforceable.[23] Unlike the FSIA, the act-of-state doctrine is judicially created and not jurisdictional. When it applies, the doctrine prevents courts from disturbing the relevant act of the foreign state.[24] The classic American statement of the act-of-state doctrine, which took root in England in 1674,[25] was set forth in 1897 by the US Supreme Court in *Underhill v. Hernandez*, in which it was stated:

> Every sovereign State is bound to respect the independence of every other sovereign State, and the courts of one country will not sit in judgment on the acts of the government of another

---

16 *Verlinden* (n. 11), at 488.

17 *Argentine Republic v. Amerada Hess Shipping Co.*, 488 US 428, 434 (1989).

18 28 USC §§ 1604–05 (1976) (limiting jurisdictional immunity); 28 USC §§ 1609–10 (1976) (limiting immunity from execution).

19 HR Rep. No. 94–1487, at 27 (1976).

20 *Rogers v. Petroleo Brasiliero, SA*, 673 F.3d 131, 140–41 (2d Cir. 2012).

21 *Rogers* (n. 20), at 854 (citing *Hilton v. Guyot*, 159 US 113, 164 (1895)) (internal quotation marks omitted).

22 *Rogers* (n. 20), at 854 (citing *Allied Bank Int'l v. Banco Credito Agricola de Cartago*, 757 F.2d 516, 522 (2d Cir. 1985)).

23 *Banco Nacional de Cuba (BNC) v. Sabbatino*, 376 US 398, 401 (1964).

24 Restatement (Revised) of Foreign Relations Law § 428 cmt c (1983).

25 *Blad v. Bamfield* (1674) 36 Eng Rep 992.

> done within its own territory. Redress of grievances by reason of such acts must be obtained through the means open to be availed of by sovereign powers as between themselves.[26]

Applying this principle, the Court in *Underhill* refused to inquire into the validity of acts committed by a revolutionary military commander, whose government had later been recognized by the United States, which were made the basis of a damages action in the United States by a US citizen who claimed that he had been unlawfully assaulted, coerced, and detained in Venezuela.[27] Building on this theory, the Supreme Court subsequently reaffirmed the act-of-state doctrine on numerous occasions and extended its application to civil suits involving personal property.[28] In its most recent authoritative enunciation of the doctrine's formulation, *Banco Nacional de Cuba v. Sabbatino* in 1964, the Court stated that: **8.13**

> [R]ather than laying down or reaffirming an inflexible and all-encompassing rule in this case, we decide only that the Judicial Branch will not examine the validity of a taking of property within its own territory by a foreign sovereign government, extant and recognized by this country at the time of suit, in the absence of a treaty or other unambiguous agreement regarding controlling legal principles, even if the complaint alleges that the taking violates customary international law.[29]

The Court in *Sabbatino* explained that the act-of-state doctrine 'arises out of the basic relationships between branches of government in a system of separation of powers', and that the policy concerns underlying the doctrine focus on the pre-eminence of the political branches—particularly the executive—in the conduct of foreign policy.[30] The applicability of the doctrine thus depends on the likely impact on international relations that would result from judicial consideration of the foreign state's act. If adjudication would embarrass or hinder the executive in a realm of foreign relations, the doctrine suggests that a court should refrain from inquiring into the validity of the foreign state's act.[31] **8.14**

The key case interpreting comity and the act-of-state doctrine in the context of sovereign debt litigation is *Allied Bank International v. Banco Credito Agricola de Cartago*.[32] **8.15**

Allied Bank arose out of the Costa Rican economic crisis of 1981, which motivated the Costa Rican government to impose restrictions on foreign exchange transactions. In an attempt to avoid defaulting on its loans, Banco Cartago petitioned the Costa Rican Central Bank for permission to continue payments. The government denied the bank's petition and notified all of the borrower banks that they would not be permitted to make any external debt **8.16**

---

26 *Underhill v. Hernandez*, 168 US 250, 252 (1897).

27 *Underhill* (n. 26), at 251.

28 *Oetjen v. Central Leather Co.*, 246 US 297, 303–04 (1918):

> The principle that the conduct of one independent government cannot be successfully questioned in the courts of another is as applicable to a case involving the title to property brought within the custody of a court... in which claims for damages were based upon acts done in a foreign country, for it rests at last upon the highest considerations of international comity and expediency. To permit the validity of the acts of one sovereign state to be reexamined and perhaps condemned by the courts of another would very certainly 'imperil the amicable relations between governments and vex the peace of nations.'

See also *Ricaud v. American Metal Co.*, 246 US 304, 309 (1918).

29 *BNC* (n. 23), at 428.

30 *BNC* (n. 23), at 423.

31 *BNC* (n. 23), at 427–8.

32 *BNC* (n. 23), at 427–8.

payments until Costa Rica restructured its national debt.[33] Allied Bank, acting on behalf of a syndicate of thirty-nine American creditors, brought suit in the US District Court for the Southern District of New York against three Costa Rican banks wholly owned by the Republic of Costa Rica.[34] The defendants argued that both Allied Bank's acceleration of its promissory notes and any recovery were precluded by the act-of-state doctrine. The District Court held that the act-of-state doctrine applied and dismissed the case.[35] The Second Circuit upheld the ruling, but on the grounds that the Court should have granted comity to the actions of the Costa Rican government.[36]

8.17 Both the District Court and the appellate court decisions were widely criticized within the banking industry and by the US government. The US government submitted a brief urging the Second Circuit to rehear the case. The United States asserted that the District Court incorrectly interpreted the act-of-state doctrine[37] and that the Second Circuit should not have applied the comity doctrine, since the actions of the Costa Rican government ran counter to US law and policy.[38] US support for the International Monetary Fund (IMF) debt restructuring programme was 'grounded in the understanding that, while parties may agree to renegotiate conditions of payment, the underlying obligations to pay nevertheless remain valid and enforceable'.[39] The US government asserted that although the United States supported Costa Rica's debt restructuring efforts, it made a distinction between public and private debt obligations. The United States was willing to restructure Costa Rica's intergovernmental obligations and continue to send aid 'to the economically distressed Central American Country',[40] but the US government asserted that 'Costa Rica's attempted unilateral restructuring of private obligations... was inconsistent with this system of international cooperation and negotiation and thus inconsistent with United States policy'.[41]

8.18 The United States also contested the District Court's dismissal of the case under the act-of-state doctrine. The government argued that the act-of-state defence was available only if the purported taking of the creditor's property occurred exclusively within the confines of the foreign state. Since the promissory notes at issue were payable in New York, the actions of the Costa Rican government had an extraterritorial effect and therefore did not fall under the act-of-state doctrine. The US government further argued that if any part of the transaction took place within the United States, then the United States has an interest in the matter and the act-of-state doctrine should not apply.[42] According to the government, the United States had an interest in ensuring that private debt held by banks doing business within the United States would be subject to the jurisdiction of US courts. If a borrower fails to make timely payments and defaults on its loans, or if the borrower unilaterally restructures

---

[33] *Allied Bank Int'l v. Banco Credito Agricola de Cartago*, 566 F. Supp. 1440, 1442 (SDNY 1983).

[34] James Thuo Gathii, 'The Sanctity of Sovereign Loan Contracts and its Origins in Enforcement Litigation' (2006) 38 Geo Wash Int'l L Rev 251, 269.

[35] *See* generally *Allied Bank Int'l* (n. 33).

[36] *See* generally *Allied Bank Int'l v. Banco Credito Agricola de Cartago*, 1984 US App. Lexis 23237 (2d Cir. 1984).

[37] Brief for the United States as *Amicus Curiae*, at 24, *Allied Bank Int'l v. Banco Credito Agricola de Cartago*, 757 F.2d 516 (2d Cir. 1985) (No.83–7714).

[38] Brief (n. 37), at 6.

[39] *Allied Bank Int'l v. Banco Credito Agricola de Cartago*, 757 F.2d 516, 519 (2d Cir. 1985).

[40] *Allied Bank Int'l* (n. 39).

[41] *Allied Bank Int'l* (n. 39).

[42] Brief (n. 37), at 25–6.

its debt obligations, then private creditors should be able to enforce the contract under New York law.[43]

The Second Circuit reheard the case in October 1984 and issued a new opinion on 18 March 1985. The Court vacated its previous decision, holding that neither the act-of-state doctrine nor comity prevented US courts from hearing the case. The Court agreed with the US government that the situs of the property at issue was located in the United States, and thus the act-of-state doctrine—which respects the acts of a foreign sovereign within its *own* territory—did not apply. The Court further noted that, in its previous decision, it had ruled based on its belief that the 'actions of Costa Rica that resulted in the prohibition of payments on external debt [were] consistent with the law and policy of the United States'.[44] After reviewing the briefs submitted by the US government, the Court reversed its position and ruled instead that although the United States supported Costa Rica's attempts to restructure its debt, it still maintained a strong public policy interest in ensuring that US-based creditors could resort to legal remedies to enforce their debt. The *Allied Bank* decision thus represents a significant, and perhaps disabling, hurdle to the comity defence in this context. To the extent that a policy motivating the foreign state's action is deemed consistent with US policy, the defence may be viable in a US court. **8.19**

C. Champerty

After the act-of-state doctrine and comity had been largely rejected as defences to the enforceability of sovereign debt in US courts, foreign states sought to combat the increase in creditor litigation resulting from the rise in trading of debt in the secondary market by invoking the champerty defence. As explained by the US Supreme Court, champerty, which is barred in some form in most jurisdictions, 'is maintaining a suit in return for a financial interest in the outcome',[45] and a champertous arrangement, as one commentator put it, is one in which a person or entity finances a legal action in return for a share of the proceeds of the lawsuit.[46] **8.20**

The doctrine of champerty has been traced back to Greek and Roman law, through the English law of the Middle Ages, and into the statutory or common law of many of the US states.[47] Historically, fear of frivolous, attorney-driven claims and of the effect of speculative suits on the judicial process led legal decision-makers to prohibit champertous agreements.[48] Today, state laws on champerty vary. In New York, there is no common law prohibition against champerty,[49] but section 489 of the New York Judiciary Law prohibits a person or **8.21**

[43] For a detailed discussion of the government's position on the applicability of the act-of-state doctrine, *see* Gathii (n. 34), at 275–7.

[44] *Allied Bank Int'l v. Banco Credito Agricola de Cartago*, 1984 US App Lexis 23237, at *9 (2d Cir. 1984).

[45] *See In re Primus*, 436 US 412, 424 n.15 (1978).

[46] Susan Lorde Martin, 'Syndicated Lawsuits: Illegal Champerty or New Business Opportunity?' (1992) 20 Am Bus LJ 485, 487.

[47] Lorde Martin (n. 46); Max Radin, 'Maintenance by Champerty' (1936) 24 Cal L Rev 48, 48–66; *see* also *Bluebird Ptnrs, LP v. First Fiduciary Bank, NA*, 94 NY.2d 726, 733–4 (2000):

> The 'champerty' concept is based on a type of French feudal tenure in land, a 'champart,' in which the fee for use of the land was neither in money nor ordinary service in kind. The tenant-by-champart was a partial owner of the land bound to share any rents and profits with the grantor, but the grantor took the risk that the crops might fail and that there would be no return. Anyone who then obtained a legal interest in that grant of land would also take a share of the profits in champart.

[48] Lorde Martin (n. 46), at 487.

[49] Indeed, the New York Court of Appeals has stated that it 'has been hesitant to find an action champertous as a matter of law': *Bluebird Ptnrs* (n. 47), at 735.

entity from acquiring debt 'with the intent and for the purpose of bringing an action or proceeding thereon'.[50] A recent amendment to section 489 restricted its application to sovereign debt cases by limiting the section's purview to items with an aggregate purchase price of US$500,000 or less.[51]

8.22 The seminal case interpreting section 489 in the context of sovereign debt litigation is *Elliott Associates, LP v. Banco de la Nacion*.[52] *Elliott* stemmed from a claim brought by Elliott Associates, an investment fund based in New York City that specializes in investing in the securities of 'distressed debtors',[53] against a Peruvian bank and the Republic of Peru. Pursuant to a 1983 agreement with its foreign creditors, Peru guaranteed the bank's debt.

8.23 In 1991, Peru entered into an agreement with the IMF to liberalize and reform its economy. Four years later, Peru and the Bank Advisory Committee for Peru agreed to a debt restructuring plan that covered 'virtually all of the external commercial debt owed by Peru and Peruvian public and private-sector debtors'.[54] Between January and March of 2006, Elliott Associates paid US$11.4 million for US$20.7 million of the working capital debt of Banco de la Nacion and Banco Popular del Peru. In 1996, shortly after Elliott Associates accumulated Peruvian debt, the Bank Advisory Committee issued the term sheet for Peru's restructuring. Of the 180 eligible creditors, only Elliott Associates and one other creditor declined to participate. After acquiring the banks' debt, Elliott Associates provided the debtors notice of its claims; the debtors responded that Elliott Associates should participate in Peru's Brady Plan.[55]

8.24 Rather than participate in Peru's restructuring, Elliott Associates filed suit in the New York Supreme Court. After the case was removed to federal court pursuant to the FSIA, the district court dismissed the complaint on the ground that Elliott Associates' purchase of the Peruvian debt violated section 489 of the New York Judiciary Law, finding that Elliott Associates 'purchased the Peruvian debt with the intent and purpose to sue', and thus committed champerty.[56]

8.25 The Second Circuit reversed, holding that 'the acquisition of a debt with intent to bring suit against the debtor is not a violation of the statute where, as here, the principal purpose of the suit is the collection of the debt acquired'.[57] The Court observed that although section 489 was enacted to prevent attorneys from purchasing debt in order to bring suit and recover legal fees from the debtor, it does not prohibit acquiring a financial stake in the outcome of a lawsuit. New York does, for example, permit contingency fees.

---

50 NY Judiciary Law § 489 (McKinney 1983).

51 NY Judiciary Law § 489 (McKinney 1983).

52 *Elliott Assocs, LP v. Banco de la Nacion*, 194 F.3d 363 (2d Cir. 1999).

53 Distressed debtors are debtors who have defaulted on payments to creditors or are at risk of defaulting.

54 *Elliott Assocs, LP v. Republic of Peru*, 12 F.Supp.2d 328, 335 (SDNY 1998), rev'd, 194 F.3d 363 (2d Cir. 1999).

55 A Brady Plan—named for former US Secretary of the Treasury Nicholas Brady—is a process through which a debtor state and its creditors renegotiate sovereign debt to avoid default. Typically, a state agrees to pay a portion of its outstanding debt while its creditors grant additional loans. In return, the debtor state implements an economic austerity programme supervised by the IMF. The terms of a Brady Plan are usually negotiated between the debtor state and the Bank Advisory Committee, which comprises a group of the largest US creditors. The members of the Bank Advisory Committee often agree to be bound by the negotiated terms, but other creditors are free to accept or reject them.

56 *Elliott* (n. 54), at 332.

57 *Elliott* (n. 52), at 372.

8.26 Relying on *Moses v. McDivitt*, a nineteenth-century case decided by the New York Court of Appeals, the Second Circuit drew a distinction between acquisition of debt for the primary purpose of litigation, and instances in which the intent to litigate is incidental and contingent. To fall within the ambit of section 489, the purchase of debt 'must be made for the very purpose of bringing... suit, and this implies an exclusion of any other purpose'.[58] Per *Moses*:

> [W]here the debt instrument is acquired for the primary purpose of enforcing it, with intent to resort to litigation to the extent necessary to accomplish the enforcement, the intent to litigate is merely incidental and contingent and does not violate the statute.[59]

8.27 After establishing the principle that a party does not violate section 489 when its 'primary goal is found to be satisfaction of a valid debt and its intent is only to sue absent full performance', the Second Circuit applied it to Elliott Associates' acquisition of Peruvian debt.[60] The Court found that Elliott Associates purchased the debt for a legitimate purpose—that is, to make a profit. The creditor's primary intent was to be paid in full, with resort to legal process only if necessary. The primary motive for purchasing the debt was thus not legal process itself. Since Elliott Associates' acquisition of debt did not fall within the scope of conduct proscribed by section 489, the Second Circuit reversed and remanded to the District Court on the issue of damages.

8.28 The Second Circuit also identified several policy reasons for ruling that purchasing distressed sovereign debt with the intent to collect via legal process does not violate section 489. First, it is in the United States' national interest for debt owed to American creditors to be enforceable. Brady Plan participation is voluntary in order to preserve the right of creditors to collect. Second, if the Court had ruled for Banco Nacion and Peru, distressed sovereign debt would be less liquid, which in turn would cause interest rates to rise and make it more difficult (or impossible) for developing countries to borrow money. Third, ruling against Elliott Associates would create a perverse incentive for sovereign debtors, because their litigating position would be stronger if they were clearly and publicly to refuse to honour their debts. Once investors received notice that a state did not intend voluntarily to pay its debt, the only reason to acquire it would be to collect through litigation—a circumstance that, if governed by the District Court's holding, would create a champerty defence. Finally, ruling for Banco Nacion and Peru would increase the risk that debtors would default, which would, in turn, increase the cost of trading distressed debt in New York. Increased costs might then lead parties to transact business in other fora.

8.29 After *Elliott*, there are few circumstances in which sovereign debtors can successfully invoke champerty as a defence against a creditor. Unless the creditor (i) is a lawyer focused more on the legal fees to be gained from seeking to collect the debt than on the debt itself, (ii) is bringing suit merely to harass the defendant state, or (iii) has expressly agreed to sue on the debt at issue, a foreign state will likely face difficulty in succeeding on a champerty defence.

D. Contract-based arguments

8.30 In addition to these principles, both creditors and foreign state debtors have claimed—or challenged—sovereign debt contract rights based on arguments relying on public policy or

[58] *Elliott* (n. 52), at 374 (citing *Moses v. McDivitt*, 88 NY 62, 65 (1882)) (internal quotation marks omitted).
[59] *Elliott* (n. 52), at 378 (internal quotation marks omitted).
[60] *Elliott* (n. 52), at 381.

other areas of law, as opposed to the terms of the underlying debt instrument. In response, courts have consistently declined to stray from the text of sovereign debt agreements and have construed such contracts in accordance with their express terms. This approach, as exemplified in *CIBC Bank & Trust Co. v. Banco Central do Brasil*,[61] is consistent with the policy of the United States of not permitting creditors or sovereign debtors 'to alter through litigation the terms of a valid debt instrument'.[62]

8.31 In *CIBC*, a creditor of Brazil who declined to participate in a Brady-type debt restructuring brought an action in the District Court for the Southern District of New York seeking to collect the full amount of its beneficial interest in the underlying debt.[63] As the creditor acknowledged, the terms of the credit agreement did not permit acceleration of the unpaid principal unless holders of 'more than 50%' consented to such action, and the creditor concededly held less than that amount. The creditor nonetheless argued that it could accelerate the principal because it held the requisite amount once the shares of Banco do Brasil, SA—an entity purportedly controlled by the debtor—were excluded. However, the debt agreement was devoid of any basis for such an exclusion. The creditor thus argued that the contract contained 'an implied covenant of good faith and fair dealing' that prohibited Banco de Brasil from retaining its shares to block the creditor's attempt to accelerate.

8.32 As in *Allied Bank*, the US government submitted a brief arguing that strict adherence to the terms of the debt instrument would be consistent with US policy. The United States observed that the *CIBC* case was the 'mirror image' of its concern in *Allied Bank*, because, as in the latter case with respect to a *debtor*, the United States 'does not wish to see a *creditor* use United States courts as a means of amending the terms of sovereign debt contracts'.[64] The US government further explained: 'It would harm the process that has evolved to deal with sovereign debt problems were creditors, in negotiating with debtors, doing so in the expectation that they could later litigate to obtain terms not in their contracts.'[65] The creditor's attempt to accelerate in *CIBC*, observed the United States, was 'an attempt to read into the contract a term restricting the rights of another creditor [Banco de Brasil]', which runs counter 'to the efforts the United States has expended since 1982 to resolve debt crisis through cooperative negotiations'.[66]

8.33 The Court in *CIBC* acknowledged that the creditor's acceleration claim was 'quite creative', but, consistent with the US government's 'plain language' argument, rejected the creditor's argument as, inter alia, incompatible with the text of the underlying contract.[67] After *CIBC*, courts have continued to adhere strictly to the language in sovereign debt agreements and have not been receptive to arguments by sovereigns that are not expressly supported by the contract, as demonstrated by the Second Circuit's decision in *NML Capital v. Republic of Argentina*.[68]

8.34 In *NML*, Argentina challenged the ability of holders of non-performing beneficial interests in floating rate accrual notes (FRANs) to enforce their beneficial interests in the underlying debt. According to the terms of the FRANs, Argentina was to pay the principal to FRANs

61 *CIBC Bank and Trust Co. (Cayman) Ltd v. Banco Central do Brasil*, 886 F.Supp. 1105 (SDNY 1995).
62 *CIBC* Brief (n. 8), 7.
63 *CIBC Bank* (n. 61), at 1107.
64 *CIBC* Brief (n. 8), 7.
65 *CIBC* Brief (n. 8), 7.
66 *CIBC* Brief (n. 8), 8.
67 *CIBC Bank* (n. 61), at 1115.
68 *NML Capital v. Republic of Argentina*, 621 F.3d 230 (2d Cir. 2010).

holders upon maturity and to make an interest payment on the notes once every six months until the principal was paid. The interest rate provision provided that the interest rate would vary based on the yields to maturity of other Argentine-issued debt; thus the riskier an investment the market considered Argentine debt, the higher the interest rates on the FRANs.

In December of 2001, to address its historic and catastrophic financial crisis, Argentina announced that it could no longer service its external debt. Argentina's announcement triggered the default provisions in the FRANs, allowing interest holders to accelerate payment of the principal. The default also made investing in Argentine debt seem particularly risky, and its yield to maturity increased accordingly. As the yield to maturity increased, so too did the interest rates that Argentina owed on FRANs rushed to maturity by the default provisions. Prior to Argentina's financial crisis, the FRANs' interest rates ranged from 9 per cent to 14.4 per cent annually; by the April 2005 maturity date, the interest rate was slightly over 100 per cent per year. **8.35**

Argentina argued on appeal that the interest rate provision should not have been enforced because it operated as an unenforceable penalty,[69] produced a substantively unconscionable result, and was contrary to public policy against exorbitant interest rates, a policy manifest in New York's usury law. The appellate court rejected each of these arguments, instead requiring the parties to adhere to the plain language set forth in the FRANs documentation.[70] **8.36**

While it is possible that, under different facts, a foreign state may be able to raise contract-based arguments in sovereign debt litigation successfully, the consistent decisions of US courts suggest that, to be accepted by a court, such an argument would have to be consistent with the plain language of the debt agreement. As the Second Circuit explained in *Allied Bank*, while it is the policy of the United States that sovereign debt crises are resolved through 'voluntary good faith negotiations between debtor and creditor', the validity of those negotiations 'ultimately depend[s] on the enforceability of international loan contracts in accordance with their terms'.[71] **8.37**

E. Litigation stays

Although sovereigns subject to jurisdiction in the United States may not be able to argue successfully that their debt obligations are unenforceable, they may be able to defer creditor litigation in times of financial distress in order to restructure their debt or otherwise stabilize their economy. Sovereign debtors defer—even though, in light of *Allied Bank*, they may not defend—such claims by invoking principles of international comity. The foremost case applying these principles in the sovereign debt context is *Pravin Banker Associates Ltd. v. Banco Popular del Peru*.[72] **8.38**

As in *Elliott*, the underlying facts in *Pravin* are tied to the Peruvian debt crisis of the 1980s, which caused Peru to default on numerous external debt obligations. After many of Peru's creditors initiated litigation against it, Peru and its Bank Advisory Committee agreed to stay all pending lawsuits 'in order to promote negotiations to resolve the entire problem of the unpaid foreign debts'. However, Pravin, which purchased from one of those litigants more than US$1 million of Peru's debt, demanded immediate payment of the principal and unpaid interest. **8.39**

---

69 *NML Capital* (n. 68), at 236 (citing *JMD Holding Corp. v. Congress Fin. Corp.*, 795 NYS.2d 502, 507 (2005)) (internal quotation marks omitted).

70 *NML Capital* (n. 68), at 238.

71 *Allied Bank Int'l v. Banco Credito Agricola de Cartago*, 757 F.2d 516, 519–20 (2d Cir. 1985).

72 *Pravin Banker Assocs, Ltd. v. Banco Popular del Peru*, 109 F.3d 850 (2d Cir. 1997).

8.40 Once it was clear that Banco Popular could not pay its creditors, Peru's central bank initiated liquidation proceedings. Pravin refused to join the Peruvian proceeding or the still-ongoing Brady Plan negotiations with the Bank Advisory Committee. Instead, Pravin sued Banco Popular and Peru for non-payment of debt in the Southern District of New York. Peru moved to dismiss, stay, or deny Pravin's motion for summary judgment, arguing that allowing the action to proceed:

> ... would reawaken all of the other lawsuits that the Bank Advisory Committee had succeeded in having stayed. It would... result in a creditor stampede to find and attach Peruvian assets, and such a stampede would, in turn, disrupt Peru's structural reform efforts.[73]

8.41 The District Court stayed the case for six months to allow the 'orderly completion' of the Peruvian liquidation proceedings.[74] Six months later, Peru argued for dismissal or an additional stay in order to allow its negotiations with the Bank Advisory Committee to run their course. Persuaded, the District Court granted an additional two-month stay. After the second stay expired, Peru again sought dismissal or a further stay, but the Court denied its motion and granted Pravin summary judgment. Peru sought to stay the judgment, but the Court rejected the motion, staying the judgment for thirty days for the sole purpose of allowing Peru to appeal the denial. After the Second Circuit rejected Peru's motion to stay, Peru appealed the denial of the motion to stay the proceedings and the grant of summary judgment, arguing that the District Court should have extended international comity to Peru's efforts to restructure its debt.

8.42 In *Pravin*, the Second Circuit held that extending comity to Peru's debt negotiations would be contrary to US policy. The Court found two potentially competing US interests at stake: first, an interest in the successful resolution of the Brady Plan negotiations between Peru and the Bank Advisory Committee; and second, an interest in ensuring that debt owed to American creditors is enforceable. The Court found the latter to be more compelling, reasoning that:

> This second interest limits the first so that, although the United States advocates negotiations to affect debt reduction and continued lending to defaulting foreign sovereigns, it maintains that creditor participation in such negotiations should be on a strictly voluntary basis.[75]

8.43 After identifying the principal US interest at stake, the Court found that extending comity to Peru and granting an additional stay of proceedings would be prejudicial to that interest. Specifically, extending comity would have denied Pravin's right to enforce the underlying debt and would have converted the negotiations between Peru and its creditors 'into the equivalent of a judicially enforced bankruptcy proceeding, for it would, in effect, have prohibited the exercise of legal rights outside the negotiations'.[76]

8.44 Despite ruling that summary judgment was appropriate, the Court found that an argument might be made that the circumstances of that case:

> ... justified a stay of the proceedings or, in the alternative, a stay of the execution of the judgment because either stay might allow the completion of Peru's negotiations with its creditors without unduly threatening the ultimate enforceability of the debt.[77]

---

[73] *Pravin* (n. 72), at 853.
[74] *Pravin* (n. 72), at 853.
[75] *Pravin* (n. 72), at 855.
[76] *Pravin* (n. 72), at 855.
[77] *Pravin* (n. 72), at 855–6.

The Court's finding is significant because it suggests a method for resolving the tension between a state's need to restructure debt and its creditors' right to payment.

The Second Circuit's holding in *Pravin* does pose a difficulty for states attempting to convince courts to stay proceedings due to Brady Plan negotiations or similar restructuring procedures,[78] but if the sovereign debtor can demonstrate an interest in favour of extending comity to those proceedings, the opinion leaves ample room for courts to grant stays of the proceedings or execution on any judgments obtained. **8.45**

3. Conclusion

Although Simone Weil was correct to label both the payment and non-payment of debt necessary for social order, the cases discussed in this chapter make clear that US courts are far from 'serenely unaware' of the interplay between 'these two contradictory necessities'. Courts have recognized that sovereign debt restructuring 'is obviously of critical importance to the economic health of a nation'[79] and that the prolonging of a sovereign's economic crisis affects not only the usual types of 'stakeholders' one finds in the context of corporate insolvency, but also tens or hundreds of millions of a foreign state's citizens. Thus, where a sovereign can demonstrate that a temporary stay of litigation is needed to create 'breathing space' during economic turmoil stemming from a financial crisis, courts may be willing to grant such relief. **8.46**

In the context of the recognition of liability, courts have consistently found that contract rights outweigh any necessity of non-payment. Foreign states' defences against the enforceability of their debt instruments in US courts have therefore been largely unsuccessful. It is only when creditor arguments stray from the terms of the underlying debt instrument and impinge upon the rights of other creditors that a foreign state may succeed in defending such claims against its creditors. **8.47**

The balance of these mutually contradictory imperatives struck by US courts is the product of their effort—with no formal guiding mechanism—to account for the numerous significant interests at stake, including the policy of the United States and the general well-being of the international economy. Although the courts' recognition of creditor contract rights has largely meant the defeat of sovereign defences to the entry of judgment, as covered elsewhere in this book, foreign state defences to the enforcement of such judgments, which are based on the strict immunity laws of various jurisdictions, including the FSIA in the United States, have sharply limited creditor remedies. Synthesizing these competing interests has been, and will remain, an ongoing challenge, but courts attuned to the various relevant interests at stake must continue to try to accommodate them appropriately. After all, nothing less than social order depends on it. **8.48**

[78] These international proceedings should be distinguished from domestic bankruptcy proceedings, with respect to which the Second Circuit affirmed the District Court's initial stay as appropriate given federal courts' 'long-standing recognition' of such proceedings: *Pravin* (n. 72), at 855–6.

[79] *EM Ltd v. Republic of Argentina*, 131 F. App'x 745, 747 (2d Cir. 2005) (summary order).

9

SPECIAL IMMUNITIES

Central Bank Immunity

Thomas C. Baxter, Jr, and David Gross[1]

1. Introduction

In 1976, the US Congress passed the Foreign Sovereign Immunities Act (FSIA).[2] In describing its findings and declaration of purpose, the Legislature wrote: **9.01**

> The Congress finds that the determination by United States courts of the claims of foreign states to immunity from the jurisdiction of such courts would serve the interests of justice and would protect the rights of both foreign states and litigants in United States courts. Under international law, states are not immune from the jurisdiction of foreign courts insofar as their commercial activities are concerned, and their commercial property may be levied upon for the satisfaction of judgments rendered against them in connection with their commercial activities. Claims of foreign states to immunity should henceforth be decided by courts of the United States and of the States in conformity with the principles set forth in this chapter.
>
> (28 USC § 1602)

For more than thirty-five years, the FSIA has 'provide[d] the sole basis for obtaining jurisdiction over a foreign state in the courts of [the United States]'.[3]

The immunity is not absolute: **9.02**

> Subject to existing international agreements to which the United States is a party at the time of enactment of this Act a foreign state shall be immune from the jurisdiction of the courts of the United States and of the States except as provided in sections 1605–1607 of this chapter.[4]

Those exceptions are hinted at in the statement of findings by Congress in § 1602: the commercial activities of foreign sovereigns and their commercial property located in the United States.

This chapter is concerned with one of these exceptions—specifically, the case in which a foreign sovereign has waived its immunity and has had a judgment entered against it. In addition, in this scenario there is property located within the United States. But there are two major **9.03**

[1] The views expressed in this chapter are those of the authors and do not necessarily reflect the views of the Federal Reserve Bank of New York or any other component of the Federal Reserve System.

[2] 28 USC §§ 1602 *et seq.*

[3] *Argentine Republic v. Amerada Hess Shipping Corp.*, 488 US 428, 443 (1989).

[4] 28 USC § 1604. The FSIA was enacted on 21 October 1976.

complications: first, the property belongs not to the sovereign, but to its central bank—that is, the property resides in a bank account held by the central bank; second, that account is located at the Federal Reserve Bank of New York, part of the Federal Reserve System, the central bank of the United States.[5]

9.04 Having laid out the factual basis in this introductory section, the chapter will examine the recent case law elucidating how sovereign immunity works with respect to a central bank holding its dollar reserves in an account at the Federal Reserve Bank. It should also be observed that it is commonplace for central banks to hold their dollar reserves at the Federal Reserve Bank. Currently, more than ninety central banks do this.[6] The discussion of the case law, however, will focus on only one: the unusual case of the Republic of Argentina and its central bank, Banco Central de la República Argentina (BCRA).

9.05 The second section of this chapter covers the history of the litigation between Argentina and its bondholders over the last ten years. After a discussion of the facts, it focuses specifically on the Second Circuit judgment of 2007, which first confronted the question of central bank immunity, and examines the legal basis for the Court's decision, including a close analysis of the different sections of the FSIA.

9.06 In the third section, the chapter looks at the second round of arguments on central bank immunity before the Second Circuit in 2011. It begins by examining whether BCRA is independent of the Republic of Argentina, and whether the existence of such independence or the strength of it matters. The section concludes with an examination of the FSIA's words 'held for its own account', and follows the Second Circuit as the Court grapples with the meaning of that phrase.

9.07 The conclusion to the chapter analyses the current state of the law of central bank immunity in light of the Argentina decisions and considers how courts may view central bank immunity in the coming years.

2. Argentina I

9.08 The litigation between the Republic of Argentina and its bondholders has been ongoing for ten years.[7] The question of central bank immunity first reached the Second Circuit Court of Appeals about six years ago.[8] The facts are taken primarily from that decision.

---

[5] The Federal Reserve Act, creating the Federal Reserve System, was passed in 1913 as a response to the Panic of 1907. The Federal Reserve System is composed of the Board of Governors (the federal government agency that is the Federal Reserve's centralized component), the twelve regional Reserve Banks (which supervise banks in their regions, conduct research on the economy, and provide financial services to banks and the US government), and the Federal Open Market Committee (the Federal Reserve's chief body for the setting of monetary policy). For more information about the structure of the Federal Reserve System, *see* <http://www.stlouisfed.org/inplainenglish/index.cfm>. For more information about the Board of Governors, *see* <http://www.federalreserve.gov/aboutthefed/default.htm>. For more information about the Federal Open Market Committee, *see* <http://www.federalreserve.gov/monetarypolicy/fomc.htm>.

[6] On behalf of the Federal Reserve System, the Federal Reserve Bank of New York offers banking and financial services to about 250 central banks, governments, and international official institutions: <http://www.newyorkfed.org/aboutthefed/fedpoint/fed20.html>.

[7] *See Lightwater Corp. v. Republic of Argentina*, 2003 US Dist. Lexis 6156 (SDNY 2003).

[8] *See EM Ltd v. Republic of Argentina*, 473 F.3d 463 (2d Cir. 2007).

A. Facts

In December 2001, in the midst of a financial crisis, the Republic of Argentina announced a temporary moratorium on its debt service payments. This caused the largest sovereign default in history.[9] Since December 2001, the Republic has not made principal or interest payments on the debt instruments at issue in the *EM Ltd* litigation discussed in this chapter. **9.09**

Certain bondholders brought suit against the Republic in the Southern District of New York in April of 2003 to recover principal and interest owed on the bonds. In the terms and conditions governing the bond, the Republic of Argentina 'irrevocably agreed not to claim and has irrevocably waived . . . immunity to the fullest extent permitted by the laws of [the] jurisdiction'. The Republic also consented: **9.10**

> . . . generally for the purposes of the Foreign Sovereign Immunities Act to the giving of any relief or the issue of any process in connection with any Related Proceeding or Related Judgment, provided that attachment prior to judgment or attachment in aid of execution shall not be ordered by the Republic's courts with respect to . . . the assets which constitute freely available reserves.[10]

In September 2003, the District Court granted summary judgment to the plaintiffs for more than US$700 million.[11] The Second Circuit affirmed the grant of summary judgment on 31 August 2004.[12]

But collecting on the judgment would prove more difficult. The plaintiffs, and other bondholders who had brought suit, but not yet received a judgment, sought to attach funds held by BCRA at the Federal Reserve Bank of New York (FRBNY). The District Court found that the Republic of Argentina had no attachable interest in the FRBNY funds, since they were the property of BCRA. The Court also found that the funds were otherwise immune from attachment under the FSIA.[13] **9.11**

B. Legal analysis

Under 28 USC § 1609: **9.12**

> Subject to existing international agreements to which the United States is a party at the time of enactment of this Act[,] the property in the United States of a foreign state shall be immune from attachment[,] arrest[,] and execution except as provided in sections 1610 and 1611 of this chapter.

Under § 1610, the FSIA's protections against attachment and execution extend to the instrumentalities of a foreign state (such as BCRA), although the protections applicable to assets of instrumentalities vary from those applicable to the assets of the foreign states themselves.[14] The Court in *EM Ltd* analysed each exception to see if it applied.

---

[9] *See*, e.g., Arturo C. Porzecanski, 'From Rogue Creditors to Rogue Debtors: Implications of Argentina's Default' (2005) 6 Chi J Int'l L 311, 317 (describing Argentina's 2001 default as 'by far the largest and potentially most complex default the world has ever known').

[10] *See* Terms and Conditions Governing Bond issued 22 June 2001, Joint Appendix.

[11] *See EM Ltd v. Republic of Argentina*, 2003 WL 22120745 (SDNY 12 September 2003), amended by *EM Ltd v. Republic of Argentina*, 2003 WL 22454934 (SDNY 27 October 2003).

[12] *See EM Ltd v. Republic of Argentina*, 382 F.3d 291, 292–94 (2d Cir. 2004).

[13] *See EM Ltd* (n. 8), at 472.

[14] *See Karaha Bodas Co., LLC v. Perusahaan Pertambangan Minyak Dan Gas Bumi Negara*, 313 F.3d 70, 82 (2d Cir. 2002) ('Section 1610 provides different regimes for sovereign states on the one hand, and their agencies and instrumentalities on the other').

9.13 Under § 1610(a):

> The property in the United States of a foreign state ... used for a commercial activity in the United States, shall not be immune from attachment in aid of execution, or from execution, upon a judgment entered by a court of the United States ... if: (1) the foreign state has waived its immunity from attachment in aid of execution or from execution either explicitly or by implication, ... or (2) the property is or was used for the commercial activity upon which the claim is based.
>
> (28 USC § 1610(a)(1)–(2))

Thus, if the FRBNY funds were the property of the Republic, § 1610(a) would apply, and the funds would be subject to attachment and execution. Similarly, under § 1610(d):

> The property of a foreign state ... used for a commercial activity in the United States, shall not be immune from attachment prior to the entry of a judgment in any action brought in a court of the United States ... if: (1) the foreign state has explicitly waived its immunity from attachment prior to judgment, ... and (2) the purpose of the attachment is to secure satisfaction of a judgment that has been or may ultimately be entered against the foreign state, and not to obtain jurisdiction.
>
> (28 USC § 1610(d))

Thus § 1610(d) allows for pre-judgment attachment of a foreign state's property used for commercial activity in the United States when the enumerated conditions are satisfied.

9.14 The Second Circuit, in its analysis, concluded that these sections did not apply, because the funds at the FRBNY were funds of BCRA, which the Court determined was a separate juridical entity from the Republic of Argentina.[15]

9.15 The Court then went even further, stating that the funds in the FRBNY account would not be attachable even if they *were* funds of the Republic, because they still do not satisfy the requirement that they be 'used for a commercial activity in the United States'.[16]

9.16 The FSIA's definition of 'commercial activity' states that '[t]he commercial character of an activity shall be determined by reference to the nature of the course of conduct or particular transaction or act, rather than by reference to its purpose'.[17] According to the US Supreme Court, '[a] foreign state engaging in commercial activities do[es] not exercise powers peculiar to sovereigns; rather it exercise[s] only those powers that can also be exercised by private citizens'.[18]

9.17 Plaintiffs argued that the funds were 'used for a commercial activity in the United States' when BCRA repaid the Republic's debt to the International Monetary Fund (IMF) in January 2006. The Court disagreed. It found that the Republic's relationship with the IMF was not 'commercial' in nature, because when Argentina borrowed from the IMF, it was exercising powers peculiar to sovereigns.[19] The Court further held that there was no evidence

---

[15] Plaintiffs, in fact, did not dispute that BCRA was a separate juridical entity from the Republic, and expressly elected not to argue that BCRA's separate juridical status should be disregarded because BCRA is the alter ego of the Republic: *see EM Ltd* (n. 8), at 479.

[16] *EM Ltd* (n. 8), at 480.

[17] 28 USC § 1603(d).

[18] *Republic of Argentina v. Weltover, Inc.*, 504 US 607, 614 (1992) (internal citations omitted).

[19] The Court went on to find that the relationship between the Republic of Argentina and the IMF was not commercial in nature for other reasons as well: *see EM Ltd* (n. 8), at 482–5.

that it was the FRBNY funds that BCRA used to repay the IMF, so it could not be said that the FRBNY funds were *used* for commercial activity under § 1610.

Finally, the Court completed its decision with a brief analysis of § 1611(b). The relevant portion of that section reads: **9.18**

> Notwithstanding the provisions of section 1610 of this chapter, the property of a foreign state shall be immune from attachment and from execution if: (1) the property is that of a foreign central bank or monetary authority held for its own account, unless such bank or authority, or its parent foreign government, has explicitly waived its immunity from attachment in aid of execution, or from execution, ...
>
> (28 USC § 1611(b)(1))

The Court noted that the FRBNY funds were immune from attachment even without reference to this section. It then pointed out that while the Republic had waived *its own* immunity in the terms and conditions, neither BCRA nor the Republic of Argentina had explicitly waived *BCRA's* immunity from attachment in aid of execution, so BCRA retained its immunity under the FSIA.

3. Argentina II

Four years later, the matters of Argentine sovereign debt and central bank immunity were back before the Second Circuit Court of Appeals.[20] Once again, plaintiff bondholders were seeking to attach the FRBNY funds. In this decision, the Court examined 28 USC § 1611(b)(1) much more closely in order to answer two questions, as follows. **9.19**

(1) Does the exercise of sovereign immunity for 'property . . . of a foreign central bank or monetary authority held for its own account' depend upon whether the central bank or monetary authority is entitled to a presumption of independence from its parent state?
(2) What is the proper meaning of the phrase 'property . . . of a foreign central bank or monetary authority held for its own account'?

A. Independence

The first question that the Court considered was whether the central bank needed to show its independence from the government before the central bank could claim sovereign immunity for its property.[21] The analysis began with a reading of the text of § 1611(b)(1). The Court reasoned: **9.20**

> [T]he text of the statute provides that the only qualification for immunity under § 1611(b)(1) is whether the property of the central bank is 'held for its own account.' We are mindful that in interpreting the statute we must 'give effect to Congress' choice of words, and understand that the text, as written,' does not create an independence requirement for the immunity of central bank assets under the FSIA. *United States v. Wilson*, 503 US 329, 342 (1992).
>
> (*NML Capital, Ltd*, 652 F.3d, at 188)

---

[20] *NML Capital, Ltd v. Banco Central de la República Argentina* 652 F.3d 172 (2d Cir. 2011).

[21] The plaintiffs, citing *First National City Bank v. Banco Para El Comercio Exterior de Cuba (Bancec)*, 462 US 611 (1983), argued that if the central bank was not independent of its parent state, then the funds should be seen as attachable interests of the Republic: *NML Capital, Ltd* (n. 20), at 172.

The Court then analysed the legislative history for any indication of Congress's intent:

> [Section 1611(b)(1)] applies to funds of a foreign central bank or monetary authority which are deposited in the United States and 'held' for the bank's or authority's 'own account'—i.e., funds used or held in connection with central banking activities, as distinguished from funds used solely to finance the commercial transactions of other entities or of foreign states.
>
> (*NML Capital, Ltd*, 652 F.3d, at 189)

There is no mention of independence in the legislative history. Finally, the Court turned to the historical context and noted that, at approximately the time that the FSIA was passed, ' "most central banks in the world functioned as departments of ministries of finance[,]" in which "the level of actual independence... was usually lower than indicated in the law" '.[22] This being the case, 'when Congress passed the FSIA, it had no reason to believe that foreign central banks and monetary authorities would be independent of their parent states because, at that time, most were not'.[23]

9.21 Countries organize their central banks in many different ways. While the central bank most usually has a separate juridical personality, there are some striking structural distinctions. Some central banks are owned entirely by their governments, while others are owned entirely by private shareholders. The nature of governmental 'control' also varies significantly. In some central banks, the chief executive officer serves at the pleasure (either de facto or *de jure*) of a governmental official, making such central banks susceptible to political considerations. In other central banks, there is no political control as such, but legislatures can influence central bank decision-making through other techniques, such as oversight hearings. For purposes of this analysis, suffice it to say that a central bank's independence of the political forms of the government is relative. In *NML Capital, Ltd*, the plaintiffs argued that BCRA was closely controlled by the Republic and that therefore it should be considered to be the Republic's alter ego.

9.22 Following its detailed analysis of the statute and the legislative history, the Court concluded that § 1611(b)(1) immunizes foreign central bank property 'held for its own account' without regard to the central bank's independence from its parent state. The Court then turned its attention to the question of whether the FRBNY funds were, in fact, the property of BCRA 'held for its own account'.

B. Held for its own account

9.23 The Court began by noting that the definition of the phrase 'held for its own account' in § 1611(b)(1) was a matter of first impression in the Second Circuit.[24] It then went on to analyse three possible definitions that the Court could adopt:

9.24 First, BCRA argued that central bank property is 'held for its own account' if that property is used for traditional central banking activities. Unfortunately, this definition is not as straightforward as it seems: '[N]o simple definition adequately describes the characteristics of all central banks.'

---

[22] *NML Capital, Ltd* (n. 20), at 189 (quoting Alex Cukierman, 'Central Bank Independence and Monetary Policymaking Institutions: Past Present and Future' (2008) 24 Eur J Pol Econ 722, 722).

[23] *NML Capital, Ltd* (n. 20), at 190.

[24] *NML Capital, Ltd* (n. 20), at 191.

> Central banks engage in a broad variety of activities in addition to typically holding their countries' reserves. The following can be regarded as central bank activities: (1) issue of notes, coin, and legal tender, (2) custody and administration of the nation's monetary reserves through the holding of gold, silver, domestic and foreign securities, foreign exchange, acceptances and other credit instruments, and IMF Special Drawing Rights, (3) establishment and maintenance of reserves of depository institutions, (4) discounts and advances to depository institutions, (5) receipt of deposits from the government, international organizations, depository institutions, and in special cases, private persons, (6) open market operations, (7) credit controls, and (8) licensing, supervision, and inspection of banks.[25]

Second, the FRBNY, appearing as *amicus curiae*, proposed an alternative definition drawn from the common law of bank deposits. Using the so-called 'plain language test,' the FRBNY suggested that property of a central bank is 'held for its own account' if it is in an account in the central bank's name. This is because 'under fundamental banking law principles, a positive balance in a bank account reflects a debt from the bank to the depositor and no one else'.[26] **9.25**

Third, the plaintiffs argued that property of a central bank is 'held for its own account' when it is held for the central bank's own profit or advantage. According to the plaintiffs: **9.26**

> [I]n the statutory phrase 'property . . . of a foreign central bank held for its own account': (1) the words 'its own' refer back to the term 'central bank' (not 'property'); and (2) the word 'for' denotes that the words that follow—'its own account'—constitute the purpose for which the property is 'held.'[27]

In analysing the competing definitions, the Court quickly disposed of the plaintiffs' suggested reading. BCRA performs numerous functions that are traditional activities of central banks, including establishing and implementing monetary policy, investing reserves, and regulating the Argentine banking system and financial system. In the view of the Court, these functions prove that the interests of BCRA could not be divided from the interests of the Republic of Argentina, so the plaintiffs' proposed definition could not be correct.[28] **9.27**

The Court then endorsed a modified central bank functions test: a combination of the 'plain language' of the statute and the 'central bank activities' test. This modified test had been proposed almost thirty years earlier by a former general counsel of the FRBNY, Ernest Patrikis: '[P]roperty of a central bank is immune from attachment if the central bank uses such property for central banking functions as such functions are normally understood, irrespective of their commercial nature.'[29] On the other hand, 'if an activity is to be regarded as commercial, as distinguished from a central bank activity, it should be an activity of the foreign central bank not generally regarded as a central banking activity'.[30] **9.28**

To summarize, the Court held that when funds are held in an account in the name of a central bank or monetary authority, the funds are presumed to be immune from attachment **9.29**

---

[25] Ernest T. Patrikis, 'Foreign Central Bank Property: Immunity from Attachment in the United States' [1982] U Ill L Rev 265, 274.

[26] *See Citizens Bank of Maryland v. Strumpf*, 516 US 16, 21 (1995) (a bank account 'consists of nothing more or less than a promise to pay, from the bank to the depositor').

[27] *NML Capital, Ltd* (n. 20), at 192.

[28] *NML Capital, Ltd* (n. 20), at 192–3.

[29] Patrikis (n. 25), at 277.

[30] Patrikis (n. 25), at 277–8.

under § 1611(b)(1). A plaintiff, however, can rebut that presumption by demonstrating with specificity that the funds are not being used for central banking functions as such functions are normally understood, irrespective of their 'commercial' nature.[31]

9.30 The Court then applied the test and found that the FRBNY funds were property of BCRA held for the central bank's own account at the FRBNY. The funds were held in BCRA's name. And the accumulation of foreign exchange reserves by BCRA to facilitate the regulation of the peso and the custody of cash reserves of commercial banks pursuant to central bank regulations are classic central banking functions. The FRBNY funds were therefore determined to be property of BCRA 'held for its own account'.

9.31 The final question that the Court considered was whether there had been an effective waiver of BCRA's immunity with respect to the FRBNY funds. Under the language of the statute, the only exception to the immunity of the property of a central bank held for its own account is where the central bank 'or its parent foreign government has explicitly waived its immunity from attachment in aid of execution, or from execution'.[32] The Court's analysis echoed its analysis in *EM Ltd*. It found that while the Republic of Argentina had explicitly waived *its* immunity in the terms and conditions governing the bonds, there had been no waiver of immunity with respect to BCRA: '[A]lthough the Republic's waiver of immunity from attachment is worded broadly, it does not appear to clearly and unambiguously waive BCRA's immunity from attachment, as it must do in order to be effective.'[33]

9.32 Because BCRA's sovereign immunity over the FRBNY funds had not been waived, and the FRBNY funds were property of BCRA held for its own account under § 1611(b)(1), the FRBNY funds were immune from attachment and restraint.

4. Conclusion

9.33 The complicated issue of Argentina's sovereign debt continues to play on in US courts. The litigation between Argentina and its bondholders is now entering its eleventh year and shows no signs of abating. In fact, the most recent argument in the matter before the Second Circuit Court of Appeals was held just a few weeks prior to writing.[34] In the ten years between April 2003 and March 2013, the litigation spawned 144 decisions in US federal courts.[35]

9.34 As for the matter of central bank immunity, the decisions by the Second Circuit Court of Appeals illustrate that: 'It is one thing to obtain a judgment against a foreign state or an agency or instrumentality, but quite another to recover on it'.[36] While the plaintiffs in the litigation have shown great resilience over the past decade, the funds of BCRA at the FRBNY seem to be safe from attachment: the US Supreme Court has declined to hear the case.[37]

---

[31] *NML Capital, Ltd* (n. 20), at 194.

[32] § 1611(b)(1).

[33] *NML Capital, Ltd* (n. 20), at 196 (quoting *EM Ltd*, n. 8, at 485, fn. 22).

[34] *See* Peter Eavis, 'Argentina's Bond Case is Being Closely Watched for Ramifications', *New York Times Dealbook*, 27 February 2013, available online at <http://dealbook.nytimes.com/2013/02/27/argentinas-bond-case-is-being-closely-watched-for-ramifications/>.

[35] *See* <https://w3.lexis.com/research2/citators/retrieve/shep/full.do?startCite=101&shepState=0_1618322888&_md5=b2f5a71bdc079ba1920855f65c781455> (subscribers only).

[36] Paul Lee, 'Central Banks and Sovereign Immunity' (2003) 41 Colum J Transnat'l L 327, 375.

[37] *EM Ltd v. Republic of Argentina*, 133 S. Ct. 23 (2012).

That denial signals a change in the law of central bank immunity for the first time in almost four decades. In analysing the question of whether the funds of a foreign central bank should be considered immune from attachment, it used to be the case that a US court would first ascertain whether the central bank was entitled to a presumption of independence from its parent state.[38] If there was no independence, then the funds in question were attachable interests of the state.[39] Under *NML Capital, Ltd*, this is no longer the case: '[T]he analysis of the immunity of a foreign central bank's property *begins* with § 1611(b)(1).'[40] An independence requirement will not be read into the statute. Going forward, the relevant analysis, when considering the matter of immunity, will focus only on whether the funds are property of the central bank 'held for its own account' under § 1611(b)(1).[41] As a result of these Argentina decisions, the law of central bank immunity in the United States under the FSIA has been simplified and improved. **9.35**

[38] *Bancec* (n. 21).
[39] *Bancec* (n. 21).
[40] *NML Capital, Ltd* (n. 20), at 190 (emphasis in original).
[41] *NML Capital, Ltd* (n. 20), at 190.

10

SPECIAL IMMUNITIES

Bank for International Settlements

Diego Devos[1]

1. Introduction

The purpose of this chapter is to illustrate the limits set on the enforcement of creditors' claims against certain sovereign entities when the assets subject to execution measures are held by an international organization as part of its core functions, protected as such by specific immunities from jurisdiction and execution. **10.01**

The Bank for International Settlements (BIS) was indeed subject to various judicial proceedings initiated by some creditors of the Republic of Argentina between 2009 and 2012 in relation to assets held on BIS books on behalf of the Central Bank of Argentina. These proceedings gave rise to final court and administrative decisions in Switzerland and in New York, which were published and reported in the press. This chapter will present an overview of these actions, given the important legal principles that have been applied in those cases that are relevant in the context of the enforcement of creditors' claims against sovereign entities. **10.02**

2. The Bank for International Settlements and its Immunities

The Bank for International Settlements[2] is an international organization created in 1930 by treaty to foster international monetary and financial cooperation between, and to serve as a bank for, central banks. **10.03**

Initially created to manage, as trustee, the war reparations due by Germany following the First World War (in particular under the so-called 'Dawes and Young bonds'), the role of the BIS evolved over time[3] to include promoting international monetary cooperation (for example through regular meetings of central bank officials, and the publication of economic and statistical reports) and facilitating the coordination of financial stability questions—namely, **10.04**

---

[1] The views expressed in this chapter are strictly those of the author and do not necessarily reflect those of the Bank for International Settlements.

[2] *See* <http://www.bis.org/>.

[3] BIS membership has also enlarged successively, in particular since the 1990s, to encompass a broader group of central banks (sixty at time of writing). On the Bank's historical evolution since its inception in 1930, *see* G. Toniolo, *Central Bank Cooperation at the Bank for International Settlements (1930–1973)* (Cambridge: Cambridge University Press, 2005), ch. 12.

as part of the so-called 'Basel process', which is the elaboration of international financial standards by various groupings of central banks and financial supervisors hosted by the BIS.[4]

10.05 In order for the BIS to fulfil its functions, it was deemed necessary that governments should not be able to exercise political influence on its operations and activities, and the states party to the 1930 Hague Agreements foresaw that only central banks should be members of the organization. Central banks perform essential sovereign functions within their respective countries, such as the definition and/or implementation of monetary policy, the imposition of minimum reserve requirements on financial institutions, the issuance of the national currency, and the management of the country's foreign exchange reserves, as well as the operation/oversight of payment systems and, in some cases, the supervision of financial institutions.

10.06 In recognition of the fact that central banks perform such important sovereign functions, many countries have granted immunities to foreign central banks, either by way of national legislation or court decisions,[5] generally with a greater degree and a wider ranging scope than the traditional *state immunity*, based on the classical distinction between state activities pertaining to sovereign functions (*acta jure imperii*), which are immune, and those that may be commercial by nature or purposes (*acta jure gestionis*),[6] which are not protected by immunities. By contrast, *central bank immunities* are most often recognized to protect, for example, any property used for central banking functions, such as the management of foreign reserves. This specific regime for central banks and other monetary authorities is expressly confirmed by the 2004 United Nations Convention on Jurisdictional Immunities of States and their Property (Article 21.1(c)), at the time of writing expected to enter into force in the near future.

10.07 Similarly, international financial institutions (IFIs) have been granted specific immunities by most countries to allow them to pursue their public interest mandates. One of the most important aspects of the privileges and immunities of international organizations, as provided in the constituent instruments and multilateral or bilateral agreements with host states, is *immunity from legal process*, which grants to the international organization immunity from domestic jurisdiction in its host state (*immunity from jurisdiction*) and immunity from corresponding enforcement measures (*immunity from execution*), without reference here to the traditional state immunity distinctions between sovereign and commercial activities, which do not apply to international organizations.[7] These immunities are granted to

---

[4] *See* BIS, 'Monetary and Financial Stability: Overview', available online at <http://www.bis.org/stability.htm>, regarding the activities of central banks and supervisory authorities meeting at the BIS as part of groupings such as the Basel Committee on Banking Supervision, the Financial Stability Board, the Committee on the Global Financial System, the Markets Committee, the Committee on Payment and Settlement Systems, the International Association of Insurance Supervisors, and the International Association of Deposit Insurance Schemes.

[5] *See* Tom Baxter and Robert Toomey, 'Legal Issues Incident to Holding Central Bank Assets Abroad', in International Monetary Fund (IMF), *IMF's Current Developments in Monetary and Financial Law, Vol. 2* (Washington DC: IMF, 2003), 450 *et seq*; C. Proctor, 'Central Banks and Sovereign Immunity' (2000) 15 JIBFL 70; C. Proctor, 'How Safe are Your Reserves?' (2006) 17(1) Central Banking Journal 42.

[6] *See* Hazel Fox, *The Law of State Immunity*, 2nd edn (Oxford: Oxford University Press, 2008), 502 *et seq*; *see* also Articles 10(1) and 19(c) of the 2004 United Nations Convention on Jurisdictional Immunities of States and their Property.

[7] *See* C. Wilfred Jenks, *International Immunities* (London: Stevens & Sons, 1961), 45; Fox (n. 6), 470.

preserve the independence of the organization from its member states and to secure its international character. Indeed, immunities ensure in general that no member state is able to interfere unilaterally through its legislative, executive, or judicial branches with the working of an international organization established to act in the common interests of its members.[8]

Consistent with the approach taken to protect international organizations in general, the Hague Convention respecting the BIS[9] established the BIS with similar privileges and immunities necessary for the performance of its functions, as confirmed by the 1936 Brussels Protocol regarding the immunities of the BIS,[10] and in the Headquarters Agreement (HQA),[11] concluded between the BIS and Switzerland on 10 February 1987.[12] **10.08**

In this respect, the BIS also provides financial services to central banks (both BIS members and non-members), international organizations, and other public institutions, by carrying out banking operations to assist them in, for example, managing and investing their international reserves, and by acting as a trustee or agent in regard to international settlements.[13] These operations should, in particular, be immune from national political, administrative, or judicial interferences. **10.09**

In terms of scope, the two following main categories of immunity protection should be distinguished. **10.10**

- *Immunity from jurisdiction*—that is, from every form of domestic judicial proceedings. Article 55(1) of the BIS Statutes and Article 4.1 HQA state that 'the Bank shall enjoy immunity from jurisdiction'. It is worth noting, however, that the BIS may waive its immunity from jurisdiction in individual cases and that such immunity from jurisdiction is, in any event, not applicable 'in civil or commercial suits, arising from banking or financial transactions, initiated by contractual counterparties of the Bank'. When the BIS is operating on the markets with financial institutions, such BIS counterparts should indeed be able to sue the BIS in court (unless an arbitration provision has been contractually stipulated, which will derogate to the competence of judicial courts).

---

[8] *See* Peter H. F. Bekker, *The Legal Position of Intergovernmental Organizations* (The Hague: Martinus Nijhof, 1994), 98 *et seq.*

[9] *See* the Hague Convention respecting the Bank for International Settlements, 20 January 1930, available online at <http://www.bis.org/about/convention-en.pdf>.

[10] *See* Article X of the Hague Agreement with Germany, 20 January 1930, which specifically grants the Bank immunity from governmental measures, as further clarified by the international treaty entitled 'Protocol regarding the immunities of the Bank for International Settlements of 30 July 1936' (the Brussels Protocol) to which some twenty-five countries have acceded to date (Australia, Belgium, Canada, Chile, China, Croatia, France, Germany, Greece, India, Ireland, Italy, Luxembourg, Mexico, New Zealand, Philippines, Poland, Portugal, Romania, Singapore, Slovenia, South Africa, Switzerland, Turkey, and the United Kingdom). Two further countries (the Netherlands and Sweden) have passed specific domestic legislation similar to the Brussels Protocol, which also extends such protection to assets subdeposited by the BIS with third parties in any of those countries.

[11] Agreement between the Swiss Federal Council and the Bank for International Settlements to determine the Bank's legal status in Switzerland of 10 February 1987, as amended by the exchange of letters of 18 December 2002 and 13 January 2003 (SR 0.192.122.971), available online at <http://www.bis.org/about/headquart-en.pdf>. Similar extensive immunities are also granted to the BIS in the host country agreements with the People's Republic of China and with Mexico, where the BIS has established local offices.

[12] The BIS has, in this respect, a legal status comparable to that accorded to the many other international organizations established in Switzerland: *see* in particular the Federal Act of 22 June 2007 on the Privileges, Immunities and Facilities and the Financial Subsidies granted by Switzerland as a Host State (SR 192.12).

[13] *See* Article 3 of the Statutes of the BIS of 20 January 1930, as amended subsequently.

- *Immunity from compulsory execution*
The purpose of these immunities is to protect both the BIS as such for its own assets,[14] as well as its central bank and international organization customers for the property and assets that they may hold at the Bank from the risk that such assets may be attached or a judgment enforced against them.
In particular, the assets held with the BIS are protected against compulsory execution pursuant to Article 55(3) of the BIS Statutes and Article 4.4 HQA, which state that:

> All deposits entrusted to the Bank, all claims against the Bank and the shares issued by the Bank shall, without the express prior agreement of the Bank, wherever located and by whomsoever held, be immune from any measure of execution (including seizure, attachment, freeze or any other measure of execution, enforcement or sequestration).[15]

10.11 As already noted, in a number of countries, central banks and international organizations, and their property and assets, directly enjoy a significant degree of immunity—in particular as regards immunity from jurisdiction and execution. The assets of central banks or international organizations should similarly not lose immunity protection when held through the BIS.

3. BIS Immunities Challenged by Holdout Bondholders Creditors of Argentina

A. Facts

10.12 On 5 November 2009, the BIS received two sequestration orders from the Basel Debt Enforcement and Bankruptcy Authority[16] to block the assets of Banco Central de la Republica Argentina (BCRA), the central bank of Argentina, in its books up to a total amount of some CHF1.25 billion in principal.

10.13 These sequestration orders were requested and obtained on an *ex parte* basis (without having the BIS or Argentina and its central bank being notified of the initiation of such proceedings) by two companies, NML Capital Ltd and EM Ltd (both headquartered in the Cayman Islands), which are creditors of the Republic of Argentina pursuant to US court decisions. Both companies are hedge funds specializing in the business of acquiring at low price (near-) defaulted bonds issued by sovereign issuers, and in particular the 1995 bonds issued by the Republic of Argentina that remained subsequently unpaid following Argentina's default in 2001, with the aim of recovering the nominal value of such bonds by way of court actions (so-called 'vulture funds'[17]).

---

[14] Article 55(2) of the BIS Statutes and Article 4(3) HQA state that 'Property and assets of the Bank shall, wherever located and by whomsoever held, be immune from any measure of execution (including seizure, attachment, freeze or any other measure of execution, enforcement or sequestration)', except, of course, if that measure of execution is sought pursuant to a final judgment rendered against the Bank by any court of competent jurisdiction (for claims due to BIS commercial counterparts or in case of waiver granted by the BIS, *see* paragraph 10.10 in the main text).

[15] And in particular of 'attachment' (*arrest*, or *séquestre*) within the meaning of Swiss law.

[16] This is the local Swiss public agency in charge of recovering claims on behalf of creditors, in particular by way of attachment.

[17] The actions initiated by the so-called vulture funds against defaulting states are well known in the context of a state's debt restructuring programmes. International financial organizations, such as the IMF or the World Bank, have stressed the importance of sovereign debt restructuring mechanisms, with the argument that these

B. Main issues under discussion

The plaintiffs basically argued as follows. 10.14

- They argued that Argentina was abusing BIS immunities—and therefore that such immunities should be disregarded by courts as is the case for any abuse of rights—by having

mechanisms benefit both the citizens of the countries whose debts are being restructured, by reducing the period of economic dislocation, and creditors, whose values are preserved to the largest extent possible. Proposals for a sovereign debt restructuring mechanism (SDRM) and collective action clauses (CAC) were made in this respect to improve restructuring processes and to avoid disruptive actions from freerider creditors (such as vulture funds). Some governments and public authorities' representatives also expressed their opposition to the action of vulture funds, which impact negatively poor and indebted countries, diminishing the impact of debt relief granted by other creditors by reducing the resources available to the country to finance development. *See*, in the United Kingdom, HM Treasury Consultation Paper, *Ensuring Effective Debt Relief for Poor Countries* (July 2009), 3 and 16: 'The UK Government has made clear its opposition to the practice of not participating in debt relief for HIPCs and litigating for the full value of the debt.' The UK Chancellor of the Exchequer also stated on 10 May 2007: 'I deplore the activities of so-called vulture funds that seek to profit from debts owed by the poorest countries of the world.' This translated eventually, in the UK, into the adoption of the Debt Relief (Developing Countries) Act 2010 to limit actions of vulture funds against heavily indebted poor countries (HIPCs) under that Act. *See* also the statement of the G-7 Finance Ministers and Central Bank Governors in Washington DC on October 2007: 'We remain concerned about the problem of aggressive litigation against HIPC countries.' *See* the Hearing before the US Subcommittee on Africa and Global Health of the Committee on Foreign Affairs of the US House of Representatives, 22 May 2007, entitled 'Vulture Funds and the Threat to Debt Relief in Africa: A Call to Action at the G-8 and Beyond'; National Bank of Belgium (NBB), *Financial Stability Review 2002*, available online at http://www.nbb.be/pub/06_00_00_00_00/06_03_00_00_00/06_03_02_00_00/FSR_2002.htm?l=en>, 118; NBB, *Financial Stability Review 2005*, available online at <http://www.nbb.be/pub/06_00_00_00_00/06_03_00_00_00/06_03_02_00_00/FSR_20050623.htm?l=en>, 163, Box 3. On sovereign debt restructurings in general, *see* Udaibir S. Das, Michael G. Papaioannou, and Christoph Trebesch, *Sovereign Debt Restructuring 1950–2010*, IMF Working Paper 12/203 (August 2012), available online at <http://www.imf.org/external/pubs/cat/longres.aspx?sk=26190.0>.

As an illustration, in 2000, a hedge fund (LP Elliott Associates), based on a Brussels court order (Court of Appeals of Brussels, 8th Chamber, 26 September 2000, in Dutch language, unpublished; Court register Nr 2000/QR/92) obtained on an *ex parte* basis, served restraining notices preventing Euroclear, the Brussels-based operator of international securities settlement system (operated at the time by the Brussels branch of Morgan Guaranty Trust), from receiving payments from, or paying out cash on behalf of, the Republic of Peru to discharge interest payments on Peru's Brady bonds held with Euroclear. In 2003, another fund (LNC Investments Inc.) served similar restraining notices to Euroclear in relation to payment interests on the Republic of Nicaragua's bonds. In Peru's case, an amicable settlement between Peru and the vulture fund was reached before the court proceedings pending in Belgium (and in the United States) were debated to the contrary. In the Nicaragua case, the Brussels Appeal Court finally lifted the attachment proceedings against Euroclear, because the latter could not be forced to operate—as decided previously by the first judge—a pro rata payment mechanism in favour of the holdout creditor, based on a debated *pari passu* provision stipulated in the issuance terms of the Nicaragua bonds to which Euroclear was not a party (Court of Appeals of Brussels, 9th Chamber, 19 March 2004, in French language, unpublished; Court register Nr 2004/1831–2003/KR/334). It will be noted that these cases have justified the adoption of special legislation prohibiting attachment and blocking measures on cash and securities accounts held with securities settlement systems private operators (such as Euroclear, Clearstream Banking Luxembourg, or some national central securities depositaries), even at the prior stage of incoming cash transfers with cash correspondents of such operators: *see*, e.g., Article 9 of the Belgian Act dated 28 April 1999 implementing the Settlement Finality Directive, as amended by a law dated 19 November 2004 (*Moniteur Belge*, 28 December 2004, p. 85854); *see* also G. Affaki and J. Stoufflet, 'Chronique de Droit Bancaire International' (2005) 101 Banque et Droit 81; Sean Hagan, 'Designing a Legal Framework to Restructure Sovereign Debt' (2005) 36(2) Georgetown J Int'l L 299, 313–5 and the related footnotes, also published in IMF, *IMF Current Developments in Monetary and Financial Law, Vol. 4* (Washington DC: IMF, 2008), 204–5; C. D. Schmerler, 'Restructuring Sovereign Debt', in James Silkenat and Charles Schmerler (eds) *The Law of International Insolvencies and Debt Restructurings* (New York: Oceana Publications, 2006), 452–6. On the *pari passu* clauses' interpretation in the light of the *Elliott* case law in particular with respect to Argentina, *see* Rodrigo Olivares-Caminal, *Litigation Aspects of Sovereign Debt in Debt Restructuring* (Oxford: Oxford University Press, 2011), 389; Rodrigo Olivares-Caminal, 'The *Pari Passu* Interpretation in the *Elliott* Case: A Brilliant Strategy but an Awful (Mid–Long-Term) Outcome?' (2013) 40 Hofstra L Rev 39.

transferred 'all of its reserves' to the BIS in order to shield them from creditors' actions,[18] following Argentina's default in 2001.

- They also developed, in Basel in November 2009, an argument that they would elaborate further in the United States[19] that the central bank of Argentina is not independent from the government and therefore that the central bank should be regarded to be the alter ego of the state, in spite of its separate legal personality. In this way, the plaintiffs justified their argument that enforcement measures could be sought by creditors of the Republic of Argentina directly against the assets of the central bank (again, notwithstanding that the hedge funds had no claims against the central bank as such).
- In support of these arguments, the funds also alleged in particular, in their various judicial submissions supported by various press campaigns, that the BCRA was holding some 98–99 per cent of its foreign reserves (amounting to some US$40 billion) in BIS books.

10.15 The perspective of the BIS, as an international organization holding central bank assets, was, of course, somewhat different.[20]

(a) It should be underlined, as a factual point, that the BIS does not hold assets on behalf of the Republic of Argentina itself, but only assets of *the central bank*, which is a distinct legal entity. The fact that a central bank would not be independent from the government, as argued by the plaintiffs in the case of the central bank of Argentina, is not uncommon[21] and should not deprive the central bank from the protections associated with its separate legal status. In any event, it is not for the BIS to enter into such distinctions for so long as the central bank is established as a separate legal entity, distinct from the state, which is what is required under its Statutes to open current accounts with the relevant central banks (Articles 21 and 24 of the BIS Statutes). Irrespectively of the existence of BIS immunities, therefore, the plaintiffs did not have an enforceable claim against the central bank of Argentina's assets deposited with the BIS.

(b) It was also factually incorrect to allege that BCRA would be holding 'practically all of the BCRA's reserves' with the BIS. When queried by the *Financial Times*, the BIS clarified in early 2010 and subsequently[22] that the exact amount of BCRA deposits could not be

---

[18] *See* also Hal Scott, *Sovereign Debt Default: Cry for the United States, not Argentina*, Washington Legal Foundation Working Paper Series No. 140 (September 2006), available online at <http://www.wlf.org/upload/Scott%20WP%20Final.pdf>, 12.

[19] *See* the alter ego motion granted in *EM Ltd v. Republic of Argentina*, 720 F. Supp. 2d 273 (SDNY 2010), overturned by the US Court of Appeals (2nd Cir.) on 5 July 2011 in *NML Capital Ltd v. Republic of Argentina*, 652 F.3d 172 (2d Cir. 2011), which held that the immunities granted to the central bank of Argentina under US federal laws for assets 'held for its own account' (§ 1611(b)(1) of the US Federal Sovereign Immunities Act) were still applicable irrespective of the alter ago/independence discussion, fuelled by the dismissal of former BCRA governor Martin Redrado in December 2009–January 2010 (on which, *see* V. Paz, 'Restructuring of Sovereign Debt and Crisis Argentina: Payment out of Central Bank Reserves' [2011] JIBLR 40).

[20] It is important to stress from the outset that the BIS did not want to take sides in litigations between the Republic of Argentina and its private creditors, to which the BIS is a third party. The BIS does not intervene, and should not be forced to intervene, in any litigation between sovereign issuers involved in the economic reorganization of their external debt and creditors seeking to enforce the contractual rights that they may have against such countries.

[21] *See* the report from the BIS Central Bank Governance Forum, *Issues in the Governance of Central Banks* (May 2009), available online at <http://www.bis.org/publ/othp04.htm>, 57 *et seq.*

[22] Later, in the *Wall Street Journal*, 22 July 2011, Mr Bolkestein, former EU Commissioner, relaying the arguments developed many times by the plaintiffs, wrote that the BIS immunities were abused by the Republic of Argentina in order to defraud Argentinian creditors by keeping almost all of that country's foreign reserves at

disclosed publicly by the BIS given the usual custodial confidentiality duties, but that 'the figures quoted by the media [90 per cent or more of Argentina's reserves, as conveyed by the plaintiffs to the press] were grossly overstated'.[23]

(c) More fundamentally, the acceptance of deposits by central bank customers, whatever their amount or proportions, and the related management of these deposits are part of the BIS core public sector missions, and as such are protected by its immunities. By maintaining all or part of their reserves at the BIS, central banks are indeed able to conduct various critical international transactions, including multilateral debt repayments, which should be freely operated without judicial disruptions (see paragraphs 10.06–10.11).

(d) Finally, as a matter of public international law, the question of an alleged abuse of BIS immunities cannot be settled by a national court, which would defeat the purposes of the immunity protection. Indeed, BIS immunities protecting customer assets cannot be reviewed and lifted by Swiss courts, and can be waived *only by the BIS itself*.[24] The question of a possible abuse of BIS immunities is governed by Article 22 HQA, which provides that the BIS will cooperate at all times with the Swiss authorities to prevent any abuse of the privileges and immunities granted to the Bank. Any instances of abuse are to be established in common agreement between the BIS and the Swiss Federal Department of Foreign Affairs (FDFA); in case of disagreement, the issue between the two parties will be referred to arbitration, under the HQA, which could ultimately force the BIS to waive its immunities.

Given these principles, the Bank responded, in two letters dated 6 and 13 November 2009, **10.16**
to the Basel City Debt Enforcement and Bankruptcy Authority and to the Supervisory Authority[25] (the higher supervisory body within the Basel City Civil Court) to deny any legal effect of such sequestration orders on the grounds of BIS' immunities.[26] The FDFA also intervened and wrote to both Basel authorities. Under applicable principles of public international law, it is indeed normally not for the international organization to claim in court the immunities to which it is entitled. If the immunities are not raised by the judge *ex officio*—as they normally should be—it is for the national authorities of the state concerned

---

the BIS. The BIS responded to these allegations by way of a letter published in the *Wall Street Journal*, 27 July 2011, available online at <http://online.wsj.com/article/SB10001424053111903591104576469960940117244.html?KEYWORDS=the+argentinian+money>, emphasizing, for example, that the BIS had no banking relationship with the Republic of Argentina and that the amounts allegedly deposited by the central bank of Argentina ('80/90% of its reserves') were in reality well below that level.

[23] *Financial Times*, 19 February 2010. In various judicial submissions, the plaintiffs referred incorrectly to IMF publicly available information (*see* IMF *Data Template on International Reserves and Foreign Currency Liquidity*, Table entitled 'Argentina: International Reserves/Foreign Currency Liquidity', available online at <http://www.imf.org/external/np/sta/ir/IRProcessWeb/data/arg/eng/curarg.pdf>) to justify their incorrect numbers. In this IMF table, there is indeed an item for the amount of reserves held at 'other national central banks, BIS and IMF' (see item A(1)(b)(i)), but it is impossible to derive the exact holdings with the BIS from this aggregated total. The (wrong) assumption made by the plaintiffs was that all reserves are placed with the BIS and none with other institutions.

[24] This is what the BIS does when, in particular, private interests (e.g. attachment of BIS staff member's salaries by private creditors) unrelated to BIS core missions are in question.

[25] That is, the Aufsichtsbehörde über das Betreibungs- und Konkursamt des Kantons Basel-Stadt.

[26] Given its immunity from jurisdiction, it will be noted that the BIS did not lodge any formal opposition to the *ex parte* order, nor did the BIS file any appeal, but it merely *denounced the illegality* of the *ex parte* sequestration order and its implementing measures to the Supervisory Authority within the Basel City Civil Court, based on articles 22(1) and 30a of the Swiss Federal Act on Debt Prosecution and Bankruptcy of 11 April 1989 (SR 281.1), which should in principle not draw the BIS into the pending judicial proceedings.

to draw the court's attention to the immunity from legal process enjoyed by the international organization.[27]

10.17 By a judgment rendered on 23 April 2010, the Basel City Supervisory Authority declared the sequestration orders null and void, in view of BIS immunities.

10.18 The plaintiffs appealed this decision before the Swiss Federal Tribunal (the Swiss supreme court). At the request of the Federal Tribunal, the BIS sent to the Tribunal in June 2010 a detailed submission letter, developing its position with respect to the illegality of the sequestration proceedings in view of its status as an international organization protected by immunities in Switzerland, without prejudice, however, to its immunity from jurisdiction.[28] The letter was supported by legal advice from two eminent experts in public international law.

C. Final decisions rendered in Switzerland

10.19 The Federal Tribunal gave its final decision on 12 July 2010,[29] confirming the nullity of the sequestration orders based on the following considerations.

(a) The BIS enjoys *full immunity* from jurisdiction and execution under its HQA, which means that the assets deposited with the BIS cannot be subject to execution measures of any kind and that the BIS cannot be involved, as a third-party custodian, in execution proceedings in Switzerland.
(b) Assets entrusted to the BIS can be sequestrated only *with the prior express agreement of the Bank*, as provided under the HQA. As a result, any enforcement decision or measure taken by debt enforcement authorities (or by courts acting in debt enforcement matters) against assets deposited with the BIS is null and void.
(c) The BIS, as an international organization, enjoys *absolute immunity* for its actions. The acceptance of deposits of central bank assets by the BIS belongs to its primary purpose (Articles 3 and 21, lit. j, BIS Statutes). The Bank requires such absolute immunity to fulfil its functions as bank to central banks.[30]
(d) National courts are not competent to review an alleged abuse of immunities, because it would imply a review of the purposes of the activities of an international organization, which would be inconsistent with the independence of such international organizations and could, in addition, call into question the impartiality of national courts. The Bank's refusal in this case to waive its immunities is therefore decisive for the national judge, according to the Tribunal.

---

[27] *See* also the opinion of the United Nations Office of Legal Affairs [1991] UNJY 319.

[28] Because the BIS enjoys immunity from Swiss jurisdiction, the BIS took the view that it should not formally be a party to the sequestration proceedings initiated by the two creditors against Argentina/BCRA (*see* n. 26) and should decline to exercise directly any recourse, including at the level of the Federal Tribunal, which could be characterized as an implicit waiver by the BIS of its immunities.

[29] Judgment 5A-360/2010 of the Federal Tribunal of 12 July 2010, BGE 136 III 379 (original version in German language); Basler Juristische Mittelungen, December 2010, at 285. *See* also online at <http://jumpcgi.bger.ch/cgi-bin/JumpCGI?id=12.07.2010_5A_360/2010>, and the French translation published in ATF 136 III 379, c. 4.1 à 4.5; JDT 2011 II, 263, with note Ed. Ph; *see* also L. Caflisch, 'La Pratique Suisse en Matière de Droit International Public 2010' [2012] RSDIE 101, in particular 127, s. 3.5.

[30] The Tribunal also emphasized that the BIS:

> . . . which serves as the bank of central banks and to that end provides for acceptance of deposits from central banks, would undoubtedly be critically impacted in the fulfilment of its function if billions in deposits from one central bank were to be sequestered or the assets and deposits entrusted to it were to have a disposal and payment freeze imposed on them by judicial order.
>
> (BGE 136 III 379, consideration 4.3.3, unofficial English translation)

(e) Article 6(1) of the European Convention on Human Rights (ECHR), which guarantees access to a judge and a right to a fair trial, is in principle applicable. However, the fact that no judge has the power to review BIS immunities is an acceptable limitation to the ECHR (such limitation must have a 'legitimate objective and be proportionate'[31]); a review by a judge would jeopardize the ability of the BIS to carry out its functions properly—in particular, the management of part of the foreign exchange reserves of a large number of countries' central banks. Indeed, the Tribunal held that:

> [I]n its function as bank of central banks, the BIS manages part of the foreign exchange reserves of a large number of countries and international financial institutions. Were Swiss courts and enforcement agencies to decide whether and to what extent central bank deposits are justified on foreign exchange policy grounds, the [BIS] would be decisively hindered in its statutory function as international settlement hub for central banks. The [BIS]'s freedom of action and the continuity of settlements among central banks in the interests of international financial stability would not be ensured. One cannot therefore speak of a breach of the Convention if the lower instance effectively refused to rule on the [BIS]'s refusal to waive immunity.[32]

Therefore the ECHR does not provide an additional remedy to the plaintiffs.

This important decision for BIS immunities—and more generally for the immunities enjoyed by international organizations based in Switzerland—is consistent with the traditional position adopted in Switzerland according to which immunities of international organizations are *absolute*[33]—that is, they cannot be waived without the express consent of the organization. **10.20**

Moreover, as indicated at paragraphs 10.06 and 10.07, the traditional distinction made with respect to *state* immunity between acts *jure imperii* (made in the exercise of sovereign authority), which enjoy unrestricted immunity, and acts *jure gestionis* (made for commercial purposes or of commercial nature), which are not covered by immunity, does not apply to international organizations, which are protected for all acts carried out in the exercise of their missions.[34] **10.21**

---

[31] *See* BGE 136 III 379, consideration 4.5.2.

[32] *See* BGE 136 III 379, consideration 4.5.3 (unofficial English translation).

[33] The author understands this to be the position of the Federal Department of Foreign Affairs; *see* Circular of the Directorate of International Law of 28 February 1994, at 4, published in *Verwaltungspraxis der Bundesbehörden* 59.157, available online at <http://www.vpb.admin.ch/deutsch/doc/59/59.157.html>. Switzerland has also enacted a Federal Act on the Privileges, Immunities and Facilities and the Financial Subsidies granted by Switzerland as a Host State (*see* n. 12) which reinforces the principle of immunities granted to international organizations based in Switzerland.

[34] *See* BGE 136 III 379, consideration 4.3.1. This view has been previously upheld by the Swiss Federal Tribunal in BGE 118 Ib 562, consideration 1a:

> International organizations enjoy absolute and complete immunity without any restriction. The so-called principle of restrictive immunity... only applies to States so that the distinction between acts performed *jure imperii* and *jure gestionis* is not relevant to international organizations.
>
> (Unofficial English translation of the original French text)

More particularly, in a sequestration case against the assets of an international organization in Geneva (the World Intellectual Property Organization, or WIPO), the Geneva Supervisory Authority of Debt Enforcement and Bankruptcy Matters upheld the organization's immunity from execution and rejected the sequestration order on the grounds that, contrary to state immunity, immunity of international organizations was absolute: Decision of 9 April 1997 (1998) 62 Bulletin des Poursuites et Faillites 220. *See* also Decision of the Swiss Federal Council of 30 October 1996 (1997) 7 RSDIE 668, following a recourse by a private Company against the decision to uphold the immunity from execution of a UN agency (the United Nations High Commissioner for Refugees, or UNHCR).

10.22 Following that decision from the Swiss Federal Tribunal, the claimants filed an administrative recourse in July 2010 with the Swiss FDFA to require the BIS to waive its immunities based on the alleged existence of an abuse. As already noted, pursuant to Article 22 HQA, the BIS and Switzerland should indeed cooperate to avoid any abuse of immunities.

10.23 In a decision dated 24 December 2010, the FDFA rejected the plaintiffs' requests on the ground that there was no element allowing Switzerland to conclude that the immunities granted to the BIS would have been abused, be it by the BIS itself or by the Argentine Republic and/or the Argentine central bank.

10.24 This decision from the FDFA was subject to an appeal to the Swiss Federal Administrative Tribunal (FAT) competent to review administrative decisions. The FAT decided on 16 August 2011[35] that it was *not* competent to review this matter, which relates to the external relations of Switzerland with an international organization,[36] and referred the case to the Swiss Federal Council (the Swiss government).[37]

10.25 The Federal Council gave its final decision on 17 October 2012, confirming that:

(a) BIS immunities are absolute and cannot be subject to enforcement measures;
(b) the acceptance of central bank deposits is part of the BIS's statutory missions; and
(c) there was no indication that BIS immunities had been abused.

The Council also confirmed that no dispute existed between the BIS and the plaintiffs (which were solely creditors of the Republic of Argentina) and that, therefore, the BIS had no obligation as a third party to put in place a dispute resolution mechanism to decide on such a dispute.[38] Finally, the Swiss Federal Council confirmed that there was no disagreement between Switzerland and the BIS as to the interpretation or the application of the HQA in this case.

10.26 The essence of the decision of the Federal Council was made public by way of official press releases[39] from the Swiss authorities.

---

[35] Judgment C-719/2011 of the Federal Administrative Tribunal of 16 August 2011.

[36] *See* article 32(1)(a) of the Swiss Act regarding the Federal Administrative Tribunal.

[37] Plaintiffs also appealed against this decision to the Swiss Federal Tribunal, which rejected in November 2011 their claim and confirmed the competence of the Swiss Federal Council to review the case: Judgment 2C-764/201 of the Federal Tribunal of 22 November 2011 [=BGE 137 I 371], available online at <http://relevancy.bger.ch/cgi-bin/JumpCGI?id=BGE-137-I-371&lang=de&zoom=OUT&system=clir>.

[38] Contrary to what was incorrectly mentioned by the Basel City Civil Tribunal (Supervisory Authority) in its appeal decision of April 2010. In reality, the BIS has put in place what is required pursuant to Article 23 HQA to avoid undue immunity protection, which is a dispute resolution mechanism for litigations of a private nature opposing the BIS to *its* counterparts. On the need for an organization to establish dispute resolution mechanisms with its private law creditors, *see* A. S. Muller, *International Organizations and their Host States* (The Hague: Kluwer Law International, 1995), 176 *et seq*: indeed, there is no immunity from jurisdiction for the BIS in 'civil or commercial suits, arising from banking or financial transactions, initiated by contractual counterparties of the Bank'. Similarly, in other private law matters regarding contracts with, for example, service providers (IT contracts, buildings, etc.), the BIS is generally offering settlement of disputes by way of contractual arbitration provisions. Disputes with shareholder central banks may be settled by the Hague Arbitral Tribunal, pursuant to Article 54 of the BIS Statutes (as happened on the occasion of disputes regarding the 2001 mandatory repurchase by the BIS of shares previously held by the public: *see* the arbitral awards rendered by the Hague Arbitral Tribunal on 22 November 2002 and 19 September 2003, reproduced on the Permanent Court of Arbitration website online at <http://www.pca-cpa.org/showpage.asp?pag_id=1157>). Employment litigations with the BIS staff are settled by the BIS Administrative Tribunal (Article 4.2 HQA; these decisions are published on the BIS website) consistent with the institutional practices of other international organizations.

[39] *See* <http://www.ejpd.admin.ch/content/ejpd/fr/home/dokumentation/mi/2012/2012-10-170.html>.

It should also be noted that, in parallel to these proceedings, other unsuccessful judicial attempts were made by the same two creditors to exert pressure on the BIS by way of criminal complaints,[40] or through discovery proceedings in the United States to access financial information regarding the BCRA accounts in BIS books,[41] all generally supported by various press campaigns.[42] **10.27**

4. Conclusions

This case has confirmed that the BIS immunities from jurisdiction and execution are essential for the exercise of the Bank's statutory mission as an international organization acting on behalf of the central banking community. **10.28**

If the BIS immunities had been subject to review by Swiss courts, this would not only have seriously endangered the continuity of BIS financial transactions and settlements on behalf of central banks and other international organizations, but it would also have called into question the Bank's role as 'bank to central banks', because it would have generated a lack of trust in the legal protection attached to the central bank assets deposited with the BIS. It would in essence have transformed the BIS into a sort of centre for recovery of private claims against central banks (and, by assimilation, against sovereign states) in view of the international foreign reserves deposited with the BIS, which is what the BIS immunities were precisely intended to prevent. **10.29**

A challenge of BIS immunities by Swiss judicial courts would also have impacted negatively other international organizations, which could have then found themselves facing similar sequestration orders, allowing a judge to decide (even on a unilateral basis through *ex parte* injunction) that their immunities should be discarded because of any abuse alleged by a third-party creditor of one of their sovereign member states. **10.30**

---

[40] For example, the BIS learned through the Swiss press early July 2011 that a criminal complaint had been lodged by the two funds against the Bank and some of its officials, alleging that it was involved in some sort of money laundering scheme by 'harbouring Argentinean state assets'. Although the BIS was (once again) never notified of this complaint, it appears that it was based on an allegation that Argentina had committed primary criminal offences by failing to pay holdout bondholders and placing its reserves at the BIS beyond their reach. This criminal complaint was rejected by the Swiss Federal Prosecutor on 22 July 2011 (through an 'Ordonnance de non-entrée en matière') given the absence of proof regarding the commission of criminal offences. The Swiss Federal Prosecutor also noted in his decision that the plaintiffs acquired Argentina bonds on the secondary market in full knowledge of Argentina's default and that the BIS should be notified of that decision to refute publicly the allegations made previously in the press.

[41] In early October 2010, the two same funds served civil subpoenas on the BIS general manager and two other BIS directors in New York and Washington, respectively, to seek financial information regarding the central bank of Argentina's accounts at the BIS. The New York Federal District Court (Hon. Judge Thomas Griesa) gave a decision on 2 September 2011 (which is now final) *quashing the subpoenas* because of lack of jurisdiction over the BIS, also considering the non-fulfilment of the geographical limits and other conditions set by US Federal Rules of Civil Procedure: *NML Capital Ltd v. Republic of Argentina*, 2011 US Dist. Lexis 99502 (SDNY 2 September 2011), available online at <http://ia600509.us.archive.org/17/items/gov.uscourts.nysd.55439/gov.uscourts.nysd.55439.docket.html>.

[42] Compare *The Economist*, 'Argentina's Debt Default: Gauchos and Gadflies', 22 October 2011, available online at <http://www.economist.com/node/21533453>, which gives a more balanced report on the Argentina litigations involving the BIS.

11

CREDITORS' REMEDIES

W. Mark C. Weidemaier and Ryan McCarl

> Asking a [sovereign] borrower to submit his fate to a judge sitting in New York or London, therefore, is sometimes viewed as equivalent to a suggestion that a mother drop her child off at King Herod's day-care centre.
>
> (Lee C. Buchheit, *How to Negotiate Eurocurrency Loan Agreements*, 2nd edn, London: Euromoney, 2006, 134)

1. Introduction

Courts in New York, London, and other major financial centres are not known for their solicitude to borrowers who have failed to repay loans. This is as true for sovereign borrowers as for private borrowers; hence Lee Buchheit's memorable analogy, likening these courts—from the sovereign borrower's perspective—to a daycare run by King Herod. **11.01**

Judging by the terms of bond contracts, investors insist on access to these courts. Sovereign bonds issued in foreign markets usually specify terms that facilitate legal enforcement, including terms waiving the sovereign's traditional immunity from suit and the immunity of its assets from execution.[1] Despite the prevalence of such contract terms, however, it is not clear why investors should care about legal enforcement. It is notoriously difficult for creditors to find and seize non-immune sovereign assets, to the extent that most academic treatments of the subject take for granted that sovereigns repay their debts not because they fear litigation, but because they wish to preserve their reputation in the capital markets or because they have some other incentive to repay.[2] **11.02**

With a few dramatic exceptions,[3] disappointed investors have rarely made successful use of the courts to recover after a sovereign default. For the most part, litigation has not resulted in meaningful payouts to holdout investors, nor has it threatened the viability of sovereign restructurings. The courts have played a minor part in the broader drama of sovereign borrowing and default. **11.03**

---

[1] W. Mark C. Weidemaier, 'Disputing Boilerplate' (2009) 82(1) Temple L Rev 1.

[2] For a summary of theories of sovereign debt repayment, *see* Ugo Panizza, Federico Sturzenegger, and Jeromin Zettelmeyer, 'The Economics and Law of Sovereign Debt and Default' (2009) 47(3) J Econ Lit 651.

[3] For example, the successful litigation by Elliott Associates, LP, against the Republic of Peru, in which Elliott obtained an order from the Court of Appeals of Brussels restraining Euroclear from receiving or distributing Peru's payments to other creditors: *see Elliott Associates, LP*, General Docket No. 2000/QR/92 (Court of Appeals of Brussels, 8th Chamber, 26 September 2000).

11.04 Recent developments, however, may herald a change in this landscape. In this short chapter, we explore the most significant of these developments: the landmark injunction in *NML Capital v. Argentina*. In a series of unprecedented decisions, federal courts in New York have approved injunctions forbidding Argentina to pay holders of its restructured debt without also paying holdout investors who did not participate in the restructuring.[4] The litigation raises a number of novel legal issues and it may call into question current restructuring techniques.

11.05 We analyse the *NML Capital* decision and consider the possibility that it heralds a significant change in the sovereign debt legal landscape. But we also raise the possibility that the decision is best understood as closely bound up with Argentina's long-standing record of defying court judgments. That record, combined with the plaintiffs' novel litigation strategy, led the courts to make an uncomfortable choice: they could allow Argentina to very publicly expose US federal courts as impotent—as essentially irrelevant to the sovereign debt markets, notwithstanding the seemingly clear legal obligations represented by the bonds—or they could embrace a novel and legally questionable remedy in a last-ditch effort to coerce compliance. So understood, the decision resulted from relatively unique circumstances and was motivated primarily by Argentina's attempt to move defaulted sovereign debt out of the reach of courts.

A. *NML Capital v. Argentina*: a brief introduction

11.06 The litigation stems from Argentina's 2001 default. The plaintiffs are investors who held out from Argentina's 2005 and 2010 exchange offers. The lead plaintiff, NML Capital (an affiliate of Elliott Associates), has obtained money judgments in a number of other lawsuits against Argentina, but so far has had little success enforcing the judgments against Argentine assets. In this lawsuit, NML took a different approach, arguing that Argentina was violating the *pari passu* clause in its bonds by paying exchange bondholders—that is, holders of restructured Argentine debt—without also paying holdout investors like NML. The district judge accepted this argument and also accepted NML's invitation to remedy the breach through an injunction providing that 'whenever [Argentina] pays any amount due under the terms of the [exchange] bonds', it must also pay plaintiffs 'the same fraction of the amount due them (the "Ratable payment")'.[5]

B. Third parties in the crosshairs

11.07 On 26 October 2012, a panel of the US Court of Appeals for the Second Circuit affirmed the injunction. That Court is presently considering how the injunction is to be enforced—a pressing question, given Argentina's apparent willingness to defy the order by continuing to pay exchange bondholders without paying the plaintiffs. A party who wilfully violates an injunction is usually held in contempt, but courts cannot impose meaningful (if any) contempt sanctions on foreign sovereigns. Thus, to give the injunction teeth, the District Court made clear that a wide range of third parties could be held in contempt if they were to act in 'active concert or participation' with Argentina in violating the injunction. These third parties include Bank of New York Mellon (the trustee for the exchange bondholders), the

[4] *NML Capital, Ltd v. Republic of Argentina* (SDNY 7 December 2011) (No. 1:08–cv–06978–TPG), ECF No. 353; *NML Capital Ltd v. Republic of Argentina* (2d Cir. 26 October 2012) (Nos 12–105(L) etc.) (NML, Second Circuit Opinion).

[5] *NML*, Second Circuit Opinion (n. 4), at 11.

registered owners of the exchange bonds, and clearing systems such as the Depository Trust Company and Euroclear.[6]

The potential impact on third parties is the most novel and important feature of the injunction. Certainly, under US law, the reach of an injunction extends beyond the enjoined party;[7] nevertheless, the enjoined party remains the primary target. Not so here. Indeed, it is fair to say that the injunction targets everyone *but* Argentina.[8] It targets financial intermediaries in the payments system, so that Argentina cannot pay exchange bondholders in the usual manner, and also targets the legal and financial advisers who might help Argentina to devise a new method of payment. In effect, Argentina is irrelevant to the injunction, the primary goal of which is to commandeer third parties in the effort to compel Argentina's compliance. **11.08**

2. The Implications of *NML v. Argentina*: A Pessimist's View

Much has been written on the possible implications of *NML v. Argentina* for sovereign restructurings.[9] We focus here on the contract term at the centre of the case: the famous *pari passu* clause, some version of which appears in nearly every sovereign bond.[10] We do not dwell on the history and evolution of the clause, nor on the widespread uncertainty as to its meaning, both of which are addressed elsewhere.[11] Instead, we address two discrete issues: first, we explore the Second Circuit's expansive interpretation of the *pari passu* clause, explaining how the Court, in effect, interpreted the clause as a promise by Argentina to never restructure; second, we show that Argentina's version of the *pari passu* clause is widely used in the sovereign debt markets. *NML v. Argentina* therefore has the potential to affect many sovereigns and to influence future restructurings. In the final section of the chapter, however, we suggest some reasons why the case may have a more limited effect. **11.09**

A. The *pari passu* clause as a promise not to restructure[12]

> The *pari passu* clause that appears in the bonds held by NML Capital and other plaintiffs is worded as follows:The Securities... shall at all times rank *pari passu* and without any preference among themselves. The payment obligations of the Republic under the Securities shall at all times rank at least equally with all its other present and future unsecured and unsubordinated External Indebtedness... **11.10**

At least two interpretations of this clause could support a finding of a breach by Argentina. The first interprets the clause narrowly as a promise that the issuing country will not formally subordinate bondholders to other, defined classes of unsecured creditor. For example, a country would violate its promise to maintain the *pari passu* ranking of debts if it were to enact a statute providing that creditor A is not to be paid anything until equally ranked **11.11**

[6] *See* Amended 23 February 2012 Order 2(f), *NML Capital, Ltd v. Republic of Argentina* (SDNY 21 November 2012) (No. 1:08–cv–06978–TPG).

[7] *See* Federal Rules of Civil Procedure 65.

[8] *See* Anna Gelpern, 'Contract Hope and Sovereign Redemption' (2013) 8(2) CMLJ 132.

[9] *See* Gelpern (n. 8); W. Mark C. Weidemaier, 'Sovereign Debt after *NML v. Argentina*' (2013) 8(2) CMLJ 123.

[10] This is true of bonds issued under foreign law (i.e. the law of a country other than the issuer). Local law bonds often do not include the *pari passu* clause.

[11] For discussion of various meanings attributed to the clause and evidence calling each into question, *see* Mark Weidemaier, Robert Scott, and Mitu Gulati, 'Origin Myths, Contracts, and the Hunt for *Pari Passu*' (2013) 38 Law & Soc Inq 72; Mitu Gulati and Robert E. Scott, *The Three-and-a-Half-Minute Transaction: Boilerplate and the Limits of Contract Design* (Chicago, IL: University of Chicago Press, 2012).

[12] Some of the ensuing discussion first appeared in Weidemaier (n. 9).

creditor B is paid in full. Argentina arguably passed just such a law. To pressure bondholders to accept its 2005 exchange offer, the country passed the so-called Lock Law, which forbade executive branch officials to reopen the exchange offer or to conduct any settlement with non-participating bondholders.[13] The Lock Law arguably violated the *pari passu* clause even under this narrow interpretation, because it amounted to a formal, legal declaration that exchange bondholders could be paid while *pari-passu*-ranking holdouts could not.

11.12 Yet if Argentina violated the *pari passu* clause by enacting the Lock Law, it is not clear what the remedy should be for its breach. Under this narrow interpretation, the clause forbids only formal (that is, legal) subordination; it does not prevent the country from making differential *payments*. As discussed in paragraphs 11.14–11.16, countries have selectively paid bondholders since the inception of the sovereign bond markets, especially in the context of debt restructurings. This makes the District Court's injunction a poorly tailored remedy for Argentina's breach. If the *pari passu* clause forbids only formal subordination, why should passage of the Lock Law result in a court order directing the country to pay all bondholders equally? The practical effect of such an order would be to enforce a promise that the country never made.

11.13 Only a broader reading of the *pari passu* clause could justify such an injunction, and the Second Circuit provided such a reading. According to that Court, Argentina's *pari passu* clause protects bondholders from more than just formal subordination. The first sentence of the clause[14] incorporates the narrow reading just described, prohibiting 'Argentina, as bond *issuer*, from formally subordinating the bonds by issuing superior debt'.[15] The second sentence, which promises to maintain the equal ranking of Argentina's 'payment obligations',[16] imposes a broader duty prohibiting Argentina, 'as bond *payor*, from paying on other bonds without paying on the [holdouts'] bonds'.[17] If the Court's reading is correct, then Argentina, in this second sentence, agreed to forgo at least a century's worth of sovereign restructuring practices.

B. *Pari passu* in historical context

11.14 In the first decades of the twentieth century, sovereigns routinely issued bonds in international capital markets. Given the ensuing economic and political turmoil, many of these bonds went into default and were later restructured. These restructurings followed some common patterns. In general, restructuring was accomplished through:

(1) a cessation of payments;
(2) an offer to resume payment on terms more favourable to the issuing country; and
(3) a resumption of payments to those (but only those) bondholders who agreed to reduce their claims.

---

[13] Argentina temporarily suspended the Lock Law to enable its second exchange offer in 2010.

[14] 'The Securities . . . shall at all times rank *pari passu* and without any preference among themselves.'

[15] *NML*, Second Circuit Opinion (n. 4), at 18.

[16] 'The payment obligations of the Republic under the Securities shall at all times rank at least equally with all its other present and future unsecured and unsubordinated External Indebtedness.'

[17] *NML*, Second Circuit Opinion (n. 4), at 18. This interpretation assigns extraordinary weight to the words 'payment obligations'. Assume (for now) that Argentina's *pari passu* clause omitted these two words. The first sentence refers only to the equal ranking of '[t]he Securities' and thus represents only a promise to maintain equality among bondholders. But this is not much protection, because Argentina could still favour other unsecured creditors (for example holders of corporate bonds guaranteed by the government). Most sovereign bonds extend such protection with respect to certain other external creditors (typically included in the definition of the term 'External Debt' or, in Argentina's case, 'External Indebtedness'). This is the function of the second sentence of Argentina's clause. But for the words 'payment obligations', then, Argentina's *pari passu* clause would be functionally indistinguishable from nearly every other *pari passu* clause in use.

Although sovereigns did not win many friends with these practices, market participants did not treat this routine restructuring process as a violation of any bond covenant. The sovereign's default consisted of its failure to pay, not its selective, post-restructuring payments to bondholders who had agreed to provide debt relief.[18] The usual remedy for default on a promise to pay is a judgment for damages, but sovereign immunity law made it nearly impossible for holdout creditors to collect.

To encourage participation in the restructuring, sovereigns routinely threatened not to pay non-participating bondholders even if an economic revival made payment feasible. Occasionally, these threats were made credible by being paired with contract terms entitling participating bondholders to share in any better deal that the sovereign might later offer to holdouts. Yet sovereigns rarely conditioned restructuring offers on substantial levels of bondholder participation and did not make use of available techniques for binding dissenters.[19] Thus even a successful restructuring left in its wake a large group of unpaid holdouts. **11.15**

The terms of a proposed restructuring were typically negotiated jointly by the borrower government and a standing committee representing bondholder interests, such as the Corporation of Foreign Bondholders (CFB) in the United Kingdom and the Foreign Bondholders Protective Council (FBPC) in the United States.[20] These committees could not consent on behalf of bondholders, but their recommendations in favour of a settlement carried a lot of weight. More importantly, the CFB and FBPC had experience interpreting sovereign bonds, and likely did so in ways that were both consistent over time and advantageous to bondholders. There is no direct evidence about how (or even whether) the CFB and FBPC interpreted the *pari passu* clause during restructuring negotiations. It is clear, however, that the *pari passu* clause made occasional appearances in sovereign bonds during this era.[21] It is also clear that the CFB and FBPC routinely negotiated restructuring proposals in which participants got paid and holdouts did not, without any suggestion that this practice might violate the terms of the underlying bonds. **11.16**

This historical evidence highlights the significance of the Second Circuit's ruling. As noted, the Court focused on Argentina's promise to maintain the equal ranking of its 'payment obligations' under the bonds, which the Court interpreted to prohibit the country, 'as bond *payor*, from paying on [restructured] bonds without paying' holdouts. Language of this sort first began to appear in sovereign bonds in the 1980s and 1990s.[22] If the Court's interpretation is correct, then sovereigns who adopted this broader formulation were promising to forgo these common restructuring practices. No longer would these countries make any payments to restructuring participants unless they also paid holdouts in full. **11.17**

[18] For discussion of these practices, *see* W. Mark C. Weidemaier and Mitu Gulati, *A People's History of Collective Action Clauses*, UNC Legal Studies Research Paper No. 2172302 (7 November 2012), available online at <http://papers.ssrn.com/sol3/papers.cfm?abstract_id=2172302>.

[19] In at least one case, a sovereign conducted a voluntary restructuring despite the fact that the relevant bonds (issued by Czechoslovakia in 1922) included a collective action clause that might have allowed the restructuring to bind dissenters: *see* Weidemaier and Gulati (n. 18).

[20] *See* Barry Eichengreen and Richard Portes, 'After the Deluge: Default, Negotiation, and Readjustment during the Interwar Years', in Barry Eichengreen and Peter H. Lindert (eds) *The International Debt Crisis in Historical Perspective* (Cambridge, MA: MIT Press, 1989); Barry Eichengreen, 'Historical Research on International Lending and Debt' (1991) 5(2) J Econ Persp 149.

[21] *See* Weidemaier et al. (n. 11).

[22] Although *pari passu* clauses made rare appearances in early twentieth-century bonds, the clauses did not include this 'payment' language. *See* Weidemaier et al. (n. 11).

C. The prevalence of Argentina's version of the *pari passu* clause

11.18 Until the 1990s, most sovereign bonds used a version of the *pari passu* clause that read something like this: 'The bonds rank, and will rank, *pari passu* with all other present and future unsecured and unsubordinated External Indebtedness.' The primary difference between this formulation and the version of *pari passu* used by Argentina is that Argentina's clause includes a promise to maintain the equal ranking of the issuer's 'payment obligations'. Bonds that do not contain such a promise may be less vulnerable to *NML*-style holdout litigation.[23]

11.19 Argentina, however, is not alone in using language that extends *pari passu* treatment to the issuer's 'payment obligations'. As Figure 11.1 details, this or functionally similar language has become more common over time, beginning in the 1990s. The figure draws from a sample of bonds issued in foreign capital markets and governed by foreign law.[24] The figure divides *pari passu* clauses into three categories:

(1) those that seem only to promise that the issuer will maintain the equal *ranking* of its bonds;
(2) those, like Argentina's, that arguably imply an equal *payment* obligation; and
(3) those that contain what amounts to an explicit promise of equal payment (for example the bonds 'rank *pari passu* in right of payment and shall be paid as such').

11.20 As Figure 11.1 indicates, the second version of the *pari passu* clause has increased in frequency since the 1990s. In this dataset, nearly half of the foreign-law-governed sovereign bonds issued after 2000 include language that is functionally similar or identical to that used

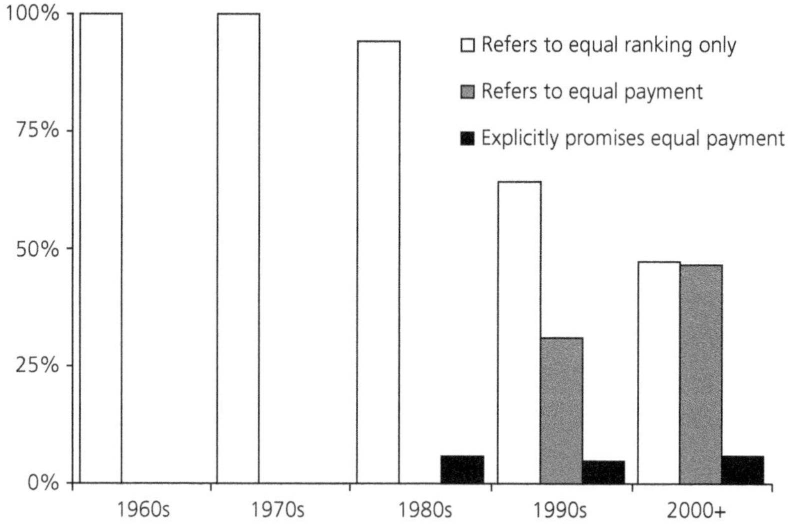

Figure 11.1 Different versions of *pari passu* over time

Source: Adapted from Mark Weidemaier, Bob Scott, and Mitu Gulati, 'Origin Myths, Contracts, and the Hunt for *Pari Passu*' (2013) 38(1) Law & Soc Inq 84.

[23] *See* n. 17.
[24] For more information on the dataset, *see* Weidemaier et al. (n. 11); Gulati and Scott (n. 11).

by Argentina. The widespread use of such language highlights the potential significance of the *NML v. Argentina* litigation for other issuers (and creditors).

D. *Pari passu* as contract pathology

NML v. Argentina may complicate future restructurings by reducing the incentive for bondholders to participate. Because there is no sovereign bankruptcy regime, sovereign issuers must persuade bondholders to reduce their claims voluntarily. The injunction approved by the Second Circuit effectively imposes a condition—full payment to holdouts—on the sovereign's ability to pay on its restructured debt. If bondholders expect such injunctions to be obeyed or enforced, they will have little reason to grant voluntary debt relief. **11.21**

Injunctions that primarily target third parties also raise other complications. *Ex ante*, legal and financial advisers and payment intermediaries cannot know whether they will be targeted by such an injunction, and as a result they may charge more for their services or limit their dealings with some sovereigns.[25] Moreover, although the plaintiffs in *NML v. Argentina* have so far limited their aim to intermediaries, it is conceivable that restructuring participants themselves could become embroiled in contempt proceedings. This may be unlikely, but it is not impossible.[26] **11.22**

The effect on third parties also undermines the equitable basis for the injunction awarded to NML. Injunctions are equitable remedies granted not as a matter of course, but at the court's discretion. NML's injunction is designed to hold exchange bondholders and payment intermediaries hostage—in effect, to force Argentina to inflict the broadest possible harm (and thus to incur the greatest reputational cost) if it insists on refusing to pay holdouts. This is a brilliant legal strategy, but the equities of such a remedy are questionable: why should investor A obtain relief that works by inflicting collateral damage on non-party investor B and on assorted non-party financial intermediaries? **11.23**

Despite these reservations, some might argue that this is exactly the bargain struck by an issuer that includes Argentina-style 'payment' language in its *pari passu* clause. If the Second Circuit's interpretation reduces incentives for bondholders to grant debt relief, it could be argued that sovereigns who adopt this version of the clause are agreeing *ex ante* to make default messy and painful. This can be understood as a costly signal that the sovereign is creditworthy and that default is less likely. At the time of the loan, a sovereign may reap the benefits of such a promise in the form of lower borrowing costs, greater market access, and the like.[27] So why should anyone object when it is later held to its promise? **11.24**

---

[25] Intermediaries might also condition the use of their services on the sovereign's representation that it has no outstanding debt subject to NML's rateable payment interpretation: *see* Gelpern (n. 8). If the sovereign's representation were to prove untrue, however, there might be no meaningful remedy. Given the prevalence of Argentina-style *pari passu* clauses, moreover, many sovereigns could not make this representation until after retiring (or revising the terms of) their outstanding debt.

[26] For example, an exchange bondholder who knew of the injunction and took active steps to facilitate Argentina's rerouting of payments (such as by voting to approve a change in the payment mechanism to route payments outside of New York) might be viewed as acting 'in active concert or participation' with Argentina: US Federal Rules of Civil Procedure 65(d)(2). NML and the other plaintiffs have not yet indicated that they would seek contempt sanctions in such a case, and it should be noted that sanctions are merely one (probably remote) possibility.

[27] There is no evidence that sovereigns obtain such benefits, but the possibility should be conceded—especially if courts begin to enforce such commitments by injunction. On the other hand, the uncertainty associated with routine enforcement might also increase borrowing costs for some or all sovereigns.

11.25 This argument is unpersuasive, not least because it is doubtful whether the words 'payment obligations' can bear so much interpretive weight.[28] Even if the interpretive point is conceded, the social utility of enforcing such promises remains questionable. The realistic alternative to a privately negotiated restructuring is often a bailout funded by taxpayers in other countries.[29] Perhaps—but only perhaps—there would be fewer sovereign defaults if borrower countries were able to commit credibly to raise restructuring costs. If a default were to occur, however, some of the costs would be transferred from investors to taxpayers, and this result is questionable on policy grounds.

11.26 For decades, the official sector has responded to debt crises by promoting 'private sector involvement' in restructurings. Although these policy initiatives have been pursued with some ambivalence (to put it mildly), they are premised on the sensible belief that lenders will act more prudently if they must internalize the losses associated with improvident loans. As interpreted by the Second Circuit, the *pari passu* clause undercuts this policy by increasing the likelihood that the costs of default will be shifted onto taxpayers. If that is the effect of the clause, it seems that courts should not go out of their way to enforce it.

3. An Alternative Story: *NML Capital* as an Outlier

11.27 Discussion thus far has assumed that *NML v. Argentina* will have lasting effects on sovereign debt markets. That assumption might prove correct even if courts do not enter *NML*-style injunctions as a matter of course. Unable to predict the likelihood or cost of such a remedy *ex ante*, financial and legal intermediaries might hesitate to deal with some sovereigns, as might some investors. Likewise, holders of distressed sovereign debt might find it difficult to assess the merits of a restructuring proposal.

11.28 It is possible, however, that *NML v. Argentina* may have a more limited impact, as this section will explain. The broader goal of the section, however, is to highlight the unsteady equilibrium that has characterized the sovereign debt markets since the doctrine of absolute sovereign immunity was abandoned in the 1970s. That doctrinal change created a tension: national courts could finally hear lawsuits against foreign sovereigns, but they remained largely powerless to enforce their judgments. In the ensuing decades, market participants dealt with this tension by ignoring it—in effect, by pretending that sovereign loans were enforceable like ordinary debt without really pushing the boundaries.[30]

11.29 *NML v. Argentina* involved a clash between a uniquely determined and creative creditor and a uniquely defiant debtor. The conflict exposed the pretence that sovereign loans are legally enforceable. It also presented the US federal courts with an uncomfortable choice: they could acknowledge impotence in the face of Argentina's extraordinary record of defiance, or they could take unprecedented steps to preserve the fiction that courts are relevant actors on the broader, fundamentally political, stage of sovereign debt. According to this characterization of the case, *NML v. Argentina* makes for great theatre, but it need not have systemic implications for the sovereign debt markets.

---

28 On this point, *see* discussion in n. 17.

29 This overlooks, of course, the effect of additional austerity on the borrower's citizens.

30 *See* Gelpern (n. 8).

A. Straddling the border of law and politics

Sovereign debt exists in an uneasy conceptual space on the border between law and politics: between the realms of enforceable legal rights and anarchic *realpolitik*. Sovereign bonds are written as contracts and, when times are good, treated as legally binding obligations. The borrower makes payments on schedule, uses the specified payment mechanism, and otherwise treats the loan documents as the definitive guide to its duties. There are good reasons for this: a sovereign that wants to borrow in the future must maintain its reputation for keeping its promises. **11.30**

Default changes the calculus. A financially distressed sovereign must choose, often in consultation with other governments and international institutions, how best to regain its financial footing. Its decisions unavoidably impose costs on third parties: its own citizens, who suffer from austerity policies; foreign taxpayers, who fund bailouts or pay to recapitalize domestic financial institutions; and private investors, who must often accept debt 'haircuts' and figure out how to manage assets the value of which has become highly uncertain. How to distribute these costs is a fundamentally political decision that cannot (and should not) be made in the loan documentation.[31] **11.31**

A key function of commercial law is to parcel out rights and duties when problems arise and normal relations go awry. In a sense, sovereign debt inverts this template. Sovereign bonds are treated like other contracts only when things are going well. An event of default triggers a conceptual shift in which political, rather than legal, concerns come to the fore. Distressed debt funds such as NML have attracted scorn—and the moniker of 'vulture fund'—by refusing to play along with this script. These funds insist that sovereign debt is enforceable as a matter of legal right, not political favour, even if the result is that successful litigants receive much larger payouts than other bondholders. **11.32**

Despite the furore over 'vulture' lawsuits, the process of litigating sovereign debt claims has traditionally preserved two key, related fictions. The first is the fiction of legal equivalence between loans to sovereign and private borrowers. Most creditors ask for a money judgment, and courts routinely enter such judgments against sovereigns who have defaulted. Except for occasional skirmishes over the scope of the sovereign's waiver of immunity, the litigation process looks much like the process for enforcing private debt. Of course, most judgments go unsatisfied, even though sovereigns always have *some* assets. But this is also true of private borrowers, who may have substantial assets that the law places out of the reach of creditors. Because unsatisfied judgments result from forces over which courts have no control, they typically do not challenge the courts' authority or prestige. Most sovereign debt lawsuits thus preserve the fiction that courts are relevant actors, even when the debtor is a sovereign nation. **11.33**

The genius of NML's litigation strategy was to take this traditional 'compromise' off the table. By asking for an injunction instead of a money judgment, NML presented the court with a stark choice: it could fashion an unprecedented injunctive remedy in the hope that Argentina would comply, or it could acknowledge its impotence in the face of Argentina's dramatic, and very public, record of defiance. **11.34**

[31] This insight underlies the earlier point that, as interpreted by the Second Circuit, the *pari passu* clause shifts some of the cost of default from investors to taxpayers. If that is how the clause functions, courts should hesitate to enforce it.

B. A uniquely defiant debtor?

11.35 For a decade, Argentina has refused to pay judgments and has taken great pains to keep non-immune assets out of creditors' reach. This is normal post-default behaviour for a sovereign borrower. But Argentina did not only refuse to pay NML and other holdouts; through its enactment of the Lock Law and its arguments in litigation, Argentina may have crossed an unspoken line, acting as if its decision whether or not to honour its contracts was a purely sovereign decision in which no foreign court had the right to interfere.

11.36 At the time of writing, the Second Circuit had recently heard the second oral argument, the point of which was to decide how much Argentina must immediately pay holdouts and to determine the range of third parties subject to the injunction. The argument was attended by an overflow crowd of lawyers, financial journalists, and Argentine public officials. To many observers, Argentina came across as a defiant lawbreaker: 'Argentina Looking Forward to Reading, Ignoring US Court's Opinion', was the caption of one prominent blog.[32] The Second Circuit judges got the same impression, twice referring to Argentina as 'contumacious' and speaking as if to a disobedient child: '[The Court] has a party in front of it who needs an order like this in order to be brought into compliance....'[33]

11.37 Argentina's arguments may have been necessitated by domestic politics, but they were not well received by the Second Circuit panel. Argentina insisted, for example, that no injunction could require it to pay holdouts more than exchange bondholders had accepted in Argentina's restructuring. This prompted one judge to ask, somewhat incredulously: '[Y]ou're telling us that... [Argentina] would not obey any order, other than the one you've just proposed?' Argentina's counsel replied that the country would not 'voluntarily obey' any other order, prompting further query from the Bench: 'What does that mean, "voluntarily obey?" I mean, we would issue an order, and I just want to be sure you're telling us that it wouldn't be obeyed.... [B]asically you're dictating what the Court would order.'[34]

11.38 Adding fuel to the fire, Argentina's counsel offered the following analogy:

> [I]f a court in Iran ordered the United States to turn over several billion dollars as damages for injuries that Iran believes it has suffered, I do not think our president and government would say yes, and would that be contumacious? In the eyes of the Iranian court, yes. Now, all I'm trying to say is that Argentina has a public policy. It is not going to and cannot prefer [NML]. And so, if that's the confrontation that the Court seeks through an injunction, that's the Court's decision.[35]

The analogy may have played well to its intended (Argentine) audience, but it is not the type of statement that federal judges are accustomed to hearing in open court.

11.39 Argentina's actions—including its passage (and brief suspension) of the Lock Law, its narrow interpretation of the *pari passu* clause, and its defiant litigation posture—may have influenced the district judge's decision to issue the injunction, as well as the Second Circuit's

---

[32] Matt Levine, 'Argentina Looking Forward to Reading, Ignoring US Court's Opinion', *Dealbreaker*, 28 February 2013, available online at <http://dealbreaker.com/2013/02/argentina-looking-forward-to-reading-ignoring-u-s-courts-opinion/>.

[33] *NML v. Argentina*, Oral Argument Transcript of 27 February 2013, at 99.

[34] *NML*, Oral Argument Transcript (n. 33), at 14–15.

[35] *NML*, Oral Argument Transcript (n. 33), at 17.

decision to uphold it.[36] The district judge seemingly interpreted Argentina's behaviour as proof that, although it had voluntarily submitted to the jurisdiction of US courts, the country ultimately believed that Argentine political officials had the last word on the legitimacy of bondholder claims. As the judge described the country's argument, it was that Argentina could 'simply declare that these [US court] judgments will not be paid . . . '.[37] The Second Circuit opinion upholding the injunction expressed similar frustration, noting that Argentina had shown 'continual disregard for the rights of its . . . creditors *and the judgment of our courts to whose jurisdiction it has submitted*'.[38] Argentina, it seems, committed two sins: it treated its debt obligations as if they were discretionary political commitments rather than binding legal obligations; and, in the process, it publicly challenged the legitimacy and efficacy of US courts.

C. A unique remedy for a unique case?

Under this alternative explanation, *NML v. Argentina* is an outlier case that resulted from NML's creative litigation strategy and Argentina's particular brand of defiance. The Second Circuit was, it is important to recall, essentially forced to choose between upholding NML's injunction and deciding the case in favour of Argentina. Although Argentina had plausible legal arguments, these arguments were intermixed with strong hints that the Court had no business interfering in the country's debt management decisions and that debt repayment is a matter of expedience, rather than legal obligation. The Second Circuit's decision, then, can be seen as an attempt to sustain the semi-fiction that sovereign bonds create legally enforceable obligations[39] and to protect its own relevance as a major player in the sovereign debt markets. By contrast, a decision in Argentina's favour would have been a tacit admission that courts are powerless to enforce debt obligations even when the sovereign has explicitly submitted to their jurisdiction. **11.40**

It is clear, however, that the Second Circuit was a reluctant player in this geopolitical drama. Some of the Court's back-and-forth with Argentina's counsel more closely resembled a diplomatic exchange than an appellate argument. At one point, while discussing the amount of money immediately due to NML, Judge Rosemary Pooler asked Argentina's counsel: '[H]ow could we be sure, if we agreed with you on a percentage, that it would be paid?'[40] Lack of trust created by the absence or weakness of binding legal enforcement mechanisms is perhaps the most common dilemma in international politics. Throughout the litigation, it has at times **11.41**

---

[36] *See*, e.g., Anna Gelpern, 'Sovereign Restructuring after *NML v. Argentina*: CACs Don't Make *Pari Passu* Go Away', *Credit Slips*, 3 May 2012, available online at <http://www.creditslips.org/creditslips/2012/05/sovereign-restructuring-after-nml-v-argentina-cacs-dont-make-pari-passu-go-away.html> (referring to Griesa J as 'exasperated'); Felix Salmon, 'Why We Might Soon See Another Argentina Default', *Reuters*, 22 November 2012, available online at <http://blogs.reuters.com/felix-salmon/2012/11/22/why-we-might-soon-see-another-argentine-default/> ('Judge Griesa . . . is mad as hell, and he's not going to take it anymore.').

[37] *See NML*, Second Circuit Opinion (n. 4), at 10 (quoting Griesa J).

[38] *NML*, Second Circuit Opinion (n. 4), at 24 (emphasis added). Later, the Court reiterated that Argentina had shown 'disregard of its legal obligations': *NML*, Second Circuit Opinion (n. 4), at 26.

[39] *Compare* David Bosco, 'The Debt Frenzy', *Foreign Policy*, 11 June 2007, <http://www.foreignpolicy.com/articles/2007/06/11/the_debt_frenzy> (noting that 'debt collecting is still a critical part of how the world's financial system works, and Argentina is putting that part of the system to the test').

[40] Transcript of Oral Argument, *NML v. Argentina*, 2d Cir. (27 February 2013), No. 12-105-CV, at 10. Argentina's counsel responded that his client, 'the [Argentinian] executive, would go to the congress and seek legislation to accomplish precisely this result'. (The exchange highlights another theoretical headache: the fact that modern sovereigns are not unitary actors; they are constrained not only by international law and politics, but also by complex domestic institutions.)

appeared that Argentina and the US courts are engaged in a game of 'chicken'—a metaphor more typically invoked to describe the incentives of sovereigns engaged in high-stakes international confrontations. In the chicken game, both parties would be better off if each were to back down, but neither wants to be the 'sucker' who swerves out of the way and is seen to have lost the contest.

11.42 After the argument, in a surprise move, the Second Circuit panel issued an invitation for Argentina to submit an alternative payment proposal that the country was willing to honour.[41] This, too, was reminiscent of a diplomatic negotiation. The judges cannot simply declare sovereign loans unenforceable; their role and training require them to issue a recognizably 'legal' opinion that recognizes sovereign loans as binding legal obligations. At the same time, Argentina has expressly stated that it will not comply with any injunction that does not meet its demands. The judges presumably wish to preserve the Second Circuit's reputation as a pre-eminent commercial court, and they likely do not relish the prospect of issuing an injunction that Argentina simply ignores. The invitation suggested that the Court would consider a range of potential orders—in other words, a compromise. Judging by Argentina's defiant response, which essentially offered to reopen the exchange offer for holdouts,[42] the Court need not have bothered.

4. Conclusion

11.43 Time will tell whether *NML v. Argentina* has a lasting impact on the sovereign debt markets. At the time of writing, the Second Circuit had not yet issued its ruling, and the injunction entered by the District Court had not yet gone into effect. The ultimate scope and impact of the injunction remain to be seen. It is clear, however, that we have not seen the last of NML-style litigation. Argentina's version of the *pari passu* clause is not unique, and copycat litigants will surely invoke the Second Circuit's interpretation of the *pari passu* clause in an effort to obtain similar injunctive relief. (Indeed, some already have.[43])

11.44 At the same time, injunctions are equitable remedies awarded at the court's discretion. In future cases, a court that wants to distinguish *NML v. Argentina* will surely find ways in which to do so. Future sovereigns may not pass laws equivalent to the Lock Law, which made it impossible for Argentina to comply with foreign court judgments. Future sovereigns also may adopt a somewhat more conciliatory litigation posture. *NML v. Argentina* does offer one clear lesson for future sovereigns that find themselves in Argentina's shoes: public relations, and the appearance of upholding the rule of law, may matter a great deal to courts.

[41] *See* Nate Raymond and Daniel Bases, 'Court Seeks Precise Payment Plan from Argentina for Bondholders', *Reuters*, 1 March 2013, available online at <http://www.reuters.com/article/2013/03/01/us-argentina-debt-idUSBRE9200YK20130301>.

[42] *See* Joseph Cotterill, 'Argentina's Gonna Make Him an Offer He Can Refuse, Part One', *Financial Times Alphaville blog*, 1 April 2012, available online at <http://ftalphaville.ft.com/2013/04/01/1442982/argentinas-gonna-make-him-an-offer-he-can-refuse-part-one/>.

[43] For example, Taiwan has brought a copycat lawsuit to collect on Grenada's defaulted debt: *Exp.-Imp. Bank of the Republic of China v. Grenada*, No. 13 Civ. 1450 (SDNY 13 March 2013) (Order on Consent).

12

SOVEREIGN ARBITRATION

Karen Halverson Cross

1. Introduction

In August 2011, an arbitration tribunal at the World Bank's International Centre for Settlement of Investment Disputes (ICSID) upheld jurisdiction to adjudicate an investment treaty claim brought by 60,000 holders of Argentine defaulted debt against Argentina. Issued just months before Greece's controversial debt restructuring in March 2012, the jurisdictional award *Abaclat v. Argentine Republic*[1] focused public attention on the use of arbitration to resolve sovereign debt disputes. This chapter reviews the use of international commercial arbitration clauses in sovereign debt contracts, and then discusses investment arbitration of sovereign debt claims, including the *Abaclat* dispute. 12.01

2. Arbitration Clauses in Sovereign Debt Contracts

A. General

In contrast with other international commercial contracts, international loan agreements, including sovereign debt contracts, rarely provide for arbitration of disputes.[2] During the early part of the twentieth century, until sovereign borrowing ceased in the wake of the Great Depression, arbitration clauses were utilized in sovereign debt contracts with some frequency. But ever since sovereign borrowing resumed in the 1960s, sovereign debt instruments tend to provide for enforcement in a court of the creditors' choosing—typically a financial centre such as New York or London.[3] The general absence of arbitration clauses from international loan agreements is interesting, in light of the difficulties associated with enforcing judgments against sovereign debtors. 12.02

[1] *Abaclat and ors (Case formerly known as Giovanna a Beccara and ors) v. Argentine Republic*, Decision on Jurisdiction and Admissibility, ICSID Case No. ARB/07/5 (4 August 2011).

[2] *See* paragraph 12.05.

[3] The sovereign debt market thrived in the early 1900s until the Great Depression. Thereafter, repeated defaults and the advent of the Second World War brought the market to a halt. By the mid-1960s, however, a number of Latin American and Asian issuers reentered the sovereign debt market. *See* S. Choi, M. Gulati, and E. Posner, 'The Evolution of Contractual Terms in Sovereign Bonds' (2012) 4 JLA 131, 150.

B. Historic use

12.03 Sovereign debt instruments issued during the early 1900s not infrequently provided for arbitration of disputes.[4] In 1939, a committee of legal and financial experts appointed by the League of Nations 'strongly' recommended that sovereign loan contracts in all cases should include an arbitration clause, at least with respect to matters of contract interpretation, and that the arbitrators should be appointed by an international body.[5]

12.04 Early sovereign debt contracts were even less enforceable against a sovereign then than they are today.[6] Mark Weidemeier contends that arbitration clauses were likely employed at the time to encourage the creditors' home state to participate in resolving any disputes arising out of the loan agreement, and to signal to investors that the state supported the loan.[7] Writing in 1957, Edwin Borchard suggested that arbitration clauses in sovereign debt contracts were likely used to address disputes over interpretation, especially difficulties in determining choice of governing law or forum.[8] As the League of Nations committee observed in 1939, courts of countries other than the debtor state 'generally declare[d] themselves incompetent' to adjudicate disputes arising out of sovereign debt contracts, and international tribunals at the time were not empowered to resolve investor–state disputes.[9] At a time when states adhered to the absolute theory of sovereign immunity, and courts were hostile to choice of law and forum selection clauses, arbitration may have been perceived as less problematic than other dispute settlement options. Whatever the justification, the historic use of arbitration clauses in sovereign debt contracts is well documented.

C. Current practice

12.05 Notwithstanding the enforcement advantages of arbitration, modern international loan agreements rarely provide for arbitration of disputes, but instead typically require the borrower to consent to the jurisdiction of the court of a creditor-friendly state such as England or New York.[10] Under the New York[11] and ICSID Conventions,[12] arbitral awards can be enforced with greater finality and broader reach than can foreign judgments.[13] Additionally, at least under US law, the exception to immunity for attachment and execution of sovereign

---

[4] M. Weidemaier, 'Contracting for State Intervention: The Origins of Sovereign Debt Arbitration' (2010) 73 Law & Contemp Probs 335, 343, Table 2; Edwin Borchard, *State Insolvency and Foreign Bondholders, Vol. 1* (New Haven, CT: Yale University Press, 1951) 36–7; League of Nations, *Report of the Committee for the Study of International Loan Contracts*, League of Nations Pub No. C.145.M.93.1939.II.A. (May 1939), Annex III.

[5] League of Nations (n. 4), paras 86–7.

[6] Weidemaier (n. 4), 337–8. The law on arbitration was still developing, and states at the time still adhered to the absolute theory of sovereign immunity.

[7] Weidemaier (n. 4), 336.

[8] Borchard (n. 4), 36.

[9] League of Nations (n. 4), paras 84–5.

[10] Philip Wood, *Law and Practice of International Finance* (London: Sweet & Maxwell, 2008), para. 32-28; Lee C. Buchheit, *How to Negotiate Eurocurrency Loan Agreements*, 2nd edn (London: Euromoney, 2000), 134–5.

[11] Convention on the Recognition and Enforcement of Foreign Arbitral Awards (New York, 10 June 1958, 330 UNTS 38) (the New York Convention).

[12] Convention on the Settlement of Investment Disputes between States and Nationals of Other States (Washington DC, 18 March 1965, 575 UNTS 159) (the ICSID Convention).

[13] K. Cross, 'Arbitration as a Means of Resolving Sovereign Debt Disputes' (2006) 17 Am J Int'l Arb 335, 358–61.

assets is somewhat broader when enforcing foreign arbitral awards.[14] Nonetheless, lenders generally prefer litigation of debt disputes, even where the debtor is a sovereign.[15]

Examples of arbitration clauses in sovereign debt contracts do exist. Loan documentation from the World Bank and other multilateral financial institutions typically provide for arbitration of disputes.[16] A few sovereign issuers, such as Brazil and El Salvador, are prohibited under domestic law from submitting to the courts of a foreign jurisdiction, and therefore agree only to arbitration of disputes.[17] Finally, English-law-governed sovereign bond instruments of certain former Eastern bloc issuers have allowed lenders the option of either litigating or arbitrating disputes in England.[18] An arbitration option was likely included in these contracts because the issuer was not subject to EU law governing the recognition and enforcement of foreign judgments.[19] Weidemaier conducted a study of enforcement-related provisions in sovereign debt contracts. Out of his sample of seventy-two sovereign bond issuers, loan documentation of only two provided for arbitration of disputes, and that of another five allowed creditors the option of arbitration or litigation of disputes.[20] **12.06**

To summarize, in contrast with general international commercial practice, for the past half-century, arbitration clauses have appeared only infrequently in sovereign debt contracts. In light of this fact, it is notable that creditors have begun to explore investor–state arbitration as a means of resolving sovereign debt claims—a development that is discussed in detail next. **12.07**

3. Investor–State Arbitration of Sovereign Debt Disputes

A. Background

i. International investment agreements (IIAs)

The first bilateral investment treaties (BITs) were concluded in 1959, when Germany, forced to rebuild its foreign investment programme after the Second World War, concluded treaties with Pakistan and the Dominican Republic.[21] Responding to a lack of meaningful protections for foreign investors under customary international law, other capital-exporting states eventually developed their own BIT programmes.[22] After the fall of the Eastern bloc, capital-exporting states continued to expand their BIT programmes and capital-importing states **12.08**

[14] Compare Foreign Sovereign Immunities Act, § 1610(a)(6) (exception to immunity from attachment for enforcing foreign arbitral awards) with § 1610(a)(2) (exception to immunity from attachment for property used for the commercial activity on which the claim is based).

[15] William W. Park, *Arbitration of International Business Disputes: Studies in Law and Practice* (Oxford: Oxford University Press, 2006), 559–60; G. Delaume, 'ICSID and the Transnational Financial Community' (1986) 1 ICSID Rev 237, 238; Cross (n. 13), 338–41.

[16] M. Boeglin, 'The Use of Arbitration Clauses in the Field of Banking and Finance: Current Status and Preliminary Conclusion' (1998) 15 J Int'l Arb 19, 24–5; Cross (n. 13), 341.

[17] M. Weidemaier, 'Disputing Boilerplate' (2009) 82 Temple L Rev 1, 28; Cross (n. 13), 341–3; O. Sandrock, 'Is International Arbitration Inept to Solve Disputes Arising out of International Loan Agreements?' (1994) 11 J Int'l Arb 33, 37 (citing older examples).

[18] Weidemaier (n. 17), 29 (referring to bonds issued by Georgia, Estonia, Poland, Slovak Republic, and Ukraine).

[19] Council Regulation (EC) No. 44/2001 on jurisdiction and the recognition of judgments in civil and commercial matters [2001] OJ L012/1; *see* Cross (n. 13), 340, fn. 22.

[20] Weidemaier (n. 17), 27.

[21] J. Salacuse, 'The Emerging Global Regime for Investment' (2010) 51 Harvard Int'l LJ 427, 433.

[22] J. Salacuse and N. Sullivan, 'Do BITs Really Work? An Evaluation of Bilateral Investment Treaties and their Grand Bargain' (2005) 46 Harvard Int'l LJ 67, 68–70.

competed to attract foreign direct investment (FDI). During the 1990s, the number of BITs worldwide more than quadrupled, from 446 in 1990 to 1,941 ten years later.[23] Free trade agreements (FTAs) also include investment chapters that mirror the provisions contained in a BIT. Referring collectively to the BITs and FTAs as international investment agreements (IIAs), by the end of 2008, the number of IIAs worldwide had increased to almost 3,000.[24]

12.09 International investment agreements provide eligible investments with powerful substantive protections. These protections typically include: guarantees of fair and equitable treatment (FET) to investments; promises to allow free transfers of investment returns; promises not to discriminate in favour of investments of nationals——that is, national treatment—or in favour of investors from third countries—that is, most-favoured nation (MFN) treatment; guarantees against expropriation without prompt, adequate, and effective compensation; and, somewhat less typically,[25] so-called 'umbrella clauses', or promises to honour contractual undertakings with respect to investments. Until recently, however, the applicability of these protections to sovereign debt instruments was uncertain. There is only one known case, *Fedax NV v. Republic of Venezuela*,[26] in which a tribunal awarded damages to the holder of sovereign debt instruments for violation of a BIT.[27] The *Fedax* tribunal briefly cited the treaty's umbrella clause, but did not discuss in any detail why Venezuela's default on the debt violated the substantive protections of the BIT.[28] The pending *Abaclat* dispute, in contrast, involves a mass sovereign debt claim alleging violation of several core provisions of the Italy–Argentina BIT.[29]

12.10 While coercive or discriminatory acts of a defaulting sovereign may provide grounds for a treaty violation, it is debatable whether declaring a moratorium on servicing debt or otherwise defaulting on a sovereign debt instrument, without more, would be found to violate an IIA's core substantive protections. According to Thomas Wälde, treaty guarantees against expropriation, of FET, and of national treatment 'do not provide an unequivocal foundation

[23] United Nations Conference on Trade and Development (UNCTAD), 'Quantitative Data on Bilateral Investment Treaties and Double Taxation Treaties', available online at <http://archive.unctad.org/Templates/WebFlyer.asp?intItemID=3150&lang=1>.

[24] UNCTAD, *Recent Developments in International Investment Agreements (2008–June 2009)*, IIA Monitor No. 3, UNCTAD/WEB/DIAE/IA/2009/8 (2009), available online at <http://unctad.org/en/Docs/webdiaeia20098_en.pdf>, 8 (citing 273 FTAs with investment chapters and 2,676 BITs).

[25] Many, but not all, investment treaties contain umbrella clauses. *See* Jeswald W. Salacuse, *The Law of Investment Treaties* (New York: Oxford University Press, 2010), 274 (citing estimates of 1,000 treaties containing umbrella clauses). Although the Italy–Argentina BIT does not contain an umbrella clause, the *Abaclat* claimants seek to incorporate one by invoking the MFN clause of the treaty: *Abaclat* Decision on Jurisdiction (n. 1), para. 242.

[26] Award, ICSID Case No. ARB/96/3 (9 March 1998).

[27] T. Wälde, 'The *Serbian Loans* Case: A Precedent for Investment Treaty Protection of Foreign Debt?' in T. Weiler (ed.) *International Investment Law and Arbitration: Leading Cases from the ICSID, NAFTA, Bilateral Treaties and Customary International Law* (London: Cameron, 2005), 383, 401. Another case, *CSOB v. Slovak Republic*, involved a dispute over sovereign debt incurred in the process of the former Czechoslovakia's breakup, but ultimately the tribunal's jurisdiction was upheld on the basis of an arbitration clause in a consolidation agreement between the parties, and not in a BIT: *Ceskoslovenska Obchodni Banka, AS v. The Slovak Republic*, Decision of the Tribunal on Objections to Jurisdiction, ICSID Case No. ARB/97/4 (24 May 1999), paras 43, 59.

[28] *Fedax* Award (n. 26), para. 29.

[29] Treaty between the Republic of Italy and the Republic of Argentina for the Promotion and Protection of Investments (Buenos Aires, 22 May 1990) (the Italy–Argentina BIT); *see Abaclat* Decision on Jurisdiction (n. 1), para. 312.

for simply enforcing sovereign debt'.[30] Similarly, notwithstanding the *Fedax* decision, Wälde has suggested that a treaty's umbrella clause should be read to apply only to abusive deployment of government power, as opposed to debt moratoria applied in a non-discriminatory way and as a means of achieving a debt restructuring in consultation with all affected creditors.[31] However, other commentators have argued that umbrella clauses should be read literally, so that any breach of contract would constitute a violation of the treaty.[32] Finally, in the context of a sovereign debt crisis, the imposition of exchange controls would be likely to violate an IIA's free transfer clause, although the transfer clause may provide an exception for financial crises, as does, for example, the Italy–Argentina BIT.[33]

As discussed at paragraph 12.21, the *Abaclat* claimants argue that Argentina's actions in connection with its default and 2005 debt restructuring were both arbitrary and unilateral.[34] In particular, Argentina's enactment of Law 26,017, concurrent with its 2005 exchange offer, might be found to be coercive. Law 26,017 prohibits the government from reopening the exchange process or entering into any other type of settlement with those bondholders that did not participate in the exchange.[35] The success of claimants' argument that Law 26,017 is expropriatory (or a violation of FET) will likely hinge on whether the law is found to have been adopted merely to enhance the credibility of the exchange offer, as opposed to as a measure targeted at uncooperative bondholders.[36] The *Abaclat* claimants also allege discriminatory treatment—that is, that Argentina afforded preferential treatment to local pension funds in violation of the national treatment obligation.[37] When dealing with a financial crisis, however, a sovereign debtor may adopt measures that violate national treatment out of legitimate considerations of economic necessity and/or political feasibility.[38] **12.11**

Even when a defaulting sovereign's actions are found to violate an IIA, the sovereign may argue that a financial crisis was an excusing event, either under the customary international law doctrine of necessity, or, if available, under a clause in the treaty.[39] Argentina successfully invoked its 2001 financial crisis as an excusing event in *LG&E Energy Corp v. Argentine Republic*.[40] One of the arbitrators on the *LG&E* tribunal, Albert Jan van den Berg, also sits on **12.12**

---

30 Wälde (n. 27), 402; *see* also M. Waibel, 'Opening Pandora's Box: Sovereign Bonds in International Arbitration' (2007) 101 AJIL 711, 742–54 (discussing decisions).

31 Wälde (n. 27), 408–9.

32 Salacuse (n. 25), 283; Andrew Newcombe and Lluís Paradell, *Law and Practice of Investment Treaties: Standards of Treatment* (The Hague: Kluwer Law International, 2009), 466.

33 Wälde (n. 27), 414–5. Article 6(3) of the Italy–Argentina BIT provides a temporary and limited exception to the free transfer guarantee in the event of exceptional balance-of-payment difficulties. *See* also Agreement between the Government of the United Kingdom of Great Britain and Northern Ireland and the Government of the Republic of Argentina for the Promotion and Protection of Investments (London, 11 December 1990), Art. 6(3) (the UK–Argentina BIT).

34 *Abaclat* Decision on Jurisdiction (n. 1), para. 312.

35 *Abaclat* Decision on Jurisdiction (n. 1), para. 79.

36 Waibel (n. 30), 746–7.

37 *Abaclat* Decision on Jurisdiction (n. 1), para. 312.

38 Waibel (n. 30), 758, fn. 262; *see* also A. Gelpern and B. Setser, 'Domestic and External Debt: The Doomed Quest for Equal Treatment' (2004) 35 Georgetown J Int'l L 795.

39 The customary international law doctrine of necessity provides a defence for actions taken to protect an essential interest against grave and imminent threats. The state must show that its response to the threat was the only means available to it and that it did not contribute to the situation of necessity: W. Burke-White and A. von Staden, 'Non-Precluded Measures Provisions, the State of Necessity, and State Liability for Investor Harms in Exceptional Circumstances', in M. Mourra (ed.) *Latin American Investment Treaty Arbitration: The Controversies and Conflicts* (The Hague: Kluwer Law International, 2008), 105, 141–2.

40 Decision on Liability, ICSID Case No. ARB/02/1 (3 October 2006).

the *Abaclat* tribunal. *LG&E* involved a claim under the United States–Argentina BIT, which contains a 'non-precluded measures' clause, or a clause providing that the treaty will not preclude a party from applying measures 'necessary for . . . the protection of its own essential security interests'.[41] Although the *LG&E* tribunal upheld Argentina's necessity defence, it relied at least in part on the non-precluded measures clause in the BIT.[42] Additionally, the *LG&E* panel excused Argentina's treaty obligations for only a temporary period, beginning with the onset of the crisis in December 2001 through to April 2003.[43] Since the BIT at issue in *Abaclat* lacks a non-precluded measures clause, any defence along these lines could be based solely on the doctrine of necessity.

12.13 To summarize, creditors that resort to investment arbitration to enforce a sovereign debt obligation will likely need to establish more than mere breach of contract, although a default alone might constitute a treaty violation if the applicable IIA contains an umbrella clause. Where the default is precipitated by a financial crisis, the sovereign debtor will most likely invoke a non-precluded measures clause in the treaty, if one exists, and/or the customary international law defence of necessity. Finally, creditors will need to demonstrate that the debt instruments fall within the scope of protected investments in the applicable IIA—a topic addressed later in the chapter.[44]

ii. Investor–state arbitration

12.14 The protections of an IIA would be less effective if an aggrieved investor were limited to enforcing those rights indirectly, through arbitration or diplomatic intervention by the home state. Historically, private parties typically lacked standing to bring claims before international tribunals; however, most IIAs grant an aggrieved investor direct enforcement rights, by providing for investor–state arbitration of disputes.

12.15 The vast majority of IIAs allow investors of one party to enforce treaty obligations against another party directly by bringing claims to arbitration.[45] Often, the treaty allows the investor to choose between ad hoc arbitration under the rules of the United Nations Commission on International Trade Law (UNCITRAL) or, if both states are party to the ICSID Convention, ICSID arbitration.[46] For example, the BIT at issue in *Abaclat* allows an investor to submit an arbitration claim either to ICSID or to ad hoc arbitration under UNCITRAL rules, if local remedies have been exhausted.[47]

12.16 ICSID arbitration awards enjoy potential enforcement advantages over other international commercial arbitration awards. In contrast to awards under the New York Convention, which require judicial recognition and enforcement (potentially subjecting the award to challenge on public policy or other grounds), an ICSID award is directly enforceable in a

[41] Treaty between United States of America and the Argentine Republic Concerning the Reciprocal Encouragement and Protection of Investment (Washington DC, 14 November 1991) (US–Argentina BIT), Art. XI. Although 'far from ubiquitous', non-precluded measures clauses regularly appear IIAs concluded by some countries, including the United States, Germany and, more recently, Canada: Burke-White and von Staden (n. 39), 108–9.

[42] *LG&E* Decision on Liability (n. 40), paras 258, 260.

[43] *LG&E* Decision on Liability (n. 40), para. 266.

[44] *See* paragraphs 12.23–12.24.

[45] Newcombe and Paradell (n. 32), 70.

[46] Newcombe and Paradell (n. 32), 72.

[47] Italy–Argentina BIT, Art. 8. The treaty allows the investor to commence arbitration if the dispute has been submitted to a local tribunal and continues for 18 months: Art. 8(3).

court of an ICSID Convention signatory state 'as if it were a final judgment of a court in that State', subject only to local law governing immunity of sovereign assets from execution.[48] Additionally, with the exception of recent awards arising out of Argentina's 2001 financial crisis, ICSID awards have generally enjoyed a high degree of voluntary compliance.[49] Although it is uncertain whether potential World Bank pressure affects the propensity of states to comply with ICSID awards, according to one commentary, the Bank's backing of ICSID 'may well be the most important factor in the ultimate success' of the ICSID regime.[50]

Notwithstanding potential enforcement advantages, however, prior to *Abaclat*, creditors seeking to enforce sovereign debt contracts did not commonly resort to ICSID arbitration. Exceptions are *Fedax* and *CSOB*.[51] Indeed, whether a sovereign debt instrument should even qualify as an 'investment', either for purposes of the ICSID Convention or for purposes of an investment treaty, has been subject to debate, as discussed at paragraphs 12.23–12.24. **12.17**

B. The *Abaclat* decision

i. Factual background

Abaclat is one of many investment arbitration claims brought against Argentina in the aftermath of its most recent debt crisis, but it was the first claim arising out of Argentina's debt default. After defaulting on its outstanding debt in 2001, Argentina succeeded in restructuring most of the debt in 2005, and restructured an additional amount in 2010. However, the holdout creditors who refused to participate in the restructurings have persevered in their efforts to enforce the defaulted debt, filing hundreds of lawsuits against Argentina in New York, Italy, Germany, and elsewhere.[52] **12.18**

Creditors have encountered significant difficulty enforcing Argentina's defaulted debt, in part because Argentina is immune from suit in some jurisdictions,[53] but more significantly because Argentina's overseas assets generally enjoy sovereign immunity against execution. US hedge funds NML Capital and EM Ltd obtained judgments on Argentine defaulted debt,[54] but tried for years without success to attach funds held by Argentina's Central Bank at the Federal Reserve Bank of New York as a means to enforce the judgments.[55] The hedge funds did succeed in attaching approximately US$3 million in a New York bank account used by an Argentine ministry to pay sellers of scientific equipment on behalf of grant beneficiaries.[56] **12.19**

---

48 ICSID Convention, Arts 54–55.

49 Cross (n. 13), 362, fn. 144 (citing sources); Michael Waibel, *Sovereign Defaults before International Courts and Tribunals* (New York: Cambridge University Press, 2011), 211.

50 E. Baldwin, M. Kantor, and M. Nolan, 'Limits to Enforcement of ICSID Awards' (2006) 23(1) J Int'l Arb 1, 21.

51 *See* paragraph 12.09 and n. 27.

52 *Abaclat* Decision on Jurisdiction (n. 1), para. 82.

53 Italy's highest court has held that, although the issuance of bonds is a private act, Argentina's unilateral extension of the payment term on its debt was a sovereign act and therefore subject to immunity: *Borri v. Argentine Republic*, Request for a Ruling on Jurisdiction, No. 6532, 27 May 2005; *cf. Republic of Argentina v. Weltover*, 504 US 607 (1992) (finding that a unilateral rescheduling of debt by Argentina was a commercial act). China still adheres to the absolute theory of sovereign immunity, including immunity from suit: *Democratic Republic of the Congo & ors v. FG Hemisphere Associates LLC*, Judgment, [2011] HKCU 1049, 8 June 2011, para. 224 (Hong Kong Court of Final Appeal).

54 *NML Capital, Ltd v. Republic of Argentina*, 652 F.3d 172, 177 n 6 (2d Cir. 2011).

55 The Second Circuit ultimately held that the Central Bank funds were 'held for its own account', and therefore immune from attachment under Foreign Sovereign Immunities Act § 1611(b)(1): *NML Capital* (n. 54).

56 *NML Capital, Ltd v. Republic of Argentina*, 680 F.3d 254 (2d Cir. 2012).

NML Capital went so far as to obtain a Ghanaian injunction to seize an Argentine naval vessel on tour in Africa,[57] which prompted Argentina to obtain a provisional order from the United Nations International Tribunal for the Law of the Sea (ITLOS) to compel Ghana to release the vessel.[58] The Second Circuit's recent decision in *NML Capital, Ltd v. Republic of Argentina*,[59] which upheld an injunction prohibiting Argentina from making payments on its restructured debt unless it pays the holdout creditor plaintiffs, has improved NML Capital's enforcement prospects.

12.20 Thousands of Argentina's holdout creditors are Italian retail investors, who purchased Argentine debt from Italian banks. After the default, when Italian regulators began investigating the sales to retail investors,[60] Task Force Argentina (TFA), a consortium of Italian banks, drafted a mandate package that it presented to Italian holders of Argentine defaulted debt, inviting the bondholders to participate in an ICSID arbitration claim against Argentina.[61] Under the terms of the mandate, any claimant who participates in the ICSID proceeding agrees to act through the legal representative appointed by TFA and is prohibited from bringing legal action against the bank that sold the debt to it.[62] Thus, by organizing and funding the arbitration, TFA effectively protected itself from the risk of lawsuits from the retail investors.[63] Although more than 180,000 bondholders accepted TFA's mandate in 2006, the size of the claimant class fell to 60,000 after Argentina's 2010 exchange offer.[64]

12.21 In September 2006, the bondholders filed with ICSID a request for arbitration against Argentina.[65] The request for arbitration alleges that, by defaulting on its debt and subsequently pursuing a 'punitive, unilateral' restructuring, Argentina violated the 1990 Italy–Argentina BIT.[66] Argentina challenged ICSID's jurisdiction over the dispute. In August 2011, the tribunal issued its decision on jurisdiction and admissibility, finding that ICSID had authority to decide the bondholders' claim. The arbitrator appointed by Argentina, Georges Abi-Saab, dissented from the majority decision in an opinion that was issued more than two months later.

ii. Decision on jurisdiction and admissibility

12.22 The *Abaclat* tribunal made two novel findings that will potentially expose sovereign debtors to future investment arbitration claims: first, that claims based on breach of a sovereign debt instrument fall within ICSID's jurisdiction; and second, that mass claims of a BIT violation can be adjudicated before an ICSID tribunal. Each of these findings is discussed in the following paragraphs.

12.23 As to the first issue, Argentina argued that the bonds on which the mass claims are based are not 'investments', either for purposes of the Italy–Argentina BIT (the asserted basis

[57] *BBC News*, 'Argentina Ship in Ghana Seized over Loans Default', 4 October 2012, available online at <http://www.bbc.co.uk/news/world-africa-19827562>.

[58] *The* ARA Libertad *Case (Argentina v. Ghana)*, Order, ITLOS Case No. 20 (15 December 2012).

[59] 699 F.3d 246 (2d Cir. 2012).

[60] *The Economist*, 'To Err Is Human', 22 July 2004, available online at <http://www.economist.com/node/2947040>.

[61] *Abaclat* Decision on Jurisdiction (n. 1), paras 65, 85.

[62] *Abaclat* Decision on Jurisdiction (n. 1), para. 86.

[63] *Abaclat* Decision on Jurisdiction (n. 1), para. 458.

[64] *Abaclat* Decision on Jurisdiction (n. 1), paras 97, 216.

[65] *Abaclat* Decision on Jurisdiction (n. 1), para. 91.

[66] *Abaclat* Decision on Jurisdiction (n. 1), para. 238.

for Argentina's consent to arbitration) or for purposes of the ICSID Convention, which limits ICSID's jurisdiction to disputes arising directly out of 'investment[s]'.[67] Rejecting Argentina's argument, the tribunal found that the sole criterion to consider in this regard is whether the bonds 'create the value' that Argentina and Italy intended to protect under their BIT.[68] Like most BITs concluded at the time, the Italy–Argentina BIT contains a very broad definition of 'investment', including in the definition 'obligations, private or public titles or any other right to performances or services having economic value'.[69] The tribunal concluded that the bonds fell within this definition, and therefore were eligible investments for the purposes of the BIT and the ICSID Convention.[70]

George Abi-Saab's dissent disputed the majority's approach to interpreting 'investment' for the purposes of determining the ICSID's jurisdiction, asserting that the term has a core meaning that cannot be waived, even by concluding a BIT.[71] In fact, other tribunals have applied additional criteria in this context—criteria such as the expected duration of the investment and its contribution to the host state's development.[72] The dissent also argued that the bonds lack a jurisdictional link to Argentina and therefore fall outside the scope of the BIT, the intent of which is to protect investments made by nationals of one party '*in the territory of the other*'.[73] Because the bonds were sold on the international financial markets, with payment taking place abroad and with choice of law and forum selection clauses designating laws and fora outside of Argentina, the debt transactions were deliberately arranged so as to have their situs located outside of Argentina.[74] **12.24**

As to the second issue, Argentina argued that its consent to investor–state arbitration in the BIT could not be construed to cover an unprecedented mass action relating to a sovereign debt restructuring. Allowance of mass claims would fundamentally change the nature of ICSID proceedings by making it impossible to evaluate the individual circumstances of each claimant, requiring the tribunal to ignore the particulars 'in favor of the lowest common denominator'.[75] In response, the tribunal found that Argentina's specific consent was not required regarding the 'form' of collective proceeding, characterizing the relevant question not as one of consent, but of whether an ICSID arbitration can be conducted in such a form.[76] It acknowledged that the ICSID framework is silent as to collective proceedings, but found that it would be 'contrary to the purpose of the BIT and to the spirit of ICSID' to interpret such silence as a prohibition.[77] Although the tribunal admitted that it would not be in a position to examine group claims in the same way as it could with individual claimants, **12.25**

[67] ICSID Convention Art. 25(1); *Abaclat* Decision on Jurisdiction (n. 1), para. 341.
[68] *Abaclat* Decision on Jurisdiction (n. 1), para. 365.
[69] *Abaclat* Decision on Jurisdiction (n. 1), para. 352.
[70] *Abaclat* Decision on Jurisdiction (n. 1), paras 361, 387.
[71] *Abaclat and ors (Case formerly known as Giovanna a Beccara and ors) v. Argentine Republic*, Decision on Jurisdiction and Admissibility, Dissenting Opinion of Professor Georges Abi-Saab, ICSID Case No. ARB/07/5, para. 46 (28 October 2011).
[72] Waibel (n. 49), 227–31; Christoph H. Schreuer, *The ICSID Convention: A Commentary*, 2nd edn (New York: Cambridge University Press, 2009), 128–34 (discussing so-called *Salini* factors).
[73] *Abaclat* Dissenting Opinion (n. 71), para. 75 (emphasis in original) (quoting the Preamble to the Italy–Argentina BIT).
[74] *Abaclat* Dissenting Opinion (n. 71), paras 78–87.
[75] *Abaclat* Decision on Jurisdiction (n. 1), paras 470–1.
[76] *Abaclat* Decision on Jurisdiction (n. 1), paras 489, 491.
[77] *Abaclat* Decision on Jurisdiction (n. 1), paras 517–19.

it weighed this consideration against the consequences of rejecting the bondholders' claims and found that the rejection could result in a 'shocking' denial of justice to the claimants.[78]

12.26 On this issue, the dissent also took a different view, arguing that the tribunal's characterization of the issue as one of admissibility was 'conceptually wrong' and that Argentina's consent to arbitrate investor claims under the BIT could not be interpreted to include mass claims actions.[79] Professor Abi-Saab relied in part on the US Supreme Court decision in *Stolt-Nielsen SA v. AnimalFeeds Int'l Corp*, which held that 'the differences between bilateral and class-action arbitration are too great for arbitrators to presume... that the parties' mere silence on the issue of class-action arbitration constitutes consent to resolve their disputes in class proceedings'.[80] He also argued emphatically that devising new procedures to handle mass claims would not only manifestly exceed the tribunal's powers, but also deprive Argentina of its due process right to 'individual adversarial examination' of the differentiated mass claims.[81]

12.27 Within days after issuing his dissenting opinion, Professor Abi-Saab withdrew from the *Abaclat* tribunal. Argentina subsequently filed a request for the ICSID to disqualify the remaining two arbitrators. This request was denied, and the arbitral tribunal was reconstituted in January 2012, with Dr Santiago Torres Bernárdez replacing Professor Abi-Saab. Since any request to annul the tribunal's decision on jurisdiction can be brought only after the tribunal issues a final award,[82] the *Abaclat* claims have proceeded to the merits. Given the size of the claimant class and the unprecedented nature of the proceeding, an award on the merits is unlikely to be forthcoming until 2014 or later.

12.28 In addition to *Abaclat*, there are two other bondholder arbitration claims against Argentina pending at the ICSID. In February 2013, one of the tribunals, *Ambiente Ufficio SpA v. Argentine Republic*,[83] issued an award upholding jurisdiction to hear the bondholders' claims. Although the tribunal's reasoning departed from that of *Abaclat* in certain respects,[84] the *Ambiente Ufficio* majority ultimately concluded, similar to the *Abaclat* majority, that the bond instruments at issue qualified as 'investments' for purposes of the ICSID Convention and the Italy–Argentina BIT,[85] that Argentina's consent to ICSID arbitration in the BIT can be construed to cover multi-party proceedings,[86] and that such proceedings are consistent with the ICSID framework.[87] However, the size of the claimant group in *Ambiente Ufficio*—reduced to ninety claimants after the 2010 exchange offer[88] —is significantly smaller than that in *Abaclat*. The *Ambiente Ufficio* majority distinguished *Abaclat* on this basis, refusing to characterize the claims at issue in *Ambiente Ufficio* as 'mass claims'.[89] Nonetheless, the majority acknowledged

---

78 *Abaclat* Decision on Jurisdiction (n. 1), paras 531, 537.

79 *Abaclat* Dissenting Opinion (n. 71), paras 126, 153.

80 *Stolt-Nielsen*, 130 S Ct 1758, 1776 (2010); *Abaclat* Dissenting Opinion (n. 71), paras 150–1.

81 *Abaclat* Dissenting Opinion (n. 71), paras 242–4.

82 Schreuer (n. 72), 921–3.

83 *Ambiente Ufficio SpA and ors (Case formerly known as Giordano Alpi and ors) v. Argentine Republic*, Decision on Jurisdiction and Admissibility, ICSID Case No. ARB/08/9 (8 February 2013).

84 For example, in contrast to *Abaclat*, the *Ambiente Ufficio* majority considered other factors beyond the definition of 'investment' in the Italy–Argentina BIT to determine whether the bonds qualified as an 'investment' for purposes of the ICSID Convention: *Ambiente Ufficio* Decision on Jurisdiction (n. 83), paras 438–9, 481.

85 *Ambiente Ufficio* Decision on Jurisdiction (n. 83), paras 482, 495, 510.

86 *Ambiente Ufficio* Decision on Jurisdiction (n. 83), paras 146, 163, 170.

87 *Ambiente Ufficio* Decision on Jurisdiction (n. 83), para. 146.

88 *Ambiente Ufficio* Decision on Jurisdiction (n. 83), para. 113.

89 *Ambiente Ufficio* Decision on Jurisdiction (n. 83), paras 120, 171.

that the *Abaclat* decision significantly influenced its own reasoning.[90] Argentina's appointed arbitrator, Dr Santiago Torres Bernárdez, dissented.[91] The jurisdictional challenge in the third case, *Giovanni Alemanni and ors v. Argentine Republic*,[92] is still pending.

C. The implications of *Abaclat* for sovereign debt

Abaclat is the first mass claim adjudicated under the ICSID Convention.[93] It is also the first known investment arbitration proceeding arising out of a sovereign debt restructuring. As discussed, the *Abaclat* tribunal interpreted the Italy–Argentina BIT as encompassing sovereign debt instruments and providing Argentina's consent to arbitrate a mass claim brought against it by 60,000 bondholders. This dramatic result may prompt states to revisit the definition of 'investment' in future IIAs. Finally, the timing of decision on jurisdiction—occurring in the midst of the European debt crisis and just months before Greece completed the largest debt restructuring in history—focused attention on the implications of the decision for future sovereign debt disputes. **12.29**

In its challenge to the *Abaclat* tribunal's jurisdiction, Argentina argued that allowing ICSID arbitration of creditor claims is not appropriate in the context of a sovereign debt restructuring, because it would complicate ongoing efforts to modernize the restructuring process.[94] The majority found this argument to be irrelevant to the question presented, noting that such policy arguments are for states to take into account when negotiating BITs, not for the tribunal to take into account 'in order to repair an inappropriately negotiated or drafted BIT'.[95] In contrast, while noting that policy considerations alone should not be determinative, the dissent raised concerns about the potentially disrupting effect of upholding jurisdiction over the bondholders' claims: **12.30**

> [I]n view of the actual profound structural crisis of the international financial system; the absence of agreed international procedures regulating State bankruptcy; and the intense international discussions and efforts to improve the sovereign debt restructuring process, the present case raises, in an acute manner, an international public policy issue about the workability of future sovereign debt restructuring, should ICSID tribunals intervene in sovereign debt disputes.[96]

TFA's involvement in organizing the claimant class in *Abaclat* may have been a unique circumstance.[97] Nonetheless, in light of increasing acceptance of contingency-fee financing of claims[98] and the tendency of hedge funds to acquire sovereign debt for a fraction of its face **12.31**

---

90 *Ambiente Ufficio* Decision on Jurisdiction (n. 83), paras 10–12.

91 Similarly to Professor Abi-Saab, Dr Torres Bernárdez dissented from the majority's conclusion that the bonds are protected investments and from its finding that Argentina consented to collective proceedings: *Ambiente Ufficio SpA and ors (Case formerly known as Giordano Alpi and ors) v. Argentine Republic*, Decision on Jurisdiction and Admissibility, Dissenting Opinion of Santiago Torres Bernárdez, ICSID Case No. ARB/08/9, paras 52–53, 502 (2 May 2013).

92 ICSID Case No. ARB/07/8 (claim registered 27 March 2007).

93 *See* S. Strong, 'Mass Procedures in *Abaclat v. Argentine Republic*: Are They Consistent with the International Investment Regime?' (2013) 3 YB Int'l Arb (forthcoming) (citing examples of other, smaller group claims adjudicated with ICSID).

94 *Abaclat* Decision on Jurisdiction (n. 1), para. 471.

95 *Abaclat* Decision on Jurisdiction (n. 1), para. 550.

96 *Abaclat* Dissenting Opinion (n. 71), para. 271.

97 *See* paragraph 12.20.

98 *See* B. Cremades, 'Third-Party Litigation Funding: Investing in Arbitration' (2011) 8(4) TDM, available online at <http://www.transnational-dispute-management.com/article.asp?key=1743>.

value in order to make a profit, the *Abaclat* decision may prompt additional investment arbitration claims, including mass claims, by creditors against sovereign debtors. Indeed, the two additional group bondholder claims currently pending at ICSID against Argentina are being funded on a contingency-fee basis.[99] On the one hand, facilitating creditor claims against a defaulting sovereign can have positive effects, such as discouraging default and promoting trust in the sovereign debt market. However, in the absence of an international bankruptcy regime that could provide a sovereign with automatic stay protection against individual creditors, encouraging investor claims may not be desirable from the policy perspective of promoting an orderly debt restructuring.

12.32 In any event, the ultimate impact of *Abaclat* remains to be seen. Even if the tribunal issues an award on the merits in favour of the creditors, Argentina is likely to seek to have the award annulled.[100] Finally, the jurisdictional challenge in the *Alemanni* case[101] is still pending. Although unlikely, it is possible that the *Alemanni* tribunal might issue a jurisdictional award that is inconsistent with *Abaclat* and *Ambiente Ufficio*. In the meantime, creditors aggrieved by the recent Greek restructuring have been assessing their options against Greece, including possible recourse to investment arbitration, as discussed next.

i. Implications for European debt crisis

12.33 In March 2012, Greece completed the largest debt restructuring in history, exchanging €197 billion of its debt for debt instruments that represent a 75 per cent loss to Greece's private creditors.[102] Greece achieved a very high participation rate in the restructuring, but by legislative fiat. Several weeks before the debt exchange, Greece's parliament adopted legislation that retroactively inserted collective action clauses (CACs) into Greek sovereign debt instruments governed by local law.[103] The effect of the legislation was to allow Greece to change the payment terms of all of its Greek-law bonds so long as two-thirds of a quorum of at least 50 per cent of all Greek-law bondholders agreed to the change.[104] The CACs were therefore triggered in order to forcibly increase the participation rate in the March 2012 debt exchange from 86 per cent to almost 96 per cent.[105]

---

[99] L. Peterson, 'World Bank Arbitration Tribunal Upholds Jurisdiction over Billion Dollar Claim by Italian Victims of Argentine Debt Default', *IAReporter*, 7 August 2011.

[100] A party can request annulment of an ICSID award on several narrowly defined grounds, including that the tribunal 'manifestly exceeded its powers', or committed a 'serious departure from a fundamental rule of procedure': ICSID Convention, Art. 52(1). Argentina has twice successfully argued that an ICSID award against it should be annulled on grounds that the tribunals manifestly exceeded their powers by failing to apply the non-precluded measures clause of the US–Argentina BIT: *Sempra Energy Int'l v. Argentine Republic*, Annulment Decision, ICSID Case No. ARB/02/16 (29 June 2010); *Enron Creditors Recovery Corp v. Argentine Republic*, Annulment Decision, ICSID Case No. ARB/01/3 (30 July 2010).

[101] *See* paragraph 12.28.

[102] R. Barley, 'Bond Swap Doesn't End Greek Crisis', *Wall Street Journal*, 10 March 2012, available online at <http://online.wsj.com/article/SB10001424052970203961204577271040570435760.html>; L. Thomas Jr, 'Next Time, Greece May Need New Tactics', *New York Times*, 9 March 2012, available online at <http://www.nytimes.com/2012/03/10/business/global/greece-debt-restructuring-deal-private-lenders.html?pagewanted=all&_r=0>.

[103] J. Zettelmeyer and M. Gulati, 'In the Slipstream of the Greek Debt Exchange', *Vox*, 5 March 2012, available online at <http://www.voxeu.org/article/slipstream-greek-debt-exchange>. About 90 per cent of outstanding Greek debt was governed by local law and therefore affected by the legislation: D. Strik, 'Proposed Greek Collective Action Clauses Law May Trigger its International Law Obligations', *Kluwer Arbitration Blog*, 24 February 2012, available online at <http://kluwer.practicesource.com/blog/2012/proposed-greek-collective-action-clauses-law-may-trigger-its-international-law-obligations/>.

[104] Zettelmeyer and Gulati (n. 103).

[105] Thomas (n. 102).

A German law firm representing non-consenting creditors whose debt instruments plummeted in value as a result of the debt exchange immediately began exploring legal action against Greece.[106] Similarly, the German investor group Deutsche Schutzvereinigung für Wertpapierbesitz eV (DSW) organized an association of Greek bondholders (Arbeitsgemeinschaft Griechenland Anleihen) and is investigating avenues of recovery for holders of Greek debt.[107] Will *Abaclat* open the floodgates to investment arbitration claims against Greece and other sovereign debtors affected by the European debt crisis? **12.34**

One issue to consider in this context is whether an intra-European Union BIT claim (an investor claim brought under a BIT concluded between two EU states) would run afoul of EU law and policy. The Lisbon Treaty, which now defines EU commercial policy as encompassing FDI,[108] calls into question the continuing legality of intra-EU BITs.[109] Although the European Commission has argued that these treaties are no longer valid because of the supremacy of EU law, investment arbitration tribunals nonetheless have upheld jurisdiction to hear investor claims under intra-EU BITs.[110] One such jurisdictional decision, *Eureko BV v. Slovak Republic*,[111] was upheld on appeal by the Frankfurt Court of Appeals, and may eventually be referred to the European Court of Justice.[112] Even if the Court of Justice were to find intra-EU treaties to be invalid as a matter of EU law, such a decision would not be binding on arbitral tribunals. However, such a decision would subject an award issued under intra-EU BITs to the risk of being set aside or refused enforcement on public policy grounds (although ICSID awards, which are directly enforceable, would not be subject to such a risk).[113] **12.35**

Most of the Greek BITs in force are with countries that are unlikely to be home to Greece's significant creditors. Greece's BIT partners include developing countries, emerging market economies such as Russia, India and China, and former Eastern bloc countries.[114] However, Greece does have BITs in force with Germany and Cyprus, countries that are home to holders of significant amounts of Greek debt.[115] In fact, in November 2012, Laiki Bank, a Cypriot holder of Greek sovereign debt, filed notice of an impending investment arbitration claim against Greece under the Cyprus–Greece BIT.[116] But in spite of reports of possible **12.36**

106 J. Wilson and G. Weismann, 'Germans Seek Lawsuits over Greek Debt Swap', *Financial Times*, 12 March 2012.

107 DSW, 'Klagemöglichkeiten in Sachen Griechenland-Anleihen' (court actions for Greek bondholders), available online at <http://www.dsw-info.de/Griechenlandanleihen.1877.0.html>.

108 Article 207 TFEU.

109 J. Kleinheisterkamp, 'Investment Protection and EU Law: The Intra- and Extra-EU Dimension of the Energy Charter Treaty' (2012) 15(1) J Int'l Econ L 85, 85–6.

110 Kleinheisterkamp (n. 109), 96.

111 Award on Jurisdiction, Arbitrability and Suspension, PCA Case No. 2008-13, 26 October 2010. Since commencing its arbitration claim, the name of Eureko BV has changed to Achmea BV.

112 S. Balthasar, 'Investment Arbitration under Intra-EU BITs: Recent Developments in *Eureko v. Slovakia*', *Kluwer Arbitration Blog*, 28 August 2012, available online at <http://kluwerarbitrationblog.com/blog/2012/08/28/investment-arbitration-under-intra-eu-bits-recent-developments-in-eureko-v-slovakia/>.

113 Kleinheisterkamp (n. 109), 108–9.

114 UNCTAD, 'Greece: Total Number of Bilateral Investment Treaties Concluded' (June 2012), available online at <http://archive.unctad.org/Templates/Page.asp?intItemID=2344&lang=1>. In fact, Slovak financial institutions recently brought a debt claim to ICSID against Greece: *Poštová banka a.s. and ISTROKAPITAL SE v. Hellenic Republic*, ICSID Case No. ARB/13/8.

115 Cyprus, for example, lost 24 per cent of its gross domestic product (GDP) as a result of the effects of Greece's debt restructuring on Cypriot creditors: G. Steinhauser, 'Cyprus Foreign Minister: Cyprus Hit Unfairly Hard by Greek Debt Restructuring', *Wall Street Journal*, 6 July 2012.

116 L. Peterson, 'Investment Treaty Arbitration against Greece Looms after Foreign Bank Gives Notice of Dispute Due to "Discriminatory" Bail-Out', *IAReporter*, 27 March 2013.

investment arbitration claims by German creditors, these creditors lack standing to bring direct claims against Greece under the Germany–Greece BIT.

12.37 Concluded in 1961, the Germany–Greece BIT was one of the earliest investment treaties.[117] The treaty guarantees eligible investments national and MFN treatment,[118] free transfer of investment returns,[119] and guarantees against expropriation.[120] Although the treaty does not include an FET clause, it guarantees full protection and security to eligible investments.[121] Most notably, however, the Germany–Greece BIT does not provide for investor–state arbitration of disputes, providing only for state-to-state arbitration of disputes regarding the interpretation or application of the treaty.[122] Therefore German holders of Greek debt seeking to enforce the treaty will be limited to pursuing such claims, if they do so at all, through the German government. To this end, German creditors have pressed the government to pursue a treaty claim against Greece on their behalf, but so far the government has declined to act.[123]

12.38 In addition to Greece, other European countries that are at heightened risk of default owing to the ongoing financial crisis—Portugal, Ireland, Italy, and Spain—similarly have BITs in force.[124] As with Greece, most of these treaties were concluded with countries that are unlikely to be home to most creditors: other developing countries, former Eastern bloc countries, or emerging market economies. Creditors may therefore try to obtain protection under these treaties through treaty shopping. 'Treaty shopping', in the investment treaty context, refers to an investor structuring its investment in such a way so as to take advantage of an IIA's protections. Many IIAs define 'investor' as including any legal person organized in accordance with the law of one of the parties to the treaty.[125]

12.39 The potential for investors to treaty shop is particularly significant in the sovereign debt context, in which debt instruments trade on the secondary market, allowing a bondholder to change nationality 'in a matter of minutes'.[126] Therefore a creditor holding distressed sovereign debt might attempt, through assignment or corporate reorganization, to invoke the protections of an IIA concluded with the issuer. For example, the Czech Republic has a BIT in force with Spain;[127] could a US holder of Spanish debt assign the debt to a Czech entity so as to enable the Czech entity to invoke, if necessary, the protections of the Spain–Czech BIT?

---

117 Treaty between the Federal Republic of Germany and the Kingdom of Greece for the Promotion and Mutual Protection of Capital Investments (Athens, 27 March 1961) (the Germany–Greece BIT).

118 Germany–Greece BIT, Arts 1(2), 2.

119 Germany–Greece BIT, Art. 4.

120 Germany–Greece BIT, Art. 3(2).

121 Germany–Greece BIT, Art. 3(1).

122 Germany–Greece BIT, Art. 11.

123 *See* I. Glinavos, *Investors vs Greece: The Greek "Haircut" and Investment Arbitration Under BITs*, available online at <http://papers.ssrn.com/sol3/papers.cfm?abstract_id=2021137>, 10.

124 *See* UNCTAD, 'Country-Specific Lists of BITs', available online at <http://archive.unctad.org/Templates/Page.asp?intItemID=2344&lang=1>.

125 Newcombe and Paradell (n. 32), 68.

126 K. Gallagher, *The New Vulture Culture: Sovereign Debt Restructuring and Trade and Investment Treaties*, IDEAs Working Paper Series No. 02/2011, available online at <http://www.ase.tufts.edu/gdae/publications/GallagherSovereignDebt.pdf>, 16–17.

127 Agreement Concerning the Protection and Reciprocal Encouragement of Investments between the Kingdom of Spain and the Czech and Slovak Federal Republic (Madrid, 12 December 1990) (the Spain–Czech BIT).

Some IIAs contain 'denial of benefits' clauses that allow the host state to deny the benefits of the treaty to an investor that is owned or controlled by a national of a non-treaty party if the investor has 'no substantial business activities' in the territory of the state under the laws of which it is organized.[128] Other IIAs narrow the definition of 'investor', requiring not only that the entity be organized in accordance with the law of a party to the treaty, but also that the entity actually does business there.[129] Subject to such treaty language, however, investment arbitration tribunals generally have allowed investors to structure their investments so as to take advantage of IIAs.[130] In *Saluka Investments BV (The Netherlands) v. Czech Republic*,[131] the tribunal expressed 'some sympathy' for the argument that a shell company set up solely to invoke the protections of an investment treaty should be denied the treaty's protections. It nonetheless ruled for the investor, reasoning that it could not impose on the treaty parties a definition of 'investor' to which they had not agreed.[132] In other words, notwithstanding the concern expressed in *Saluka* regarding treaty shopping, arbitral decisions so far tend to allow it, so long as such practice is consistent with the applicable treaty language.[133] 12.40

As for the hypothetical example suggested in paragraph 12.39, the Spain–Czech BIT lacks a denial of benefits clause and defines 'investor' (in the case of a legal person) by reference to the territory in which the company is 'located', in addition to the law under which the company is established.[134] Thus a Czech holder of Spanish debt that acquired the debt in anticipation of a potential violation[135] of the BIT by Spain would be likely to be able to invoke the protections of the Czech–Spanish BIT, so long as it could demonstrate that it is organized under Czech law and 'located' in the Czech Republic. 12.41

On the other hand, even if our hypothetical Czech bondholder were to prevail in an enforcement action against Spain under the Spain–Czech BIT, in awarding damages the tribunal likely would take into consideration the circumstances surrounding the bondholder's acquisition of the debt, including its knowledge that the debt was at substantial risk of default. Investment treaties protect the 'legitimate expectations' of an investor. In the sovereign debt context, awarding recovery of the debt's full nominal value would be unlikely to reflect its fair market value at the time of acquisition and thus arguably would provide the investor with a windfall.[136] 12.42

The example of *Rosinvestco UK Ltd v. Russian Federation*[137] is instructive. The claimant, an affiliate of the hedge fund Elliott International, acquired shares in Yukos Oil in late 2004, 12.43

[128] NAFTA Art. 1113(2).

[129] *See*, e.g., Agreement between the Hellenic Republic and the Government of the Republic of India on the Promotion and Reciprocal Protection of Investments (Athens, 26 April 2007) (the India–Greece BIT), Art. 1(3)(b); Newcombe and Paradell (n. 32), 68.

[130] Schreuer (n. 72), 292.

[131] Partial Award (17 March 2006).

[132] *Saluka Investments* Partial Award (n. 131), paras 240–1.

[133] Schreuer (n. 72), 290–2 (citing decisions); Newcombe and Paradell (n. 32), 69 (same); *cf. TSA Spectrum de Argentina, SA v. Argentine Republic*, Award, ICSID Case No. ARB 05/5 (19 December 2008), para. 262 (piercing the corporate veil to determine 'foreign control' of an investor for purposes of ICSID Convention Art. 25(2)(b)).

[134] Spain–Czech BIT Art. 1(2)(b).

[135] A bondholder would not have standing unless it were an investor at the time that the treaty violation took place: *Daimler Financial Services AG v. Argentine Republic*, Award, ICSID Case No. ARB/05/1 (22 August 2012), para. 145.

[136] Waibel (n. 30), 755–7; Wälde (n. 27), 419–20; Daniella Strik, 'Investment Protection of Sovereign Debt and Its Implications on the Future of Investment Law in the EU' (2012) 29(2) J Int'l Arb 183, 196.

[137] Final Award, SCC Arbitration V (079/2005) (12 September 2010).

shortly before Russia carried out a series of actions that led to the company's bankruptcy. Claimant sold its economic interest in the shares to its affiliate in the Cayman Islands, but repurchased the interest in 2007.[138] The tribunal found that the participation agreement concluded between the claimant and its affiliate did not deprive it of investor status under the UK–Soviet BIT,[139] and that Russia's actions amounted to an expropriation.[140] However, the tribunal limited damages to US$3.5 million—a tiny fraction of the amount claimed.[141] It reasoned that, by the time the claimant acquired the shares, the market had 'priced in' the likelihood of the Russian government's actions with respect to Yukos.[142] The tribunal found that the claimant had made a 'speculative investment consistent with the modus operandi of Claimant and the Elliott Group'.[143] Additionally, since the claimant had no real economic interest in the shares while the participation agreement was in effect, the value of the claimant's investment was calculated as of the date of the agreement's termination in 2007.[144]

12.44 To summarize, notwithstanding *Abaclat*, the likelihood that a flood of investment arbitration claims will arise out of the European debt crisis is relatively modest. The conformity of intra-EU BITs with EU policy remains somewhat uncertain. Most BITs concluded by Greece and other European debtor countries are with treaty partners that are unlikely to be the creditors' home state. A principal exception, the Germany–Greece BIT, does not provide for investor–state arbitration. The possibility remains that creditors will treaty shop, for example by transferring their debt to bondholders located in a treaty state in anticipation of a sovereign default or restructuring. But in such a case, taking account of the investor's legitimate expectations at the time that it acquired the debt would very possibly limit any compensation awarded to the investor under the applicable BIT.

D. IIA clauses excluding or limiting protection of sovereign debt

12.45 As discussed,[145] an issue that split the majority and dissent in *Abaclat* was whether a sovereign debt instrument issued on the international financial markets constitutes an 'investment' for purposes of the ICSID Convention or the Italy–Argentina BIT. The *Abaclat* majority answered this question by focusing solely on the BIT's definition of 'investment'. This focus on the BIT calls into question whether a narrower treaty definition would be desirable as a matter of policy. Older IIAs, including the 1990 Italy–Argentina BIT, typically define 'investment' very broadly; since the early 1990s, many IIAs define 'investment' with greater precision. In particular, a growing number of IIAs expressly exclude sovereign debt from the definition of 'investment', or add provisions to the treaty that subject sovereign debt to special treatment.

12.46 Perhaps the first example of a sovereign debt exclusion from an IIA is the investment chapter of the North American Free Trade Agreement (NAFTA). The Agreement expressly excludes from the definition of 'investment' any loan to, or debt security of, a 'state enterprise'.[146]

---

138 *Rosinvestco* Final Award (n. 137), para. 5.
139 *Rosinvestco* Final Award (n. 137), para. 323.
140 *Rosinvestco* Final Award (n. 137), para. 633.
141 *Rosinvestco* Final Award (n. 137), para. 676.
142 *Rosinvestco* Final Award (n. 137), para. 665.
143 *Rosinvestco* Final Award (n. 137), para. 669.
144 *Rosinvestco* Final Award (n. 137), para. 673.
145 *See* paragraphs 12.23–12.24.
146 North American Free Trade Agreement (NAFTA) (Washington DC, Ottawa, ON, and Mexico City, 17 December 1992, 32 ILM 289 (1993)), Art. 1139.

Daniel Price, a principal US negotiator of NAFTA, emphasized that NAFTA's drafters, while intending to define 'investment' very broadly, made a deliberate decision to carve out sovereign debt:

> [T]he scope of Chapter 11, as is the case with most bilateral investment treaties, is enormously broad. This is not an accident. The parties did not stumble into this. The parties did not inadvertently do this. This was a carefully crafted definition. Where parties wanted to carve something out, such as public debt, they did. The carve-out is there.[147]

NAFTA does not exclude all public debt from the definition of 'investment'; only loans to or debt of a 'state enterprise'. Since the conclusion of NAFTA, however, Mexican IIAs tend to exclude not only state enterprise debt, but also all public debt.[148] US IIAs, in contrast, generally do not exclude sovereign debt from the definition of 'investment'.[149] Although Canada's 2004 model Foreign Investment Protection Agreement excludes sovereign debt,[150] several BITs that Canada concluded since 2004 do not retain the exclusion.[151] **12.47**

In contrast to the exclusions described in the previous paragraph, several IIAs contain provisions that subject sovereign debt to special treatment. For example, the US–Chile FTA[152] excludes the rescheduling of Chile's debts from the investment protection guarantees contained in the agreement, except for national treatment, MFN treatment, and investor–state arbitration.[153] Similarly, the US–Colombia FTA[154] imposes temporal restrictions on claims (other than alleged breaches of national or MFN treatment) brought by a US investor against Colombia with respect to sovereign debt restructuring.[155] These provisions, however, may be vulnerable to attempts by investors to use the MFN clause to incorporate more investor-friendly provisions from other treaties. For example, a creditor arguing that a Chilean sovereign debt default expropriated its investment might invoke the more favourable treatment available under the UK–Chile BIT, which does not exclude sovereign debt rescheduling from its expropriation guarantee.[156] **12.48**

On the other hand, it is debatable whether an MFN clause would apply to treaty provisions that limit investor–state dispute settlement of sovereign debt claims. Investment arbitration tribunals have disagreed over whether the MFN clause in an IIA may be invoked **12.49**

---

147 D. Price, 'Chapter 11: Private Party vs Government, Investor–State Dispute Settlement: Frankenstein or Safety Valve?' (2000) 26 Canada–US LJ 107, 109.

148 Agreement between the United Mexican States and the Republic of Austria on the Promotion and Protection of Investments (Paris, 18 February 1998) (the Mexico–Austria BIT), Art. 1(2); *see* also Table 12.1.

149 US Department of State, 2004 Model Bilateral Investment Treaty, Art. 1; US Department of State, 2012 US Model Bilateral Investment Treaty, Art. 1.

150 Canada Model 2004 Foreign Investment Protection Agreement, Art. 1.

151 *See*, e.g., Agreement between Canada and the Czech Republic for the Promotion and Protection of Investments (Prague, 6 May 2009) (the Canada–Czech BIT), Art. I(d); Agreement between the Government of Canada and the Government of Romania for the Promotion and Reciprocal Protection of Investments (Bucharest, 8 May 2009) (the Canada–Romania BIT), Art. I(g).

152 United States–Chile Free Trade Agreement (Miami, 6 June 2003) (the US–Chile FTA).

153 US–Chile FTA, Annex 10-B.

154 United States–Colombia Free Trade Agreement (Washington, 22 November 2006) (the US–Colombia FTA).

155 US–Colombia FTA, Annex 10-F. Any claim must be brought after 270 days have elapsed and may not be brought while restructuring negotiations are ongoing.

156 *See* Agreement between the Government of the United Kingdom of Great Britain and Northern Ireland and the Government of the Republic of Chile for the Promotion and Protection of Investments with Protocol (Santiago, 8 January 1996) (the UK–Chile BIT), Art. 4.

to circumvent limitations in the treaty on a state's consent to investor–state arbitration.[157] Therefore the temporal limitations on investor–state arbitration claims contained in the US–Colombia FTA might be upheld by a tribunal in spite of the FTA's MFN clause.

12.50 Table 12.1 contains a non-exhaustive list of IIA provisions that exclude sovereign debt or subject sovereign debt to special rules. Over half of the fifty-seven agreements listed in the table are Mexican IIAs. In contrast to the provisions described in the preceding paragraphs, an IIA that excludes sovereign debt from the definition of covered investment similarly excludes it from the scope of that treaty's MFN clause. All but one of the treaties listed in the table were concluded by at least one Latin American party.

Table 12.1 IIA provisions excluding sovereign debt or subjecting sovereign debt to special treatment

Agreement/parties	Year agreement signed	Provision	Type of provision
NAFTA (Canada, US, Mexico)	1992	Art. 1139	Definition of investment excludes loans to or debt of a state enterprise
Mexico–Colombia–Venezuela FTA	1994	Art. 17–01	Definition of investment excludes debt obligations of, or the granting of loans to, the state or a state enterprise
Mexico–Costa Rica FTA	1994	Art. 13–01	Definition of investment excludes debt issued by the state or a state enterprise
Mexico–France BIT	1994	Art. 1(1)	Definition of investment excludes debt issued by the state or a state enterprise
Cuba–Bolivia BIT	1995	Art. 1.1	Definition of investment excludes debt of a state enterprise
Mexico–Switzerland BIT	1995	Art. 1(3)	Definition of investment excludes debt issued by the state or a state enterprise
Canada–Chile FTA	1996	Art. G-40	Definition of investment excludes loans to, or debt securities issued by, the state or a state enterprise
Mexico–Argentina BIT	1996	Art. 1(a)(x)	Definition of investment excludes debt issued by the state or a state enterprise
Mexico–Nicaragua FTA	1997	Art. 16–01	Definition of investment excludes loans to or debt of a state enterprise
Mexico–Austria BIT	1998	Art. 1(2)	Definition of investment excludes loans to, or debt issued by, the state or a state enterprise
Mexico–Chile FTA	1998	Art. 9–01	Definition of investment excludes loans to, or debt issued by, the state or a state enterprise
Mexico–Germany BIT	1998	Art. 1(1)	Definition of investment excludes debt issued by the state or a state enterprise
Mexico–Netherlands BIT	1998	Art. 1(2)	Definition of investment excludes debt issued by the state or a state enterprise
El Salvador–Nicaragua BIT	1999	Art. 1	Definition of investment excludes debt issued by the state or a state enterprise

[157] *See*, e.g., *Daimler* Award (n. 135), para. 268; *cf. Daimler Financial Services AG v. Argentine Republic*, Dissenting Opinion of Judge Charles N. Brower, ICSID Case No. ARB/05/1, paras 23–6 (15 August 2012).

Agreement/parties	Year agreement signed	Provision	Type of provision
Mexico–Italy BIT	1999	Art. 1.1(c)	Definition of investment excludes debt issued by the state or a state enterprise
Mexico–Portugal BIT	1999	Art. 1(1)	Definition of investment excludes debt issued by the state or a state enterprise
Mexico–Uruguay BIT	1999	Art. 1(1)	Definition of investment excludes debt issued by the state or a state enterprise
Mexico–Denmark BIT	2000	Art. 1(1)	Definition of investment excludes debt issued by the state or a state enterprise
Mexico–Greece BIT	2000	Art. 1(1)	Definition of investment excludes debt issued by the state or a state enterprise
Mexico–El Salvador–Guatemala–Honduras FTA	2000	Art. 14–01	Definition of investment excludes debt issued by the state or a state enterprise
Mexico–Korea BIT	2000	Art. 1(1)	Definition of investment excludes debt issued by the state or a state enterprise
Mexico–Sweden BIT	2000	Art. 1(3)	Definition of investment excludes debt issued by the state or a state enterprise
Peru–Cuba BIT	2000	Art. 1.1	Definition of investment excludes debt issued by the state or a state enterprise
Mexico–Cuba BIT	2001	Protocolo Ad: Art. 1	Definition of investment excludes debt issued by Mexico or a state enterprise of Mexico
Mexico–Czech Republic BIT	2002	Art. 1.2	Definition of investment excludes debt issued by the state or a state enterprise
Chile–US FTA	2003	Annex 10-B	Excludes Chile's debt restructuring from treaty obligations, except for MFN treatment, national treatment, and dispute settlement
CAFTA–DR (US, Dominican Republic, Honduras, Nicaragua, Costa Rica, Guatemala, and El Salvador)	2004	Annex 10-A	Excludes a Central American party's or the Dominican Republic's debt restructuring from treaty obligations, except for MFN treatment, national treatment, and dispute settlement
		Annex 10-E(3)	Imposes temporal restrictions on investor–state arbitration by a US investor of claims involving short-term sovereign debt
Mexico–Australia BIT	2005	Art. 1(a)(x)	Definition of investment excludes debt issued by the state or a state enterprise
Mexico–Iceland BIT	2005	Art. 1(2)(d)	Definition of investment excludes debt issued by the state or a state enterprise
Peru–Belgium BIT	2005	Art. 1.2	Definition of investment excludes debt issued by the state or a state enterprise
Uruguay–US BIT	2005	Annex G	Imposes temporal restrictions on investor–state arbitration of claims involving sovereign debt
Colombia–Switzerland BIT	2006	Ad Art. 1 (1)(c)	A payment obligation from, or a credit to, the state or a state enterprise is not considered an investment

(*Continued*)

Table 12.1. *Continued*

Agreement/parties	Year agreement signed	Provision	Type of provision
Colombia–US FTA	2006	Art. 10.28, n. 13	Definition of investment excludes loans issued by the state to another treaty party
		Annex 10-F	Investor bears burden to show default or non-payment of sovereign debt violates treaty
			Imposes temporal restrictions on investor–state arbitration of claims involving sovereign debt restructuring, except for claims alleging violation of MFN treatment or national treatment
Mexico–Panama BIT	2006	Art. 1.6	Definition of investment excludes debt issued by the state or a state enterprise
Mexico–Spain BIT	2006	Art. 1.4	Definition of investment excludes debt issued by the state or a state enterprise
Mexico–Trinidad BIT	2006	Art. 1.5(j)–(k)	Definition of investment excludes loans to, or debt issued by, the state or a state enterprise
Mexico–UK BIT	2006	Art. 1	Definition of investment excludes debt issued by the state or a state enterprise
Peru–Canada BIT	2006	Art. 1	Definition of investment excludes loans to, or debt issued by, the state or a state enterprise
Peru–US FTA	2006	Art. 10–28, n. 13	Definition of investment excludes loans issued by the state to another treaty party
		Annex 10-F	Investor bears burden to show default or non-payment of sovereign debt violates treaty
			Imposes temporal restrictions on investor–state arbitration of claims involving sovereign debt restructuring, except for claims alleging violation of MFN treatment or national treatment
Azerbaijan–Croatia BIT	2007	Art. 1.1	Definition of investment excludes debt instruments issued by the state or state enterprise
Colombia–Peru BIT	2007	Art. 42	Definition of investment excludes: (i) loans issued by the state to another treaty party; and (ii) public debt operations
Honduras–El Salvador FTA	2007	Art. 10.01	Definition of investment excludes debt obligations of, or the granting of loans to, the state or a state enterprise
Mexico–India BIT	2007	Art. 1(7)(c)-(d)	Definition of investment excludes loans to, or debt instruments issued by, the state or a state enterprise
Mexico–Slovakia BIT	2007	Art. 1.10(c)-(d)	Definition of investment excludes loans to, or debt instruments issued by, the state or a state enterprise
Panama–Costa Rica FTA	2007	Art. 10.40	Definition of investment excludes debt obligations of, or the granting of a loan to, the state or a state enterprise

Agreement/parties	Year agreement signed	Provision	Type of provision
Australia–Chile FTA	2008	Art. 10.1(j)(iii)	Definition of investment excludes debt instruments issued by the state or a state enterprise
Colombia–Canada FTA	2008	Art. 838, n. 11	Definition of investment excludes: (i) loans issued by the state to another treaty party; and (ii) public debt operations of the state or a state enterprise
Peru–Singapore FTA	2008	Art. 10.1, n. 10–3	Definition of investment excludes loans issued by the state to another treaty party
		Art. 10.18	Investor bears burden to show default or non-payment of sovereign debt violates treaty
			Imposes temporal restrictions on investor–state arbitration of claims involving sovereign debt restructuring, except for claims alleging violation of MFN treatment or national treatment
Colombia–China BIT	2008	Art. 1(1.1)	Definition of investment excludes public debt operations
Mexico–China BIT	2008	Art. 1	Definition of investment excludes loans to, or debt instruments issued by, the state or a state enterprise
Mexico–Belarus BIT	2008	Art. 1.5(c)	Definition of investment excludes loans to, or debt instruments issued by, the state or a state enterprise
Colombia–Belgium BIT	2009	Art. 1(2.1(a))	Definition of investment excludes public debt operations
Colombia–India BIT	2009	Art. 1(2.1)	Definition of investment excludes public debt operations
Peru–China FTA	2009	Art. 126, n. 11	Definition of investment excludes loans issued by the state to another treaty party
		Annex 8	Investor bears burden to show default or non-payment of sovereign debt violates treaty
			Imposes temporal restrictions on investor–state arbitration of claims involving sovereign debt restructuring, except for claims alleging violation of MFN treatment or national treatment
Colombia–UK BIT	2010	Art. 1(2)(b)(i)	Definition of investment excludes public debt operations
Colombia–Japan BIT	2011	Art. 1	Definition of investment excludes debt to the state or a state enterprise
Peru–Mexico FTA	2011	Art. 11.1	Definition of investment excludes debt instruments issued by the state or a state enterprise

Note: BIT = bilateral investment treaty; CAFTA-DR = Dominican Republic–Central America Free Trade Agreement; FTA = free trade agreement; MFN = most-favoured nation; NAFTA = North American Free Trade Agreement

12.51 Although the number of treaties that exclude sovereign debt from their scope probably comprises a relatively small percentage of all IIAs, that percentage may grow—particularly in light of the notoriety surrounding the *Abaclat* decision. In 2005, the International Institute for Sustainable Development (IISD) developed a model investment agreement designed to promote sustainable development, and to achieve a balance of rights and duties among investors, home countries, and host countries. To that end, the IISD model agreement excludes sovereign debt and state enterprise debt from the treaty's definition of 'investment'.[158]

4. Conclusion

12.52 It remains to be seen whether the investment treaty regime will provide a viable alternative to court enforcement of sovereign debt contracts. Although Wälde predicts that international investment tribunals are likely to be more responsive to the interests of sovereign debtors than money-centre domestic courts have been,[159] Waibel suggests that a shift from litigation to investment arbitration of such disputes may limit a state's flexibility to respond to sovereign debt crises and make creditors less inclined to participate in a voluntary restructuring.[160] Similarly, Louis Wells contrasts investment arbitration practice unfavourably with that of the World Trade Organization (WTO) Dispute Settlement Body, a multilateral institution that has generated a relatively coherent body of decisions and the governing agreements of which include various escape clauses.[161]

12.53 There have been multiple proposals to establish a multilateral mechanism to resolve sovereign debt disputes. In 2001, the International Monetary Fund (IMF) proposed amending its Articles of Agreement to create a framework for restructuring sovereign debt: a sovereign debt restructuring mechanism (SDRM).[162] The proposal envisaged establishing a tribunal to resolve disputes arising out of the restructuring process and, if requested by the debtor and approved by a supermajority of creditors, imposing a temporary stay on enforcement actions during the restructuring process.[163] In the face of opposition, the IMF eventually ceased work on the SDRM proposal in 2003.[164]

12.54 More than sixty years before the SDRM proposal, the League of Nations similarly considered establishing a permanent international tribunal to resolve sovereign debt claims.[165] In 1935, faced with a wave of sovereign debt defaults, the League of Nations adopted a resolution designating a committee, comprising mostly European financial and legal experts, to examine ways in which to improve sovereign debt contracts and to prepare model provisions,

---

158 H. Mann, K. von Moltke, L. Peterson, and A. Cosbey, *IISD Model International Agreement on Investment for Sustainable Development* (April 2005), available online at <http://www.iisd.org/investment/capacity/model.aspx>, Art. 2(C).

159 Wälde (n. 27), 421, fn. 100.

160 Waibel (n. 30), 757–8.

161 Louis T. Wells, 'Property Rights for Foreign Capital: Sovereign Debt and Private Direct Investment in Times of Crisis', in K. Sauvant (ed.) *Yearbook on International Investment Law & Policy* (New York: Oxford University Press, 2009–10), 486–8.

162 S. Hagan, 'Designing a Legal Framework to Restructure Sovereign Debt' (2004–05) 36 Georgetown J Int'l L 299, 300–1.

163 IMF, *Proposed Features of a Sovereign Debt Restructuring Mechanism* (12 February 2003), reprinted in Hagan (n. 162), 394–402.

164 Hagan (n. 162), 301.

165 League of Nations (n. 4); *see* also Borchard (n. 4), 37–9; Waibel (n. 49), 324–6.

'if necessary, with a system of arbitration' for such contracts.[166] The committee was presented with a draft League of Nations Convention for the establishment of an International Loans Tribunal, the decisions of which on disputes arising out of sovereign debt contracts would have the same force as if rendered by a national court of last instance in any state acceding to the Convention.[167] Certain features of the draft Convention resemble the ICSID Convention—particularly the provision relating to the enforceability of the tribunal's awards. But the draft Convention, unlike the investment treaty regime, was designed exclusively to address the problem of resolving sovereign debt disputes and envisaged establishing a tribunal available to debtor states, as well as creditors.[168]

As with the SDRM proposal, the League of Nations' proposal was never implemented. **12.55** The committee was of the view that concluding an international convention to establish an international loans tribunal would be unrealistic under 'present circumstances' (the report was issued just months before Germany's invasion of Poland). Therefore the committee did not examine the draft proposal in detail, merely including it as an annex to the committee report.[169]

As the League of Nations' proposal illustrates, the challenges associated with resolving claims **12.56** arising out of sovereign debt defaults have existed for many decades. A multilateral solution would be the most effective way in which to resolve these challenges, by preventing a rush on the defaulting sovereign's assets, ensuring enforceability of the resulting awards, and resolving disputes in a manner that balances investor rights against the long-term developmental interests of the sovereign debtor. The European debt crisis and the Second Circuit's recent *NML Capital* decision against Argentina[170] have prompted calls to revive the SDRM proposal.[171] Unfortunately, notwithstanding renewed interest, it is unlikely that international consensus to adopt such a multilateral solution will be achieved any time soon.

166 League of Nations (n. 4), paras 1–2.
167 League of Nations (n. 4), Annex IV, para. (viii).
168 League of Nations (n. 4), Annex IV, para. (vi).
169 League of Nations (n. 4), para. 92.
170 *See* paragraph 12.19.
171 R. Wigglesworth and A. Beattie, 'Bankruptcy Regime for Nations Urged', *Financial Times*, 6 January 2013.

Part III

COMPLICATING FACTORS

13. Restructuring in a Monetary Union: Legal Aspects 177
Antonio Sáinz de Vicuña

14. Restructuring in a Monetary Union: Economic Aspects 195
Daniel Gros

15. Sovereign Debt and Banking Crises: An 'Arial View' 205
Anna Gelpern

16. International Lender of Last Resort : A Floor of Support for Troubled Sovereign Debt 219
Adam Lerrick

17. Odious Debt 233
Sir William Blair

18. Sovereign Contingent Liabilities 241
Lee C. Buchheit and G. Mitu Gulati

13

RESTRUCTURING IN A MONETARY UNION

Legal Aspects

Antonio Sáinz de Vicuña[1]

1. Introduction

13.01 The introduction of the euro in 1999 signified a profound change in the history of monetary law. Seventeen member states of the European Union (EU)[2] today share a single currency and a single interest rate policy. Until 2012, bonds issued by member states in that currency area were considered to be risk-free assets, weighted zero for the purposes of calculating the capital ratio of credit institutions.[3] The global financial crisis that commenced in 2007 mutated into a sovereign debt crisis in 2010 in some member states of the euro area, in part as a result of the fiscal support provided to their respective banking sectors.

13.02 The Hellenic Republic was the first country to be affected by the crisis, as its sovereign bond market started to dry up by the end of 2009. A programme of reforms was agreed by the EU and the International Monetary Fund (IMF), which included austerity measures such as tax increases, savings in the public sector, the sale of state assets, pension and labour reforms, and, importantly, the funding of such programmes by way of loans from other euro area members. Following a political agreement among euro area leaders, it was considered appropriate that private investors in Greek sovereign bonds should also share—together with taxpayers and pensioners—part of the burden of redressing Greece's fiscal position.

13.03 The first proposed solution to the Greek sovereign debt problems was the so-called 'reprofiling' of Greek bonds (that is, the maintenance of principal and interests with an extension of maturities), so as to provide some breathing space in which to carry out the necessary reforms. However, it soon became apparent that 'reprofiling' was not enough: private investors also needed to contribute by taking a haircut on principal. At the Eurogroup level, it was

---

[1] The views held in this chapter are the personal views of the author and do not represent the European Central Bank (ECB). This chapter was completed in March 2013 and thus any subsequent legal development is not considered. The author thanks Rosa Lastra for comments.

[2] The seventeen member states, known as the 'euro area', are Austria, Belgium, Finland, France, Germany, Ireland, Italy, Luxembourg, The Netherlands, Portugal, Spain, Greece, Slovenia, Cyprus, Malta, Slovakia and Estonia. Other non-EU countries using the euro as legal currency are Andorra, Kosovo, Monaco, Montenegro, San Marino, and the Vatican. Denmark, Latvia, and Lithuania keep their currencies pegged to the euro through the Exchange Rate Mechanism (ERM2), and Bulgaria does so by way of a currency board. Latvia will formally adopt the euro in 2014.

[3] This is still the case under the Basel III Accord.

considered important that such private sector involvement (PSI) be voluntary, so as to avoid the trigger of credit default swaps (CDSs) or further downgrades in Greece's rating.[4]

13.04 The concept of risk-free assets, one of the paradigms of modern finance on which confidence is built, was substantially affected in the EU by the Greek PSI, which was termed by all EU leaders as 'unique and exceptional'.

13.05 This chapter explains how a sovereign debt restructuring in a monetary union differs from the general case of other sovereign debt workouts. It points to some specific and somehow unprecedented issues that the Greek PSI case brought with it, and recommends further normative steps.

2. Sovereign Debt Restructuring in the Case of a State Participating in the European Monetary Union: Elements of Differentiation Vis-à-Vis other Sovereign Debt Restructurings

13.06 Historically, sovereign bond workouts have, in almost all cases, involved single states, not parties to a regional currency union.[5] Unprecedented issues arose as a result of the decision of the Hellenic Republic,—a full member of the European Monetary Union (EMU)—to proceed, in the course of February and March 2012, with a restructuring of its outstanding sovereign bonds. But what are the elements that make such a process different from the 'ordinary' cases of single states with full monetary competences? Six differentiating factors can be identified, as follows.

A. Impossibility of devaluing the currency

13.07 Very often,[6] for loans granted or bonds issued in the domestic currency, states have a policy of allowing a devaluation of their currency so as to facilitate full repayment of the nominal amount of their bonds. Greece, for example, formally devalued the drachma in 1882, 1928, 1953, 1985, and 1998, all of these instances benefiting the state by reducing the cost of servicing and repayment of outstanding drachma debt.[7] When, in 2012, the Hellenic Republic faced the need to obtain debt relief, it could not resort to devaluation: its currency was the euro and monetary policy for members of the euro area is the exclusive competence

[4] A binding modification of bond contracts would enter into the market definition of 'restructuring event' for CDSs governed by the International Swaps and Derivatives Association (ISDA) standard agreement, triggering settlement of insured amounts.

[5] Three states of the East Caribbean Currency Union—namely Antigua and Barbuda (2010), Dominica (2004), and Grenada (2005)—had external debt renegotiations. Twelve states participating in the two African regional monetary unions (the Central African Economic and Monetary Community, and the Economic and Monetary West African Union) also had their external debt renegotiated. In most of these cases, such renegotiations took place in the context of the Paris Club, because their only creditors were public ones; still, a few of them that also had commercial loans had them rescheduled in the context of the London Club. In no case did it concern bonds placed and traded in international markets.

[6] According to a 2012 IMF Working Paper, between 1800 and 2007 there were 150 cases of yearly inflation beyond 20 per cent allowing for de facto reduction of debt denominated in local currency: *see* Udaibir Das, Michael Papaioannou, and Christoph Trebesch, *Sovereign Debt Restructurings 1950–2010: Literature Survey, Data, and Stylized Facts*, IMF WP/12/203 (August 2012), available online at <http://www.imf.org/external/pubs/cat/longres.aspx?sk=26190.0>.

[7] Greece had a long history of defaults on its foreign loans, starting with its independence loans from Great Britain in 1824 and 1825, then further international loans in 1832, which had to be renegotiated following a default on the principal in 1843, as well as interest payments suspension. From 1848, it suspended conversion

of the EU. The major part of the public debt of the Hellenic Republic was denominated in euro. Had Greece been outside the monetary union, it could have devalued its currency (the Greek drachma was the national currency in the Hellenic Republic before the adoption of the euro). Such devaluation would have helped Greece to reduce the real cost of servicing and repaying the debt. Neither could Greece resort to an inflationary policy that could have softened the debt burden, since the euro is governed by the European Central Bank (ECB), which has a clear non-inflation mandate.

The EMU's primary objective is price stability—that is, the maintenance in the medium term of the purchasing power of the currency (Article 127.1 TFEU). Both devaluation and a policy aimed at inflation (favouring debtors) would hinder the pursuit of such an objective. A deliberate inflationary policy effected by a central bank assuages the indebtedness of the sovereign when debt is denominated in its national currency. In the case of the EMU, this is not possible, because the independent ECB carries out an anti-inflationary monetary policy and ensures—and has ensured since 1999—the primacy of price stability. **13.08**

B. Impossibility of imposing restrictions on movements of capital

When a sovereign debt crisis occurs, there is an associated capital flight (that is, the phenomenon of capital leaving the country). To counteract such capital flight, sovereign states normally impose exchange controls.[8] However, in the EU since 1999,[9] such tools have been only exceptionally permitted: **13.09**

- vis-à-vis non-EU countries temporarily and subject to a Community procedure (that is, not by an individual member state);[10] or
- for specific reasons, such as taxation avoidance, financial stability in cases of mergers and acquisitions of financial institutions, statistical purposes, or for public policy or public security.[11]

of banknotes into gold or silver, allowing devaluation by banknote printing. Greece's outstanding debt was not settled until 1878. Greece was, for a short while, able to tap foreign capital again, until in 1893 it defaulted on interest payments, leading in 1897 to the formation of an international committee with capacity to influence Greek public finances and debt management, which led Greece to join the gold standard in 1910 and the Latin Monetary Union, and obtaining foreign finance to fund the 1912–13 Balkan Wars. Following the Great War and the Asia Minor War, financed by internal inflation, the League of Nations again intervened to assist in restoring orderly Greek public finances, establishing the Bank of Greece. This led to a subsequent pegging of the drachma to the sterling pound, then to the US dollar, thereafter to the sterling pound again, with regular devaluations and exchange controls. Exchange controls remained in place until 1995. Greece joined the Exchange Rate Mechanism of the EU in 1999, leading to the euro in 2001. For a full monetary history of Greece, *see* Sophia Lazaretou, *Greek Monetary Economics in Retrospect: The Adventures of the Drachma* (Athens: Bank of Greece, 2003).

[8] Article VI(3) of the IMF's Articles of Agreement states that 'Members may exercise [capital controls] as are necessary to regulate international capital movements', but restrictions to payments for current transactions (i.e. current account convertibility) are subject to an IMF procedure. Article VIII(2) gives external effect to such restrictions. All EU member states are bound by these provisions.

[9] Exchange controls in the EU were prohibited by Council Directive of 24 June 1988, the content of which was reflected in the Maastricht Treaty (now Arts 63–66 TFEU). Greece was exceptionally given three more years in which to eliminate capital controls, so the general EU prohibition to use such instruments applied to Greece only in 1995. Member states could, however, unilaterally and subject to a Community procedure, adopt 'defensive measures' in cases of difficulties. This possibility, contained in the Treaty signed at Maastricht (Arts 109h and 109i, later renumbered as Arts 119 and120), was time-limited: paragraph 4 of those provisions stated that such possibility for unilateral 'defensive measures' (i.e. capital restrictions) expired at the start of Stage Three of EMU, because a monetary union cannot admit limitations to the free flow of money within the currency area. Since 1999, therefore, such restrictions have no longer been possible within the EMU. In addition, in 1999, the euro was declared by the IMF to be a 'freely usable currency', thus eligible for the special drawing rights (SDRs) basket.

[10] Article 66 TFEU.

[11] Article 65.1(b) TFEU, e.g. the prosecution of fraud and crime.

An internal market like the one in the EU—and even more so a monetary union based on a currency-wide money market—is incompatible with capital barriers, except in very specific cases.[12] A fiscal crisis like the one the one affecting Greece leads to an important outflow of bank deposits, which cannot be legally addressed by way of exchange controls. 'Money' comprises not only central bank money ('M0'), but also commercial bank money ('M1'); both need to be fully fungible within a monetary zone, and be undifferentiated by the holders and users of such money. The introduction of exchange controls would have disrupted such fungibility, and denaturalized the current concept of 'money' as encompassing both M0 and M1 money.

C. Impossibility of monetizing the sovereign's debt

13.10 Individual states may get financial help from their central banks in a budget-related crisis (for example excessive deficits and indebtedness); this is not legally possible in the euro area. One of the pillars of EMU is the prohibition on central banks financing the public sector[13] under Article 123 TFEU.[14] Sovereign debt crises outside the euro area can be smoothed by means of the central bank funding the state. The prohibition of this 'monetary financing'[15] is therefore not a universal rule and may not apply to countries outside the EU.[16] In addition to its economic rationale,[17] indeed a basic tenet of central bank independence, in the case of EMU such prohibition is an essential tool to ensure the neutrality of the central bank vis-à-vis conflicting fiscal and economic policies by participating member states.

13.11 If Greece were not a participant in EMU, the Bank of Greece might have alleviated the fiscal needs of the Hellenic Republic and, in doing so, facilitated a downward path of the external value of the drachma, helping the government in its servicing and repayment of public debt.

D. Impossibility of being bailed out by other Union members

13.12 It is not infrequent, with regard to the external obligations of developing countries, that the developed ones condone part of the outstanding debt. As a continuation of a practice that existed in colonial times, fiscal transfers often take place in the relations between the developed and developing world, whereby the former—including many EU member

---

[12] Article 65 TFEU.

[13] The only two exceptions to that rule being: (i) credit institutions controlled by the public sector, which may obtain central bank liquidity on terms identical to private credit institutions; and (ii) the financing of state obligations vis-à-vis the IMF. In addition, the United Kingdom is authorized to maintain the 'Ways and Means' credit facility of the Bank of England with the British government (s 10, Protocol 15 on Certain Provisions Relating to the United Kingdom, attached to the TFEU).

[14] Further developed by Council Regulation (EC) No. 3603/93 of 13 December 1993 (OJ L332, 31.12.1993).

[15] The media tends to refer to such activity as 'printing money', in spite of the fact that it does not necessarily entail an increase in banknote circulation.

[16] In fact, some major central banks have, in the course of the current financial crisis, decided to foster the economy by granting credit to their respective government, in what has been termed 'quantitative easing' (e.g. the Federal Reserve System, the Bank of England, the Bank of Japan). This instrument is prohibited for EU countries, except for the UK under its specific TFEU Protocol.

[17] The monetary philosophy since the 1980s, overturning decades of Keynesian economics, requires central banks to be independent from government and to serve the primary objective of ensuring the stability of the purchasing power of the currency that they issue. Should central banks finance governments, such objectives would be put at risk, because they would become subordinate to political decisions and, in addition, fiscal discipline would be weakened.

states—agree to condone totally or partially the outstanding debt of the latter, either in the context of the Paris Club or of multilateral programmes.[18]

In theory, given the relatively small size of the Greek economy within the larger euro area, it may have been considered that a partial forgiveness of Greek debt, subject to reform conditions, would be a price worth paying for the maintenance of the euro. However, another basic pillar of EMU is the so-called 'no-bailout rule',[19] according to which there are no fiscal transfers among participating states in the single currency. These transfers are prohibited to prevent taxpayers from one state financing the public services of another. This pillar is thus based on fundamental constitutional reasons. **13.13**

However, this rule is not absolute; regional integration organizations usually provide for some mutual fiscal transfers. Fiscal transfers have occurred in the EU since its very origin in the 1950s; indeed, there are a series of structural funds that have provided for regular fiscal transfers aimed at mitigating the economic divergences within the EU and fostering convergence,[20] as well as allowing for common EU policies. Such fiscal transfers are based on EU law and, although comprising ever-growing amounts, have never been contested.[21] If Greece had not been subject to the no-bailout rule, some other sources of foreign aid would have been available—as was indeed the case throughout earlier episodes of its troubled financial history. **13.14**

The Treaty on the Functioning of the European Union (TFEU) lays down the no-bailout rule in Article 125.[22] The Court of Justice of the European Union (CJEU) has had the opportunity of interpreting the provision in the recent *Pringle* case,[23] whereby an Irish parliamentarian had questioned the compatibility of the European Stability Mechanism (ESM)—a fund owned by the euro area member states, analysed elsewhere in this book—with Article 125 TFEU. The Court assessed the objective of this provision and considered that: **13.15**

(a) ESM lending is conducive to a return to fiscal discipline of the borrowing state thanks to the conditionality attached to it, and thus consistent with one of the objectives of Article 125 TFEU—namely, fiscal discipline for all EU member states; and
(b) the ESM, in its lending, does not replace the Hellenic Republic in its liabilities vis-à-vis its creditors, but rather 'adds' to its liabilities. Lending is thus legally permissible, whilst 'condoning', or 'paying for another', is not.

---

[18] For example, the IMF and World Bank have sponsored the Highly Indebted Poor Countries (HIPC) initiative.

[19] In international meetings, this is sometimes referred to as the 'own house in order (OHIO) rule'.

[20] The European Regional Development Fund (FEDER), the European Social Fund (ESF), the European Agricultural Guarantee Fund (EAGF), the European Agricultural Fund for Rural Development (EAFRD), the European Fisheries Fund (EFF), and the Cohesion Fund.

[21] The odd exception being the UK, which has received a sizeable rebate of its contributions to the EU budget since the time that Margaret Thatcher headed the British government. Ms Thatcher infamously demanded, at the EU Summit at Fontainebleau in 1985: 'I want my money back!'

[22] It reads:

> The Union shall not be liable for or assume the commitments of central governments, regional, local or other public authorities, other bodies governed by public law, or public undertakings of any Member State, without prejudice to mutual financial guarantees for the joint execution of a specific project. A Member State shall not be liable for or assume the commitments of central governments, regional, local or other public authorities, other bodies governed by public law, or public undertakings of another Member State, without prejudice to mutual financial guarantees for the joint execution of a specific project.

[23] *Pringle case*, Case 370/12, Judgment dated 27 November 2012.

The Court therefore concluded that the ESM loans do not contradict Article 125 TFEU.

13.16 Greece has benefited from financial assistance from fellow euro area member states and from the IMF, although such assistance has at times been given reluctantly and there have also been legal challenges.[24] Since May 2010, a number of mechanisms and initiatives at the EU level and at the level of the member states have been aimed at tackling or alleviating the Greek debt problems. Some funds came directly from the EU budget and from a loan provided by a syndicate of euro area member states.[25] The European Financial Stability Facility (EFSF)[26] was established as a temporary facility (the 'first rescue fund' of the euro area); then the 'permanent' ESM was established. The IMF—which, as Lastra argues in her chapter in this volume, is now firmly inserted in the EU process—has been involved throughout the Greek debt crisis (as part of the troika),[27] providing financial assistance to the Hellenic Republic so that it can restructure its public finances, subject to strict conditionality and external monitoring. The Court in *Pringle* stated that, to the extent that no substitution of Greece's liabilities vis-à-vis its creditors has taken place, the establishment of the ESM and its lending facilities do not breach Article125 TFEU.

E. Impossibility of redenominating the sovereign debt into a new or revived national currency

13.17 A state within a monetary union is a 'part of a whole'. Regional monetary unions tend to aim at eternity. The dream of a universal currency that would be based in gold and silver led, in the nineteenth century, to the Latin Monetary Union and to the Scandinavian Monetary Union, at a time when universal standards of measurement were being agreed.[28] In the twentieth century, EMU was construed as the final stage of a gradual process, with the final objective of ensuring a single market that would not suffer from the currency fluctuations and exchange control regimes that had hampered a common and stable measure of value, and thus a 'clear and stable system' for the pricing of goods and services, and of Community policies. The process started with the Werner Plan of the 1970s, went through

[24] In addition to the *Pringle* case, a group of German professors and parliamentarians questioned the constitutionality of Germany's support to Greece on basically two grounds: that such support escaped democratic control; and that it had the potential of having inflationary effects hindering the fundamental right to property. On 7 September 2011, the German Constitutional Court rendered its judgment dismissing the three joined claims, but requiring a case-by-case approval by the German Parliament of financial supports under the European Financial Stability Facility (EFSF). A similar complaint was introduced in 2012 before the same Court, asking for an interim injunction to stop the ratification process of the ESM by Germany; it was rejected on 12 September 2012. Final judgment on the constitutionality of the ESM ratification by Germany is pending.

[25] It was a voluntary loan: one euro area member state, Slovakia, decided not to participate in such syndicated lending.

[26] The EFSF was established in Luxembourg as a company by shares in June 2010.

[27] The so-called 'Troika missions' (EU, IMF, and ECB).

[28] The General Conference on Weights and Measures was established in Paris in 1875, and now comprises ninety-three member or associated states, and established global measures (plus their subdivisions and multiples) such as the metre, the litre, the gram, the carat, the degree celsius, the ampere, the bar, the farad, the volt, the watt, etc. The Latin Monetary Union (LMU) was established in 1866 with the same aim: a common definition of national currencies in terms of gold and silver, so as to allow their global use. Up to eleven European countries plus Venezuela adopted the LMU standards. The LMU was followed by the Scandinavian Monetary Union in 1876, with a common gold definition of the Scandinavian currencies. The respective founding treaties did not foresee a time limit for such unions; they were created for eternity. The national central banks of signatory states have had to labour to preserve the metallic definitions since their start, in particular against market speculators from London and Frankfurt betting against their stability. The upheavals of the global monetary system in the aftermath of the First World War finally brought the unions to an end.

a phase of monetary coordination and mutual support—the EMS and its Exchange Rate Mechanism (ERM)—which failed in the early 1990s, and culminated in the monetary union with the euro, itself a process with subphases and clear deadlines.

The EMU provisions in the TFEU do not foresee any mechanism for exiting the monetary union: euro area member states have transferred their monetary powers to the Union level for good. But not necessarily for eternity: there is the possibility, foreseen in Article 50 of the Treaty on the European Union (TEU), of leaving the EU altogether, in which way member states might 'recover' their monetary powers. Article 50 TEU foresees the exit from the EU after the conclusion of a treaty fixing the conditions for such exit. A euro area country leaving the EU would have to include in such 'exit treaty' the monetary aspects of such withdrawal. Much was said about the prospect of Greece exiting the euro; indeed, the media even coined a term for it, 'Grexit'. The fact remains, however, that there is no legal basis for an EMU country to leave the euro and remain in the EU. The unilateral exit of Greece from the euro without the use of Article 50 TEU would have been illegal and would have created a decade of litigation. Thus this is not an option to assuage sovereign crises among euro area member states. On a smaller economic scale, the same issue arose in relation to the Cypriot crisis of 2013, with the same conclusion. 13.18

F. Increased risk of contagion within members of the currency area

Individual states are masters of their own fate regarding their public debt. States that share a common currency within a monetary union are subject to an element outside their control: market perception of the impact of the fiscal behaviour of one upon another. Sovereign crisis in an individual state normally has a limited effect on other states; in a monetary union, the closer financial links between members and the integration of their financial markets lead to a market sentiment that may be termed 'herding behaviour'.[29] Indeed, the experience in some euro area member states in 2011–12 provides ample evidence in this regard. An event in Italy—perhaps a political upheaval—can have an impact on the pricing of Spanish bonds, for example, and vice versa. The pro-cyclical behaviour of the market—fed by the pro-cyclical behaviour of credit rating agencies and of the financial media—tends to amplify such effects beyond any rational dimension, leading to the establishment of a kind of 'domino' effect along the lines of 'The next in line is . . . '. Furthermore, the hypothesis of Greece leaving the euro meant for many market players and the financial media that the euro, as a currency, was doomed altogether—in spite of other EMU participants being in comparatively better shape. A kind of 'panic' or 'hysteria' in markets, and the resulting herding behaviour, led CDS prices to rise or fall in a very volatile manner depending on the news from one or another state; facts were simplified, and news affecting one euro area state were mixed in a unscientific hotchpotch, triggering unfounded negative market behaviour vis-á-vis other euro area states. Sovereigns with less indebtedness and lower deficit than others received occasional undeserved and merciless treatment by the market—hence 'contagion'. 13.19

[29] When, in 1994, Mexico suffered a balance-of-payments crisis, triggering a devaluation of the peso and an international rescue package, its effects extended to the whole of Latin America, in what was then named the 'Tequila effect', whereby market players simplified facts in an unscientific manner and considered all Latin American countries to be similar to Mexico. The same dynamics, in more intense proportions, applied to the euro area.

3. Analysis of Some Legal Issues Arising in the Restructuring of the Sovereign Debt of the Hellenic Republic in 2012

13.20 Although sovereign debt restructuring has been with us for a long time, debt restructuring in the euro area is a rather novel issue and so are the legal challenges involved in such restructuring.

A. 'Negative pledge clauses' and maintaining the eligibility of Greek government bonds as central bank collateral throughout the debt exchange process

13.21 Greek government bonds (GGBs) have been eligible collateral for access to Eurosystem operations since the Hellenic Republic entered the euro area in January 2002. Following the debt exchange proposed by Greece in 2012, such GGBs suffered a rating downgrade into 'selective default' and, irrespective of their external 'junk' rating, were bound to be the subject of a 'haircut' in the exchange. This made the GGBs clearly ineligible as Eurosystem collateral, because the Treaty requires the collateral to be 'adequate'. Declaring it 'ineligible' would have jeopardized the whole Greek banking system (leading to a non-functioning interbank market). With a view to mitigating that risk, the Hellenic Republic offered to the Eurosystem several means of temporarily enhancing the quality of the GGBs as collateral; many had to be rejected because of 'negative pledge clauses' (NPCs) among the issuances of GGBs outside Greece. Such NPCs prohibit the issuer encumbering assets to the benefit of some, but not all, of the same-ranking creditors. Allowing a pledge of Greek assets to further enhance the GGBs given as collateral to the Eurosystem risked triggering breaches of NPCs, leading to the acceleration of maturities, default, and cross-default, with catastrophic consequences.

13.22 An agreement was entered into on 21 March 2012 whereby:

(a) the Eurogroup in Brussels[30] accepted the use of the EFSF to provide the Hellenic Republic with EFSF bonds on loan, which would be made available to the Eurosystem for exchange against GGBs obtained by it in the case of a counterparty default during the GGBs' exchange period;
(b) the ECB in Frankfurt accepted the 'adequacy' of such modality of 'credit enhancement', which had the legal nature of a 'buyback offer'—that is, it was purely contractual and did not create any 'security' in the legal sense, and thus was consistent with usual NPCs.

In practice, no counterparty defaulted on its borrowings from the Eurosystem during the exchange period, so the collateral enhancement was not put to test.

B. Question of a voluntary participation of the Eurosystem in a collective action clause process

13.23 The GGBs had been taken as Eurosystem collateral since 2001 and thus the Eurosystem was affected by the activation of the collective action clause (CAC) in the Greek PSI. Also,

---

30 The Eurogroup Statement of 21 February 2012 reads:

> The Eurogroup considers that the necessary elements are now in place for Member States to carry out the relevant national procedures to allow for the provision by EFSF of a buy back scheme for Greek marketable debt instruments for Eurosystem monetary policy operations.

since May 2010, the Eurosystem had carried out secondary market purchases of GGBs in order to mitigate the malfunctioning of that market and to preserve the monetary transmission mechanism. These secondary market interventions were named the Securities Markets Programme (SMP), and the ECB made very clear its pure monetary policy concept aimed at keeping the repurchase (or 'repo') market alive by offering a potential 'buyer of last resort' to counterparties with a portfolio of GGBs.[31]

The Eurosystem was thus an important holder of GGBs when the PSI negotiations started. Whether the GGBs held by the Eurosystem would participate in the projected debt exchange significantly affected the level of the haircut to be proposed. The following considerations were important for the final decisions adopted. 13.24

i. Against participation in the Private Sector Involvement

Public nature of the ECB's portfolio The Eurosystem's portfolios of GGBs had been the result of its public basic mandate: monetary policy and price stability. Unlike private investors, GGBs among Eurosystem members were either the result of their admittance as eligible collateral or of the SMP market interventions. Private investors had made an investing decision balancing risks and profit; the ECB had acted in performance of its basic mandate, disregarding any lucrative consideration. 13.25

The Private Sector Involvement meant to address the private sector The proposal to carry out a debt exchange was termed 'private sector involvement' precisely to refer to the 'private sector'; until the PSI was agreed, only the public sector had supported Greece, by way of fiscal measures and the European funding mechanisms, and by the large Eurosystem support to the Greek banking system. The overall idea was that the 'private sector' had to share part of the financial burden; otherwise, European taxpayers would be financing private investors. If the Eurosystem had been drawn into the Greek PSI, the aim of the PSI would have been subverted, since the losses in the Eurosystem would have impacted upon the budget of euro area member states—that is, upon taxpayers. 13.26

Monetary financing considerations The monetary financing prohibition was an important consideration: the Eurosystem would be in breach of Article 123 TFEU if it were in any manner to cooperate with a mechanism that pumped central bank money into the purse of the Greek Treasury. Because Eurosystem GGBs had been acquired with central bank money, a haircut in favour of the issuer would have had the economic effect of a monetary financing in breach of the Treaty.[32] 13.27

---

[31] The SMP was fully explained in a speech made by ECB President Trichet in Vienna on 31 May 2010, available online at <http://www.ecb.europa.eu/press/key/speaker/pres/html/index.en.html>. *See* also the speech made by ECB President Jean-Claude Trichet on 20 May 2010, available online at <http://www.ecb.europa.eu/press/key/speaker/pres/html/index.en.html>, in which he said:

> Our present monetary policy stance is appropriate. Our decisions taken on 9 May have confirmed it. We are not engaging in any form of 'quantitative easing'. The 'Securities Markets Programme' is designed to ensure an effective functioning of the monetary policy transmission mechanism by helping to resolve a malfunctioning of some segments of the euro area debt securities markets. The liquidity provided through this programme is withdrawn in its entirety through tenders of term deposits.

[32] On 6 September 2012, the Governing Council of the ECB decided to put in place a new monetary policy instrument, aimed at allowing the ECB to correct the occasional malfunctioning of the sovereign debt market and the shortcomings of the Securities Market Programme (SMP), which would be terminated, by way of targeted market interventions on the sovereign bond market of countries under an EU/IMF programme.

13.28 **Consistency of stance** The ECB had been consistently and publicly opposed to the idea of a sovereign debt exchange in the EU; fundamental considerations of anchoring confidence in the world of finance required every sovereign to honour its signature. If a European sovereign were to fail to honour its commitments, the whole edifice based on trust would fall. The financial system is based on the existence of risk-free financial assets,[33] and sovereign bonds of developed economies had hitherto been such assets. These considerations led the Eurogroup to include in all public statements the mantra that the Greek PSI was an exceptional and unique case, and to remind European states to honour their signatures, and led also to the basic condition that any sovereign debt exchange would be 'voluntary'. Accepting the contribution of its important amount of GGBs to the proposed debt exchange was seen by the ECB as inconsistent with its previous and public stance against a PSI in Europe.

ii. In favour of participation in the exchange

13.29 **Bonds fungibility** The GGBs in Eurosystem portfolios were marketable bonds fungible with GGBs held by private investors, and therefore with same rights and conditions. An exemption to the Eurosystem would contradict such fundamental fungibility.

13.30 **No preferred creditor status** An exemption to the Eurosystem may be seen as a recognition of 'preferred creditor status' (PCS) with no legal basis. Such a status, not enshrined in hard law, is globally recognized for public sector loans from public lenders that precisely lend where the market is not able to lend (for example, at long-term, low interest rates, for non-profitable public infrastructures or social projects, in fragile political environments, etc.). International public financial institutions such as the IMF, regional development banks,[34] and the European rescue funds[35] are generally recognized as benefiting from PCS. Because of the monetary financing prohibition, the Eurosystem was not—and could not be—a lender to the Greek state, because it lends only to banks; thus it escaped the usual PCS perimeter.

This new instrument, named an 'outright market transaction' (OMT) was announced, together with the commitment by the ECB to 'accept the same (*pari passu*) treatment as private or other creditors with respect to bonds issued by euro area countries in accordance with the terms of such bonds'. This statement was meant to say that if bonds acquired under the OMT had have CACs, the Eurosystem would basically play under the same rules as other bondholders. However, other bondholders are not subject to the Treaty prohibition of monetary financing—so what to do in the unlikely case of another PSI case when a CAC is activated? Can the Eurosystem agree to negotiated haircuts? An answer could be that, if the vote of the Eurosystem were not necessary to achieve the supermajority needed to accept such a haircut, abstention would be a solution. If, on the contrary, the vote of the Eurosystem were necessary for such a supermajority, it is suggested that compliance with Article 123 would mean a duty to minimize the monetary financing effect of a debt haircut. Confronted with a possible debt default if haircuts are not agreed, the Eurosystem should aim at keeping the monetary financing effect to the minimum. If a default would entail a monetary financing effect of a bigger size, a negotiated haircut could mitigate it (e.g. Argentina's unilateral offer of 25 cents to the dollar in 2001, while perhaps an earlier negotiated haircut may have avoided it). Thus, in such a hypothetical situation, the duty of the Eurosystem under Article 123 of the Treaty would be to influence the CAC vote so as to minimize the haircut to the best possible extent, whilst achieving the objective of an eventual return of the member state—subject to EU/IMF conditionality—to the market.

[33] Since the demise of gold and silver as kind of risk-free assets. The successive Basel 'Accords' on capital adequacy have retained, until this day, the zero weighting of sovereign bond holdings for regulatory capital weighting purposes.

[34] At least six international financial institutions (IFIs) were identified as lenders to Greece: the IMF; the European Investment Bank (EIB); the European Bank for Reconstruction and Development (EBRD); the European Company for the Financing of Railroad Rolling Stock (Eurofima); the Black Sea Community Development Bank; and the Council of Europe Development Bank.

[35] The EFSF and ESM, but also lending by the Union under the 'solidarity' emergency budget (Art. 122(2) TFEU).

Subordination An exemption from the PSI would have negative market effects for other EMU states, because it could be perceived to have created a precedent case of 'subordination' of normal investors vis-à-vis Eurosystem portfolios, making future borrowings by sovereigns more expensive. 13.31

Jurisdictional limits A legal exemption of the Eurosystem Greek-law GGBs could not extend itself to the English-law GGBs held by the Eurosystem. English-law GGBs had been acquired in the secondary market or taken as collateral with the inbuilt CACs, whereby the ECB had, as any other bondholder, implicitly accepted the possibility of their activation. 13.32

The final decision by the ECB's Governing Council and the Eurogroup sought to balance all of these arguments. Both accepted a financially neutral exchange of the Eurosystem GGBs for equivalent GGBs, whereby the Governing Council agreed to earmark the profits arising from such GGBs' portfolios for their use by member states as compensation for a reduction of interest rates charged to Greece in the EFSF loans. 13.33

4. Legal Framework for Debt Issuance by States Participating in the European Monetary Union

The Greek sovereign crisis of 2010, the absence of a legal framework to deal with it, and the political decision not to allocate the whole burden of the rescue only to the taxpayers motivated the need to revisit the current framework for sovereign debt issuance of euro area member states, and the general introduction of CACs. 13.34

Collective action clauses—analysed elsewhere in this volume—had existed in the London bond market since 1879, as a civilized way in which to organize collective decision-making when there is a plurality of creditors, ensuring also that the collective interest dominates over private—often *insolidaire*—interests.[36] The CAC resurfaced as an outcome of the Argentinian crisis, when the IMF decided in 2002 to establish a 'G-10 Working Group on Contractual Clauses' aimed at recommending the use of CACs, for which the London practice served as a basis, to all international sovereign issuers.[37] 13.35

Some demands to link the use of such CACs by sovereign issuers to eligibility conditions to IMF funding did not prosper. But their introduction into issuances placed in the New York and European markets since 2003 was easily accepted by investors, who had seen the uncertainties and shortcomings of the Argentinian debt exchange process, as well as the damage done to a possible return to the market by Argentina out of the disruptive actions of holdout creditors. In 2003, the EU supported the use of CACs for international issuances,[38] as well 13.36

[36] *See* Lee Buchheit and G. Mitu Gulati, 'Sovereign Bonds and the Collective Will' (2002) 51 Emory LJ 1317.

[37] *See* IMF, *Collective Action Clauses: Recent Developments and Issues* (March 2013), available online at <http://www.imf.org/external/np/psi/2003/032503.htm>.

[38] A statement of the President of the Ecofin, April 2003, reads:

> The EU will use contractual provisions based on the framework developed by the G10, and where necessary in accordance with applicable law and adjusted to local practice, in their central government bonds issued under a foreign jurisdiction and/or governed by a foreign law by the end of this year.

as the IMF and World Bank.[39] Many European countries[40] have introduced CACs into their international issuances since 2002.

13.37 The G-10 refrained from recommending globally a fully harmonized CAC model. A group of trade associations produced, in February 2003, a set of model CACs for bonds issued in New York and London markets.[41] However, CACs are negotiated individually for every issuance, without a globally accepted prescribed set of terms; as a result, majorities needed for several decisions, aggregation clauses, disenfranchisement provisions, etc., show a relatively wide diversity. Some authors[42] opined that a certain diversity was tolerable, if the basic parameters were respected.

13.38 In 2010, a political decision was taken in the EU to create a framework whereby bondholders would have to support part of the costs of the restructuring of the public finances of the sovereign issuer. In May 2010, the member states of the euro area agreed to lend money to the Hellenic Republic in a collective effort to facilitate the adoption of fiscal austerity measures, the increase in tax collection, and the orderly privatization of part of the assets owned by the Hellenic Republic, plus a number of structural reforms aimed at putting the Greek public sector in a financially sustainable shape. And they simultaneously took the decision that, in principle, sovereign bondholders should bear a part of the costs.

13.39 In November 2010, the Eurogroup decided that 'standardised and identical Collective Action Clauses (CACs) will be included in the Terms and Conditions of all new euro area government bonds', as a way in which to ensure that, in the future, bondholder creditors of the euro area sovereigns should—in the unlikely event of another sovereign crisis in Europe—share the burden of the restructuring measures by accepting a rescheduling of their credits negotiated under a harmonized, generally agreed CAC system. In doing so, the political leaders of the euro area followed the Economic and Financial Affairs Council (Ecofin) statement of April 2003 imposing upon themselves the use of CACs. On 2 February 2012, the Treaty Establishing the ESM was signed by seventeen euro area member states, Article 12(3) of which states: 'Collective action clauses shall be included, as of 1 January 2013, in all new euro area government securities, with maturity above one year, in a way which ensures that their legal impact is identical.'

13.40 On 26 March 2012, the standardized CACs to be applied as of 1 January 2013 were made public by Ecofin.[43] Their content builds upon international practice, and therefore is conceptually aligned and broadly consistent with existing CACs, although it differs in a number of particular respects.[44] Since the CACs apply only as of 2013, for a time pre-existing

[39] *See* Communiqué of the International Monetary and Financial Committee (April 2003), available online at <http://www.imf.org/external/np/sec/pr/2013/pr13129.htm>, and the IMF Guidelines for Public Debt Management (March 2001), available online at <https://www.imf.org/external/np/mae/pdebt/2000/eng/index.htm>.

[40] Namely, Romania, Greece, Sweden, Austria, Cyprus, Estonia, Hungary, Italy, Lithuania, Poland, Slovakia, and the UK.

[41] *See*, e.g., the London model, available online at <http://www.icmagroup.org/assets/documents/310103%20Final%20Model%20Clauses%20and%20Code%20of%20Conduct.doc.PDF>.

[42] F. Elderson and M. Perassi, 'Collective Action Clauses in Sovereign Foreign Bonds: Towards a More Harmonised Approach' (2003) 2 Euredia 239.

[43] *See* Ecofin, 'Euro Area Model CAC 2012', available online at <http://europa.eu/efc/sub_committee/cac/cac_2012/index_en.htm>.

[44] *See* a legal assessment of variations vis-à-vis the CAC model hitherto used in the London market, available online at <http://www.linklaters.com/pdfs/mkt/london/A14950441_0_11_120508_CAC_client_memo_MND.pdf>.

sovereign bonds without CACs coexist with post-2013 bonds with the new CACs—and these coexist with English-law-governed bonds with different terms and conditions again. To meet the political requirement that 'the legal impact [of CACs] is identical', Ecofin[45] discussed and dismissed several options, as follows.

(a) *The use of a EU legal Act*—This road was not further pursued because no clear legal basis existed in the Treaty.
(b) *The incorporation of the model CACs as an Annex to the ESM Treaty*—This option suffered from a lack of flexibility in that it would freeze the CACs once and forever; any adaptation that might prove necessary in the future would require an amendment to the ESM Treaty. It was also improper to include in an international treaty a mandatory provision belonging to the contractual domain.
(c) *The separation of the CACs from the general terms and conditions of sovereign issuances, and submission of the CAC (not the overall issuance) to the law and jurisdiction of a single predetermined EU member state*—This private international law technique—known as *dépeçage*—would have provided a single legal system for the interpretation and enforcement of the CACs, irrespective of the sovereign issuer. Identical application of the CACs across Europe would have been achieved. However, it was not accepted on the ground that it was considered politically unacceptable for a sovereign to submit itself to the laws and jurisdiction of a foreign state in all of its debt sovereign issuances, both domestic and international.[46]

The euro area member states finally settled on the idea of formatting the CACs as a sufficiently elaborated and detailed 'common terms of reference' so as to ensure consistent application by all, but documented in an informal manner, available on the Commission's website; euro area member states would use such terms as a rule, but because of its lack of legal format, adaptations might be possible. Because, under this model, the CAC would be only a clause in the terms and conditions of each issuance, domestic or international, the CAC would be subject to the law and to the courts under which the issuance was made—albeit that this entails a risk that the application of the CACs might not be 'identical' everywhere. Such risk was, however, considered to be within an acceptable level, since the prospect of another case of rescheduling the sovereign debt of a EU member state was becoming remote as a result of reforms being introduced[47] in the euro area and because any judgment by a national court on the standardized CACs should, in all reasonable logic, take into account judgments of courts of justice located in other jurisdictions on the same kinds of clause. **13.41**

A substantial majority of bonds issued by European sovereigns are issued under the law of the issuer and subject to its domestic courts. Under the agreed CAC model, the same terms **13.42**

[45] The CACs were discussed in the Sub-Committee of EU Sovereign Debt Markets, reporting to Ecofin: *see* online at <http://europa.eu/efc/sub_committee/index_en.htm>.

[46] *See* Antonio Sáinz de Vicuña y Barroso, 'Identical Collective Action Clauses for Different Legal Systems: A European Model', in Klaus-Albert Bauer, Andreas Cahn, Patrick S. Kenadjian (eds) *Collective Action Clauses and the Restructuring of Sovereign Debt*, Institute for Law and Finance Series (Berlin: De Gruyter, 2013), 15–24.

[47] The start of a financially powerful and operationally flexible European Stability Mechanism (ESM), together with the enhanced governance of the fiscal discipline and of the macroeconomic convergence of euro area member states (the arrangements known as the 'six-pack', the 'two-pack', and the Treaty on Stability, Coordination and Governance, nicknamed the 'Fiscal Compact'), plus the plans agreed in the Summit and in the Euro Area Summits of June, September, October, and December 2012 for a Financial Union, a Fiscal Union, and an Economic Union.

apply to all euro area sovereigns, irrespective of whether issuances are subject to national law and domestic jurisdiction, or are international.

13.43 It is submitted that risks for investors are higher in the case of domestic issuances, since—in a major crisis—the sovereign may use its capacity to enact legislation to alter or amend the terms of its issuance unilaterally, including the inserted CACs,[48] and also because a domestic court may be subject to and may have to apply national laws that provide for procedural privileges to the sovereign, such as immunity from execution, or budgetary laws that delay or otherwise affect the enforcement of judgments—for example by requiring budgetary consent—or may in any other manner favour or protect the sovereign.

13.44 The credibility of CACs depends on the avoidance of the legislative arm of the sovereign using its power to change their terms or otherwise influence their application in any manner. The enforcement of the CACs should be outside the powers of the issuing sovereign. Would that be an ideal case for an international jurisdiction?

13.45 Article 37 of the ESM Treaty provides for the jurisdiction of the CJEU for disputes about the interpretation of the ESM Treaty; however, the *locus standi* for such jurisdiction is limited to the signatories to the ESM Treaty—that is, the euro area member states—and the ESM itself. That means that individual holders of sovereign bonds cannot sue the issuing sovereign in the CJEU, but only in the national court designated in the terms and conditions of such bonds. Whether such designated national court may seek a preliminary ruling from the European Court is to be answered in the negative, since:

- there is no provision for this in the ESM Treaty;
- the text of the CACs is located outside the ESM Treaty and thus is not part of it; and
- the interpretation of the CAC is related neither to the interpretation of the ESM Treaty nor to EU law.

13.46 The proposal that was suggested—and finally rejected—when the ESM Treaty was being discussed by Ecofin was to submit the CACs—only the CACs and not the other clauses of a sovereign debt issuance (that is, the *dépeçage* method)—to the arbitration of the Permanent Court of Arbitration (PCA) in The Hague.[49] That Court is a body established in 1899 under public international law, the statute of which provides for fact finding, arbitration, and conciliation in disputes involving various possible combinations of states, state entities, private parties, and international organizations. It has pre-established arbitration rules and a permanent Secretariat to administer them. It has a long track record of arbitrating disputes between bondholders and public issuers.[50] It has its seat in the Peace Palais of the International Court of Justice (ICJ) in The Hague, and it could provide a neutral forum for the interpretation of CACs in which biases in favour of the issuing sovereign could not be even conceived. The rejection of that idea came out of the desire to keep public debt under existing practices, where a national court is designated or implicit.[51]

---

48 On 23 February 2012, the Parliament of the Hellenic Republic adopted Law 4050/2012 on Amendment of Securities Issued or Guaranteed by the Greek Government by Consent of the Bondholders, which affected the public debt issued under Greek law and subject to Greek courts.

49 *See* online at <http://www.pca-cpa.org>.

50 *See* list available online at <http://www.pca-cpa.org/showpage.asp?pag_id=1029>.

51 The allegation was even made by an EU member state that submission of the sovereign issuer to international arbitration was unconstitutional.

5. Idea of Establishing a Statutory Framework for Debt Restructuring within a Regional Monetary Union

In line with the evolution of debt recovery in the case of private debtors, it is submitted 13.47 that the day will come on which proper insolvency procedures for sovereigns will exist. Painful negotiations under CACs and litigation by dissatisfied creditors will be replaced by a pre-established mechanism that will organize in a neutral manner the workouts of states in financial difficulty. The image of speculative holdout bondholders (the so-called 'vulture funds') escaping sensible rescheduling proposals and trying to seize assets of the sovereign all around the globe should never be repeated; these are reminiscent of times of wilderness—of a hunting spirit rather than protecting the common good. The IMF tried a statutory approach in 2002–03 with its Sovereign Debt Restructuring Mechanism (SDRM).[52] Regrettably, the proposal did not obtain enough support within the IMF. It would have made a difference when the Greek sovereign workouts were addressed in 2010, by offering legal certainty, and ensuring that backdoor manoeuvring and intransparent tactical games were avoided. The current sovereign crisis in Europe has triggered renewed initiatives for such pre-established arrangements.[53] The final destination in this domain is without doubt a permanent procedural and institutional system to minimize damages, to ensure fairness of treatment, and to protect the general interest.

In the context of EMU, a statutory system for sovereign debt workouts can be built upon the 13.48 already-existing institutional set-up with a Court of Justice, an independent Commission, a powerful ESM as possible financier of fiscal consolidation, and the expert advice of the ECB (in particular because of the impact of such crises on banking systems). The European Council and Parliament, as EU legislators, may establish the legal framework; otherwise, a revision of the ESM Treaty may include such a framework.[54] The necessary elements to be included in this framework are:

(a) an orderly procedure, from start to end;
(b) the capacity to stay any creditor's proceedings against the sovereign and to join all individual claims into the general proceedings;
(c) the perimeter of what is a sovereign debt (only the state, or the public sector);
(d) the amount and classes of sovereign debt;
(e) the list of creditors;

---

[52] *See* n. 7.

[53] *See* <http://www.iir-hu.de/en/veranstaltungen/tagungen/intl-conference-legal-procedure/>; B. Weder di Mauro and J. Zettelmeyer, 'European Debt Restructuring Mechanism as a Tool for Crisis Prevention', *Vox*, 26 Novermber 2010, available online at <http://www.voxeu.org/article/european-debt-restructuring-mechanism-tool-crisis-prevention>; F. Gianviti, A. O. Krueger, J. Pisani-Ferry, A. Sapir, and J. von Hagen, *A European Mechanism for Sovereign Debt Restructuring: A Proposal* (October 2010), available online at <http://www.indiana.edu/~econdept/workshops/Fall_2010_Papers/EMSDR_191010.pdf>. The establishment in 2010 by the International Law Association (ILA) of a Sovereign Insolvency Study Group aimed at proposing improvements to the insufficient legal framework for sovereign debt workouts.

[54] This is the proposal of Lee C. Buchheit, G. Mitu Gulati, and Ignacio Tirado, *The Problem of Holdout Creditors in Eurozone Sovereign Debt Restructurings* (January 2013), available online at <http://papers.ssrn.com/sol3/papers.cfm?abstract_id=2205704>.

(f) the ranking and preference of creditors (for example bondholders, lenders, private or official, etc.), making legally clear some as yet unclear concepts such as *pari passu*,[55] PCS,[56] etc.;
(g) voting and majorities for the rescheduling;
(h) the universal binding effect of agreements;
(i) the terms of the immunity of the state from holdout creditors' actions; and
(j) the exclusive jurisdiction of the Court to decide on claims against the sovereign.

13.49 Clearly, until the current financial crisis is over, any initiative to put in place a statutory regime in Europe for sovereign debt workouts is to be kept on hold. Markets may receive any news in that direction as a premonition of future renegotiation exercises, in spite of European leaders expressing loudly and clearly the message that the Greek case is 'unique and exceptional' and will never be repeated. The more recent troubles of Cyprus demonstrate the hard reality that the crisis is not yet over, although clearly the mechanisms are now in place to navigate through the waves created by economic imbalances. This is why an immediate new and clear institutional and legal architecture for sovereign debt restructuring would be premature and counter-productive; only when the situation is calmer and sounder could such reforms go ahead.

6. Conclusions

13.50 The sovereign debt crisis of a country sharing a currency in a regional monetary union has peculiarities that need to be taken into account and which differentiate the treatment of a sovereign debt restructuring in such a setting from the general debt workouts of countries that issue their own currencies. The absence of powers to devalue, to use internal inflation, and to establish exchange controls, and (at least in the European case) the prohibition on bailouts by other states, on the use of the 'monetary financing' tool, or on exiting the currency union do considerably complicate the solution to such a crisis.

13.51 In particular, the role of the central bank of the regional monetary union as liquidity provider to the banking system in the context of a debt restructuring raises two question:

- can it take sovereign bonds from a state undergoing a restructuring as collateral; and
- if the central bank holds sovereign bonds in its portfolio, arising from its statutory duties, does it benefit from PCS?

This chapter has described the experience of the Eurosystem in the case of the Greek sovereign bond renegotiations.

[55] The concept of *pari passu* is still unclear and controversial. For some, it means the duty to distribute any debtor payment equally among all creditors of the same ranking (*NML v. Argentina* 699 F.3d 246 (2d Cir. 2012)), while for others it refers only to an obligation not to subordinate *ex post* a certain class of creditor (*see* the very authoritative paper on this issue dated 1 March 2005 from the Financial Markets Law Committee of the Bank of England, available online at <http://www.fmlc.org/Pages/papers.aspx>; *see* also Lee Bucheit's seminal article 'The *Pari Passu* Clause *sub Specie Aeternitatis*' (1991) 10 Int'l Fin L Rev 11, and his later 'The *Pari Passu* Clause in Sovereign Debt Instruments' (2004) 53 Emory LJ 763).

[56] The concept of PCS is clear on its substance—a superior ranking vis-à-vis other creditors—but unclear in its remit; public sector institutions as creditors tend to be included in the concept, but the contours of such preference on whom and of which quality are undefined.

Finally, the question is raised whether the manner of addressing sovereign debt workouts merits normative improvement. The general introduction of CACs in sovereign bonds, following the English model and after Argentina's difficult experience, is a good step forward. As of January 2013, CACs are a general feature of bonds issued by euro area member states. The Greek experience of an ad hoc law introducing a CAC on Greek-law-governed bonds showed the need to have that instrument generally available as a matter of course, irrespective of the Greek PSI being *unique and exceptional*, never to be repeated in Europe. But, overall, what is still missing in our global financial market is a set of clear rules on sovereign debt rescheduling. The IMF proposal in 2003 to have a statutory system for such workouts is a good starting point. When the current financial crisis is over, Europe once more might offer an example to the world by organizing such a system. Entering into such discussions during the course of the ongoing crisis, however, may raise market concerns and deteriorate the 'reflective nature and academic atmosphere' that should govern the preparation of this missing piece of global financial architecture. **13.52**

14

RESTRUCTURING IN A MONETARY UNION

Economic Aspects

Daniel Gros

1. Introduction

Sovereign debt management does not take place in an ideal world. It is determined to a large extent by the structure of the financial system and the economic fundamentals of the country concerned. The economics and politics of any restructuring of sovereign debt also depend on these factors, and particularly on who holds the debt at the time it is to be restructured. **14.01**

It matters greatly whether the debt is held by foreigners or residents. In principle, all domestic residents are subject to the full taxing powers of the national government. **14.02**

The only restraints on the domestic taxation power of the sovereign are provided by international treaties and, in Europe, by European Union (EU) rules, but neither provides much protection when the sovereign is in difficulties. This implies that, in principle, a government could always find ways in which to expropriate domestic bondholders. **14.03**

Domestic debt (debt owed to residents) is more rarely restructured. This has both economic and political reasons. **14.04**

From an economic point of view, restructuring domestically held debt does not increase the resources available for the country as a whole: what the government gains is lost by the private sector. This becomes apparent when the debt is held by the domestic banking system, which usually has a very low loss-absorption capacity. This could also be observed in the case of Greece, where formally the domestic banking system had to accept losses in the public sector involvement (PSI) operation, but then had to be recapitalized immediately. **14.05**

From a political point of view, restructuring foreign-held debt is also easier because foreign residents do not vote, whereas foreign creditors always provide a convenient target for populist parties. **14.06**

An exception to the rule that foreign debt is a more attractive target for restructuring is that debt owed to foreign official institutions is (openly) restructured even more rarely than domestic debt. The claims of the International Monetary Fund (IMF) are regarded traditionally as 'super senior'. But even the bonds bought by the European Central Bank (ECB) on the open market were de facto exempted from the Greek PSI operation, although *ex ante* one could have argued that the ECB should not be treated differently from any private sector investor. This exceptional treatment of foreign official credits was justified by the fact that **14.07** it was mostly provided when the country was already in a crisis. But official creditors could be treated as 'super senior' also because they usually accounted only for a small part of the overall debt. This is no longer the case for Greece, whose remaining debt is overwhelmingly owed to official creditors.

14.08 These background conditions regarding the structure of debt holdings determine when and how a sovereign restructures its debt. The legal framework tends to adapt to these background conditions, and in particular to the key role of sovereign debt in financial markets. This is particularly true of the euro area, where the balance sheets of banks tend to be linked to the sovereign, so that if one is restructured, the other has to be restructured too (or be bailed out).

14.09 This chapter discusses the economic aspects of sovereign debt restructuring by first showing how economic and monetary union (EMU) changes the usual concordance between foreign debt and foreign currency debt. The second section then shows how financial market integration should lead to most sovereign debt being held abroad. The third section presents a concrete proposal for how the euro area's financial system could be made more resilient to a sovereign restructuring. The chapter ends with a conclusion.

2. Sovereign Debt in a Monetary Union

14.10 Sovereign debt issued in a monetary union creates particular challenges that result from the fact that the usual distinction between domestic and foreign currency debt no longer applies.

14.11 The 'normal' case in so-called 'advanced' countries was that of a government issuing its debt in the currency of the country and selling it mainly to residents. Under these conditions, a restructuring is extremely rare, because the government would have to default on its own voters and because inflation represents a softer way in which to reduce the debt-service burden.

14.12 The other extreme used to be the case for 'less developed' countries with insufficient domestic savings, where the government had to issue debt in a foreign currency to be able to sell it to foreigners. Under these conditions, restructuring becomes rather more likely, because it is the only way in which to alleviate an excessive debt burden and because it expropriates the assets of foreigners who cannot vote.

14.13 However, within a monetary union, the usual equations—Domestic debt = Domestic currency debt = Inflation risk and Foreign debt = Foreign currency debt = Default risk—no longer apply.

14.14 Moody's argues that, in a world without capital controls, it no longer makes sense to rate domestic currency and foreign currency debt separately. But it also notes, in the context of foreign-currency government debt, that: 'One of the hallmarks of sovereign default is a high proportion of foreign-currency-denominated debt. On average, the foreign-currency government debt ratio was 75.9% for the 20 sovereigns covered in our 2010 sovereign default study.'[1]

[1] Moody's analysis is historical in nature, describing the phenomenon as reflecting:

> ... the original sin phenomenon, wherein a sovereign must rely on external creditors because its domestic capital market is too shallow to borrow in foreign currency because its domestic currency is not convertible. Moreover, macroeconomic or balance-of-payments shocks, or both, can lead to a currency crisis and large depreciation, which increase both the debt-servicing costs and debt burden of a sovereign in local currency terms.

Under EMU, a formerly rare 'asymmetric' case becomes more common. Under a fiat currency standard, it is rare that the sovereign issues foreign currency debt to its own residents. This used to be the case only in countries in which the trust in the domestic currency has been completely destroyed. However, this now becomes the normal case in the euro area when residents buy the debt of their own governments. **14.15**

There is no need to consider the even rarer case in which domestic currency debt is held by foreign residents. This is the case on a large scale only for the United States, which has the 'exorbitant privilege' of being able to indebt itself massively to foreigners in its own currency. The euro is also an important reserve currency, but this does not provide any individual euro area sovereign with a similar 'privilege', because no single euro area sovereign can control the value of the euro. **14.16**

Given the importance of both the currency and the nature of the creditor, it is useful to consider both aspects separately, as is done in Table 14.1. **14.17**

It is apparent that debt in the domestic currency is subject much more to inflation risk than default risk because a government can never be forced to default formally on its debt as long as it controls the printing press. By contrast, a government might be forced to default on foreign currency debt, for example if it cannot roll over large repayments coming due. The risk for bondholders thus changes from inflation risk to default risk when the sovereign no longer controls the currency of its debt. This is exactly what happened with the start of EMU: no individual member country can control the ECB, which is actually forbidden to provide 'monetary financing' to any government and even the EU institutions. **14.18**

In theory, it might not matter whether the purchasing power that an investor can obtain from an investment in government debt is reduced by inflation or an outright default. But in reality the switch from inflation risk to default risk matters greatly. First of all, the nature of the risk is different. Inflation eats away the real value under most circumstances in a gradual manner, whereas a default has a much more abrupt impact. In the extreme, it is 'all or nothing' (that is, no default or close to nothing when a default materializes, given that the recovery rates in sovereign defaults tend to be low). A second reason why inflation risk is different is that it tends to be less disruptive for financial markets, which normally operate in nominal terms.[2] **14.19**

Table 14.1 Domestic and foreign currency debt: a taxonomy

		Does the sovereign control the currency?	
		Yes => Inflation risk	No=> Default risk
Is debt owed to subjects under control of the sovereign?	Yes => Default zero sum game for country	'Normal' case: Domestic-currency debt held by residents	Foreign-currency debt held by residents
	No => Default alleviates burden on country	US exorbitant privilege: Domestic-currency debt held by foreigners	EMU (or emerging market debt): Foreign-currency debt held by foreigners

[2] Inflation-indexed debt is widely available, but has never become dominant except in times of high and persistent inflation.

14.20 Another part of the reality that determines policy in the euro area is that some individual member countries alone account for a sizeable fraction of the euro area's economy, while at the same time the federal level does not dispose of any significant fiscal resources. This distinguishes the euro area from the United States, where the federal level has the largest budget and no individual state is large enough to represent a systemic risk for the entire area.

3. Who Holds Sovereign Debt in Europe?

14.21 Within a fully integrated monetary union, one would expect sovereign debt to be dispersed throughout the common currency area, with investors everywhere allocating similar shares to different countries. For small euro area member countries, this would imply that almost all public debt is held abroad—even if one neglects euro debt holdings abroad.[3] For example, for a country such as Greece, Ireland, or Portugal, each of which account for less than 5 per cent of the euro area's debt markets, one would expect 95 per cent of all debt to be held outside the country if there were absolutely no home bias. Even for the largest euro area country, Germany, which accounts for less than 30 per cent of the eurozone economy (and a similar share of its public debt given that the German debt-to gross-domestic-product (GDP) ratio is not far from the average), 70 per cent of public debt should be held abroad if there were no home bias.

14.22 This implies that one would expect that most euro area countries should fall in the cell in the lower right-hand side of the matrix in Table 14.1, which represents the highest default risk: de facto foreign currency debt held by foreign residents.

14.23 Over the first ten years of EMU, the trend was indeed in this direction, with the proportion of government debt held abroad rising significantly for all countries, as shown for the larger euro area member countries in Table 14.2. Before EMU, most public debt was held domestically, with the share of domestic investors amounting in most cases to about three-quarters of the total. During the first decade of EMU, the proportion held by foreign residents increased steadily as the introduction of the euro fostered financial market integration (and the temporary illusion that all euro area government debt was in the same class). By 2008–09, the proportion held abroad had more than doubled, reaching two-thirds in the case of Greece. With the onset of the crisis, the home bias has increased again, with foreign holdings falling from 50 per cent to 40 per cent of the total for Italy, and even more in the case of Spain where, by the end of 2012, non-residents held only 29 per cent of the total—not much more than when Spain still had the peseta. There are a number of reasons for this return of the 'home bias'. First of all, financial institutions face different incentives: in the countries with high risk premia, financial institutions had an incentive to invest in high-yielding domestic government debt because this offset, at least partially, their higher refinancing costs and nobody could be held responsible for not foreseeing the default of its own government. Moreover, governments naturally encouraged this tendency of their own banks to support the market for their own debt.

[3] From the point of view of any individual euro area country, it does not matter whether the rest of the world also perceives euro area public debt to be fully fungible.

Table 14.2 Share of total public debt held by non-residents (%)

	Pre-EMU (1997)	Peak (2008–09)	2012
Germany	25	No peak	58
France	17	62	55
Italy	20	50	40
Spain	25	51	29
Greece	25	67	n/a

Source: BRUEGEL dataset (December 2012)

By contrast, the share of German public debt held abroad has continued to increase even after the onset of the crisis, probably mainly owing to holders from third countries—often, central banks that did not want to take any risk with their euro foreign exchange reserves. **14.24**

Another important factor in any restructuring is whether the debt holders are able to support any losses. When a large proportion of sovereign debt is held by leveraged financial institutions, a restructuring becomes a danger for financial stability. Unfortunately, this proved to be the Achilles heel for the euro area recently, as the proportion held by financial institutions seems to be very large. **14.25**

The ECB reports the euro area averages for 2011: about a quarter of government debt was held by resident banks;[4] another 12 per cent by other resident financial institutions (mostly insurance companies); only 8 per cent by non-financial residents (including households); and over 50 per cent by non-residents (most within the euro area itself). One has to assume that, among non-residents, the share held by financial institutions is at least as large as among domestic holdings. This implies that only less than a fifth of total sovereign debt is held by non-financial holders—which are presumably those most capable of absorbing losses. **14.26**

Compared to the very large balance sheets of the banking sector in the eurozone (total assets are three times larger than GDP), holdings of government debt are not that large. Holdings of government debt now account on average for about 6 per cent of the total assets of the euro area banking system, and this ratio is actually somewhat lower than ten years ago. **14.27**

This shows that it is not so much the absolute amount of government debt held by banks, but the risk in relation to their very limited capacity to absorb losses as measured by their capital, which is about the same order of magnitude as their government debt holdings, given that banks have to hold capital equal to about 6–8 per cent of their (risk-weighted) assets. **14.28**

However, it is unlikely that all euro area governments would restructure their debt simultaneously and therefore the real risk is the concentration of banks' holdings on their own governments. In some countries, bank holdings of their own government's debt is equivalent to two or three times the capital of the banking system. This implies that any restructuring would immediately make the domestic banking system insolvent. **14.29**

[4] The real exposure of banks to a sovereign cannot be measured only by looking at holdings of government securities, since a significant part of these holdings is often covered by credit default swap (CDS) protection.

4. Strengthening Financial Market Resilience

14.30 Banks occupy a special position in financial markets. Especially in the euro area, they intermediate most savings, but they also provide public services like the payment system. Thus the stability of the banking system is, and will remain, an overriding policy objective in Europe.

14.31 This implies that the large amount of government debt on banks' balance sheets complicates any restructuring of sovereign debt.[5]

14.32 Why do euro area banks hold so much government debt? A large part of the answer is that they are encouraged by regulation to do so.[6] Under the internationally agreed Basel capital rules, banks do not have to hold any capital against claims on their own government that are *in their own currency* because the own government's debt is regarded as riskless. The rationale for zero-risk weights under normal conditions is clear: when the country has its own currency, the government can, in extremis, always order the central bank to print enough money to be able to service its debt. This might create inflation, but in nominal terms government debt should thus be riskless.

14.33 However, no national government can command the printing press in the euro area. The ECB is actually forbidden to provide monetary financing to any government, or even to the EU authorities. When monetary and fiscal authorities are distinct, default risk on sovereign debt is not zero because debt denominated in euro constitutes de facto 'foreign currency' debt.

14.34 This was recognized by economists at the start of EMU, but at the time a sovereign insolvency was considered by the EU authorities (and member states) to be out of the question. In the EU legislation that translated the Basel rules into EU law, it was thus stipulated that any debt issued by a member state and 'denominated and funded in the domestic currency' of that state should be regarded as riskless. Annex VI to the EU Directive on the 'taking up and pursuit of the business of credit institutions' recites:

> **1.2 Exposures in the national currency of the borrower**
> 4. Exposures to Member States' central governments and central banks denominated and funded in the domestic currency of that central government and central bank shall be assigned a risk weight of 0%.[7]

14.35 This was the case even before EMU. The legal fiction employed when the euro was introduced was simply to argue that, from a legal point of view, the euro became the domestic currency of all participating member states in EMU. The economic reality was (and remains), of course, the opposite, in the sense that the euro is not under the control of any individual member state—but the legal fiction was attractive because it provided member states with cheaper access to funding.

---

[5] In principle, the same considerations should apply to other financial intermediaries. But no other important class of intermediary is subject to runs like banks. In particular, insurance companies, which also hold large amounts of government debt, do not pose the same immediate risks of systemic crisis, since their clients are locked into long-term contracts.

[6] Another reason is that governments have not tried to sell their obligations directly to households.

[7] The 2006 recast of the Directive is available online at <http://eur-lex.europa.eu/LexUriServ/LexUriServ.do?uri=OJ:L:2006:177:0001:0200:en:PDF>.

The experience of the eurozone clearly illustrates the implications of this economic reality. A first corollary is that 'runs' on government debt become possible within the euro area because a large part of government debt usually has to be refinanced within rather short periods, whereas the key asset of the government—namely, the power to levy taxes—represents a rather long-term asset. As argued by Kopf[8] and de Grauwe,[9] this implies that even a solvent government could run out of funds and thus be forced into insolvency if it cannot refinance itself in the market. This cannot happen in a country with its own currency because the national central bank could always step in and provide the government with liquidity. Within the euro area, the ECB is not allowed to do so.[10] **14.36**

A second, related implication is naturally that any national government can become formally insolvent because it can no longer force the national central bank to finance its deficits and inflate the debt away if the political cost of servicing the debt through taxes (or lower expenditure) becomes too large. **14.37**

The case of Greece is instructive in this respect: If the debt of the Greek government had been denominated in the drachma, the outcome of the crisis would most probably have been quite different: the drachma would have devalued massively and inflation would over time have eroded the real value of the government debt.[11] Moreover, if Greece had not been in the eurozone, most of its public debt would probably have been held by domestic institutions. The fallout from its problems on the euro area would have been quite limited. **14.38**

Greece did avoid a formal government default, but the reduction of Greek sovereign debt that was finally agreed 'voluntarily' in early 2012 shows that private investors, including banks, can experience heavy losses on sovereign debt. A presumption of zero risk weights goes against the facts. **14.39**

It is also clear that the euro area's political authorities themselves do not expect that Greece will remain forever a 'special and unique' case, as it was called in the Conclusions of the European Council of 23–24 June 2011. That private investors in public debt might again make losses has been effectively announced in the constitution of the euro area's rescue mechanism. Article 12(2) of the Treaty establishing the European Stabilization Mechanism (ESM) requires that, under certain circumstances, private creditors should be involved in providing relief to sovereigns whose debt levels have become unsustainable. Given the Greek precedent and this legal norm, the credit risk of sovereign debt cannot be said to be zero. The regulatory framework for banks must be consistent with other legal norms and this requires that this credit risk be taken into account in the determination of capital requirements for banks. **14.40**

---

[8] *See* Christian Kopf, *Restoring Financial Stability in the Euro Area*, CEPS Policy Brief, (March 2011), available online at <http://www.ceps.eu/book/restoring-financial-stability-euro-area>.

[9] Paul De Grauwe, *Governance of a Fragile Eurozone*, CEPS Working Document (May 2011), available online at <http://www.ceps.eu/book/governance-fragile-eurozone>.

[10] In reality, the ECB has actually been providing assistance to governments under its Securities Market Programme (SMP), under which it first bought government bonds of Greece, Portugal, and Ireland, and later those of Italy and Spain. The SMP has now been stopped, but the outright monetary transactions (OMT) programme announced in September 2012 amounts in essence to the same.

[11] One would, of course, also expect that the Greek government would not have been able to accumulate the same amount of public debt under the drachma. Interest rates might have increased much earlier, forcing the government to rein in its deficit much earlier.

14.41 But what should be the basis for determining capital requirements for sovereign debt? Any risk weights (which would probably have to be introduced after the crisis has at least somewhat abated) should be based on 'objective' criteria, rather than ratings.

14.42 Experience has shown that ratings tend to follow market developments and that the ratings methodology is not well suited to anticipate problems.

14.43 In concrete terms, this could take the following form: the risk weights on government debt (in euro) could be set as a function of objective factors (debt/deficit), instead of ratings. For example, the risk weight could remain at zero if the debt remains below 60 per cent of GDP and the deficit remains consistent with the target of the Fiscal Compact—namely, a structural deficit of no more than about one half of 1 per cent of GDP. But the capital requirement would increase by 2 percentage points for each point by which the debt ratio exceeds the 'reference' value of the Treaty. The capital requirement could also be increased (in percentage point terms) by a multiple of the times the deficit (as a percentage of GDP) exceeds the target value set in the Fiscal Compact. This would give countries with debt ratios far exceeding the 60 per cent of GDP level a strong incentive to reduce debt as quickly as possible.

14.44 In addition, the risk weights should be linked to the stages of the excessive deficit procedure (for example, if the procedure is launched, the risk weight is increased by 50 percentage points). For each additional stage, the excessive deficit procedure is ratcheted up; the risk weighting would be automatically increased further. This would provide the prohibition of excessive deficits with real teeth even without the need to impose fines.

14.45 Moreover, government securities provide collateral when banks are borrowing from the ECB. The ECB should also apply these objective criteria in determining the haircuts it applies, instead of the ratings categories that it now uses.

14.46 Introducing positive risk weights for government debt will not be enough to prevent crisis because of the 'lumpiness' of sovereign risk. Experience has shown that sovereign defaults are rare events—but the losses are typically very large (more than 50 per cent) when default does materialize. Even with a risk weight of 100 per cent, banks would have capital to cover losses of only 8 per cent. Risk weights would thus have to become extremely high before they could protect banks against realistic scenarios.[12] This suggests that the more important aspect is *diversification*.

14.47 All regulated investors (banks, insurance companies, investment funds, pension funds) have rules that limit their exposure to any single counterparty to a fraction of their total investment or capital (for banks). Under the European Union's 'large exposure' rule, banks cannot lend more than 25 per cent of their own capital to any one borrower, but this limit does not apply to sovereign debt (especially within the eurozone for banks).[13] The result of this lack

[12] In the language of bankers, the 'loss given default' (LGD) tends to be large.

[13] This exemption from the exposure limits has its 'internal' logic if one considers public debt (issued in the 'domestic' currency of the issuer government) as riskless. This is also the way in which it is formulated in the so-called 'large exposure rules'. Article 113 of the Capital Adequacy Directive recites:

> 3. The following exposures shall be exempted from the application of Article 111(1):
> (a) asset items constituting claims on central governments or central banks which, unsecured, would be assigned a 0% risk weight under Articles 78 to 83.

See <http://eur-lex.europa.eu/LexUriServ/LexUriServ.do?uri=CONSLEG:2006L0048:20100330:EN:PDF>.

of exposure limits has been that banks in the periphery have too much debt of their own governments on their balance sheets, which has led to the deadly feedback loop between sovereigns and banks: any restructuring of sovereign debt would bankrupt the domestic banking system.

Another indirect advantage of introducing exposure limits on sovereign debt holdings is that northern European investors, which typically cannot avoid government debt (such as investment funds and life insurance companies), have also concentrated their holdings nationally, leading to the fall in government bond yields not only in Germany, but also throughout northern Europe and in some cases even to negative yields. Today, this might appear a prudent strategy, but this situation increases the vulnerability of the system to any reversal of fortunes. Moreover, if northern investors were required to diversify their holdings, there would be a natural demand for southern European bonds. **14.48**

Introducing exposure limits now (during a crisis period) is much less pro-cyclical than introducing capital requirements. The simplest way in which to smooth the transition would be to grandfather the existing stocks, but to apply exposure limits to new investments in government bonds. **14.49**

A concrete way in which to ensure risk diversification would be to eliminate the exemption for sovereign debt under the so-called 'Large Exposure Directive'. Banks could then not hold more than 25 per cent of their capital in government bonds of any single sovereign (to be applied during a transition period only to flows). **14.50**

Even if the zero risk weights for sovereign debt are abandoned and diversification limits are imposed, some preference for sovereign as opposed to private debts will persist because sovereign debt securities tend to be more liquid than private debt securities. This greater liquidity of sovereign debt is a natural consequence of the fact that most euro area sovereigns have a larger volume of securities outstanding than any corporation. Because banking regulation will require banks to hold a larger proportion of liquid assets, they might still have relatively large amounts of government debt on their balance sheets. However, the definition of liquid assets should not be made by category (that is, all public debt is liquid), but by effective level of liquidity as measured by bid–ask spreads and the amounts actually exchanged under normal conditions. Here, again, the existing proposals for the implementation of the so-called 'net stable funding' ratio are likely to be deficient because they classify public debt as liquid, thus de facto mandating a large share of public debt to be held by banks instead of concentrating on their effective degree of liquidity. **14.51**

5. Concluding Remarks

Two factors make a sovereign restructuring more likely: if the debt is in foreign currency and if it is owed to foreigners. The first is definitely the case in the euro area, because no individual country prints euros. The second was the case at the start of the crisis because, during the first decade of EMU, debt holdings had become more dispersed. There has been a partial increase in the home bias since then, but in the long run one would expect diversification to lead again to large cross-border holdings. **14.52**

Unfortunately, the euro area's financial system is also vulnerable to any restructuring, given the large holdings of government debt by banks that have a small capital base. The official **14.53** policy line is to make future restructuring as unlikely as possible by imposing strict limits on government deficits. It remains to be seen whether this goal will be reached given that debt levels are still hovering close to 100 per cent of GDP in many countries and growth prospects remain dim.

14.54 It is thus important to make the financial system more resilient. This chapter has shown that this could be done by recognizing that government debt is no longer riskless in a monetary union and by forcing banks to diversify their holdings so that a restructuring no longer represents a danger to the stability of the system as a whole.

15

SOVEREIGN DEBT AND BANKING CRISES

An 'Arial View'

Anna Gelpern[1]

1. Introduction: Font Matters

It has been a distinctive, yet unremarked-upon, pattern: each time European officials unveil bold new measures to end the Crisis, a few draft pages in Arial 12pt font appear on the Social Science Research Network (SSRN) website. Within hours, the draft is downloaded thousands of times, sending ripples across the blogosphere before lodging in a pink paper column and in the side of said officials. The authors, Lee Buchheit and Mitu Gulati, make roughly the same argument each time: policymakers have three to five options to solve the problem before them. One of these does more harm than good. Coincidentally, it is the chosen one. The draft then charts a path out of the hole. Sometimes, the officials take the path—eventually;[2] at other times, they keep digging. **15.01**

Buchheit and Gulati's latest intervention followed the launch of a programme for Cyprus.[3] The Cypriot banking system was eight times the size of the island's economy and tottering on the brink from exposure to Greece. As a condition of financing the government, Europe insisted that bank depositors pay a burden-sharing 'tax'. The tax would contain the crisis in the banking sector and spare the holders of government bonds. The announcement would showcase Europe's commitment to sharing losses with private creditors, and to breaking the bond between banks and national governments. **15.02**

It took three pages in Lee Buchheit's trademark font to demolish the plan and lay out an alternative. What came to be called 'the botched Cyprus bailout' was doomed from the start: after paying the deposit tax, people would have pulled the rest of their savings, brought down the banking system, and forced the government to intervene on a much larger scale. **15.03**

---

[1] The author is grateful to the many colleagues who have commented on early versions of this chapter, to the editors of this volume and to Will Chamberlain for valuable research assistance. Portions of this contribution have appeared in the Foreign Policy Association (FPA) *Great Decisions* in 2011 and on CreditSlips.org.

[2] *See*, e.g., Jeromin Zettelmeyer, Christoph Trebech, and G. Mitu Gulati, *The Greek Debt Exchange: An Autopsy*, Peterson Institute for International Economics Working Paper No. 2013/13/8 (August 2013), available online at <http://papers.ssrn.com/sol3/papers.cfm?abstract_id=2144932>, 33; Lee C. Buchheit and G. Mitu Gulati, *How to Restructure Greek Debt*, Working Paper (May 2010), available online at <http://papers.ssrn.com/sol3/papers.cfm?abstract_id=1603304>, 7–10.

[3] *See* Lee C. Buchheit and G. Mitu Gulati, *Walking Back from Cyprus*, Working Paper (March 2013), available online at <http://papers.ssrn.com/sol3/papers.cfm?abstract_id=2235359>.

Buchheit and Gulati instead proposed to extend uninsured deposits over €100,000 into five- and ten-year certificates of deposit, and to reschedule €8.2 billion in government debt. This combination would have filled more than half of the programme financing gap without touching the insured depositors.

15.04 Their prescription flowed from the insight that governments and financial systems are communicating vessels: strength or weakness in one flows to the other, and back. This chapter elaborates the implications of this insight and considers the bank–government link in recent financial crises. It is far from unique to Europe, although it does not always result in feedback effects, or the 'doom loop' that has made headlines of late. As capital movements have become more rapid and global, the abiding connection between banks and governments has turned more destructive. The policy goal is to reduce the risk of destruction and harness the connection in the name of financial stability. In conclusion, this chapter suggests several avenues for policy reform and further research.

2. Far from Europe

15.05 On 27 January 2011, Standard & Poor's (S&P) downgraded Japan's government debt, which then stood at nearly double the size of the Japanese economy.[4] The prime minister apparently learned about the downgrade from a foreign journalist. His flub instantly became iconic—but it was also overblown: the downgrade had little meaning for most of Japan's creditors. For regulated domestic financial institutions, holding almost 70 per cent of Japanese government bonds, for government pension funds, and for the Japanese central bank, there were few practical consequences from the S&P pronouncement. At the extreme, the value of the debt to these creditors was a function of regulatory say-so, and their prospects of repayment, a function of domestic politics. Only foreigners, holding just over 5 per cent, might have had reason to listen to S&P.[5]

15.06 This anecdote is at once happy, sad, and symptomatic of an old relationship at the heart of modern finance. It is about banks and governments, which are both inseparable and doomed to bring each other down. On the bright side, they are each other's indispensable safety net; on the dark side, government debt default can ravage financial systems and banking crises can bring down governments.

15.07 Until recently, bank and government debt problems were seen as related, but distinct. Banking crises were bad for the economy and hence for public finances.[6] Rulers running short on funds have turned to banks since time immemorial, which did not imply the death of regulated institutions, nor the start of a self-destructive spiral. Bank and government debt

[4] Standard & Poor's, 'Japan (Unsolicited Rating)', 2 April 2011 (indicating the 27 January 2011 credit rating downgrade to AA–); *see* IMF, *Japan: Staff Report for the 2010 Article IV Consultation*, IMF Country Report No. 10/211 (July 2010), available online at <http://www.imf.org/external/pubs/ft/scr/2010/cr10211.pdf>, 27, 32; Lindsay Whipp and Mure Dickie, 'S&P Downgrades Japan on Debt Worries', *Financial Times*, 27 January 2011, available online at <http://www.ft.com/cms/s/0/095efb70-29f3-11e0-997c-00144feab49a.html#axzz1I5eYizo3>.

[5] Whipp and Dickie n. 4; *see* Ministry of Finance of Japan, *Debt Management Report 2010*, available online at <http://www.mof.go.jp/english/jgbs/publication/debt_management_report/2010/>, ch. 3 at 20.

[6] *See*, e.g., Carmen M. Reinhart and Kenneth S. Rogoff, *This Time Is Different: Eight Centuries of Financial Folly* (Princeton, NJ: Princeton University Press, 2009), 141–73; Ben S. Bernanke, 'Non-Monetary Effects of the Financial Crisis in the Great Depression' (1983) 73 Am Econ Rev 257, 263–7.

crises travelled along distinct paths, required different prophylactic measures *ex ante*, and different solutions *ex post*. For modern banks, solvency regulation has been the principal bulwark against failure; resolution, the principal way to limit collateral damage from failure. For governments, fiscal prudence has been the accepted prophylactic; belt-tightening (adjustment) and debt restructuring, the standard solutions.

The five case studies that follow reveal the blurry boundary between bank and government crises. In Asia, Europe, and the Americas, events now known as either banking or government debt crises often had elements of both. Some could have gone either way; policy and political choices determined their path. In all cases, governments were as indispensable for resolving banking crises as banks were for resolving sovereign debt crises. More recently, the feedback loop between bank and sovereign distress appears to have intensified, prompting calls for radical measures to break the bank–government link. Some of the measures proposed so far may adjust, elaborate, or displace the link; none would break it. **15.08**

3. Banks or Governments

Accounts of banking crises start with a credit boom, during which private institutions (perhaps operating under loose monetary conditions) make imprudent loans financed by fragile short-term borrowing.[7] An economic downturn might deliver a shock to bank assets; market panics might make it impossible for banks, as a group, to roll over maturing liabilities. Policymakers then face a choice: to let private losses fall where they may, to redistribute them among private actors, to absorb some losses on behalf of their taxpayers, or to make them a problem for another government. **15.09**

A. Korea 1997

Korea's was a traditional banking crisis story. Its banks had borrowed from abroad to finance risky domestic corporate loan portfolios. When the currency crisis in Thailand and Indonesia spread to Korea in late 1997, the banks could not roll over their short-term debts to foreign financial institutions. As they repaid these foreign loans, the banks drained Korea's hard currency reserves. A blanket government guarantee of all bank liabilities failed to stem the outflow. At year end, finance officials in Europe, Japan, and the United States had to cajole their banks to renew loans to Korean banks to avoid imminent default. **15.10**

By then, more than half of all Korean banks were operating with insufficient capital.[8] At the height of the crisis in 1998, close to a third of all Korean firms were insolvent; more than half were illiquid.[9] Also in 1998, foreign lenders agreed to a formal restructuring of their claims on Korean banks. In exchange, they got debt guaranteed by the government of Korea. By **15.11**

---

[7] Reinhart and Rogoff (n. 6), 144–5.

[8] Ajai Chopra, Kenneth Kang, Meral Karasulu, Hong Liang, Henry Ma, and Anthony Richards, *From Crisis to Recovery in Korea: Strategy, Achievements, and Lessons*, IMF WP 01/154 (October 2001), available online at <http://www.imf.org/external/pubs/ft/wp/2001/wp01154.pdf>, 38.

[9] Stijn Claessens, Simeon Djankov, and Giovanni Ferri, 'Corporate Distress in East Asia: The Effect of Currency and Interest Rate Shocks', *Public Policy for the Private Sector*, January 1999, available online at <http://siteresources.worldbank.org/EXTFINANCIALSECTOR/Resources/282884-1303327122200/172claes.pdf>, Table 1.

October 2000, the government had absorbed resolution costs to the tune of 22 per cent of gross domestic product (GDP).[10]

15.12 Despite this extraordinary spending, Korea's government exited the crisis with debt at 18 per cent of GDP: double the pre-crisis level of 9 per cent, but still very low by international standards.[11] The Korean banking crisis did not bring down public finances in part because government debt was low at the outset, the size of the banking sector was manageable in retrospect,[12] and the economy's growth potential was high.[13]

15.13 The Asian financial crisis is usually described as originating in the private corporate and financial sectors. Poor lending and borrowing decisions by banks left countries like Korea exposed to external shocks that demanded government intervention. On the other hand, it is also true that bank lending and borrowing practices channelled government economic policy.[14] Although bank debts did not bankrupt the Korean national treasury, they did nearly drain the central bank's foreign exchange reserves.[15] Breathing space for the eventual restructuring came courtesy of foreign governments using 'moral suasion' to maintain their own banks' exposure to Korea.[16] The story shifts easily from one of a private sector crisis and exceptional public intervention to one of long-term symbiosis and mutual assured destruction. It is also a transnational story, in which governments across jurisdictions leveraged their relationships with regulated institutions for the sake of financial stability.

15.14 A decade on, Korea's ability to cushion the fall of its banks looked unusual—almost quaint.

B. Iceland 2008

15.15 Between 2003 and 2007, Iceland—a country of about 300,000 inhabitants and an economy of about US$12 billion—transformed from a fishing hub into a major international financial centre. It had five main commercial banks, of which the three largest (accounting for 90 per cent of the banking system) borrowed tens of billions of dollars short-term on the international capital markets. Unchecked by regulators, they amassed speculative and illiquid

---

[10] Chopra et al. (n. 8), 44.

[11] IMF World Economic Outlook Database (April 2013), available online at <http://www.imf.org/external/pubs/ft/weo/2013/01/weodata/weoselgr.aspx> (select 'Advanced Economies' country group; then click 'Clear All' and select 'Korea'; then, under 'Government finance', select 'General government gross debt: Percent of GDP'; select 'Start Year' 1995 and 'End Year' 2000; then click 'Prepare Report').

[12] Commercial bank assets stood over 150 per cent of GDP in Korea in 1996, compared to 136 per cent in the European Union at the time: Carl-Johan Lindgren, Tomás J. T. Baliño, Charles Enoch, Anne-Marie Gulde, Marc Quintyn, and Leslie Teo, *Financial Crisis and Restructuring: Lessons from Asia*, IMF Occasional Paper 188 (1999), available online at <http://www.imf.org/external/pubs/ft/op/opfinsec/op188.pdf>, 11, 13, Box 3. By 2011, bank assets in Europe were closer to 300 per cent of GDP, and exceeded 700 per cent in Cyprus and Ireland: Stefano Borgioli, Ana C. Gouveia, and Claudio Labanca, *Financial Stability Analysis: Insights Gained from Consolidated Banking Data for the EU*, ECB Occasional Paper Series No. 140 (January 2013), available online at <http://www.ecb.int/pub/pdf/scpops/ecbocp140.pdf>, 15, chart 1; IMF, *European Union: Publication of Financial Assessment Program Documentation*, IMF Country Report No. 13/67 (March 2013), available online at <http://www.imf.org/external/pubs/ft/scr/2013/cr1367.pdf>, 6.

[13] *See* Chopra et al. (n. 8), 76–7 and Table 10. *See* also Ashoka Mody and Damiano Sandri, 'The Eurozone Crisis: How Banks and Sovereigns Came to be Joined at the Hip' (2012) 27 Econ Pol'y 199, 206 (weak growth prospects can intensify banking crises).

[14] *See* Chopra et al. (n. 8), 8–10.

[15] *See* Mark Allen, Cristoph Rosenberg, Christian Keller, Brad Setser, and Nouriel Roubini, *A Balance Sheet Approach to the Financial Crisis*, IMF Working Paper 02/210 (December 2002), available online at <http://www.imf.org/external/pubs/ft/wp/2002/wp02210.pdf>, 17–18. *See* also Paul Blustein, *The Chastening: Inside the Crisis that Rocked the Global Financial System and Humbled the IMF* (New York: Public Affairs, 2001), 124–7.

[16] *See* Blustein (n. 15), 192–202.

investments abroad. In 2004–06, these banks sought to diversify their funding sources and to expand their retail deposit base.[17] Buoyed by permissive cross-border expansion rules in the European Economic Area (EEA),[18] they attracted deposits from a wide range of sources, including local governments in Britain and retirees in the Netherlands; however, the bulk of Icelandic bank funding still came from the wholesale capital markets. Bank assets grew from roughly equal to more than ten times the size of the economy in just three years. More than half were abroad, but even assets in Iceland were nearly four times the size of the economy on the eve of the crisis. Over 80 per cent of bank liabilities and just under 80 per cent of their assets were denominated in foreign currencies.[19]

When global financial markets collapsed in the fall of 2008, the currency fell by 40 per cent; **15.16**
the banks could no longer refinance their debts and were taken over by the government, beginning October 6. The legislature enacted emergency measures authorizing the government to 'ring fence' domestic assets and liabilities of the banking system, and retroactively granted depositors preference over other bank creditors. Fearing losses to depositors in the United Kingdom, the British government famously invoked anti-terrorism legislation to freeze Icelandic bank assets in the UK, accelerating wholesale collapse of the banking sector in Iceland.[20] Iceland's government fell shortly thereafter.

With the blessing of the International Monetary Fund (IMF), the authorities imposed **15.17**
capital controls and proceeded to restructure the banks. Some smaller ones were sold or liquidated; the largest were split along national lines. Three new banks established with government capital got the domestic assets and domestic liabilities; the old, failed banks retained the foreign assets and liabilities. Domestic deposits received a blanket government guarantee. Some foreign creditors of the old banks were able to swap their debt into new bank equity. Government debt went from 30 per cent to 120 per cent of GDP, mostly owing to economic contraction from the crisis.[21] The net direct costs of bank restructuring have been estimated at about 20 per cent of GDP, attributable in important part to central bank financing for the banking system on the eve of the crisis.[22] Negotiations over allocating the losses continue five years later (at the time of writing); some foreign creditors stand to lose nearly all of their investment.[23]

---

[17] *See* IMF, *Iceland: 2008 Article IV Consultation*, IMF Country Report No. 08/367 (December 2008), available online at <http://www.imf.org/external/pubs/ft/scr/2008/cr08367.pdf>, 4, Box 1.

[18] House of Commons Treasury Committee, *Banking Crisis: The Impact of the Failure of the Icelandic Banks*, HC 402 (April 2009), available online at <http://www.publications.parliament.uk/pa/cm200809/cmselect/cmtreasy/402/402.pdf>, 110–11. The EEA comprises EU member states plus Iceland, Norway, and Liechtenstein.

[19] *See* IMF (n. 17), 3, 28, Table 3.

[20] *See* Althingi Special Investigation Commission, *Causes of the Collapse of the Icelandic Banks: Responsibility, Mistakes, and Negligence* (April 2010), ch. 21, available online at <http://www.rna.is/media/skjol/RNAvefurKafli21Enska.pdf>, 89; House of Commons Treasury Committee (n. 18), 41–2.

[21] IMF, *Iceland: 2010 Article IV Consultation*, IMF Country Report No. 10/305 (October 2010), available online at <http://www.imf.org/external/pubs/ft/scr/2010/cr10305.pdf>, 33, Table 7; IMF, *Iceland:* Ex Post *Evaluation of Exceptional Access under the 2008 Stand-By Arrangement*, IMF Country Report No. 12/91 (April 2012), available online at <http://www.imf.org/external/pubs/ft/scr/2012/cr1291.pdf>, 14.

[22] IMF, *Iceland: 2010 Article IV Consultation* (n. 21), 33, Table 7; IMF, *Iceland:* Ex Post *Evaluation* (n. 21), 14. *See* also Friðrik Már Baldursson, 'Iceland's Programme with the IMF 2008–11', *Vox*, 8 November 2011, available online at <http://www.voxeu.org/article/iceland-s-programme-imf-2008-11>.

[23] IMF, *Iceland:* Ex Post *Evaluation* (n. 21), 13–4, 19; *see* also Richard Milne, 'Iceland's Creditors Braced for Losses', *Financial Times*, 2 May 2013, available online at <http://www.ft.com/intl/cms/s/0/298407e8-b19a-11e2-b324-00144feabdc0.html#axzz2VNIxdAlC>.

15.18 In retrospect, the fall looks inevitable. Iceland started out with low government debt—but no government can guarantee liabilities remotely approaching ten times the size of its economy and no central bank can hold enough foreign currency to finance capital outflows on the scale that threatened Iceland. When the government could not compensate everyone, it chose to pay its own citizens ahead of foreign creditors, including ordinary Europeans who put money in Iceland's banks.

15.19 The UK and Dutch governments were unwilling to see their nationals lose hard-earned savings in Iceland. They compensated their depositors and sued Iceland's government for compensation—a bid to turn bank debt (deposits) into sovereign debt.

15.20 In 2013, the European Free Trade Area (EFTA) Court rebuffed their claims.[24] It ruled that Iceland's treaty obligations were limited to establishing a deposit insurance scheme; funding the scheme was another matter. The upshot of the decision was that Icelandic banks had every right to take deposits across Europe with a private and utterly underfunded deposit insurance scheme; creditors took the risk and paid the price.[25] While many observers decried the Court's formalistic approach,[26] others greeted the decision as a strike against bailouts.[27] From now on, they said, private creditors would have to live with the consequences of their investment decisions.

15.21 It was a stretch to describe the ruling as a victory for private responsibility. Although some bank creditors will surely suffer large losses, a large group of depositors was simply rescued by a different cast of government characters. Rather than adding to Iceland's debt stock, Icelandic bank liabilities migrated onto UK and Dutch government books.

15.22 In late 2008, Iceland seemed like an anomaly: its private banking sector had grown so monstrously large so quickly that it simply swallowed up the country, government, and all. It did so using a quirk in the European treaty framework, which did not require countries to fund or backstop deposit insurance, and which was subsequently validated by a court's reading of the treaties.

15.23 The dramatic details obscure the ways in which Iceland was rather ordinary. Outsized banking sectors have become the norm in Europe, with assets more than three times the size of national economies on average.[28] Offshore financial centres such as Cyprus and Switzerland have banking sectors far bigger than the average;[29] Luxembourg's banks dwarf the rest

---

[24] *See* Case E-16/11, *EFTA Surveillance Authority v. Iceland*, 2013 WestlawNext 178 (28 January 2013).

[25] *See EFTA Surveillance Authority* (n. 24), 19–23.

[26] *See*, e.g., Tim Young, 'Editorial: EFTA Court's Icesave Ruling Leaves European Deposit Insurance in Tatters', *Central Banking*, 31 January 2013, available online at <http://www.centralbanking.com/central-banking/opinion/2240651/opinion-efta-courts-icesave-ruling-leaves-european-deposit-insurance-in-tatters>.

[27] *See*, e.g., *Financial Times*, 'Editorial: Saga Ends with Icesave Redemption', 29 January 2013, available online at <http://www.ft.com/intl/cms/s/0/78b96684-6a21-11e2-a80c-00144feab49a.html#axzz2VNIxdAlC>.

[28] *See* European Central Bank, *EU Banking Structures* (September 2010), available online at <http://www.ecb.int/pub/pdf/other/eubankingstructures201009en.pdf>, 10, Chart 3.

[29] *Compare* European Central Bank, 'Aggregated Balance Sheet of Euro Area Monetary Financial Institutions, Excluding the Eurosystem: December 2012', available online at <http://www.ecb.int/stats/money/aggregates/bsheets/html/outstanding_amounts_2012-12.en.html> (showing that Cypriot Banks held total assets of €128.1 billion at the end of 2012) *and* Swiss National Bank, *Monthly Bulletin of Banking Statistics* (February 2013), available online at <http://www.snb.ch/en/iabout/stat/statpub/bstamon/id/statpub_bstamon_hist>, 28 (showing that Swiss banks held total assets of 2.83 trillion Swiss francs) *with* IMF, *World Economic Outlook Database* (April 2013), available online at <http://www.imf.org/external/pubs/ft/weo/2013/01/weodata/index.aspx>, (showing that Cyprus' 2012 GDP was €14.8 billion and Switzerland's 2012 GDP was 548 billion Swiss francs.)

at nearly twenty times the size of the economy.[30] These are products of economic policy choice and regulation as much as, or more than, they are market mutations. Similarly, while Iceland's deposit insurance scheme might seem laughable in retrospect, few funded schemes can withstand complete collapse of a banking system. And as the EFTA Court noted, once the system collapses, governments choose how they go about restructuring, even if it means stiffing the foreigners in favour of their own voters. The fact that governments will rescue their people and institutions, but try to stick other governments with the bill, is also hardly unusual: crises from Mexico in 1982 to the United States in 2008 saw policymakers debating whether and how to push losses from their financial institutions onto other people's taxpayers.[31]

4. Governments or Banks

It generally takes a big banking sector to bring down a national treasury. Loss on relatively small holdings of public debt can wipe out bank equity. This is because, compared to other firms, banks are thinly capitalized.[32] If banking system capital is at 8 per cent of risk-weighted assets, a default on government debt, or even a big drop in its value, can quickly leave the system undercapitalized and many banks insolvent. **15.24**

Government debt stood at over 10 per cent of banking system assets in six out of the twenty-four high-income countries last surveyed by the IMF, with Japan leading the pack at nearly 25 per cent and Italy at nearly 15 per cent, in line with Greece before its debt restructuring.[33] The United States was not one of the six, but would easily make the list if bank holdings of government-sponsored enterprise (GSE) debt were included.[34] All US government obligations stood at more than 13 per cent of the assets in the US banking system in March 2013.[35] In developing countries where capital markets are shallow and lending to the private sector limited, government securities may be the only game in town. **15.25**

[30] Borgioli et al. (n. 12), Chart 1.

[31] *See* Report of Anton R. Valukas, Examiner, *In re Lehman Bros. Holdings Inc.,* 439 BR 811 (SDNY 2010) (No. 08-13555(JMP)), at 703–10 (discussing Lehman); Congressional Oversight Panel, *June Oversight Report: The AIG Rescue, Its Impact on Markets, and the Government's Exit Strategy* (10 June 2010), available online at <http://www.gpo.gov/fdsys/pkg/CPRT-111JPRT56698/html/CPRT-111JPRT56698.htm>, 92–3 (discussing AIG).

[32] *See* generally Anat Admati and Martin Hellwig, *The Bankers' New Clothes* (Princeton, NJ: Princeton University Press, 2013) (discussing why banks have higher leverage than other firms).

[33] *See* IMF, *Global Financial Stability Report: Old Risks, New Challenges* (April 2013), available online at <http://www.imf.org/External/Pubs/FT/GFSR/2013/01/pdf/text.pdf>, 133, Fig. 3.7. *See* also Serkan Aslanalp and Takahiro Tsuda, *Tracking Global Demand for Advanced Economy Sovereign Debt,* IMF Working Paper No. 12/284 (December 2012), available online at <http://www.imf.org/external/pubs/ft/wp/2012/wp12284.pdf>, 32, Fig. 15.

[34] Federal Deposit Insurance Corporation (FDIC) statistics for GSEs cover the Federal National Mortgage Association, the Federal Home Loan Mortgage Corporation, the Federal Home Loan Bank System, the Farm Credit Banks, the Banks for Cooperatives, the Federal Agricultural Mortgage Corporation, the Student Loan Marketing Association, the College Construction Loan Insurance Association, and any of their affiliated or member institutions, and any other GSE as designated by the Secretary of the Treasury: *see* 12 USC § 1828(s)(5) (2013), citing the Financial Institutions Reform, Recovery, and Enforcement Act (FIRREA) of 1989, § 1404(e)(1)(A), Pub. L. No. 101–73, 103 Stat. 183. Investors have long bought GSEs' debt as a proxy for the debt of the federal government even before the takeovers of Fannie Mae and Freddie Mac in 2008.

[35] Figure taken from <http://www.federalreserve.gov/releases/h8/current/>.

15.26 Bank holdings of government debt often increase in the run-up to financial crisis.[36] Like other investors, banks may see government debt as a safe haven in times of market turbulence and risk aversion; in other cases they may come under pressure from the government to act as its lenders of last resort when all other creditors have left. For example, US bank holdings of US Treasury securities nearly doubled between 2008 and 2010 according to Federal Reserve data. Portuguese bank lending to the Portuguese government more than doubled in the two years preceding its turn to the IMF.[37]

15.27 Regulation and supervision can help to obscure—or soften—the impact of public debt problems on the financial sector. Where they applied in ordinary times, borrower concentration limits and activities restrictions might be suspended in crisis; asset values might perk up from a newly discovered accounting treatment; wafer-thin capital cushions may be deemed 'good enough' under the circumstances.

15.28 Argentina offers a particularly rich case study of government debt in the banking system and the way in which direct financial involvement by the government can interact with regulation on bank balance sheets.

A. Argentina 2001

15.29 To most outside observers, Argentina's government debt default in late 2001 subsumed and overshadowed its banking crisis. Quite apart from their exposure to sovereign credit risk, banks were vulnerable to the effects of economic contraction and currency depreciation: if the peso's 1:1 peg to the US dollar were to break down, bank borrowers' wealth would shrink and their mammoth books of dollar loans would go into default. But the government presented a distinct source of danger for the banks.

15.30 At the height of the crisis, Argentina's public debt ratios were several times the size of those of Korea or Iceland.[38] Despite a succession of bank runs in the year before default, the government relied on domestic banks and pension funds, along with funds from the IMF, to fill its growing financing gap. Bank credit to the public sector doubled as foreign creditors ran for the hills, while credit to the private sector shrank. The US$5.1 billion that Argentina borrowed from the IMF that year helped to sustain the wobbling currency peg amid rampant capital flight: domestic depositors moved US$16 billion offshore; short-term external creditors of the banks pulled another US$13.4 billion.[39] Banks' sources of funding shrank as their vulnerability to government default grew.

---

[36] Serkan Arslanalp and Takahiro Tsuda, *Tracking Global Demand for Advanced Economy Sovereign Debt*, IMF Working Paper 12/284 (December 2012), available online at <http://www.imf.org/external/pubs/ft/wp/2012/wp12284.pdf>, 31–2 and Figs 14–15.

[37] Banco de Portugal, *Statistical Bulletin* (May 2013), available online at <http://www.bportugal.pt/en-US/Estatisticas/PublicacoesEstatisticas/BolEstatistico/Publications/B3.pdf>, Table B.3.7.1, column 11. According to press reports at the time, the turn to the IMF was apparently prompted by something of a buyers' strike among domestic institutions.

[38] *See* IMF, *Argentina: 2002 Article IV Consultation*, IMF Country Report No. 03/226 (July 2003), available online at <http://www.imf.org/external/pubs/ft/scr/2003/cr03226.pdf>.

[39] Brad Setser and Anna Gelpern, 'Pathways through Financial Crisis: Argentina' (2006) 12 Global Governance 465, 479; Nouriel Roubini and Brad Setser, *Bailouts or Bail-ins? Responding to Financial Crises in Emerging Markets* (Washington DC: Peterson Institute, 2004) 8, Table 1.1, and 131, Table 4.3.

Argentina could have used IMF borrowing to cushion the impact of devaluation and public debt restructuring on local banks.[40] Instead, it gambled for resurrection, apparently at the banks' expense. By the end of 2001, the government needed bank holidays and capital controls to keep the remaining deposits in the banking system. After default, the government continued to use banks to cushion the effects of the crisis on other parts of the economy: for example, it converted dollar loans and deposits into pesos at asymmetric rates, so that bank owners faced a 40 per cent gap between their assets and liabilities. It eventually filled the gap with new government bonds, which enjoyed favourable regulatory treatment and were serviced while foreign bonds remained in default.[41] The approach helped debtors; it also reflected the government's unwillingness to nationalize the banking system when bank owners threatened to walk away. **15.31**

In sum, a depression, a currency collapse, and a government debt crisis combined to bring down Argentina's banks. Regulation and supervision allowed the government to finance itself from the banks when no other private creditors would lend to it. On the other hand, more regulatory forbearance and new government debt issued post-default kept the banking system on life support while the economy recovered, until deposits could be freed without risking a run. When the government was ready to restructure its foreign debt, domestic banks that held about half of it boosted creditor participation. **15.32**

In Korea, the government stood behind Korean banks and their foreign creditors. In Iceland and Argentina, foreign creditors of the banks and the sovereign, respectively, absorbed losses from the combined bank–government insolvency. In all cases, loss allocation was an iterative process involving multiple political actors, stretching over multiple regulatory cycles. **15.33**

B. The Third World debt crisis 1982

What came to be known as the 'Third World debt crisis' of the 1980s could have—but did not—become the 'First World banking crisis' to rival the Great Depression. Between August 1982 and October 1983, twenty-eight governments from Latin America, Africa, Asia, and Eastern Europe suspended payments and initiated rescheduling talks over their obligations to commercial banks in the United States, the UK, and Germany, among others. In 1982, when Mexico started the wave of suspensions and restructurings, loans to the most heavily indebted governments represented over 130 per cent of all capital in US banks, 85 per cent of all capital in British banks, and over 31 per cent of all capital in German banks.[42] The nine largest US banks were exposed to the tune of 194 per cent of their capital—over 44 per cent for Mexico alone. **15.34**

Like other banking crises, this one originated with a credit bubble. The oil price shocks in the 1970s led to spikes in dollar revenues of energy-exporting countries and a corresponding rise in 'petrodollar deposits' in major financial centre banks. The banks invested the deposits in high-yielding loans to governments and private sector borrowers in developing countries. In the early 1980s, a global recession and rising interest rates in the United States made it **15.35**

[40] IMF, *Debt-Related Vulnerabilities and Financial Crises: An Application of the Balance Sheet Approach to Emerging Market Countries* (July 2004), available online at <http://www.imf.org/external/np/pdr/bal/2004/eng/070104.htm>, 26.

[41] Roubini and Setser (n. 39), 272.

[42] William Cline, *International Debt Re-Examined* (Washington DC: Peterson Institute, 1995), Tables 2.10–2.12.

impossible for developing-country borrowers to refinance these dollar debts. At the same time, banks in major financial centres were under stress, their capital worn thin with recession, and their loan-loss provisions too low to absorb the looming defaults.

15.36 Sovereign debtors and their creditors' governments faced a dilemma: if the debtors were to default or pursue debt principal reduction, major banks in the United States and Europe would have been exposed overnight as insolvent, potentially triggering deposit runs, and economic and social dislocation in creditors' countries. If the banks' home governments and principal regulators had pursued early debt restructuring, they would have had to backstop their banks to mitigate the consequences. Instead, the creditors' governments helped to broker negotiated arrangements with each debtor, whereby bank syndicates refinanced sovereign debts as if they were dealing with a temporary liquidity problem. The debtors also received financing from multilateral creditors and promised policy reform. Such arrangements had to be renegotiated frequently, adding to the sovereign debt stock: foreign bank claims on the most heavily indebted countries went up by nearly a third between 1982 and 1987, while economic growth stagnated. Over the same period, banks in New York, London, and Frankfurt were rebuilding capital and provisions.[43]

15.37 The tide turned in 1989, when the idea that developing-country debt stocks were unsustainable became actionable and politically acceptable. Banks could absorb principal writedowns with relatively modest regulatory forbearance. In March of that year, US Treasury Secretary Nicholas F. Brady gave a famous speech in which he recognized publicly for the first time that full debt repayment would stunt growth in these debtor countries; this signalled major policy change on loss allocation.[44] His initiative led to restructuring agreements with substantial principal reduction, led again by Mexico, including the forgiveness of some US$60 billion in debt,[45] much of which fell on banks and their shareholders.[46] Debt relief was conditioned on dramatic economic reforms, including large-scale privatization and liberalization in many developing countries.

15.38 The delay in principal reductions and the resulting long-term costs for debtors' economies was a function of many complex factors. However, there is little doubt that the health of leading international commercial banks was a key factor in treating the crisis as one of temporary borrower illiquidity. The burden of debt distress initially fell on the debtors in the form of higher debt stocks and domestic economic adjustment, and only later on the banks in the form of debt write-offs. As in other crises, loss allocation among banks and governments took multiple iterations of regulatory forbearance, public financing, and intergovernment negotiation.

5. Back to Europe (the Doom Loop)

15.39 The eurozone crisis has made the distinction between banking and public debt crises harder to sustain. The combination of very large national banking sectors, strained fiscal resources,

---

43 Cline (n. 42), 70–1.

44 Nicholas F. Brady, Secretary of the Treasury, 'Remarks to the Brookings Institution and the Bretton Woods Committee Conference on Third World Debt' (10 March 1989), available at <http://digitalcollections.library.cmu.edu/awweb/awarchive?type=file&item=441057>.

45 Cline (n. 42), 17.

46 Ross P. Buckley, 'The Facilitation of the Brady Plan: Emerging Markets Debt Trading from 1989 to 1993' (1997) 21 Fordham Int'l LJ 1802, 1804–5 and fn. 17.

financial integration, and the inability of national governments to print money have made it virtually impossible for member states to contain crises in their banks or to limit the impact of government debt distress on their banking systems.[47] Persistent home bias in sovereign debt holdings helped to make national banking systems in the most vulnerable member states especially exposed to their governments' debt problems.[48] However, banks can fall victim to their sovereigns' debt problems even when they do not hold too much of their government's debt: to the extent that markets counted on national governments to back their banks, weak public finances showed, among other things, diminished backstop capacity.[49] An early and stark illustration of the loop dynamic came from Ireland.

At the height of the global financial crisis in 2008, Ireland's financial system buckled under **15.40** the weight of bad real estate loans. When it collapsed, the system stood at eight times the size of the Irish economy. Partly under external pressure, the government extended a blanket guarantee to all Irish bank liabilities, nationalized a large bank, and recapitalized much of the remaining banking system, bringing about partial nationalization. A national asset management company bought distressed real estate assets off bank books and replaced them with government debt. Irish government debt stock rose from 25 per cent of GDP in 2007 to nearly 120 per cent in 2012.[50] Some estimated the government's contingent liabilities at over 200 per cent of GDP.[51] Economic fallout from the crisis would have pushed up Irish government debt in any case; the bank rescue tipped it into dangerous territory.[52] Even as guarantees expired and bank restructuring proceeded apace, nearly a third of all Irish bank loans were non-performing in 2012—by far the highest level in Europe.[53]

---

[47] *See*, e.g., Maurice Obstfeld, *Finance at Center Stage: Some Lessons of the Euro Crisis*, Working Paper (March 2013), available online at <http://www.princeton.edu/economics/seminar-schedule-by-prog/macro-s13/FinanceCenterStage.pdf>; Paul de Grauwe, 'The Governance of a Fragile Eurozone' (2012) 45 Aus Econ Rev 255; S. Gerlach, A.Schulz, and G. B.Wolff, *Banking and Sovereign Risk in the Euro Area*, CEPR Discussion Paper No. 7833 (May 2010), available online at <http://efa2010.unicp.net/provide_paper.php?pid=367>; Mody and Sandri (n. 13).

[48] *See*, e.g., IMF, *Greece:* Ex Post *Evaluation of Exceptional Access under the 2010 Stand-By Arrangement* (5 June 2013), available online at <http://www.imf.org/external/pubs/cat/longres.aspx?sk=40639.0> (attributing the delay in Greek debt restructuring partly to Greek bank exposure to their sovereign).

[49] For theories of transmission between governments and banks, *see* Viral V. Acharya, Itamar Drechsler, and Philipp Schnabl, *A Pyrrhic Victory? Bank Bailouts and Sovereign Credit Risk*, National Bureau of Economic Research Working Paper 17136 (June 2011), available online at <http://www.nber.org/papers/w17136>; Patrick Bolton and Olivier Jeanne, 'Sovereign Default Risk and Bank Fragility in Financially Integrated Economies' (2011) 59 IMF Econ Rev 162. For an empirical investigation, *see*, e.g. Chiara Angeloni and Guntram B. Wolff, *Are Banks Affected by Their Holdings of Government Debt?*, Bruegel Working Paper 2012/07 (March 2012), available online at <http://www.bruegel.org/publications/publication-detail/publication/717-are-banks-affected-by-their-holdings-of-government-debt/>. *See* also Bank for International Settlements, *The Impact of Sovereign Credit Risk on Bank Funding Conditions*, Committee on the Global Financial System Paper No. 43 (May 2011), available online at <http://www.bis.org/publ/cgfs43.pdf>.

[50] IMF, *Ireland: Staff Report for the 2012 Article IV Consultation* (21 August 2012), available online at <http://www.imf.org/external/pubs/ft/scr/2012/cr12264.pdf>, 37, Table 4.

[51] Angelo Baglioni and Umberto Cherubini, *Marking-to-Market Government Guarantees to Financial Systems: An Empirical Analysis of Europe*, Preliminary Draft (10 November 2010) available online at <http://papers.ssrn.com/sol3/papers.cfm?abstract_id=1715405&download=yes>, 13, Table 6.

[52] IMF (n. 40); *see* also Karl Whelan, *ELA, Promissory Notes and All That: The Fiscal Costs of Anglo Irish Bank*, Revised Draft (September 2012), available online at <http://www.karlwhelan.com/IrishEconomy/Whelan-PNotes-September2012.pdf>.

[53] IMF, *European Union: Publication of Financial Sector Assessment Program Documentation—Technical Note on Progress with Bank Restructuring and Resolution in Europe*, IMF Country Report No. 13/67 (March 2013), available online at <http://www.imf.org/external/pubs/ft/scr/2013/cr1367.pdf>, 14.

15.41 At first, the Irish case was seen primarily as one of bailouts gone wrong. Ireland and Iceland, whose financial systems imploded at about the same time, showed that bank bailouts could sink public treasuries. Iceland drew the line on guarantees to protect its own; Ireland did not—perhaps could not. In both countries, insolvencies across an outsized banking sector were bound to have a spectacular impact on public finances, even though both countries started with low government debt. In Iceland, the distribution battles between the government and its banks took place largely behind the wall of capital controls. Irish banks remained internationally active and soon fell victim to the debt problems of the government that saved them. On learning that they had to pay extra to pledge their government debt as collateral for European clearing houses, Irish banks chose instead to dump the sovereign bonds.[54]

15.42 Europe—and Ireland in particular—holds the dubious prize for testing the logical implications of bank–government ties. When neither banks, nor governments, can fully cushion each other's falls, when no fairy godmother materializes with transfers or deep-pocketed creditors from abroad, and when governments are committed to avoiding default and maintaining open capital flows, the link between banks and governments becomes a suicide pact—or the 'doom loop'.

6. Conclusions

15.43 The case studies in this chapter illustrate some ways in which bank–government links operate in a crisis. Three themes recur.

(a) Banks and governments are indispensable partners in one another's crises. The relationship holds with or without 'twin' bank–government crises, which are rare, and apart from the feedback 'doom loop'. In particular, bank and government liabilities seem to migrate easily between bank and government books as the crisis deepens, and as part of its resolution.
(b) Related to the first theme, private bank balance sheets emerge as public policy conduits. Japan and Korea highlight the fact that this function is not limited to crisis; however, it becomes particularly stark in crisis. Banks sprout new assets and liabilities, which might be valued in brand new ways in the name of financial stability.
(c) When banks are internationally active, they come to mediate the distribution of losses among governments. Governments want private creditors to bear the consequences of their risk-taking, but feel compelled to shield their own nationals, and try to get other governments to pick up the tab.

15.44 Policy response to this abiding link between banks and governments is a mix of palliative and denial. It starts with a story of the relationship as a symptom of underdevelopment and crisis, one of aberration and redemption. Reforms are then sold as projects for getting banks off government dole and getting governments out of banking—as in the Dodd–Frank Act's promise that taxpayers 'shall bear no losses' from bailing out insolvent banks,[55] and

[54] David Oakley and Sam Jones, 'Bond Sell-off Takes Ireland Closer to Tipping Point', *Financial Times*, 10 November 2010, available online at <http://www.ft.com/intl/cms/s/0/41815768-ecfa-11df-9912-00144feab49a.html#axzz2Vk2nkWCR>.

[55] 12 USC § 5394(c) (2010).

the European banking union's 'imperative to break the vicious cycle between banks and sovereigns'.[56] Such statements are misleading at best: Dodd–Frank elaborates the process by which governments may support a broader range of financial institutions, while Europe substitutes the regional government for national ones in the bank–government marriage. Both try to limit government support for financial institutions and other governments, and to raise its price *ex ante*. This is renegotiation, not divorce—and properly so, since attempts to renounce bailouts by rule have yet to survive a crisis.[57] Still, there remains the relationship that dare not speak its name.

Acknowledging the pervasive and enduring nature of bank–government ties reframes the policy task. Instead of outlawing bailouts, the focus shifts to the precise terms of loss-sharing between banks and governments, and among governments, in crisis—and the incentive effects of this allocation in good times. Decisions about the terms of the bargain must be intelligible to the public and democratically accountable, if only because of their enormous consequences for distribution, in both good times and bad. The democratic imperative in turn raises a host of research and policy questions. For example, to what extent should government promises of support for banks—and banks' tacit backing of governments—be made explicit on bank and government balance sheets? Should bank and government claims on one another occupy a special place in the claims hierarchy—and if so, what should that place be? Should regulatory privileges for government debt be abolished—or made more explicit and institutionalized? Considering the limits on the enforcement of government promises (amply demonstrated elsewhere in this volume), what is the right commitment device to ensure that governments deliver on their promises of debt repayment, liquidity support, and recapitalization—and that banks pay a fair price for the benefits they receive? How might government commitments to one another (for example to share losses in cross-border bank resolution) fare in such a newly transparent regime? And how might the answers to such questions affect the structure of the financial sector, and the behaviour of banks and governments, going forward? **15.45**

The answers are far beyond the scope of this chapter. For now, describing the bank–government relationship with its cross-border dimensions as something other than an aberration to be stamped out or swept under the rug might prompt a humbler look at crisis management and regulation. Reforming the relationship to limit its worst dysfunctions, and to render it intelligible and accountable to the public in whose name it exists, will take more than official declarations. Harnessing its stabilizing potential is an even bigger challenge. 'Walking back from Cyprus' will take a while—and, on the bright side, many more drafts in Arial 12pt font. **15.46**

[56] Euro Area Summit Statement, Brussels European Council (29 June 2012).

[57] *See* Consolidated Version of the Treaty on the Functioning of the European Union (TFEU), Arts 123, 125, 30 March 2010, 2010 OJ (C 83) 99. *See* also Jonathan Tomkin, 'Contradiction, Circumvention, and Conceptual Gymnastics: The Impact of the Adoption of the ESM Treaty on the State of European Democracy' (2013) 14 Ger LJ 169, 180–1 (explaining how Arts 123–5 of the Lisbon Treaty have been functionally abandoned); Adam Levitin, 'In Defense of Bailouts' (2011) 99 Geo LJ 435, 299 (explaining how governments have generally ignored the law when engaging in lender-of-last-resort activity) and at 487 (explaining how bankruptcy can be a 'procedure' for a bailout). But *cf.* John B. Taylor, 'Preface', in John B. Taylor and Kenneth E. Scott (eds), *Bankruptcy not Bailout* (Stanford, CA: Hoover Institution, 2012), ix, ix–xii (proposing to replace bailouts with a new bankruptcy mechanism).

16

INTERNATIONAL LENDER OF LAST RESORT

A Floor of Support for Troubled Sovereign Debt

Adam Lerrick

Doing nothing is usually best.

(General Edmund Allenby, *Lawrence of Arabia*)

We couldn't just sit back and do nothing.

(European Central Bank President Draghi, *Der Spiegel*, 29 October 2012)

1. Introduction

As economic history repeats itself, so does the saga of troubled sovereign debt. All but the most hardened libertarian will concur that the official sector should step in when markets fail to function. It is the 'how' and the 'how much' that are under dispute. In the final tally, does escalating official intervention moderate or exacerbate the cycle of crises in a global system? **16.01**

The course of crisis follows a familiar path. Markets wake up to an unpleasant surprise and prices fall. As investors mark to market and lenders call for margin and collateral liquidation, the need for cash spirals from the centre of the crisis to unrelated asset classes. Panicked markets drive prices below rational valuation. Investors refuse to buy bonds of sound issuers and sell whatever can be sold. Solvent, but illiquid, borrowers are forced into default as financing costs spin out of control. Bank capital is wiped out by collapsing asset values. Politicians and bankers confuse the end of *their* world with the end of *the* world. Central banks abandon their principles. And still another bailout renews investor licences to gamble with taxpayer money. **16.02**

The fire brigade metaphor is the official sector's mantra with which to justify a two-decade stream of lavish loans that have transferred more than US$1 trillion in sovereign debt and banking failures from private sector investors to protesting taxpayers: when the global system is burning, bring in the fire engines with tanks of liquid money to contain the flames; the arson team can ferret out causes at a later date. Critics, such as German central banker Juergen Stark, retort: What if 'the water damage [is] bigger than the fire damage'?[1] What if long-term distress is the price of short-term relief? **16.03**

---

[1] Noah Barkin and Andreas Framke, 'Special Report: A Fight for the Soul of the ECB', *Reuters*, 6 October 2012, available online at <http://www.reuters.com/article/2011/10/06/us-europe-stark-idUSTRE79512G20111006>.

16.04 Repeated intervention subverts the incentives that are the moving force of market behaviour. Investors are invited to a casino in which the rule is: 'When you win, you win, and when you lose, you don't pay.' Sovereigns are issued credit cards co-signed by a doting parent to indulge spoiled electorates with a lifestyle their productivity cannot deliver. When there is no longer a penalty for bad choices, the link between reward and risk is severed. The cycle of crisis and its damages are renewed on an ever-ascending scale.

16.05 The official sector must move out of the shadows of financial prehistory—when big banks and governments collaborated to manage markets—and accept the realities of a rough-and-ready, profit-driven global trading room, which they neither like nor understand. For the arbiters of the world economy, a new definition of crisis governs: high interest rates for overborrowed nations. 'Cajole, conciliate, and coerce, but never commit to a fixed policy to guide investors' sums up the official sector response. Compromise solutions have been one-off, incomplete, and temporary. Today's numbers on trader screens reflect expectations of the future. Low bond prices signal that investors have failed to find the long-term stability that they seek.

16.06 Instead of a series of patches on the present, the official sector must set fixed rules for the future. It must learn to work with markets, not try to control them. In a new role that is crucial, but narrowly defined, it must build and enforce a predictable framework in which incentives can safely function, investors are protected from disaster, but prevented from shifting the cost of their mistakes to taxpayer accounts, and sovereigns that enjoy official support are compelled to keep their word.

16.07 On the continuum between total bailout and abandoning the market to chaos, there is a place where the official sector can step in and siphon panic from the system. Setting an official floor of support under asset prices insures investors against catastrophic loss, but not against all loss. When risk-taking and loss-taking are rejoined, the global system will stabilize.

2. A Third Party in a Two-Party Game

16.08 An Italian technocrat at a European institution votes to spend German taxpayer money to bail out a hedge fund holding unpayable bonds of an insolvent Greek government because it will lower Italy's cost of funds and improve the capital ratios of Italian banks. Is this the plot of a bad crime novel about global finance? No, a real-time tale of what happens when the official sector sits down at a negotiating table meant for two.

16.09 Sovereign debt settlement should be simple. It is a zero-sum game with two players: Whatever the debtor government gains, the private sector creditors lose. Within the legal framework of the bond contract, they battle to divide the cost of failure. The government weighs its social debt to its people against its financial debt to its bondholders. At stake are higher taxes, fewer public services, and asset sales. Finance ministers strive to minimize debt, start borrowing again, and, hopefully, survive the next confidence vote. Profit-driven creditors want to go home with the least loss on balance sheets or a large performance fee on speculative gain. The bargaining chips are cash, reduced principal, lower interest rates, and longer maturities. It is all arm's length and it is all about money.

16.10 Enter the official sector in haste, always late and carting a hefty load of policy baggage. Now a simple two-dimensional game morphs into a three-dimensional quagmire. The first words spoken—a call for 'voluntary market-friendly solutions'—transform adversaries into colluders. The interests of the debtor government and its private sector creditors are now aligned as they unite to shift the cost of their mistakes onto the *deus ex machina* who has descended upon the stage with bags full of other people's money.

Creditors, already '100 per cent bailed in' by their own faulty choices, are emboldened to up the ante. They threaten market mayhem and a withdrawal of capital—not only for their debtor, but also for a wide spectrum of countries and banks. Posturing and public relations pay off, and the price of their bonds jumps. **16.11**

Sovereign debtors are glad to offer more as long as someone else is footing the bill. When market debt migrates to official balance sheets, the new obligations do not weigh heavily on national treasuries. Foreign taxpayer funds are cheap. Official loans cost a fraction of private sector capital. Crucially, the sovereign debtor is often its own largest creditor. Domestic banks, insurance companies, and politically sensitive pension funds are large holders of government bonds. The smaller the writedown, the smaller the need to recapitalize banks and to shore up voters' retirement. Unsaid, but implicit in the deal, if crisis returns, official sector interest rates will be lowered and maturities extended at the stroke of a pen after a summit dinner. Repayment is in the distant and hazy future. **16.12**

For the third party at the table, cost is the least of concerns. Taxpayers too various and too distant to demand an accounting will pay. Fear dominates: fear of systemic meltdown; fear that trouble in one state will raise debt burdens for many; fear of capital drying up from markets to nations; fear of mission failure and career mis-steps; fear of the next election. Overpaying a few billion is just a rounding error. The fate of the failing economy and the suffering of its people, once primary to the process, becomes a sideshow to the policy main event. **16.13**

For the markets, failure cannot be cloaked in double-speak. 'Default' is when a debtor pays its creditors less or later than originally promised. 'Bailout' is when official money is poured in to pay the cost of private sector mistakes. New cash and cash equivalents of lowered interest rates and extended maturities on old official loans, all shift the burden from investors to taxpayers. Interest-rate differentials between nations reflect risk differentials and not 'faulty monetary transmission mechanisms'. 'Voluntary exchanges' and 'market-friendly solutions' do not hide coercion of lenders. No one voluntarily takes a loss. Protestations of 'solidarity' do not conceal transfers between nations. Losses can be moved around, but no magic trick can make them disappear. In the end, either taxpayers or investors must settle the account. **16.14**

3. For an International Lender of Last Resort: Incentives, Discipline, and Control of Risk

More than a century ago, Walter Bagehot proposed what remains the classic formula for confronting market crisis: a lender of last resort (then the nation's central bank) stabilizes markets and sound financial institutions in distress by lending freely at a penalty interest rate against good collateral.[2] In Bagehot's world, the context was domestic and government bonds were the ultimate 'good collateral'. But what if the sovereign itself is overextended? In a global market, what 'good collateral' can a distressed government offer? How does an international lender of last resort (ILOLR) support troubled governments without resorting to the inflationary printing press? **16.15**

An official sector floor of support that guarantees minimum values for assets in times of stress can replicate the Bagehot lender of last resort on a global scale, and lend the cash **16.16**

[2] Walter Bagehot, *Lombard Street: A Description of the Money Market* (London: Henry S. King, 1873).

and credibility that faltering governments temporarily lack. Setting intervention prices at a discount to normal market levels is the floor's equivalent to Bagehot's penalty interest rate. A commitment to sound policy is the government's 'good collateral'.

16.17 The floor of support can accomplish much without overstretching official resources or exposing taxpayers to undue risks. For investors, it contains losses to painful, but manageable, limits. For borrowers, it buys time in which to set their economies back on track. For the global system, it can remedy market failure and stop panic before it starts, while it restores liquidity and the flow of funds to sound nations. As market forces discipline sovereigns to borrow less and compel investors to curb risk, the cycle of crisis will moderate.

16.18 A promise to pay by a credible institution with deep pockets can obviate the need to pay. Since floor-of-support prices are set at discounts to rational expectations of asset values, calls on official funds will be limited. The official sector assumes the execution risk that governments will renege on their promises; if these commitments are fulfilled, no funds will be spent. But all intervention has an inherent risk of loss. Just as a national central bank may hold an impaired asset if the collateral posted as security for a loan to a domestic bank deteriorates, the security value of sound policy for the ILOLR declines if the government reneges on its reforms. Support will be cut off going forward, but, just as in the domestic bank context, commitments to the markets must be honoured on assets that have now declined in value. To restrain contagion and stabilize markets, the ILOLR follows Bagehot's formula by lending 'around the insolvency' not 'into the insolvency'. Offers of support are extended to all endangered nations that meet its 'good collateral' criterion.

16.19 But who, then, is the ILOLR? Or will it be the plural—lender*s*? Once, for nations in trouble, the International Monetary Fund (IMF) was the central source of support; now, the vast global marketplace and the crisis needs of industrialized economies and of the growing powers of the emerging world outstrip the Fund's resources. Today, the IMF provides value with its *imprimatur* not with its money; in recent years, it assumed just 15 per cent of Europe's US$650 billion crisis funding. The eurozone and the larger European Union provide a template that will be replicated. Coalitions of governments, central banks, and international agencies will combine skills and funds to protect their mutual interests. Time, geography, and occasion will dictate whether the European Stability Mechanism (ESM) or the Chiang-Mai Initiative, which pools the reserves of thirteen Asian central banks, or agencies yet to be formed will underwrite the intervention.

16.20 How the floor of support adapts to answer the needs of three classic events of capital market distress is next addressed. When instability pervades capital markets, a floor for secondary market prices will preserve the flow of private sector funds. When market access has been closed, a floor for recovery values on new bond issues will restore funding to solvent, but illiquid, governments. When debts are unsustainable, a floor for defaulted bond prices will make restructuring timely and complete.

4. A Floor of Support to Preserve the Flow of Private Sector Funds[3]

16.21 The crisis is this: for valid reasons or otherwise, markets have lost faith in the debt of weak members of the Atlantis Monetary Union and their cost of borrowing is rising to

[3] The proposal of a central bank floor of support to maintain stability in sovereign bond markets was originally outlined in A. Lerrick, 'How to Save the Euro', *Wall Street Journal*, 2 December 2011, available online at <http://online.wsj.com/article/SB10001424052970203833104577070561141739048.html>.

unsustainable levels. The Atlantis Central Bank (ACB) steps into the secondary market with a floor of support that stands ready to buy unlimited quantities of bonds at predetermined prices for all governments that commit to fiscal solidity. Costs of financing stabilize, while overspending by governments is contained by a painfully high inflation-adjusted interest rate. The ACB never has to buy a single bond. Its strong word and even stronger balance sheet suffice. Market tranquillity is restored.

What central banks should and should not do is violently debated by economists the world over and never more so than in a currency union, in which a whole roster of member governments are looking over the shoulder of a joint monetary authority. Purists argue that the central bank mandate is first and only to safeguard price stability. Activists embrace an expanded mission to promote employment, to increase lending, and to improve social welfare. **16.22**

Finance ministers, who believe that membership in a currency club entitles them to the same low cost of funds as their more solvent neighbours, clamour for the union's central bank to turn on the monetary printing press and to buy up every weak government bond until yields are driven down to windfall rates. Intervention in the secondary market of sovereign bonds has always been a standard tool of monetary policy, but narrowly directed at the rates of inflation and economic growth. Purists condemn secondary market bond purchases with a goal of lowering a government's cost of funds as inflationary monetization of deficit and debt. Activists retort that muddled interest rates set by a mistaken market need correction. **16.23**

Correctness aside, massive direct intervention in the secondary market is an inefficient way in which to force the cost of new funds down. Trillions of questionable assets might suddenly move from the private sector to the central bank's balance sheet and conflict its choices as both a creditor and the guardian of price stability. But, in a panic, stabilizing the value of the entire stock of outstanding debt may be the only effective tool to calm markets. **16.24**

Central banks need not choose between market chaos and monetary integrity. A floor of support can provide a clear rule of intervention that does away with the uncertainty that leads to market disruption, while an inflation-adjusted intervention rate that leans against economic cycles will resolve objections of monetary expansion. A new outright monetary transactions (OMT) programme from the European Central Bank (ECB) mirrors the format of the floor of support, but chooses flexibility over the precision that quiets uncertainty and lacks safeguards against inflationary financing of government deficits.[4] **16.25**

Under the floor-of-support structure, the central bank would publicly announce that it stands ready to buy at a 5 per cent *inflation-adjusted* yield all bonds of all governments with a proven, not just promised, commitment to fiscal reform. Strong conditionality would **16.26**

[4] In August 2012, President Mario Draghi announced a sweeping mission statement for the ECB. The Bank stood ready to 'do whatever it takes' and to buy unlimited amounts of member government bonds in the secondary market at a price unset, at a time unstated, and under conditions unspecified. Bond prices jumped as investors and politicians applauded. A programme of continuous fiscal reform was added as a condition to intervention.

The programme's title, 'Outright Monetary Transactions', cloaked its real intent of lowering funding costs for weak members with the pretext that differences in market rates do not reflect true creditworthiness, but an unjustified fear that troubled nations might leave the monetary union. But for markets, default and redenominating government bonds in a national currency are both broken promises with the same credit risk. Different costs of funds for identical companies on different sides of the Italian–Austrian border are not evidence of a 'faulty monetary policy transmission mechanism', but reflect the risks of their respective governments.

underpin the central bank support. If governments backslide, central bank purchases automatically end. The floor-of-support price is counter-cyclical, falling as the inflation rate rises and leaning against monetary expansion. Buying sound government bonds at a 5 per cent real rate of interest cannot be inflationary over the medium term.

16.27 Each month, a rolling twelve-month inflation rate will reset the central bank floor-of-support level for five–ten-year government bonds. At an inflation rate of 3 per cent, sovereign interest rates would be capped at 8 per cent. For a seven-year bond with a 7 per cent coupon, this translates to a central-bank-guaranteed price of 95 per cent of nominal amount. If inflation were to rise to 4 per cent, the same bond would have a guaranteed value of 90 per cent. If inflation were to fall to 2 per cent, the guaranteed minimum value would be 100 per cent. If inflation jumps, the counter-cyclical impact of the floor of support gains force. At 6 per cent inflation, the central bank interest rate cap rises to 11 per cent and the price guarantee on the same bond falls to 81 per cent.

16.28 Figures 16.1 and 16.2 detail the impact of the floor-of-support intervention rule for the governments of Spain and Italy during the 2010–12 eurozone crisis.

16.29 For investors, the central bank has set a bottom to the market that protects against panic-induced losses linked to market failure, but not against rational losses linked to bad decisions.

16.30 For weak governments, borrowing costs are painful, but sustainable, keeping pressure on politicians to restore sound finances. The government will remain solvent because the cost of the high real interest rates applies only to new financing, not to its entire existing stock of debt. Because tax revenues track inflation, the impact of the central bank counter-cyclical intervention rule on government budgets will be cushioned.

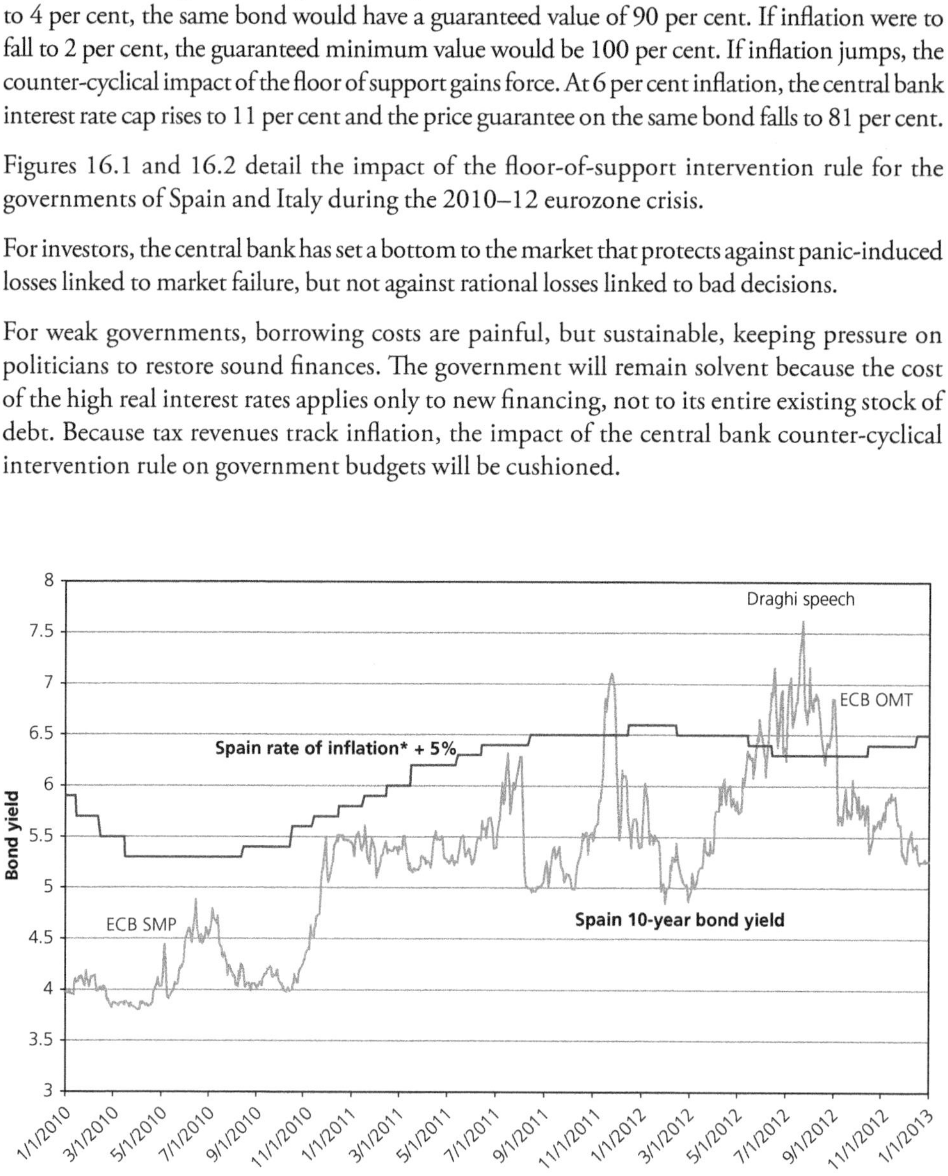

Figure 16.1 Real interest rate floor of support: Spain

* Annual rate of consumer price inflation excluding energy prices

Sources: Bloomberg; Eurostat

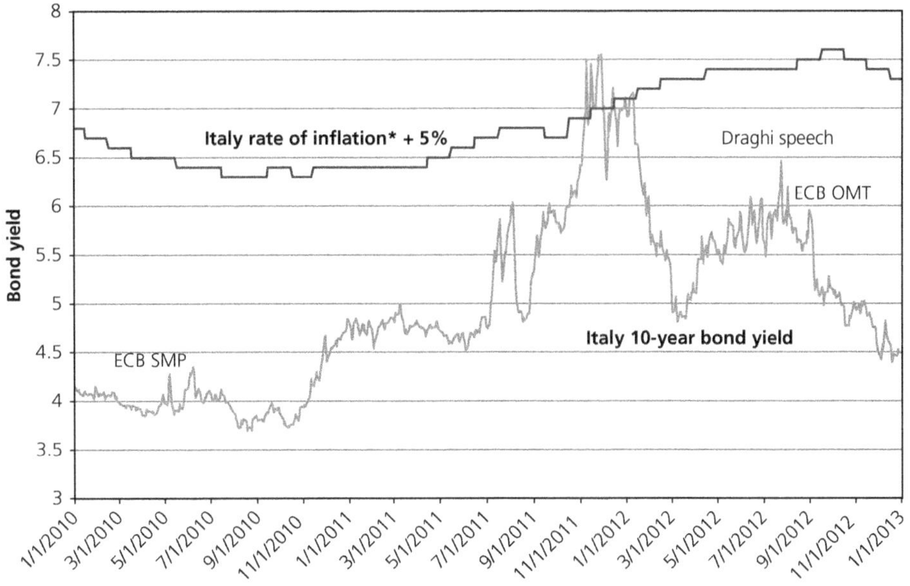

Figure 16.2 Real interest rate floor of support: Italy

* Annual rate of consumer price inflation excluding energy prices

Sources: Bloomberg; Eurostat

For the financial system, the central bank's fully funded promise guarantees liquidity and supports collateral values for loans. For the currency itself, the clearly defined counter-cyclical rule ensures stable inflation and exchange rates. **16.31**

Central banks are designed to stand up when markets fail to function. The floor of support meets the criteria of a classic lender of last resort—lending in a crisis against good collateral at a penalty interest rate. The inability of a government with a sound fiscal programme to obtain funds at a 5 per cent real interest rate is a crisis. An interest rate of 5 per cent above inflation is a penalty. The government's execution, not the promise, of a credible fiscal policy is good collateral. **16.32**

5. A Floor of Support to Restore Private Sector Investment Flows[5]

The crisis is this: the Kingdom of Olives has based its spending on boom-time revenues and now faces mounting fiscal deficits that markets fear will lead to insolvency. As borrowing costs escalate, the government is months late in honouring everyday supplier bills: hospitals are short on drugs; rubbish is uncollected in the streets. To buy time and to restore credit while Olives mends its ways, the Regional Financial Stability Facility writes a floor of support into the Kingdom's new bonds that insures a substantial recovery value if default occurs. Capital returns at affordable rates, public sector bills are paid, and businesses get credit. **16.33**

[5] The proposal of an official floor of support guaranteeing minimum recovery values for sovereign bonds in the event of default was originally outlined in A. Lerrick, *An EFSF Floor of Support to Achieve Eurozone Stability while Maintaining Discipline*, American Enterprise Institute Research Paper (September 2011).

16.34 There are no small losses in sovereign debt. The record shows that, when governments default, the toll is 50–70 per cent down for the private sector. Where countries are willing to commit to reform, the official sector issues a floor-of-support umbrella policy against catastrophic loss on new bonds that sets a limit to investor risk: 70 per cent of capital value will be guaranteed to the bondholder. Government failure to honour fiscal promises will trigger cancellation of insurance for future borrowing and a return to costly stand-alone rates.

16.35 This floor of support replicates a centuries-old insurance industry formula that protects against the risk of catastrophic loss—fire and flood that destroy a house and traffic pile-ups that total a truck. Against affordable risks, the policyholder self-insures with deductibles.[6] As the stand-in for the insurance company, the taxpayer moves to a preferred creditor status. When the investor's first loss is added to expected recovery values under default, the taxpayer exposure is reduced to a fraction of the nominal commitment.

16.36 New bonds issued by crisis governments would carry their standard terms and conditions except that:

- the interest rates on the bonds will be below stand-alone market levels; and
- in the event of a default by the issuing government, the official sector will guarantee the investor's ability to sell the bond at a predetermined minimum 70 per cent of nominal amount on its maturity date. The minimum value guarantee can take the form of a put option or a loan to the distressed government specifically dedicated to repurchase bonds.[7]

16.37 Targeting the appeal of primary market bonds is an efficient use of scarce official resources. It lowers the cost of new financing flows without expending large sums to raise the value of the entire stock of secondary market debt.

16.38 The floor of support increases the effectiveness of official sector resources without borrowing and without magnifying the risk of loss. Every €1 of official funds mobilizes €6–9 of new financing for distressed governments.

16.39 Four factors create the leverage. Only the last 70 per cent of the nominal amount of government bonds is covered. Payment is distant at the maturity date of the bonds. The probability of default is less than 100 per cent. If default does occur, recovery values reduce losses. The effective value of the official sector commitment determines the resources necessary and can be measured continuously:

$$\text{(Floor of support} - \text{Minimum recovery)} \times \text{Net present value (NPV) of nominal commitment} \times \text{Probability of default}$$

[6] An alternative 'first loss' protection formula, offered by the European official sector, has it backwards. Picking up the first 20 per cent of losses, which investors may not welcome, but can weather, still leaves the bondholder exposed to the massive losses of default that hit seldom, but with hurricane force. The risk for the taxpayer is magnified. If any default occurs, the taxpayer will be wiped out. There is no reason for taxpayers to subsidize an affordable credit risk that belongs on private sector balance sheets.

[7] The floor of support differs from standard credit default swap (CDS) protection in three ways: (a) the payment upon default is 70 per cent of nominal amount versus 100 per cent under a standard CDS contract; (b) the payment upon default is made on the maturity date of the bond, not at the time of default, as under a standard CDS; and (c) there is no up-front payment by the investor. A standard CDS requires the overwhelming majority of the cost to be paid up-front. Over a range of recovery values from 40 per cent to 60 per cent in the event of a default, the value of the floor of support on a ten-year maturity bond is 30–40 per cent of the value of a standard CDS.

Example
Official floor of support: 70% of nominal amount of bonds supported
Accreted NPV of nominal official sector commitment: 82.14% of nominal commitment
Credit default swap (CDS) determined probability of default over remaining life: 39.8%
Minimum expected recovery upon default: 30% of nominal amount of bonds
Effective value of official sector commitment: (0.70 – 0.30) × 0.8214 × 0.398 = 13.1% of nominal amount of bonds supported
Efficacy of official sector resources: 1 ÷ 0.131 = 7.6 times

Table 16.1 details the effective resource commitment and the leverage of official funds under a floor of support over a range of expected recovery values and time horizons.

Table 16.1 Effective commitment of official sector and resource efficacy*

End of year	CDS-based probability of default over remaining life (%)	Accreted NPV of nominal official 70% commitment (% of nominal amount of bonds)	Official resources to stand behind effective value of commitment (% of nominal amount of bonds)			Efficacy of official resources (bonds supported/official resources)		
			Recovery rate			Recovery rate		
			0%	30%	40%	0%	30%	40%
0	51.4	52.9	27.2	15.5	11.7	3.7	6.4	8.6
1	47.8	54.4	26.0	14.9	11.1	3.8	6.7	9.0
2	43.9	55.9	24.5	14.0	10.5	4.1	7.1	9.5
3	39.8	57.5	22.9	13.1	9.8	4.4	7.6	10.2
4	35.9	59.1	21.2	12.1	9.1	4.7	8.2	11.0
5	31.5	60.8	19.2	10.9	8.2	5.2	9.1	12.2
6	25.9	62.6	16.2	9.3	6.9	6.2	10.8	14.4
7	19.9	64.3	12.8	7.3	5.5	7.8	13.7	18.2
8	13.4	66.2	8.9	5.1	3.8	11.3	19.7	26.3
9	6.6	68.1	4.5	2.6	1.9	22.2	38.9	51.9
10	0.0	70.0	0.0	0.0	0.0	n/a	n/a	n/a

*Based on a 70 per cent floor of support, a 2.85 per cent ten-year zero-coupon bond cost of official sector financing, and 19 September 2011 CDS prices for Italy

The liquidity demands of the programme must be closely monitored. As the floor of support expands leverage, the nominal amount of commitments could temporarily exceed available cash if a default were to trigger payouts to investors. The official sector can guard against cash shortfalls by limiting leverage and diversifying the maturities of the bonds insured. 16.40

Example of liquidity demand
Default at the end of year 9 of floor-of-support programme
Recovery of 30% in year 12
Total nominal amount of bonds supported: €633 billion
Official floor-of-support nominal commitment: €443 billion (633 × 0.70)
Official sector resource requirement (effective value of commitment based upon 30% recovery): €253 billion (633 × (0.70 – 0.30))
Official sector liquidity demand for two years from commitment drawdown at ten-year maturity date of bonds until recovery in year 12: €190 billion (633 × 0.30)

Table 16.2 details the official sector liquidity requirement under a floor-of-support structure.

Table 16.2 Liquidity requirement of official floor of support*

Default at end of year	Floor of support bonds supported (€bn)	NPV of nominal official commitment (€bn)	Total recovery (€bn)	Recovery before drawdown of official commitment (€bn)	Official resources committed (€bn)	Official liquidity requirement (€bn)
0	633	335	190	190	145	0
1	633	344	190	190	154	0
2	633	354	190	190	164	0
3	633	364	190	190	174	0
4	633	374	190	190	184	0
5	633	385	190	190	195	0
6	633	396	190	190	206	0
7	633	407	190	190	217	0
8	633	419	190	190	229	0
9	633	431	190	0	241	190
10	633	443	190	0	253	190
11	n/a	443	190	n/a	253	190
12	n/a	443	190	n/a	253	0

*Based on a default on €633 billion of floor of support bonds, a 70 per cent floor of support, a 30 per cent recovery rate upon default, a two-year recovery period, and a 2.85 per cent official sector cost of funds

16.41 Keeping pressure on spendthrift politicians is crucial for the success of fiscal reform. As countries improve, markets will respond with lower rates on new floor-of-support bonds. Conversely, failure to meet reform promises will lead to cancellation of the programme and high stand-alone rates on borrowing. As an option to enhance performance incentives, the official sector can charge a fee to borrowing governments equal to a percentage of the difference between the interest rate on the floor-of-support bonds and the government's stand-alone market rates.

6. A Floor of Support to Underpin an Orderly Restructuring[8]

16.42 The crisis is this: the Republic of Manana has indulged voters with social overspending until its debt measures far more than it can ever hope to repay. Only a massive writedown will restore solvency. The Global Monetary Fund underwrites a floor of support in the form of a cash bid that guarantees a minimum market value for Manana's distressed bonds during the

[8] The proposal of an official floor of support in a sovereign debt restructuring was originally outlined in A. Lerrick and A. Meltzer, 'Beyond IMF Bailouts: Default without Disruption', *Financial Times*, 9 May 2001, and in A. Lerrick and A. Meltzer, 'Blueprint for an International Lender of Last Resort' (2003) 50(1) JME 289. This section is an adaption of the description of the structure outlined in A. Lerrick and S. Srivastava, 'Default without Disruption: Simulation of a Sovereign Debt Restructuring' (2004) 1(1) JRF 79, which detailed a simulation of a sovereign debt restructuring utilizing an official floor of support.

restructuring. Panic is prevented, while restructuring proceeds. Professional holdouts search for other targets. Manana completes the exchange in a quick three months, with a 97 per cent participation rate. There are no calls on official promises to pay. A solvent Manana returns triumphantly to the markets.

Illiquidity for investors is the trigger for panic when borrowers begin to fail. The floor of support restores a well-functioning market in distressed debt during restructuring because it guarantees to creditors the ability to sell claims for a fixed cash price significantly above trough levels of past crises.[9] The arbitrage and financing opportunities created will draw in a whole new universe of investors. The turbulent path of market prices during Ecuador's 1999 default, when prices collapsed to 2 per cent of nominal value, is what the official sector fears and the floor of support precludes. (See Figure 16.3.)[10] **16.43**

For restructuring to succeed, a credible threat of imminent default is a prerequisite. Voluntary writedowns are wishful thinking; no investor ever volunteers to take a loss. The government of the debtor country and the official sector make six announcements simultaneously, as follows. **16.44**

- All payments of principal and interest on the debt to the private sector will be suspended.
- A fixed minimum restructured value (maximum loss) is set for an exchange for new bonds. The final value may rise above the minimum as debtor and creditors negotiate.
- A programme of economic policies that substantiates the economy's ability to support the minimum restructured value of the debt is detailed.

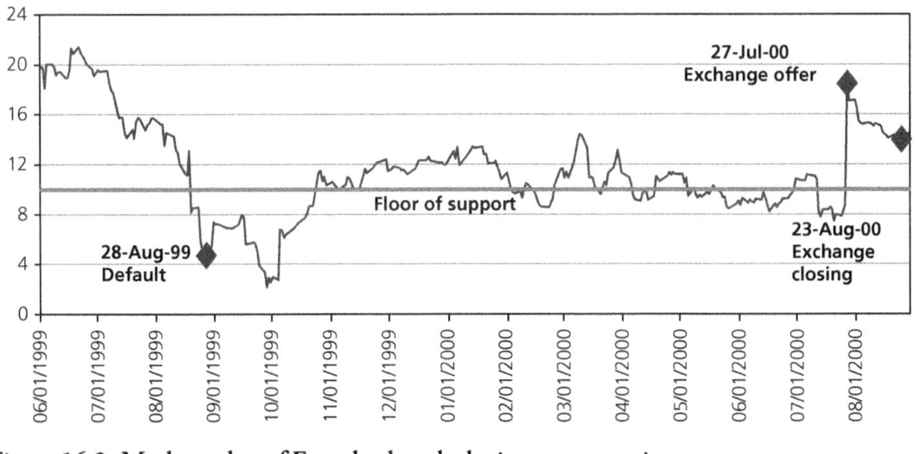

Figure 16.3 Market value of Ecuador bonds during restructuring

Sources: Bear Stearns; Bloomberg; Merrill Lynch

[9] The guarantee can take the form of a put option directly to the official sector or a loan to the distressed government dedicated to repurchase its bonds.

[10] During the fifteen trading days prior to the default on 28 August 1999, prices of Ecuador's US$1.4 billion collateralized discount bonds due 2025, stripped of their US Treasury collateral, fell from 14.5 per cent of principal amount to 5 per cent. Over the succeeding month, prices collapsed further to 2 per cent of principal amount. Stability returned after the initial panic, with prices rebounding to the 10–12 per cent range. When the terms of the restructuring were announced on 27 July 2000, prices jumped from 8 per cent to 18 per cent of principal amount. At the closing of the restructuring, prices settled at 14.5 per cent.

- A floor-of-support line of credit from the official sector to the government will permit debt holders to sell distressed claims for a fixed cash price set at a 15–20 per cent discount to the government's minimum offer.
- The exchange for new bonds will be offered within three months, at which point official support will end.
- To forestall contagion, the official sector stands ready to lend around the default to other economies if disruption spreads.

16.45 Illiquid distressed bonds are now transformed into highly marketable collateral. Banks will lend not against the bonds' intrinsic value, but upon the AAA on-demand cash value of the official bid. New investors will be attracted to leverage the official bid as collateral for borrowing and increase their returns. Demand for the bonds will push the market price above the official bid. Old creditors, who prefer cash, will not wait for the exchange and will unload their bonds in the market. Few, if any, funds will be demanded from official coffers.

16.46 Suppose that *p* is the par value of the country's bonds, *mrp* is the minimum restructured value and *smrp* is the official cash support bid. Since *smrp* is guaranteed by the official sector while the country's exchange offer is outstanding, an arbitrage opportunity is present during the term of the offer. An arbitrageur can buy the bonds at a price above *smrp*, use the bonds as collateral for a bank loan, and make the exchange for new bonds valued at or above *mrp* at the end of the ninety-day restructuring period. Banks would be willing to lend close to *smrp*, because the collateral could be sold for cash to the official sector at any time for this amount.

Example
p = 100
mrp = 50%
smrp = 40%

With a 95 per cent loan to collateral value and a purchase price of 49 per cent of nominal amount per bond, arbitrage yields an annualized return of 40 per cent over a three-month restructuring period. Even without leverage, annualized returns would be 40 per cent on a cost of 46 and 28 per cent on a cost of 47.

16.47 Vulture funds that invest at the end of a collapse with a view to holding out for preferential treatment are thwarted. By precluding excessive price declines, the floor of support ups the required investment and lowers returns. If the price of the defaulted bonds with a minimum restructured value of 50 falls only to 48, as opposed to 20 in a panic, a potential holdout's investment is more than doubled and the maximum total profit from extracting the full 100 face value falls from 400 per cent to 108 per cent, not even counting the always-significant collection costs. For a recovery time horizon of two to three years, the potential annual return is more than halved from 60–100 per cent to just 28–44 per cent.

16.48 Calls on official resources will be limited if realism prevails. The overly optimistic projections of growth, reform, and sustainable debt that have been used to justify past bailouts will be restrained by a set of new incentives. In a floor-of-support restructuring, both borrower and official sector will be motivated to choose conservative estimates that add up to a substantial writedown. Containing creditor demands for official cash and avoiding the high cost to the economy of repeated default will be the new goals.

7. Toward a Credible International Lender of Last Resort

Markets hate surprises: surprises cause panic. Now, the spectacle of a fearful official sector, charged with the stability of the global system, has raised uncertainty to shock-prone levels. **16.49**

Time and again, principle has been sacrificed for expediency, as central banks and international agencies have bent the rules and embraced the 'once unthinkable'. Rescue loans to Cyprus, Greece, Ireland, Portugal, and Spain flouted a key provision of the euro's founding treaty that forbade the transfer of debt between national treasuries. The ECB moved beyond its inflation-fighting mandate when it saddled its balance sheet with a troublesome €200 billion asset and soaked up weak eurozone government bonds to lower fiscal financing costs. A century of US bankruptcy law was reversed in the reordering of Chrysler debt when secured bank lenders were pressured by the White House to cede place to unsecured union pensions. Banana republic behaviour by advanced democracies and multilateral agencies proves that the rule of law will be violated if a sufficiently large crisis looms. **16.50**

Signals are often so confused that a team of fortune tellers is needed to interpret official announcements. Loans granted in the early morning hours of an all-night summit speak of transient compromise and reversal down the road. Caveats of a 'unique and exceptional event' negate the precedents that guide private sector investment flows. Collective action clauses that streamline the management of debt are called forth at whim: one day inserted retroactively in bonds and exercised to force a harsh agreement; next, dismissed in favour of overly friendly accord; then, made obligatory for all new bond issues. Fear of frightening investors ends by frightening investors away. Speculators remain to profit. **16.51**

Halfway measures do not buy even halfway cures. They delay the reckoning and prolong the suffering, while root causes fester and return in a stronger mutation. Only 'doing nothing', or as close to 'nothing' as world opinion permits, will teach markets to stop leveraging up capital in the conviction that bailouts that are decried in principle will be embraced in practice and that taxpayer earnings will be transferred to investor pockets. **16.52**

The International Lender of Last Resort must speak with a clear voice and commit to a clear rule. Known parameters equip the private sector to measure risk and invest capital. The German policy of *Ordnungspolitik* provides a template: rule enforcement that never hesitates or waivers; action that is predetermined and automatic; case-by-case tampering forbidden. **16.53**

A rule is only as strong as the credibility of the official sector and the good faith of threatened governments. Credibility requires resources of the magnitude to face down the most brutal and broad-based collapse. Credibility requires the conviction to stand up and commit these resources when crisis comes. Credibility requires the stomach to jettison distressed economies that fail to make good on policy reform and the integrity to refuse to mask insolvency with the banal excuse of illiquidity. **16.54**

Credibility must be permanently earned—crisis by crisis. Only time and a consistent record of promises fulfilled will flatten the volatile graph of market expectations and ensure to sound sovereigns an abundance of affordable funds for growth. **16.55**

17

ODIOUS DEBT

Sir William Blair

1. Introduction

Debts are legal constructs—their effect depends on the law that governs the debt. They can be repaid according to their terms, or they can be rescheduled by way of contractual variation or novation. They can become time-barred under the applicable prescription rules and they can become worthless through inflation. But they cannot vanish of their own accord. A fundamental principle of the rule of law is that, where legally enforceable, debts will be enforced. This applies as much to sovereign debt as to any other kind of debt. 17.01

The theme of this chapter has to do with the role of the law in tackling specific aspects of sovereign debt that render the debt *unenforceable* in whole or in part under ordinary principles of private law. It goes on to review the terms of a *lex specialis* that results in a limited form of statutory unenforceability. The law in question is the United Kingdom's Debt Relief (Developing Countries) Act 2010, which remains, it is believed, the only example of its kind. 17.02

The subject was broached in a well-known article published in *Duke Law Journal* in March 2007 by Lee Buchheit and two co-authors, G. Mitu Gulati and Robert. B. Thompson, under the somewhat forbidding title, 'The Dilemma of Odious Debts'.[1] The inimitable style of Lee Buchheit is evident from the article's epigraph, quoting the Scottish novelist Alexander McCall Smith—one of a number of literary allusions that make the text eminently readable. However, the subject matter is a serious one: namely, the liability of states for tainted debts entered into by corrupt governments. 17.03

The term 'odious debt' may (as the article suggests) be one of public international law, but it is not much used in English law, currently at least, and certainly has no technical meaning—but the words speak for themselves and, since much international sovereign lending is traditionally issued under English law, this chapter provides a response from that perspective. 17.04

The heart of the matter is stated at the beginning of the article. Public international law, say the authors, requires that states and governments succeed to the debts incurred by their predecessors, however ill-advised those borrowings may have been. There are situations, they continue, in which applying this rule of law strictly can lead to a morally reprehensible result. The example given is forcing future generations of citizens to repay money borrowed in the state's name by, and then stolen by, a former dictator. 17.05

---

[1] Lee C. Buchheit, G. Mitu Gulati, and Robert B. Thompson, 'The Dilemma of Odious Debts' (2007) 56 Duke LJ 1201.

17.06 The authors conclude, however, that there is no doctrine of public international law vitiating so-called 'odious debts'. This conclusion, it is considered, is plainly correct. However, that does not imply that the sovereign borrower in such a position is necessarily without remedy. As the authors point out, debt is meaningful only so far as it is enforceable and defences exist under US law that could be used to address many, although admittedly not all, cases of allegedly odious debts.

17.07 The authors surmise that such defences exist under other legal systems. The point is made in this chapter that this is correct as a matter of English law: there is, in fact, a recent and widely reported case that demonstrates this. It was in part publicity attaching to the case that led the UK to enact the Debt Relief (Developing Countries) Act 2010, albeit addressing a different problem. This is where the recovery of sovereign debt through the courts would be unduly onerous for a particular class of heavily indebted poor country (HIPC), as defined under the International Monetary Fund (IMF) and World Bank's HIPC Initiative.

17.08 As will be seen, the 2010 Act does not provide a general statutory defence for impoverished sovereign debtors. Further, unlike in the case of the so-called 'odious debt', the debt itself has been incurred perfectly properly. There is no question of unenforceability under applicable legal principles. The problem arises because of the inability of the country concerned to repay it—or, more precisely, since inability to pay is a routine phenomenon for which every legal system provides, the lack of any international system to allow for sovereign insolvency, despite the suggestions that have been made from time to time.

2. The Position of an Assignee of the Debt

17.09 The point made in the Buchheit article is that private law may provide adequate means of challenging odious debts if and when the creditor comes to enforce. Buchheit and his co-authors take the example of the case in which the creditor knows, or suspects, that a loan purportedly for the state is, in fact, to be used for the personal enrichment of the dictator. They posit a claim in the American courts by a creditor to recover the loan against the state now ruled by a successor—and hopefully better—government, and argue that there is no need for recourse to public international law. The state is amply protected under domestic private law doctrines, which preclude parties who are the knowing accessories to fraud from benefiting from the fraud.

17.10 When looked at in that way, it is clear that the example extends beyond enforcement in the American courts. The same kinds of doctrine are surely applied in most, if not all, courts of countries where the rule of law is observed.

17.11 The fraudulent accessory doctrine, in whatever form domestic law recognizes it, is readily applicable where the original lender knows or suspects that the loan is in fact to be applied for nefarious purposes. What is the position upon assignment?

17.12 A number of different scenarios may arise and it is worth identifying two of them. The first is where an *improperly* advanced debt (for example the loan purportedly to the state, but in fact for the dictator's personal purposes) is assigned to an assignee that is not itself in bad faith. Can that party enforce free of the effects of the fraud?

17.13 This is an important point, since so much sovereign debt is assignable and assigned. Consider the example given in the Buchheit article—that is, a debt purportedly for the purposes of the state, but which the lender knows (or suspects) is for the dictator's personal benefit. Private law, as has been seen, will effectively preclude enforceability. But what if the debt is assigned? How does the sovereign stand against an assignee who takes in good faith?

The first point to make is that someone who *suspects* wrongdoing is not in good faith, even if he or she does not actually *know* of the wrongdoing. There is vast body of case law on this subject, articulating doctrines such as constructive notice, but that is a broad summation of the principle. Suppose, however, that the assignee neither knows nor suspects of the wrongdoing. **17.14**

Here, it is necessary to distinguish between assignable and negotiable debt. The law merchant developed, at an early stage, the doctrine of negotiability in connection with bills of exchange. The effect of negotiability is that a good faith transferee of a negotiable debt instrument takes free of defects in the title of the original creditor. **17.15**

When he came to draft the Bills of Exchange Act 1882 (which remains the current statute in the UK), Sir Mackenzie Chalmers did not include bonds or other debt securities because he felt that the law was still in the course of development. However, the case law shows that such instruments will be treated by the courts as negotiable if they are treated as such in the market.[2] **17.16**

In the case of other debt, another basic legal principle comes into play. Axiomatically, the assignee of a debt can be in no better position vis-à-vis the debtor than was the original creditor. The obligation of a debtor to repay cannot differ merely because the debt is owed to a different party, following assignment. In such a case, therefore, the answer in principle is that such private law defences as were available against the original creditor remain available against an assignee. **17.17**

A second scenario is the case in which the debt was *properly* advanced. No question arises of any fraud at the time of the loan. But the debt is thereafter assigned in circumstances in which the assignment itself is tainted. Clearly, fraud or other improper behaviour concerned with an assignment raises different considerations from those just discussed, in that the relations between assignor and assignee are distinct from those between either of those parties and the debtor. In other words, fraud in the assignment may not have any connection with, or effect upon, the debtor's liability, although it may affect who can enforce it. **17.18**

However, in practice, the position may not be so simple and similar issues are capable of arising on assignment, as is illustrated by the case discussed next. **17.19**

3. Turning Metal into Gold: A Case of Alchemy

In *Donegal International Ltd v. Republic of Zambia*,[3] a case decided by the English Commercial Court following a lengthy trial, the facts were as follows. **17.20**

In 1979, Romania loaned Zambia US$15 million for the purchase of agricultural equipment—to be precise, Romanian tractors. The tractors never appear to have worked **17.21**

[2] For a review, *see* William Blair, 'Negotiability and Estoppel' (1988) 1 JIBL 8.

[3] [2007] 1 Lloyds Rep 397. The author of this chapter declares an interest, having acted as lead counsel for the Republic of Zambia in the case.

very well, but that is beside the point. The transactions were unimpeachable and in effect provided aid to Zambia by way of a soft loan.

17.22 In keeping with the nature of the transaction, there was minimal documentation. There was no jurisdiction provision or governing law provision, and no waiver of sovereign immunity on the part of Zambia. Presumably, no one ever expected to enforce the loan and anyone would have been hard pressed to do so, had they wanted to.

17.23 Soft it may have been, but it was still a loan. After the fall of Ceausescu in 1989, fraternal relations no longer took pride of place and Romania began to press for repayment (not being a Paris Club member).

17.24 In December 1998, a memorandum of understanding (MOU) was agreed by which Zambia would buy back the debt for 12 per cent. This beneficial treatment reflected the amount paid under an earlier World-Bank-funded scheme. The deal agreed was for payment of US$3.5 million reflecting accrued interest, payable over the next twelve months.

17.25 At this point in time, a Washington-based hedge fund stepped in and, acting through a special purpose vehicle (SPV) called Donegal, offered the Romanians US$3.2 million, but payable immediately. The Romanian government signed up, was paid, and assigned the debt to Donegal.

17.26 But, given the contractual position, the debt was effectively worthless, because it was effectively unenforceable. The assignment was, in reality, dependent on the goodwill of the Zambian government to recognize it—a point that the Governor of the Central Bank of Zambia made when recommending that the country did not engage with the fund.

17.27 However, in February 1999 and in controversial circumstances, an official in the Ministry of Finance provided Donegal with a letter from the government that acknowledged the company as having full and beneficial title. The letter concluded:

> In the event that we receive written notice from Donegal or subsequent holders that the Debt has been assigned, this Ministry will forthwith confirm in writing to the relevant assignees that such assignees had been registered as beneficial holders for the Debt.

In other words, the government not only expressly endorsed the assignment to Donegal, but also undertook to recognize any subsequent assignees.

17.28 It was Zambia's case at trial that the letter had been obtained by the payment of a bribe. However, as the trial judge pointed out, this is a serious allegation and, after a careful review of the evidence, the judge found that bribery had not been proved.

17.29 What happened next is that, armed with the acknowledgement, the fund set about trying to persuade Zambia to pay up. In July 2002, steps were under way to bring litigation against the country to recover the sum of US$42 million. There were a number of problems with this prospective litigation. One was that the figure depended on applying a rate of interest of 12 per cent debt, on the basis that the Zambian government had agreed such a rate. The judge found that no contractually binding agreement was reached.[4]

[4] *See Donegal* (n. 3), [326].

Another was choice of forum. In the event, proceedings were begun in the British Virgin Islands (BVI), where Donegal was incorporated. Since the contract of loan between Romania and Zambia had no connection with the BVI, there was no apparent basis for jurisdiction. However, the proceeding did give Donegal some leverage in its discussions with Zambia. 17.30

On a Saturday in April 2003, a representative of Donegal came to the Ministry of Finance with a settlement agreement, which the minister signed. The judge described it as 'an extraordinary way for the Government to conclude an important agreement'.[5] 17.31

The significance of the settlement agreement, however, was that it converted the original Romanian debt to something with a real value. The settlement agreement was subject to English choice of law and jurisdiction, and Zambia waived sovereign immunity. The agreement recorded the debt as being US$45 million (allowing for accruing interest at the alleged contractual rate). The settlement amount was US$15 million payable over three years. But, in case of a missed payment, the whole sum of US$45 million became due. 17.32

Over the next few months, US$2.5 million was paid, but payments were then missed by the Zambians. The claim was brought in the English court on the settlement agreement for the full amount of US$45 million. (The debt, it will be recalled, had been acquired for US$3.2 million.) 17.33

4. The Lessons to Be Learned

The facts, as found by the court, are a matter of record. What do they tell us about the hypothesis in the Buchheit article? In the *Donegal* case, the original lending was without reproach: it was essentially a soft loan from one government to another for the purchase of agricultural equipment. The case shows that, although the original lending may be unimpeachable, a vitiating factor of the kind discussed by the authors may arise on assignment. Zambia's complaint was made in respect of the circumstances surrounding the assignment and thereafter. Had the bribe allegation been proved, the fund's claim would have failed in its entirety. 17.34

In the event, Donegal recovered the sum of US$15 million, the agreed settlement figure, rather than US$45 million, which the settlement agreement recorded as being the amount of the debt. This result followed the application of another private law principle—namely, the doctrine of 'penalty'. As applied in English law, it holds that whilst the courts will enforce a genuine pre-estimate of damage that the parties have agreed, payment of a penal sum payable on default is not enforceable. 17.35

The case therefore serves as a useful illustration of the thesis in the article. At the enforcement stage, private law can be capable of providing adequate remedies in the case of a lender knowing or suspecting impropriety, or by an assignee in a similar position. Private law also contains other doctrines capable of mitigating unconscionable agreements—in this case, the rule against penalties. 17.36

Another point that arises from the case is a practical one. Zambia disputed the claim, and fought the case through trial on the facts and law. Although it achieved less than it had argued 17.37

[5] *See Donegal* (n. 3), [404].

for, the outcome was seen to be a fair one. In any event, payment was made by the state in accordance with the court order. A state will be in a much weaker position if it allows judgment to go by default and seeks to raise counterarguments at the enforcement stage.

5. The Debt Relief (Developing Countries) Act 2010

17.38 The *Donegal* case created considerable disquiet, and was a factor leading to the enactment in the UK of the Debt Relief (Developing Countries) Act 2010. On any view, this is a fairly remarkable piece of legislation—particularly coming from a creditor nation, the law of which is commonly used in international financial transactions.

17.39 As already noted, although prompted by the *Donegal* case, the Act addresses an entirely different kind of question. What it seeks to do, in essence, is to place limits on the enforceability of foreign sovereign debt in the English courts by reference to the HIPC Initiative. Between thirty and forty countries are included within this initiative, or potentially eligible. The details are beyond the scope of this chapter, but are readily accessible through public sources.

17.40 Laudable though the aim of legislation was, it posed a considerable legislative challenge, not least because HIPC is an initiative, not a set of rules. In the event, it is quite tightly circumscribed in its scope. The following features of the statute may be noted.

(a) It covers (i) public debt (ii) incurred prior to the enactment of the Act, (iii) which is covered by the HIPC Initiative, (iv) held externally, (v) not arising from the supply of goods or services, and (vi) with a maturity of over a year.
(b) It extends to foreign judgments and arbitral awards in respect of such debts, and includes debt subject to a negotiated agreement (as in the *Donegal* case).
(c) It applies regardless of governing law.
(d) The UK courts are prohibited from enforcing the debt beyond the HIPC terms applicable to the debt. In other words, for the purposes of enforceability, claimant creditors will be subject to the HIPC writedown. This is the essential feature of the legislation.
(e) There are various 'balancing' provisions. For example, in the event of a default after a restructuring, the HIPC formula is applied to the original amount of the debt.
(f) The Act does not apply unless the debtor has offered to make a payment comparable to HIPC terms.
(g) There is a sunset clause in the legislation. However, in May 2011, a year after its enactment, the Act was extended to have a permanent effect by the incoming Parliament, reflecting the fact that it had cross-party support. It nonetheless continues to apply *only* to pre-commencement debt; it does *not* apply to debts incurred after the enactment of the legislation.

17.41 This last exclusion of post-enactment debt is an important proviso. It was included because the UK did not wish to be alone in the approach that it took. Nevertheless, although other countries talked of such an enactment, it does not yet seem to have been followed elsewhere.

6. Postscript

17.42 No one needs convincing of the breadth of the contribution that Lee Buchheit has made in the field of sovereign debt. It extends far beyond the geopolitical challenges of sovereign restructuring.

In another article entitled 'Law, Ethics and International Finance',[6] Buchheit pointed out that the law—by which he meant public international law—requires successor governments to honour the obligations incurred by their predecessors, with very few exceptions. He continued: 17.43

> Morality and fairness, however, balk at the idea of forcing the citizens of a country to repay debts that may have only benefitted a kleptomaniacal former dictator. The trick, of course, is finding a way to relax the strict legal rule to avoid the morally repugnant result, without abandoning altogether the principle that sovereign-debt contracts are intended to be legally binding undertakings.

An outcome by which the law can accommodate an ethical approach in this respect may be a long way off, but it is surely worth pursuing? 17.44

6 Lee C. Buchheit, 'Law, Ethics and International Finance' (2007) 70 Law & Contemp Probs 1.

18

SOVEREIGN CONTINGENT LIABILITIES

Lee C. Buchheit and G. Mitu Gulati

1. Introduction

It is a truth universally acknowledged, that a sovereign borrower in possession of an uncomfortably large stock of debt, must be in want of camouflage. And since the commencement of the financial crisis in 2008, many sovereigns seem to have found it—in the form of contingent sovereign liabilities. **18.01**

In every situation in which a sovereign lends its credit support to facilitate a borrowing by a third party, the sovereign will have had a choice. The alternative to guaranteeing the debt of the third party is for the sovereign to borrow the money in its own name and on-lend the proceeds to that entity. The difference is that a direct liability appears on a sovereign's own balance sheet; a contingent liability probably will not. In the last five years, as the need to finance Great Recession stimulus measures has swollen the debt-to-gross-domestic-product (GDP) ratios of many developed countries, sovereigns have sought to camouflage the true extent of their liabilities by resorting to the issuance of contingent, rather than direct, obligations.[1] **18.02**

2. Sovereign Comfort

A benignant sovereign may bestow its credit support to a third party in a variety of ways, as follows. **18.03**

A. Explicit sovereign guarantees

At one end of the spectrum will be an explicit contractual guarantee by the sovereign expressed in words like these: **18.04**

> The Republic hereby unconditionally and irrevocably guarantees (as primary obligor and not merely as surety) the punctual payment when due, whether at stated maturity, by acceleration or otherwise, of all obligations of the Obligor now or hereafter existing under this Agreement....

[1] *See*, e.g., Landon Thomas Jr, 'State Debt Guarantees that are Hidden Add to Worries in Europe', *New York Times*, 5 February 2013; Christopher Spink, 'Contingent Sovereign Liabilities a "Landmine"' [2012] Int'l Fin Rev 1935; David Reilly, 'Time to End the Fiction of "Frannie"', *Wall Street Journal*, 21 August 2012. Reilly writes:

> That [a new requirement that Fannie Mae and Freddie Mac pay all of their profit to the US government as a dividend] bolsters the argument that Fannie and Freddie should be included on the government's balance sheet. Of course, that is politically unpalatable: The inclusion of their combined $5.3 trillion in liabilities would balloon the nearly $16 trillion in total federal debt outstanding and breach the debt ceiling.

Such an explicit guarantee will sometimes come with all of the trappings of an independent, separately enforceable, legal obligation on the part of the sovereign guarantor: representations; covenants; waiver of sovereign immunity; choice of foreign governing law; submission to foreign court jurisdiction; and appointment of an agent for service of process abroad.

18.05 Explicit sovereign guarantees may also be extended by operation of law. Some—but only some—deposit insurance schemes benefit from the full faith and credit of the host sovereign. In some countries, certain state-owned enterprises will, by law, carry the full faith and credit of their sovereign in their borrowing activities.

B. Implicit sovereign assurances

18.06 The other side of the spectrum of sovereign credit support consists of nothing more than a background shadow—a figurative (perhaps even a literal) wink, nod, and reassuring smile to the prospective investor. These are normally situations in which the primary obligor is so closely associated with the sovereign in the mind of the market (such as a political subdivision or an important state-owned enterprise) that lenders to the primary obligor are passively encouraged in the belief that the sovereign could never tolerate a circumstance in which the primary obligor tarnishes the reputation of the sovereign by defaulting on its debts. Nothing is ever said openly about sovereign credit support in these situations, but the perceptive investor is expected to see the warm arm of the sovereign wrapped in a reassuring manner around the shoulder of the debtor.

C. In between

18.07 Between these two extremes of unambiguously explicit sovereign guarantees and gauzily implicit sovereign reassurances are many gradations, including the following.

- *Partial guarantees*—The sovereign agrees to cover only a portion of the amount payable by the primary obligor.
- *Indemnities*—The sovereign agrees to indemnify the creditor for any residual loss, but only after all efforts to recover the debt from the primary obligor have been exhausted.
- *Keepwells*—The sovereign's promise to the lender is limited to an undertaking that the primary obligor will, at all times, have a positive net worth (often expressed as a nominal amount), but the sovereign is free to achieve this objective of solvency in any way it wishes (by recapitalizing the primary obligor, assuming or paying some of its debts, lending money to the primary obligor, etc.).
- *Comfort letters*—An aptly named instrument, the comfort letter, in its most innocuous form, merely assures the lender that the sovereign is aware that the primary obligor is borrowing the money, that the sovereign does not object to the transaction, and that the obligor continues to enjoy the affections of the sovereign.

18.08 The remainder of this chapter will deal only with explicit sovereign guarantees. For obvious reasons, it is impossible to identify or quantify implicit guarantees because they exist only in the eye of the beholder.[2]

---

[2] This vagueness about whether a particular loan does or does not enjoy the credit support of the sovereign carries its own risks. In a distressed debt context, a lender that thinks itself the beneficiary of an implicit sovereign guarantee is apt to howl if the sovereign orphans the primary obligor and allows the loan to go into default. The United Arab Emirates, burned by just this reaction during the Dubai financial crisis of 2009, subsequently changed its policy to ensure that there would be no future misunderstandings about which loans to state-linked enterprises did, and which did not, enjoy government support: *see* Camilla Hall, 'Abu Dhabi Tightens Rules for Debt Issued to State-Linked Businesses', *Financial Times*, 23 October 2012, 15.

3. Contingent Charms

The principal charm (for the guarantor) of a contingent obligation lies precisely in its contingent nature: no one can be sure, at the time that the debt is incurred, whether it will be paid by the primary obligor without recourse to the guarantor. This feature allows guarantors, with the blessing of the accounting profession, to treat the resulting liabilities as off balance sheet unless and until something happens down the road that makes it probable that the guarantee will, in fact, be called. For sovereigns already groaning under dangerously bloated debt-to-GDP ratios, this accounting treatment allows the sovereign to continue to raise capital on the strength of the sovereign's credit standing while not visibly increasing the size of the sovereign's own stock of debt. The only catch is that the loans must be directed in the first instance to a third party (the primary obligor) under the cover of the sovereign guarantee. That third party may be related to the sovereign (a state-owned enterprise, for example), or it may be a private sector entity whose activities the sovereign wishes to encourage. A construction project undertaken by a private sector entity in the tourism industry is a good example. **18.09**

Accounting standards differ somewhat in how they describe the circumstances that allow a guarantor to keep a contingent liability off of its own balance sheet. For corporate borrowers, the International Accounting Standard (IAS) 37 directs that if a present obligation 'may, but probably will not, require an outflow of resources' from the guarantor, it need not be 'recognized' on the balance sheet of the guarantor, but should be disclosed in financial statements as a contingent liability.[3] Where the likelihood of an outflow of resources from the guarantor is 'remote', even the need for financial disclosure is omitted.[4] **18.10**

The general principle established by Eurostat (the statistical office of the European Union) for presenting the accounts of EU member states is broadly similar. As long as a state guarantee is not called by beneficiary, the liability is recorded only on the balance sheet of the primary obligor, not that of the sovereign.[5] Eurostat recognizes a 'special case' exception to this general principle in situations in which need for the government to make debt service payments on the loan is open and notorious from the outset. The Eurostat Manual describes the circumstances in the following terms: **18.11**

> Even though the liability is issued by the enterprise itself, it may be right away considered with certainty as an actual government liability if the following conditions are fulfilled:
> - the law authorizing issuance of the debt specifies the government's obligation of repayment.
> - the budget of the State specifies each year the amount of repayment.
> - this debt, issued by the enterprise, is systematically repaid by the State (interest and principal).
>
> The liability must then be recorded directly—as soon as at issuance—in the government financial account and balance sheet, and not in the enterprise's. Its amount must be taken into account in the government debt.[6]

---

[3] IASB Guidance on Implementing IAS 37, Tables, *Provisions and Contingent Liabilities*.

[4] IAS 37, para. 28.

[5] Eurostat, *Manual for Government Deficit and Debt: Implementation of ESA95* (2012 edition), available online at <http://epp.eurostat.ec.europa.eu/portal/page/portal/product_details/publication?p_product_code=KS-RA-12-003>, II.4.3.2(1).

[6] Eurostat (n. 5), II.4.3.2(2).

A Note on the Database

The statistical information in this chapter is based on a survey of sovereign guaranteed bonds issued between 1 January 1965 and 1 July 2013, which bonds appear on three publicly available databases (Dealogic, Perfect Information, and Thomson One Banker).[7] The prospectuses and offering circulars for a total of 885 sovereign guaranteed bonds appearing on these databases were reviewed.

This is *not* the total universe of sovereign guaranteed bonds. The databases used are commercial and therefore usually include only those bonds that the database operators believe will be of interest to paying customers. The information derived suggests that those customers tend to be foreign rather than local investors (domestic investors are often less concerned with legal terms, having other mechanisms with which to police and monitor the behaviour of their sovereign). In other words, what is reported on in this chapter is probably both a small and biased (towards the interests of foreign investors) subset of the universe of sovereign guaranteed bonds, the exact size of which is entirely a matter of speculation.

It is nevertheless the authors' belief that the results reveal general trends in the issuance of these instruments over time, particularly in the areas of greatest relevance to the subject of this chapter—that is, number of issuances (relative to direct sovereign bonds), governing law, submission to court jurisdiction, and waiver of sovereign immunity.

4. The Explosion of 2008–12

18.12 The data reviewed suggests that there was an explosion in the number of sovereign-guaranteed bonds issued after the onset of the financial crisis in 2008, particularly in Europe. Using publicly available information (see 'A Note on the Database'), the results are shown on Figure 18.1.

18.13 Figure 18.2 reports a different, but equally striking, perspective: it focuses on the bonds and guarantees for the six euro area nations that were generally perceived to be at the heart of the crisis starting in late 2009—that is, Greece, Italy, Ireland, Portugal, Spain, and Belgium. These are also the six early entrants to the European Monetary Union (EMU) who have not traditionally been AAA-rated (in contrast to, for example, Germany and France). For these six nations, Figure 18.2 reports both the numbers of sovereign bonds and guaranteed bonds issued during the quarter-century between 1 January 1988 and 1 July 2013. As the European crisis worsens during the 2009–12 period, the issuance of guaranteed bonds, particularly in comparison to regular sovereign bonds, mushrooms.

18.14 An excellent study released by Houlihan Lokey in May 2012[8] concluded that sovereign loan/bond guarantees in Europe as of end 2010 (a category that did not include other forms of

[7] The bonds available from Bloomberg, a fourth data source, were also examined, but found to include no bonds that had not already been accessed from one of the other databases.

[8] Houlihan Lokey, 'The Increasing Risks Posed by Contingent Liabilities: How to Measure and Manage Them', Presentation at the 2012 Meeting of the Private Sector with the Paris Club and with Representatives of Non Paris Club Bilateral Creditors (September 2012), available online at <http://www.iif.com/emp/dr/>.

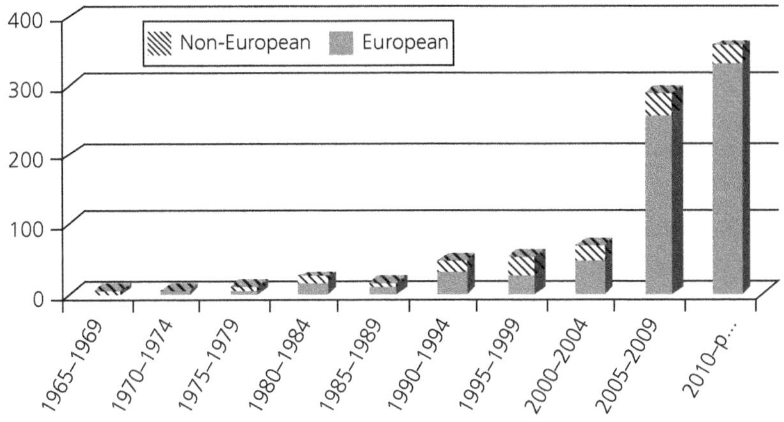

Figure 18.1 Number of bonds with sovereign guarantees (1 January 1965–1 July 2013)

Note: N = 885

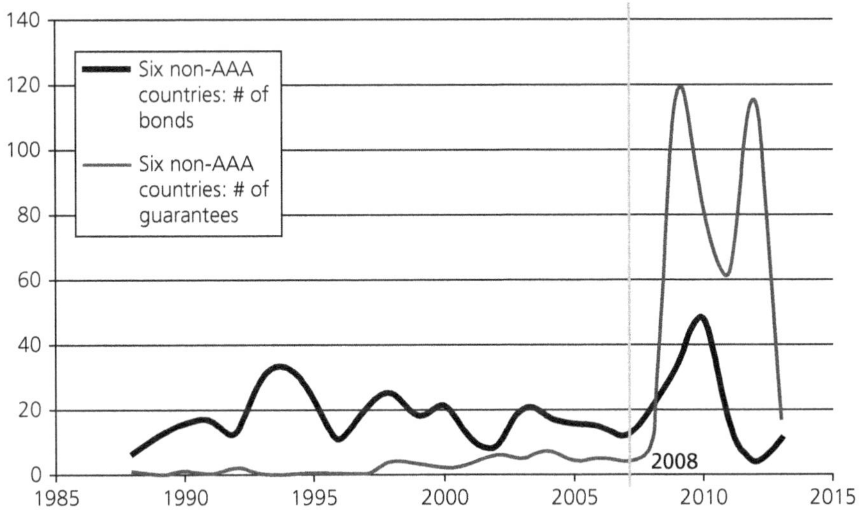

Figure 18.2 Numbers of bonds versus guaranteed bonds for six non-AAA early euro area entrants (1 January 1988–1 July 2013)

sovereign contingent exposure such as umbrella guarantees or deposit insurance schemes) represented, on a GDP-weighted average, 13.1 per cent of European GDP. In some countries, contingent exposure approached 30 per cent of GDP. The trend noted in the Houlihan study was upward; the aggregate size of guarantees outstanding in 2013 is undoubtedly significantly larger than it was in 2010.

There are two explanations for this dramatic rise in the popularity of contingent sovereign obligations. The first, as discussed, is the desire of overindebted developed countries to minimize further strains on their debt-to-GDP ratios. The off-balance-sheet accounting treatment of contingent obligations permits this. The second explanation relates to the methods by which the European Central Bank (ECB) has been prepared to provide liquidity **18.15** assistance to banks in the eurozone. A bank in need of liquidity may either borrow money directly from the ECB's discount window by posting eligible collateral for the loan, or it may borrow the funds from its own central bank through the emergency liquidity assistance (ELA) programme. These latter funds, however, are ultimately also sourced from the ECB and the Eurosystem, and require the posting of eligible collateral by the borrowing bank.

18.16 Peripheral European banks that had exhausted their store of eligible collateral for these programmes came up with an ingenious solution: they manufactured eligible collateral.[9] The bank issues a debt instrument to itself (there is no third-party purchaser of the instrument), takes the instrument to its local ministry of finance and obtains a government guarantee, and then uses the instrument as collateral for a new borrowing from ECB's discount window or the ELA.[10]

18.17 In July 2012, the ECB is reported to have grown alarmed at the size of the manufactured collateral that it was accepting at its discount window. The ECB accordingly capped the amount of 'specially tailored bonds' that could be used for this purpose by eurozone banks at the level that each bank had outstanding at the time the new policy was announced.[11]

5. Precedents

18.18 One of the remorseless laws of sovereign debt management is that size brings risk. If a component of a sovereign's debt stock is of negligible size, that component can sometimes escape a debt restructuring. For example, with only a couple of exceptions, sovereign bonds were not restructured in the 1980s debt crisis. The reason? Emerging market sovereign bond issues were rare in the period before the crisis began in 1982, and the cost–benefit analysis weighed heavily in favour of exempting those few bonds from the restructurings that engulfed commercial bank loans and bilateral credits in that decade. But, by the late 1990s, bonds had replaced bank loans as the main component of the debt stocks of many emerging market countries. Bond restructurings therefore became inevitable in countries with insupportable debt loads.

18.19 If this remorseless law is indeed remorseless, it suggests that any country carrying a significant stock of contingent sovereign obligations will eventually need to address those liabilities if a generalized restructuring of the country's debt becomes necessary. Unfortunately, there are few historical precedents to guide such an exercise.

18.20 In the sovereign debt restructurings of the 1980s, the aggregate number of sovereign guarantees was small. This allowed them to be ignored in the debt workouts of that era. The

---

[9] The Cypriot Ministry of Finance charmingly refers to instruments issued for the sole purpose of ECB/ELA discounting as 'collateral for liquidity extraction from the European Central Bank': Republic of Cyprus, Ministry of Finance, *Public Debt Management Annual Report 2011* (March 2012), available online at <http://www.mof.gov.cy/mof/pdmo/pdmo.nsf/All/FF9F9CCE6F27A2DCC225782B002F21CC/$file/Annual%20Report%202011.pdf>, 35.

[10] *See* Sonia Sirletti and Elisa Martinuzzi, 'Italy Banks Said to Use State-Backed Bonds for ECB Loans', *Bloomberg*, 21 December 2011, available online at <http://www.bloomberg.com/news/2011-12-20/italian-banks-are-said-to-use-state-guaranteed-bonds-to-receive-ecb-loans.html>.

[11] *See* Marc Jones, 'ECB Caps Use of State-Backed Bonds as Collateral', *Reuters*, 3 July 2012, available online at <http://uk.reuters.com/assets/print?aid=UKBRE8620V920120703>; Joseph Cotterill, 'ECB Collateral Shift du Jour', *FT Alphaville blog*, 3 July 2012, available online at <http://ftalphaville.ft.com/2012/07/03/1070271/ecb-collateral-shift-du-jour/>.

normal approach was to include a contingent liability in the restructuring only if the beneficiary called on the guarantee before the restructuring closed. But no pressure was placed on beneficiaries to call on their guarantees. This set a precedent that has been followed in most sovereign debt restructurings of the last thirty years.[12]

One notable exception was Grenada's restructuring in 2005, when the government's contingent exposure equalled about 10 per cent of its direct liabilities. Grenada warned in the disclosure document for its restructuring that any contingent obligation called by a beneficiary after the restructuring closed would be settled by the delivery of consideration having a net present value (NPV) equal to what the lender would have received had the guarantee been called in time to be included in the main restructuring.[13] **18.21**

The most recent precedent, Greece in 2012, is mixed. Although the Hellenic Republic had hundreds of outstanding state guarantees at the time that it announced its debt restructuring in February of 2012, only thirty-six of those instruments were made eligible for inclusion in the workout.[14] The distinguishing characteristic of the included instruments was that they fell within Eurostat's 'special cases' exception to the general rule of off-balance-sheet treatment.[15] In effect, Eurostat had already concluded that the liabilities were central government debt and had to be shown as such for Eurostat reporting purposes. Accordingly, they were also made eligible for the restructuring of the central government's direct debt. **18.22**

Interestingly, although the main Greek debt restructuring was facilitated by Greek legislation that retrofit a collective action mechanism on that portion of the debt stock governed by Greek law (93 per cent of the total), this legislation did *not* attempt to sweep in the Greek government guarantees of the guaranteed bonds that were declared eligible for the restructuring, nor did the Greek legislature attempt to pass separate legislation dealing with the government's local law guarantees. The Greek authorities therefore avoided the legal and operational complications that would have attended an attempt to restructure sovereign guarantees in a more coercive way. **18.23**

6. The Restructurer's Dilemma

If a country that is forced to restructure its outstanding (direct) indebtedness also has a significant amount of contingent obligations coming due during the period covered by that restructuring, there are a limited number of options: **18.24**

(a) hope that the primary obligor will have the resources to pay the debt without a call on the guarantee;
(b) hope that the beneficiary of the guarantee will voluntarily roll over the debt at maturity;
(c) honour the guarantee if it is called by paying the debt in full; or
(d) dishonour the guarantee and attempt to restructure the liability when it matures.

[12] *See* Lee C. Buchheit and G. Mitu Gulati, 'The Treatment of Contingent Liabilities in a Sovereign Debt Restructuring', in J. LaBrosse, R. Olivares-Caminal, and D. Singh (eds) *Financial Crisis Containment and Government Guarantees* (Cheltenham: Informa Law, 2013).

[13] *See* Lee C. Buchheit and Elizabeth Karpenski, 'Grenada's Innovations' (2006) 21(4) J Int'l Banking Reg 227, 231.

[14] Twenty series of these guaranteed bonds (totalling €4.88 billion) were governed by Greek law; the other sixteen series (totalling €4.97 billion) were governed by foreign law.

[15] *See* paragraph 18.11.

18.25 Option (a) is, of course, the sovereign's preferred choice. But a natural selection process is always at work in guarantees. Had the primary obligor been perceived as fully creditworthy on its own, it would not have needed sovereign credit support in order to raise capital at a tolerably low interest rate. The very presence of a sovereign guarantee is thus a sign that the primary obligor might not be good for the money when it comes due.

18.26 Option (b), a voluntary rollover, is the sovereign's second-best choice. Naturally, this requires the cooperation of either an indulgent or a captive beneficiary. The 'liquidity extraction bonds'[16] that have been issued by European banks for the purpose of accessing the ECB's discount window or the ELA programme presumably fall into the category of 'captive beneficiary'. Demanding repayment of the loan to the discounting bank on its maturity date would, in most of these situations, be pointless. Demanding payment from the sovereign guarantor of the guaranteed bonds pledged to secure the loan would be inconsistent with the official sector's bailout programme for the country. The result is a captive beneficiary that has little choice but to roll over the loan and the accompanying collateral for the loan.

18.27 Option (c), to pay up, can have several problems. The first, of course, is money—a commodity that is rarely in abundant supply when a sovereign is compelled to restructure its debts. Even if the cash is available, paying the beneficiary of a state guarantee in full while all of the sovereign's direct creditors have been forced to take losses will naturally delight the former and enrage the latter. Finally, it is unlikely that the financial predicates underlying the restructuring will have assumed payment in full of maturing contingent liabilities during the adjustment period. If those contingent liabilities are of a significant size, a policy of paying them may torpedo the entire programme.

18.28 Option (d), to attempt an ad hoc restructuring of a contingent liability when it matures, raises the predictable issues of feasibility, cost, and intercreditor equity. It would also inevitably prolong the perception that the country remains mired in a debt crisis.

18.29 The restructuring of a contingent obligation is more complicated than the same exercise for direct sovereign debt. For one thing, until the guarantee is called by the beneficiary, it remains contingent; the guarantor is rarely in a position to force such a call. This gives the beneficiary the option of attempting to ride out the sovereign's restructuring of its direct obligations in the hope that, after that main restructuring closes, the sovereign will be reluctant to plunge back into another debt crisis by dishonouring a call on the guarantee.

18.30 Moreover, even if beneficiaries can be persuaded to call upon their guarantees, they are in a fundamentally different position from the sovereign's direct creditors. By definition, the holder of a sovereign-guaranteed bond benefits from the credit of both the primary obligor *and* that of the sovereign guarantor; in the jargon, the creditor is holding 'two-name paper'. Giving such a creditor the same deal as that offered to direct creditors of the sovereign would effectively attribute no value to the credit of the primary obligor. But any attempt to sweeten the terms of the restructuring for contingent sovereign creditors in order to compensate those holders for the surrender of their claim against the primary obligor requires someone to put a monetary value on that second credit risk. This could be a delicate and politically sensitive task when the primary obligor is a state-owned or state-controlled enterprise.

[16] *See* n. 9.

In short, the restructurer's dilemma is that contingent liabilities, if they are of any material size, cannot safely be left *out* of a sovereign debt restructuring, nor can they easily be included *in* a sovereign debt restructuring. This problem was not a problem for so long as contingent liabilities represented only a small part of the debt stocks of affected countries. But for many countries that period ended with the commencement of the financial crisis in 2008. The problem will therefore be unavoidable in at least some of the sovereign debt restructurings yet to come. **18.31**

In the bankruptcy of a corporate borrower in the United States (let us call it 'Acme Corporation'), the value of any contingent claims against Acme that are not expected to be crystallized before the bankruptcy proceeding ends may be estimated for the purposes of allowing the beneficiary's claim to be filed in the insolvency proceeding (see US Bankruptcy Code §502(c)(1)). This is done to avoid unduly prolonging the administration of Acme's estate or forcing the administrator to establish a reserve against the claim. If it appears that the primary obligor will be able to pay the debt out of its own resources (without requiring a call on Acme's guarantee), then the beneficiary's claim in Acme's bankruptcy may be estimated at zero or close to it. **18.32**

7. Restructuring Sovereign Contingent Obligations

How hard would it be to cast the net of a sovereign debt restructuring wide enough to catch the sovereign's contingent obligations? **18.33**

A. Voluntary offers

If the debt restructuring is conducted as a purely voluntary exchange—that is, no use of collective action clauses (CACs), embedded or retrofit— and involves delivery of new debt instruments of the sovereign in exchange for outstanding sovereign guaranteed bonds, the holders of contingent sovereign paper can be expected to ask for a sweeter deal than that offered to the direct creditors. The justification will be that this additional consideration is needed to compensate for the creditors' surrender of a claim against the first name (the primary obligor) of their two-name paper. Apart from the politically delicate job of deciding whether the incremental credit risk of a parastatal on a debt instrument is worth a nickel or a dime or something more, different values would logically need to be assigned for each of the primary obligors—a tedious and possibly controversial task. **18.34**

The alternative would involve restructuring each guaranteed bond in a manner that maintains the primary obligor as the first name on the paper. This could be done either by exchanging each old guaranteed bond for a new guaranteed bond with the same parties, or else attempting to modify the terms of that old bond within its four corners (no exchange). This approach would address the concern about the loss of the creditor's claim against the primary obligor, but it could significantly complicate the mechanics of the restructuring. For one thing, it would be tantamount to a separate restructuring for each guaranteed bond. Because the primary obligors would continue as a credit risk on the restructured debt instruments, the securities laws in many jurisdictions would require separate disclosure for each of those primary obligors in the exchange offer. Instead of issuing a single series of sovereign bonds for exchange with existing debtholders, the restructuring would involve the issuance, listing, and administration of multiple series of bonds, each corresponding to an underlying guaranteed debt instrument. **18.35**

B. Less-than-voluntary offers

18.36 A debt restructuring that does not rely exclusively on persuasion to bring creditors into the deal will face its own set of problems with contingent sovereign obligations.

i. Collective action clauses (CACs)

18.37 One immediate question will be whether the terms of the guarantee will need to be amended separately from, or in parallel with, a modification of the terms of the underlying debt instrument. If the underlying instrument does not include a CAC of some kind, its amendment—and the corresponding amendment of the related guarantee—would presumably require the unanimous consent of each debtholder. Even where the underlying debt instrument contains a CAC, however, the related sovereign guarantee almost certainly will not. Research suggests that CACs are almost never incorporated in sovereign guarantees.

18.38 Somewhat more common, but still quite rare, is the instance in which the CAC appearing in the underlying bond permits changes to the accompanying sovereign guarantee. As Figure 18.3 shows, of the guaranteed bonds with CACs in the database on which the research was based, fewer than 10 per cent permitted modifications by a supermajority vote of creditors to both the underlying bond *and* the accompanying guarantee.

18.39 Why should contract drafters who were cautious enough to put CACs into their bonds have felt it unnecessary to incorporate a similar feature in the accompanying guarantees? The most plausible explanation is that the drafters simply did not see the need to do so. The guarantee promises payment of the bond on the dates and in the amounts due. If the creditors agree to amend the terms of the bond, this argument goes, the terms of the guarantee will automatically wrap around those modified terms.

18.40 This assumption may be a bit too facile. For one thing, the wording of the guarantee could be crucial. For example, a Republic of Turkey sovereign guarantee in the database recites that: 'The intention and purpose of this Guarantee is to ensure that the Bondholders . . . shall receive the amounts payable as interest and principal as and when due and payable *according*

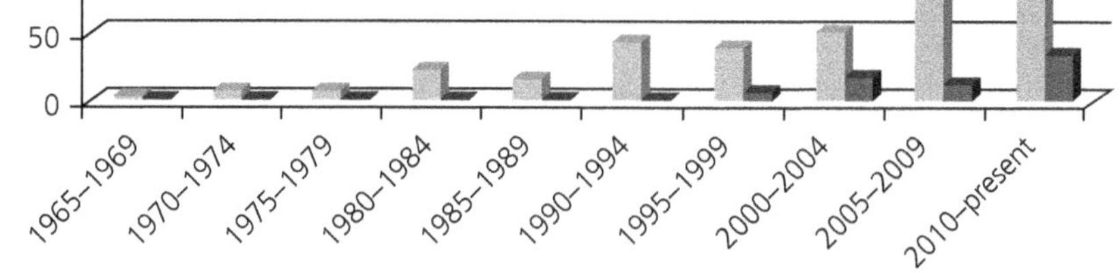

Figure 18.3 Number of sovereign guarantees with CACs mentioning guarantee modification (1 January 1965–1 July 2013)

to the Issue Terms...'[17] No mention is made of a possible modification to the original issue terms. It is therefore not clear whether an amendment to the terms of the underlying bond would automatically result in a corresponding amendment to the accompanying guarantee.

More importantly, the amendment of a sovereign-guaranteed bond through the use of a CAC is still an unusual event and would raise novel legal issues. **18.41**

If a supermajority of bondholders can alter the terms of an underlying bond through a CAC, but no similar contractual flexibility exists to modify the terms of the related sovereign guarantee, can a disaffected minority of bondholders insist on payment by the guarantor of the amounts originally due under the bond? The argument *against* permitting such a claim focuses on the words of the guarantee promising payment 'when due' of the primary obligor's obligations under the bond. If those obligations are extended or reduced in a manner permitted by the terms of the bond (through the exercise of the CAC), the argument goes, the guarantee should automatically wrap around the amended terms. **18.42**

The argument in *favour* of allowing those disgruntled creditors to insist on strict performance of the guarantee has several components. **18.43**

(a) First, these guarantees are often deliberately set up to be free-standing, separately enforceable instruments; the guarantor is frequently described as being liable as a 'primary obligor and not merely as surety' of the underlying obligation. If a supermajority of bondholders wishes to modify the terms of the underlying obligation, the presence of a CAC may allow them to sweep along a disaffected minority at that level. But absent a CAC in the guarantee, the consent of each beneficiary of the guarantee would appear to be required to effect a parallel amendment of that instrument.
(b) Second, had the drafter of the guarantee wanted to permit its terms to be modified with less than the unanimous consent of the beneficiaries, this would have been easy to do. Under normal principles of contract interpretation, a court would not read such a modification clause into the document.
(c) Finally, many guarantees contain language similar to the following:

> The liability of the Guarantor hereunder shall be absolute and unconditional irrespective of any change in the time, manner or place of payment, or any other term of, the [underlying obligation].[18]

This situation (a conflict between a 'collective action' amendment of an underlying obligation and the modification of an accompanying guarantee) is not well developed in US law for the simple reason that collective action modification clauses fell out of favour in corporate debt instruments in the United States in the 1930s, and have only recently (since 2003) begun to appear in sovereign debt instruments governed by the law of a US jurisdiction. In a **18.44**

[17] Central Bank of the Republic of Turkey, DM200,000,000 7 per cent Deutsche Mark Bearer Bonds of 1987/1992, irrevocably and unconditionally guaranteed by the Republic of Turkey (emphasis added).

[18] This language is included in a guarantee to ensure that the guarantor is not released if the lender agrees to vary the terms of the underlying obligation: *see* Raymer McQuiston, 'Drafting an Enforceable Guaranty in an International Financing Transaction: A Lender's Perspective' (1993) 10 Int'l Tax & Bus Lawyer 138, 156 ('Common law courts have ruled consistently that a variation or change in the terms of the underlying loan agreement without the guarantor's consent... justifies a release of the guarantor from its obligations'). That said, a bondholder might argue that the language could equally be seen as preserving a bondholder's claim against the guarantor to perform the unamended terms of the underlying instrument unless that lender has also agreed to amend the guarantee.

traditional US amendment clause requiring the unanimous consent of all creditors for a change to payment terms, the issue does not arise; by definition, every holder will have consented to the change.

ii. Governing law

18.45 A sovereign fortunate enough to have its guarantees governed by its own law may (subject to constitutional constraints) be able to encourage holders of its contingent obligations to accept a restructuring by threatening to pass domestic legislation containing a sentence along these lines:

> All guarantees issued by the Republic of Ruritania in respect of debt obligations of third parties that are eligible to participate in the [Ruritanian restructuring] shall, if called by the beneficiary at any time after the closing of the [Ruritanian restructuring], be satisfied and discharged in full by delivery to the creditor of consideration equivalent to that offered in the [Ruritanian restructuring].

18.46 The effect of such a provision would be to remove any incentive on the part of the beneficiary of a state guarantee to refrain from calling on the guarantee at the time of the main restructuring. It is thus a statutory expression of the warning that Grenada gave in 2005 to the holders of its contingent obligations.[19] In a debt restructuring, a local law guarantee thus provides the sovereign with considerable leverage.

18.47 One of the most startling conclusions of the empirical research has been the split between the law chosen to govern the underlying debt instruments and the governing law of the related sovereign guarantee. The contrast between Figure 18.4 (number of sovereign guarantees by law of the bond) and Figure 18.5 (number of sovereign guarantees by law of the guarantee) shows that while the fraction of guaranteed bonds governed by foreign law has been increasing at a rapid rate (particularly in the period post 2010), the shift toward foreign law has not been anywhere near as marked in the guarantee contracts themselves.[20]

18.48 It is likely that an important reason for the dramatic shift toward foreign law in Figure 18.4 is the Greek restructuring of 2012, because that restructuring highlighted the added risks for the holders of debt instruments governed by local law.[21] However, Figure 18.5 shows that those lessons have not been fully absorbed. A significant percentage of the guarantees issued since 2010—even guarantees given in respect of foreign-law-governed bonds—continue to specify local law as the governing law. That said, this percentage is decreasing rapidly.

iii. Waiver of immunity

18.49 All creditors of sovereigns face the daunting challenge of enforcing their claims against a recalcitrant debtor, but most benefit from an express waiver by the sovereign of any entitlement that the sovereign (or its property) may enjoy based on sovereign immunity. Figure 18.6 suggests, however, that such express waivers of immunity are far less common in sovereign guarantees than one might have thought.

---

19 *See* paragraph 18.21.

20 The number of bonds used for Figures 18.4 and 18.5 is smaller than the number used for the other graphs reported in the chapter because it is based on incomplete information—in particular, with respect to a subset of Italian sovereign-guaranteed bonds issued after 2009.

21 The Greek Parliament retrofit a collective action mechanism on its local law debt stock in early 2012 in order to facilitate a restructuring of those obligations: *see* Jeromin Zettelmeyer, Christoph Trebesch, and Mitu Gulati, 'The Greek Debt Exchange: An Autopsy', *Economic Policy* (forthcoming).

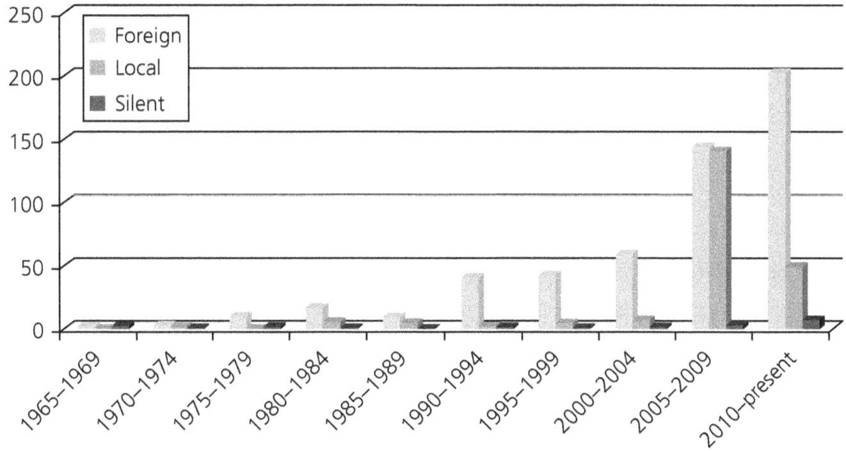

Figure 18.4 Number of sovereign guarantees by law of the bond (1 January 1965–1 July 2013)

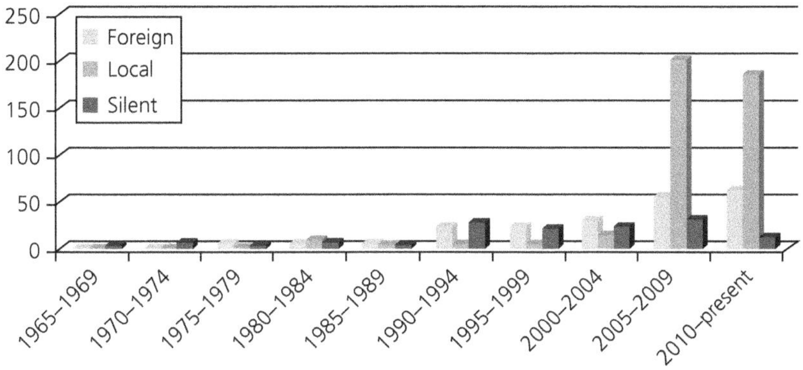

Figure 18.5 Number of sovereign guarantees by law of guarantee (1 January 1965–1 July 2013)

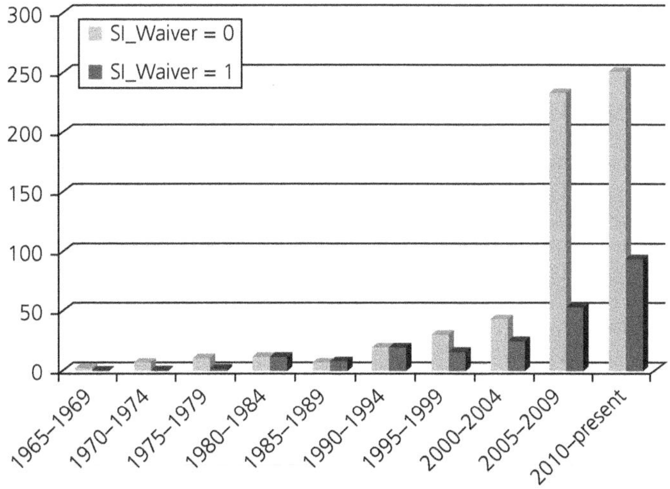

Figure 18.6 Number of sovereign guarantees with waiver of immunity by sovereign guarantor (1 January 1965–1 July 2013)

18.50 The absence of an express waiver of immunity does not make it impossible to enforce a guarantee against a defaulting sovereign, but it will make the enforcement process more difficult. Sovereigns can be expected to remind the beneficiaries of their guarantees of this likely difficulty as a means of encouraging those beneficiaries to join a general restructuring.

8. Conclusions

18.51 The following conclusions can therefore be drawn.

- In a number of important countries, sovereign guarantees have become so prevalent that they cannot be ignored in any future debt workouts that may be needed for those countries.
- Exactly how the contingent portion of a sovereign's debt stock is to be addressed in such a restructuring remains a mystery. There are very few precedents and no good precedents.
- For a while at least (until existing bonds mature and are replaced by new issues with more pro-creditor provisions), some sovereigns will benefit in a debt restructuring from the prelapsarian innocence shown in the contract drafting patterns that prevailed before 2010 in areas such as governing law and waiver of immunities.
- One thing seems certain: the presence of a significant number of contingent liabilities in a sovereign's debt stock will present major complications for the architects of a debt restructuring for that country, not least of which will be psychological. The need to address contingent liabilities will force everyone—creditors, official sector sponsors, and citizens—to watch with alarm as formerly off-balance-sheet liabilities come rushing on to the sovereign's balance sheet, just in time to be restructured.

Part IV

ECONOMICS OF SOVEREIGN BORROWING

19. **Why Governments Default** 257
Willem H. Buiter and Ebrahim Rahbari

20. **Sovereign Debt Markets** 287
Gene Frieda

21. **Borrowing and Debt: How Do Sovereigns Get into Trouble?** 309
Arturo C. Porzecanski

19

WHY GOVERNMENTS DEFAULT[1]

Willem H. Buiter and Ebrahim Rahbari

1. Introduction

From an economic perspective, default is any change in the stream of current and future payments on a debt contract that makes it less valuable to the creditor than the execution of the contractually agreed payments stream.[2] Default is probably as old as debt itself, because, as with virtually any intertemporal contract, the net present (discounted) value (NPV) of abiding by the terms of the contract (its continuation value) changes over the life of the contract for the parties involved and may well become negative for one or more of the parties. In the case of debt contracts, the debtor has his fun up-front, when it gains control over the resources that it borrows. Servicing the debt, interest, and repayment of principal is the unpleasant part of the debt contract for the borrower. Why would any borrower ever repay a debt once the continuation value of the debt contract turns negative? 19.01

In the case of a debt contract involving a private borrower, one obvious answer is that third-party enforcers—including, but not limited to, the courts—provide the incentives to repay. But in the case of a sovereign borrower, third-party enforcement is the exception rather than the rule: sovereigns choose to service their debt rather than are forced to do so by a third party. That then raises the question why sovereigns do not choose to default more often or indeed—since the lack of third-party enforcement of sovereign debt contracts is rather evident to the (potential) creditors—why *any* sovereign debt should be deemed sustainable and why anyone would willingly be a creditor to a sovereign. The answer, of course, is that it is often in the sovereign's interest to honour its debt obligations, primarily because the costs of sovereign default—to the sovereign debtor—can be substantial. But these costs are also not infinitely high. So we are squarely in the realm of *choice*: sovereigns, on the whole, *choose* to service their debt or *choose to default*. The choice aspect of sovereign default tends to be given too little weight in assessments of debt sustainability. 19.02

2. Enforcement of Private Debt Contracts

For most contracts between private parties, there are two types of contract enforcement: third-party enforcement by some external entity not a party to the contract; and 19.03

---

[1] The views and opinions expressed are those of the authors only, and do not represent the views and opinions of Citigroup.

[2] *See* the Appendix for an attempt to formalize this notion.

self-enforcement. Today, in reasonably advanced market economies with a modicum of rule of law, third-party enforcement is mainly performed by the state, through the courts, bailiffs, and the other servants of law and order. But the coercive power of the state is not the only source of coercive power capable of enforcing contracts; organized crime, vigilantes, and other non-state enforcers can also play that role.

19.04 Self-enforcement relies on debt service being in the perceived self-interest of the borrower even after the initial transfer of resources from the creditor to the borrower has taken place and without the benefit of the *deus ex machina* of an effective third-party or external enforcer. One self-enforcement mechanism could be honour or honesty. In the ancient (and quite possibly mythical) world of 'my word is my bond', people choose to honour their debts because it was the right thing to do. Even if you could get away with defaulting on your debt, and thus be better off from a material point of view in every period and in every state of nature, you would not do so, because it would be wrong or immoral to do so. In much of modern economics, short shrift is given to the imperative of 'doing the right thing' as a motive for human action. In most non-cooperative game theory under uncertainty and asymmetric information, honesty is a tactical option, not an intrinsically valued form of behaviour or a compulsion.[3] You tell the truth if it is advantageous to do so; you lie if lying pays. George Washington and his hatchet would not last long in modern non-cooperative game theory. Truth telling and commitment (which, for our purposes, can be taken to be the same thing) may, of course, have evolutionary value if communities with widespread honesty, in which most members use honest signalling, can develop and sustain cooperative arrangements based on trust that are not open to communities full of opportunistic liars.[4]

19.05 Self-enforcement of private debt contracts when economic agents are conventional selfish and opportunistic economic automata (that is, without a capacity for credible commitment based on truth telling and keeping commitments as forms of compulsive behaviour) requires that a sequential (by backward induction) cost–benefit analysis of default versus continued contractual debt service yield contractual debt service as the rational outcome. The costs of default include reputational costs if the defaulting debtor cannot become anonymous following a default. Debt default, in a world with imperfect and asymmetric information, may be interpreted as a powerful signal of the 'type' of the borrower—one with a higher propensity to default, other things being equal, than borrowers who have not (yet) defaulted. A standard consequence of, or punishment for, default is exclusion from future access to borrowing for at least a while and a high likelihood of higher borrowing costs even after borrowing becomes possible again. The cost of restricted future market access will be higher to a borrower weighing the pros and cons of default the more likely it is to wish to borrow again at some point in the future. More variable and uncertain future income streams and investment opportunities will therefore increase the cost of default.

19.06 In addition, the creditor or parties associated with the borrower may inflict damage on the person or property of the defaulting borrower. Clearly, in the case of borrowing from the

---

[3] For an extensive treatment, *see*, e.g., Drew Fudenberg and Jean Tirole, *Game Theory* (Cambridge, MA: MIT Press, 1991).

[4] *See* A. Pinar Osizik and Kyle I. Harrington, 'The Effects of Tags on the Evolution of Honest Signalling', in Terence Soule and Jason H. Moore (eds) *Genetic and Evolutionary Computation Conference (GECCO), Philadelphia, PA, USA, July 7–11, 2012, Companion Material Proceedings* (New York: ACM, 2012), 345–52; Kevin J. S. Zollman, Carl T. Bergstrom, and Simon M. Hutteger, 'Between Cheap and Costly Signals: The Evolution of Partially Honest Communication' (2013) 280(1750) Proc R Soc B 1471–2954.

Mafia or other criminal lenders ('loan sharks'), the distinction between self-enforcement and third-party enforcement gets blurred: the lender or its agents ensure that the cost–benefit analysis of continued contractual debt service versus default favours the continued debt service outcome by threatening the borrower and/or his nearest and dearest with loss of life, limb, or property. Indeed, it is possible to see third-party enforcement as simply a special case of self-enforcement, in which a very high cost of default motivates choice informed by a rational, selfish cost–benefit analysis. In this view, third-party external enforcement, even by the state, is shorthand for a bundle of costs of default: the notoriety of a court case; fear of arrest and of debtors' prisons in an earlier age; fines; disqualification from certain activities, occupations, or professions; damage to one's credit rating; and the wider damage to one's reputation and social standing.

A. A special case: social or collective contract enforcement

An interesting form of informal private debt contract enforcement that is neither traditional self-enforcement nor conventional third-party enforcement by the state or the henchmen of an unfriendly loan shark is the collective, or group, enforcement of debt contracts found, for example, in the micro-lending by the Grameen Bank in Bangladesh. These uncollateralized loans are made to groups of poor, mainly rural, borrowers. Peer pressure within the group is used to enforce repayment and to maintain or improve the credit standing of the group.[5] Peer pressure can, of course, cover a wide range of behaviour, from disapproval and Amish-style shunning, to threats to persons or property. **19.07**

3. Sovereign Default

The standard view in the academic economic literature of sovereign debt contract enforcement is that it relies entirely on self-enforcement. Sovereign means '*Dieu et mon droit*' ('I'll do as I please'). There is no higher authority, no third party, which can enforce sovereign debt contracts against the will of the sovereign, unless the sovereign has voluntarily yielded the substance of sovereignty by agreeing to the adjudication of disagreements over its debt contracts by a foreign court. However, even in the case of sovereign debt contracts under foreign law, the enforcement powers of the foreign courts tend to be limited, even when the sovereign is weak and short of international goodwill. Very few observers believe, for instance, that the Argentine government will pay in full the holdout creditors who rejected the restructuring offers made by Argentina since its default in 2001, regardless of how the US Court of Appeals for the Second Circuit (New York) rules on the judgment of Judge Thomas P. Griesa, a federal judge for the US District Court for the Southern District of New York, who determined that the Argentine government must pay these holdouts *pari passu* with the creditors that agreed to the debt restructurings.[6] **19.08**

Since gunboat diplomacy went out of fashion a while ago (probably after the Venezuelan debt crisis of 1902), creditors no longer count on warships to assist in debt collection.[7] **19.09**

---

5 *See* David Bornstein, *The Price of a Dream: The Story of the Grameen Bank* (New York: Oxford University Press, 2005).

6 *See* Gene Bolton, *WRH Archives: Debt Restructuring in Argentina* (Washington, DC: Council on Hemispheric Affairs, 2013).

7 In 1902, the United Kingdom, Germany, and Italy imposed a naval blockade on Venezuela, which was in default on its foreign debt. Soon after this intervention, Venezuela reached an agreement with its foreign bondholders and began meeting its obligations again.

Even trade sanctions—the moderate face of gunboat diplomacy—are rarely used to collect sovereign debt and when they are used that way, as in the case of Cuba, they tend to be ineffective or even counterproductive. Instead, sovereign debt contract enforcement relies on a cost–benefit analysis that is, in many ways, similar to self-enforcement of private contracts—without the sharp edges (knuckledusters and crushed kneecaps) sometimes found in the informal enforcement of private contracts.

19.10 For modern sovereigns, it is almost exclusively self-enforcement that induces them to service their debt. One aspect of self-interest is common between private and sovereign creditors: just like private creditors, sovereign creditors may wish to borrow again in the future; default will restrict their access to finance in the future and/or raise the cost of doing so.[8] For example, a one standard-deviation increase in haircuts has been found to be associated with a 50 per cent lower likelihood of re-accessing international capital markets in any year after the restructuring.[9] For both sovereign and private creditors, there are also real resource costs (legal, administrative, and time costs) that are associated with dealing with default and its aftermath.

19.11 There are two key differences between sovereign default and private default that affect the cost of sovereign default, and thus the likelihood of strategic sovereign default, in perhaps surprising ways. Both relate to systemic externalities from sovereign default. The first type concerns financial stability and macroeconomic externalities vis-à-vis the domestic private sector from sovereign default, caused by contagion or excessive risk concentration. The second type concerns *rule of law externalities* from sovereign default.[10]

A. Financial stability and macroeconomic externalities

i. Contagion and concentration risk

19.12 Much has been made recently in the euro area of non-market links (that is, links through a mechanism other than formal, explicit, financial or contractual exposures, one-way or

[8] Much of the discussion in the previous section dealt with externally held debt. But qualitatively, much the same arguments hold for domestic debt, as long as it is either foreign-currency-denominated or the domestic sovereign has no control over its central bank, as is the case in the euro area. In their book, *This Time is Different: Eight Centuries of Financial Folly* (Princeton, NJ: Princeton University Press, 2009) C. M. Reinhart and K. S. Rogoff show that, although externally held debt is more likely to be defaulted upon than domestically held debt, both have been defaulted on with some regularity—and even more frequently if we extend the definition of default to include any deliberate NPV reduction in the real value of the public debt, including through higher inflation (unanticipated or anticipated, in combination with financial repression). To ignore domestically held debt because we owe it to ourselves is bad economics. Those who own the debt (typically older and richer) are different from those who pay for servicing the debt through taxation or cuts in public spending (typically younger and poorer). Domestic bondowners have more in common with foreign bondowners than with domestic taxpayers. Servicing both externally held debt and domestic debt requires a dual transfer: for externally held debt, it is the internal transfer from the domestic taxpayer/public spending beneficiary to the state and the external transfer from the state to the foreign creditor; for internally held debt, there is one internal transfer from the domestic taxpayer/public spending beneficiary to the state and a second internal transfer from the state to the internal bondholder/creditor.

[9] *See* J. Cruces and C. Trebesch, *Sovereign Defaults: The Price of Haircuts*, Center for Economic Studies/ Ifo Institute Working Paper No. 3604 (October 2011), available online at <http://www.econstor.eu/bitstream/10419/52478/1/669443050.pdf>. There is also some evidence that market penalties for default may have fallen somewhat compared to previous decades (*see* G. Gelos, R. Sahay, and G. Sandleris, 'Sovereign Borrowing by Developing Countries: What Determines Market Access?' (2011) 83(2) J Int'l Econ 243–54), even though, given the relative rarity of defaults and the wide diversity of post-default experiences, we should be careful not to overinterpret these data.

[10] Of course, there are also externalities to other sovereigns.

two-way) between a sovereign and private sector entities—in particular banks, other systemically important financial institutions, and sometimes also private non-financial corporations. Sovereign default in a country can lead to a reassessment of sovereign default risk in other countries. Sovereign default could plausibly lead to a reassessment by actual and potential creditors of the creditworthiness of connected private sector entities or of other sovereigns quite independent of the existence of links through formal, explicit, contractual or financial exposures. Not all such 'contagion' would necessarily be blind: sovereign default in a country may lead to reassessments of the value of deposit insurance for banks (often implicitly sovereign-backed, although formally backed by the banking industry only), of other explicit or implicit guarantees provided by the government to private sector entities that are deemed too big, too systemically important, or too politically connected to fail. It could also lead to different assessments of fiscal risks in other countries.

In addition, there is the *direct* financial exposure of these non-government entities to the sovereign that may cause them to be affected by sovereign default—a problem that is aggravated by the high concentration in the exposure of many euro area banks to their domestic sovereign. **19.13**

Concentration risk is an important feature of the current European financial crisis. At least until the start of the Greek sovereign phase of the European crisis in 2010, national bank supervisors and regulators in the European Union (EU) and in the euro area in particular had failed singularly to prevent a very high concentration in their banks of exposure to European sovereigns in general, and to Greek risk—and Greek sovereign risk—in particular. Ironically, this supervisory and regulatory failure may well have been the result in part of an attempt to correct an earlier widespread supervisory and regulatory error that was highlighted by the North Atlantic financial crisis: the low share of liquid assets on the balance sheets of the banks. Under Basel III and assorted national add-ons, national supervisors and regulators have been pressing the banks in their jurisdictions to hold more liquid assets. Eurozone sovereign debt was viewed as liquid and safe by supervisors and regulators, and therefore also by the banks. This ignored two fundamental truths: first, that no sovereign is completely safe; and second, that there are large variations in the default risk associated with different sovereigns, even among the EU and euro area sovereigns. **19.14**

Since 2010, the repatriation of periphery sovereign debt from the rest of the EU to the banks in the periphery has substantially increased the exposure of euro area periphery banks to their own sovereigns. The desire by core euro area banks to dispose of periphery sovereign debt meshed nicely with financial repression in the periphery, where officials (ministries of finance, treasuries, national central banks, national supervisors and regulators) forced their domestic banks to hold more domestic sovereign debt and at lower yields than they would have voluntarily, all in the name of funding the sovereign at affordable yields. One leg of the so-called sovereign–bank link (the financial repression of domestic banks to fund a domestic sovereign whose solvency was questionable) thus inevitably created another (the excessive exposure of domestic banks to the creditworthiness of the domestic sovereign). **19.15**

Until the excessive concentration of holdings of high-risk sovereign debt in the balance sheets of euro area periphery and soft-core banks is remedied, either by spreading this risk voluntary by selling the debt to a wider range of private investors, or by socializing the risk, partly or completely, a sovereign default by a euro area member state could undermine the viability of euro area periphery banks and cause further systemic distress. **19.16**

19.17 However, even with the concentration risk present in the euro area, sovereign default is likely to be less systemically damaging from a financial perspective than the failure of a large, complex, cross-border financial institution like Lehman Brothers. One reason for this is that, as former Citicorp Chairman Walter Wriston pointed out (in a much misinterpreted statement):

> Countries don't go out of business... The infrastructure doesn't go away, the productivity of the people doesn't go way, the natural resources don't go away. And so their assets always exceed their liabilities, which is the technical reason for bankruptcy. And that's very different from a company.[11]

19.18 Note that Wriston did not say that banks and other private creditors cannot go broke by lending to sovereigns or that sovereigns do not default. His statement, which is correct, means that, when the sovereign defaults, as they have often done historically, the country over which they are sovereign does not get wound up, broken up, or liquidated, with physical, human, and financial assets sold at fire-sale prices by creditors who fear they may miss out in the rush for the exit. The sovereign default tends to be followed by a form of 'Chapter 11 lite'[12]—very lite—with the debtor firmly in control of the real assets, human and physical, of the nation. The country remains open for business. The assets within its jurisdiction can typically not be attached. As regards doing cross-border business, both the sovereign and likely also the private entities of a state where the sovereign has defaulted recently will operate on a cash-in-advance basis. But even Argentina has continued to trade internationally following its repeated defaults, and its people and government officials have continued to travel freely internationally.

ii. Rule-of-law externalities

19.19 The 'rule of law' externality associated with sovereign default is potentially seriously damaging to the long-run growth and prosperity prospects of a country. A private default on a formal debt contract is (supposed to be) settled under the rule of law by a transparent legal process involving some or all of the following: arbitration; the courts; administrators; conservators; arbitrators; bailiffs; and other law enforcement agencies. Private defaults are (supposed to be) resolved under the rule of law and according to the law, and do not therefore undermine the rule of law or the subset of the rule of law that deals with contracts—what, in rather idolatrous terms, is sometimes called the 'sanctity of contracts'. This may well be one of the reasons why the ad hoc bailouts of systemically important financial institutions during the recent crisis provoked such strong emotions. Another example of a private debt restructuring that violated natural justice was the proposed de facto bail-in (through a tax levy) of insured depositors in both solvent and insolvent banks, in the version of the Cyprus rescue programme originally agreed by the Cypriot government and the troika,[13] but subsequently rejected unanimously by the Cypriot Parliament. The fact that the senior unsecured bank bondholders escaped the axe under the ultimately rejected proposal compounded the flaws

[11] Cited by IMF, 'Money Matters: An IMF Exhibit—The Importance of Global Cooperation; Debt and Transition (1981–1989)', available online at <http://www.imf.org/external/np/exr/center/mm/eng/mm_dt_01.htm>.

[12] Chapter 11 being the chapter of the US Bankruptcy Code that provides for the reorganization of a debtor's business affairs and assets on bankruptcy.

[13] That is, the European Commission, the International Monetary Fund (IMF), and the European Central Bank (ECB).

in the original deal.[14] It was perceived by many as a perversion of the rule of law, the social contract, and the fundamental principles of a market economy, which require the imposition of hard budget constraints on all obligors and respects seniority rankings.

When the state itself defaults on its obligations, the rule of law inevitably is harmed. Social capital and trust are corrupted—sometimes destroyed. When the state, the very party to the social contract that is supposed to enforce contracts impartially, is itself involved in a breach of contract, respect for all contracts and respect for the rule of law are undermined. The answer to the question '*Quis custodies ipsos custodes?*' ('Who will guard the guardians?') is, of course, '*Nemo*' ('No one'). It is therefore essential that the sovereign allows, in its cost–benefit analysis of rational or strategic default, for the damage done by opportunistic sovereign default to respect for the law, and thus to the social fabric that differentiates a contract-based market economy under the rule of law from a predation and force-based anarchic economy under the law of the jungle. **19.20**

Governments, the political elites, and sometimes even the polity as a whole tend to be aware of the long-term social cost of this weakening of the rule of law promoted by discretionary sovereign recourse to default. This is why voluntary sovereign default tends to occur mainly in two kinds of countries. The first are countries that have been shocked and traumatized by extraordinary events that have harmed their capacity to service external and/or internal debt, and which also are highly unlikely to be repeated. The market's perception of the sovereign's creditworthiness is likely, under such conditions, to worsen but little as a result of a sovereign default. The West German internal sovereign default of 1948 is an example of a sovereign default that probably did not create a precedent that raised citizens' and other market participants' subjective likelihood of future defaults by the West German sovereign.[15] The same holds true for the West German external default of 1953, when the 1953 London Debt Agreement settled Germany's external debts from the interwar period.[16] **19.21**

The second kind of country that chooses sovereign default is deeply polarized and internally divided, with little social capital, weak and corrupt political institutions, and ineffective political leadership. Greece's two sovereign defaults in 2012 fit this template. Prior to these recent Greek sovereign debt restructurings, there had been no sovereign defaults in Western Europe, North America (excluding Mexico), Japan, Australia, or New Zealand since the (West) German sovereign defaults of 1948 and 1953. **19.22**

B. Default and the sovereign debt Laffer curve

In certain circumstances, a default can result in a positive-sum outcome from a social perspective, relative to the alternative where default is avoided. This can happen if the total resources available to creditor and debtor (and to society as a whole) are higher following default than in the absence of default. The case of a sovereign default when the sovereign is on **19.23**

[14] *See* also Hugo Dixon, 'Cyprus Bank "Resolution" a Bad Joke', *Reuters*, 3 April 2013, available online at <http://in.reuters.com/article/2013/04/03/breakingviews-cyprus-idINDEE93206P20130403>.

[15] Central to the West German sovereign default of 1948 on the domestic debt was a currency reform. Prices and recurrent liabilities were converted at par from old Reichsmarks (RM) to new Deutschemarks (DM), domestic government debt was written off, and other nominal financial claims were converted at an average rate of RM6.5 to DM1.

[16] The Agreement wrote down the overall external debt by about 50 per cent and granted the debtors a significantly longer repayment period. Some debt service payments were even postponed until such time as Germany was reunified.

the wrong side of the 'sovereign debt Laffer curve' is an example. If very severe fiscal austerity or very high inflation are the only alternatives to sovereign default, then default may be the lesser evil. If the alternative to bank default is shifting the losses to the taxpayers, both fairness and intertemporal incentives (the prevention or mitigation of moral hazard) may call for default, provided that this can be implemented in a reasonable orderly manner and does not threaten systemic financial stability. More generally, the social costs of 'debt overhang' can exceed the costs of default in situations in which debt is excessive.

19.24 Figure 19.1 shows the relationship between the market value of the debt and its notional or face value. For simplicity, the units chosen are such that the market value of one unit of face value debt is 1 if there is no risk of default. The face value, or notional value, of the debt is denoted *D* and the market value, *PD*, where *P* is defined in the Appendix by equation A5. In Figure 19.1, $P = 1$ if the probability of default is zero. As shown in Figure 19.1, a larger stock of debt by face value or notional value *D* will, as soon as the probability of default becomes non-zero (at a face value of debt *A* in Figure 19.1), increase the market value less than one for one. If the probability of default increases fast enough with the face value of the debt outstanding, the market value of the debt can decline if the face value of the debt rises beyond a certain level (at point *B* in Figure 19.1). The 'slippery slope of the debt Laffer curve' is the segment of the curve to the right of point *B*. Assume a debtor country has landed itself on a point such as *C*. Clearly, a partial default on the debt, reducing it to any amount in face value greater than *F*, but less than *C*, will make the creditors better off (the market value of their claims on the debtor country is higher than it would have been without the default, although, of course, less than it would have been if the debtor had somehow been able to stick to the terms of the contract, given by point *E* on the 45-degree line), while the debtors are also better off, if there are costs to them that are increasing with the face value of the debt.

19.25 Distortionary taxes required to service the debt could be one mechanism ensuring that sovereign debtors are better off when the face value of their debt is reduced, even if its market value increases. Another example is the adverse effect of a bad sovereign credit rating (associated with

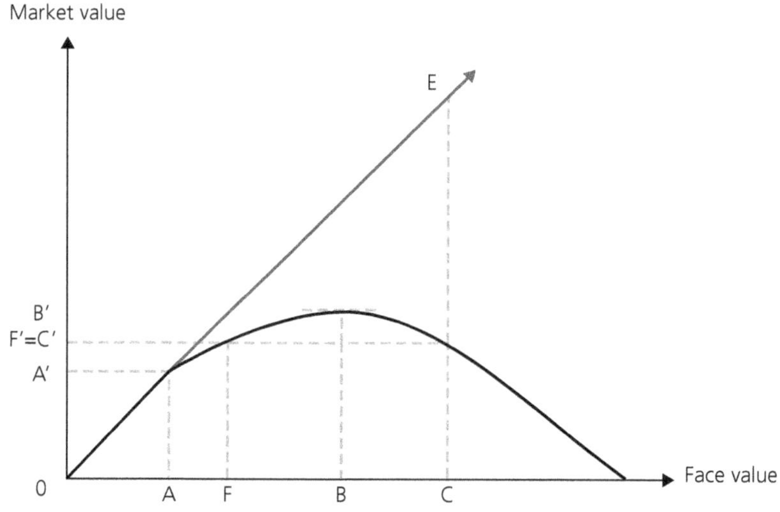

Figure 19.1 Sovereign debt Laffer curve
Source: Citi Research

a large face value of the sovereign debt) on the credit ratings and access to funding of the private agents in its jurisdiction. Even if a sovereign partial default or debt restructuring does not create a Pareto improvement where both debtor and creditors are better off, it can still be socially efficient in the weaker 'utilitarian' sense that the total resources available to both creditors and debtors (and of the wider society of which they are part) can increase as a result of a (partial) default or sovereign debt restructuring. (Note that this illustration leaves out the social cost of rule-of-law externalities associated with voluntary, strategic, or opportunistic sovereign default.)

4. So Why Do Governments Default?

Unless you are on the wrong side of the sovereign debt Laffer curve, the costs of sovereign default in the form of systemic externalities and impairing future access to capital markets provide powerful incentives to make sovereign creditors whole. But it would be wrong to suggest that sovereigns default only when it is absolutely unavoidable. In fact, it would be more appropriate to say that governments, for the most part, default because they *choose to default*. In rich countries at least, sovereign defaults are opportunistic, strategic, or 'rational'. This applies to the EU member states that are, since the eruption of the North Atlantic financial crisis in August 2007, struggling to varying degrees with sovereign debt sustainability problems. In these countries, sovereign default is the outcome of a cost–benefit analysis undertaken by an agent incapable of credible commitment. The government, as manager of the state, cannot credibly commit its successor government, nor can it credibly commit itself during its remaining term in office, to a contingent sequence of future actions unless these happen to be time-consistent (and part of what game theorists call a 'subgame perfect equilibrium'). The issue is willingness to pay (perhaps *collective* willingness to pay) rather than ability to pay. And since it is willingness to pay rather than ability to pay that matters, political and political economy factors (rather than purely economic factors) are of crucial importance in assessing public debt sustainability. 19.26

There are exceptions to the characterization that sovereign default usually constitutes a choice to default. These include the sovereigns of the very poorest countries, such as Haiti following the 2010 earthquake, the countries benefiting from the 2005 Heavily Indebted Poor Countries (HIPC) Initiative under which the International Monetary Fund (IMF), the International Development Association (IDA) of the World Bank, and the African Development Fund (AfDB) cancel all of their claims on countries that reach the 'completion point'—the stage at which a country qualifies for full and irrevocable debt relief—or countries as poor as the HIPC beneficiaries that have not (yet) benefited from relief under the Initiative, including Cambodia, Tajikistan, Chad, Eritrea, and Sudan.[17] 19.27

[17] As of February 2013, there were thirty-five 'completion point' countries that had reached the completion point under the Enhanced HIPC Initiative: Afghanistan; Burkina Faso; Burundi; Central African Republic; Democratic Republic of Congo; Ethiopia; The Gambia; Ghana; Guinea-Bissau; Liberia; Madagascar; Malawi; Mali; Mozambique; Niger; Rwanda; São Tomé and Príncipe; Sierra Leone; Tanzania; Togo; Uganda; Benin; Bolivia; Cameroon; Comoros; Republic of Congo; Côte d'Ivoire; Guinea; Guyana; Haiti; Honduras; Mauritania; Nicaragua; Senegal; and Zambia. *See* IMF, *The Multilateral Debt Relief Initiative*, IMF Factsheet (April 2013), available online at <http://www.imf.org/external/np/exr/facts/mdri.htm>.

It is sometimes argued that, even in very poor countries, sovereign default is most likely voluntary rather than involuntary, because even in very poor countries the value of a nation's natural resources, physical capital, net foreign financial assets, and human capital (the NPV of its labour income) exceeds the face value of the sovereign debt. This rather distorts the normal meaning of words such as 'voluntary' and 'choice'.

A. Arithmetic of fiscal sustainability: 'won't pay' and 'can't pay' insolvency

19.28 Even though this enters the realm of political economy, a bit of arithmetic can go some way to illustrate the drivers of debt sustainability. The arithmetic of public debt dynamics is simple, but inexorable. In this section, the net non-monetary debt of the augmented general government (the consolidated general government and central bank) is referred to as the *public debt*.[18] The evolution of public debt can then be expressed by means of the following equation (which is, in fact, an identity):

$$\Delta d \equiv -s + \left(\frac{r-\gamma}{1+\gamma}\right)d \qquad (1)$$

where:

s is the augmented general government primary (non-interest) surplus as a share of gross domestic product (GDP);
r is the effective real interest rate on the outstanding public debt;
γ is the growth rate of real GDP;
d is the public-debt-to-GDP ratio at the beginning of a period;
Δd the 'change in' the public-debt-to-GDP ratio between the end and the beginning of a period.

19.29 To keep the ratio of net public debt to GDP constant, the augmented general government's primary surplus as a share of GDP has to satisfy:

$$s = \left(\frac{r-\gamma}{1+\gamma}\right)d \qquad (2)$$

If the real interest rate on the outstanding public debt exceeds the real growth rate of GDP (as seems likely in many advanced economies today and as will likely be the case in the future for an even wider range of advanced economies, when at last we exit the era of extraordinarily low safe real interest rates produced by the global savings glut, excess capacity in the advanced economies, the zero lower bound on nominal interest rates, and the provision of near-infinite liquidity at those rates), the government needs to generate adequate primary surpluses (positive values of s of sufficient magnitude) to stop the debt burden from rising.

19.30 We can express solvency through a very similar equation to (2). Define variables with an over-bar as the 'permanent' equivalent of their equivalent without a bar—that is, for example $\bar{\gamma}$ would be the permanent growth rate of real GDP. For simplicity, for now, think of *permanent* roughly as the 'expected future long-run average'. Any sustainable fiscal–financial–monetary programme of the sovereign has to satisfy the condition that the outstanding public debt cannot exceed the present discounted value of current and future expected primary surpluses of the augmented general government. Let us express this relationship as:[19]

[18] Net debt is gross debt *less* financial and non-financial assets. By 'non-monetary debt', we mean any liabilities of the government and central bank other than the monetary base.

[19] Equation (3) strictly holds only if s, r, and γ are both known with perfect foresight and are constant over time. However, an alternative formulation for (3) can be found at the expense of substantial additional notational complexity.

$$\bar{s} \geq \left(\frac{\bar{r}-\bar{\gamma}}{1+\bar{\gamma}}\right)d \tag{3}$$

The minimum value of the primary surplus (as a share of GDP) that will ensure solvency for the sovereign, $\bar{s}^{\min}$, can then be defined as: 19.31

$$\bar{s}^{\min} = \left(\frac{\bar{r}-\bar{\gamma}}{1+\bar{\gamma}}\right)d \tag{4}$$

If the long-run effective real interest rate on the public debt exceeds the long-run growth rate of real GDP, $\bar{s}^{\min}$ will be positive in any country with a positive outstanding stock of (net) public debt—that is, the country would, on average, have to run future primary augmented general government surpluses. For instance, a country with a 100 per cent net public-debt-to-annual-GDP ratio, an expected long-run growth rate of real GDP of 2 per cent per annum, and an average effective real interest rate on the public debt of 3 per cent would have to run an average 1 per cent of GDP primary surplus in the future. 19.32

The key question is therefore whether $\bar{s}^{\min}$ is feasible, economically and politically.[20] The primary surplus (as a share of GDP), s, is the difference between revenues, τ (mainly taxes), plus seigniorage, σ (the change in the monetary base), and public spending, g, all expressed as shares of GDP: 19.33

$$s = \tau + \sigma - g \tag{5}$$[21]

Higher taxes are distortionary and costly to extract. Lower public spending can hurt growth when public spending cuts fall on productive infrastructure spending and essential 'intermediate' public administration goods and services. Fiscal tightening will weaken effective demand through the usual Keynesian channels and attempts to raise seigniorage revenue will, sooner or later, result in higher inflation. Indeed, estimates of the maximum amount of seigniorage that can be extracted in the major advanced economies when inflation is fully anticipated (and therefore reflected in market nominal interest rates as long as these are not capped by official action) are very low: typically, no more than 2 per cent of GDP.[22] Unanticipated inflation can, of course, be used to reduce the real cost of servicing nominally 19.34

[20] Primary surpluses should be thought of here in a broad sense, incorporating stock-flow adjustments in public debt (such as asset sales and privatizations or bailouts) even if they are not, according to common accounting conventions, captured by primary surpluses in government financial statements.

[21] If M is the stock of base money, P is the GDP deflator, and Q is the real GDP, then $\sigma \equiv \frac{\Delta M}{PQ}$.

[22] *See* Willem H. Buiter and Ebrahim Rahbari, *Looking into the Deep Pockets of the ECB*, Citi Economics Global Economics View (February 2012), available online at <http://blogs.r.ftdata.co.uk/money-supply/files/2012/02/citi-Looking-into-the-Deep-Pockets-of-the-ECB.pdf>; Willem H. Buiter, *The Role of Central Banks in Financial Stability: How Has it Changed?*, Paper presented at the 14th International Banking Conference organized by the Federal Reserve Bank of Chicago and the European Central Bank in Chicago, IL, 10–11 November 2011.

denominated, domestic-currency-denominated, fixed-interest-rate public debt, and so can the combination of inflation (anticipated or unanticipated) and financial repression.

19.35 Whatever the efficiency costs of higher taxation, lower public spending, and wealth levies through (unanticipated) inflation, it is their political costs that are likely to turn out to be the binding constraint on raising the permanent augmented primary surplus (as a share of GDP). The anti-austerity protests in the euro area periphery have made it clear that both raising taxation and reducing public spending can be very unpopular—indeed, prohibitively so for any government interested in political survival. We can define $\bar{s}^{\max}$, the maximum feasible primary surplus, reflecting economic, technical, *and political* limits. This also allows us to define the associated maximum sustainable level of (net) public debt:

$$\bar{d}^{\max} = \left(\frac{\bar{r} - \bar{\gamma}}{1 + \bar{\gamma}}\right)^{-1} \bar{s}^{\max} \tag{6}$$

B. A historical digression

19.36 Historically, before the nineteenth century, the norm everywhere (including in the countries now characterized as advanced economies) was that sovereign risk tended to be worse than the credit risk of leading merchants or private bankers.[23] Prior to the Industrial Revolution, sovereigns everywhere defaulted regularly. Although many sovereigns in what are now called 'emerging markets' and developing countries continued to default throughout the nineteenth and twentieth centuries, in the advanced industrial countries, sovereign default had not happened since the (West) German defaults of 1948 and 1953 until the Greek defaults of 2012.

19.37 This absence of sovereign defaults in the advanced economies for almost sixty-five years has come to be viewed as the norm, rather than as something to be explained or possibly even as something rather unusual or even anomalous. Is there a risk that the advanced economies could return to the sovereign default patterns from before the nineteenth century?

19.38 The poor credit rating and performance of sovereigns in Western Europe before the nineteenth century should not come as a surprise. Prior to the modern age of broad-based income taxes, indirect taxes, and taxes on property, the sovereign's revenue sources were limited: seigniorage (revenue from coinage, which was limited in a world with commodity money rather than paper or electronic fiat money); a range of in-kind or corvée (labour supplied without pay) taxes; import and export duties, and their local equivalent; tolls; scutage;[24] tallage;[25] aids;[26] Danegeld;[27] carucage;[28] assorted excises; transactions and transfer taxes; a range of property taxes and poll taxes, including inheritance taxes and death duties; the sale of monopolies; fines; confiscation of wealth; and plunder. Although the taxes were many, the revenues were low.

---

23 *See* Reinhart and Rogoff (n. 8).

24 A payment in lieu of military service.

25 A tax on feudal dependants.

26 A tax paid by a vassal to his lord in feudal times.

27 A medieval land tax used to fund military expenditures (originally to pay off the raiding and invading Danes).

28 A land tax that replaced Danegeld in England.

Early examples of income taxes can be found—notably, the income tax introduced by Emperor Wang Mang of the Xin Dynasty in CE 10. When he was overthrown in CE 23, that income tax experiment came to an end. The modern era of income taxes starts with the December 1789 Budget of Pitt the Younger, which introduced a temporary income tax to finance the war effort against France. It was indeed abolished in 1802 during the peace of Amiens, reintroduced when hostilities started again in 1803, and abolished again in 1816, a year after the battle of Waterloo. Its reintroduction in 1842 by Sir Robert Peel has not yet been followed by another abolition. **19.39**

In the United States, income tax was first imposed in July 1861 to help to pay for the American Civil War. It was abolished in 1872, revived in 1894, and again abolished in 1895, when it was declared unconstitutional by the Supreme Court. Since the ratification of the 16th Amendment to the US Constitution in 1913, there has been a federal income tax in the United States. **19.40**

Unlike excises or duties on individual commodities, which go back at least to 2000 BCE, broadly based sales taxes, including multi-stage turnover taxes such as value added tax (VAT), date to the First World War or more recent times. **19.41**

Income taxes (personal and corporate), levied on labour income, interest income, dividends, and capital gains, and including a range of social security taxes, together with broadly based indirect taxes (sales taxes, turnover taxes, multi-stage turnover taxes such as VAT, excises and duties) and broadly based property taxes, permitted the funding of general government spending programmes that now range, in advanced industrial countries, from just above 30 per cent of GDP to just below 60 per cent. The euro area average is around 50 per cent of GDP (see Table 19.1). **19.42**

The reasons for the absence of completely (default) risk-free sovereigns among the advanced economies (or anywhere else), despite the massive growth of sovereign tax capacity, are three. **19.43**

First, demand for public spending in advanced economies has, since the Great Depression and especially since the end of the Second World War, grown even faster than the capacity to tax and has now outstripped the capacity to raise revenues in a way that: (a) is politically acceptable to the polity; and (b) does not materially damage incentives to work, to educate oneself, and to take risk as a saver, investor, or entrepreneur. **19.44**

Second, in a number of countries with high public debt burdens and large primary structural deficits (see Table 19.2), political polarization has increased to the point at which even if everyone recognizes the unsustainability of the fiscal programme and the need for, and desirability of, early fiscal tightening, agreement on such a sustainability-restoring programme may be postponed as each interest group tries to minimize its share of the total burden of adjustment. There is a rich non-cooperative game theory literature on 'wars of attrition' that rationalizes such individually rational, but collectively disastrous, behaviour.[29] Fiscal adjustment could possibly be delayed for long enough to trigger an eventual sovereign debt crisis. Even if the war of attrition between different groups of (potential) taxpayers and (potential) **19.45**

[29] *See* J. Maynard Smith, 'Theory of Games and the Evolution of Animal Contests' (1974) 47 J Theor Biol 209; D. T. Bishop and C. Cannings, 'A Generalized War of Attrition' (1978) 70 J Theor Biol 85; K. Chatterjee, J. G. Reiter, and M. A. Nowak, 'Evolutionary Dynamics of Biological Auctions' (2012) 81 Theor Popul Biol 69.

Table 19.1 Selected countries: general government expenditure, 1870–1996 (% of GDP)

	Late nineteenth century	Pre-First World War	Post-First World War	Pre-Second World War	Post-Second World War			Twenty-first century		
	c.1870	1913	1920	1937	1960	1980	1990	2000	2010	2012
Australia	18.3	16.5	19.3	14.8	21.2	34.1	34.9	34.7	36.6	36.6
Austria	10.5	17.0	14.7	20.6	35.7	48.1	38.6	51.9	52.6	51.1
Canada	n/a	n/a	16.7	25.0	28.6	38.8	46.0	40.8	43.0	41.0
France	12.6	17.0	27.6	29.0	34.6	46.1	49.8	51.7	56.6	56.6
Germany	10.0	14.8	25.0	34.1	32.4	47.9	45.1	45.1	47.7	45.0
Italy	13.7	17.1	30.1	31.1	30.1	42.1	53.4	45.9	50.4	50.7
Ireland	n/a	n/a	18.8	25.5	28.0	48.9	41.2	30.7	64.9	41.6
Japan	8.8	8.3	14.8	25.4	17.5	32.0	31.3	37.3	38.9	41.3
New Zealand	n/a	n/a	24.6	25.3	26.9	38.1	41.3	34.9	40.1	37.3
Norway	5.9	9.3	16.0	11.8	29.9	43.8	54.9	41.5	44.9	43.4
Sweden	5.7	10.4	10.9	16.4	31.0	60.1	59.1	52.7	50.6	50.1
Switzerland	16.5	14.0	17.0	24.1	17.2	32.8	33.5	34.4	32.7	32.7
UK	9.4	12.7	26.2	30.0	32.2	43.0	39.9	34.3	46.7	43.5
US	7.3	7.5	12.1	19.7	27.0	31.4	32.8	33.7	42.4	40.2
Average	**10.8**	**13.1**	**19.6**	**23.8**	**28.0**	**41.9**	**43.0**	**40.7**	**46.3**	**43.6**

Note: Data for late nineteenth century corresponds to 1870 or closest year available for all columns. Data corresponds to the general government, except for Austria 1920 and Sweden c. 1870, for which it refers to the central government.

Sources: For pre-2000 data, V. Tanzi and L. Schuknecht, *Public Spending in the 20th Century: A Global Perspective* (Cambridge: Cambridge University Press, 2010); for post 2000 data, IMF World Economic Outlook Database.

claimants on public spending does not postpone fiscal adjustment until a sovereign default is the only option, the delays in adjusting are likely to make the total cost of adjustment larger. Greece and the United States would be prime examples of such polarized societies.

19.46 Third, as part of the widespread erosion of social capital (in the sense of trust between government and citizen, between members of rival political parties and between citizens), tax administration has become less effective in many advanced economies, with rapid growth of the underground (or 'grey') economy, and in tax avoidance and tax evasion.[30]

19.47 Globalization has contributed to this, by providing new avenues for people and corporates to shield their income and wealth from the tax authorities, but the phenomenon is older than that. Tax enforcement is costly. It is effective only if tax compliance is both a social norm and an internalized objective of most citizens, enforced by the law (and informed random auditing), by social disapproval for evasion and avoidance, and by the small voice of individual

[30] *See*, e.g., Joel Slemrod, 'Cheating Ourselves: The Economics of Tax Evasion' (2007) 21(1) J Econ Persp 25; Joel Slemrod and Shlomo Yitzhaki, 'Tax Avoidance, Evasion and Administration', in A. Auerbach and M. Feldstein (eds) *Handbook of Public Economics, Vol. 3* (Amsterdam: North-Holland, 2002), 1423–70; Joel Slemrod and Naomi Feldman, 'War and Taxation: When Does Patriotism Overcome the Freerider Impulse?', in Isaac W. Martin, Ajay K. Mehrota, and Monica Prasad (eds) *The New Fiscal Sociology: Taxation in Comparative and Historical Perspective* (Cambridge: Cambridge University Press, 2009), 138–54.

Table 19.2 Selected countries: general government primary balance, 2012 (% of GDP)

	Primary balance (% of GDP)	Cyclically adjusted primary balance (% of GDP)
Australia	−2.5	−2.4
Austria	−0.5	−0.3
Belgium	−0.7	−0.5
Canada	−2.7	−2.2
Denmark	−3.9	−2.7
Finland	−1.9	−0.8
France	−2.2	−0.7
Germany	2.4	2.3
Greece	−1.2	2.1
Iceland	1.5	1.0
Ireland	−4.6	−2.9
Italy	2.3	4.0
Japan	−9.3	−8.4
Netherlands	−2.9	−1.5
Norway	11.7	−8.6
Portugal	−0.8	1.0
Spain	−7.9	−2.6
Sweden	−1.3	−1.4
Switzerland	0.7	0.8
UK	−6.1	−3.3
US	−6.4	−4.4

Sources: IMF Fiscal Monitor Database; Citi Research

conscience. Such equilibrium is vulnerable to defection. If a sufficient number of taxpayers default from the 'pay what you owe' equilibrium, others will wonder why they should pay both their own taxes and a share of the taxes of those who avoid and/or evade their fair contributions. If enough defect, there can be a tipping point after which only the foolish and the unlucky pay their taxes in full.

The incidence of tax avoidance and evasion appears to have risen everywhere in Europe and in the United States since the Second World War, and also appears to be higher as one moves further south and east in Europe. Among the worst affected countries are Greece and Italy. Although the size and growth of the informal sector/shadow economy/grey economy is driven not only by taxation, but also by regulatory avoidance and evasion, the cross-sectional evidence from Table 19.3 and time-series evidence for the advanced economies[31] is also indicative of the extent of tax compliance and the quality of tax administration. **19.48**

[31] *See* Friedrich Schneider and Dominik Enste, *Shadow Economies around the World: Sizes, Causes, and Consequences*, IMF Working Paper No. 00/26 (February 2000), available online at <http://www.imf.org/external/pubs/ft/wp/2000/wp0026.pdf>; Friedrich Schneider and Dominik Enste, 'Shadow Economies and Corruption All over the World: Revised Estimates for 120 Countries', *Economics, The Open-Assessment E-journal*, 27 October 2009.

Table 19.3 Size of the shadow economy in twenty-five high-income OECD countries in 2006 (% of GDP)

Rank	Country	Shadow economy
1	United States	7.0
2	Switzerland	7.6
3	Austria	7.6
	Luxembourg	8.2
4	New Zealand	8.8
5	Japan	8.8
6	Netherlands	9.5
9	Australia	9.8
10	UK	10.6
	France	10.8
11	Canada	11.5
13	Ireland	12.7
14	Germany	13.3
15	Finland	13.3
16	Denmark	13.4
17	Norway	14.2
18	Sweden	14.3
19	Slovakia	15.5
	Czech Republic	16.0
	Belgium	16.8
20	Spain	19.2
21	Portugal	19.4
22	Italy	21.6
	Hungary	22.5
	Slovenia	23.6
23	Greece	24.0
	Poland	24.4
	Malta	25.3
	Cyprus	25.6
	Latvia	26.1
	Turkey	27.2
	Estonia	28.2
	Lithuania	28.5
	Croatia	29.0
	Romania	29.1
	Bulgaria	31.9

Source: Friedrich Schneider, *Size and Development of the Shadow Economy of 31 European and 5 other OECD Countries from 2003 to 2013: A Further Decline* (April 2013), available online at <http://www.econ.jku.at/members/Schneider/files/publications/2013/ShadEcEurope31_Jan2013.pdf>.

19.49 Only in the last few years have there been signs that at least some of the more egregious forms of tax evasion and tax avoidance may be on the retreat. Robust exchanges between the US government and the German government, on the one hand, and the governments of leading European tax havens such as Switzerland and Liechtenstein, on the other, have resulted in material erosion of bank secrecy—a cornerstone of tax evasion and avoidance. The recent demise of Cyprus as a euro area tax haven has accelerated the trend towards ending bank secrecy in the EU, in European nations encircled by the EU and in the UK crown dependencies, and in overseas territories in the Channel Islands and the Caribbean. This could lead to a step improvement in tax-collection capacity and could create new, less demand-destroying revenue opportunities through wealth levies, including tax amnesties that may prove valuable to such countries as Italy.

C. Political feasibility of sustainable fiscal–financial–monetary policy

19.50 The previous section highlighted the social and political forces that, together with factor endowments, technology, and other economic characteristics of a nation determine the bounds on the values that public debt and primary balance ratios can assume. These dry algebraic symbols can hide a lot of human drama.

19.51 From the foregoing analysis, the relevant solvency criterion is thus whether $d \leq \bar{d}^{\max}$ (or $\bar{s}^{\max} \geq \bar{s}^{\min}$), in which case the sovereign would be solvent, or $d > \bar{d}^{\max}$ ($\bar{s}^{\max} < \bar{s}^{\min}$), which would signify insolvency. Solvency thus requires that the minimum primary surplus necessary to sustain the existing debt is also feasible—in particular politically feasible. Since the definitions of $\bar{d}^{\max}$ and $\bar{s}^{\max}$ explicitly include political limits to raising primary surpluses, it is apt to think of insolvent here mostly as unwilling to pay.[32] Of course, 'won't pay' insolvency is what is relevant for a number of advanced economies today, which have high levels of debt, but also high levels of per capita income (far away from subsistence levels) and wealth. The notion that these countries would not be able to eliminate large primary or overall deficits, or to service outstanding levels of debt, is, for the most part, a logical and economic nonsense, even with zero future growth.

19.52 Equation (5) expressed the sustainable level of debt as a function of the effective permanent interest rate $\bar{r}$, the permanent growth rate $\bar{y}$, and the maximum sustainable level of the primary surplus $\bar{s}^{\max}$. Thus anything that affects $\bar{r}$, $\bar{y}$, or $\bar{s}^{\max}$ should affect how much debt a country can sustain—which would be a large number of political, social, cultural, and financial, as well as economic, factors, which vary both across countries and over time.[33]

[32] It is also possible to define a maximum feasible primary surplus excluding political factors, say, $\overset{-\max}{s}$, with an associated maximum sustainable level of debt, $\overset{-\max}{d}$. By construction, it holds that $\bar{s}^{\max} < \overset{-\max}{s}$ and $\bar{d}^{\max} < \overset{-\max}{d}$. Strictly speaking, 'won't pay' insolvency would be given by $\bar{d}^{\max} < d < \overset{-\max}{d}$ (or $\bar{s}^{\max} < \bar{s}^{\min} < \overset{-\max}{s}$) and 'can't pay' insolvency, by $\overset{-\max}{s} < \bar{s}^{\min}$ or $d > \overset{-\max}{d}$.

[33] As for the interest rate charged, issuing a major international vehicle and reserve currency, such as the dollar, tends to keep required returns low, as does greater home bias by domestic investors. High private savings can magnify the effect of the home bias on the interest rate, while financial repression may be more effective in such circumstances as well. Of course, attitudes towards risk and risk itself, including economic risk, political risk, inflation risk, and other risks, would affect required yields too. Finally, the determinants of growth

19.53 Politics and policy can have an effect on all three variables, but political economy considerations are especially pertinent when considering the feasibility of raising primary surpluses. A high level of social capital (the absence of perceptions of corruption, a sense of solidarity, etc.) and a well-organized and competent tax administration, perceived as fair and non-partisan by the citizens, should allow more tax revenues to be obtained, other things being equal, and at relatively low cost. A high share of foreign-owned debt, on the other hand, may make it more difficult to find the political support necessary to generate and sustain large primary surpluses, mostly for the benefit of making foreign creditors whole. It is somewhat ironic that one of the greatest fiscal consolidations in recent history (Greece in 2012) was attempted in a country that must have scored among the worst according to these three criteria. Of course, intensely political choices are also involved in deciding who or what will be taxed, or whose spending will be cut, when trying to raise primary surpluses—that is, to determine the composition of fiscal tightening. The IMF recently noted that, for the median country in the sample that it studied, the maximum annual primary surplus achieved was 6½ per cent of GDP for advanced economies since the 1950s, but that that maximum fell to 3½–4 per cent of GDP for five-year moving averages and to 2¾–3¼ per cent of GDP for twenty-year averages.[34]

D. What about liquidity?

19.54 No discussion of default would be complete without discussing liquidity. To discuss liquidity, let us first distinguish between insolvency and default. Sovereigns (just like companies or households) can be insolvent ($d > \bar{d}^{max}$ or $\bar{s}^{max} < \bar{s}^{min}$), yet avoid default by being bailed out—a hope that undoubtedly exists among a few sovereigns in the euro area currently. On the other hand, countries may default on their obligations because they cannot meet their debt service obligations (interest and/or principal), sometimes despite the fact that they are fundamentally solvent. Put more precisely, even though there exists at least one interest rate $\bar{r}$ that is an equilibrium interest rate (in the sense that the sovereign default risk premium embodied in $\bar{r}$ *ex ante* will match the *ex post* likelihood of default if $\bar{r}$ is indeed the interest rate paid by the sovereign) and that is consistent with government solvency $d < \bar{d}^{max}$ or $\bar{s}^{max} > \bar{s}^{min}$, there also exists at least one other interest rate $\bar{\bar{r}} > \bar{r}$, which is also an equilibrium interest rate, but for which the sovereign is insolvent—that is, $d > \bar{d}^{max}$ or $\bar{s}^{max} < \bar{s}^{min}$.

are a literature of their own, which points out the major drivers of economic growth in the medium and long terms: *see*, e.g., Willem H. Buiter and Ebrahim Rahbari, *Global Growth Generators: Moving beyond 'Emerging Markets' and 'BRIC'*, Citi Economics Global Economics View (February 2011), available online at <http://www.econ.uzh.ch/faculty/groupzilibotti/Conferences/2011Nov21Demo/E_Rahbari.pdf>; Robert Barro and Xavier Sala-i-Martin, *Economic Growth*, 2nd rev'd edn (Cambridge, MA: MIT Press, 2003). It is, however, important not to misinterpret the arithmetic effect of higher growth on the fiscal debt burden and the level of sustainable debt. It is true that, other things being equal, higher growth reduces the public-debt-to-GDP ratio more rapidly. It also raises revenues, which may appear to provide a painless way of generating larger primary surpluses. However, through human psychology and political entrepreneurship, higher growth also raises the pressures for increased public spending. Other things being equal, a large amount of private assets should allow the government to levy higher taxes or to reduce public spending without running material risks of endangering the physical well-being of the population.

34 *See* IMF, *Fiscal Monitor: Fiscal Adjustment in an Uncertain World* (April 2013), available online at <http://www.imf.org/external/pubs/ft/fm/2013/01/fmindex.htm>.

We call an instance of inability to meet debt service obligations despite being fundamentally solvent 'illiquidity'. Of course, countries can also fail to meet debt service commitments due when they are fundamentally insolvent. We call failure to meet debt service payments due 'default', both when the debtor is solvent and when it is insolvent. 19.55

In order to illustrate illiquidity, we return to our discussion of the interest rate $\bar{r}$. Earlier in the chapter, $\bar{r}$ was referred to as the 'permanent real interest rate on public debt', to be understood as an expected long-term average. That does not quite pin down $\bar{r}$. In fact, $\bar{r}$ is the interest rate (or, more precisely, the 'average' or permanent value of a sequence of interest rates over time) that discounts the stream of primary surpluses appropriately (in a self-validating or equilibrium sense, reflecting not only default risk, but also all other types of risk, such as liquidity, inflation, and expropriation, which investors would be expected to price in). If more than one self-validating or equilibrium sequence of interest rates exist, $\bar{r}$ corresponds to the lowest permanent or long-run average value of these multiple equilibrium-interest-rate sequences. 19.56

This elaboration of the definition of $\bar{r}$ is not (only) an exercise in pedantism. With a positive level of outstanding (net) public debt, there always exists a value of $\bar{r}$ high enough (potentially infinite) to make any positive level of debt unsustainable—and that interest rate would also be self-validating. Suppose investors assume that the sovereign is certain to default and correspondingly charge a very high interest rate; that very high interest rate then, in turn, makes the debt unsustainable, validating the expectation of default. Even excluding a self-fulfilling 'bad equilibrium', there may be multiple good equilibria (consistent with a low *ex ante* and *ex post* likelihood of default). We define $\bar{r}$ as the lowest such equilibrium interest rate and henceforth treat the 'good' equilibrium as unique. 19.57

Now define $\bar{r}^{\max}$ as the highest interest rate at which the sovereign is still solvent—that is: 19.58

$$\bar{r}^{\max} = \bar{\gamma} + (1+\bar{\gamma})\left(\frac{\bar{s}^{\max}}{d}\right) \qquad (7)$$

Illiquidity is then defined as $r > \bar{r}^{\max} > \bar{r}$—that is, the interest rate at which the sovereign would be able to borrow exceeds the maximum interest rate at which it would be solvent, *even though the sovereign is solvent* in the sense that its debt would be sustainable, if it were charged the interest rate $\bar{r}$. This definition not only captures situations in which investors charge an unreasonably high interest rate, but can also encompass a scenario when the sovereign is cut off from markets altogether (in which case, it would face an infinite immediate interest rate).

Illiquidity clearly happens. 'Good' and 'bad equilibria' arise typically in models of bank runs in which banks have a serious maturity or duration mismatch between their assets and liabilities. Typically, banks have mostly long-maturity, illiquid assets with few liquid reserves. They also have short-maturity liabilities, such as deposits withdrawable on demand and subject to a 'sequential service constraint', under which deposits are redeemed on a 'first come, first served' basis out of the scarce liquid reserves. Assets that have to be sold prior to maturity can be sold only at a huge loss. Such models of bank runs describe well the position of a sovereign whose liabilities are either denominated in foreign currency or which cannot force its central bank to act as lender of last resort should the sovereign be threatened with a sudden market 19.59

funding stop. Sovereigns too have mostly highly illiquid assets (the net present discounted value of future taxes and the net present discounted value of future spending cuts) and shorter-maturity liabilities.

19.60 Illiquidity can be the result of contagion, for example a sudden shift, following a sovereign default or restructuring in one country, of the markets' 'focal point' for other countries' sovereign risk from a virtuous equilibrium to a vicious equilibrium. Historically, there have been many examples of nations with a lot of foreign-currency-denominated liabilities that have suffered a 'bank-run' style rush for the exit by foreign creditors whose foreign-currency bond exposure or loans to the country matured. This can cause a sovereign default either if the foreign exposure is sovereign exposure or if the foreign exposure is by private institutions deemed, by the sovereign, too systemically important to fail, but which also turn out to be too big to save. A sovereign rescue attempt can then result in sovereign default. This almost happened in Iceland in 2008, where the sovereign at the last moment decided not to risk its own solvency by guaranteeing the unsecured debt of its cross-border banks. It happened in Ireland, where European Financial Stability Facility (EFSF) loans to the sovereign have been restructured several times since they were first issued. Even at issuance, the interest rates on these loans were likely below the risk-adjusted cost of funding to the creditor nations.

19.61 If this depiction sounds all too familiar—and recalls the rants of some European policymakers against unreasonable investors or greedy speculators—a word of caution is probably in order: they probably happen less often than might be thought, at least for advanced economies. For default to result from illiquidity or contagion, two conditions need to be satisfied: first, the sovereign does not have sufficient liquid assets to meet the debt service obligations that are due (otherwise, the sovereign can pay out of its own pocket); and second, no adequate lender of last resort exists. The first condition may be met relatively often, as has already been noted.

19.62 On the other hand, the second condition may not be met very often. In countries in which the bulk of the sovereign's liabilities are denominated in domestic currency, the domestic central bank can usually act as a lender of last resort.[35] Foreign currency liquidity can be harder to obtain, but international institutions, such as the IMF, the European Stability Mechanism (ESM), or the international development banks, or ad hoc or systematic arrangements with foreign central banks (say, through foreign currency swaps), can provide foreign-currency liquidity, often at no-to-short notice and on acceptable terms. This is the rule rather than the exception for advanced economies (emerging markets have long complained that the terms of access to such sources of liquidity had been unduly harsh for them during many crises in the past).

19.63 More often than not, what *looks* like illiquidity is really a reassessment of risks based on learning. An example is the reassessment of sovereign risk for nations other than Greece, based on the observation of Greece's two sovereign debt restructurings with public sector involvement (PSI) in 2012, which were the first sovereign defaults in the euro area since its creation in 1999 (and in Western Europe since the West German defaults in 1948 and 1953). It has been impressive, in most financial crises since the 1980s, including the latest stage of the eurozone financial crisis that started in 2010, how little contagion there has been

[35] Legal provisions, such as Article 125 of the Lisbon Treaty in the EU, may complicate a central bank's lender-of-last-resort function for sovereigns, but usually only at the expense of higher legal bills and inefficient financial arrangements.

as a result of blind fear and panic. Although there has been jitteriness and nervousness galore, the markets—and creditors in general—have on the whole been highly discriminating and selective as regards the sovereigns singled out for special attention. Countries with sound fiscal fundamentals have not been tested in this crisis.

Since the initiation of the long-term refinancing operations in November 2011 and February 2012, and especially since the announcement of the outright market transaction (OMT) programme in September 2012, the risk that blind contagion could drive otherwise solvent sovereigns into default and out of the eurozone has been lowered materially. The European Central Bank (ECB)/Eurosystem is now acting as lender of last resort for euro area banks and sovereigns. This does not, of course, eliminate either sovereign default risk for fundamentally insolvent sovereigns or bank failures, recoveries, recapitalizations, and resolutions for fundamentally insolvent banks. **19.64**

E. Politics of debt sustainability analysis

Political economy factors matter greatly for sovereign debt sustainability, as this chapter has made clear. Perhaps less obviously, politics also play a major role in sovereign debt sustainability *assessments*. Such assessments are part of the bread-and-butter business of many international organizations and development banks, including the IMF, the World Bank, the European Commission, and related bodies. These organizations are usually picked both because of the financial resources they have at their disposal and for their human resources, as well as an institutional and organizational knowledge base that should allow them to form an objective assessment of appropriate policy choices, as well as debt sustainability. **19.65**

Given the large number of factors (including social, cultural, and political factors, not only economic and financial ones) that affect debt sustainability, such assessments are fiendishly hard. Mistakes tend to be made and over time—hopefully—some learning occurs. Some of the relatively recent lessons learned are that it is not only public debt, but also private debt, that matters for sovereign debt sustainability (as a result, for example, of the latter's tendency to migrate to the sovereign balance sheet when things go bad), and that it is important to distinguish more carefully between cyclical and structural drivers of government balances. On the whole, the financial, human, and organizational resources would seem adequate at these institutions to the task at hand. The guidelines for carrying out these assessments also usually look rather appropriate. For example, the IMF's approach to debt sustainability is summarized by the Fund itself in the following way: **19.66**

> The [IMF] framework consists of two complementary components: the analysis of the sustainability of total public debt and that of total external debt. Each component includes a baseline scenario, based on a set of macroeconomic projections that articulate the government's intended policies, with the main assumptions and parameters clearly laid out; and a series of *sensitivity tests* applied to the baseline scenario, providing a *probabilistic upper bound* for the debt dynamics under various assumptions regarding policy variables, macroeconomic developments, and financing costs. The paths of debt indicators under the baseline scenario and the stress tests allow to assess the vulnerability of the country to a payments crisis.
>
> DSAs [debt sustainability analyses] should however not be interpreted in a mechanistic or rigid fashion. Their results must be *assessed against relevant country-specific circumstances*, including the particular features of a given country's debt as well as its policy track record and its policy space.... the frameworks have been regularly refined with a view to—among

other elements—bringing a greater discipline to the analysis and responding to the *changing economic and financial environment.*[36]

19.67 The summary suggests that the IMF's experts are aware of the many facets that assessing debt sustainability has, of the inherent margins of error, and of the differences over time and between countries. Political factors are not explicitly mentioned and thus do not get the special attention that they deserve. But that omission still does not explain why the IMF (and the troika) got it so wrong in the case of Greece (at least in its original debt sustainability projections) and in Portugal, too, to name but the two most obvious examples of DSAs that looked wildly over-optimistic even at the time that they were performed.

19.68 The answer is, of course, that politics are to blame here, too. In May 2010, when the original memorandum of understanding (MOU) for the first Greek adjustment programme was agreed, the Greek government's euro area sovereign creditors-to-be (which account for 22 per cent of the IMF capital and votes—see Table 19.4) simply let it be known that they had no appetite for a Greek debt restructuring, because they had no appetite for another round of bailouts of their own insufficiently capitalized and excessively Greece-exposed banks. And the IMF, being the shareholder-friendly organization that it is, responded to its board putting pressure on its management to put pressure on its staff, by coming up with forecasts that not only included wildly optimistic GDP and budget deficit forecasts, but also defined 120 per cent of GDP (in 2020) as the threshold for debt sustainability (see Figures 19.2 and 19.3). Based on the IMF's guidelines, one should assume that this was a country-specific threshold, reflecting the special characteristics and fiscal capacities of the Greek economy. But it bore an uncanny resemblance to the level of public debt in Italy at the time (Italy's general government gross debt-to-GDP ratio has since risen to 127 per cent of GDP in 2012, according to the IMF, and is due to exceed 130 per cent of GDP this year, again according to the IMF).

19.69 The IMF has since regretted that it was so easily convinced to make its forecasts fit the preferences of some of its shareholders and the issue has reportedly, on several occasions, raised a few grunts from other parts of its membership, including the non-European advanced economies and some emerging markets. It has since also spoken out much louder on the issue of debt sustainability, and not only in Greece, but also, and quite emphatically, in the case of Cyprus. In addition, Greece has, since the unfortunate 'all clear' of May 2010, already undergone two formal debt restructurings, with the IMF's blessing. Trust in the objectivity of the troika programmes forecasts has yet to be fully restored, however—and the politicization of DSAs continues.

19.70 It would be wrong, of course, to single out the IMF for the political influences on technical, seemingly objective, assessments. National governments tend to use economic forecasts as mere debating tools. Many other multilateral or international institutions fare, or would fare, no better—certainly not the main European institutions, such as the European Commission or the ECB. Even though the latter may, at times, have been swayed more by institutional orthodoxy and concern about the size of its own balance sheet than by

[36] *See* IMF, 'Debt Sustainability Analysis: Introduction' (March 2013), available online at <http://www.imf.org/external/pubs/ft/dsa/> (emphasis added).

political considerations, this detail has not benefited its objectivity. The recent remarks by European Commissioner Rehn and ECB Executive Board Member Asmussen about ending the 'troika'—by which they really mean to kick the IMF out—can therefore hardly be regarded as good news.[37]

Table 19.4 Selected countries: IMF votes

Country/area	IMF votes	
	Number	% of total
Austria	21,876	0.87
Belgium	46,789	1.86
Cyprus	2,319	0.09
Estonia	1,676	0.07
Finland	13,375	0.53
France	108	4.29
Germany	146,392	5.81
Greece	11,755	0.47
Ireland	13,313	0.53
Italy	79,560	3.16
Luxembourg	4,924	0.2
Malta	1,757	0.07
Netherlands	52,361	2.08
Portugal	11,034	0.44
Slovakia	5,012	0.2
Slovenia	3,487	0.14
Spain	40,971	1.63
Euro area	**456,709**	**22.44**
Bulgaria	7,139	0.28
Czech Republic	10,759	0.43
Denmark	19,651	0.78
Hungary	11,121	0.44
Latvia	2,158	0.09
Lithuania	2,576	0.1
Poland	17,621	0.7
Romania	11,039	0.44
Sweden	24,692	0.98
United Kingdom	108,122	4.29
European Union	**671,587**	**30.97**
China	95,996	3.81
Japan	157,022	6.23

Sources: IMF; Citi Research

[37] Martina Stevis, 'ECB Official Sees Eventual End to IMF Involvement in Euro Crises', *Wall Street Journal*, 8 May 2013, available online at <http://online.wsj.com/article/SB10001424127887323744604578470523613305046.html>.

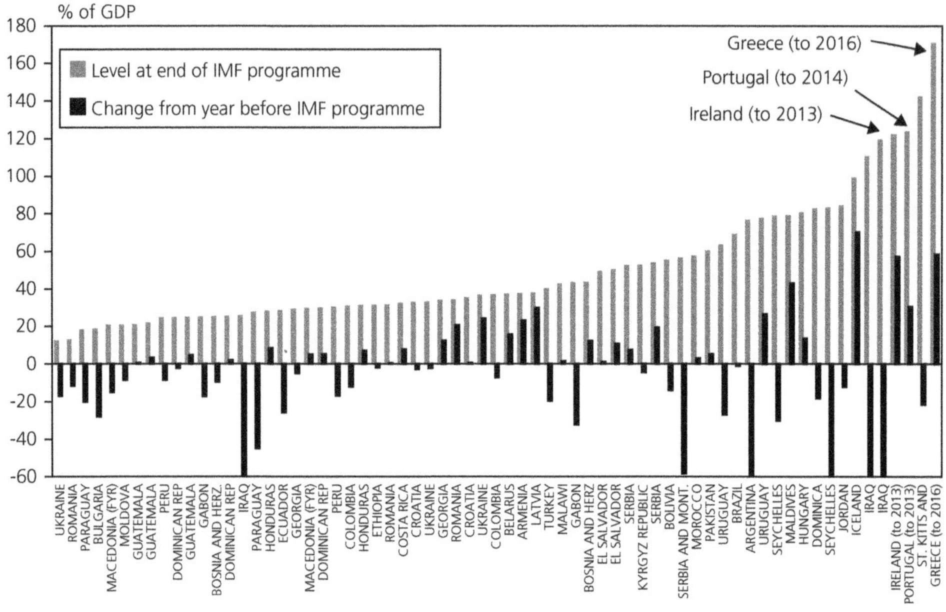

Figure 19.2 Selected countries: government debt–to–GDP ratio before and after IMF General Resource Account (GRA) programmes, 2002–16

Note: Data from IMF Monitoring of Fund Arrangements (MONA) database, updated with latest World Economic Outlook projections for Greece, Ireland, and Portugal. Some countries appear more than once if they had more than one programme. Greece's first programme has been combined with the second one.

Sources: IMF; Citi Research

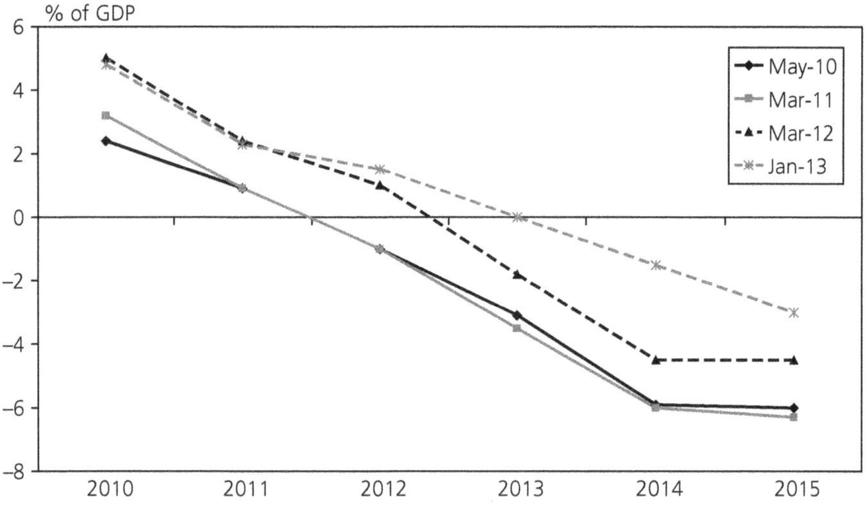

Figure 19.3 Greece: IMF projections of primary balance (% of GDP)

Note: Values correspond to projections on the general government primary balance produced by the troika on the specified date.

Sources: IMF, *Greece: Staff Report on Request for Stand-By Arrangement* (May 2010); IMF, *Third Review under the Stand-By Arrangement: Staff Report* (March 2011); IMF, *Request for Extended Arrangement under the Extended Fund Facility: Staff Report* (March 2012); IMF, *First and Second Reviews under the Extended Arrangement under the Extended Fund Facility: Request for Waiver of Applicability, Modification of Performance Criteria, and Rephasing of Access—Staff Report* (January 2013); Citi Research

5. The Political Economy of When and How to Default as a Sovereign

At the outset, this chapter defined default as any change in the stream of current and future payments on a debt contract that makes it less valuable to the creditor than the execution of the contractually agreed stream. There are many ways in which to get there—and still quite a few that do not get stamped as default by the rating agencies or the International Swaps and Derivatives Association (ISDA), which has the role of deciding whether a particular transaction constitutes a 'credit event' for credit default swaps (CDSs). The staple of a 'short back and sides' (a haircut to the face value of the principal) is only one of a dizzying variety of options, including maturity lengthening, coupon reductions, or the change of any other of the price or non-price terms of the debt contract. **19.71**

Both sovereign default (or debt restructuring) and the details of the restructuring of private sector debt are often the outcome of a complex web of legal, accounting, and other considerations, as well as of financial ones. But there are two major differences: first, political considerations play a much larger role when sovereign debt restructuring is the name of the game; and second, when it comes to sovereign default, the 'rules of the game' can potentially change during the process. If the creditors (as well as the debtor) are public entities, political and popular considerations in the creditor countries seem to suggest almost lexicographic preferences between debt restructurings that do not involve face-value haircuts (but with potentially very large NPV losses through lengthening of maturities or coupon reductions, and/or deferrals) and debt restructurings with face-value haircuts. Political considerations in the debtor countries often also support ways in which to restructure the debt that may not be designated formal defaults at all. Hence the idea of dressing up defaults as 'voluntary' debt exchanges (but with 'voluntary' interpreted in the 'army' sense) or, even better, cajoling domestic financial institutions through financial repression into rolling over or expanding their commitments to hold sovereign debt when—at the terms being offered—they would have no interest in doing so. **19.72**

The 'rules of the game' also often change during sovereign debt restructuring processes. This is particularly true for debt issued under domestic jurisdiction. In those cases, it often takes only an Act of Parliament to change certain terms of the contract or the seniority of claims. For these reasons, it is more commonplace that, in sovereign debt restructurings, certain creditors receive preferential treatment relative to others, with the most common beneficiaries being other public sector entities, systemically important private actors, and other politically sensitive or powerful entities. The deft manoeuvre through which the ECB and the national central banks of the Eurosystem avoided taking losses on their exposures to the Greek sovereign through the Securities Market Programme (SMP) in 2012 is a textbook example of changing the de facto seniority ranking of different classes of creditor. Of course, private debt restructurings are not fully devoid of such political interventions, because governments sometimes find it opportune to involve themselves in private debt restructuring processes when their outcome is of some popular interest. Recent examples include mortgage foreclosure processes in many countries, including Ireland, Italy, and Spain, and the bankruptcy of General Motors in 2009. **19.73**

The moderately good news for investors is that, partly because a sovereign default allows the country to continue operating as a 'going concern', the recovery rates following sovereign **19.74** defaults tend to be quite high. There are exceptions—notably, defaults that take the form of repudiations, as with Russia's Tsarist debt, West Germany's Nazi-era debt, and Cuba's Batista era debt. And, of course, Argentina's 2001–02 default left at least 70 per cent of the creditors with just 30 cents on the dollar. But these were the exceptions, until Greece, in March 2012, defaulted on about €200 billion worth of sovereign or sovereign-guaranteed bonded debt and imposed a haircut of over 70 per cent on the bondholders.

19.75 One study[38] of thirty-five sovereign debt renegotiations during the period 1986–2007 considered only *ex post* default and preemptive renegotiations, and excluded episodes of delays in payment such as Paraguay in 2003, and Venezuela in 1995, 1998, and 2005, and the swap agreement for Peru in 2000. Table 19.5 shows the recovery rates found for this recent sample of sovereign defaults.

19.76 There are also differences between sovereign default and private default in the timing of default. Again, for sovereigns, politics can come into play. A new government under high debt sustainability pressure may want to default as quickly as possible (assuming that it views default as ultimately inevitable), while an incumbent government may have a desire to try to postpone default until after the next election, or simply to delay it in the hope for a better tomorrow—more like the way in which private corporates faced with material default risk behave.

19.77 Sovereign debtors also usually tend to have a greater ability to stave off default for a little while longer, if they are so inclined. This is because they tend to have access to some additional sources of financing, be it through financial repression of domestic banks or other captive entities in the domestic private sector, through the central bank, or through the benevolence (or naivety) of friendly foreign sovereigns, central banks, or international institutions.

19.78 For private debtors, on the other hand, there is also an element of choice, but access to liquidity tends to be much more limited once solvency is in doubt, so delaying the day of reckoning is harder. In addition, delayed filing of insolvency by corporates is a criminal offence in many countries and creditors can file for insolvency under some conditions, further limiting the scope for postponing private default.

19.79 It is thus the case that, for sovereign creditors more than for private creditors, the timing of default is the result of the bargaining between creditors and debtors. Creditors may be private or public and, often enough, these creditors share with the debtor government a preference for postponing default. If the private creditors are banks, they may prefer, for a substantial period of time and for a variety of reasons, rolling their commitments over or evergreening their loans to realizing their losses. This type of behaviour was evident following both the Latin American debt crisis and in Europe in 2010 and beyond.

6. Conclusions

19.80 Sovereign defaults have been rare in advanced economies in recent decades, despite the fact that third-party enforcement plays almost no role for sovereign debt. The dearth of defaults

[38] Tamon Asonuma, *Sovereign Default and Renegotiation: Recovery Rates, Interest Spreads and Credit History* (April 2009), available online at <https://editorialexpress.com/cgi-bin/conference/download.cgi?db_name=NASM2009&paper_id=288>.

Table 19.5 Sovereign bond exchanges since 1997

Initial default date	Country	Distressed exchange details	Distressed exchange date	Debt in exchange			Loss (%)		
				US$ bn	% of total debt	% GDP	Nominal haircut*	Loss as measured by trading prices or NPV of cash flows	Loss as measured by:
Aug-98	Russia	LC debt (GKO and OFZ)	May-99	8.3	4.5	3.1	29	46res., 62 non-res.; devl. 95	NPV of cash flows
	Russia	FC debt (MIN FIN III)	Feb-00	1.3	0.7	0.7		75	Trading prices
	Russia	FC debt (PRIN and IAN)	Aug-00	29.1	16.4	16.3	36	90	Trading prices
Sep-98	Ukraine	LC T-bills held domestically	Sep-98	4.5	30.0	9	34	18	NPV of cash flows
	Ukraine	LC T-bills held by non-residents	Sep-98	0.4	2.8	0.8		59	NPV of cash flows
	Ukraine	FC Chase-Manhattan loan	Oct-98	0.1	0.7	0.2		31	NPV of cash flows
	Ukraine	FC ING bond and Merrill Lynch bond	Aug-99	0.4	2.0	1	45	38	NPV of cash flows
	Ukraine	FC eurobonds	Mar-00	1.6	8.3	5.1	5	31	Trading prices
Jul-99	Pakistan	Eurobonds	Dec-99	0.6	1.2	0.9		48	Trading prices
Aug-99	Ecuador	External debt and FC domestic bonds	Aug-00	7	49.5	41.5	40	56external, 9 domestic	Trading price (external); NPV (domestic)
Mar-00	Cote d'Ivoire	Brady bonds	Apr-10	2.8	18.7	12.4	20	82	Trading prices
Nov-01	Argentina	Domestic debt	Nov-01	64.4	49.6	22.6		83	Trading prices
	Argentina	External debt	Feb-05	79.7	41.7	52	66	71	Trading prices
Jun-02	Moldova	Eurobond	Oct-02	0.04	3.2	2.7		40	Trading prices

(*Continued*)

Initial default date	Country	Distressed exchange details	Distressed exchange date	Debt in exchange			Loss (%)		
				US$ bn	% of total debt	% GDP	Nominal haircut*	Loss as measured by trading prices or NPV of cash flows	Loss as measured by:
Jan-03	Paraguay	Domestic debt due in 2003–06	Jul-04	0.1	6.5	2.6		8	NPV of cash flows
May-03	Uruguay	LT FC bonds (external and domestic)	May-03	5.4	56.8	39.6		34	Trading prices
Jul-03	Nicaragua	CENI bonds FC-denom. payable in LC	Jul-03	0.3	6.1	8.2		n/a	n/a
	Nicaragua	CENI bonds FC-denom. payable in LC	Jul-08	0.3	12.5	5.4		51	NPV of cash flows
Jul-03	Dominica	LC bonds (domestic and external)	Jun-04	0.1	44.5	42.4	30	53	NPV of cash flows
H2–04	Cameroon	Domestic debt	H1–05	1	10.5	6.5		n/a	n/a
Dec-04	Grenada	Global bond and domestic debt	Nov-05	0.3	65.1	48.9		35	Trading prices
Apr-05	Dominican Republic	International bonds	May-05	1.1	16.7	5.1		5	Trading prices
Dec-06	Belize	Private external debt	Feb-07	0.5	51.6	45.8		24	Trading prices
Jul-08	Seychelles	External debt	Jan-10	0.3	29.6	36.8	50	70	Trading prices
Dec-08	Ecuador	Global bonds	May-09	3.2	25.3	5.9	65	72	Trading prices
Feb-10	Jamaica	Domestic debt	Feb-10	7.9	56.5	63.7		10	Trading prices
Jan-11	Cote d'Ivoire	Treasury bills (short-term)	Dec-11	1.3	8.5	5.4		5	NPV of cash flows
	Cote d'Ivoire	Eurobond coupon	In progress	0.1	0.6	0.4		25	Trading prices

Initial default date	Country	Distressed exchange details	Distressed exchange date	Debt in exchange			Loss (%)		
				US$ bn	% of total debt	% GDP	Nominal haircut*	Loss as measured by trading prices or NPV of cash flows	Loss as measured by:
Nov-11	St Kitts and Nevis	Domestic bonds and external debt	Mar-12	0.1	12.8	19.7	50	62	NPV of cash flows
	St Kitts and Nevis	Domestic loans (debt-land swap)	Apr-12	0.3	30.3	46.6		n/a	n/a
Mar-12	Greece	Greek and foreign law bonds	Mar-12	273.4	55.2	94.2	54	76	Trading prices
Sep-12	Belize	2029 superbond	In progress	0.5	48.0	37.3	In progress	In progress	Trading prices
Exchange Average				16	24	21			
Country Average				22	33	30			

*Largest nominal haircut shown if new instruments had different haircuts.

Note: CENI = *Certificados Negociables de Inversion* ('investment certificates'); FC = foreign currency; GKO = *Gosudarstvennoye Kratkosrochnoye Obyazatyelstvo* ('government short-term commitment'); IAN = interest arrears note; LC = local currency; MIN FIN III = Ministry of Finance International bonds; OFZ = *Obligatsyi Federal'novo Zaima* ('federal loan obligation'); PRIN = principle note

Sources: Moody's; IMF; Federico Sturzenegger and Jeromin Zettelmeyer, *Haircuts: Estimating Investor Losses in Sovereign Debt Restructurings, 1998–2005*, IMF Working Paper No. WP05/137 (July 2005)

is therefore almost exclusively explained by the strength of self-enforcement by sovereigns in averting default and the systemic externalities that come with it, as well as by the fact that revenue-raising capabilities had risen for decades until relatively recently. Even though sovereign defaults are rare, we should not neglect the element of choice that is involved: Sovereigns mostly choose whether or not to default, and political economy rather than 'naked' economics can explain not only the incidence of default, but also often the timing and nature of it.

19.81 These considerations lead to deep scepticism that the absence, until very recently, of defaults in advanced economies will continue in future years. Of course, we already witnessed two formal debt restructurings by Greece in 2012—involving both PSI and official sector involvement (OSI)— and a number of additional OSIs (through maturity lengthening and coupon reductions of officially held debt) in Ireland and Portugal. It is almost certain that more sovereign defaults, involving both PSI and OSI, will follow. Not only are levels of public debt high and growth prospects relatively modest in many advanced economies, but also, more importantly, demands for public spending have managed to continue to grow, even when the ability of governments to raise revenues efficiently started to decline, as social capital eroded. The political economy in many highly indebted advanced economies also argues for a much higher future risk of debt restructuring, as disaffected voters, both in the periphery (austerity resistance) and in the core (bailout resistance), resist making sacrifices for the benefit of making sovereign creditors (domestic and foreign) whole. A Santa Claus may sometimes appear, but it is doubtful that his gift sack will be big enough. It is therefore likely that we will see at least a few more sovereign debt restructurings in the euro area in the next few years.

19.82 When these occur, they will probably primarily take the form of a lengthening of maturities, with haircuts at most in coupon payments or interest rates and with possible deferral of interest payments, but without face-value haircuts. Such restructuring does, of course, involve an NPV loss or haircut, but for reasons that are often hard to fathom (and which mainly seem to reflect poor auditing, accounting, accountability, regulatory, and tax standards, rules, and practices), many investors prefer between two equal NPV haircuts the one with the lowest face-value haircut. The logic of these 'soft' defaults will likely be pushed quite far, with some maturities promising to pay nothing forever—an instrument with full face value and zero NPV.

20

SOVEREIGN DEBT MARKETS

Gene Frieda

The progress of the enormous debts which at present oppress, and will in the long-run probably ruin, all the great nations of Europe has been pretty uniform.

(Adam Smith, *The Wealth of Nations*)

1. Introduction

The fund managers who best understood market developments between August 2007 and the collapse of Lehman Brothers just over a year later framed the growing earthquake as a classic bank run. In response, they bought three assets: gold; the dollar; and US treasuries. Buying the currency and the sovereign debt of the country at the heart of the subprime storm was hardly intuitive, but these simple choices underscored the dynamic evolution of sovereign debt crises—past, present, and future. **20.01**

By the time the global financial crisis reached full bloom in September 2008, the market had largely forgotten about sovereign credit risk. Excluding Japan, advanced economy debt and fiscal deficits were the smallest in a generation. Sovereign debt levels in the emerging markets had been in steady decline since the early 2000s to generationally low levels of 33 per cent of gross domestic product (GDP) by 2008. Sovereign external debt was viewed by many as more akin to an interest rate than a credit product and any attempt to speculate against a sovereign's external debt was quickly met by a 'wall of money', the popular term for a massive pool of global savings that was being recycled by mostly emerging market countries. As one trader put it in 2006, there were no more bearish sovereign traders active in the markets; they had either been fired or had moved into risk management. Sovereign spreads could seemingly move only one way relative to US treasury yields: tighter. The crisis that ensued was yet another reminder that financial history has tended to repeat over centuries. **20.02**

This chapter examines the remote and proximate causes of sovereign debt crises from the perspective of a market participant. It seeks to characterize the borrowers and lenders in sovereign debt markets in a modern context, replete with sophisticated derivatives markets, historically unprecedented levels of financial integration, and creaking international and European monetary systems. **20.03**

On the supply side, the pecking order among sovereign borrowers has been turned on its head within the space of two decades. For most of the past century, the main sovereign borrowers were emerging markets that ran large fiscal and current account deficits. These deficits required external financing, which was in short supply. **20.04**

20.05 Thirty years after Mexico kicked off a new wave of sovereign debt problems, emerging market governments now routinely pay back far more than they borrow annually from external debt markets. They often run current account surpluses, and can issue debt in their own local currency and with local law covenants. Instead, the sovereign debt market is now dominated by the advanced economies. The better description may be the 'decrepit economies', given that populations are ageing rapidly, potential GDP growth is rarely above 2 per cent per annum, and debt burdens from past crises are of alpine proportions.

20.06 This chapter argues that five factors—divergent economic growth prospects, first in favour of advanced economies in the 1980s and 1990s, and later in favour of the emerging markets; declining interest rates; the rise of self-insurance; the reintegration of China into the world trading system; and US monetary policy—have been responsible for today's potholed sovereign borrowing landscape.

20.07 While much has been made of the surge in the supply of government debt, the demand side has received insufficient attention. Despite huge fiscal deficits and 40–60 per cent increases in public sector debt levels as a share of GDP, sovereign bond yields are at or near record lows, and not only in advanced economies, but in the emerging markets as well. Using newly available data sets, this chapter also examines changes in the composition of the sovereign debt investor base through the prism of government solvency risk.

20.08 After breaking down the demand side of the sovereign borrowing market by domicile—foreign and domestic—and by institutional type—central banks, banks, and non-banks (sovereign wealth funds and institutional investors)—the scene is set for a more in-depth discussion of how recent crises have developed. Sovereign debt crises are not particularly unique in history; as such, the chapter looks at lessons that have and have not been learned by market participants and governments alike. It also discusses some of the unique challenges that have already begun to arise in a post-Bretton Woods[1] world that cannot distinguish as neatly as it did in the past between 'borrower' and 'lender'.

20.09 Yet to survey the landscape in the wake of the global financial crisis, one cannot help but be struck by the generally low cost of sovereign borrowing. European periphery economies are the exceptions, rather than the rule.[2]

20.10 To conclude, this chapter attempts to answer a basic question to a remarkable fact: the scale and breadth of sovereign indebtedness has reached multi-century extremes, yet the cost of borrowing for sovereigns globally is at record low levels in real and nominal terms. Is such pricing a reflection of good lessons learned from past crises and more prudent sovereign behaviour, or is it the inevitable consequence of predatory sovereign behaviour, particularly from central banks, which aims to resolve cases of de facto insolvency through financial repression?

[1] Peter Garber, 'The Collapse of the Bretton Woods Fixed Exchange Rate System', in M. Bordo and B. Eichengreen (eds) *A Retrospective on the Bretton Woods System: Lessons for International Monetary Reform* (Chicago, IL: University of Chicago Press, 1993).

[2] For the purposes of this chapter, the periphery economies of the euro area refer to Greece, Ireland, Italy, Portugal, and Spain.

2. Sovereign Borrowing: The Last Thirty Years

The real story about the shifting coalface of the sovereign borrowing market relates to economic growth rather than the absolute size of the debt. At the turn of the millennium, there was much discussion about the famine besetting government debt markets. Strong economic growth inflated the public coffers and, as is so often the case in financial booms, market participants and policymakers projected an accelerated decline in government debt well into the future. As the year 2000 approached, US President Bill Clinton famously declared that the United States would reduce the public debt to zero by 2015.[3] As a share of GDP, US government debt had been shrinking steadily from a peak of 72.4 per cent in 1993 to 61 per cent at the time of Clinton's declaration. The debt ratio troughed just over a year later and at the time of writing is expected to reach 115 per cent of GDP by the end of 2015.[4] 20.11

The false confidence of the United States was gutted less than a decade later by the onset of the global financial crisis in 2008. In the ultimate about-face, it was suddenly a number of advanced economies that had to go begging for cash, first on the capital markets, and later to the International Monetary Fund (IMF) and other supranational lenders. By 2012, Greece was declared in selective default on its debt as it underwent a 'voluntary' restructuring of its sovereign debt. Portugal and Ireland were in formal macroeconomic stabilization programmes funded by the IMF and the European Financial Stability Fund (EFSF), and Spain and Italy faced the imminent prospect of being shut out of debt capital markets. 20.12

Despite the well-known problems of advanced economies, their share of total government debt remained remarkably stable at between 83 per cent and 86 per cent. Between 2000 and 2012, advanced economy sovereign debt grew 60 per cent in dollar terms, while emerging market sovereign debt grew 90 per cent. Yet the debt-to-GDP ratio of the emerging markets declined steadily, while that of the advanced economies ballooned. The difference, of course, was growth: advanced economies grew 71 per cent over the period in dollar terms, while the size of emerging market economies more than trebled. As a result of this stellar growth, emerging market debt ratios have declined steadily over the past decade. 20.13

Declining interest rates have been the single most important driver of the growth backdrop, and in turn the oscillating fortunes of sovereign borrowers, over the past three decades. At the risk of vast simplification, the assault of Paul Volcker, then chairman of the US Federal Reserve Bank (the Fed), on high US inflation in 1979 marked the start of a sustained thirty-year decline in global inflation. However, the corresponding recession was enough to tip several heavy-borrowing emerging market sovereigns over a debt cliff, starting with Mexico's declaration of a standstill arrangement in 1982. 20.14

While the next decade was a lost one for most non-Asian emerging markets, inflation rates continued to fall steadily in the advanced economies through the 1990s. And as they fell, real interest rates declined in tandem. Real one-year US treasury yields declined from 8 per cent in mid-1984 to an average of 4 per cent during 1985–89 and to 1.6 per cent during 1990–94. 20.15

[3] *BBC News*, 'Exorcising the US National Debt', 30 June 1999, available online at <http://news.bbc.co.uk/1/hi/business/380923.stm>.

[4] IMF, *World Economic Outlook Database* (October 2012), available online at <http://www.imf.org/external/pubs/ft/weo/2012/02/weodata/index.aspx>.

20.16 The 1990s marked a new dawn for the emerging markets. But in an eerie parallel to the experience of the advanced economies starting in 2007, the decline in real interest rates, coupled with significant capital account and financial sector liberalization, sparked a credit boom in Russia, Latin America, and much of Asia. A surprise bout of policy tightening by the US Federal Reserve in 1994 kicked off a multi-year period of crises within these emerging economies, driven in large part by a reversal in capital flows. Asset bubbles burst, economic growth collapsed, and currencies devalued substantially. Several sovereigns—most notably, Indonesia, Russia, and Argentina—also defaulted on their debt.

20.17 The decline in real advanced economy government borrowing rates was not solely a function of tamed inflation. The re-emergence of solid fiscal anchors also played a crucial role in lowering debt and deficits ahead of the global financial crisis. Fiscal consolidation in the United States was followed by a similar effort in Europe ahead of the launch of monetary union in 1999. Sovereign borrowing needs declined and most countries experienced falling debt levels as a share of GDP in the early 2000s. The emerging markets followed suit, albeit in many cases only after the severe financial crises and IMF-supervised stabilization programmes. Fiscal consolidation generated positive feedback effects on sovereign creditworthiness, disinflation efforts, and thus borrowing costs, creating a virtuous cycle of declining interest rates known as the 'Great Moderation'.

20.18 The Great Moderation was anything but moderate where private debt levels were concerned. Private debt levels in the United States and Europe went up by 46 per cent of GDP in the decade to 1999, and by a further 61 per cent in the following decade. Echoing the 1997 Asian bubble, the crisis that began with US subprime real estate in 2007 would have similar consequences: collapsing economic growth not only created large fiscal deficits, but also led to massive contingent liabilities for governments. In the span of ten years, the advanced and emerging market economies had effectively swapped places.

3. Macro Drivers of Demand for Sovereign Debt

20.19 The Great Moderation reshaped the demand side of the sovereign debt market in ways that enabled a massive and generalized increase in sovereign indebtedness. A series of factors intersected in the late 1990s and early 2000s, leading to fast growth in sovereign bond demand.

20.20 In the advanced economies, declining real interest rates and inflation increased demand for credit and duration risk. Effectively, lower interest rates enabled sovereigns to run sustainably higher levels of debt. Despite the large increase, the United States, which hosted the most liquid sovereign debt market in the world, was emblematic in managing to extend the average weighted maturity of its debt from forty-three months in 1982 to sixty-seven months in 1991.[5] Even Italy, which was experiencing a meteoric rise in debt levels from 54 per cent of GDP in 1980 to 105 per cent in 1992, managed to triple the average life of its debt to three years.

---

[5] US Department of the Treasury Office of Debt Management, *Fiscal Year 2012 Q1 Report*, available online at <http://www.treasury.gov/resource-center/data-chart-center/quarterly-refunding/Documents/TBAC%20Discussion%20Charts%20Feb%202012.pdf>.

Private sector demand for credit also accelerated as interest rates fell. US private (household and corporate) debt rose, on average, from 105 per cent of GDP in 1980 to 129 per cent of GDP by 1989. Reflecting a desire for diversification, as well as greater appetite for credit risk, advanced economy investors also began to cast their eyes abroad for other sovereign debt opportunities, initially focusing on other highly rated advanced economy sovereigns. **20.21**

While advanced economies saw their sovereign bond markets develop quickly through the 1980s, the emerging market economies were stuck in the dumps. The Soviet Union was effectively bankrupt and near collapse. And much of Latin America was stuck in a perpetual debt purgatory, with sovereigns and their main private creditors, US and European commercial banks, in a decade-long stand-off. **20.22**

All of this changed with Mexico's restructuring of the debts it owed to commercial banks into Brady bonds. The launch of the first Brady programme for Mexico in March 1989 marked the dawn of a new era in emerging market sovereign borrowing.[6] Presaging a trend that would reach extremes with the trancheing of subprime mortgage debt, the introduction of Brady bonds allowed commercial banks to exchange their claims for tradeable securities. Whereas before banks extending loans to emerging market sovereigns had been stuck with the risk on their balance sheets, come what may, they could now transfer as much of the exposure as they desired at any given point in time, subject to market liquidity considerations. Another seventeen emerging market economies would subsequently agree to restructure their commercial bank debts into tradable bonds. **20.23**

4. Emerging Market Self-Insurance and the Rise of China

Between 1994 and 2002, two major developments, one cyclical and the other structural, set the stage for the role reversal between advanced and emerging economies. At the end of 1994, Mexico succumbed to a sustained bout of massive capital flight and allowed its currency to devalue. Only recourse to a special loan package from the United States and the IMF staved off sovereign default. Contagion to Brazil and Argentina followed, but both managed to fend off pressure on their currency pegs, at least temporarily. **20.24**

The Mexican crisis turned out to be a warm-up exercise for what followed in Asia less than three years later. The successful speculative attack on the Thai baht peg to the US dollar in July 1997 blossomed into a wider currency crisis across Asia. An early beneficiary of the first round of outflows from developed to emerging economies, Asia experienced an investment-led boom that fuelled equity and real estate bubbles reminiscent of the Japanese bubble a few years earlier. But whereas Japan's bubble had been domestically financed in yen, the Asian emerging market bubble was financed with foreign currency. And once the bubble burst, the economic consequences were far more severe as Asian exchange rate pegs collapsed. **20.25**

The ensuing economic downturns were on par with depressions and fundamentally changed Asian behaviour toward financial stability. As with most currency crises, exchange rates overshot on the downside and then recovered, aided by a marked improvement in current **20.26**

[6] John Clark, 'Debt Reduction and Market Re-Entry under the Brady Plan' (1993–94) 18(4) FRBNY Quarterly Rev 38.

account positions. But this time around, central banks intervened more actively to prevent rapid exchange rate appreciation. Foreign reserves were rapidly rebuilt to pre-crisis levels and then began to grow precipitously. Self-insurance against external shocks became the mantra, even after foreign reserve cushions surpassed any realistic level of what could be deemed prudentially sufficient.

20.27 As Asian cyclical developments were leading to a behavioural shift in favour of large foreign reserve balances, China was beginning to emerge from a deep slumber. The trade opening of China to the outside world had begun with Deng Xiaoping's reforms of the late 1980s, but China's economy was starting to reach a globally significant scale as the Asian crisis hit. The lack of capital account liberalization spared China the worst effects of the currency crisis. Between 1985 and the onset of the Asian crisis in 1997, China's economy more than tripled in size to US$950 billion.

20.28 By the time of its entry into the World Trade Organization (WTO) in 2002, the Chinese economy was worth US$1.3 trillion and, in dollar terms, was doubling in size every five-and-a-half years. Nothing much changed in terms of the GDP growth, but China's WTO membership led to explosive growth in the country's current account surplus, from a five-year average of US$25 billion per annum in 2002 to a peak of US$412 billion by 2008. Together with strong foreign direct investment (FDI), large speculative 'hot money' inflows betting on Chinese property price appreciation, and a fixed exchange rate, foreign reserves ballooned as well, from US$185 billion at the end of 2001 to more than US$1 trillion by early 2007. Chinese foreign reserves surpassed the US$2 trillion mark in 2009 and the US$3 trillion mark in 2011.

5. Surfing the China Wave

20.29 Commodity exporters, most of which were emerging markets that had borrowed heavily in the sovereign external debt market in the past, experienced a sharp reversal of fortune born of China's inexorable rise. Commodity prices had collapsed alongside the burst of the Asian investment bubble in the late 1990s. The price of a barrel of Brent crude oil fell over 60 per cent to a low of US$9.55 between early 1997 and the end of 1998. Copper prices fell by nearly 50 per cent over the same period. Oil prices surpassed levels seen at the height of the Asian bubble within a year of their post-crisis trough. And by late 2004 the cost of a barrel of oil was double that of the pre-crisis peak, having reached US$52 a barrel, and would double again by early 2008. Copper prices surpassed their previous peak in 2004 and would triple again over the following four years.

20.30 Like China, the commodity exporters began to accumulate foreign reserves quickly. Since many of the commodity exporters, particularly in the Middle East, ran fixed exchange rate pegs to the dollar, the resulting accumulation of foreign reserves was automatic. For others, ranging from Russia to Brazil, the choice to accumulate reserves was more discretionary, but nonetheless natural given past histories of fixed or crawling pegs to hard currencies. As shown later, the consequences of China's rise fundamentally changed the nature of central banks as managers of foreign exchange reserves.

20.31 China's entry into the global trading system in 2002 brought a seemingly inexhaustible supply of cheap labour into the world's economy. The sharp decline in interest rates globally had already served to crowd private sector activity. In the United States, as private sector demand for cheap credit surged, asset prices started to rise precipitously in two distinct phases. Between 1995 and 2001, the bubble was concentrated in equity markets. From 2003, the bubble shifted to real estate. But in contrast to previous asset price bubbles, the rise in prices did not spill over to goods markets, thanks in large part to China's ever-growing supply of cheap manufactured goods. Consumer price inflation, accordingly, remained low.

US monetary policy adapted during the real estate bubble. Where the Federal funds target rate had largely tracked a rules-based specification of monetary policy through the 1990s, low consumer price inflation now allowed the Fed to maintain loose monetary policy well into the first decade of the 2000s, even as house prices went through the roof. **20.32**

There were warning signs in a large and growing US current account deficit, but China and the increasingly cash-rich commodity exporters were only too happy to buy dollars in almost unlimited quantities in order to prevent their exchange rates from appreciating too rapidly, or at all in the case of the many commodity exporters that formally pegged their currencies to the dollar. From 2002 on, the trade-weighted dollar began a steady multi-year depreciation to record low levels. **20.33**

At the macro level, the traditional reflexivity between advanced economy and emerging market sovereign borrowing trends was again exerting itself: as the borrowing needs and costs for advanced economy sovereigns declined through the late 1990s and into the 2000s, capital went in search of yield elsewhere. **20.34**

6. The Apparent End of 'Original Sin'

Whereas previous cycles dating back to the nineteenth century had seen reflexive shifts in favour of and against emerging market sovereign borrowers, the combination of macroeconomic stability, strong growth, and an extreme search for yield generated the greatest shift of all in sovereign borrowing trends. For the first time in the post-Bretton-Woods era, many emerging markets regained access to regular issuance of long-term sovereign debt in their own currencies. **20.35**

'Original sin', the inability of sovereigns to borrow internationally in their own currency, foreshadowed much of the history of debt crises in many emerging (and some now developed) economies.[7] But with the steady rise in foreign exchange reserves and strong economic growth, the supply of sovereign external debt began to dwindle. **20.36**

As discussed at paragraph 20.57, one temporary solution to the disappearing supply of sovereign external debt was the launch of sovereign credit default swaps (CDSs)—a form of insurance contract that gave the seller exposure to the default risk of an underlying sovereign obligation denominated in foreign currency and contracted under international law. **20.37**

Investor demand for longer-dated local currency debt nonetheless grew as yields on all forms of sovereign external debt diminished. With the onset of the global financial crisis, advanced economy central banks embarked on a race to the bottom in policy rates. As yields in the United States, United Kingdom, Japan, and euro area converged toward zero and sovereign spreads over **20.38**

[7] Barry Eichengreen and Ricardo Hausmann, *Exchange Rates and Financial Fragility*, National Bureau of Economic Research (NBER) Working Paper No. 7418 (November 1999), available online at <http://www.nber.org/papers/w7418>.

US treasuries continued to narrow, cash poured into local currency emerging market sovereign debt as a yield alternative, while at the same time many advanced economies such as Canada, Sweden, Australia, and New Zealand experienced similar inflows to their local debt markets as investors sought 'safe haven' alternatives to the debased US dollar and the fragile euro.

20.39 The rise in local currency funding by emerging market governments marked a dramatic shift in the balance of power back to sovereign debtors and away from creditors. Whereas, in advanced economies, domestic-currency-denominated debt formed 93 per cent of total central government debt in the period 1991–2010, the share of domestic debt in emerging markets was a mere 49 per cent.[8] Nonetheless, the change over twenty years was remarkable, with the share of domestic to total government debt rising from 38 per cent in the mid-1990s to the low 60s by 2010. The average maturity of emerging market domestic debt has increased to more than ten years in 2011 from only five years in 1995.

20.40 The rise in the share of domestic debt marked more of a return to normalcy than a new precedent. The share of domestic debt had declined precipitously after 1960 from a peak of 73 per cent owing to high and often hyperinflationary periods during the 1970s and 1980s. The trend was particularly pronounced in Latin America, where the share of domestic debt fell as low as 30 per cent at the end of the 1980s. During this period, dependence on external debt created a much higher propensity for debilitating sudden stops in capital flows, which in turn caused a wave of currency crises and sovereign defaults.

20.41 The relevance of the shift toward local currency funding within the emerging markets to incidents of sovereign debt crises is evident from summary statistics on incidence of default. Rogoff and Reinhart show how the incidence of default on local debt has been as high as the incidence of default on external debt over the period 1800–2010.[9] External debt probabilities are higher in the pre-fiat money period ending 1939, at 20 per cent versus 12 per cent for domestic debt. But in the period since, domestic debt default risk has been higher, as governments have expropriated wealth through high inflation.

20.42 Ultimately, emerging market governments have capitalized on post-crisis fear of excessive advanced economy indebtedness by shifting their funding bases toward domestic debt. In doing so, they have regained their ability to inflate away debt in the event of future financial stress and also to change local law covenants in government bond contracts as a means to restructure their liabilities. Quietly, the future nature of sovereign debt crises in the emerging markets has undergone a dramatic shift accordingly.

7. Sovereign Debt Demand Dynamics

20.43 Changes on the demand side have also had a profound effect relative to previous financial cycles, as alluded to earlier. These changes can be characterized as part of an interdependent process of global financial integration and domestic financial market deepening. To put in context the scale of the changes in demand for sovereign debt, advanced economy sovereign bond yields are at or near record lows despite a 49 per cent rise in debt as a share of GDP over the space of five years. For most emerging markets governments, borrowing rates are also at record low levels.

---

[8] Carmen Reinhart and Ken Rogoff, *The Forgotten History of Domestic Debt*, NBER Working Paper No. 13946 (April 2008), available online at <http://www.nber.org/papers/w13946.pdf>.

[9] Reinhart and Rogoff (n. 8).

Shifts in the composition of the sovereign investor base led to markedly lower borrowing costs, both for advanced and emerging market governments. Compositional changes were generally positive in their first iteration—arguably a natural process of market maturation and financial stability. But as will be shown, the shifting investor base eventually created systemic risks of a breadth and scale not seen since the Great Depression. **20.44**

The demand side of the sovereign borrowing market can be broken down by domicile—foreign and domestic—and by institutional type—central banks, banks, and non-banks (sovereign wealth funds and institutional investors). Shifting demand dynamics among these six players reflect a variety of macro and micro developments in the pre- and post-crisis periods. **20.45**

First, just as emerging market governments were becoming less dependent on external sovereign borrowing in the early 2000s, emerging market central banks were becoming important sovereign lenders. Dollars accumulated from foreign exchange intervention were initially used to pay down external debt, but as the supply of external debt shrank, central banks found that they had undesirably large concentrations of their foreign reserves in dollars and euros. With little yield and heavy concentration risk, they felt comfortable shifting funds into less liquid, higher yielding 'safe' assets—normally AAA-rated sovereign debt of other advanced economies. **20.46**

But the pools of foreign currency assets were becoming so large as to exceed any reasonable level of hard currency holdings for precautionary purposes. Accordingly, many set up separate agencies called 'sovereign wealth funds'[10] in order to manage the assets for the purpose of long-term taxpayer gain. These funds for future generations were willing to take greater risk in search of larger returns. Their mandates extended, in many cases, beyond traditional sovereign debt, but a core component of their investment mandate was higher yielding non-dollar sovereign debt. **20.47**

Aggregate foreign ownership of advanced economy sovereign debt rose from US$5 trillion to nearly US$12 trillion between 2004 and 2012. Some 40 per cent of the increase was driven by foreign (mostly emerging market) central banks and sovereign wealth funds. **20.48**

Second, the investor base for sovereign debt was changing with the advent of the institutional investors, including insurance companies, pension funds, and investment funds. Structural reforms to pension systems, in favour of fully funded, defined-contribution pension schemes, put fresh onus on individuals to build their own retirement savings. By 2011, the weighted average size of pension fund assets in Organisation for Economic Co-operation and Development (OECD) economies had reached 72 per cent of GDP, or US$21 trillion, up from 67 per cent in 2001. **20.49**

Holdings of sovereign debt as a share of total assets vary widely from country to country, but the key trend was a substantial increase in foreign ownership of sovereign debt. Foreign non-bank purchases accounted for a quarter of the US$6.5 trillion rise in aggregate foreign ownership of advanced economy sovereign debt between 2004 and 2012.[11] **20.50**

[10] Andrew Rozanov, 'Who Holds the Wealth of Nations?' (2005) 15(4) Central Banking 52.

[11] Serkan Arslanalp and Takahiro Tsuda, *Tracking Global Demand for Advanced Economy Sovereign Debt*, IMF Working Paper No. 12/284 (December 2012), available online at <http://www.imf.org/external/pubs/cat/longres.aspx?sk=40135>.

20.51 Despite generally superior demographic trends, the emerging markets have also shifted toward fully funded pension schemes. Emerging market pension fund assets have grown 70 per cent over the decade to 2011, reaching US$1.5 trillion. Assets are expected to double again within five years.[12] While tiny compared to advanced economy pension savings, the growth of these assets within the emerging markets has arguably been the most important driver of demand for longer maturity local-currency-denominated sovereign debt.

20.52 Third, the role of banks shifted from one of primary creditor to a secondary position as originator and intermediator. With deregulation and the development of risk-trancheing derivative instruments, banks could offload credit exposure to others rather than maintain the risk entirely on their own balance sheets. The diversification of the investor base for sovereign debt away from banks presaged a change in the nature and resolution of later sovereign debt crises.

20.53 Whereas, prior to the 1990s, lending to emerging market sovereigns had been primarily the domain of commercial banks, there now arose a new class of bespoke investing in emerging markets dominated by the non-banks. Emerging market governments would issue debt denominated in hard currency, mostly in dollars, to a variety of investors ranging from hedge funds to insurance companies. Banks still warehoused some of the sovereign exposure, not least as a result of the importance of such debt for collateral in derivatives and funding transactions. But their main role became origination and intermediation.

20.54 In the four years preceding the global financial crisis, foreign banks accumulated no new net exposure to advanced economy sovereign debt. But in the four years after mid-2008, they accumulated some US$1.5 trillion in highly rated sovereign debt. Even including the broad bias toward 'safe' government debt in the wake of the crisis, this vast sum amounted to a mere 8 per cent of total foreign purchases of advanced economy sovereign debt between 2004 and 2012.

20.55 Similarly in the emerging markets, the traditional role of domestic banks as the primary holders of domestic government debt gradually declined as markets were deregulated and private pension systems developed. Whereas government debt in advanced economies with prudent fiscal policies formed around 10 per cent of total assets, the share in emerging markets was typically 20–40 per cent at the start of the 2000s.[13] Reduced exposure of banks to sovereign debt naturally created greater insulation from any bout of sovereign stress. Put another way, the expansion of the investor base precluded the need for governments to rely on banks as instruments of financial repression, regardless of their fiscal stance.

20.56 Domestic banks in advanced economies were generally big players in the sovereign debt market in the run-up to the crisis, and their demand for high-quality sovereign debt jumped predictably after the onset of the shock. The rise was most visible in the periphery economies of the euro area, not least because of the extent to which ratings downgrades destroyed the regulatory risk weight advantage for holding one's own sovereign debt. By the end of 2011, more than 90 per cent of the domestic banking sector's total sovereign debt holdings of

[12] Vital Meschoulam, Carolina Ramirez, and Robert Habib, *EM Rates—(R)evolution, Part II: The Ascent of Local Pension Funds*, Morgan Stanley Research Paper (February 2013).

[13] Michael Kumhof and EvanTanner, *Government Debt: A Key Role in Financial Intermediation*, IMF Working Paper No. 05/57 (March 2005), available online at <http://cdi.mecon.gov.ar/biblio/docelec/fmi/wp/wp0557.pdf>.

Portugal, Spain, Italy, and Greece was that of the same sovereign parent. While the home bias toward domestic debt was a global phenomenon after 2007, the concentration of domestic sovereign debt within domestic banks in the euro area periphery soon set up a vicious negative feedback loop between banks and sovereigns.

8. Financial Weapons of Mass Destruction

A related financial product development stemmed from, and subsequently fed back to, the rising demand for sovereign debt. Financial derivatives started modern life in the 1970s, but, starting in the mid-1990s, growth in derivative markets skyrocketed. In 1997, the first CDS was developed by JP Morgan as a means of dividing and parcelling out credit risk in a more efficient fashion to different types of investor.[14] As the supply of tradeable emerging-market hard-currency sovereign debt ebbed in the mid-2000s, demand for higher yielding paper spawned the advent of single-named sovereign CDSs and later baskets of sovereign CDSs in the form of collateralized debt obligations (CDOs). **20.57**

In design, CDSs are an insurance contract whereby the seller offers insurance against a credit event to the buyer. In return, the buyer pays the 'writer' of protection an insurance premium, normally determined by the risk premium on sovereign bonded debt (plus a small premium for the credit risk of the counterparty).[15] If there is a credit event on the reference obligation—in this case, a sovereign bond—then the CDS seller is required to pay the buyer the difference between the face value of the bond (normally par) and the recovery value on the bond. The difference between a true insurance contract and a CDS is that the counterparties to the bilateral transaction need not have any economic exposure to the underlying credit. Sovereign CDS contracts form around a tenth of the US$30 trillion-plus CDS market.[16] **20.58**

Prior to the global financial crisis, investors were starved for yield and thus sought to sell protection as a means by which to gain credit exposure to various governments. The demand was so strong that, for many sovereigns at various points in time, CDS spreads were narrower than those of the underlying reference obligation (the bond). Investors would rather have owned bonds, but they simply were not available—or at least were not available in the desired size. **20.59**

The frenzy for yield exposure reached extremes with the development of sovereign CDOs and first-to-default baskets, in which investors (sellers of protection) received a slight yield premium to the sum of the constituent sovereign parts in return for selling 'correlation risk'. **20.60**

In calm times, the premium for correlation risk was small because the various sovereigns were relatively uncorrelated. But, in periods of stress, the correlation risk would rise. The investor was exposed to the credit risk on the first sovereign in the constituent basket to default.[17] If **20.61**

---

[14] Gillian Tett, *Fool's Gold* (London: Abacus, 2009).

[15] For more details on the operational aspects of CDSs and the sovereign CDS market in particular, *see* Patrick Augustin, *Sovereign Credit Default Swap Premia* (April 2012), available online at <http://papers.ssrn.com/sol3/papers.cfm?abstract_id=2055346>.

[16] *BIS Quarterly Review*, September 2012, available online at <http://www.bis.org/publ/qtrpdf/r_qt1209.htm>.

[17] First-to-default baskets were popular with German Landesbanks, which turned out to be some of the earliest buyers of these products: *see* M. El Morsalani, *Correlation Trading: Facts and Challenges*, Financial Workshop Ulm (September 2005), available online at <http://www.mathematik.uni-ulm.de/finmath/confpage/papers/elmorsalani.pdf>.

nine of the ten sovereigns in a CDO had very low probability of default, but one of the ten happened to be Argentina, then, in a time of stress, the spread on the basket would converge from being a weighted average yield of the ten sovereign credits to the single sky-high yield of the distressed credit. At least one could theoretically hedge this risk by going short on the bonds (or buying single-named CDSs) of the individual sovereign. However, if the basket contained two distressed sovereigns, then hedging was almost impossible.

20.62 CDS contracts were particularly attractive to banks and investors alike because they were contracts for differences. Instead of paying US$100 for a bond with a cash of US$100, the buyer was required to deposit only a small margin at the start of the trade, and then the buyer and seller would exchange a variation margin on an ongoing basis, depending on the daily change in the price of the contract.

20.63 While time series data on sovereign CDS contracts is even shorter than the short history of the contracts, the Bank for International Settlements (BIS) reported US$1.26 trillion in single-named sovereign CDSs outstanding as of December 2005. By mid-2012, the amount outstanding had almost tripled to US$2.85 trillion. Sovereign CDSs pushed the market to extremes, reducing perceived credit risk excessively in the run-up to the crisis and exacerbating it in the crisis wake.

20.64 Kazakhstan epitomized the extremes, in both directions, to which the sovereign CDS market could evolve. In the run-up to the global financial crisis, the country had no sovereign bonded debt, but because of a rapidly growing economy and the promise of unlimited oil wealth, investors asked investment banks to write protection on the Kazakh sovereign. Credit default swaps always contain references to legal debt obligations of the sovereign. No matter that Kazakhstan had no such obligations. Investors were willing to sell one-year protection for as little as 18 basis points (bps) and five-year protection for a mere 33bps in mid-2007. Banks were generally comfortable being on the other side of the trade as a hedge against large and growing credit exposures to Kazakh banks. The hedges were, of course, proxies rather than precise, and would fail to protect the investment banks if Kazakh financial institutions were to go bust and the Kazakh sovereign, which had no debt in the first place, would emerge unscathed.

20.65 In the second half of 2007, it became clear that Kazakh banks had over-leveraged themselves. The banks could no longer finance themselves in international markets and the outstanding bonded debt became extremely illiquid. Both investment banks and end-investors rushed to hedge themselves against the risk of a financial sector collapse by purchasing sovereign protection. All were desperate to avoid showing any exposure to Kazakhstan on their balance sheets. If pushed, the logic that they expressed in buying one year CDS protection at spreads as high as 2,075bps was that if the Kazakh banks were to collapse, the sovereign would issue a bond and promptly default on it, thereby validating the existence of the CDS contracts.

20.66 It should be clear from the foregoing that the number of creditors to any sovereign has tended to increase with the growth in the CDS market, exacerbating the potential for coordination failures in the wake of a credit event and indeed the risk of sovereign default. Effectively, buyers of Kazakh sovereign CDSs had no interest in insuring themselves against default, per se, because there were no underlying obligations on which to default. A similar dynamic developed in the CDS market of Kazakh banks, in which buyers bought protection in sizes well beyond any economic interest they had.[18] As a result, the European Union has since banned the naked buying of CDS protection on sovereigns.

But whereas the intent of the CDS market is supposedly to allow better apportionment of credit risk, the ability to hedge lending exposure through the CDS market can also increase the probability of sovereign default. Similar to the originate-to-distribute model that fed the growth of the US subprime lending bubble, recourse to CDS hedging can lead to excessive and imprudent lending on the basis that any fees and short-term gains from such lending can be protected from future loss. **20.67**

9. Europe: A Microcosm of Past, Present, and Future Crises

The euro area, a group of seventeen European countries that share a single currency, deserves special mention, given its unique features. The euro area arguably lies at the crossroads of crises past and crises of the future. Seventeen European countries share a common currency, but retain fiscal sovereignty. In the run-up to the launch of the single currency in 1999, a minority of commentators warned that a group of seventeen countries with distinct structural features, including differences in labour and product market flexibility, markedly different income levels, and competing national and supranational regulatory structures, would be prone to extreme imbalances.[19] **20.68**

Prior to 1999, a similar tendency of some European countries to run excessively loose fiscal policies and then devalue their way out of trouble became one of the major motivations for seeking a common union. Several countries, including Germany, sought some form of political and fiscal union as well, but having failed to secure agreement, member countries settled for second-best. The Stability and Growth Pact (SGP) set out fiscal and debt criteria to which countries pledged adherence. Sanctions were threatened for those countries that violated the SGP. **20.69**

The monitoring and sanctions regimes within the SGP failed miserably—particularly when the pact proved unenforceable against the euro area's largest members, Germany and France. But the even greater problem was that the SGP failed to take into account broader macroeconomic considerations. A country experiencing a real estate bubble that temporarily inflated the tax base and another country in the midst of a depression would have been treated equally under the SGP. **20.70**

Two primary deficiencies became clear only belatedly after the onset of the global financial crisis. First, the early warnings about structural deficiencies were proven correct, particularly in recognizing that the SGP took no account of a build-up in broader macroeconomic imbalances. Spain and Ireland had been model pupils in terms of headline budget deficits and debt reduction, but their banking sectors ballooned with inflated real estate assets, on which the eventual losses were partially assumed by the state. Ireland and Spain entered monetary union with debts equal to 48 per cent and 62 per cent of GDP respectively. Their debt ratios fell to 25 per cent and 36 per cent of GDP by 2007. Five years on, Ireland's debt ratio stood at 117 per cent of GDP, while Spain was not far behind at 91 per cent. In both cases, it will take years to work off a debt overhang that was supposed to be impossible under the tenets of the SGP. **20.71**

[18] Gillian Tett, 'Insight: Kazakh Bank Falls Foul of CDS', *Financial Times*, 30 April 2009.
[19] Bernard Connolly, *The Rotten Heart of Europe* (London: Faber and Faber Ltd, 1995).

20.72 Second, as the scale of the sovereign's contingent liabilities to the banking sector became clear, there was a loss of confidence in sovereign creditworthiness. The experience of Greece, Portugal, Ireland, Spain, and Italy was markedly different from that of the United States and the United Kingdom for one simple reason: the US and UK had their own central banks that could print currency. As the housing bubble burst in the US and the collapse of Lehman Brothers created a panic around global investment banks, the US injected massive amounts of liquidity into the financial system, taking US treasuries and equivalent US government agency securities as collateral. The UK acted in tandem and, as a result, large capital outflows resulted in a weaker currency than in tighter liquidity conditions.

20.73 The euro area periphery economies also benefited from liquidity injections by the European Central Bank (ECB), but because the central bank could not play the role of fiscal backstop to its sovereign members, doubts quickly emerged as to whether periphery governments would be able to afford to backstop the country's banks. A vicious cycle developed whereby banks, many of which were dependent on wholesale markets to fund large portions of their assets, found themselves unable to access the private market. They sought recourse to ECB lending, but the reputational risk of being seen as dependent on such borrowing—and indeed margin calls from wholesale creditors—forced banks to start liquidating assets rapidly. As the value of the assets fell sharply and funding access remained constrained, the value of the bank's equity declined sharply. Many governments stepped in to provide support in the form of hard capital or government guarantees, but the size of the support kick-started a cycle of credit downgrades, which in turn led to higher margin requirements on banks' wholesale borrowings.

20.74 If the story of the European periphery sounds familiar, that is because it echoes the wave of sudden stops in capital flows to emerging markets during the 1980s and 1990s. Investors ignored the fact that common currency did not mean independent monetary authority. If there was a positive difference, the ECB had no legal capacity to backstop governments, but was still superior to emerging market central banks in its willingness to provide 'foreign' euros to replace flight capital from the country.

20.75 Even then, the ECB encountered constraints on its ability to provide support. A periphery economy that lost private financing could replace the lost financing only if its banks had ECB-eligible collateral.[20] At the start of the crisis, the pool of eligible collateral was large, but as capital flight accelerated, many banks found themselves running short of ECB-eligible collateral. As sovereign and bank credit ratings fell, haircuts on existing borrowings, including from the ECB, went up and, for some, large portions of the collateral pool were rendered ineligible for ECB lending operations once ratings fell below investment grade.

20.76 An ominous precursor to the troubles can be seen in the share of 'own' government in total government debt held by European banks. Despite rapid economic and financial integration during the first decade of monetary union, banks domiciled in Portugal, Spain, Italy, and Greece held between 70 and 99 per cent of their government debt holdings in the debt of their parent sovereign.[21]

---

[20] For a broader discussion on how ECB treatment of government debt as collateral contributed to the build-up of risk in the European periphery, *see* Peter Boone and Simon Johnson, 'Europe on the Brink', Peterson Institute for International Economics Policy Brief No. PB11–13 (July 2011), available online at <http://www.iie.com/publications/pb/pb11-13.pdf>.

[21] Arslanalp and Tsuda (n. 11).

The problems experienced within the European Monetary Union (EMU) are, in many respects, a microcosm of the broader challenges faced within the sovereign debt market in the years ahead. On the positive side, changes in bank regulation will create more demand for sovereign debt. As an example, market estimates of a liquidity coverage ratio of 57 per cent for thirty large bank holding companies will require between US$500 billion and US$1 trillion in mitigating actions, most of which will come from increased holdings of highly rated sovereign debt.[22] Demand from pension funds will continue to grow. **20.77**

However, without something closer to full fiscal integration, the highly indebted eurozone periphery economies face a long period of slow growth as public and private sectors deleverage. Also in contrast to the emerging markets, which now have reasonably low debt levels, demographic pressures have already begun to exert a significant negative impact on their budgets. Accordingly, the eurozone periphery will continue to face pressures typical of the emerging markets in the 1990s that ran pegged currency regimes. In that environment, creditors will retain significant leverage over debtors. **20.78**

Moreover, efforts to reform the euro area have led to repeated policy contradictions and broken promises. There remains an inherent conflict between debt sustainability and the political prerogative against sovereign default. Reflecting this conflict, Greek private sector involvement (PSI) is still noted by European leaders as an isolated case, yet from 1 January 2013, all newly issued euro area sovereign debt will carry collective action clauses (CACs). The collateral damage of broken political promises is enduring to investor sentiment, reinforcing the home bias toward euro area sovereign bonds. **20.79**

The ECB's outright monetary transactions (OMT) facility, whereby the ECB will buy sovereign debt in the secondary market in return for a country meeting IMF-approved conditionality, creates similar conflicts. After having protected itself on grounds of monetary financing from losses associated with the Greek debt restructuring, the ECB has pledged that its purchases will be *pari passu* with the private sector.[23] This pledge is not legally embedded in any treaty. **20.80**

Moreover, sovereign loans from the European Stability Mechanism (ESM), the supranational organization set up by the euro area to provide financial assistance to its members in times of crisis, remain formally senior to all creditors bar the IMF, unless an exception is made by the Eurogroup. Where seniority can be juggled so effortlessly, and by no less than creditors empowered to change laws (in contrast to the IMF), investor concerns are likely to rise in times of stress. **20.81**

Relative to the ESM, the private sector's subordination to the IMF is different for two key reasons: first, the rules of the game tend not to change frequently and there is less political interference in the process of administering conditionality; and second, the IMF makes no such promise that sovereign default is forbidden. It normally conducts a debt sustainability analysis (DSA), determines whether debt is sustainable, requires a restructuring if it is not, and then lends *ex post*. An IMF loan is accordingly equivalent to a reasonably credible belief that the country is solvent, but illiquid. Its track record is hardly unblemished, but, relative **20.82**

[22] US Department of the Treasury, Office of Debt Management (n. 5).
[23] ECB, 'Technical Features of Outright Monetary Transactions', Press Release, 6 September 2012, available online at <http://www.ecb.europa.eu/press/pr/date/2012/html/pr120906_1.en.html>.

to the ESM, there is less moral hazard embedded in an IMF loan that implicitly accepts that the sovereign can still go bust.

20.83 For the euro area as a whole, the common factors with emerging markets are not so remote. Like emerging markets, all European member states in the monetary union, except perhaps Germany, can be considered reliant at some significant level on external funding. While they may fund themselves primarily in their own currency, a large share of their creditors is foreign, a non-negligible share of their debt is under foreign law covenants, and both have banking systems that are intimately linked to their own sovereign as a result of their large holdings of domestic government bonds.

20.84 Perhaps most importantly, neither the periphery economies of Europe nor the emerging markets are any better insulated from positive and negative global financial shocks. As the BIS has recently highlighted,[24] financial cycles can run far longer than traditional business cycles, and indeed attempts to smooth the business cycle continue to play a key role in exacerbating and extending financial imbalances.

20.85 The final factor of note is the reflexivity of sovereign borrowers and creditors within the euro area. Periphery imbalances were largely financed by capital flows from core euro area countries, including Germany, France, the Netherlands, and Austria. When trouble hit, core creditors exerted their political power to protect their taxpayers from loss. Much of the capital that fled the euro area periphery was core country savings that returned home. Germany complained as its liabilities to the Eurosystem went up, even though the increase largely reflected the substitution of private German lenders to the periphery for public lending via the ECB. Just as there has been little focus on the demand side of the sovereign debt market, there has been similarly inadequate focus on excessive savings imbalances and how savings can distort asset prices, inclusive of sovereign credit risk, as they seek a foreign home.

10. Lessons Learned, Ignored, and Forgotten

20.86 The preceding story details a remarkable reversal of fortunes in the sovereign bond market from the borrowers' perspective over the past thirty years. the less developed economies of the 1980s have become a group of dynamic emerging economies in the 1990s and 2000s, while the advanced economies of the 1980s have become the decrepit economies of the twenty-first century. Sovereign debt dependency has shifted accordingly—and indeed ironically—from the poor to the rich countries.

20.87 Optimists will argue that countries have learned much from the crises of the past thirty years and acted aggressively to mitigate future risks on three major fronts, as follows.

(a) *Macro stabilization policies*—Prudent budget policies anchored the progress made by monetary policy in minimizing actual and expected inflation. After the frontal assault on high inflation at the start of the 1980s, central banks shifted to explicit inflation targeting as their primary objective. Advanced economy central banks started the trend and, after their own wave of crises in the 1990s, emerging market monetary authorities followed suit. The growth of pension funds in both the advanced and emerging

[24] Claudio Borio, *The Financial Cycle and Macroeconomics: What Have We Learnt?*, BIS Working Paper No. 395 (December 2012), available online at <http://www.bis.org/publ/work395.htm>.

economies has also been an example of forward-looking policies aimed at addressing worsening demographics.

(b) *Self-insurance*—Recognizing the risks associated with dependence on external borrowing, many emerging markets have built large war chests of foreign exchange reserves as insurance against future shocks. Global foreign exchange reserves were equivalent to 15 per cent of global GDP at the end of 2012, up from less than 5 per cent in 1995.[25] In a similar vein, many governments of commodity-exporting economies have saved, rather than spent, the fruits of the commodity price booms that have accompanied China's rapid ascent. In both cases, the resulting savings pools have bolstered sovereign credit ratings as the risk of booms followed by busts has diminished.

(c) *Debt management*—Building on the successes of macro stabilization efforts, debt managers responded to growing investor appetite for longer duration and local-currency-denominated debt. Broader and deeper sovereign debt markets have accordingly reduced the risk of a debt crisis, particularly in the larger emerging markets. The average maturity of emerging market government debt reached nearly twelve years in 2011, up from five years in 1995.[26] Dependency on external borrowing has declined and, outside the particular case of the euro area periphery countries, confidence in sovereign debt, as measured by price and volume, is seemingly at a record high. Broadly defined, foreign ownership of advanced and emerging market debt is at all-time high levels.

11. The Fallen Saints of Original Sin

A fourth factor, the unconventional monetary policies of advanced economy central banks, is at least as important in understanding why the threat of sovereign debt crises has not necessarily become more remote, despite positive progress just noted. **20.88**

The fine line between unconventional monetary policy and fiscal dominance was probably crossed long ago in the larger advanced economies. Fiscal dominance occurs when a government browbeats its central bank into financing an otherwise unsustainable fiscal deficit. Put differently, if the central bank were not drafted into the service of its sovereign, the government would likely go bust at some point in the not-too-distant future. **20.89**

Investors have learned to cheer the episodic jumps from one round of quantitative policy easing to the next, as central banks buy up more and more sovereign debt. They fail to recognize that their claims on the government are likely being subordinated to the central bank, as investors discovered to their chagrin in Greece. And they are short-sighted in their assumption that central banks will engineer an exit from their roles as financier of last resort to governments without recourse to an inflation spiral that will wipe out the claims of the domestic private sector and foreign creditors alike. **20.90**

Referring back to the 'original sin' of governments that cannot borrow in their own currency, it should be clear that advanced economy monetary policies will have a profound effect on the likelihood and nature of sovereign debt crises in the future. **20.91**

[25] IMF, 'Currency Composition of Official Foreign Exchange Reserves (COFER)', available online at <http://www.imf.org/external/np/sta/cofer/eng/>.

[26] Meschoulam (n. 12).

20.92 First, the positive policy regime that advanced economies prescribed for emerging markets has been undermined. Advanced economies, via the IMF, preached macroeconomic religion to the emerging markets through the crises of the 1990s and early 2000s. Most emerging market governments were forced to accept three anchors—fiscal prudence, floating exchange rates, and single-mandate monetary policy regimes oriented around low inflation—as part of their bailout packages. Those good students who managed to avoid crisis adopted the policies willingly.

20.93 But with the onset of the global financial crisis, the advanced economies have run roughshod over their own advice. Fiscal deficits remain large, with at best a promise that the deficits will self-correct as soon as economic growth returns. Monetary subordination to fiscal policy is the new orthodoxy. Short-term investment decisions around sovereign debt are often based on which central bank will buy the most amount of debt. Emerging market policy regimes, less well anchored and often with less institutional protection, are deteriorating accordingly.

20.94 Second, unlimited monetary policy stimulus has become a substitute for governmental actions to fix unsustainable budget policies. There is nothing like an acute crisis to steer a country and its people onto a more prudent path of macroeconomic policy in the future—a fact to which many emerging markets beset by recent crises can attest. There is no question that the policy response of advanced economy central banks has mitigated financial pain, warded off potential sovereign and private sector bankruptcies, and improved economic growth outcomes in the short run. Attempts to mitigate market failures, such as in the US securitization market, were particularly helpful. The longer the duration and the larger the share of domestic debt in the total sovereign debt stock, the greater will be the temptation to inflate away unsustainable debts. Similarly, the larger the share of foreign ownership of the domestic debt stock, the less will be the net loss to a given economy from inflating away the debt.[27]

20.95 Third, in taking the cost of debt service down to zero and promising to buy ever more sovereign debt, central banks have reduced the incentives of both the public and the private sectors to pay down excessive debt. The progress of advanced economy private sectors in deleveraging has been modest, despite the large size of sovereign fiscal deficits. In many economies, aggregate debt levels have continued to rise rather than fall. Why should creditors to sovereign governments care if the private sector chooses to remain indebted or instead pays down its debts? The crisis has shown that a sovereign creditor often ends up being a bank creditor as well. As private sector debts go bad, the leveraged capital of the banking system disappears. If investors lose confidence in the banks, the banks are nationalized by the government in order to avoid a systemic loss of confidence. Sovereign creditors should thus have learned from the global financial crisis that, at some level, the banks are a contingent liability of the government.

20.96 Finally, work on the financial crisis architecture has shifted away from international lenders of last resort and mechanisms to mediate and resolve sovereign debt crises, towards efforts to squeeze more juice out of monetary policy. A key area of neglect in the run-up to the global financial crisis was the speed with which growth in global capital flows outpaced the growth

[27] There is much discussion about the United States' willingness to inflate away its debts. Foreign ownership of the debt is substantial and the debt stock is almost entirely denominated in US dollars. However, because the weighted average maturity of marketable debt is only sixty-four months, any bout of inflation would need to be sharp and sudden to succeed in inflating away this debt.

in multilateral safety nets. Efforts were mobilized in 2009 to augment the lending capacity of the IMF to US$1 trillion. In the event, the effort was only partially successful, but even with US$1 trillion it is not clear that the IMF has sufficient resources to deal with a financial crisis in one or more large advanced economies—or indeed in a few mid-sized emerging markets that experience simultaneous stress.

The failure of sovereign lender of last resort structures to keep up may seem less important as debt management has shifted toward domestic, rather than foreign currency, borrowing. But that is wishful thinking on several grounds. The history of sovereign debt crises tells a story of marginal, rather than absolute, funding problems. A country might be able to fund 80 per cent of its borrowing in domestic currency, but if it cannot cover the remaining 20 per cent in foreign currency, the government can quickly go bust. But if the government loses market access, the international lender of last resort normally needs to cover several years' worth of borrowing requirements, plus any rollover of existing government debt. As an example, full three-year bailout of Spain and Italy would exhaust all of the resources of the ESM and a substantial portion of existing IMF resources. Together, these countries count for less than 5 per cent of global GDP. **20.97**

Moreover, the earlier description of factors affecting the demand and supply of sovereign debt does not distinguish between cause and effect. There is some evidence that the recent decline in net external borrowing by emerging markets and the consequent ability to embark upon countercyclical macroeconomic policies is the result of lower fiscal deficits and debt, and not a reduction in original sin.[28] Hausmann and Panizza find that, for a sample of sixty-five countries, the average currency mismatch fell from 56 per cent in 1999 to 27 per cent in 2008. Some 69 per cent of the decline can be explained by lower external debt, with just under a quarter of the fall the result of higher foreign currency reserves. The decline in original sin was responsible for the residual 7 per cent. **20.98**

The key point—and indeed warning for the future—is that most emerging markets have managed to increase their reliance on domestic-currency-denominated funding, but they remain heavily reliant on foreigners for their funding. Many governments are still a hostage to the fortunes of animal spirits in the form of fickle foreign investor demand for their bonds. It is likely that, once the interest rates of the largest advanced economies in general and the United States in particular start to normalize toward higher levels, many countries will again find themselves suffering from access to less plentiful and more expensive foreign capital. But at the same time these governments have achieved an unprecedented transfer of leverage over their foreign creditors in a remarkably short period of time. These two factors will lead to conflict between debtors and creditors in the future. **20.99**

12. The Limits of Conflict Resolution

Important developments in the dispersion of sovereign creditors will play a significant role in how future conflicts are managed, and indeed whether, for the first time in a century, **20.100**

[28] Ricardo Hausmann and Ugo Panizza, *Redemption or Abstinence? Original Sin, Currency Mismatches and Countercyclical Policies in the New Millennium*, Center for International Development at Harvard University (CID) Working Paper No. 194 (February 2010), available online at <http://www.hks.harvard.edu/var/ezp_site/storage/fckeditor/file/pdfs/centers-programs/centers/cid/publications/faculty/wp/194.pdf>.

sovereign debt disputes are played out in fields that extend beyond the legal system. The broadening out of the sovereign investor base is generally a positive phenomenon. In the past, concentrated risks in the hands of a few creditors have often led to significant financial contagion to other economies. As before, pension funds and sovereign wealth funds have already played an important role since the onset of the global financial crisis in stabilizing certain markets, banking systems, and economies. But the limitations of these long-term investments, and the potential for unintended consequences, should not be underestimated.

20.101 Sovereign wealth funds and traditional central bank foreign reserve assets are increasingly assumed to be a 'given', once they invest. But these investments cannot be both self-insurance and long-term external capital, except perhaps by luck. It is far from inconceivable that a financial shock in one country might force the government to start to liquidate its holdings of foreign reserve assets in order to support the domestic economy. Other creditors may respond to a larger seller by selling as well, at which point a self-fulfilling panic can develop.

20.102 Two examples, one real and the other hypothetical, underscore the potential conflict between domestic and foreign stability objectives. First, between June 2010 and June 2011, ten-year Spanish government bond spreads rose from 72bps over German Bunds to 250bps—levels not seen since 1996. IMF data shows that foreign central banks were the primary sellers of Spanish government debt during this period, preceding a more generalized loss of foreign confidence in Spain from 2011.[29]

20.103 The theoretical example is even more frightening. China has experienced rapid growth in the size of its financial sector in recent years. Until 2008, the size of the sector was transparent, well captured in the official data on commercial banks. But, since 2008, a shadow financial system has exploded in size. Parts of the system are regulated, albeit more loosely in banks, and other parts are so opaque as to make size estimates almost impossible. The range of shadow banking assets is estimated to be between 33 per cent and 64 per cent of GDP. When combined with the formal banking sector, the size of the financial sector is somewhere between 161 per cent and 192 per cent of GDP, equivalent in US dollars to a range of US$13.1 trillion–US$15.7 trillion.

20.104 Against this mountain of liabilities, the Chinese central bank has US$3.3 trillion in foreign reserves and sovereign wealth fund assets estimated at US$500 billion. The assets of the sovereign wealth fund are mainly in the form of share and private equity investments, making them relatively illiquid. And the vast majority of the central bank's foreign reserves are held in government debt. Imagine a scenario in which China had to sell a third of its foreign reserves in order to recapitalize its banking system. An exodus of historic proportions would likely ensue from government bond markets globally, as China's financial stress was exported to other countries, and indeed unsuspecting private investors, as they suffered subsequent stress.

20.105 Nor are geopolitical considerations inconsequential. In 2011, national central banks of the Eurosystem were exempted from the 'voluntary' restructuring of Greek government debt. The Chinese central bank was not—much to its chagrin, having played a constructive role by purchasing bonds after the initial loss of confidence in Greece. Separately, Russia, Venezuela, and Iran have sought to use the sale of US assets as a political and financial weapon.

[29] Arslanalp and Tsuda (n. 11), and author's calculations.

13. Hostages to Benchmarks and Ratings

The long-term pension, and related mutual fund, investment industry is also a hostage to fortunes over which the industry has little control, no matter how well due diligence is performed. If the growth of the pension and mutual fund industry were likened to the transformation of a ship from tanker to supertanker, the development of sovereign credit ratings and benchmark bond indices would service the role of compass and true north marker, respectively. Sovereign credit ratings were a stamp of approval that a country met certain macroeconomic and political criteria to ensure that the probability of default on its sovereign debt was above a minimum threshold. Benchmark bond indices, in turn, created baskets of sovereign bonds that could be copied by portfolio managers with mandates to invest in a certain category of bonds. **20.106**

For example, JP Morgan's emerging market bond index was created in 1992 after the issuance of the first Brady bond by Mexico.[30] The index became the standard for emerging-market-dedicated sovereign bond investors. The basket of bonds is a function of debt outstanding, subject to minimum liquidity criteria, for each sovereign that qualifies, based on a minimum credit rating. Since the mandate of many investment funds requires passive tracking of the benchmark index, exposure to sovereign debtors automatically rises with increasing debt levels and automatically falls when (and not before) the country loses the minimum credit rating required to stay within the benchmark index. **20.107**

By definition, the long-term sovereign credit ratings do not change frequently. They tend to lag changes in fundamental conditions until it is clear that those conditions are likely to be sustained. When ratings are on the rise, and particularly when they cross the key investment grade threshold that allows entry into an elite club of the benchmark indices tracked by a much larger pool of investment capital, the passive funds cannot invest until the rating change takes place. But the greater concern is when ratings are falling and passive investors are constrained from reducing their holdings until the moment at which ratings go below a certain threshold and the sovereign is disqualified from participation in the bond index. At that point, there is a cascade of selling that can become systemically destabilizing.[31] **20.108**

14. Conclusion

Perhaps the clearest conclusion from this description of sovereign debt markets is the growing complexity of collective action problems in the resolution of future crises. In the wake of the global financial crisis, central banks have underwritten a chronic growth environment to avoid acute failures. Persistently weak economic growth and high debt levels are a recipe for **20.109**

---

[30] Tina Vandersteel, *Emerging Markets Bonds Index Plus Methodology*, JP Morgan Securities Emerging Markets Research (12 July 1995).

[31] An important offshoot to the ratings problem relates to the eligibility of government debt as collateral for central bank and private market repurchase agreements. As the rating on a sovereign bond falls and the bond is deemed to be riskier, the haircut (or the cash margin against a loan that a borrower wishes to secure using government bonds as collateral) on the government bond goes up. Indeed, at some level of distress, the government bond may no longer be deemed eligible as collateral. Since central banks normally make loans only against collateral, a bank without access to central bank-eligible collateral will quickly go bust. This chapter largely ignores the extensive role played by government bonds as collateral in such transactions, but the seminal link between credit ratings, banks, and sovereigns should be clear.

conflict, between creditors and debtors, between countries and between political extremes within countries.

20.110 The delineation between sovereign borrower and sovereign lender has been muddied by the growing power of sovereign wealth funds and central bank reserve managers. The policy anchors that enabled the rapid rise of the emerging markets are just as rapidly being eroded. The nature of the shift in power away from foreign creditors and in favour of sovereign debtors creates powerful political incentives in both advanced and emerging economies to inflate away debt.

20.111 There is still no commonly agreed sovereign debt restructuring mechanism. The size of international sovereign lending has outgrown the capacity of the existing financial architecture to backstop cases of illiquidity. And where groups of countries have shown willingness to create their own architectures, as has been the case in Europe with the creation of the EFSF and its successor, the ESM, classic principal–agent problems have tended to make problems more acute, more costly, and thus more difficult to resolve.

20.112 But perhaps these worries are overblown, given the breadth of the decline in real government borrowing costs to record low levels. While there are few certainties in life or markets, the physics of the sovereign borrowing market has remained steady. Gravity always prevails. The question is not whether excessively indebted countries repudiate their debts, but how. To quote Barry Eichengreen, shifts happen.[32] When they do, the players often misjudge their changes in fortune. The history of these shifts among sovereigns is that tension tends to be managed poorly.

[32] Barry Eichengreen 'Global Shifts', Paper prepared for the Bank of Finland 200th Anniversary Symposium, Helsinki, 5–6 May 2011.

21

BORROWING AND DEBT

How Do Sovereigns Get into Trouble?

Arturo C. Porzecanski

1. Introduction

Sovereign debt issuance serves as the primary means for governments to finance their expenditures, and particularly to cover gaps between cash outlays and inflows from genuine revenues, such as those derived from taxation. Under normal circumstances, government bonded debt is highly liquid and is priced to yield the least of any comparable securities, in accordance with the perception that it is the easiest to trade and the most unlikely to experience a default. A secondary function of public debt is to provide a benchmark for all other issuers (such as municipalities, banks, and corporations), as well as for investors (whether institutional or retail), enabling them to price and trade all other, non-sovereign bonds. This reference role is predicated on the usually safe assumption that the yield curve for sovereign bonds sets a lowest-risk floor for all such securities, above which every other security will be priced (in yield or spread terms) depending on its perceived liquidity and default risk. **21.01**

How much public debt should be issued? In principle, it makes good macroeconomic sense to allow government budget outcomes, and thus debt issuance, to fluctuate in reflection of the business cycle, fulfilling a stabilizing, anti-cyclical role. During economic downturns, governments should accept revenue declines (for example owing to lower personal and corporate incomes) and certain spending increases (for example on unemployment benefits and other social safety-net programmes), and thus there is nothing wrong with them running smaller budget surpluses, or even operating deficits, because the economy needs to be supported during such dips. By the same token, during boom times, governments ought to refrain from cutting tax rates and from spending all additional revenues, thereby allowing swelling fiscal incomes to reduce budget deficits or to generate operating surpluses, because the economy does not need to be boosted and, in fact, it may have to be restrained. The case for such fiscal flexibility was first made by the disciples of John Maynard Keynes in the 1940s, and it began to be accepted and implemented in Europe and North America after the Second World War—initially, to rein in post-war inflation through restrictive fiscal policies, rather than to boost aggregate demand and create jobs through government largesse.[1] **21.02**

[1] From the late 1920s until his death in 1946, Keynes supported using public works projects to stimulate aggregate demand at appropriate points in the business cycle, but contrary to the legend that his disciples

21.03 In the ensuing decades, however, and especially since the 1970s, most governments have not engaged in the kind of symmetrical, sound fiscal behaviour that would deliver a low *average* level of public indebtedness over the long run. They have instead tended to run smaller budgetary deficits during good economic times and larger deficits during bad times. It is this 'deficit bias' that accounts for the enormous accumulation of sovereign indebtedness that has arisen in most countries around the world—in absolute terms and often also relative to rising export earnings, fiscal revenues, or gross domestic product (GDP). The problem is that the larger and heavier the burden of the public debt—all else being equal—the greater the risk that debt-servicing difficulties will be encountered.

21.04 There are other circumstances under which sovereigns can get into trouble, often on short notice, at seemingly sustainable levels of indebtedness. A first reason is the existence of contingent liabilities that suddenly come to life, burdening a sovereign with large-scale obligations that undermine its creditworthiness. The unexpected need to provide fiscal resources to compensate bank depositors affected by a systemic banking crisis, or to pay for humanitarian relief and infrastructure reconstruction-related costs (for example in the wake of armed conflict, or a seismic or weather-related calamity), can easily lead to a destabilizing jump in the public debt. A second reason is currency mismatches, such as when a government or the banking system under its protection experiences large losses in the wake of a massive currency devaluation, because too many liabilities (relative to assets) were denominated in foreign currencies and suddenly became very costly to keep servicing in full. A third reason is maturity mismatches, encountered when governments (and potentially also systemically important banks and corporations) rely on short-term funding to cover long-term needs, usually because long-maturity financing is too costly or downright unavailable. This can lead to refinancing problems when maturing obligations cannot easily be rolled over, or else to large unfunded gaps when sizeable maturities come due, or when lines of credit are withdrawn during a period when new financing is hard to obtain.

21.05 These and other deleterious circumstances to be discussed later in the chapter explain why sovereign debt crises are usually precipitated by adverse economic or political events that trigger a loss of confidence on the part of creditors just when the government is most vulnerable to a disruption in access to financing. Indeed, it is the sudden development of a large gap between the amount of funding demanded by the government and the supply of funding willingly delivered by bondholders and other creditors, that tends to spawn the kind of 'perfect storm' that ends in a sovereign debt crisis. It is a sovereign's actual or perceived inability to pay maturing obligations that typically precedes a request for debt or debt-service relief—and, in the worst of cases, which leads to an outright default.

21.06 There are exceptional circumstances, however, when unwillingness, rather than inability, to pay is the underlying cause of a sovereign default, the purpose of which is to extract unwarranted debt relief concessions from creditors. In these rare cases, governments are disinclined to shoulder the political costs of raising the revenues, or of cutting the expenditures, necessary to generate the fiscal resources to service the public debt on contracted or reasonably modified terms. This reluctance often makes the governments in question ineligible for financial assistance from the International Monetary Fund (IMF) and other

(and also his critics) created, he did not advocate that governments should actually run budget deficits: Roger E. Backhouse and Bradley W. Bateman, 'Keynesianism', in Steven N. Durlauf and Lawrence E. Blume (eds) *The New Palgrave Dictionary of Economics Online*, 2nd edn (Basingstoke: Palgrave Macmillan, 2008).

multilateral lending agencies, because they would likely insist on the adoption of unpopular economic stabilization and reform measures—to enhance the government's ability to pay its obligations in the future. A telltale sign of unwillingness to pay is the refusal to tap even existing—sometimes ample—fiscal or central bank reserves to help to meet payments falling due. Argentina since late 2001, Ecuador in 2008–09, and Belize in 2012 provide vivid examples of sovereigns exhibiting unwillingness to pay.[2]

2. Budgetary Outcomes

Ever since the early 1970s, budgetary deficits and mounting public indebtedness have **21.07** become the norm in most countries around the world. Even before the financial crisis of 2008 hit, fiscal balances in both advanced and developing economies had been in the red in each of the prior thirty years, with an average deficit of about 3 per cent of GDP per annum for both groups.[3] While there was an improvement in the overall fiscal positions of the advanced economies during the economic boom of the 1990s, it was quickly reversed in the years starting in 2001; the crisis of 2008 then ushered in a five-year period during which twenty-four out of thirty advanced economies were awash in red ink. From 2008 through 2012, the advanced economies, as a group, registered overall deficits that averaged the equivalent of more than 6½ per cent of GDP per annum.[4]

One researcher has tabulated the proportion of years during which each of the advanced **21.08** economies ran a fiscal deficit during the period 1960–2011.[5] In principle, such observations should account for about half of the years involved, but the record shows that only a handful of countries conformed to the expected pattern: Denmark, New Zealand, and Sweden, with Norway being an outlier because it ran mostly surpluses in the wake of outsized, yet unspent, oil-related revenues. For all other countries, with the exception of Finland, fiscal deficits in fact were registered in at least four years out of every five, with two countries (Italy and Portugal) managing to run deficits in every single year. And countries such as Austria, Greece, and France last achieved a budgetary surplus in the early 1970s. Thus the advanced countries, much more so than the developing ones, have demonstrated that fiscal deficits can be—and have been—the rule with few exceptions during five decades in a row.

[2] *See* Arturo C. Porzecanski, 'From Rogue Creditors to Rogue Debtors: Implications of Argentina's Default' (2005) 6(1) Chi J Int'l L 311; Lee C. Buchheit and G. Mitu Gulati, 'The Coroner's Inquest' (2009) 28 Int'l Fin L Rev 2 ('It was the first time in modern history that a sovereign debtor had demanded that its external commercial creditors write off most of their claims...without advancing a plausible argument that financial distress warranted such extraordinary debt relief'); Arturo C. Porzecanski, 'When Bad Things Happen to Good Sovereign Debt Contracts: The Case of Ecuador' (2010) 73 Law & Contemp Probs 251; Edward Al-Hussainy and Ariane Ortiz Marrufo, *Belize Debt Restructuring: 2007 vs 2012* (1 October 2012), published by Moody's Investors Service and available online at <https://www.moodys.com/credit-ratings/Belize-Government-of-credit-rating-600046797>.

[3] Manmohan S. Kumar and Teresa Ter-Minassian, 'Fiscal Discipline: Key Issues and Overview', in Manmohan S. Kumar and Teresa Ter-Minassian (eds) *Promoting Fiscal Discipline* (Washington DC: International Monetary Fund, 2007), 1.

[4] IMF, *Fiscal Monitor: Taking Stock—A Progress Report on Fiscal Adjustment* (Washington DC: International Monetary Fund, 2012), available online at <http://www.imf.org/external/pubs/ft/fm/2012/02/pdf/fm1202.pdf>, 77. The six countries that proved the exception to the rule were Hong Kong, Korea, Norway, Singapore, Sweden, and Switzerland.

[5] Charles Wyplosz, 'Fiscal Rules: Theoretical Issues and Historical Experiences', in Alberto Alesina and Francesco Giavazzi (eds) *Fiscal Policy after the Financial Crisis* (Chicago, IL: University of Chicago Press, 2013), 495–530.

21.09 In most developing economies, budgetary deficits likewise became the rule during the past several decades, the long-running exception being the major Middle East oil exporters with small populations (for example Kuwait, Oman, Qatar, and Saudi Arabia). In the early or mid-2000s, some of the new oil exporters and a few non-oil-commodity-exporting nations were finally able to balance their government budgets and to start running fiscal surpluses (for example Angola, Chile, Kazakhstan, Peru, and Russia), but even they slipped back into deficit, albeit temporarily, in 2009. During 2009–12, the thirty leading developing countries, as a group, recorded overall fiscal deficits averaging about 2¾ per cent of GDP per year.[6]

21.10 The international prevalence and persistence of budgetary deficits, and the accompanying rise in public sector indebtedness prior to the budget-busting financial crisis of 2008, have spawned political-economy writings proposing reasons why government officials in so many countries may have exhibited such a 'deficit bias'. Many different hypotheses have been advanced to explain the phenomenon, but none has prevailed over all others when tested empirically.

21.11 Deficit biases may arise because of information asymmetries, as when the electorate is uninformed about the path of public finances, allowing elected officials to engage in riskier fiscal behaviour than otherwise. Another reason may be that politicians' fear of losing elections (or re-elections) tends to prompt them to make even unwise promises of higher spending or lower taxes—because they certainly *are* more popular with voters than promises to tighten the fiscal belt. In certain situations, there may also be an incentive for an incumbent party concerned about losing to increase spending and pile on debt in order to tie the hands of the opposition party, should it end up winning power. Since public spending projects and targeted tax breaks tend to favour small groups, both lobbyists and legislators may not give due consideration to the full budgetary costs of their decisions. There may be intergenerational transfer problems, such as when neither the electorate nor the political elite cares sufficiently about the fate of future generations, prompting 'spend now, tax later' attitudes.[7] In sum, there has been no dearth of potential explanations for the observed 'deficit bias'—just as there has been no shortage of prescriptions for how to deal with it, as will be discussed later in the chapter.

3. Contingent Liabilities and Currency Mismatches

21.12 The steady accumulation of sovereign indebtedness is usually insufficient to engender a crisis, and the greater risk is that of a sudden, destabilizing jump in the public debt arising out of contingent liabilities or currency mismatches that undercut actual or perceived creditworthiness.[8] Examples of contingent liabilities that impose a heavy burden on government balance sheets, and lead to unexpectedly higher government spending, are decisions to pay the costs of resolving systemic banking crises, to provide rescue packages for municipal or state-related enterprises in dire straits, or to rebuild housing and critical infrastructure in the

[6] IMF (n. 4), 81.

[7] For a discussion of deficit-bias hypotheses, *see* Lars Calmfors and Simon Wren-Lewis, 'What Should Fiscal Councils Do?' (2011) 26(68) Econ Pol'y 649.

[8] 'Most debt explosions have little to do with recorded deficits but arise from contingent liabilities often associated with past policies or with inherent vulnerabilities in a country's debt structure': *see* Camila F. S. Campos, Dany Jaimovich, and Ugo Panizza, 'The Unexplained Part of Public Debt' (2006) 7(3) EMR 228.

aftermath of a devastating war, earthquake, or hurricane.[9] Currency mismatches that likewise have an immediate impact on the fiscal accounts arise, for instance, from having to confront the suddenly higher cost of servicing the government's foreign-currency-denominated debts, and possibly also those of systemically significant banks and corporations, in the wake of a surprisingly large currency devaluation.

The important explanatory role of such shocks to sovereign creditworthiness has been quantified in numerous studies. The standard analytical procedure followed is to decompose changes in the level of public debt relative to GDP by identifying the impact of: **21.13**

(a) the gap between government revenues and spending, excluding the cost of interest payments—the so-called 'primary fiscal balance';
(b) the gap between the average interest rate paid on debt and the average growth rate of GDP; and
(c) all other relevant factors lumped together and referred to as 'stock-flow adjustment (or reconciliation) residuals'.[10]

This last category reflects currency valuation effects operating on the stock of debt plus the impact of spending recorded separately (say, as investment), the assumption of debts of non-governmental entities, the booking of privatization or other capital gains, and the drawdown or build-up of government savings.

Currency valuation changes have tended to play a negligible role in explaining debt accumulation cycles in advanced economies, because traditionally their public and private sectors have been able to fund themselves solely or mostly by issuing securities denominated in their local currency. That is not the case in developing countries, which, until a decade ago, featured mostly shallow domestic capital markets that could not meet the long-term funding needs of governments, banks, and corporations via the placement of securities denominated in their own currency. However, the costs of banking crises, and of war- and disaster-related expenses, have loomed large in the sovereign debt history of both advanced and developing nations. **21.14**

The recent analysis of a new, historical database on sovereign debt identified sixty episodes of large debt increases in nineteen advanced economies during a century-and-a-quarter (1880–2007), most (forty-four) occurring during the absence of war conditions. After decomposing them into contributions from the primary fiscal balance, the interest-growth differential, and the stock-flow adjustment term, it became apparent that nearly half of debt surges were explained by large stock-flow adjustments, which figured prominently in fifty of the sixty instances.[11] **21.15**

[9] For advanced countries, the direct loss of capital stock attributable to specific natural disasters usually does not exceed a few percentage points of GDP, but for developing economies this direct impact can reach the equivalent to more than 10 percentage points of GDP—and for small islands it can be worth 100 per cent or more of their GDP, such that uninsured reconstruction costs can derail their debt sustainability. *See* Eduardo Borensztein, Marcos Chamon, Olivier Jeanne, Paolo Mauro, and Jeromin Zettelmeyer, *Sovereign Debt Structure for Crisis Prevention*, IMF Occasional Paper No. 237 (2004), available online at <http://www.imf.org/external/pubs/nft/op/237/op237.pdf>, 33–5.

[10] For a good summary of the mathematics behind debt dynamics, *see* Julio Escolano, *A Practical Guide to Public Debt Dynamics, Fiscal Sustainability, and Cyclical Adjustment of Budgetary Aggregates*, IMF Technical Notes and Manuals (January 2010), available online at <http://www.imf.org/external/pubs/ft/tnm/2010/tnm1002.pdf>.

[11] The debt surges averaged 44 percentage points of GDP, and were actually higher during peacetime (46 percentage points) than during wartime (38 percentage points): *see* S. M. Ali Abbas, Nazim Belhocine, Asmaa El-Ganainy, and Mark Horton, 'Historical Patterns and Dynamics of Public Debt: Evidence from a New Database' (2011) 59(4) IMF Econ Rev 717, and for the statistical results cited, *see* 737–8.

21.16 Another recent and comprehensive study of public debt dynamics over the 1950–2011 period—this one covering both advanced and developing countries—confirmed that events besides the accumulation of fiscal deficits have played an important role, particularly in the latter group of countries. Whereas the mean and median values for advanced economies showed that fluctuations in the primary balance, interest rate growth differentials, and stock-flow changes each explained roughly a third of the variance of changes in their debt ratios, in the case of developing economies, their debt changes were far more unstable and in most cases were explained largely by the volatility in the stock-flow residual.[12]

21.17 In particular, the adverse consequences of banking crises for sovereign debt and creditworthiness have been observed abundantly around the world. A study that looked at the experience of 154 countries between 1980 and 2006 concluded, for instance, that banking crises were associated with a significant and long-lasting increase in government debt. The effect has been a function of the severity of the crisis: for crises classified as severe, comparable to the post-2007 ones in terms of output losses, banking crises were followed by a medium-term, average jump of about 37 percentage points in the government debt-to-GDP ratio. This ratio tended to surge even more in fragile countries with a worse initial fiscal position and a higher share of foreign debt—probably because of currency mismatches.[13]

21.18 The nexus between governments and banks has turned toxic for both parties in plenty of instances on every continent, with the recent troubles in the periphery of Europe being only the latest and largest-scale example. The extension of blanket guarantees to depositors, bail-outs of senior or foreign creditors, purchase of bad debts from banks, and recapitalizations of financial institutions have often combined to deliver a huge blow to sovereign creditworthiness. The case of Ireland is dramatic: three-fifths of the increase in that government's net debt position, from the equivalent of less than 20 per cent of GDP in 2007 to a peak of over 100 per cent in 2012, was caused by the (largely unforeseen) costs of bank support decisions—a case of contingent liabilities truly gone wild.[14] Without extraordinary financial support from its European partners and the IMF, the Irish government would surely have faced severe debt-servicing difficulties.[15]

21.19 At the same time, asset bubble deflations, economic recessions, and other adverse economic or political shocks have been known to undermine many a banking system, because banks are highly exposed to sovereign debt both through direct holdings and indirectly through implicit government guarantees. Therefore, when sovereign creditworthiness deteriorates, the banking system usually suffers consequences. The case of Greece is dreadful: as a result of the country's worsening fiscal crisis, Greek banks lost a third of their private-sector deposits between late 2009 and late 2012; their non-performing loans skyrocketed from 5 per cent of

---

[12] Paolo Mauro, Rafael Romeu, Ariel Binder, and Asad Zaman, *A Modern History of Fiscal Prudence and Profligacy*, IMF Working Paper No. WP/13/5 (January 2013), available online at <http://www.imf.org/external/pubs/ft/wp/2013/wp1305.pdf>; for the statistical results cited, *see* 30–1.

[13] Davide Furceri and Aleksandra Zdzienicka, 'The Consequences of Banking Crises for Public Debt', in Banca d'Italia, *Fiscal Policy: Lessons from the Crisis—Workshops and Conferences* (February 2011), available online at <http://www.bancaditalia.it/pubblicazioni/seminari_convegni/Fiscal_Policy/6_Fiscal_Policy.pdf>, 627–47.

[14] IMF, *Ireland: Eighth Review under the Extended Arrangement*, IMF Country Report No. 12/336 (November 2012), available online at <http://www.imf.org/external/pubs/ft/scr/2012/cr12336.pdf>.

[15] Prior instances of contingent liabilities or the recognition of obligations causing a sharp increase in the public debt include Canada in 1999–2000, Egypt in 2003, Greece in 2002 and 2004, and Japan in 1998 and 2006.

gross loans in 2008 to around 25 per cent by late 2012—possibly rising beyond 30 per cent in 2013; and the Greek government default and debt exchange in March 2012 depleted the banks' capital base, rendering them economically insolvent and generating enormous recapitalization needs of around €50 billion, of which some €35 billion were directly attributable to the sovereign's own woes.[16]

The fallout from currency mismatches has sometimes been massive on governments and systemically significant banks and corporations in many developing economies. The origin of the problem is that, historically, foreign-currency-denominated loans and bonds have frequently been a major source of funding—particularly of scarce medium- and long-term funding—for sovereigns and large financial and non-financial corporations in developing economies with stunted domestic capital markets. Whenever reliance on such funding is heavy, unforeseen currency devaluations can wreak havoc on the balance sheets and income statements of all concerned—because the cost of servicing such obligations increases suddenly by the extent of the devaluation.[17] This is why currency mismatches have been not only a major contributor to many sovereign and financial crises in developing economies, but also a feature that has increased the cost of crisis resolution—especially when governments are moved to support flagship banks and companies in the aftermath of their exchange rate losses. **21.20**

Two cases from a decade ago vividly illustrate the point.[18] In early 2002, the authorities in Argentina abandoned a fixed exchange rate regime whereby one peso was convertible into one dollar. The currency lost two-thirds of its value during 2002 and, because the government's public debt was overwhelmingly denominated in currencies other than pesos—in fact, at the end of 2001, 97 per cent of it was contracted in US dollars, European currencies, or Japanese yen—the peso-equivalent cost of the debt tripled virtually overnight. The ratio of the public debt to GDP skyrocketed from about 55 per cent at the end of 2001 to 165 per cent at the close of 2002, such that the obligations could not possibly be serviced on their original terms.[19] A reputable debt decomposition analysis estimated that currency valuation losses accounted for nearly two-thirds of this jump.[20] **21.21**

The devaluation also hit major companies very hard, because they had huge net liability positions in foreign currency. To help to prevent widespread bankruptcies, the authorities **21.22**

---

[16] Greek banks had to exchange their holdings of government bonds at a huge discount, thereby incurring enormous losses: IMF, *Greece: First and Second Reviews under the Extended Arrangement under the Extended Fund Facility*, IMF Country Report No. 13/20 (December 2012), available online at <http://www.imf.org/external/pubs/ft/scr/2013/cr1320.pdf>; Moody's Investors Service, 'Greece: Banking System Outlook Remains Negative', Announcement, 1 August 2012.

[17] Just as governments usually cannot raise taxes enough to cover the higher cost of servicing their foreign-currency obligations in the wake of a massive devaluation, neither can companies raise their prices much. On the contrary, since such devaluations are often destructive of consumer and investor confidence, they tend to have a contractionary effect on economic activity, and thus they undermine government revenues and business sales. Only governments, banks, and corporations that have hedged themselves, or are naturally hedged by having substantial earnings or assets in foreign currencies, can withstand currency fluctuations without harm.

[18] Other cases in which sudden exchange rate depreciations had a large impact on fiscal solvency are Egypt in 2003, Iceland in 2001, and Israel in 2002.

[19] Argentina Ministerio de Economía y Finanzas Públicas, *Boletín Fiscal 2º Trimestre 2012* (November 2012), available online at <http://www.mecon.gov.ar/onp/html/boletin/2dotrim12/2dotrim12.pdf>, Table 67. Argentina defaulted on its debt obligations starting in December 2001.

[20] Federico Sturzenegger and Jeromin Zettelmeyer, *Debt Defaults and Lessons from a Decade of Crises* (Cambridge, MA: MIT Press, 2006), 123.

decreed that debtors could repay their domestic bank loans at the prior one-to-one exchange rate, thereby shifting a large part of the burden of the devaluation onto the banking system—and ultimately to the government and its creditors and taxpayers, since the banks were partially compensated for the resulting losses with special-issue public debt.

21.23 The massive devaluation and default in Argentina, and particularly a freeze on bank deposits decreed in order to stem a run on that nation's banking system, caused extensive collateral damage in neighbouring Uruguay. Many well-off Argentines had sizeable deposits in Uruguay's banks that they started to repatriate and news of this began to induce a stampede by Uruguayan depositors as well. The authorities in Uruguay took a number of measures to cope with the banking emergency, including letting the exchange rate depreciate rapidly, such that it lost nearly half its value during 2002. Since 83 per cent of the public debt as of end-2001 had been denominated in foreign currencies, the collapse of the Uruguayan peso led to a one-year jump in the ratio of debt to GDP from about 45 per cent to 95 per cent as of the close of 2002, and it has been estimated that a third of that increase resulted from the government's currency mismatch.[21] In the event, Uruguay was forced by its state of affairs to request financial support from Washington DC (in 2002) and debt relief from its creditors soon thereafter (in 2003).

4. Maturity Mismatches and High Coupons

21.24 Debt vulnerabilities are also a function of the maturity profile and the level of coupon (interest) payments. The higher the share of maturing or short-term debt, the greater the risk that refinancing risks will be encountered once domestic or external circumstances suddenly deteriorate, and lenders and investors turn risk-averse. In fact, empirical studies have found short-term debt to be a leading indicator of vulnerability to international financial crises, because governments are rendered more susceptible to debt rollover crises, and also by giving rise to vicious cycles stemming from the two-way interaction between debt levels and interest rates.[22]

21.25 Whenever the average maturity of the stock of debt is low, the debtor can become the victim of creditor panics triggered by shifts in market sentiment. Sudden changes in international interest rates, commodity prices, exchange rates, or other factors such as contagion effects and political news can impact the cost of funds relatively quickly. A sovereign, bank, or corporation with large maturities or a high level of short-term debt may swiftly find itself in a situation in which rising bond yields give rise to perceptions of debt unsustainability, which in turn increase the default risk premium and thus the coupons that must be offered to obtain financing—hence the self-fulfilling prophecy. This is precisely what happened in the wake of an unexpected tightening of US monetary policy in the early 1980s under Federal Reserve Chairman Paul Volcker, which helped to precipitate sovereign debt crises throughout Latin America and beyond, or after the unexpected failure of Lehman Brothers in September 2008, which triggered banking crises in many European countries, the banks of which were overly reliant on short-maturity interbank funding.

---

[21] Banco Central del Uruguay, *Deuda del Sector Público Global* (September 2012), available online at <http://www.bcu.gub.uy/Estadisticas-e-Indicadores/Documents/Finanzas-Publicas/resdspg.pdf>, Table 4; Sturzenegger and Zettelmeyer (n. 20), 154.

[22] Borensztein et al. (n. 9), 14.

Likewise, the larger the share of floating- or adjustable-rate debt, the higher the risk that the cost of indebtedness will increase in the aftermath of a spike in bond yields prompted by a tightening in monetary policy at home or abroad, the prospect of higher inflation, or the perception of an increased risk of default. Sometimes, sovereigns encounter both problems simultaneously. When it becomes difficult to refinance maturing obligations or to roll over lines of credit that are expiring—no matter the reason—the cost of funding can suddenly jump and prompt concerns about debt sustainability, thereby scaring away even those lenders and investors who had been willing to provide financing. An extended maturity structure and borrowing mostly locked in at low coupons, therefore, can help to cushion against temporary shocks that adversely affect economic output, tax revenues, and credit conditions—and thus decrease the vulnerability of a government's overall liability position. **21.26**

Why have some governments at times relied heavily on short-maturity debt, or on funding at variable rather than fixed interest rates? For the same reasons that banks have on occasion relied too much on interbank funding, or corporations have depended too heavily on suppliers' credits and working-capital loans: because short-term debt is usually cheaper and easier to obtain than long-term debt—certainly so whenever the normal term structure (yield curve) prevails. Besides, short-term funding may be the only variety that is on offer to debtors considered to be very risky—except, of course, for the concessional loans and grants for which the governments of low-income countries usually qualify, such as from foreign aid agencies or the World Bank's International Development Association (IDA). Governments in Ireland, Greece, and Portugal issued only short-dated debt in 2011–12, and did so because they were reluctant to validate, and lock in, the very high yields demanded in longer-dated bonds by investors who were nervous about these countries' creditworthiness and also about the possibility of a break-up of the eurozone. **21.27**

The cases of Mexico in 1994 and Russia in 1998 serve to illustrate the perils described here. In both instances, there was a problem with maturity mismatches involving domestic government debt that was popular with foreign investors. In Mexico, the mismatches helped to precipitate a financial crisis and a major devaluation, but a default was avoided because the government was able to adopt emergency economic policies that elicited large-scale financial support from the IMF and the US government. In Russia, the mismatches likewise contributed to a financial crisis and a major devaluation, but the crisis included a default on the government's part because the authorities were unable to adopt the economic policy measures necessary to keep qualifying for a financial lifeline thrown by the IMF.[23] **21.28**

Throughout 1994, Mexico was buffeted by a series of very negative developments that undermined investor confidence and led to capital flight at a time when the economy was dependent on external financing, because it was running a large imbalance between exports and imports of goods and services. The year began with news of a guerrilla uprising in the southern state of Chiapas and was followed by: the assassination of the leading presidential candidate to replace the incumbent in August elections; abductions and murders involving business and religious leaders; the assassination of the head of the ruling party; and a stunning, although short-lived, year-end offensive by the Zapatista guerrillas in Chiapas. The government's policy response was completely inadequate to the task: neither fiscal nor **21.29**

[23] For general background on both episodes and the IMF's involvement, *see* James M. Boughton, *Tearing down Walls: The International Monetary Fund 1990–1999* (Washington DC: International Monetary Fund, 2012), chs 7 (Russia) and 10 (Mexico).

monetary policies were tightened—this at a time of rapidly rising interest rates in the United States—and the exchange rate was not allowed to depreciate enough to discourage capital flight. As a result, the authorities ended up losing most of their hard-currency reserves and thus, by the end of the year, they had to allow for a massive currency devaluation.[24]

21.30 Matters were aggravated by the government's view throughout 1994 that it could satisfy what was perceived as a temporary surge in demand for dollars by issuing enormous quantities of short-term debt (mostly at ninety-one-day maturities) indexed to the exchange value of the US dollar (*tesobonos*), instead of the usual treasury bills in pesos (*cetes*). Besides, as long as the currency was not devalued meaningfully, it appeared to be a cost-effective funding strategy for the government: since holders of *tesobonos* would be compensated for any potential devaluation, these bills could be sold with much lower coupons than peso instruments. By the close of 1994, *tesobonos* accounted for over half of total public debt, up from less than 5 per cent at the start—and virtually all (the equivalent of nearly US$30 billion as of end-2004) matured within twelve months. It was this maturity mismatch that brought the government to the edge of default, because its dollar reserves at the end of 1994 were down to a fraction (a fifth) of the *tesobonos* coming due in 1995.[25]

21.31 The Russian financial crisis of mid-1998 was rooted in a fundamental policy inconsistency between high fiscal deficits (on the order of 6½ per cent of GDP on average during 1995–98) and a quasi-fixed exchange rate that became increasingly overvalued. In the face of various adverse shocks to the balance of payments, and absent a supportive fiscal policy, the central bank lost half its international reserves in the year to August 1998 trying to prevent the ruble's devaluation. The fiscal deficit was the result of chronically low tax revenues, mainly because of tax breaks and energy subsidies granted to enterprises that could not cope with the transition from communism to capitalism. The main adverse shocks were: a loss of investor confidence in the wake of the Asian financial crisis; a precipitous drop in world oil prices, affecting Russia's leading export; unreliable political support in the legislature (the Duma) for the Boris Yeltsin administration's corrective measures; and related decisions by the IMF to withhold its loan disbursements to Russia (in late 1997 and after July 1998).[26]

21.32 An aggravating factor was the government's massive issuance of government short-term commitments (*Gosudarstvennoye Kratkosrochnoye Obyazatyelstvo*, or GKOs), zero-coupon bonds denominated in rubles with short maturities, such that, by May 1998, nearly three-quarters of the government's ruble-denominated debt had a maturity of less than one year. This exposed the government to extreme rollover pressures, not only because of the volume of GKOs that were maturing all of the time, but because the coupons that had to be paid on new issues soared during the first half of 1998 as sentiment deteriorated. The combination of annualized yields jumping from about 30 per cent to almost 95 per cent by June, and redemptions coming due, meant that debt-service payments on GKOs came to exceed the ruble equivalent of US$1 billion per week. Initially, the main GKO holders were domestic

---

[24] Jeffrey Sachs, Aaron Tornell, and Andrés Velasco, 'The Collapse of the Mexican Peso: What Have We Learned?' (1996) 11(22) Econ Pol'y 13.

[25] Harold L. Cole and Timothy J. Kehoe, 'A Self-Fulfilling Model of Mexico's 1994–1995 Debt Crisis' (1996) 41(3–4) J Int'l Econ 309; Banco de México, *Informe Anual 1994* (Mexico, DF: Banco de México, 1995), 74 and 162; Banco de México, *Informe Anual 1995* (Mexico, DF: Banco de México, 1996), 187.

[26] Homi J. Kharas, Brian Pinto, and Sergei Ulatov, 'An Analysis of Russia's 1998 Meltdown: Fundamentals and Market Signals' [2001] BPEA 1; David Owen and David O. Robinson (eds) *Russia Rebounds* (Washington DC: International Monetary Fund, 2003).

banks, but foreign investors soon became an important segment of the market, accounting for between one third and one half of holders, depending on the use and abuse of various investment schemes. In the event, a default on GKOs was announced on 17 August 1998, and the government ended up imposing huge losses on investors, with large Moscow-based commercial banks pushed into insolvency and having to default on their own external obligations because of their holdings of GKOs.[27]

Most governments have since learned not to be 'penny-wise and pound-foolish' by taking on short-maturity or adjustable-rate indebtedness. A wide consensus has emerged in the literature on the benefits of fiscal insurance, and sovereign debt managers have paid greater and greater attention to reducing the exposure of their debts to maturity and interest-rate risks. The lengthening of the maturity structures that has taken place over the last two decades is clear evidence of the increased awareness of such risks.[28] Moreover, many governments in developing countries have fostered the growth of domestic capital markets, largely through improved macroeconomic policies and structural reforms, including the partial privatization of pension plans. This has enabled them to issue domestic-currency bonds instead of relying on short-term financing from domestic or foreign banks. These domestic capital markets have also provided a useful financing source for large banks and corporations. **21.33**

However, the recent case of Greece demonstrates that a benign debt structure is insufficient to shelter a sovereign from the worst-case scenario of investor demand evaporating completely. At the end of 2009, the Greek public debt was structured very favourably by advanced-economy standards—yet that was not good enough to prevent the catastrophic default that took place twenty-seven months later. **21.34**

5. Access to Financing

Greece illustrates the point that sovereigns encounter debt difficulties when their financing needs—be they relatively large, medium, or small—cannot be satisfied if investor confidence collapses. At that point, funding for even a shrinking fiscal deficit becomes extremely difficult, as does the refinancing of maturing obligations. Once creditor banks and other institutional investors have panicked and are bent on cutting their exposure to sovereign risk, bond yields will shoot up in the secondary market and auctions of new government debt will fail. The sovereign may try to get by for a while on the basis of prior fiscal savings (if they exist), the sale of state-owned assets (if they can be privatized promptly), the delay of payments to suppliers and civil servants, and above all recourse to emergency financing from a lender of last resort such as the IMF—or some combination of all of the aforementioned—but, unless confidence is soon regained through economic or political announcements and measures that address the underlying causes of the confidence crisis, the government is likely to start running out of cash, and possibly also of international reserves, and will end up defaulting. **21.35**

[27] Niko Gobbin and Bruno Merlevede, 'The Russian Crisis: A Debt Perspective' (2000) 12(2) Post-Communist Economies 141; IMF, *Sovereign Debt Restructurings and the Domestic Economy: Experience in Four Recent Cases* (February 2002), available online at <http://www.imf.org/external/np/pdr/sdrm/2002/022102.pdf>.

[28] Alessandro Missale, 'Sovereign Debt Management and Fiscal Vulnerabilities', in BIS, *Threat of Fiscal Dominance?*, BIS Papers No. 65 (May 2012), available online at <http://www.bis.org/publ/bppdf/bispap65.pdf>, 157–76.

Therefore the issue of access to financing—or lack thereof—is at the heart of any analysis of sovereign debt sustainability.

21.36 The accepted version of why Greece entered into a debt crisis that culminated in a gigantic sovereign default (in March 2012) is that the country was fiscally mismanaged for a long time. It had failed to carry out needed structural reforms that could have preserved the country's creditworthiness if and when conditions in the eurozone deteriorated. Consequently, even before the global financial crisis of late 2008 hit, the country was 'an accident waiting to happen' according to some farsighted European Union (EU) officials and private sector economists.[29]

21.37 In reality, Greece's road to fiscal disaster was never straightforward—and there was no historical inevitability about it, either. In the five decades through 2009, successive governments in Greece had managed the country's public finances without a hitch, including servicing a very high level of public debt that averaged the equivalent of nearly 100 per cent of GDP during half a century. That included a track record of very prudent liability management, such that, as of end-2009, only 10 per cent of government debt had a residual maturity of less than one year, three-quarters of the public debt featured fixed-rate coupons and they were very low (the average interest rate paid was 4.2 per cent), and virtually all obligations (99.6 per cent of total) were denominated in euros, the national currency.[30] At the time, the government was not running currency or maturity mismatches, contingent liabilities were not a problem, and the cost of the debt was quite manageable.

21.38 What eventually sunk Greece was the erosion of investor confidence that began in December 2009, prompted by initial hesitation on the part of newly elected Prime Minister George Papandreou to take corrective fiscal measures, which elicited downgrades from all three of the leading credit-rating agencies because the fiscal deficit had reached double digits that year. The situation was aggravated by inertia and indecision that gripped eurozone governments in subsequent months with regard to whether and how to assemble an emergency stabilization programme for Greece underwritten by the EU and the IMF. But October 2010 brought about a major turning point: German Chancellor Merkel and French President Sarkozy agreed, in Deauville (France), that private investors would have to 'contribute' to future European sovereign bailouts. This was the price exacted by Germany to set up a larger, permanent bailout fund to replace the European Financial Stability Facility (EFSF), because, according to Merkel, the existing rules had allowed too much moral hazard to creep into

---

[29] 'Ever since its last-minute inclusion in the single currency in 2001, Greece has been considered by many in Brussels to be an accident waiting to happen': *see The Telegraph*, 'Greek Crisis: Athens to Ashes', 29 April 2010, available online at <http://www.telegraph.co.uk/finance/financialcrisis/7649803/Greek-crisis-Athens-to-Ashes.html>. For a similar appraisal dating from well before the failure of Lehman Brothers, *see* Mark Landler, 'As Euro Nears 10, Cracks Emerge in Fiscal Union', *New York Times*, 1 May 2008, available online at <http://www.nytimes.com/2008/05/01/world/europe/01euro.html> ('Greece, said Thomas Mayer, the chief European economist at Deutsche Bank, is an "accident waiting to happen" ').

[30] Ministry of Finance, *Hellenic Republic Public Debt Bulletin*, No. 56 (December 2009), available online at <http://www.minfin.gr/content-api/f/binaryChannel/minfin/datastore/14/90/39/14903996c439862738744b8790877f25b03da784/application/pdf/pdb_2009_12_20100219.pdf>. The weighted-average residual maturity of Greek government debt was eight years as of end-2009, the second-longest among advanced economies after the United Kingdom: IMF, *Fiscal Monitor* (November 2010), available online at <http://www.imf.org/external/pubs/ft/fm/2010/fm1002.pdf>, 27. The average implicit interest rate was calculated by the author from Eurostat, *Government Finance Statistics: Summary Tables 1996–2010* (December 2011), available online at <http://epp.eurostat.ec.europa.eu/portal/page/portal/product_details/publication?p_product_code=KS-EK-11-002>, 13.

the eurozone bond market. However, this decision triggered a tidal wave of concern among bondholders—that they would suffer losses on government securities issued by countries (such as Greece) receiving financial assistance from their eurozone partners.[31]

As the IMF would admit in a July 2011 report, the very protracted public debate in Europe over how to deliver financial support to eurozone members would take a heavy toll on Greece. It would not only propel Greek bond yields ever higher, but by encouraging an exodus of bank deposits and also, via rating downgrades, by decreasing the value of Greek collateral with the European Central Bank (ECB), it would force Greek banks to post additional collateral when they could least afford it. And the only way in which they could do that was by calling in loans, thereby provoking a major credit crunch that would aggravate the country's deepening recession.[32] The steeper-than-expected economic contraction, for its part, would cause tax revenues to underperform, which meant that the government would always be under pressure to cut spending further to meet the pre-established fiscal deficit targets. This austerity mindset elicited more social and political unrest, which scared away remaining investors, particularly given an understandable cascade of downgrades on the part of the credit-rating agencies. This is the confidence-destroying, downward spiral into which Greece was pushed by circumstances largely out of its control—a spiral that had not come to an end as of early 2013. **21.39**

It was in the midst of this vicious cycle that the ECB, EU, and IMF (the so-called 'troika') decided—first gingerly in mid-2011 and then ferociously in early 2012—that Greece's debt burden was unviable and thus that the government had to obtain massive debt relief from its creditors. In the beginning, the 'haircut' demanded of investors was in the order of 20 per cent on a net present value (NPV) basis, but in the end the figure imposed by the troika was above 70 per cent—by far the largest, and also among the most punishing, default in sovereign debt history. The trend of Greek government bond yields speaks volumes about what happened to investor demand during the intervening twenty-seven months: whereas, in December 2009, the market-clearing median yield of two-year government paper was below 3.5 per cent, by the final month of 2010 it had jumped to almost 12 per cent, and by December 2011 it had skyrocketed to 145 per cent.[33] Investor confidence had been utterly destroyed. **21.40**

While Greece is an extreme case, recent events throughout the periphery of Europe demonstrate that sovereigns, just like their banks, can be the object of creditor runs—whether self-inflicted or not. This highlights the importance of minimizing budgetary deficits as a rule, and the wisdom of generating fiscal savings whenever economic times are good and government revenues swell, in order to infuse confidence in investors ahead of any economic, political, or financial shocks that may materialize. **21.41**

There is a large empirical literature on the determinants of long-term bond yields in advanced economies, and most of it concludes that higher levels of fiscal deficits and public debt tend to raise interest rates—and particularly so when expectations of future fiscal outcomes **21.42**

[31] Arturo C. Porzecanski, 'Behind the 2012 Greek Default and Restructuring', in Eugenio A. Bruno (ed.) *Sovereign Debt Restructuring: Legal, Financial and Regulatory Aspects* (London: Globe Law and Business, 2013), 33–48.

[32] IMF, *Greece: Fourth Review under the Stand-By Arrangement*, IMF Country Report No. 11/175 (July 2011), available online at <http://www.imf.org/external/pubs/ft/scr/2011/cr11175.pdf>.

[33] Porzecanski (n. 31); data on yields on two-year Greek government bonds courtesy of Bloomberg.

change. One reputable study of thirty-one advanced and emerging economies over the period 1980–2007 found that higher fiscal deficits and public debt raised long-term nominal bond yields in both types of economies. Moreover, countries with higher initial deficits and debt levels experienced correspondingly larger increases in bond yields when their fiscal position deteriorated.[34] Evidently, investor appetite for government bonds is itself a function of fiscal outcomes and prospects.

21.43 Recent results based on a novel, high-frequency panel dataset for twenty-six emerging economies between 2005 and 2011 show that whenever global risks were perceived as low, domestic bond yields were influenced mostly by domestic considerations (inflation and economic growth expectations). This suggests that, in tranquil times, bond investors focused mostly on risks related to the domestic business cycle. However, when spooked by an increase in international uncertainty, investors took default risks more seriously, and expectations regarding fiscal outcomes played a significant role in determining changes in domestic government bond yields. Every percentage point expected worsening in the fiscal balance in relation to GDP raised yields by 30 basis points (bps), and every additional 10 percentage points in the expected ratio of debt to GDP raised domestic yields by 60bps.[35] Given the ebb and flow of global conditions, these findings underscore the need for governments in emerging economies, in particular, to behave in a fiscally prudent manner. In order to anchor the confidence of investors once market conditions deteriorate, they must earn and deepen that confidence the rest of the time.

6. Indicators of Debt Sustainability

21.44 The most commonly cited indicators of potential debt problems are ratios of public debt to GDP, or else of public- and private-sector foreign debt to total export earnings. The latter ratio was especially popular until a decade ago, because the financial crises that earned worldwide notoriety in the 1980s and 1990s involved defaults mainly on loans extended by foreign banks, or on bonds purchased chiefly by foreign investors. It was thought that the ability of governments, banks, and corporations to service their cross-border liabilities, especially in countries with artificial exchange rate regimes, depended on a country's capacity to generate foreign exchange through exports of goods and services. In recent years, however, ratios of debt to exports have gone out of fashion for several good reasons, as follows.

(a) The emergence of domestic capital markets and financial liberalization measures have enabled foreign investors to take substantial positions in domestic debt instruments denominated in local currencies, thus erasing the relevance of the distinction between 'foreign' and 'domestic' debt.
(b) The ability of economic agents in any one country to access foreign exchange is less dependent on export earnings, and more a function of net capital flows and the current account (the difference between exports and imports of goods, services, and transfers).

[34] Emanuele Baldacci and Manmohan Kumar, *Fiscal Deficits, Public Debt, and Sovereign Bond Yields*, IMF Working Paper No. WP/10/184 (August 2010), available online at <http://www.imf.org/external/pubs/cat/longres.cfm?sk=24130.0>.

[35] Laura Jaramillo and Anke Weber, *Bond Yields in Emerging Economies: It Matters What State You Are In*, IMF Working Paper No. WP/12/198 (August 2012), available online at <http://www.imf.org/external/pubs/ft/wp/2012/wp12198.pdf>.

(c) In the past two decades, a number of governments have defaulted on domestic, as well as on cross-border, obligations, and thus a more comprehensive measure of their financial obligations and burden is warranted as part of an assessment of debt sustainability and creditworthiness.

Ratios of debt to GDP or exports both have a number of shortcomings, however. They provide a static snapshot of the relative size of obligations at any given point in time, but they do not convey a trajectory—never mind a forward-looking judgement of capacity to pay. Also, such ratios reveal nothing about contingent liabilities, currency or maturity mismatches, the cost of servicing the debt, or the nature and behaviour of the investor base. For example, there are low-income countries with high debt ratios, but their interest burdens are light and their maturity profiles are very benign—because they are the beneficiaries of loans granted on concessional terms by official bilateral and multilateral agencies. And there are middle-income countries with low debt ratios, but which are prone to economic and political instability, or else to wild swings in their export earnings, capital flows, and exchange rates, such that they are vulnerable. In sum, as one of the leading credit-rating agencies recently concluded after a review of the historical evidence, while defaults are correlated with rising debt burdens, a high debt-to-GDP ratio is neither a necessary nor a sufficient condition for a sovereign to default.[36] **21.45**

The unreliability of ratios of debt to GDP or to exports as predictors of sovereign defaults is revealed by Table 21.1, which documents the lack of any useful relationship between them and past instances of default. During the calendar year before nineteen defaults took place during 1998–2012, whether on foreign or domestic debt or both, ratios of public debt to GDP ranged from a low of 27 per cent (Ecuador 2008) to a high of 236 per cent (Nicaragua 2003), with a sample median of 79 per cent. The prior-year ratio of foreign debt (public plus private sector) to total export earnings, for its part, ranged from a modest 54 per cent (Ukraine 1998) to a maximum of 560 per cent (Nicaragua 2003), with a sample median of 180 per cent. Equally random are the values of these ratios for countries that have yet to default. For example, Japan has the highest ratio of public debt to GDP of any country in the world—it has averaged more than 200 per cent since 2009—and at the same time countries deemed quite risky by the credit-rating agencies (including Cambodia, Honduras, Paraguay, and Venezuela) have ratios below 40 per cent.[37] And yet many judgements have been expressed about the sustainability (or not) of a given country's public or foreign debt, particularly by official bodies such as the IMF, on the basis of ratios like these that have no predictive power, certainly not out of their proper historical, institutional, economic, and political contexts. **21.46**

More sophisticated empirical research has found, however, that, once various control variables are incorporated, the larger and heavier the burden of the public debt, the greater the risk that debt-servicing difficulties will be encountered. One reputable study analysed the relationship between the probability of experiencing a debt crisis and the ratio of public debt to GDP using a pooled sample of fifty-five low- and middle-income countries during **21.47**

[36] Moody's Investors Service, 'The Causes of Sovereign Defaults: Ability to Manage Crises Not Merely Determined by Debt Levels', 2 November 2010.

[37] Moody's Investors Service, *Moody's Statistical Handbook: Country Credit* (November 2012). The median public debt-to-GDP ratio for twenty-six governments rated 'B1' to 'C' by Moody's was likewise below 40 per cent in 2012, and the median foreign debt-to-total-exports ratio stood at 90 per cent.

Table 21.1 Defaults on public debt and key debt ratios

Country	Date of default	Debt affected	Public debt-to-GDP prior year (%)	Foreign debt-to-exports prior year (%)
Russia	Aug-98	FC & LC	54.7	121.1
Ukraine	Sep-98	FC & LC	29.9	54.3
Pakistan	Jul-99	FC	76.2	345.0
Ecuador	Aug-99	FC & LC	61.4	301.8
Ukraine	Jan-00	FC	61.0	91.8
Côte d'Ivoire	Mar-00	FC	89.8	244.4
Argentina	Nov-01	FC & LC	45.6	380.0
Moldova	Jun-02	FC	84.0	196.4
Uruguay	May-03	FC & LC	94.7	324.9
Nicaragua	Jul-03	FC & LC	235.7	560.4
Grenada	Dec-04	FC & LC	78.8	206.2
Dominican Rep.	Apr-05	FC	36.9	74.8
Belize	Dec-06	FC	103.6	164.4
Seychelles	Jul-08	FC	130.1	137.1
Ecuador	Dec-08	FC	26.7	108.8
Jamaica	Feb-10	LC	142.8	260.3
Côte d'Ivoire	Jan-11	FC	66.4	84.3
Greece	Mar-12	FC & LC	165.4	n/a
Belize	Aug-12	FC	83.6	134.3

Note: FC = foreign currency; LC = local currency

Source: Author's calculations based on the following public sources: default data from Moody's Investors Service, 'Sovereign Default and Recovery Rates, 1983–2012H1' (30 July 2012), 10–11, and from 'Investor Losses in Modern-Era Sovereign Bond Restructurings' (7 August 2012), 7; debt/GDP data from IMF, 'Historical Public Debt Database' (September 2012); debt/exports data from World Bank, 'International Debt Statistics Database' (2013).

1971–2002 and three control variables. It found that while a debt ratio of 40 per cent was associated with a 20 per cent probability of facing a crisis in the following year, a debt-to-GDP ratio of 80 per cent was paired with a 50 per cent probability and a ratio of 100 per cent was correlated with a sample probability of 63 per cent. However, there did not appear to be obvious cut-off points for the range of sustainable debt ratios because debt crises have occurred, as demonstrated earlier in the chapter, at a very wide range of debt ratios.[38]

21.48 There are good reasons why the degree of fiscally responsible behaviour does not correlate with the relative size of the public debt. In some countries, fiscal responsibility decreases, while in others it is strengthened, as the debt ratio rises to high and potentially risky levels. Social attitudes and historical precedents concerning the seriousness with which debt

[38] Harald Finger and Mauro Mecagni, *Sovereign Debt Restructuring and Debt Sustainability: An Analysis of Recent Cross-Country Experience*, IMF Occasional Paper No. 255 (April 2007), available online at <http://www.imf.org/external/pubs/cat/longres.cfm?sk=19634.0>, 14–15.

obligations are regarded may determine different degrees of 'willingness to pay', explaining why some nations fit the profile of 'serial defaulters' at debt levels that are relatively low.[39]

The shortcomings of static indicators have given rise to more dynamic assessments of debt sustainability based on medium-term simulations of the debt-to-GDP and other ratios given certain macroeconomic forecasts and fiscal policy assumptions. One approach is to calculate the primary fiscal outcome (the difference between genuine revenues and non-interest expenditures) consistent with a stabilization of the debt-to-GDP ratio. If the observed primary balance is less than the debt-stabilizing balance, then the current path of fiscal policy implies an increasing ratio of debt to GDP, and the difference between the two quantifies the degree of belt-tightening needed. Judgement can then be passed on whether such fiscal austerity is politically and otherwise attainable, given what else is known about the country in question. **21.49**

Another approach involves making a fiscal forecast over the medium term (generally, five–ten years) assuming historical or plausible macroeconomic conditions, and then developing alternative scenarios in which the base case is subjected to shocks such as a jump in bond yields, an economic slowdown, or an exchange-rate adjustment. The purpose is to see by how much and for how long the fiscal accounts would be derailed, and thus what would happen to the ratio of debt to GDP or to exports assuming no constructive fiscal policy response. The next level up in terms of sophistication is to incorporate a 'guesstimate' of the nature and extent of a likely budgetary course correction in the wake of an unfavourable shock, which can be based on historical experience and various economic and institutional fundamentals of the fiscal policy process.[40] That usually yields a more realistic story of what could happen to public finances in a forecast that contemplates both shocks and responses to them. **21.50**

In the absence of reliable 'sustainability thresholds', however, such estimates per se do not allow for judgements on the viability of any particular fiscal path. Uncertainty about future macroeconomic conditions and potential fiscal policy reactions inevitably weakens the basis for drawing compelling policy conclusions using scenario analyses. Crucial factors are often missed, such as judgements about the loyalty of the investor base, the availability of refinancing options, and the danger from contingent liabilities. Assessments of the appropriateness of a country's debt burden should reflect the history of fiscal responsibility, the vision and degrees of freedom of its policymakers, and the professionalism and thus credibility of a country's institutions (for example the central bank and budgetary agencies). This is probably why a World Bank study of 132 low- and middle-income countries covering the 1970–2002 period confirmed that countries with better policies and institutions were able to carry substantially higher debt burdens than countries with worse policies and institutions—and without increasing the risk of debt distress.[41] **21.51**

---

[39] 'The contrast between the histories of the nondefaulters and those of the serial defaulters ... is stunning. Default can become a way of life.... [S]erial default may owe to a vicious cycle in which default weakens a country's institutions, in turn making subsequent default more likely': Carmen M. Reinhart, Kenneth S. Rogoff, and Miguel A. Savastano, 'Debt Intolerance' [2003] BPEA 1.

[40] Oya Celasun, Xavier Debrun, and Jonathan D. Ostry, *Primary Surplus Behaviour and Risks to Fiscal Sustainability in Emerging Market Countries: A 'Fan-Chart' Approach*, IMF Working Paper No. WP/06/67 (March 2006), available online at <http://www.imf.org/external/pubs/ft/wp/2006/wp0667.pdf>.

[41] Aart Kraay and Vikram Nehru, 'When is External Debt Sustainable?' (2006) 20(3) The World Bank Econ Rev 341.

21.52 The IMF, World Bank, and all other official lending institutions routinely conduct debt sustainability studies. Using a framework designed for countries with regular access to world capital markets, the IMF makes judgements about countries' capacity to borrow and service debts without compromising their own stability or that of other Fund members.[42] The Fund and the Bank have another framework tailored for low-income countries, intended to estimate repayment risks and to help governments to prevent unviable debt burdens—especially when they have already been granted debt relief by official lenders.[43] In reflection of the difficulty of predicting debt sustainability, however, these institutions have had to tinker with their methodology every couple of years, and they are still far from reliable. Both the Fund and the Bank have failed to predict many debt crises ahead of time, and the root of the problem is that any approach based on past performance is often of limited relevance in terms of predicting the future, while the nature and likelihood of any scenarios imagining what the future might bring are, by definition, unknown.[44]

21.53 The credit-rating agencies and analysts throughout the financial industry likewise attempt to anticipate debt sustainability problems by similar means. The rating agencies publish their methodologies, which involve a combination of quantitative and qualitative judgements intended to capture the capacity, as well as the willingness, of sovereigns to meet their debt obligations. This is an improvement over what the official multilateral agencies are doing, because no quantitative model can adequately capture the complex web of political, economic, financial, and social factors that lead a government to default on its debt.[45] Their analysis incorporates indicators of institutional effectiveness and political risk, economic structure and growth prospects, the size and nature of international assets and liabilities, fiscal performance and resilience, and monetary and exchange-rate flexibility.[46] As one of the agencies has acknowledged, a sustainable public debt burden varies across countries and over time, and hence there is no simplistic relationship between the stock of government debt or debt service (whether relative to GDP or government revenue) and sovereign creditworthiness or ratings. Likewise, there is no given level of external indebtedness that becomes unsustainable and results in debt default.[47] And yet their methodologies have also evolved through time in reflection of past failures to foresee debt-servicing problems or close calls—whether in the 1920s–1930s, in Asia during the late 1990s, or in Europe in recent years.[48]

---

42 The framework for market-access countries was introduced in 2002 and has been subsequently refined several times to incorporate lessons learned: *see* IMF, *Staff Guidance Note on Debt Sustainability Analysis for Market Access Countries* (July 2008), available online at <http://www.imf.org/external/np/pp/eng/2008/070308a.pdf>.

43 The joint World Bank–IMF Debt Sustainability Framework (DSF) was introduced in 2005 and has been modified multiple times: *see* World Bank and IMF, *Revisiting the Debt Sustainability Framework for Low-Income Countries* (January 2012), available online at <http://www.imf.org/external/np/pp/eng/2012/011212.pdf>.

44 *See* the discussion of the 'impossibility principle' in Charles Wyplosz, 'Debt Sustainability Assessment: Mission Impossible' (2011) 2(3) Rev Econ & Inst 1.

45 Moody's Investors Service, *Sovereign Bond Ratings* (September 2008), available online at <https://www.moodys.com/researchdocumentcontentpage.aspx?docid=PBC_109490>.

46 Standard & Poor's, *Sovereign Government Rating Methodology and Assumptions* (June 2011), available online at <http://www.standardandpoors.com/spf/upload/Ratings_EMEA/2011-06-30_CBEvent_Criteria GovSovRatingMethodologyAndAssumptions.pdf>.

47 Fitch Ratings, *Sovereign Ratings Criteria* (August 2012), available online at <http://www.fitchratings.com/creditdesk/reports/report_frame.cfm?rpt_id=685737>.

48 For example, Iceland's foreign-currency sovereign debt was rated AA until 2007–08 (subsequently downgraded to BB+/BBB–), and Greece was rated A until late 2009 (subsequently downgraded to Default). For an analysis of how poorly the rating agencies also fared in the interwar years, *see* Marc Flandreau, Norbert Gaillard, and Frank Packer, *To Err is Human: Rating Agencies and the Interwar Foreign Government Debt Crisis*, BIS Working Papers No. 335 (December 2010), available online at <http://www.bis.org/publ/work335.pdf>.

The most challenging aspect of all of these attempts at forecasting debt sustainability or creditworthiness is how to anticipate changes in market perceptions of sovereign default risk, and thus shifts in the demand for the bonds issued by various governments. These changes take place because investors become more or less risk-averse, or because certain asset classes are in or out of fashion, or because investment horizons turn short or long. Years, and sometimes decades, of benign appraisal by the financial markets and the credit-rating agencies can come to a surprisingly abrupt end. At times, investors appear to differentiate among countries in accordance with their respective credit profiles, but on occasion investors get caught up in entry or exit modes that recognize no borders and disregard country fundamentals. Moreover, there is substantial endogeneity in the way in which markets assess sovereign risk: the mere perception of illiquidity or even insolvency (arising, say, from an adverse exogenous shock to government revenues or expenditures, or to political instability) can initiate a vicious cycle whereby rising, and eventually unsustainable, bond yields lead to market illiquidity and actual insolvency. This is why debt sustainability can be said to be largely in the eye of the beholder: it depends on investor beliefs about what the future will bring.[49] Unless governments listen and react constructively to what the financial markets are telling them, swings in investor preferences can alter significantly their ability to fund themselves—and thus their margin of manoeuvre to avoid an adverse credit event. **21.54**

7. Conclusions

A history of 'deficit bias' on the part of most governments during the past several decades, pockmarked by destabilizing swings in investor sentiment, has popularized the notion that both fiscal behaviour and investor attitudes should be anchored by the adoption of national fiscal rules. A fiscal rule imposes a long-lasting constraint on fiscal policy through numerical limits, usually on deficit financing, debt levels, or public spending. Fiscal rules typically aim to correct distorted incentives, and to contain pressures to overspend—particularly in good times—so as to ensure fiscal responsibility and debt sustainability over the long term. The objective is also to banish doubt or ambiguity about the willingness of governments to follow a prudent fiscal path that will enable them to keep paying their debts. In the presence of a constrained public purse, and in the context of greater predictability for investors in government debt, there should be far fewer opportunities for a gap to develop between the amount of funding demanded by the government and the supply of funding willingly delivered by bondholders and other creditors. **21.55**

Two decades ago, whatever fiscal rules were in existence constrained mostly the fiscal activities of sub-sovereign (for example provincial or municipal) governments, but by now more than eighty countries—especially members of currency unions and emerging market economies—have instituted them in order to constrain their own national governments.[50] The latest fashion in fiscal rules is to combine rigid sustainability objectives with flexibility to accommodate economic shocks, and thus many of the more recently adopted rules set budget targets in cyclically adjusted terms, following the examples set by Chile and Switzerland a **21.56**

[49] Jean-Pierre Landau, 'Policies on Sovereign Debt' (2012) 16 BDF FS Rev 191.

[50] Nina Budina, Tidiane Kinda, Andrea Schaechter, and Anke Weber, *Fiscal Rules at a Glance: Country Details from a New Dataset*, IMF Working Paper No. WP/12/273 (November 2012), available online at <http://www.imf.org/external/pubs/cat/longres.aspx?sk=40101>. In 1990, only five countries (Germany, Indonesia, Japan, Luxembourg, and the United States) had fiscal rules in place that covered at least the central government level.

decade ago. The bulk of national expenditure, balance, and debt rules are embedded in statutory norms, and those designed for currency zones (in Africa, the Caribbean, and Europe) are mostly supranational rules established by international treaties. The supporting institutional arrangements vary, but increasingly fiscal councils or independent committees are providing key budgetary assumptions, methodologies, and supervision.[51]

21.57 The jury is still out on whether fiscal rules can actually help to prevent excessive borrowing and sovereign debt crises. A recent review of their past effectiveness concludes that they are neither necessary nor sufficient to achieve fiscal discipline, but that they help.[52] It would appear that rules with more encompassing design features have been associated with better fiscal performance, but it is also clear that the mere introduction of fiscal rules has not guaranteed success unless there were steep financial or political costs associated with breaking the rules. This is one of the clear lessons of the abject failure of Europe's Stability and Growth Pact (SGP) in terms of strengthening debt sustainability ahead of the financial crisis of 2008—especially in the periphery countries of the eurozone.

21.58 The SGP fiscal framework, which fleshed out the policy provisions laid down by the Maastricht Treaty of 1992, was introduced in 1998 and revised in 2005. However, enforcement failures were the Achilles' heel of the SGP.

(a) Many governments—including the largest members of European Monetary Union (EMU)—did not follow the instructions to strive for underlying fiscal balance over the business cycle, and they were unsuccessful in keeping deficits below their ceilings. More generally, before the crisis hit, many member governments did not sufficiently use the good economic times to build up public finance buffers, as demanded by the SGP.[53]
(b) Laxity in applying the SGP to the larger countries had a negative demonstration effect on the newer members and, with the lower likelihood of being sanctioned, fiscal policy became less disciplined—especially around the eurozone's periphery.
(c) Many governments followed the letter, but not the spirit of the SGP, and thus they routinely incorporated overly optimistic budgetary assumptions, engaged in creative accounting and misreporting, and pursued electorally motivated fiscal policies with expansionary biases.[54]

---

[51] Andrea Schaechter, Tidiane Kinda, Nina Budina, and Anke Weber, *Fiscal Rules in Response to the Crisis: Toward the 'Next-Generation' Rules*, IMF Working Paper No. WP/12/187 (July 2012), available online at <http://www.imf.org/external/pubs/ft/wp/2012/wp12187.pdf>.

[52] Wyplosz (n. 44).

[53] The SGP complemented the 3 per cent of GDP deficit limit and 60 per cent of GDP debt ceiling by requiring countries to strive for a medium-term fiscal objective (MTO). Originally, countries were urged to attain a common 'close-to-balance or in surplus' position, interpreted as a deficit no larger than 0.5 per cent of GDP over the cycle, to provide sufficient cyclical room to allow for the kicking in of automatic stabilizers during downturns without breaching the 3 per cent limit. After the 2005 revision, countries were able to set their own MTOs based on sustainability factors, within certain limits including a maximum 1 per cent of GDP deficit. If an excessive deficit were deemed to exist, countries would be obliged to undertake corrective policies within a defined time frame under the Excessive Deficit Procedure (EDP). Non-complying countries were supposed to be subject to increasingly stringent surveillance, which could culminate in the imposition of financial penalties: *see* IMF, *Fiscal Rules: Anchoring Expectations for Sustainable Public Finances* (December 2009), available online at <http://www.imf.org/external/np/pp/eng/2009/121609.pdf>, 42–3.

[54] Roel Beetsma, Benjamin Bluhm, Massimo Giuliodori, and Peter Wierts, 'From Budgetary Forecasts to *Ex Post* Fiscal Data: Exploring the Evolution of Fiscal Forecast Errors in the European Union' (2013) 31(4) Contemp Econ Pol'y 795; Roel Beetsma, Massimo Giuliodori, and Peter Wierts, 'Planning to Cheat: EU

Since fiscal rules are not a panacea, and all of the economic, political, and financial forces that impact on sovereign creditworthiness cannot possibly be controlled, chances are that some governments will encounter debt-servicing difficulties when they least expect it. Certainly, to the extent that nations adhere to market-friendly policies that foster investor confidence and prosperity, and generate the budgetary revenues, export earnings, and capital inflows necessary to keep servicing debt obligations, their fiscal resilience will be enhanced. Sound liability-management practices can also make a major contribution to creditworthiness, because when the public debt exhibits a risk-averse currency, interest rate, and maturity structure, it should be able to withstand the temporary harm done by a natural disaster, or a sudden deterioration in financial market conditions or the terms of foreign trade. And last, but not least, prudential regulations, and sensible monetary and exchange rate policies, can make a major difference in terms of minimizing contingent liabilities arising out of the banking system, state-owned enterprises, and other risk pockets in the economy, thereby preventing a destabilizing jump in the public debt. These are the lessons from painful experience. **21.59**

Fiscal Policy in Real Time' (2009) 24(60) Econ Pol'y 753; Jeffrey Frankel and Jesse Schreger, 'Over-Optimistic Official Forecasts and Fiscal Rules in the Eurozone' (2013) 149(2) Review of World Economics 247; Timothy C. Irwin, *Accounting Devices and Fiscal Illusions*, IMF Staff Discussion Note No. SDN/12/02 (March 2012), available online at <http://www.imf.org/external/pubs/ft/sdn/2012/sdn1202.pdf>; Jürgen von Hagen and Guntram B. Wolff, 'What Do Deficits Tell Us about Debt? Empirical Evidence on Creative Accounting with Fiscal Rules in the EU' (2006) 30(12) J Bank Fin 3259.

Part V

PROPOSALS TO REFORM SOVEREIGN DEBT SYSTEMS

22. **Statutory Sovereign Debt Resolution Mechanisms** 333
Rodrigo Olivares-Caminal

23. **Debt Restructuring and Economic Recovery** 359
Sean Hagan

24. **Corporate Bankruptcy Law and State Insolvencies** 387
Philip R. Wood QC (Hon)

25. **European Collective Action Clauses** 399
David Billington

26. **Eurozone Financial Rescue and Stabilization Measures, and their Legal Foundations** 417
Andrew Yianni and Nikita Aggarwal

27. **UNCTAD Principles on Responsible Sovereign Financing** 443
Juan Pablo Bohoslavsky and Yuefen Li

28. **Sovereign Debt in the Light of Eternity** 463
Lee C. Buchheit

22

STATUTORY SOVEREIGN DEBT RESOLUTION MECHANISMS

Rodrigo Olivares-Caminal[1]

> [A] country does not go bankrupt.
>
> (Walter B. Wriston, 1982)[2]

> It must, on principle, still be possible for a State to go bankrupt.
>
> (Wolfgang Schäuble, 2010)[3]

1. Introduction

22.01 As a result of the use of bonds to finance sovereign deficits, capital markets have become more efficient and diversified. However, there are a number of serious downsides when a country faces unsustainable debt, including that creditors become increasingly numerous, anonymous, and difficult to coordinate, and a variety of debt instruments subject to different governing laws, with no single statutory legal framework applicable, coexist (encouraging creditors in a distress scenario to hold out or sue for better terms).[4]

22.02 While there is widespread agreement for a revamped sovereign debt restructuring process, there is also disagreement over what the actual process should be.[5] So far, in the sovereign debt restructuring episodes, the major issue of concern has been the issue of holdout creditors. However, a recent study suggests that the problem of holdouts has been overestimated, since of the thirty-four sovereign bond exchanges since 1997, only two have been affected by holdout creditors.[6]

---

[1] All opinions expressed in the chapter are personal and should not be attributed to any institution with which the author is, or has been, affiliated.

[2] Walter B. Wriston (former chairman of Citibank, who was regarded as the single most influential commercial banker of his time), 'Banking against Disaster', *New York Times*, 14 September 1982.

[3] Wolfgang Schäuble (Germany's Minister of Finance), 'Why Europe's Monetary Union Faces its Biggest Crisis', *Financial Times*, 11 March 2010.

[4] *See* International Monetary Fund, *Proposals for a Sovereign Debt Restructuring Mechanism (SDRM)*, IMF Factsheet (January 2003), available online at <http://www.imf.org/external/np/exr/facts/sdrm.htm>.

[5] Randall Dodd, 'Sovereign Debt Restructuring' (2002) 9(1–4) Financier 1, available online at <http://www.financialpolicy.org/dscsovdebt.pdf>.

[6] Elena Duggar, Richard Cantor, and Bar Oosterveld, *The Role of Holdouts Creditors and CACs in Sovereign Debt Restructuring*, Moody's Investors Service Sovereign Default Series (10 April 2013), available online at <http://www.moodys.com/research/Sovereign-Defaults-Series-The-Role-of-Holdout-Creditors-and-CACs--PBC_150162>.

22.03 The following sections examine in further detail the statutory proposal of the International Monetary Fund (IMF)—that is, the Sovereign Debt Restructuring Mechanism (SDRM). This analysis will be followed by consideration of the statutory developments in the European Union (EU) as result of the sovereign debt crisis in Greece and other peripheral countries. Finally, some concluding remarks will be made, including some possible considerations for reform.

2. The Sovereign Debt Restructuring Mechanism (SDRM)

22.04 Recently, the debate on reform of the international financial architecture has been centred on how to ensure orderly sovereign debt restructuring.[7] In this sense, the IMF believes that incentives are lacking to help countries with unsustainable debt to resolve the problem promptly and in an orderly fashion.[8] This drives up the cost of default—that is, it is harmful to the country, its citizens, and the international community.[9]

22.05 Therefore, since domestic bankruptcy law serves as a useful model in the distressed/insolvency context, the IMF started considering a sovereign debt restructuring mechanism in 2001.

22.06 It was Sachs[10] who reignited the discussion in 1995 with an influential paper on international bankruptcy procedures for sovereigns.[11] Moreover, Schwarcz,[12] in 2000, elaborated on the idea and proposed a convention to avoid reliance on the IMF.

22.07 The IMF proposed a 'twin-track' mechanism known as the SDRM, which was based on two complementary approaches, and aimed to create a more orderly and predictable process for sovereign debt restructuring. First, a contractual approach to debt restructuring would be facilitated by the enhanced use of certain contractual provisions in sovereign debt

---

[7] *See* IMF (n. 4).

[8] Anne Krueger, 'International Financial Architecture for 2002: New Approach to Sovereign Debt Restructuring', Speech at the National Economists' Club Annual Members' Dinner, 26 November 2001, available online at <http://www.imf.org/external/np/speeches/2001/112601.htm>.

[9] IMF (n. 4), 7.

[10] *See* Jeffrey Sachs, 'Do We Need an International Lender of Last Resort?', Frank D. Graham Lecture, Princeton University, 20 April 1995, available online at <http://academiccommons.columbia.edu/catalog/ac:124041>:

> There is considerable confusion as to how the principles of bankruptcy should translate to the case of sovereign borrowers, ie governments. In the international context there is little formal law covering state insolvency, and certainly no bankruptcy code. Therefore, the question is mostly a normative one—how should international practice, and specifically IMF practice, be arranged in view of the lessons of bankruptcy law.

[11] According to Kenneth Rogoff and Jeromin Zettelmeyer, *Early Ideas on Sovereign Bankruptcy Reorganization: A Survey*, IMF Working Paper No. WP 02/57 (March 2002), available online at <http://www.imf.org/external/pubs/ft/wp/2002/wp0257.pdf>, the idea of a bankruptcy procedure for sovereigns can be traced back at least to 1776, when Adam Smith stated, in his *An Inquiry into the Nature and Causes of the Wealth of the Nations*:

> When it becomes necessary for a State to declare itself bankrupt, in the same manner as when it becomes necessary for an individual to do so, a fair, open and avowed bankruptcy is always the measure which is both least dishonorable to the debtor, and least harmful for the creditor.

[12] Steven L. Schwarcz, 'Sovereign Debt Restructuring: A Bankruptcy Reorganization Approach' (2000) 85 Cornell L Rev 956.

contracts.[13] Second, the establishment of a universal statutory framework would create a legal framework for collective decisions by debtors and a supermajority of its creditors.[14] As the IMF explained, the central objective is to put countries and their creditors in a better position to restructure unsustainable sovereign debt in an orderly and timely manner.[15] Although a country could access the SDRM after default, ideally the SDRM would encourage a country with unsustainable debt and its creditors to restructure before default becomes the only option.[16] It is worth stressing that the SDRM would have applied only to sovereign debt governed by foreign law or debt subject to the jurisdiction of foreign courts.[17]

According to the IMF, the objectives of the SDRM are:[18] **22.08**

- to put countries and their creditors in a better position to restructure unsustainable sovereign debts in an orderly and timely manner;
- to benefit citizens of the countries whose debts are being restructured because the period of economic dislocation is reduced;
- to benefit creditors since their asset values are preserved; and
- to increase the efficiency and stability of the global financial system by creating a more predictable environment for workouts in cases of unsustainable debt burdens.

A formal SDRM would need to be built on the following four key objectives.[19] **22.09**

- *Deterring disruptive litigation*—That is, it would aim to prevent creditors from obtaining relief through national courts, for example by granting a legal stay or a standstill to avoid holdouts, rogue creditors, freeriders, and distress investors from disrupting negotiations that could lead to a restructuring agreement.
- *Protecting creditor interests*—It would provide a guarantee that the debtor country would act responsibly during the course of any standstill.
- *Priority financing*—It would encourage private lenders to provide fresh money during the restructuring procedure to facilitate ongoing economic activity.
- *Majority restructuring*—Restructuring agreements reached by the parties should be binding to all of them, and not only to the majority who have agreed to them.

In order to achieve these objectives, the IMF proposed an SDRM with the following features: **22.10**

- supermajority voting;[20]
- a mechanism that would deter disruptive litigation;[21]

---

[13] IMF, *IMF Board Discusses Possible Features of a Sovereign Debt Restructuring Mechanism*, IMF Public Information Notice (PIN) No. 03/06 (7 January 2003), available online at <http://www.imf.org/external/np/sec/pn/2003/pn0306.htm>.

[14] IMF (n. 13).

[15] IMF (n. 4), A.2.

[16] IMF (n. 4), 8.

[17] *See* International Law Association (ILA), *Report of the International Monetary Law Committee* (Berlin 2004), available online at <http://www.ila-hq.org/en/committees/index.cfm/cid/22>, 6.

[18] IMF (n. 4).

[19] Krueger (n. 8).

[20] Supermajority voting will resolve the new terms of the restructuring agreement and prevent minority creditors from blocking an agreement or enforcing the terms of the original debt contracts: *see* IMF (n. 4).

[21] In the 2003 version of the SDRM, the IMF replaced the original idea of an automatic stay by a mechanism to deter disruptive litigation by creditors during the debt restructuring negotiations. This notwithstanding, no further specification has been made: *see* IMF (n. 4).

- good faith negotiations;[22]
- transparency requirements;[23]
- grant of seniority to new lenders;[24] and
- the establishment of a dispute resolution forum.[25]

22.11 The SDRM was designed to help only sovereign states whose debts were unsustainable. The process would allow states to reorganize their finances and activities to restore debt payments. The SDRM would allow creditors to decide collectively on a restructuring, although ultimately a debtor cannot use the SDRM without the consent of a supermajority of its creditors.[26]

22.12 In April 2002, the International Monetary and Financial Committee (IMFC) endorsed the work performed in the elaboration of the SDRM and encouraged the IMF to continue to examine the legal, institutional, and procedural aspects of two approaches, which could be complementary and self-reinforcing:

- a statutory approach, which would enable a sovereign debtor and a supermajority of its creditors to reach an agreement binding all creditors; and
- an approach, based on contract, which would incorporate comprehensive restructuring clauses in debt instruments.[27]

22.13 The features of the SDRM have changed since it was first proposed. Table 22.1[28] summarizes the evolution of the main characteristics of the proposals made between 2001 and 2003. It is important to note that the sovereign debt restructuring regime proposed by the IMF would not be substantially different from a contractual approach, because it would be 'creditor-centred' rather than 'IMF-centred'.[29]

A. Inclusion of other creditors, the preferred status of the Fund, and the special treatment of heavily indebted poor countries (HIPCs)

22.14 Other relevant matters included under the umbrella of the SDRM involve the treatment to be given to other debt—that is, domestic debt, Paris Club debt, and IMF and other official sector debt.

---

[22] *See* IMF (n. 4). Creditors would have assurance that the debtor will negotiate in good faith and will pursue policies—most likely designed in conjunction with financial support from the IMF—that will help to protect the value of creditor claims and limit dislocations in the economy.

[23] *See* IMF (n. 4). The SDRM would establish transparency requirements that would, among other things, enable creditors to have information about how other creditors are being treated during the restructuring process.

[24] *See* IMF (n. 4). Creditors could agree to give seniority and protection from restructuring to fresh private lending, in order to facilitate ongoing economic activity through the continued provision of trade and other types of credit.

[25] *See* IMF (n. 4). A dispute resolution forum would be established to resolve disputes that may arise during the voting process or when claims are being verified.

[26] *See* IMF (n. 4), qus D.3 and D.4.

[27] *See* IMF, 'Communiqué of the International Monetary and Financial Committee of the Board of Governors of the International Monetary Fund', Press Release No. 02/22, 20 April 2002, available online at <http://www.imf.org/external/np/sec/pr/2002/pr0222.htm>.

[28] *See* Marcus Miller, *Sovereign Debt Restructuring: New Articles, New Contracts–or No Change?*, International Economic Policy Briefs No. PB02-3 (April 2002), available online at <http://www.iie.com/publications/pb/pb02-3.pdf>.

[29] *See* Nouriel Roubini, *Private Sector Involvement in Crisis Resolution and Mechanisms for Dealing with Sovereign Debt Problems*, Paper prepared for the Bank of England Conference on the Role of the Official Sector and Private Sector in Resolving International Financial Crises, London, 23–24 July 2002.

Table 22.1 Key features of SDRM[1]

Mechanism	Legal stay	Financing reorganization	Restructuring debt	Restraining holdouts
SDRM1[2]	Capital controls + Automatic stay	Preferred creditors + Limited IMF lending	Negotiations supervised by IMF + IMF programme	Supermajority voting + Arbitration?
SDRM2[3]	Payments standstill + Short stay, which may be renewed upon the decision of a super-majority vote of creditors	Preferred creditor status for new money	Negotiations supervised by neutral agency + IMF programme	Supermajority voting across all classes
SDRM – 3[4]	Stay upon the decision of a supermajority vote of creditors	Preferred creditor status for new money upon the decision of a supermajority vote of creditors	Negotiations with creditors + IMF programme	Supermajority voting across all classes

Sources: [1] SDRM1 and SDRM2 are from a table included in Marcus Miller, *Sovereign Debt Restructuring: New Articles, New Contracts—or No Change?*, International Economic Policy Briefs No. PB02-3 (April 2002), available online at <http://www.iie.com/publications/pb/pb02-3.pdf>; [2] Anne Krueger, 'International Financial Architecture for 2002: New Approach to Sovereign Debt Restructuring', Speech at the National Economists' Club Annual Members' Dinner, 26 November 2001, available online at <http://www.imf.org/external/np/speeches/2001/112601.htm>; [3] Anne Krueger, 'New Approaches to Sovereign Debt Restructuring: An Update on Our Thinking', Institute for International Economics Conference on Sovereign Debt Workouts: Hopes and Hazards, Washington DC, 1 April 2002, available online at <http://www.imf.org/external/np/speeches/2002/040102.htm>; [4] IMF, *Proposals for a Sovereign Debt Restructuring Mechanism (SDRM)*, IMF Factsheet (January 2003), available online at <http://www.imf.org/external/np/exr/facts/sdrm.htm>.

According to the IMF, the inclusion of domestic debt in the SDRM should be considered on a case-by-case basis, since foreign or non-resident investors may be willing to provide substantial debt reduction only if they know that domestic creditors are shouldering a fair share of the burden too.[30] **22.15**

With regard to Paris Club debt, there has been some inclination by the IMF to exclude these claims from the formal framework of the SDRM. This notwithstanding, it should be borne in mind that Paris Club minutes of agreements usually include a 'comparability of treatment provision'[31] and a 'pull-back clause'[32] to ensure that the debtor will not agree better terms **22.16**

[30] IMF (n. 4).

[31] For example, the 'comparability treatment provision' included in Pakistan's agreed minutes with the Paris Club on 30 January 1999 reads as follows:

> In order to secure comparable treatment of its debt due to all its external public or private creditors, the Government of the Islamic Republic of Pakistan commits itself to seek from . . . bond holders the reorganization of bonds. This reorganization will be done on terms comparable to those set forth in the present Agreed Minute. The Government of the Islamic Republic of Pakistan commits itself not to accord any category of creditors a treatment more favourable than that accorded to the Participating Creditor Countries.

[32] For example, the 'pullback clause' included in Pakistan's agreed minutes with the Paris Club on 30 January 1999 reads as follows:

> The participating Creditor Countries will review the implementation of the conditions stated . . . for the comparability of treatment between all external creditors; if the Participating Creditor Countries determine that these conditions are not substantially fulfilled, they will declare the provisions set forth [in the present agreed minutes] null and void.

with its private creditors, and that if it does, then it is entitled to exit the agreement reached with the debtor.

22.17 As widely known, the 'lender of last resort' (LOLR) role of the central bank remains the major rationale for most central banks around the world, both in developed and developing countries.[33] The LOLR role is to provide credit in emergency situations. The IMF has acted as *international* lender of last resort (ILOLR) towards its member states during economic and/or financial crises, for example during the financial assistance packages interventions in Mexico (1994), Russia (1994), and Asia (1997), or more recently taking part in the assistance provided to Cyprus, Greece, Ireland and Portugal in the context of the European Union.

22.18 Since the IMF is not a commercial organization seeking profitable lending opportunities and often lends at a time when other creditors are reluctant to do so—and at interest rates that are below those that would be charged at that juncture by the private sector[34] —preferred creditor status (PCS) should be assigned to this lending. The IMF has clearly explained that the ILOLR role benefits not only Fund members, but also official and private creditors alike, by allowing the Fund to assist member countries in regaining a sustainable financial path and helping to promote orderly resolutions to debt problems, when necessary.[35] As noted by Lastra, the IMF plays different roles by wearing different 'hats'. Among these are that of an 'honest broker' or arbiter between creditors and debtors, that of primary lender by means of providing financial assistance to countries experiencing balance-of-payment needs, as preferred creditor with an interest at stake, as ILOLR, as crisis manager, and as standard setter.[36] Combining the IMF claims with commercial claims in a workout would fundamentally undermine the Fund's capacity to play those vital roles in future.[37]

22.19 These reasons are the rationale for the de facto priority claimed by and implicitly assigned to the IMF, World Bank, and other official sector debt.[38] A recent New York court decision has acknowledged and reconfirmed the IMF's super-priority.[39] However, Bolton and Skeel Jr contend that this de facto priority is partly an illusion, because the IMF has generally agreed to roll its loans over when the sovereign is unable or unwilling to pay.[40]

22.20 The possibility of obtaining debtor-in-possession (DIP) financing is a feasible alternative to financing restructurings in replacement of the ILOLR. It is an alternative in terms of privatizing the source of money—that is, shifting the source of funds from international organizations

[33] *See* Rosa M. Lastra, *Legal Foundations of International Monetary Law* (Oxford: Oxford University Press, 2006), 491–8. *See* also Rosa M. Lastra, 'Lender of Last Resort, an International Perspective' (1999) 48(2) Int'l Com L Quarterly 340.

[34] IMF (n. 4).

[35] IMF, *Financial Risk in the Fund and the Level of Precautionary Balances* (February 2004), available online at <http://www.imf.org/external/np/tre/risk/2004/020304.pdf>.

[36] Lastra, *Legal Foundations* (n. 33), 499.

[37] IMF (n. 4).

[38] *See* Nouriel Roubini and Brad Setser, *The Reform of the Sovereign Debt Restructuring Process: Problems, Proposed Solutions and the Argentine Episode*, Paper prepared for the Institute for International Economics/ Institut Francais des Relations Internationales Conference on Improving the Sovereign Debt Restructuring Process, Paris, 9 March 2003, 4; Lastra, *Legal Foundations* (n. 33), 486; Schwarcz (n. 12); Steven L. Schwarcz, 'Idiot's Guide to Sovereign Debt Restructuring' (2004) 53 Emory LJ 1189; IMF (n. 4); IMF (n. 35).

[39] *See NML Capital, Ltd, v. Republic of Argentina*, Second Circuit Court of Appeals, 12-105(L), (23 August 2013).

[40] Patrick Bolton and David Skeel Jr, 'Redesigning the International Lender of Last Resort' (2005) 6 Chi J Int'l L 177.

to private lenders. It should be noted as an example that, in 1992, Macy's (a US department store) obtained new working capital in the form of a US$600 million loan through DIP financing only three weeks after filing its petition under Chapter 11 of the US Bankruptcy Code, while Russia had to wait more than a year to obtain any financing.[41] Shifting the source of funding from the ILOLR to the capital markets will foster intercreditor coordination and will reduce moral hazard. This change of source of credit for the sovereign will not diminish current creditors' status, since the IMF, World Bank, or other official sector debt already has de facto priority over non-secured creditors. It is worth stressing, however, that the IMF was not proposing an insolvency mechanism for countries because '[a] country cannot go bankrupt';[42] rather, the IMF was promoting a mechanism to facilitate debt workout negotiations that differed from insolvency laws because it did not include an automatic stay on the enforcement of creditors' rights, there is no ultimate sanction of liquidation, policies are not supervised by a bankruptcy court, and creditors cannot insist on a change in management.[43]

Finally, the debt problems of low-income countries are being dealt with under the Highly Indebted Poor Countries (HIPCs) Initiative.[44] Debt relief under the Initiative was launched jointly by the IMF and the World Bank in 1996.[45] In 1997, this initiative was linked to the Poverty Reduction and Growth Facility (PRGF) and a trust administered by the IMF was set up—that is, the HIPC–PRGF Trust.[46] In 1999, the international community recognized the need for a concerted effort to deal with the external debt problem of certain countries (mostly African) and revamped the HIPCs Initiative to provide faster and deeper debt relief to allow HIPCs to reach a level of sustainability.[47] In late 2005, the IMF's Executive Board approved the Multilateral Debt Relief Initiative (MDRI) involving a total debt relief to HIPCs and those countries with per capita income below US$380 and outstanding debt to the IMF at end-2004.[48] On the same date, the Exogenous Shocks Facility (ESF) was also **22.21**

---

41 *See* Jeffrey D. Sachs, 'IMF, Reform Thyself', *Wall Street Journal*, 21 July 1994.

42 *See* Lex Rieffel, *Restructuring Sovereign Debt: The Case for Ad Hoc Machinery* (Washington DC: Brookings Institution Press, 2003), 289. *See* also Wriston (n. 2), in which the phrase was coined.

43 IMF (n. 4).

44 According to the IMF's glossary of selected financial terms, the HIPCs Initiative was adopted in 1996 and provides exceptional assistance to eligible countries to reduce their external debt burdens to sustainable levels, thereby enabling them to service their external debt without the need for further debt relief and without compromising growth. It involves multilateral, Paris Club, and other official and bilateral creditors. To be eligible for the Initiative, countries must: (i) have established a strong track record of performance under programmes supported by the IMF's Poverty Reduction and Growth Facility (PRGF) and the International Development Association (IDA); (ii) be IDA-only and PRGF-eligible; (iii) face an unsustainable debt burden; and (iv) have developed a Poverty Reduction Strategy Paper (PRSP). In 2005, the HIPC Initiative was supplemented by the Multilateral Debt Relief Initiative (MDRI), which allows for 100 per cent relief on eligible debts of countries completing the HIPC Initiative process. *See* <http://www.imf.org>.

45 *See* IMF, Debt Relief under the Heavily Indebted Poor Countries (HIPC) Initiative', IMF Factsheet (April 2013), available online at <http://www.imf.org/external/np/exr/facts/hipc.htm>.

46 Instrument to establish—under Article V(2)(b)—the Poverty Reduction and Growth Facility Trust, Decision No. 8759—(87/176) ESAF, 18 December 1987, as amended.

47 The HIPCs include: Afghanistan; Benin; Bolivia; Burkina Faso; Burundi; Cameroon; Central African Republic; Chad; Comoros; Côte d'Ivoire; Democratic Republic of the Congo; Eritrea; Ethiopia; Ghana; Guinea; Guinea-Bissau; Guyana; Haiti; Honduras; Liberia; Madagascar; Malawi; Mali; Mauritania; Mozambique; Nicaragua; Niger; Republic of Congo; Rwanda; São Tomé and Príncipe; Senegal; Sierra Leone; Somalia; Sudan; Tanzania; The Gambia; Togo; Uganda; and Zambia.

48 *See* IMF, *IMF Executive Board Agrees on Implementation Modalities for the Multilateral Debt Relief Initiative*, Public Information Notice (PIN) No. 05/164 (8 December 2005), available online at <http://www.imf.org/external/np/sec/pn/2005/pn05164.htm>; IMF, *The Multilateral Debt Relief Initiative (MDRI)*, IMF Factsheet (30 September 2012), available online at <http://www.imf.org/external/np/exr/facts/mdri.htm>.

approved as a part of the PRGF Trust to support HIPCs in the event of economic shocks caused by rising oil prices, natural disasters, contagion of conflicts or crisis in neighbouring countries, etc.

22.22 Since the SDRM deals with issues concerning sovereign debt to private sector creditors, it is more relevant to those countries that have borrowed on international capital markets, which is usually not the case with HIPCs.[49]

B. The shortcomings and criticisms of the SDRM

22.23 Under the SDRM, a supermajority of the creditors, regardless of the bond issue or loan obligations held, would be able to vote to accept new terms of payment under a restructuring agreement and minority creditors would be bound by the decision of the majority.[50] Consequently, a dispute resolution forum would be created for different purposes, such as verifying claims, guaranteeing the integrity of the voting process that led to the restructuring, and adjudicating disputes among creditors. Thus, to grant a legal stay binding on all parties, the mechanism must have the force of law universally.[51] Otherwise, creditors would be able to sue the debtor state in their own jurisdiction, in the jurisdiction governing the bond issuance, or in the jurisdiction of the debtor state. Obtaining a convention or a treaty binding all countries would be likely to take a very long time. In 2002, an IMF official stated that 'even with unanimous political support this approach could not be in place for at least two or three years'.[52] This IMF officer was not aware that, two years later and owing to the criticism and scepticism towards the SDRM, another IMF officer would expressly state that '[t]he debate on the Sovereign Debt Restructuring Mechanism [SDRM] has been shelved for the time being'.[53] Some critics believe the process could take decades 'and could end up being ineffective if too many nations refuse to join [in]'.[54]

22.24 The imposition of standstills and the use of majority voting in debt restructuring agreements binding on a dissenting minority require an amendment to the IMF's Articles of Agreement. In order to amend the Articles, two criteria have to be met:

(a) the amendment must be supported by a two-thirds majority of members; and
(b) the number of members voting for the amendment must hold at least an 85 per cent of the voting power.[55]

---

49 IMF (n. 4).

50 Barry Eichengreen and Ashoka Mody, *Is Aggregation a Problem for Sovereign Debt Restructuring?* (January 2003), available online at <http://emlab.berkeley.edu/users/eichengr/research/aeapapers&proceedings5jan15-03.pdf>.

51 Krueger (n. 8).

52 Krueger (n. 8).

53 IMF, 'Interview with Mark Allen: IMF Needs to Do Far More to Help Countries Learn from Each Other's Successes and Failures' (2004) 33 (7) IMF Survey 97, available online at <http://www.imf.org/external/pubs/ft/survey/2004/041204.pdf>. In the same sense, *see* international press articles (*The Economist*, 'Dealing with Default', 8 May 2003; Paul Blustein, '"Bankruptcy" System for Nations Fail to Draw Support', *Washington Post*, 2 April 2003; Alan Beattie, 'Brown Plan to Reform Global Financial System Meets Opposition', *Financial Times*, 14 April 2003).

54 Owen C. Pell, 'Nations Need Bankruptcy Process', *CBS MarketWatch*, 8 February 2002, available online at <http://www.whitecase.com/files/Publication/b5fcea31-cb8e-4845-8a4a-e05570d0c9d8/Presentation/PublicationAttachment/a4d59aef-4348-441b-8ba3-e3424b567f43/article_nations_need_bankruptcy_process_pell.pdf>.

55 *See* IMF Articles of Agreement, Art. XXVIII(a).

The US has a decisive vote in amending the IMF's Articles of Agreement since its quota[56] — that is, the country's economic position relative to other members—entitles it to 421,961 votes, which represent 16.75 per cent of the total members' voting rights. Therefore if the US does not vote in favour of the amendment, the second criteria cannot be attained. In order for the country to vote in favour of the amendment, the US Congress must approve the change. There is no indication, however, that there would be sufficient political support for the SDRM in the US Congress.[57]

Even if a binding treaty were adopted, the IMF would have serious decisions to make. Would the treaty be binding on pre-existing bonds—that is, would it have retroactive effect? A twofold analysis should be made: on one hand, it can be easily argued that the default and the need to use the SDRM occurred after the adoption of the treaty; on the other, the terms and conditions of the debt instruments giving rise to the rights of the bondholders were 'agreed' prior to the adoption of the treaty. Regarding the latter, it is worth mentioning that Article 28 of the 1969 Vienna Convention on the Law of Treaties sets the non-retroactivity of treaties as a general rule, unless otherwise established. Moreover, the Permanent Court of International Justice (PCIJ) has held, in *Phosphates in Morocco*,[58] that: **22.25**

> ... the only situations or facts falling under the compulsory jurisdiction [the main issue at stake in this case] are those which are subsequent to the ratification [of the treaty] and with regard to which the dispute arose, that is to say, those which must be considered as being the source of the dispute.

Under US law, a retroactive law is not unconstitutional unless it: (i) is in the nature of an *ex post facto* law; (ii) impairs the obligation of contracts; (iii) divests vested rights; or (iv) is constitutionally forbidden. A treaty instituting the SRDM with retroactive effects would definitively manifest (ii) and (iii), making it unconstitutional.

Notwithstanding these practical difficulties in implementing the SDRM, the IMF believes that, as the result of a greater predictability in the restructuring progress afforded by the adoption of the SDRM, an improvement in the functioning of international capital markets should be expected.[59] However, according to Heise,[60] while an SDRM would make the process of restructuring easier and faster, this may create an environment in which governments do not try their hardest to avoid defaults in the first place. As sovereign debt always has the potential to lead to 'opportunistic defaults' (unwillingness to pay as opposed to inability to **22.26**

[56] As of 25 March 2011, the US quota is SDR42,122.4 million. Special drawing rights (SDR) are an international reserve asset created by the IMF in 1969 as a supplement to existing reserve assets. *See* IMF, *IMF Quotas*, IMF Factsheet (March 2013), available online at <http://www.imf.org/external/np/exr/facts/quotas.htm>.

[57] Patrick Bolton, *Toward a Statutory Approach to Sovereign Debt Restructuring: Lessons form Corporate Bankruptcy Practice Around the World*, IMF Working Paper No. 03/13 (January 2003) , available online at <http://www.internationalmonetaryfund.com/external/pubs/ft/staffp/2002/00-00/pdf/bolton.pdf>, 27–8.

[58] *Phosphates in Morocco (Italy v. France)* 1938 PCIJ (Ser. A/B) No. 74 (14 June), 10–48.

[59] IMF (n. 4); IMF (n. 13).

[60] Michael Heise, 'An Improved International Finance Architecture Contributions from the Official and Private Sector', Speech at the Conference for New Sovereign Debt Restructuring Mechanisms: Challenges and Opportunities, Berlin, 21–22 February 2003, available online at <http://www.dse.de/ef/sdrm/heise.htm>.

pay),[61] a restructuring that is too 'easy' or 'orderly' (with little or no cost to the debtor) may not be socially efficient.[62] As Krueger[63] stated:

> [T]he Fund's involvement would be essential to the success of such a system [referring to the SDRM]. We are the most effective channel through which the international community can reach a judgment on the sustainability of a country's debt and of its economic policies, and whether it is doing what is necessary to get its balance of payments back into shape and to avoid future debt problems.

22.27 What would happen if a sovereign state were to obtain an agreement with its creditors through an SDRM and thereafter default again? It should be noted that although the SDRM is based on the US Chapter 11, there is no ultimate sanction of liquidation and creditors cannot insist on a change in management. A twice-defaulting country would demonstrate that the SDRM is not a panacea, and it would call into question the IMF's ability to provide supervision.

22.28 Further, establishing a quasi-judicial entity under the IMF would likely be a time-consuming and difficult process.[64] In addition, many countries fear that the introduction of statutory and even contractual mechanisms for debt restructuring would impair their access to international capital markets and discourage capital flows.[65]

22.29 Thus it is apparent that the SDRM has some shortcomings and many enemies. Its enemies include the private financial sector—especially representatives of different actors in the international bond market—and developing countries, which feel no ownership of the proposal and express even less enthusiasm for it. In addition, it is unclear where developed countries stand or whether they stand together.[66] The question, then, is whether an institutional change in the international financial system providing for orderly sovereign debt restructuring is needed.[67]

22.30 Despite its shortcomings, the SDRM does provide some benefits. It is innovative in bringing debtors and bondholders together whether or not bonds contain collective action clauses (CACs). It is also innovative because it secures greater transparency and provides a mechanism for dispute resolution.[68] The SDRM goes further than the CAC restructuring approach by not requiring separate decisions from the holders of individual bond series or

61 *See* Arturo Porzecanski, 'When Bad Things Happen to Good Sovereign Debt Contracts: The Case of Ecuador' (2010) 73 Duke L & Contemp Probs 251; Yuefen Li, Rodrigo Olivares-Caminal, and Ugo Panizza, 'Avoiding Avoidable Debt Crises: Lessons from Recent Defaults', in Carlos A. Primo-Braga and Gallina A. Vincelette (eds) *Sovereign Debt and the Financial Crisis: Will This Time be Different?* (Washington, DC: World Bank, 2010), 252; Lee C. Buchheit and Mitu Gulati, 'The Coroner's Inquest' (2009) 29(9) Int'l Fin L Rev 22.

62 *See* Roubini (n. 29).

63 Krueger (n. 8).

64 Mark Jewett, 'Legal Approaches and Procedures', Speech at the Conference for New Sovereign Debt Restructuring Mechanisms: Challenges and Opportunities, Berlin, 21–22 February 2003, available online at <http://www.dse.de/ef/sdrm/jewett.htm>.

65 Yilmaz Akyüz, 'Some Reflections on SDRM', Speech at the Conference for New Sovereign Debt Restructuring Mechanisms: Challenges and Opportunities, Berlin, 21–22 February 2003, available online at <http://www.dse.de/ef/sdrm/akyüz.htm>.

66 *See* Barry Herman, 'The International Community Should Continue Work on a Mechanism for Restructuring Sovereign Debt', Speech at the Conference for New Sovereign Debt Restructuring Mechanisms: Challenges and Opportunities, Berlin, 21–22 February 2003, available online at <http://www.inwent.org/ef-texte/sdrm/herman.htm>.

67 Roubini (n. 29).

68 Akyüz (n. 65)

other creditors and allowing a single vote to restructure multiple debt instruments. The vote is an aggregate of the votes of the creditors holding participating debt instruments. Thus it permits the debtor and its creditors to act as if all of the debt (in bonds and other debt instruments) were governed by a single CAC.[69] This aggregation mechanism has been incorporated in the new debt instruments issued in Uruguay's 2003 debt reprofiling. Some other debt instruments issued after Uruguay's incorporation also included this feature. In particular, the standard CAC adopted by euro area member states includes this feature. Therefore if the SDRM is not applicable retrospectively, the wide spread of CACs and the possibility of series aggregation can replicate these advantages.

Although the adoption of the SDRM could be considered a positive step in debt restructuring, the effects of the SDRM could also be achieved through the broader use of CACs in a decentralized market-oriented approach, as proposed by Taylor ('using the tools we already have'),[70] or perhaps using them more creatively and more confidently to promote orderly workouts, as proposed by Buchheit and Gulati.[71] When CACs are not available, creative contractual sweeteners are required to enhance the degree of participation in the exchange offer. **22.31**

According to Cohen and Portes,[72] the SDRM proposal was shelved specifically because it would have required an amendment to the IMF's Articles of Agreement. However, Lastra contends that a more modest alternative could be a 'creative' interpretation of Article VIII(2)(b) as a means of imposing a stay on creditors.[73] This position is also supported by Francotte[74] and Gianvitti.[75] The latter argues that an interpretation under Article XXIX can be reached to create uniformity of interpretation within the courts of IMF members.[76] **22.32**

This notwithstanding, the SDRM remains a live issue, since the IMF has not given up on it even though its development has been halted.[77] Yet, as Sgard stated,[78] the fact that the SDRM proposal was eventually shelved does not imply that it has lost any political or historical significance, since it indeed highlights the range of possible solutions that dominant states are ready to consider. **22.33**

Although a market-oriented approach has worked in the restructuring cases of, among others, Pakistan, Ukraine, Ecuador, Argentina, Uruguay, and Belize, the view of the IMF is **22.34**

---

69 IMF (n. 4).

70 John B. Taylor, 'Sovereign Debt Restructuring: A U.S. Perspective', Remarks at the Conference 'Sovereign Debt Workouts: Hopes and Hazards?' before the Institute for International Economics, Washington, DC, 2 April 2002, available online at <http://www.iie.com/publications/papers/paper.cfm?ResearchID=455>.

71 Lee C. Buchheit and G. Mitu Gulati, 'Sovereign Bonds and the Collective Will' (2002) 51(4) Emory LJ 4.

72 Daniel Cohen and Richard Portes, 'Dealing with Destabilizing "Market Discipline"', Paper prepared for the Bank for International Settlements/Federal Reserve Bank of ChicagoConference on 'Market Discipline: The Evidence across Countries and Industries', Chicago, IL, 30 October–1 November 2003, available online at <http://faculty.london.edu/rportes/research/FRBC-BIS220104.pdf>, 5.

73 Lastra, *Legal Foundations* (n. 33), 481.

74 *See* Pierre Francotte, 'The Fund Agreement in the Courts', in Robert Effros (ed.) *Current Legal Issues Affecting Central Banks, Vol. 1* (Washington DC: IMF, 1992), 14.

75 *See* François Gianvitti, 'The Reform of the International Monetary Fund', in Rosa M. Lastra (ed.) *The Reform of the International Financial Architecture* (London: Kluwer Law, 2001), 102.

76 *See* Gianvitti (n. 75), 102.

77 Ross P. Buckley, *Deficiencies in the International Financial System and Their Impact on the Poor*, Paper prepared for the Foundation for Development Cooperation.

78 Jérôme Sgard, 'The Renegotiation of Sovereign Debts and the Future of Financial Multilateralism', Paper presented at the Fifth Pan-European Conference of the Standing Group on International Relations, The Hague, 9–11 September 2004.

that the costs at present are too high and too disruptive to the international community as a whole.[79] As previously discussed, Buchheit and Gulati[80] contend that the existing collective decision-making provisions in sovereign bonds can, if used more confidently and creatively, replicate certain features of domestic corporate bankruptcy—that is, automatic stays, cram-downs, and, DIP financing—but not its coordination feature. Coordination among different series of bonds was resolved in Uruguay's debt reprofiling by the aggregation mechanism in which amendments to any terms (including payment terms) was incorporated into one or more series of bonds simultaneously.[81] Aggregation is becoming a standard to follow when incorporating CACs in debt instruments. More importantly, the proposed SDRM excludes the IMF, as well as other official sector debts, and is inclined to exclude the Paris Club and domestic creditors. An approximately similar degree of coordination to the SDRM can be achieved by the use of CACs.[82]

22.35 Probably the most difficult aspect of the SDRM is not a technical one, but the political one. The next section analyses what has been done in the EU to address the euro area sovereign debt crisis.

3. The European Stability Mechanism: An Institution Designed to Avert Financial Crises

22.36 The severe international financial crisis and economic downturn that was sparked by problems in the US subprime mortgage market and compounded by the failure of Lehman Brothers led to a widening in budget deficits and ratios of higher public debt to gross domestic product (GDP) in many countries. This reflected not only lower public sector revenues and increased expenditures to shore up aggregate demand, but also led to a need to lend support to troubled financial institutions and to create measures to check the risk of financial panic.

22.37 As the financial and economic situation worsened, investors became increasingly risk-adverse and risk evaluation became very difficult. In a number of countries, the turmoil in the banking sector seems to have been tempered only by large infusions of government financial intervention that, in turn, aggravated the sovereign debt picture. For some European countries, the deterioration in borrowing conditions seemed to go beyond what underlying economic fundamentals might have called for in more normal times.

22.38 The euro area member states (EAMSs) are of particular interest, because they have been at the epicentre of the EU sovereign debt crisis and there have been important spillover effects from one EAMS to another, to the point at which the stability of the euro area as a whole has been called into question. Greece, Ireland, Portugal, Spain (for the banking sector), and Cyprus, for example, have had to seek financial assistance from the EU, other EAMSs, the IMF, the European Central Bank (ECB), and non-EAMSs countries in attempts to rectify public sector finances and to reduce their debt burden in an orderly manner.

---

[79] IMF (n. 4).

[80] *See* n. 71.

[81] In order to approve the amendment, a double majority is required: 85 per cent of the aggregate principal amount of all affected series; and 66⅔ per cent of each specific series.

[82] *See*, among others, Eichengreen and Mody (n. 50).

The introduction of the euro was accompanied by increased intra-eurozone financial interdependence and, as it has turned out, some financial fragility and risks that have become apparent only under crisis conditions. Thus a euro-area-specific issue seems to have emerged as a component of the broader evolving international state of affairs. 22.39

The EU institutional reaction to recent European financial distress scenarios in the sovereign context is addressed in the following paragraphs. In particular, it will focus on providing a critical analysis of the treaty that created the European Stability Mechanism (ESM), an intergovernmental organization under international public law, and some suggestions regarding the challenges going forward. 22.40

A. Initial responses

In early May 2010, Greece and the European Commission (acting on behalf of the EAMSs) entered into a memorandum of understanding (MOU) for a programme to correct fiscal and external imbalances, and to restore confidence.[83] The programme's financing requirements would be covered by the EAMSs and the IMF to facilitate Greece's reaccess to capital markets. The estimated 'public financing gap' for the entire length of the programme was €110 billion,[84] to be covered by means of an intergovernmental framework involving pooled matching bilateral loans provided by the EAMSs in the amount of €80 billion,[85] and an IMF Standby Arrangement in the amount of €30 billion.[86] Greece would draw on these resources throughout the programme period on an eight-to-three ratio for each disbursement.[87] The coordination and management procedures were set out in an intercreditor agreement.[88] 22.41

Following the execution of these agreements, the Economic and Financial Affairs Council (Ecofin)[89] met to address the Greek situation, which had broader eurozone implications. 22.42

[83] *See* section 5 of the MOU between the European Commission, acting on behalf of the EAMS and the Hellenic Republic, dated 3 May 2010 (unpublished, on file with the author).

[84] *See* section 23 of the MOU (n. 83).

[85] The Loan Facility Agreement was entered into on 8 May 2010 by the Kingdom of Belgium, Ireland, Kingdom of Spain, French Republic, Italian Republic, Republic of Cyprus, Grand Duchy of Luxembourg, Republic of Malta, Kingdom of the Netherlands, Republic of Austria, Portuguese Republic, Republic of Slovenia, Slovak Republic, Republic of Finland and the bank KfW (acting on behalf of the Federal Republic of Germany), as lenders, and the Hellenic Republic as borrower (and the bank of Greece as the agent of the borrower). The lenders, in all of their functions, rights, and obligations under the Loan Facility Agreement, act through and are represented by the EC, and have agreed to act in a coordinated manner and to channel communications (to the EC) through the Euro Working Group Chairman. The release of subsequent loans is conditioned upon the EAMS (except Greece) deciding favourably, after consultation with the ECB on the basis of the findings of verification by the EC, that the implementation of the economic policy of Greece accords with the adjustment programme or any other conditions laid down in the Council Decision on the basis of Articles 126(9) (EU Council Recommendations in re Budget Deficits) and 136 (Specific Provisions for Member States whose Currency is the Euro) TFEU and the MOU.

[86] Greece requested a Standby Arrangement in an amount equivalent to SDR26,432.9 million (€30 billion) for a period from 9 May 2010 to 8 May 2013, which was approved on 9 May 2010.

[87] *See* n. 83. The eight-to-three ratio has to do with the contribution ratio of the programme to which the EAMSs contributed €80 billion and the IMF, €30 billion.

[88] The intercreditor agreement was entered into on 8 May 2010 between the Kingdom of Belgium, Federal Republic of Germany, Ireland, Kingdom of Spain, French Republic, Italian Republic, Republic of Cyprus, Grand Duchy of Luxembourg, Republic of Malta, Kingdom of the Netherlands, Republic of Austria, Portuguese Republic, Republic of Slovenia, Slovak Republic, and Republic of Finland (unpublished, on file with the author).

[89] The Economic and Financial Affairs Council is commonly known as 'Ecofin' and is composed of the economics and finance ministers of the EU member states, as well as budget ministers when budgetary issues are discussed. It meets once a month and covers EU policy in areas such as economic policy coordination,

The Council decided to adopt a comprehensive package of measures directed at preserving financial stability in Europe.[90] These measures included the establishment of two additional sources of financial assistance to complement the initial ad hoc loan facility agreed with Greece, as follows.

- The European Financial Stabilization Mechanism (EFSM) is a mechanism based on Article 122(2) of the Treaty on the Functioning of the European Union (TFEU), which foresees financial support for member states in difficulty resulting from factors beyond their control.[91] It consists of an intergovernmental agreement to provide financial assistance of up to €60 billion, subject to terms and conditions similar to those mandated by the IMF in the context of a joint EU–IMF support package. The EFSM was to operate independently of the facility providing medium-term financial assistance for non-EAMS balance-of-payments disequilibria.
- The European Financial Stability Facility (EFSF) is a temporary credit-enhanced special purpose vehicle (SPV), with minimal capitalization, created to raise funds from capital markets on its investment grade rating, with the objective of providing financial assistance to distressed EAMSs at lower interest rates than otherwise would be available to them. On 26 October 2011, heads of state or government of the EAMSs agreed to enlarge the capacity of EFSF based on two approaches: partial credit enhancement to primary sovereign bonds issued by an EAMS; and the creation of one or more co-investment funds (CIFs) to allow the combination of public and private funding to enlarge the resources available to the EFSF's financial assistance instruments.[92] Financial support to EAMSs through the EFSF would be on comparable terms to the stability support loans that were advanced by EAMSs to Greece on an ad hoc basis prior to the establishment of the EFSF.

22.43 In October 2010 (after financial assistance had been provided to Greece, and while economic and financial conditions continued to deteriorate), the EU Council agreed on the need for a permanent crisis prevention mechanism to help to safeguard the financial stability of the euro area as a whole.[93] It was resolved that consultations should be undertaken towards a limited Treaty amendment for this purpose, but not for modifying the so-called 'no bailout' clause included in Article 125 TFEU.[94] In December 2010, the EU Council agreed that there was a need for EAMSs to establish a permanent stability mechanism—that

economic surveillance, monitoring of EU member states' budgetary policy and public finances, the euro (legal, practical, and international aspects), financial markets and capital movements, and economic relations with third countries. One of the most important tasks of Ecofin (jointly with the European Parliament) is to prepare and adopt the budget of the European Union on a yearly basis. *See* <http://www.consilium.europa.eu/policies/council-configurations/economic-and-financial-affairs?lang=en>.

[90] *See* Council of the European Union, 'Extraordinary Council Meeting: Economic and Financial Affairs, Brussels, 9–10 May 2010', Press Release No. 9596/10 (Presse 108) (May 2010), available online at <http://www.consilium.europa.eu/uedocs/cms_data/docs/pressdata/en/ecofin/114324.pdf>.

[91] As noted in Council Regulation (EU) No. 407/2010, these difficulties may be caused by a serious deterioration in the international economic and financial environment. *See* Council Regulation (EU) No. 407/2010 (OJ L 118/1).

[92] *See Euro Summit Statement*, Brussels, 26 October 2011, available online at <http://www.consilium.europa.eu/uedocs/cms_data/docs/pressdata/en/ec/125644.pdf>, 6, para. 19.

[93] European Council, *Conclusions of the European Council, 28–29 October 2010*, EUCO 25/1/10 (REV 1), CO EUR 18 (CONCL 4), 30 November 2010, available online at <http://www.consilium.europa.eu/uedocs/cms_data/docs/pressdata/en/ec/117496.pdf>.

[94] *See* n. 92.

is, the ESM. Under the Conclusions of the European Council[95] and EU Council Decision 2011/199/EU, it was resolved to add a paragraph to Article 136 TFEU to establish a permanent stability mechanism for EAMSs,[96] at which the chapter looks next.

B. The European Stability Mechanism (ESM)

The Treaty establishing the features of the ESM was finalized in February 2012 and came into force in October 2012, when instruments of ratification, approval, or acceptance were deposited by EAMS signatories whose initial subscriptions represented no less than 90 per cent of the total capital subscriptions.[97] **22.44**

The ESM is to be an international financial institution[98] based in Luxembourg.[99] It will mobilize funding and provide financial assistance, under strict economic policy conditionality, to its members, when they are threatened or experiencing severe financing problems.[100] Its underlying raison d'être is to help to assure euro area financial stability, in the context of macro-economic adjustment programmes, taking into account the severity of the economic and financial imbalances of the EAMSs.[101] **22.45**

The Treaty begins by restating the importance of the EU framework and its economic governance rules (for example the Stability Growth Pact, or SGP, and the macroeconomic imbalances framework and economic governance rules of Europe, including the Treaty on Stability, Coordination and Governance), whereby the ESM is to be seen as a backstop mechanism to help to safeguard the financial stability of the euro area as a whole. **22.46**

Use of the ESM is to be limited to extreme circumstances; access to financial assistance is subject to strict economic policy conditionality, accompanied by a macroeconomic adjustment programme, and a rigorous analysis of public debt sustainability is mandatory. Like the EFSM and EFSF, the ESM will call for active participation of the IMF on both technical and financial aspects. It is important to stress that one of the Recitals of the Treaty states that financial assistance to the Treaty's contracting parties (ESM members) will be limited to cases in which regular access to market financing is impaired.[102] Thus lending is restricted to circumstances in which no conventional party would be willing to lend[103]—that is, the ESM **22.47**

[95] European Council, *Conclusions of the European Council, 24–25 March 2011*, EUCO 10/1/11 (REV 1), CO EUR 6 (CONCL 3), 10 January 2011, available online at <http://www.consilium.europa.eu/uedocs/cms_data/docs/pressdata/en/ec/120296.pdf>.

[96] *See* European Council Decision 2011/199/EU of 25 March 2011 amending Article 136 of the Treaty on the Functioning of the European Union with regard to a stability mechanism for Member States whose currency is the euro, 6 April 2011 (OJ L 91/1), available online at <http://eur-lex.europa.eu/LexUriServ/LexUriServ.do?uri=OJ:L:2011:091:0001:0002:EN:PDF>. The following paragraph has been added to Article 136 TFEU:

> The Member States whose currency is the euro may establish a stability mechanism to be activated if indispensable to safeguard the stability of the euro area as a whole. The granting of any required financial assistance under the mechanism will be made subject to strict conditionality.

[97] *See* Art. 48 ESM Treaty.

[98] *See* Art. 1(1) ESM Treaty.

[99] *See* Art. 31(1) ESM Treaty.

[100] *See* Arts 3 and 12 ESM Treaty.

[101] *See* Art. 12 ESM Treaty.

[102] *See* Recital 13 ESM Treaty.

[103] It is worth noting that, theoretically speaking, there could always be someone willing to lend if the associated risk is properly priced. So far, during the EU sovereign debt crisis, when financing rates have gone above a 7 per cent return (and have remained at such rate or increased), official financial assistance has been provided.

will be acting as ILOLR. The role of ILOLR is usually played by the IMF,[104] but the Recital states that the ESM will enjoy preferred creditor status in a similar fashion to the IMF, while accepting the preferred creditor status of the IMF over the ESM.[105] It is worth noticing that IMF creditor priority has not been formally established anywhere and is de facto. The Treaty is the first formal document in which it has been officially acknowledged. The Treaty has created a second super-priority creditor, although one that is subordinate to the IMF.

22.48 The required funding is obtained either by issuing financial instruments, by entering into financial or other agreements with third parties, and/or by means of arrangements with ESM members.[106] The ESM shall use risk management tools to minimize potential adverse outcomes.[107]

22.49 The ESM has an authorized capital stock of €700 billion[108] divided into paid-in shares (€80 billion)[109] and callable shares (€620 billion).[110] If an ESM member fails to meet the required payment under a capital call,[111] an appeal will be made to all other ESM members to cover the shortfall,[112] thereby ensuring that the ESM receives the total amount of required paid-in capital. Experience with the EFSF, which has required a capital increase and the use of leverage to increase its financing capacity as the crisis worsened, suggests that, to reassure markets, it would have been prudent to have provided the ESM with a more substantial capital base and/or allowed a more flexible approach.

22.50 The capital participation of ESM members is based on their central banks' subscription to the ECB's capital, pursuant to Article 29 of Protocol (No. 4) of the Statute of the European System of Central Banks (ESCB) and the ECB.[113] The ESM will assume tasks that would have been previously performed by the EFSM and EFSF.[114] Total lending outstanding will have an initial ceiling of €500 billion and, given the ESM's limited capital, in order to increase the eurozone's financial support capability, a temporary overlap between the ESM and EFSF has been agreed. Although the total lending capacity has been limited to €500 billion, its firepower could go beyond that as a result of the EFSF's capacity maximization resolved on 26 October 2011 (that is, partial credit enhancement and CIFs).

---

[104] Regarding the ILOLR role of the IMF, *see* Sachs (n. 10); Charles W. Calomiris, 'The IMF's Imprudent Role as Lender of Last Resort' (1998) 17(3) Cato Journal 275; Stanley Fischer, 'On the Need for an International Lender of Last Resort' (1999) 13 J Econ Persp 85; Adam Lerrick and Allan H. Meltzer, 'Blueprint for an International Lender of Last Resort' (2003) 50 JME 289; Giancarlo Corsetti, Bernardo Guimarães, and Nouriel Roubini, *The Tradeoff between an International Lender of Last Resort to Deal with Liquidity Crisis and Moral Hazard Distortions: A Model of the IMF's Catalytic Finance Approach*, IMF Seminar Series Research Paper 03/149 (June 2003).

[105] *See* Recital 13 ESM Treaty.

[106] *See* Art. 3 ESM Treaty.

[107] *See* Art. 21(3) ESM Treaty.

[108] *See* Art. 8(1) ESM Treaty.

[109] *See* Art. 8(2) ESM Treaty.

[110] *See* Art. 25(2) ESM Treaty.

[111] *See* Arts 8(4) and 9 ESM Treaty.

[112] *See* Art. 25(2) ESM Treaty.

[113] OJ C 115, 9 May 2008, 230.

[114] There will be a transitional period between the establishment of the ESM and until the phasing out of the EFSF. During this time, the consolidated ESM and EFSF lending shall not exceed €500 billion (*see* Art. 39 ESM Treaty), also subject to the authorization of the board of governors in assuming the rights and obligations of the EFSF (Art. 40 ESM Treaty).

The governance structure of the ESM is complicated because it comprises a board of governors, a board of directors, and also establishes the position of a managing director with specific tasks. The board of governors is in charge of setting the guidelines and policies of the ESM, while the board of directors is entrusted with the day-to-day operations of the ESM in accordance with the Treaty and its by-laws.[115] Considering the division of responsibilities, an analogy can be made with the governance structure of a company regarding shareholders' meetings and their role, as well as board of directors' meetings and their agenda. However, each ESM member, irrespective of its percentage participation, has only one vote. Each ESM participant appoints one member to the board of governors,[116] while, in turn, each governor appoints a member to the board of directors;[117] board appointments are revocable at any time.[118] Appointments to both boards also include the appointments of alternates, in case of absence of the principal or impossibility to participate. Both the board of governors and the board of directors require a double threshold quorum of two-thirds of the members, with voting rights representing at least two-thirds of the voting rights.[119] Decisions made by the board of governors can be adopted either by mutual agreement (that is, unanimity, although abstentions do not prevent a mutual agreement decision)[120] or an 80 per cent qualified majority.[121] It is worth stressing that the Treaty contemplates an emergency voting proceeding for situations in which the EU Commission and the ECB conclude that a failure to urgently adopt a decision to grant or implement financial assistance can threaten the economic and financial sustainability of the euro area. In these cases (that is, under an emergency voting proceeding), the grant of financial assistance, the economic policy conditionality, and the choice of instruments has to be adopted by unanimity, meeting the requirement of a qualified majority of 85 per cent of the votes cast.[122] Decisions of the board of directors can be adopted by mutual agreement, qualified majority, and/or simple majority.[123] **22.51**

Any ESM member who fails to comply with its financial obligations (for example paid-in shares, calls of capital, or reimbursement of the financial assistance) will not be able to exercise its voting rights until the situation is rectified.[124] **22.52**

The managing director is the legal representative of the ESM, and will chair the meetings of the board of directors and shall participate in the meetings of the board of governors.[125] **22.53**

There will be an auditing board comprising five independent members not taking instructions from the ESM governing bodies, the ESM members, or any other public or private body.[126] The accounts will be subject to external audit.[127] The members of the auditing board are appointed by the board of governors, and shall include two members from the supreme **22.54**

115 The ESM by-laws are going to be adopted by the board of governors (*see* Art. 5(7)(c) ESM Treaty).
116 *See* Art. 5(1) ESM Treaty.
117 *See* Art. 6(1) ESM Treaty.
118 *See* Arts 5(1) and 6(1) ESM Treaty.
119 *See* Art. 4(2) ESM Treaty.
120 *See* Art. 4(3) ESM Treaty.
121 *See* Art. 4(5) ESM Treaty.
122 *See* Art. 4(4) ESM Treaty.
123 *See* Art. 4(2) ESM Treaty.
124 *See* Art. 4(8) ESM Treaty.
125 *See* Art. 7 ESM Treaty.
126 *See* Art. 30(1) and (2) ESM Treaty.
127 *See* Art. 29 ESM Treaty.

audit institutions of the ESM members and one from the European Court of Auditors (ECA).[128]

22.55 ESM financial assistance for stability support can consist of: precautionary financial assistance;[129] financial assistance for the recapitalization of financial institutions of an ESM member;[130] loans;[131] a primary market support facility;[132] and/or a secondary market support facility.[133] All these types of stability support are subject to strict conditionality, which may range from a macroeconomic adjustment programme to a continuous respect of pre-established eligibility conditions.[134]

22.56 ESM members undertook an irrevocable and unconditional obligation to provide their respective contributions to the authorized capital stock,[135] which also is the limit of their liability.[136] The board of governors has the mandate to establish a reserve fund and, if required, other funds.[137] In the event of ESM losses, these shall be covered by (in order of priority): (i) the reserve fund; (ii) the paid-in capital; and (iii) the appropriate amount of the authorized unpaid capital, which shall be called in if needed[138] to cover a shortfall between the paid-in capital and the total subscribed capital.[139]

22.57 Any new member state adopting the euro will become an ESM member with full rights and obligations as from the entry into force of a decision of the EU Council taken in accordance with Article 140(2) TFEU.[140] New ESM members will be admitted on the same terms and conditions as existing ESM members,[141] and shall receive shares in the ESM in exchange for their capital contributions.[142]

22.58 The Treaty encourages EU member states, EAMSs, and non-EAMSs to provide financial assistance on an ad hoc basis (for example Denmark, Sweden, and the United Kingdom provided bilateral assistance to Ireland to complement the EFSM–EFSF–IMF programme).[143] In such cases, the EAMSs (that is, ESM members) will grant equivalent creditor status to those involved in bilateral lending alongside the ESM.[144] Recital 14 of the Treaty reads: '[EAMSs] will support equivalent creditor status of the ESM and that of other States lending bilaterally in coordination with the ESM.' The wording is not very clear and it can lead to conflictive views regarding the creditor status of other bilateral lenders. It can be understood that third parties (for example a non-EAMS or even a non-European state) lending on a bilateral basis can be equalled to the preferred creditor status of the ESM.

---

128 *See* Art. 30(1) ESM Treaty.
129 *See* Art. 14 ESM Treaty.
130 *See* Art. 15 ESM Treaty.
131 *See* Art. 16 ESM Treaty.
132 *See* Art. 17 ESM Treaty.
133 *See* Art. 18 ESM Treaty.
134 *See* Arts 12(1) and 13(3) ESM Treaty.
135 *See* Art. 8(4) ESM Treaty.
136 *See* Art. 8(5) ESM Treaty.
137 *See* Art. 24(1) ESM Treaty
138 See Art. 25(1) ESM Treaty.
139 *See* Art. 9(3) ESM Treaty.
140 *See* Art. 2(1) ESM Treaty.
141 *See* Arts 2(2) and 44 ESM Treaty.
142 *See* Art. 2(3) ESM Treaty.
143 *See* Recital 9 ESM Treaty.
144 *See* Recital 14 ESM Treaty.

Non-EAMSs providing financial assistance on an ad hoc basis will participate as observers in the ESM meetings when financial assistance and monitoring are discussed, and will have access to all available information in this respect.[145] **22.59**

The twenty-seven EU member states authorized the EAMS to request the EU Commission and the ECB to perform the tasks required by the Treaty.[146] The Commission and the European Council are entrusted with post-programme surveillance within the framework established by Articles 121 and 136 TFEU.[147] **22.60**

Any disputes concerning the interpretation and application of the Treaty arising among the ESM members, or between them and the ESM, should be submitted to the board of governors.[148] If the decision of the board of governors is contested, the dispute shall be submitted to the jurisdiction of the Court of Justice of the European Union (CJEU), following the criteria set forth in Article 273 TFEU.[149] **22.61**

The procedure for the granting of the financial assistance is as follows.[150] **22.62**

(a) An ESM member makes a formal request for financial assistance to the chairperson of the board of governors.
(b) Upon receipt of a request, the chairperson will request the European Commission (in liaison with the ECB) to:
    (i) assess the existence of a risk to the financial stability of the euro area as a whole;[151]
    (ii) undertake (jointly with the IMF) a debt sustainability analysis (DSA) of the ESM member in distress;[152] and
    (iii) assess the financing needs of the ESM member[153] and the type of private sector involvement required (that is, maintenance of exposure or a reprofiling/restructuring).[154]
(c) Based on the Commission's assessment, the board of governors may decide to grant—in principle—financial assistance to the ESM member.[155]
(d) If the decision of the board of governors is favourable, the Commission (jointly with the IMF and in liaison with the ECB) will negotiate with the ESM member an MOU detailing the economic policy conditionality, contained in a macroeconomic adjustment programme, to be attached to the financial assistance.[156]
(e) The draft MOU will be considered by the board of governors and, subject to its approval, the Commission will sign the MOU on behalf of the ESM.[157]

---

145 *See* Arts 5(4), 6(3), and 38 ESM Treaty.
146 *See* Recital 10 ESM Treaty.
147 *See* Recital 17 ESM Treaty.
148 *See* Art. 37(2) ESM Treaty.
149 *See* Art. 37(3) ESM Treaty.
150 *See* Art. 13 ESM Treaty.
151 *See* Art. 13(1)(a) ESM Treaty.
152 *See* Art. 13(1)(b) ESM Treaty.
153 *See* Art. 13(1)(c) ESM Treaty.
154 *See* Recital 12 ESM Treaty.
155 *See* Art. 13(2) ESM Treaty.
156 *See* Art. 13(3) ESM Treaty.
157 *See* Art. 13(4) ESM Treaty.

(f) The board of directors will approve the financial assistance agreement drafted by the managing director, detailing the technical aspects of the financial assistance and the disbursement of the first tranche.[158]

(g) A warning system will be put in place by the ESM to ensure that it receives the repayments due under financial assistance in a timely manner.[159]

(h) The Commission (jointly with the IMF and in liaison with the ECB) will be entrusted with monitoring the compliance with the economic policy conditionality attached to the financial assistance.[160] A mutual agreement decision by the board of directors, based on the monitoring performed by the European Commission, is required prior to any further tranche disbursement in the case of financial assistance for the recapitalization of financial institutions or loans.[161]

22.63 An additional feature, as a complementary measure to safeguard the stability of the euro, is the mandatory inclusion of standardized and identical CACs as of July 2013 in the terms and conditions of all new euro area government securities with maturities of more than one year.[162] This measure was brought forward and came into force on 1 January 2013. It is ironic that a treaty was required to do this, despite the April 2003 statement by EU member states of their intention to lead by example.[163] That same year, the Ecofin Chairman (a former Minister of Economy and Finance of Greece) stated that 'EU Member States will no longer issue such bonds without any CACs'.[164] It may be that the Treaty is not the most suitable place for the inclusion of such a provision. The inclusion of CACs is something on which the EU, as a whole, has been working since 2003 and it may be that the requirement would be more appropriately included elsewhere, where it would have broader application. Nevertheless, such an initiative should be welcomed, although extended to non-EAMSs.

C. A critical analysis of the ESM

22.64 The ESM is another step in strengthening the economic aspect of the Union and should be welcomed as the latest edifice in the international architecture to prevent and/or minimize the effects of financial crises. However, the foregoing analysis suggests that considerable room for improvement remains. The new mechanism does not significantly change what the IMF could do, except that it creates a European-centred institution. The latest draft of the ESM Treaty has reduced the private sector involvement. In addition, the granting of preferred creditor status can produce a crowding-out effect.

22.65 The financing capacity of the ESM clearly seems to be at odds with a realistic appraisal of potential requirements. The different pools of financial assistance that have been temporary created until the ESM became operative collectively exceed the ESM's financing capacity.

---

[158] *See* Art. 13(3) and (5) ESM Treaty.

[159] *See* Art. 13(6) ESM Treaty.

[160] *See* Art. 13(7) ESM Treaty.

[161] *See* Arts 15(5) and 16(5) ESM Treaty.

[162] *See* Art. 12(3) ESM Treaty.

[163] *See* Ecofin, *Implementation of the EU Commitment on Collective Action Clauses in Documentation of International Debt Issuance*, ECFIN/CEFCPE(2004)REP/50483, Brussels, 12 November 2004, available online at <http://europa.eu/efc/sub_committee/pdf/cacs_en.pdf>.

[164] Statement by Mr Christodoulakis, Minister of Economy and Finance of Greece, in his capacity as Chairman of the EU Council of Economic and Finance Ministers, to the International Monetary and Financial Committee, 12 April 2003. Ironically, perhaps, not all post-2003 Greek government bonds included a CAC.

Additionally, some observers have estimated that, in a scenario of distress involving countries such as Italy or Spain, the €700 billion maximum capacity of the ESM would be insufficient to calm financial markets if others were to enter into the turmoil.[165] It has been suggested that at least €1 trillion may be required.[166]

The ESM's scope for action may be too restrictive. The EFSF, the temporary SPV created to provide liquidity assistance, potentially has greater capacity owing to its maximizing lending techniques (that is, partial credit enhancement to primary sovereign bonds issued by an EAMS and the creation of one or more CIFs). However, it is worthy of note that the Treaty authorizes the ESM board of governors to reassess and eventually increase the authorized capital stock.[167] Table 22.2 provides a comparison between the scopes of the EFSF and ESM. In both cases, there are references to 'old' and 'new', or 'I' and 'II', when referring to the EFSF and ESM, to highlight the difference of powers and capacities that were originally granted and subsequently amended as result of the worsening of the crisis (and the need to grant a greater firepower to these institutions). **22.66**

It should also be kept in mind that extensive financial assistance from the ESM could inadvertently reduce the supply of funds from private lenders, since their claims would be subordinate to those of the ESM, as an ILOLR. So far, the ILOLR role has been fulfilled by the IMF. On the other hand, bilateral and private creditors may see their positions enhanced, by virtue of the assistance provided by the ESM to the EAMSs and the associated policy conditionality. While the ESM will be providing ILOLR lending and therefore should be granted priority, its priority will not be exempt from challenges in courts of law, since it is not pre-established, but rather imposed by the Treaty. On a more practical note, to the extent that it diminishes perceived repayment prospects, the preferred creditor status assigned to the ESM (jointly with, although inferior to, that of the IMF) may reduce the private sector demand for sovereign debt and thereby increase public sector financing costs. Since it is possible that the Treaty will be amended to broaden the financing capacity, or 'firepower', of the ESM (and probably its scope as well), it may also be advisable to delete the reference to the preferred creditor status, which may offer little by way of protection and may undermine support efforts. **22.67**

The role of the ESM vis-à-vis that of the IMF raises some questions. The ESM has been designed to work very closely with the IMF. For example, upon the request for ESM stability support by a distressed EAMS, the European Commission, together with the IMF and in liaison with the ECB, will assess the actual financing needs of the EAMS. Then, the Commission and the IMF (jointly with the ECB) will negotiate an MOU with the EAMS, outlining a macroeconomic adjustment programme. The Commission and the IMF (jointly with the ECB) will be responsible for monitoring compliance with policy conditionality. Thus there is a close relationship between the ESM (and the EU institutions) and the IMF. In common with the IMF, the ESM will be providing financial assistance in exchange for conditionality. In conclusion, one might ask whether it is appropriate to create another international organization, under public international law with super-priority, which will **22.68**

---

[165] Adrian Blundell-Wignall, 'Solving the Financial and Sovereign Debt Crisis in Europe' (2011) 2 OECD Journal of Financial Market Trends 1, available online at <http://www.oecd.org/dataoecd/14/25/49481502.pdf>.

[166] John McDermott, 'China to Europe: That's Sure a Nice EFSF that You Have there', *FT Alphaville blog*, 28 October 2011, available online at <http://ftalphaville.ft.com/2011/10/28/715586/china-to-europe-thats-a-sure-nice-efsf-you-have-there/?Authorised=false>.

[167] *See* Art. 10 ESM Treaty.

Table 22.2 EFSF AND ESM Main Features Comparison Table

	EFSF I (old)	EFSF II (new)	ESM I (old)	ESM II (new)
Face value	€440 billion	€780 billion	€700 billion (€80 billion paid-in + €620 billion callable)	€700 billion (€80 billion paid-in + €620 billion callable)
Effective lending capacity	€255.5+/- billion	€440 billion	€500 billion	€500 billion
Over-guarantee	120%	165%	n/a	n/a
Lending capacity maximization	n/a	Partial guarantee on securities issuances by member states + CIFs	n/a	n/a
Purpose	(1) Provide temporary financial assistance by the issuance of debt instruments (2) In exceptional circumstances, intervene in the debt primary market (3) Not authorized to intervene in the secondary market (4) Not able to provide precautionary credit lines	Financial assistance by way of: (1) loan disbursements; (2) precautionary facilities; (3) facilities to finance the recapitalization of financial institutions in an EAMS through loans including non-programme countries; (4) facilities for the purchase of bonds in the primary and secondary markets	Financial assistance in the form of loans conditioned to strict economic policy conditionality under macroeconomic adjustment programme, a rigorous analysis of public debt sustainability, and PSI	Financial assistance by way of: (1) loan disbursements; (2) precautionary facilities; (3) facilities to finance the recapitalization of financial institutions in an EAMS through loans including non-programme countries; (4) facilities for the purchase of bonds in the primary and secondary markets
In force?	No	Yes	No (amended before entering into force)	October 2012

replicate some of the functions of the IMF, but lack its experience, credibility, resources, and long-established ad hoc super-priority.

4. Perfecting the Status Quo

22.69 This section will analyse a particular aspect of Iraq's debt restructuring in 2002, which provides a very interesting feature that can be replicated for other restructuring episodes. Its most salient feature is that it can be used to replicate some features of the SDRM without requiring the amendment of the IMF's Articles of Agreement or the adoption of a new treaty.

Also, the second part of this section will analyse whether the features developed in Iraq can be replicated in a similar fashion at the euro area level through the ESM.

A. A backdoor SDRM

The Iraqi debt restructuring has shown that, in extreme cases, a sovereign can make a request to the United Nations Security Council (UNSC) to issue a resolution to prevent creditors from seizing assets during a short restructuring period. In the case of Iraq, this was done by means of the Security Council Resolution No. 1483/03 of 22 May 2003. This resolution shielded Iraq from possible seizures or attachments of its oil reserves until 31 December 2007. Security Council Resolution No. 1546/04, dated 8 June 2004, decided that the provisions of paragraph 22 of Resolution No. 1483/03 (the shielding of assets) shall continue to apply, with the exception that the privileges and immunities provided in that paragraph shall not apply with respect to any final judgment arising out of a contractual obligation entered into by Iraq after 30 June 2004.[168] 22.70

Since UNSC resolutions—in favour of which the US voted—are not self-executing and did not confer rights on US citizens that are judicially enforceable in US domestic courts in the absence of implementing legislation,[169] the US president enacted Executive Order No. 13,303[170] —on the same date as UNSC Resolution No. 1483/03. The only substantial difference between both pieces of legislation is that the US Executive Order does not have an expiration date regarding the shielding of the Iraqi assets. On 29 November 2004, Executive Order No. 13,364 was enacted to protect central bank assets.[171] 22.71

As noted by Gelpern,[172] the 'great powers' stand ready to give less fortunate governments extraordinary legal protections in extreme legal circumstances. It is very important to trace a line between what has been happening in the SDRM arena and the adoption of UNSC Resolution No. 1483/03 in order to stress the real importance of the latter. As explained earlier in the chapter, scholars, practitioners, and IMF officials agree that the SDRM proposal has been shelved. One particular scholar is very clear in this respect, stating that the 'IMF Board officially shelved the proposal as politically unfeasible'.[173] This shelving was effected on 11 April 2003 in a document entitled *Report of the Managing Director to the International Monetary and Financial Committee on the IMF's Policy Agenda*.[174] Therefore it can be argued that only forty days after the SDRM was shelved, an ad hoc SDRM was adopted by UNSC Resolution No. 1483/03 of 22 May 2003. Although creditors can obtain final judgments, they are not able to enforce them against oil reserves (or central bank reserves). It is worth 22.72

[168] The rationale behind this resolution is to extend immunity to Iraqi obligations with the exception of those entered by the new government. 30 June 2004 is the date of the transfer of sovereignty back to the Iraqi citizens.

[169] *See Diggs v. Richardson*, 555 F2d 848 (DC Cir. 1976).

[170] Executive Order 13,303 Protecting the Development Fund for Iraq and Certain other Property in which Iraq Has an Interest, 68 Fed Reg 31931 (28 May 2003).

[171] Executive Order No. 13,364 Modifying the Protection Granted to the Development Fund for Iraq and Certain Property in which Iraq Has an Interest and Protecting the Central Bank of Iraq, 69 Fed Reg 70177 (29 November 2004). Other relevant executive orders regarding the protection of assets in the US include Executive Order 13,315, dated 28 August 2003, and Executive Order 13,350, dated 29 July 2004. Finally, on 22 May 2006, in accordance with § 202(d) of the National Emergencies Act (50 USC 1622(d)), the US President decided to extend the national emergency protecting the Development Fund for Iraq and certain other property in which Iraq has an interest for a year.

[172] Anna Gelpern, 'What Iraq and Argentina Might Learn from Each Other' (2005) 6(1) Chi J Int'l L 393.

[173] Gelpern (n. 172), 399.

[174] *See* IMF, *Report of the Managing Director to the International Monetary and Financial Committee on the IMF's Policy Agenda* (April 2003), available online at <http://www.imf.org/external/np/omd/2003/041103.htm>.

noting that oil reserves—the main asset targeted by UN resolutions—account for more than 75 per cent of Iraqi's total sources of income.[175]

22.73 Within an ad hoc legal framework of sovereign debt restructuring, this can be an alternative SDRM to that proposed by the IMF. It is referred as an 'ad hoc SDRM' because it replicates one its most important features—that is, the legal stay—which is the only feature that so far has not been achieved contractually. The IMF can eventually endorse a sovereign request with the UNSC.

B. An ESM add-on

22.74 With the continuous deterioration of the sovereign debt portfolio of the EAMSs, it is not impossible that the 'unique and exceptional' nature of the Greek restructuring[176] in relation to the private sector involvement might need to be repeated. The differentiating element is that the debt instruments of other EAMS are not majorly governed by their own domestic laws, as was the case in Greece and which facilitated the retrofitting of CACs. Therefore constraining holdout creditors might not be a simple task.

22.75 Buchheit et al.[177] argue that EAMSs can immunize the assets of an EAMS (held within the EU) in a similar fashion to what was done in the Iraqi case by means of a simple addition to the ESM Treaty—that is, the inclusion of an Article granting immunity from judicial process to the assets and revenue streams of any EAMS who is receiving stability support from the ESM. The aim of this provision would be to prevent any form of attachment, garnishment, execution, injunctive relief, or similar forms of judicial process by any claimant who was eligible to participate in a restructuring exercise under a 'private sector involvement' initiative as part of an ESM provision of financial assistance. The authors also explain that such immunity from process would protect the provision of financial support for the restabilization of the economy, but shall automatically expire when all amounts due to the ESM have been repaid in full.

22.76 Another important element highlighted by Buchheit et al.[178] is that such a measure would not be effective if it were not replicated by other EU member states (although non-EAMS), such as the UK. In this sense, the authors argue that the UK might wish to incorporate such immunities into its own law to prevent driving financial transactions away from London. However, this might not be a simple task, since it might have a retroactive effect on previous debt obligations, and would clash with the sanctity of contracts and the respect for the rule of law.

5. Concluding Remarks

22.77 As evidence demonstrates, episodes of sovereign bond restructuring have been resolved quickly, without severe creditor coordination problems, and involving little litigation—the

[175] *See* Iraq—Letter of Intent, Memorandum of Economic and Financial Policies, and Technical Memorandum of Understanding, Baghdad, 24 September 2004, available online at <http://www.imf.org/external/np/loi/2004/irq/01/index.htm>.

[176] *See* Council of the European Union, *Statement by the Heads of State or Government of the Euro Area and EU Institutions*, Brussels, 21 July 2011, available online at <http://www.consilium.europa.eu/uedocs/cms_data/docs/pressdata/en/ec/123978.pdf>, para. 6; *Euro Summit Statement*, Brussels, 26 October 2011, available online at <http://www.consilium.europa.eu/uedocs/cms_data/docs/pressdata/en/ec/125644.pdf>, para. 15.

[177] Lee C. Buchheit, G. Mitu Gulati, and Ignacio Tirado, *The Problem of Holdout Creditors in Eurozone Sovereign Debt Restructurings*, Duke Law School Working Papers (January 2013), available online at <http://scholarship.law.duke.edu/faculty_scholarship/2808/>.

[178] Buchheit et al. (n. 177).

only significant exception being Argentina, a 'serial defaulter' and a 'rogue debtor'. So why mend something that is not broken? The exchange offers of Pakistan (1999), Ukraine (1999), Ecuador (2000), Uruguay (2003), Argentina (2005–10), and Belize (2006) can be used to demonstrate that exchange offers work. In all of these cases, the degree of creditors' participation in the exchange offers has been above 90 per cent. As previously noted, of the thirty-four sovereign bond exchanges since 1997, only two have been affected by holdout creditors.[179]

The ad hoc market-centred voluntary approach of exchange offers should be endorsed. However, it can benefit from complementary contractual sweeteners (to entice creditors to participate) and the use—if required—of exit consents (to increase the degree of participation of those creditors that were not convinced by the contractual sweeteners). If CACs are already included in the debt instruments, they can simply be resolved by the required contractual majority. **22.78**

In addition, a backdoor SDRM can be considered for exceptional circumstances, but should not be the rule. However, without the geopolitical element of Iraq, it seems difficult to imagine the UNSC adopting another resolution shielding the assets of another sovereign—although, technically, it is not impossible. The proposed add-on on the ESM can work as a backdoor SDRM for EAMSs. This notwithstanding, it should probably be kept as a last resort rather than included as an *ex ante* policy in the Treaty, since it could undermine sovereign lending conditions and practices. The SDRM, the UNSC resolution, or the backdoor SDRM for EAMS can achieve a creditor stay. This will complement existing reorganization financing (although it is provided only by the official sector—otherwise priority will not be granted). The other desired features of the SDRM—that is, restructuring and holdout constraint—can be achieved by the use of CACs. Another option, less coercive than a Treaty amendment (either *ex ante* or *ex post*), is building an automatic stay within the four corners of the bond. Table 22.3 illustrates how contracts can be used to replicate the main features of the SDRM. **22.79**

Table 22.3 SDRM main features and how to replicate them

Legal stay	• Contractually within the terms of the bond
	• Through a UN Security Council Resolution (Iraq)
	• Amending the ESM Treaty
Financing reorganization	• Official sector preferred creditor status
	• Using an IFI to raise money from the capital markets (EFSF/ESM)
	• DIP financing[1]
Restructuring debt	• CACs
	• In the absence of CACs, exit consents + contractual sweeteners
Restraining holdouts	• CACs or contract stay

[1] *See* Rodrigo Olivares Caminal, John Douglas, Randall Guynn, Alan Kornberg, Sarah Paterson, Dalvinder Singh, and Hilary Stonefrost, *Debt Restructuring* (Oxford: Oxford University Press, 2011), paras 11.313–11.35.

[179] *See* n. 6.

22.80 The SDRM has a strong political element and many detractors. It still has to overcome political resistance towards it and to resolve some shortcomings—mainly the fact that the underlying element of an insolvency regime is not there: the possibility of intervening and/or liquidating the debtor after a reorganization arrangement has failed. Without the 'stick', the dynamics of an insolvency regime that are attempted to replicate with the SDRM are inevitably doomed.

6. Corollary

22.81 Since this volume is a *liber amicorum* for Lee Buchheit, it is apt to finish this chapter acknowledging the obvious: it is he who has been behind most of the sovereign debt developments. For example, it was Buchheit who first used the exit consent technique in the sovereign debt context. It was also Buchheit who designed and introduced several of the contractual sweeteners to enhance the degree of creditor participation. Also, it was he who was behind the six cases that have been mentioned in this chapter to demonstrate that the current ad hoc restructuring techniques can—to certain extent—guarantee at least a 90 per cent degree of participation. He also was the mastermind behind the Iraqi restructuring, Uruguay's spotless debt reprofiling and Greece's CACs retrofitting. The other more controversial issues, such as the *pari passu* litigation, the design of the SDRM, or the drafting of the ESM Treaty, did not involve Buchheit directly, but it is unlikely that any correlation can be coincidental.

23

DEBT RESTRUCTURING AND ECONOMIC RECOVERY

*Sean Hagan**

1. Introduction

The financial crisis that swept through the global economy in 2008 was unprecedented, both in terms of its depth and the range of countries affected. Aftershocks are still being felt, both in the United States, where it continues to be a drag on growth, and in Europe, where it has revealed serious flaws in the euro architecture. While the manifestations of the crises have varied, the problem of overindebtedness is a constant theme. The range of sectors affected by excessive leverage is very broad: not only have the balance sheets of the sovereign, banking, and corporate sectors been placed under stress, but also—and perhaps for the first time—the overindebtedness of the household sector has acquired systemic dimensions. And, as is always the case, problems in one sector have had an adverse affect on others: the excessive debt of the corporate and household sectors has weakened the financial position of the banks. Moreover, to the extent that bank weaknesses have become so severe that governments have had to bail them out, the problem of overindebtedness has shifted to the sovereign. **23.01**

Faced with these problems, the challenges for economic policymakers have been daunting. There is abundant research to demonstrate that a recovery from a recession caused by a banking crisis involving excessive leverage is far more difficult than a recovery from a normal cyclical recession.[1] Efforts by governments, banks, firms, and households to 'deleverage' and repair their balance sheets take time, and these efforts, while necessary, constrain demand and accordingly slow growth. Although accommodating monetary policy has played an important role in supporting economic activity during this period, there is an understandable limit to the creativity—and courage—of central bankers. A prolonged period of very low interest rates can encourage excessive risk taking and, accordingly, sow the seeds of the next crisis.[2] Fiscal policy is also of limited utility for two distinct reasons: first, the ability of the government to provide a stimulus to the real economy is constrained by its own debt overhang; and second, as governments try to address their own overindebtedness through **23.02**

---

* Sean Hagan is General Counsel and Director of the Legal Department with the International Monetary Fund (IMF). The views expressed in this article are those of the author and do not necessarily reflect the views of the IMF.

[1] *See* Carmen M. Reinhart and Kenneth S. Rogoff, *This Time is Different: Eight Centuries of Financial Folly* (Princeton, NJ: Princeton University Press, 2011), 162–73.

[2] International Monetary Fund, *Global Financial Stability Report* (April 2013), available online at <http://www.imf.org/external/pubs/ft/gfsr/>, 2.

fiscal consolidation, they have recognized that there are limits to how far fiscal austerity can be relied upon to achieve this objective. At some point, austerity can become counterproductive since, by slowing growth, it reduces the tax revenues that are relied on to pay down government debt.[3]

23.03 Given these constraints, there is a growing recognition that greater reliance will need to be placed on debt rescheduling and, where necessary, debt reduction. This is not to suggest that debt restructuring should be undertaken across the board and without regard to the specific circumstances of the debtor. On the contrary: the long-term stability of the financial system requires a credible commitment to contractual terms. But in circumstances in which a determination has been made that a particular firm, individual, or government does not have the capacity to repay its debts, it is imperative that a restructuring take place as soon as possible. Although the allocation of losses to creditors that arise from this process will be painful, experience demonstrates that delaying the restructuring of unsustainable debt only exacerbates this pain. More importantly, for policymakers, it can undermine economic recovery.

23.04 Reducing delays in the restructuring of unsustainable debt requires policy action on a number of fronts. For example, banks are often reluctant to engage in the debt restructuring process simply because the recognition of a loss on their balance sheets will have adverse capital implications. For this reason, vigilant supervision by bank regulators is a necessary feature of any effective debt restructuring strategy. However, delays—and inefficiencies—in the debt restructuring process are also attributable to weaknesses in the legal and institutional frameworks that guide this process. This chapter identifies some of the key weaknesses in the frameworks applicable to corporations, bank, households, and sovereigns, and identifies some avenues for reform, including, in particular, the following.

- *In the corporate context*, much progress has been made in achieving international convergence on the optimum design of liquidation and rehabilitation provisions. However, as is discussed later in the chapter, a key challenge is how to apply—and modify—these frameworks in the context of a systemic crisis.
- *With respect to the restructuring of banks*, the crisis has created important momentum towards the adoption of national rescue and resolution frameworks that seek to allocate losses to unsecured creditors in a manner that safeguards financial stability. The chapter goes on to discuss why the development of a framework for cross-border cooperation is essential if these bank resolution frameworks are to have a chance of success.
- *Regarding household insolvency*, the crisis revealed the extent to which the absence of a framework to write down mortgages so as to reflect the actual market value of property has imposed a significant cost on economic growth, including in the United States. The chapter identifies possible reform measures that could address this weakness.
- Last, but certainly not least, the chapter discusses the *restructuring of sovereign debt*, an area in which—notwithstanding the robust policy debate that has been ongoing over the past fifteen years—there continues to be considerable uncertainty as to when a sovereign should initiate a restructuring and how the restructuring process should unfold from that point onwards.

[3] For example, the need for policymakers in both the United States and the eurozone to be more accommodating with fiscal policy is emphasized in IMF, *World Economic Outlook* (April 2013), available online at <http://www.imf.org/external/pubs/ft/weo/2013/01/>.

2. Corporate Debt Restructuring in the Context of a Systemic Crisis

A. Lessons from the Asian crisis

Over fifteen years ago, economic policymakers learned an important, albeit difficult, lesson. During the Asian crisis, weaknesses in the insolvency frameworks of countries such as Thailand, Indonesia, and Korea undermined their capacity to eliminate a massive external debt overhang in the corporate sectors of these economies.[4] The persistence of this overhang undermined the recovery not only of the real economy, but also of the banking system, which continued to be overwhelmed by a large pool of non-performing loans that could not be resolved. As a consequence, considerable effort was devoted to reforming the rehabilitation and liquidation chapters of the corporate insolvency laws of the countries in this region. Moreover, the relevant governments also actively supported relatively well-structured out-of-court restructuring frameworks.[5] **23.05**

Largely as a result of this experience, the international community began to devote an extraordinary amount of energy to distilling best practices in this area and promoting the adoption of these practices internationally. In 2003, the United Nations Commission of International Trade Law (UNCITRAL) completed its *Legislative Guide on Insolvency Law*, a carefully negotiated document that reflects a surprising amount of international convergence around the key principles that should underpin an effective corporate insolvency system.[6] This effort has been supported by the both the International Monetary Fund (IMF) and the World Bank, which have been actively promoting reform in this area in the context of their Financial Sector Assessment Programmes (FSAPs), which are designed to identify and address vulnerabilities in the financial sectors of their member countries.[7] **23.06**

Notwithstanding the benefits of all of this work, the Asian crisis highlighted an important question: can a legal and institutional framework designed to address the failure of individual enterprises also assist in resolving crises of systemic proportions, in which a significant portion of the corporate sector is in distress? **23.07**

The first challenge is to manage expectations as to how quickly meaningful progress in insolvency reform can be achieved. While a law can be revised or drafted quickly, institutional reform is a much more time-consuming process. Indeed, perhaps more than any other legal framework, the effectiveness of an insolvency system is totally dependent on a strong institutional infrastructure, and, in particular, an independent and competent judiciary. Very **23.08**

[4] *See* William C. Hunter, George. G. Kaufman, and Thomas H. Krueger (eds) *The Asian Financial Crisis: Origins, Implications and Solutions* (Boston: Kluwer Academic Press, 1999) for a comprehensive discussion of the causes of the Asian crisis in a compilation of papers presented at a conference co-sponsored by the Federal Reserve Bank of Chicago and the International Monetary Fund, 8–10 October 1998.

[5] For a general discussion of insolvency reform during the Asian crisis, *see* Sean Hagan, 'Insolvency Reform and Economic Policy' (2001) 17 Conn J Int'l L 63.

[6] UNCITRAL Working Group on Insolvency Law, *Legislative Guide on Insolvency Law*, 24th Session, UN Doc. A/CN.9/WG.V/WP.54 (2001), available online at <http://www.uncitral.org/uncitral/en/uncitral_texts/insolvency/2004Guide.html>.

[7] *See* IMF Legal Department, *Orderly and Effective Insolvency Procedures: Key Issues* (1999), available online at <http://www.imf.org/external/pubs/ft/orderly/>; World Bank Working Group on Rehabilitation, *Building Effective Insolvency Systems* (September1999), available online at <http://siteresources.worldbank.org/GILD/ConferenceMaterial/20154457/Developing%20Countries%20-%20Rehabilitation%20Working%20Group.pdf>.

few elements of the law are self-executing. The difficulty, of course, is that the process of institutional reform is far more complicated than that of legislative reform. In the case of the judiciary, for example, while the judges' lack of familiarity with the legal and commercial concepts that underlie the law will hamper its predictable application, there are often more fundamental issues that need to be addressed. Providing judges with training in the area of insolvency will have limited impact if the institution lacks independence or is corrupt.

23.09 As a means of mitigating institutional weaknesses, consideration can be given to increasing the automaticity of the law, for example by providing for specific and objective criteria in critical areas, such as the type of protection to be provided to secured creditors during the period of the stay. Moreover, in order to avoid undue delays, deadlines can be set forth in the law with respect to the rendering of critical decisions, such as the determination of whether proceedings should commence once a petition has been filed. However, it would be neither feasible nor appropriate to try to exclude the judiciary entirely from the process. Not only would such an approach raise constitutional concerns, but it would also constitute a short-sighted approach to reform. As discussed earlier, an effective insolvency system relies upon the effective application of other commercial laws, particularly those relating to the enforcement of secured and unsecured credit, all of which require the intervention of an effective judiciary.

23.10 Given the volume of cases and the general lack of familiarity with the insolvency system, all of the IMF-supported adjustment programmes during the Asian crisis provided for the establishment of relatively structured out-of-court frameworks that are generally referred to as the 'London Approach'. While it was understood that most of the negotiations would take place within this framework, it was also recognized that the formal system still had to play a role in providing incentives for negotiations in at least two respects: first, the threat of the initiation of liquidation was needed to bring debtors to the table; and second, the voting provisions of the rehabilitation law were needed to threatened potential holdouts. In that latter context, efforts have been made to design the laws in a manner to allow for 'pre-negotiated' or 'pre-packaged' rehabilitation plans.[8]

23.11 A final challenge has been the issue of local shareholders. The implementation of an insolvency law during a crisis is always complicated by the pressure that vested interests often bring to bear. Since the introduction of new laws or the amendments to these laws apply to existing debt, introducing new rules to address an outstanding debt overhang makes the legislative process a politically charged one. But there are also more specific issues. In circumstances in which a large portion of the corporate sector is in distress, the continued participation of existing shareholders may be critical for the future rehabilitation of many of the enterprises. Accordingly, it is important that incumbent management have an opportunity—and perhaps even the first opportunity—to present a rehabilitation plan to the creditors for approval. But what happens if the existing shareholders are not cooperative and, for example, present plans that provide for the creditors to reduce the value of their

[8] While, in some countries, the verification of claims process has been easy, in others, it has been more complicated. In particular, some countries require the use of a relatively formal and time-consuming verification of claims process that must precede the stage at which a rehabilitation plan is proposed and voted upon, thus making it difficult to propose a plan immediately after the commencement of proceedings. In these countries, efforts have been made to modify the verification-of-claims rules to allow for an accelerated verification procedure that will ensure that plans can be voted upon shortly after they are proposed.

claims without the shareholders having to surrender any equity? Under some laws, the failure of the debtor's plan to attract adequate creditor support will automatically lead to liquidation of the enterprise. Under other—more modern—systems, there is another option: namely, the creditors themselves can present a plan that, among other things, can result in the creditors effectively acquiring the company and stripping existing shareholders of all equity. The latter approach, of course, is consistent with the objective of maximizing the value of claims of creditors—that is, if the company is fundamentally viable, creditors will obtain a better return through rehabilitation than through liquidation.

Nevertheless, although the possibility of creditor plans has been incorporated into laws of some emerging market countries, it raises a number of difficulties. First, it is a concept that is entirely alien in countries where many of the enterprises are closely held and, in some cases, have been owned and operated by the same family since their establishment. Second, in circumstances in which the creditors in question are foreign, there is a concern that the use of creditor plans will become a means by which a large section of the corporate sector will be owned by foreigners. Third, where the state has become a creditor by virtue of its acquisition of loans through the bank restructuring process, it can mean that the state itself will hold a significant amount of equity, which could result in the effective nationalization of a large portion of the enterprise sector. While these issues do not invalidate the need to introduce the concept of creditor plans as a matter of 'best practice', they do highlight the infeasibility of a wholesale transfer of ownership of the enterprise sector in the context of a systemic crisis. **23.12**

B. Corporate insolvency and the 2008 crisis

When the crisis erupted in 2008 in central and eastern European countries, the problems were reminiscent of those faced during the Asian crisis ten years earlier. As in Asia, countries such as Hungary, the Ukraine, and Latvia had experienced explosive growth that had been fuelled by foreign borrowing.[9] Unfortunately, this growth created an unsustainable increase in prices, which undermined the competitiveness of these economies and led to a sudden collapse in confidence in these economies among foreign investors. As in the case of Asia, this lack of confidence resulted in capital outflows and, because the authorities did not have adequate resources to meet these, the exchange rate suffered a large depreciation. Importantly, since much of the borrowing incurred by the banking, corporate, and household sector had been denominated in foreign exchange, this depreciation resulted in the overindebtedness of large portions of the banking and corporate sector.[10] **23.13**

[9] IMF, *Hungary: Request for Stand-By Arrangement—Staff Report*, IMF Country Report No. 08/361 (November 2008), available online at <http://www.imf.org/external/pubs/ft/scr/2008/cr08361.pdf>, including 'Hungary: Letter of Intent' at 40; IMF, *Ukraine: Request for Stand-By Arrangement—Staff Report*, IMF Country Report No. 08/384 (December 2008), available online at <http://www.imf.org/external/pubs/ft/scr/2008/cr08384.pdf>, including 'Letter of Intent and Memorandum of Economic and Financial Policies' at 45; IMF, *Latvia: Request for Stand-By Arrangement—Staff Report*, IMF Country Report No. 09/3 (November 2008), available online at <http://www.imf.org/external/pubs/ft/scr/2009/cr0903.pdf>, including 'Latvia: Letter of Intent' at 60.

[10] Notwithstanding the similarities with the Asian crisis, however, there are important differences. First, the problems in Asia were triggered exclusively by a loss of confidence in the policies of those countries. In central and eastern Europe, the outflows have also been exacerbated by the deleveraging process that occurred at a global level as a result of the problems experienced in a number of developed countries, such as the United States and the United Kingdom. Second, during the Asian crisis, the stabilization programme was achieved through a combination of external financing from the IMF (and other official creditors) and economic adjustment. Although there had been widespread insolvency in the banking and corporate sectors, there was no need to rely on exchange controls. In central and eastern Europe, however, this has not always been the case. Most notably,

23.14 It was recognized at the outset that the restructuring of corporate debt owed to non-residents was a necessary element in any economic recovery strategy of these countries. As in the Asian crisis, government intervention supported the restructuring process in three areas. First, it established a legal and institutional framework that would support the rehabilitation and liquidation of enterprises, primarily through the adoption of insolvency laws and the strengthening of the judicial system. Second, and relatedly, the government established out-of-court frameworks that facilitated such restructurings, albeit in the shadow of the formal insolvency system. Finally, to the extent to which the sovereign became a creditor to the corporate sector by virtue of its acquisition of liabilities through the bank restructuring process, it also played a leading role in the negotiation strategy, sometimes through the leverage gained by stronger legal enforcement powers that had been conferred upon it in the enabling legislation.

23.15 As in the Asian crisis, the IMF has been actively assisting the countries of central and eastern Europe to implement this strategy in the context of the economic reform programmes that it had been financing.[11] This strategy has also been of relevance for a number of euro area countries, including Portugal and Greece.[12] It is fair to say that the lessons of Asia and some of the distinguishing features of the crisis of 2008 have resulted in adjustments to the overall approach in a number of respects.

23.16 The first adjustment relates to the nature of public intervention. During the Asian crisis, the prevailing view was that, as a matter of principle, public funds should not be used to support corporate restructuring. There was a concern that such intervention would engender moral hazard: by shielding both creditors and corporate debtors from their losses, it would only encourage risky behaviour going forward. While public funds were used to support the restructuring of the banking sector, this was considered an appropriate step given both the systemic implications of the collapse of the banking sector and the pre-existing public exposure arising from the deposit guarantee system.

23.17 Looking at the challenges currently faced by the IMF's members regarding the overindebtedness of their corporate sectors, there are several reasons why there is recognition that a more robust role for the government may be necessary going forward. At the outset, one

---

in Iceland, the authorities have had little choice but to rely on comprehensive exchange controls to staunch capital outflows and thereby ensure the effectiveness of the stabilization programmes. While these controls were in place before the Fund approved the relevant standby arrangement, the IMF recognized that, at least in the short term, these controls were necessary given the fact that the amount of external financing being provided, even when coupled with the economic adjustment being implemented, was outstripped by the level of capital outflows.

[11] For countries in which insolvency reform was, or is, an explicit part of the programme, *see* IMF, *Republic of Latvia: Request for Stand-By Arrangement*, IMF Country Report No. 09/3(January 2009), available online at <http://www.imf.org/external/pubs/cat/longres.aspx?sk=22586.0>; IMF, *Republic of Moldova: Article IV Consultation... and First Reviews under the Extended Arrangement and under the Three-Year Arrangement under the Extended Credit Facility*, IMF Country Report No. 10/234 (July 2010), available online at <http://www.imf.org/external/pubs/cat/longres.aspx?sk=24079.0>; IMF, *Republic of Serbia, Letter of Intent, Memorandum of Economic and Financial Policies, and Technical Memorandum of Understanding* (April 2009), available online at <http://www.imf.org/external/np/loi/2009/srb/043009.pdf>; IMF, *Ukraine Request for Stand-By Arrangement*, IMF Country Report No. 10/262 (August 2010), available online at <http://www.imf.org/external/pubs/cat/longres.aspx?sk=24137.0>.

[12] *See* IMF, *Greece: Letter of Intent, Memorandum of Economic and Financial Policies, and Technical Memorandum of Understanding* (March 2012), available online at <http://www.imf.org/external/np/loi/2012/grc/030912.pdf>; IMF, Portugal: *Letter of Intent, Memorandum of Economic and Financial Policies, and Technical Memorandum of Understanding* (May 2011), available online at <http://www.imf.org/external/np/loi/2011/prt/051711.pdf>.

needs to acknowledge that recent events have demonstrated that moral hazard concerns have been superseded by others. The level and depth of government intervention in industrial countries, including financial intervention, has been unprecedented. As evidenced by US intervention in the automobile industry in 2009, this intervention has been extended to the corporate sector.[13] It is difficult to continue to apply the principal of moral hazard rigidly in emerging markets when it is being applied rather more flexibly elsewhere.

The fact is that even if government is successful in putting in place a corporate debt restructuring framework through the establishment of both a formal and out-of-court system, the question remains as to whether it will actually be used. Although an effective system should give creditors the legal leverage they need to bring debtors to the table, experience demonstrates that many creditors will prefer to bide their time until the economy recovers sufficiently to strengthen the debt-servicing capacity of the debtor. Of course, if all creditors take this position, the overall restructuring process will be delayed, thereby undermining the recovery. The problem may be viewed as a form of market failure. This problem is exacerbated by the fact that, in many of these countries, there is very little experience with corporate debt restructuring. **23.18**

Given these factors, it is relatively clear that the government may need to provide additional incentives beyond an insolvency framework in order to catalyse the restructuring process. Whether these incentives are financial or regulatory in nature will depend on the situation of the country in question. For example, in some cases, it may be possible for the government to provide financing incentives in the form of guarantees on the restructured claims. There are challenges in implementing this approach. Among other things, it will be important to ensure that guarantees are not simply used to prop up non-viable institutions. Moreover, the feasibility of this approach will depend on the amount of fiscal space available to the government. In some central and eastern European countries, this problem has been complicated by the fact that there is also pressure on the sovereign to support the restructuring of consumer debt.[14] **23.19**

One final lesson has been learned from the Asian crisis that the Fund is trying to bring to bear in Europe: when contemplating the design and implementation of a corporate restructuring strategy in the context of a systemic crisis, it is necessary to consider not only the instruments that will be the most effective, but also the sequencing of the strategy. In particular, it is unreasonable to expect that there will be a restructuring of corporate sector debt before macroeconomic stabilization has been achieved. While values and prices are uncertain, creditors and debtor are unlikely to be in a position to conclude agreements. Moreover, one needs a minimum level of stability in the banking sector before a corporate restructuring strategy can be implemented. Such stability may require significant recapitalization. Unless banks are in a financial position to write down the value of their loans, they will not be in a position to agree to the level of debt reduction that will be necessary to ensure the viability of the corporation in question. **23.20**

[13] *See* description of US support to the automobile industry in Mark J. Roe and David Skeel, 'Assessing the Chrysler Bankruptcy' (2009–10) 108 Mich L Rev 727.

[14] For a description of the economic context for corporate debt restructuring in the wake of the 2008 crisis, *see* Thomas Laryea, *Approaches to Corporate Debt Restructuring in the Wake of Financial Crisis*, IMF Staff Position Note SPN/10/02 (January 2010), available online at <http://www.imf.org/external/pubs/ft/spn/2010/spn1002.pdf>.

3. The Resolution of Financial Institutions in a Cross-Border Context

23.21 When the financial crisis erupted in 2008, the response by economic policymakers followed along two distinct paths. First, measures were adopted that were designed to mitigate the effects of the crisis. These measures included fiscal stimulus, expansionary monetary policy, and, in some countries, large-scale intervention in the financial system. Second, even at the earliest stages of the crisis, there were initiatives to design reform measures that would prevent these types of crises from recurring in the future.[15] With respect to the crisis in the banking system, there was a painful awareness that these two distinct efforts were effectively operating at cross-purposes: while bailouts were need to ensure that weaknesses in several large or interconnected financial institutions did not threaten the stability of the entire system, there was recognition that such bailouts made it more—rather than less—likely that such a crisis would recur. Unless creditors of these institutions were forced to bear the costs of the risk that they incur, they would continue to ignore such risks.

23.22 In principle, this problem could be readily addressed by applying the type of legal framework that is generally applicable to companies: by restructuring the obligations of viable financial institutions and liquidating nonviable institutions, moral hazard problems would be avoided—as would the fiscal problems created by government bailouts. The difficulty is that the application of the general corporate insolvency law to financial institutions is problematic for a number of reasons relating to financial stability, including the fact that a number of features of the corporate insolvency process would not be feasible given the speed at which the bank resolution process need to take place.[16]

23.23 In light of these considerations, since the 2008 crisis erupted, policymakers have given priority to the development of resolution frameworks that were adequately tailored to financial institutions—that is, to the development of frameworks that would provide for the imposition of losses on shareholders and creditors while, at the same time, preserving the essential operations of the institutions, thereby safeguarding financial stability.

23.24 From the very outset, however, it has been recognized that this was not a problem that could be solved exclusively through a domestic policy response Since most of the systemically important financial institutions operate on a global basis, an uncoordinated application of resolution systems by national authorities would make it much more difficult both to secure the continuity of essential business operations and to ensure that both shareholders and creditors bear an appropriate share of the financial burden of the resolution process. Indeed, there is a stark contrast between the globally integrated way in which firms operate and the exclusively domestic way in which they are resolved. On the one hand, a large international financial group is likely, for efficiency purposes, to organize itself with centralized functions for the entire group, such as capital, liquidity, and risk management. Thus a subsidiary in a country, while legally distinct, may have no de facto independence from its parent or

[15] *See*, e.g., G-20, *Declaration on Strengthening the Financial System*, London, 2 April 2009, available online at <http://www.g20.utoronto.ca/2009/2009ifi.pdf>; *see* also G-20, *Leaders Statement*, Pittsburgh Summit, 24–25 September 2009, available online at <http://www.g20.utoronto.ca/2009/2009communique0925.html>.

[16] *See* IMF, *Overview of the Legal and Institutional and Regulatory Framework for Bank* (April 2009), available online at <http://www.imf.org/external/np/pp/eng/2009/041709.pdf>, 16.

affiliates located elsewhere. As a result of this interconnectedness, however, weaknesses in one of these affiliates can adversely affect the entire group. On the other hand, the resolution frameworks that operate in such times of distress are distinctly national in scope and apply to distinct parts of the group rather than the group as whole. Since bank resolution frameworks are currently established by national authorities, they are directly enforceable only vis-à-vis those institutions—or branches of institutions—operating in their territory. While this problem could be mitigated through cooperation among national authorities, the authorities are often not empowered to engage in such cooperation.

Indeed, experience demonstrates that the more integrated financial groups become, the **23.25**
more disruptive uncoordinated local resolution actions are likely to be. First, such actions can actually precipitate a crisis: if, during a period of stress, the host jurisdiction requires the transfer of assets to cover the liabilities of a branch, this action may actually destabilize the bank in the home jurisdiction. Second, in circumstances in which the home jurisdiction is trying to organize a rescue of the entire group, the unwillingness—or inability—of the host jurisdiction to cooperate may both destroy value and undermine financial stability. If, for example, the national authorities in the home jurisdiction wish to preserve business continuity through a purchase and assumption transaction (for example transfer of certain assets and liabilities to a bridge bank), these efforts will be undermined if the authorities who have jurisdiction over the branch do not allow for the necessary transfer of assets and focus exclusively on a liquidation to satisfy stakeholders in that branch.

In contemplating how to address this problem, the official sector recognized that the estab- **23.26**
lishment of a comprehensive legal framework that would implement full 'universality' was not feasible.[17] Under such an approach, jurisdictions would incur, through a new multilateral treaty, substantive obligations that would, in effect, require the host authorities to defer to the home authorities with respect to any resolution of a financial institution. It was recognized that, at least in the medium term, it was very unlikely that all key jurisdictions would be willing to sacrifice the degree of national sovereignty to implement such an approach. Moreover, implementing full universality would not necessarily solve the identified problem, since this approach applies only to single entities (that is, a parent bank and its branch). This would be an important shortcoming since the problems arising from cross-border interconnectedness—as described earlier—also apply to separate legal entities within a group.[18]

At least theoretically, an alternative approach would have been the other extreme: since it is **23.27**
not feasible to match global institutions with a global legal framework, one could consider 'de-globalizing' financial institutions so that they match existing national legal frameworks. Subsidiaries would need to be financially and operationally independent of their parents so that the resolution of one would not cause distress in the other. This approach would, of course, mean that firms would need to give up the efficiencies of operating on a global basis. More fundamentally, de-globalization of financial institutions would have undermined the ability of emerging markets and low-income countries to access credit markets. Moreover,

[17] Within the IMF, this discussion takes place on the basis of a paper entitled *Resolution of Cross-Border Banks: A Proposed Framework for Enhanced Co-ordination* (June 2010), available online at <https://<http://www.imf.org/external/np/pp/eng/2010/061110.pdf>.

[18] For a comprehensive discussion of the legal and institutional issues that arise in the context of cross-border resolution, *see* Rosa Lastra (ed.) *Cross Border Insolvency* (Oxford: Oxford University Press, 2011), 201.

the 2008 crisis has revealed that some degree of interconnectedness can support crisis resolution in these markets. In particular, financial support provided by parents to subsidiaries operating in member countries experiencing a financial crisis was very beneficial.[19]

23.28 Avoiding these approaches, the official sector settled on a middle option—one that would rely on cooperation among national authorities in the application of their own legal frameworks, but which would not require a complete surrender of sovereignty by these authorities. Elements of this approach were first recommended by the Cross-Border Bank Resolution Group of the Basel Committee on Banking Supervision (BCBS) in March 2010.[20] An elaborate framework for implementing this approach was developed by IMF Staff in June 2010 in its paper *Resolution of Cross-Border Banks—A Proposed Framework for Enhanced Co-ordination*.[21] Building on these efforts, the Financial Stability Board (FSB) proposed a more detailed framework in its *Key Attributes of Effective Resolution Regimes for Financial Institutions*,[22] which was endorsed by the G-20 during its 2011 meeting.[23]

23.29 The approach proposed by the BCBS, the IMF, and the FSB involves the establishment of an enhanced coordination framework that would be agreed among countries that are in a position to adhere to its various elements. As elaborated in the *Key Attributes*, the enhanced cooperation framework consists of several self-supporting elements.

(a) Domestic laws would be modified so as to authorize national authorities to cooperate with foreign jurisdictions.
(b) Participating countries would achieve a minimum level of harmonization in the design of their resolution frameworks.
(c) Finally, a procedural framework would be established that would facilitate coordination for global systemically international financial institutions (G-SIFIs).

In addition to the above, an issue identified in the IMF paper is the need to establish a framework for financial burden sharing among relevant jurisdictions. Each of these is now briefly described.

A. Empowering national authorities to cooperate

23.30 The FSB's *Key Attributes* provides that national law should 'empower and strongly encourage' the national resolution authority to act in a manner that achieves a 'cooperative solution with foreign resolution authorities'. While this provision would preclude national legislation from requiring unilateral 'ring fencing' of the local entity in all circumstances, it falls short of actually imposing a cooperation requirement: domestic regulators would continue to have the latitude to choose to refuse to cooperate with a foreign resolution authority when such cooperation is judged to be inconsistent with their mandate both to pursue domestic

---

[19] This support was enhanced through the European Bank Co-ordination Initiative (known as the 'Vienna Initiative'), which was launched in 2009. For a description of the Vienna Initiative, *see* European Bank for Reconstruction and Development (EBRD), available online at <http://www.ebrd.com/pages/research/publications/factsheets.shtml>.

[20] *See* BCBS, *Report and Recommendation of the Cross-Border Bank Resolution Group* (March 2010), available online at <http://www.bis.org/publ/bcbs169.pdf.>

[21] *See* IMF (n. 17).

[22] FSB, *Key Attributes of Effective Resolution Regimes for Financial Institutions*(October 2011), available online at <http://www.financialstabilityboard.org/publications/r_111104cc.pdf>.

[23] G-20, *Communiqué: G-20 Leaders Summit*, Cannes, 3–4 November 2011, available online at <http://www.whitehouse.gov/the-press-office/2011/11/04/cannes-g-20-communique>.

financial stability and to protect the creditors of the domestic institution. In this respect, there is no surrender of sovereignty. At the same time, and as is discussed in the relevant IMF paper, it is recognized that, in circumstances in which the foreign resolution authority in question has adhered to other elements of the cooperation framework—including the harmonization of key substantive aspects of the resolution regime—there would be a presumption that cooperation would, in fact, further the interests of domestic stability and domestic creditors.[24]

Interestingly, the delicate balance between encouraging cooperation, on the one hand, and preserving national sovereignty, on the other hand is reflected in § 210 of the US Dodd–Frank Act of 2009, which directs the Federal Deposit Insurance Corporation (FDIC) as follows: **23.31**

> The Corporation, as a receiver for a covered financial company, shall co-ordinate, to the maximum extent possible, with the appropriate foreign financial authorities regarding the orderly liquidation of any covered financial company that has assets or operations in a country other than the United States.[25]

B. Harmonization of resolution frameworks

It is recognized that resolution authorities would, as a practical matter, exercise their new-found authority to coordinate with foreign resolution authorities only if they had sufficient confidence in the capacity of their counterparts—and that such confidence would be enhanced if there were convergence among various jurisdictions regarding the design of their resolution frameworks. To that end, both the FSB and the IMF recommended that the design of the domestic legal framework for the resolution of financial institutions include a number of critical features, including, in particular, the following.[26] **23.32**

- *Early intervention*—It is critical that there be some consistency among jurisdictions regarding the trigger that allows for intervention and that this trigger enable the authorities to take action before balance-sheet insolvency.
- *Broad resolution powers*—In order to achieve the objective of resolving institutions in a manner that preserves critical operations, it is critical that the national legal framework give the resolution authority robust resolution powers, including:
  (a) the authority to take control of the institution, and to remove and replace senior management;
  (b) the capacity to conclude mergers and acquisitions, and transfers to other institutions (including bridge banks), without third-party consent; and
  (c) the capacity to temporarily suspend termination provisions contained in financial contracts.
- *Creditor safeguards*—Since these broad resolution powers interfere with property and contractual rights, it is important that the safeguards—including judicial review of the actions of the resolution authority within carefully circumscribed limits—be included in the design of the legal framework. Among these safeguards is the rule that compensation be provided to a creditor to ensure that it is no worse off in resolution that it would have been if the institution had failed and gone into liquidation.

24 IMF (n. 17), 18.
25 Section 210(a)(1)(N) Dodd-Frank Wall Street Reform and Consumer Protection Act of 2009.
26 *See* IMF (n. 17), 19–21; *see* also FSB (n. 22), 7–12.

- *Non-discrimination*—Cross-border coordination will be possible only if national resolution authorities have the assurance that domestic laws do not discriminate against creditors on the basis of nationality, location of claim, or the jurisdiction in which it is payable. Domestic depositor preference based on the nationality or location of the depositor would be inconsistent with this principle.

23.33 Regarding the substantive issues that are raised by the harmonization element of the *Key Attributes*, two are of particular interest.

23.34 First, while most of the resolution powers identified reflect best practices in this area, at least one was novel: the recommendation that the regulators have the capacity to 'bail in' unsecured creditors and shareholders. This authority would enable the regulator to conduct a mandatory conversion of the claims of unsecured creditors into equity, thereby relying on creditors to recapitalize the institution in question. Relative to other resolution tools, which envisage a restructuring in the context of some form of liquidation, bail-in authority would involve a 'going concern' restructuring that allows for the continuity of the original legal entity. The objective of this approach is to maximize the possibility that critical operations would continue in a distressed firm, thereby limiting the risk of financial instability. As yet, there is limited experience with the application of bail-in authority. It should be noted that, while the Dodd–Frank Act gives the FDIC the authority to restructure the claims of unsecured creditors unilaterally into equity, this would occur with respect to the newly created entities that have been formed as part of the resolution process—that is, while bail-in would occur, it would do so in the context of the exercise of the FDIC's liquidation authority.

23.35 Second, harmonization of creditor priorities proved to be a difficult issue. This was an area that had been identified in the IMF paper as being an important condition for cross-border coordination. In particular, if the priority rules in the home country do not recognize a priority given in the host country to its insured depositors and deposit guarantee scheme, this difference may undermine the incentive of the host country to cooperate and will more likely result in it seeking a purely domestic solution. However, the *Key Attributes* do not require such harmonization, reflecting the difficulty in achieving a consensus on a very contentious question. Rather, with respect to this issue, the *Key Attributes* have had to settle with the requirement of transparency: 'The treatment of creditors and ranking in insolvency should be transparent and properly disclosed to depositors, insurance policy holders and other creditors.'[27]

C. Coordination procedures

23.36 Given the speed at which intervention must occur if it is to achieve the objective of both ensuring burden sharing and maintaining financial stability, it was recognized that credible coordination procedures would need to be established *ex ante*. In the midst of a meltdown, there is little time to improvise on how to collaborate and any uncertainty would merely increase the odds that national authorities would resort to ring fencing. For this reason, considerable effort has been made to establish a robust framework for coordination with respect to G-SIFIs, which would build upon the contingency planning that is being done at

[27] *See* FSB (n. 22), 13.

the national level in a number of countries. The most important features of this framework, which is set forth in detail in the *Key Attributes*, may be summarized as follows.

i. Crisis management groups

At the heart of the coordination framework are the crisis management groups (CMGs) that are to be established by each home and host jurisdiction for G-SIFIs, and which are to comprise all of the regulatory agencies that are responsible for the resolution of systemic financial institutions—that is, supervisory authorities, central banks, resolution authorities, finance ministries, and the authorities responsible for any guarantee scheme applicable to financial institutions.[28] **23.37**

ii. Cooperation agreements

The *Key Attributes* envisage that, with respect to G-SIFIs, each of the CMGs will enter into institution-specific cooperation agreements that provide a roadmap on how coordination among the respective institutions will take place in the event of the need for a resolution of the institution in question. Within each CMG, it is envisaged that a lead agency would be identified—an important feature given the fact that a financial group is often likely to be subject to the jurisdiction of a number of different agencies. Moreover, the coordination agreements entered into among the CMGs are required to define the respective roles of the authorities during the crisis. In particular, host jurisdictions are required to commit that they will make every effort to cooperate with the actions being taken by the home jurisdiction and, in particular, will 'not pre-empt resolution actions by home authorities while reserving the right to act on their own initiative if necessary to achieve domestic stability in the absence of effective means of the home authority'.[29] This text further reflects—as discussed earlier—the attempt to balance delicately the need to achieve effective cooperation with the recognition that host jurisdictions would not be willing to surrender national sovereignty of the resolution of entities within their jurisdiction. Finally, in addition to setting forth a roadmap on how a crisis would be handled, the cooperation agreements are required to commit to regular meetings that will assess, among other things, new information for the purposes of assessing the continued appropriateness of the envisaged roadmap.[30] **23.38**

iii. Recovery and resolution plans/resolvability assessments

As a substantive matter, the cooperation commitments will centre on how the cooperating jurisdictions will implement the recovery and resolution plans that each systemic financial institution will be required to prepare. The *Key Attributes* identify the necessary elements of these plans and the fact that they must be subject to a resolvability assessment to be undertaken by the home jurisdiction, in cooperation with the host jurisdiction. Where a corporate group is concerned, the home jurisdiction would prepare an assessment of the group, while the host jurisdiction would prepare an assessment of the subsidiary that is consistent with the former assessment. The objective of the resolvability assessment is to 'evaluate the feasibility of resolution strategies and their credibility in light of the likely impact of the firm's failure on the financial system and the overall economy'.[31] **23.39**

[28] *See* FSB (n. 22), 14.
[29] *See* FSB (n. 22), 24.
[30] FSB (n. 22), 22.
[31] FSB (n. 22), 15.

iv. Sharing of information

23.40 Given the fact that the cooperation agreements are institution-specific, it was recognized that cooperating jurisdictions would most likely need to share with each other confidential information regarding the specific firms in question. For this reason, the *Key Attributes* provide that domestic laws should empower national resolution authorities, subject to the receipt of confidentiality safeguards, to share information with cooperating jurisdictions regarding the recovery and resolution plans that have been prepared with respect to the firms in their jurisdictions.[32]

D. Financial burden sharing

23.41 Although a key objective of a robust cross-border resolution framework is to minimize the need for a bailout by the public sector, experience demonstrates that the resolution process may, indeed, require some public funding, even if this funding is only temporary. However, unlike in the context of corporate debt restructuring, the frameworks applicable to financial institutions generally do not provide for the debtor- in possession (DIP) financing that would provide the basis for liquidity support during the resolution process.[33] Among other things, the resolution process—by necessity—moves so quickly that the private sector will not be able to act with sufficient speed to mobilize the needed financial support—particularly where, as often will be the case, there is turmoil in the market that places strain on other financial institutions. In these circumstances, the public sector may have no choice but to provide the necessary funding, either from the ministry of finance or the central bank—with the risk that the resolution process fails and the public sector is not repaid in full.

23.42 In light of these points, a key issue that arises in the design of a cross-border resolution framework is the issue of burden sharing. Home countries are likely to be unable—or unwilling—to absorb the entire cost of rescuing or resolving a large international group. While the allocation of the financial burden between the home jurisdiction and the host jurisdiction can be reached after the crisis, this approach does not provide the home jurisdiction with any certainty during the crisis, and this uncertainty may undermine its incentive to take prompt and effective action. For this reason, the IMF paper stressed that an important element of any cross-border resolution framework would be the reach of an *ex ante* agreement on how the financial cost of public intervention would be allocated. Ideally, these agreements would be institution-specific and would be integrated into the cooperation agreements. Short of that, and at a minimum, there should be some *ex ante* agreement on the criteria that would guide the allocation of cost in the event of a cross-border resolution. Among the possible criteria identified in the IMF paper were: the relative systemic importance of the group across jurisdictions; the relative contribution from the deposit guarantee scheme and any other resolution funds; and the relative distribution of losses across jurisdictions.[34]

23.43 Of course, it is recognized that reaching agreement on burden-sharing issues is politically sensitive given the fact that a primary objective of a cross-border resolution framework is to avoid public bailouts. Nevertheless, given the critical—albeit limited role—that public funding plays in the resolution framework, this is not an issue that can be avoided.

---

32 FSB (n. 22), 14.

33 For a general discussion of DIP financing in the context of corporate restructuring, *see* IMF (n. 7).

34 IMF (n. 17), 24–5.

4. Household Debt and its Systemic Implications

23.44 One of the novel features of the financial crisis of 2008 is that the debt overhang in the household sector was of such a magnitude that developing a framework to address the problem became not only a social priority, but also a macroeconomic imperative. While institutions such as the IMF had extensive experience in assisting members to restructure corporate, banking, and sovereign debt, establishing mechanisms to address unsustainable household debt presented novel challenges. Unlike in the corporate and banking context, for example, there are no internationally recognized best practices that can serve as a guide. The causes of the problem varied. In Hungary and Poland, for example, the need for a restructuring arose, in part, because of the devaluation in the local currency, which made it impossible for many homeowners to service foreign-currency-denominated mortgages.[35] In the United States and Ireland, the problem arose primarily from a collapse of property prices, which, following years of an excessive credit boom in the housing sector, resulted in families having negative equity in their homes.[36]

23.45 Whatever the causes of the problem, the economic consequences of allowing the debt overhang in the household sector to persist has become painfully obvious. First, this debt—as with unsustainable corporate debt—threatened the balance sheets of banks by increasing the volume of non-performing loans. Resulting weaknesses in the financial position of the banks led to a sharp reduction in the availability of credit, thereby undermining economic growth. Second, the 'wealth' effect of households having less—and in some cases negative—equity as a result of a sharp decline in household prices has a negative impact on consumption, which also affects growth. Lower growth increases unemployment, further depressing household income—thereby exacerbating the downward spiral.[37]

23.46 Faced with problems of this magnitude, the question is not whether the government should intervene, but rather what should be the nature and scope of this intervention. It has been recognized that allowing the problem to be resolved exclusively by the 'market' through widespread foreclosures on defaulted household debt was not a viable strategy. Apart from the social cost of such an approach, in some cases it merely exacerbated the economic problem: since foreclosures are relatively inefficient in terms of recovery, they put further downward pressure on prices, therefore increasing both general uncertainty and the stress on bank balance sheets.

23.47 In that context, an extremely difficult—and politically sensitive—issue has been how to restructure mortgage debt, including, in particular, mortgage debt where the value of the property has declined to the point at which it is less than the value of the loan. In these circumstances, it would

[35] *See* IMF, *Hungary* (n. 9); IMF, *Poland: Request for Stand-By Arrangement.*

[36] *See* IMF, *United States: 2012 Article IV Consultation*, IMF Country Report No. 12/213 (August 2012), available online at <http://www.imf.org/external/pubs/ft/scr/2012/cr12213.pdf>; IMF, *Ireland: 2012 [US] Article IV and Seventh Review under the Extended Arrangement—Staff Report* (September 2012), available online at <http://www.imf.org/external/pubs/cat/longres.aspx?sk=26248.0>; see also IMF, *Ireland: Ninth Review under the Extended Arrangement*, IMF Country Report No. 13/93 (April 2013), available online at <http://www.imf.org/external/pubs/ft/scr/2013/cr1393.pdf>.

[37] For a general discussion of the macroeconomic implications of overindebteness in the household sector, *see* Luc Laeven and Thomas Laryea, *Principles of Household Debt Restructuring*, IMF State Position Note SPN/09/15 (June 2009), available online at <http://www.imf.org/external/pubs/ft/spn/2009/spn0915.pdf>.

appear to be in the interest of the debtor, the creditor and the economy more generally for the unsecured portion of the property to be restructured along with all other unsecured debt—that is, for there to be a write-down of the mortgage principal. However, such an approach is generally not permitted under the legal frameworks applicable to household debt.

23.48 Indeed, a very notable example of a country that has suffered as a result of this deficiency is the United States.[38] Problems in the housing sector were a primary contributor to the 2008 crisis and there is a general consensus that the decline in housing prices—which has been exacerbated by reliance on foreclosures—is one of the principle reasons why growth in the United States was so anaemic in 2012. Between March 2011 and April 2012, more than 2.6 million foreclosures were initiated and more than 900,000 homes were actually sold in foreclosure. Apart from depressing house prices, the 'wealth' effect of these enforcement measures undermined not only consumer demand, but also local and state tax bases. As a means of finding an alternative to the foreclosure process, the US government launched a series of initiatives designed to encourage voluntary mortgage write-downs. The viability of a voluntary approach has been undermined by a number of factors, including the fact that a significant amount of the mortgage debt has been securitized. Specifically, as a result of the securitization process, it is the servicer of the mortgage loan, rather than either the loan originator or the holders of the mortgage-backed security, which has the primary power to decide whether a delinquent mortgage goes into foreclosure or is restructured. Unfortunately, a loan servicer does not have the financial incentive or the legal capacity under the relevant 'pooling' agreement to initiate—or even agree to—a mortgage restructuring.

23.49 Given the important impact that mortgage restructuring could have on the US economy, the IMF Staff recently lent its voice to the growing call for the introduction of a legal framework that would support mandatory mortgage restructuring. The IMF Staff's views are reflected in a paper prepared in the context of what is referred to as the 'Article IV Consultation' with the United States, the annual exercise that involves an assessment by the IMF of whether its member's policies are consistent with their obligations under the Fund's charter, its Articles of Agreement. These include the obligation to promote domestic stability, which require members, among other things, to 'direct their domestic economic and financial policies toward the objective of fostering orderly economic growth with reasonable price stability'.[39]

---

[38] In the United States, the economic consequences of these deficiencies are described in IMF, *United States* (n. 36), 98–9.

[39] Article IV(1)(a)(ii) IMF Articles of Agreement. The full text of Article IV(1) reads as follows:

Section 1. General obligations of members

Recognizing that the essential purpose of the international monetary system is to provide a framework that facilitates the exchange of goods, services, and capital among countries, and that sustains sound economic growth, and that a principal objective is the continuing development of the orderly underlying conditions that are necessary for financial and economic stability, each member undertakes to collaborate with the Fund and other members to assure orderly exchange arrangements and to promote a stable system of exchange rates. In particular, each member shall:

(i) endeavor to direct its economic and financial policies toward the objective of fostering orderly economic growth with reasonable price stability, with due regard to its circumstances;
(ii) seek to promote stability by fostering orderly underlying economic and financial conditions and a monetary system that does not tend to produce erratic disruptions;
(iii) avoid manipulating exchange rates or the international monetary system in order to prevent effective balance of payments adjustment or to gain an unfair competitive advantage over other members; and
(iv) follow exchange policies compatible with the undertakings under this Section.

The discussion of these issues in the context of the US Article IV Consultation reflected a judgement of the Staff that failure to address the foreclosure crisis was of relevance to domestic stability of the US economy.

The IMF staff's proposal to introduce a mandatory framework to restructure mortgage debt built on the work done by the National Bankruptcy Conference (NBC), a non-profit organization comprising lawyers, law professors, and judges who are leading experts in the area of bankruptcy.[40] In essence, the proposal would entail modifying Chapter 13 of the US Bankruptcy Code to allow for a modification of mortgages that apply to a debtor's principal residence.[41] It is important to emphasize that such a modification would be designed to be consistent with the broader principles that underlie the US bankruptcy system. Specifically, and whether it be in the corporate or household context, a secured creditor is normally treated differently from—and preferentially to—unsecured claims, but only to the extent that the value of the collateral is equal to the value of the creditors' claim. The value of the secured creditor's claim is normally determined at the timing of the filing of the bankruptcy petition. If the collateral is worth less than the secured claim, the claim is 'bifurcated' into a secured claim equal to the value of the collateral and an unsecured claim for the remaining amount. The secured portion of the claim must be paid in full or fully cured during the term of the repayment plan confirmed by the court, while the unsecured claim is paid pro rata with other unsecured claims and generally written down. Under the existing law, however, even if the value of the house is less than the value of the mortgage loan, there is no bifurcation: provided that the loan is a first residential mortgage, no portion of the loan—including the unsecured portion—can be modified without the lender's consent.[42] The NBC proposal, which was supported in the IMF Staff paper, would involve—among other things—the elimination of the prohibition on the modification of first residential mortgages: the bankruptcy court could strip such mortgages down to the fair market value of the residence as of the bankruptcy petition and re-amortize them over a period not to exceed thirty years.[43] **23.50**

The mortgage industry has generally opposed any proposals that would involve the elimination of the 'special protection' given to residential mortgages.[44] When this protection was originally introduced in 1978 in the context of the overall reform of the Bankruptcy Code, the industry argued that it was necessary in order to ensure an adequate flow of credit into the housing market. Consistent with that position, the argument against the elimination of this provision was that, by shifting additional risk to lenders, it would increase the cost of home mortgages and undermine credit availability. Concerns have also been expressed about potential abuse by debtors—including wealthier debtors—who might file for bankruptcy for the purpose of achieving this relief, and then benefit from a windfall if they sell their property after the housing market has recovered and their houses have appreciated in value. **23.51**

---

[40] For a description of the NBC's composition and mission, *see* NBC, 'Our Mission', available online at <http://www.nationalbankruptcyconference.org/mission.cfm>.

[41] A description of the NBC's proposal is included in the 30 October 2007 Testimony of Richard Levin, Vice Chair of the NBC, given before Subcommittee on Commercial and Administrative Law of the House Judiciary Committee, available online at <http://www.nationalbankruptcyconference.org/images/Levin%20 Testimony%2010_07.pdf>.

[42] *See* § 1322(b)(2) US Bankruptcy Code.

[43] *See* IMF, *United States* (n. 36), 107–8.

[44] The mortgage industry has been constantly against any proposal to allow any modifications of mortgages in Chapter 13: *see* <http://mortgagebankers.org/files/AU/IssueBriefs/CramDownIssueBrief.pdf>.

23.52 The arguments made by the mortgage industry are not entirely convincing. If the mortgage is stripped down to the value of the property, the mortgage lender is still getting what it would have received had the borrower not filed for bankruptcy and the lender exercised its foreclosure rights. Moreover, the provisions of Chapter 13 are designed to prevent the type of 'strategic' bankruptcy filings that are the concern of mortgage lenders. For example, there is a cap on the amount of individual debt and a detailed review by the court of the entire financial situation of the debtor. Moreover, the NBC proposal contained provisions that would be designed to ensure that, in the event of an appreciation of the property after the modification, the secured creditors would be able to recapture some of the equity. For example, under the proposal, if the debtor sells the property within a year after the principal is reduced at a price that is in excess of the value determined during bankruptcy, 50 per cent of the difference is payable to the lender.

5. Restructuring Sovereign Debt: An Unresolved Problem

23.53 During the period 2000–03, there was an intensive debate as to whether the framework for restructuring sovereign debt needed to be modified, and if so, how.[45] It is fair to say that the crisis of 2008 has rekindled that debate. As noted in the introduction, although the crisis created distress in the corporate, bank, and household sectors, the sovereigns' own balance sheet, at least initially, were spared. However, as a result of combination of factors, including the fact that the bailout of the banking system in a number of countries simply shifted the debt problems to the sovereign, the problem of sovereign debt has become a primary—if not *the* primary—focus of concern in a broad range of advanced economies. As these countries struggle to address their overindebtedness with a number of tools—including both loose monetary policy and fiscal austerity—the subject of sovereign debt restructuring has once again become a central part of the policy debate.

23.54 Although this subject raises complex—and politically sensitive—issues, they may be distilled into two broad questions: first, when should a sovereign debt restructuring take place; and second, in those cases in which it is needed, how should it proceed? Answering these questions is difficult precisely because, as will be discussed next, sovereign debt is *sui generis* and, accordingly, many of the approaches that have been discussed earlier in this chapter regarding corporate, banking, and household debt are simply inapplicable.

A. When should a sovereign restructure its debt?

23.55 The problem of overindebtedness of a sovereign is hardly new. With the globalization of capital markets, advanced economies and creditworthy emerging market economies have been able to access private capital with relative ease, either indirectly, through the banking sector, or directly, through the issuance of bonds. As is often the case, as the indebtedness of these countries increases, markets may begin to become concerned about the capacity of the member to continue to service its debt and, as a result, will increase the interest rates that are charged on the amounts that the country needs to continue to service its debt. Depending on the circumstances of the country, however, these increases may simply exacerbate the

[45] For a discussion of the scope of this debate—and its motivations—*see* Sean Hagan, 'Designing a Legal Framework to Restructuring Sovereign Debt' (2005) 36(2) Georgetown J Int'l Law 299.

concern within the market about the sovereign's debt-servicing capacity and, at some point, the cost of borrowing becomes so prohibitive that the sovereign effectively loses access to the markets.

In circumstances in which a sovereign has lost access to private finance, it will normally turn to the IMF for financial support so as to enable it to continue to service its debt. Under its charter, the Articles of Agreement, the IMF may provide financing to a member country only when it has satisfied itself that the member is undertaking the adjustment measures that the IMF judges to be necessary to address its underlying problems. These measures must be implemented within a time frame that provides the IMF with the assurance that the member will be able to repay the Fund in accordance with the maturity structure of IMF financing, which is typically three to five years.[46] These requirements give rise to what is referred to as IMF 'conditionality'.[47] **23.56**

The precise nature of the adjustment measures that form part of IMF conditionality will depend on the circumstances of the member. While the consolidation of public finances is normally an important part of the package (through a combination of a reduction in expenditures and an increases in revenues), there is a limit to the degree to which fiscal measures can be relied upon before they begin to become counterproductive: at some point, excessive fiscal austerity will undermine demand and growth, thereby adversely affecting the revenue base.[48] Indeed, for many countries, the only sustainable solution to addressing the problem of overindebtedness *is* growth: a country that is growing fast enough will effectively be able to grow out of its debt, which is why an assessment of the sustainability of a member's debt level is normally determined by reference to the ratio of debt to gross domestic product (GDP). In circumstances in which growth can no longer be fuelled by borrowing because of the market's concerns, the only durable basis for such growth is the introduction of measures that enhance the country's competitiveness. In circumstances in which a country has its own currency, this can be achieved through a devaluation of the currency. However, where a country forms part of a currency union and, accordingly, this instrument cannot be relied upon, a country will have no choice but to adjust through what is referred to as an 'internal devaluation'. Under this approach, competitiveness is enhanced through measures designed to lower prices and increase productivity. Indeed, lowering prices is a particular priority for overindebted countries given the fact that the inflow of capital arising from this borrowing **23.57**

---

[46] Article V(3)(a), which gives the Fund the authority to provide balance-of-payments financing, reads as follows:

> (*a*) The Fund shall adopt policies on the use of its general resources, including policies on stand-by or similar arrangements, and may adopt special policies for special balance of payments problems, that will assist members to solve their balance of payments problems in a manner consistent with the provisions of this Agreement and that will establish adequate safeguards for the temporary use of the general resources of the Fund.

[47] The Fund adopts decisions of general applicability ('policies') that guide the design and implementation of IMF conditionality, which include the Guidelines on Conditionality. *See* IMF, *Selected Decisions and Selected Documents of the International Monetary Fund*, 36th Issue (Washington DC: IMF, 2011), available online at <http://www.imf.org/external/pubs/ft/sd/2012/123111.pdf>.

[48] There has been a rich debate on the extent to which fiscal consolidation—austerity—can be relied upon to reduce overindebtedness: *see*, e.g., Martin Wolf, 'Banks are on a Eurozone Knife-Edge', *Financial Times*, 23 April 2013, available online at <http://www.ft.com/intl/cms/s/0/035c1b2e-8d37-11e1-8b49-00144feab49a.html#axzz2SiI8oQTK>. *See* also IMF (n. 3).

will normally have exacerbated the increase in prices that have undermined competitiveness. The adjustment measures that are needed to achieve this internal devaluation include labour market reform and the measures that deregulate sectors of the economy that were protected from the forces of completion.[49]

23.58 When a member is losing or has already lost market access, the purpose of the IMF's support is normally of a 'catalytic' nature—namely, the financing provided by the IMF, coupled with the formulation and implementation of a credible economic adjustment programme, is designed to restore market access by giving lenders confidence that the debtor will, in fact, have the capacity to service its existing debt burden. There are situations, however, in which this approach is no longer feasible because the member's debt is so large that it is judged to be 'unsustainable'—that is, a judgement is made that, under any reasonable assumptions, the member's debt-to-GDP ratio is most likely going to continue to rise in the medium term, no matter what adjustment measures are introduced and no matter how much financing is provided by the Fund. As already noted, there are limits to the degree to which fiscal consolidation can address overindebtedness, since an excessive dose of austerity will only worsen debt dynamics by undermining growth. Moreover, where debt is unsustainable, financing by institutions such as the IMF may actually exacerbate the problem because it is merely adding to the debt burden. In these cases, the only solution—short of the provision of grant financing—is for a debt restructuring to take place that results in a reduction in the net present value (NPV) of the debt.

23.59 Accordingly, when the IMF determines that a member's debt is unsustainable, it is precluded from continuing to provide financing unless steps are being taken to ensure sustainability, which will normally require a debt restructuring.[50] Judgements about sustainability are just that—judgements, which, by necessity, involve the exercise of considerable discretion. The advantage of a framework that relies on discretion is that it has given the Fund the flexibility

---

[49] It is recognized that, while in the medium term such policies increase competitiveness and therefore growth, these measures may reduce demand in the short term as a result of, for example, the reduction of the minimum wage.

[50] The requirement of debt sustainability as a condition for Fund financing is explicitly set forth in the policy on exceptional access, which applies in circumstances under which the Fund's exposure exceeds 200 of a member's quota. The relevant provision of the decision provides that all of the following criteria be satisfied:

(a) The member is experiencing or has the potential to experience exceptional balance of payments pressures on the current account or the capital account, resulting in a need for Fund financing that cannot be met within the normal limits.

(b) A rigorous and systematic analysis indicates that there is a high probability that the member's public debt is sustainable in the medium term. However, in instances where there are significant uncertainties that make it difficult to state categorically that there is a high probability that the debt is sustainable over this period, exceptional access would be justified if there is a high risk of international systemic spillovers. Debt sustainability for these purposes will be evaluated on a forward-looking basis and may take into account, inter alia, the intended restructuring of debt to restore sustainability. This criterion applies only to public (domestic and external) debt. However, the analysis of such public debt sustainability will incorporate any potential contingent liabilities of the government, including those potentially arising from private external indebtedness.

(c) The member has prospects of gaining or regaining access to private capital markets within the timeframe when Fund resources are outstanding.

(d) The policy program of the member provides a reasonably strong prospect of success, including not only the member's adjustment plans but also its institutional and political capacity to deliver that adjustment.

(IMF (n. 47), 456–7)

to provide very large amounts of money to heavily indebted countries on the basis of an assessment that, notwithstanding the size of the member's indebtedness, the debt-to-GDP ratio of the particular country concerned can be stabilized by the implementation of an effective macroeconomic adjustment programme—that is, notwithstanding the loss of market access, the debt is sustainable and can be paid on its original terms. Avoiding a restructuring in these circumstances limits the cost both for the country and the system more generally.[51]

However, this flexibility also has its disadvantages: the exercise of discretion in this context can result in an excessively sanguine view of the debt dynamics—that is, there are circumstances in which the debt is judged to be sustainable even though there are a number of factors that indicated that it is probably not. The tendency to 'give sustainability the benefit of the doubt' reflects, in large part, the confluence of incentives that is typically in place when judgements need to be made as to whether to restructure sovereign debt. First, countries generally want to avoid a restructuring because of the economic dislocation that may occur, particularly in circumstances in which the domestic banks hold a significant amount of the debt in question.[52] Second, private creditors also have an interest in avoiding a restructuring since they would prefer to paid on the original terms. Finally, other countries—and the official creditor community—may be concerned about the contagion effect of a restructuring—particularly where the debtor's economy is closely integrated into those of other countries—as is the case with a currency union. Accordingly, all of these actors may have an interest in having the IMF continue to provide financing in the absence of a debt restructuring. **23.60**

As understandable as this incentive structure may be, it is short-sighted. For the debtor, delaying the inevitable restructuring will only amplify the shock when the day of reckoning arrives—particularly where the banking system acquires even more debt during the interim and, accordingly, is even more insolvent. Moreover, the uncertainty created by the debt overhang will depress growth and investment. For the private creditors, those who have not 'exited' will find that they suffer a greater loss than would have been the case, since now there are fewer creditors to bear the burden. Finally, for the official community, the result of such delay is that a large portion of private creditors are simply bailed out, which only serves to exacerbate moral hazard. **23.61**

Ensuring that unsustainable debt is restructured earlier rather than later will, in the final analysis, require a modification of IMF lending policy. As noted, under the current policy, the central criterion relied upon to determine whether or not IMF financing will be made contingent upon a debt restructuring is that of debt sustainability. Can the discretion that is relied upon for purposes of the application of this criterion be further constrained? This is not a new debate. Over the years, alternative 'triggers' have been discussed, including, for example, the use of firm limits on the amount of access that can be provided to a country.[53] Such an approach would have the benefit of certainty: in circumstances in which the member needed financing above such access limits, the financing would need to come **23.62**

---

51 The benefits of an early and orderly restructuring of sovereign debt were discussed extensively at the time the SDRM was explored: *see* Anne Krueger and Sean Hagan, 'Sovereign Workouts: An IMF Perspective' (2005–06) 6 Chi J Int'l L 203.

52 Indeed, countries are normally tempted to 'gamble for resurrection' by adopting extreme measures that are designed to avoid the economic and political pain of a debt restructuring: *see* Krueger and Hagan (n. 51), 207.

53 Andy Haldane and Mark Kruger, *The Resolution of International Financial Crises: Private Finance and Public Funds* (November 2001), available online at <http://www.bankofengland.co.uk/publications/Documents/other/financialstability/boeandboc.pdf>.

through the relief provided by a debt restructuring. However, as also noted, retaining some degree of discretion has the advantage of the IMF being able to provide large financing packages to those countries that, notwithstanding their debt, the IMF assesses as having the capacity to grow out of their debt—that is, those countries whose debt is sustainable. This loss of flexibility would bring a cost not only for the country, but also for the system. At the time of writing, the IMF has initiated a review of its policies and practices in this area, to determine whether it is possible to impose greater discipline in its lending policies so that restructurings occur only when necessary, but that, when necessary, they occur as soon as possible.[54]

B. How should a restructuring take place? Collective action problems

23.63 When the judgement has been made—as difficult as that judgement may be—that a sovereign's debt is unsustainable and, accordingly, will need to be restructured, all stakeholders have an interest in ensuring that the restructuring take place in a relatively orderly and predictable manner. Over the past fifteen years, there has been a relatively heated discussion as to whether there is an adequate legal framework to ensure that this can happen. The chief concern identified by proponents of reform have been collective actions problems—namely, although private creditors as a group would stand to benefit from agreeing to a restructuring of unsustainable debt as soon as possible, individual creditors may believe that it is in their best interests to decline, to participate in the hope of receiving payment under the original terms. Of course, to the extent that creditors as a group perceive that individual creditors may hold out, it will undermine their own incentive to participate in the restructuring in light of the intercreditor concerns that would arise. Moreover, holdout risks might undermine the debtor's willingness to initiate the restructuring process, given the possibility that broad creditor support would not be achieved.[55]

23.64 Collective action problems are a form of market failure and, of course, are also of relevance in the context of any insolvency proceeding—corporate, banking, and household. In those cases, the problem is generally addressed by statutory provisions that limit the ability of individuals to enforce their claims, and enable a restructuring that has been agreed by a qualified majority of creditors to be made binding on all creditors. The collective action problems confronting a sovereign are somewhat unique, however, and have been greatly shaped by the developments in financial and legal developments in at least two respects.[56]

23.65 First, over the past twenty years, the composition of creditors has changed significantly. The restructuring of sovereign debt that took place during the 1980s primarily involved commercial banks and, although the process was not free of difficulties, collective action problems were somewhat limited. Even though much of the debt was in default, litigation was rather limited. Moreover, there was broad support among banks with respect to the terms of a restructuring agreement, which were negotiated under the control of the bank steering committees. The constructive approach followed by banks reflected not only the fact that

---

[54] *See* IMF, *Sovereign Debt Restructuring: Recent Developments and Implications for the Fund's Legal and Policy Framework* (April 2013), available online at <http://www.imf.org/external/np/pp/eng/2013/042613.pdf>.

[55] For further discussion regarding holdout issues, *see* Hagan (n. 45), 311–24.

[56] As described by UNCITRAL (n. 6), these are common features of any well-designed corporate rehabilitation law.

they were regulated institutions under the influence of the official sector, but also the fact that many of them had longer-term relationships with the sovereign debtor.[57]

However, with the emergence of the sovereign bond market as the primary source of financing for sovereigns, the restructuring process has become far more complicated. In particular, collective action problems have been exacerbated not only because of the large number of creditors, but also because of their composition. Many of the institutions who purchase these bonds on the secondary market are unregulated and have no long-term relationship with the sovereign. As credit purchasers rather than credit providers, their singular objective is to maximize the value of their claims. In some cases, these creditors can actually facilitate the restructuring process. For example, a creditor that has purchased its claim on the secondary market at a very steep discount will be in a much better position to agree to significant debt reduction than a creditor who purchased the claim at its face value. However, there are a relatively small group of credit purchasers (often referred to as 'vultures') who have developed a strategy of not participating in a debt restructuring and instead suing the sovereign for full recovery.[58] **23.66**

The second development relates to changes in the legal environment—changes that have effectively enhanced the leverage of holdout creditors, thereby undermining the restructuring process. As a general matter, it has become relatively straightforward to get a judgment against a sovereign as result of the erosion of the traditional concept of sovereign immunity.[59] It is far more difficult, however, to collect on that judgment. Only certain classes of asset are generally available for attachment and they need to be within the jurisdiction of the court that is issuing the attachment order.[60] In light of this important limitation, creditors **23.67**

---

[57] There were notable exceptions to this collaborative approach. For example, the most notable was when Fidelity Union Trust of New Jersey refused to participate in a restructuring agreement that had been reached between Costa Rica and all other members of the syndicate. It sued Costa Rica through the agent, Allied Bank. The ensuing litigation had important implications regarding the development of the doctrine of 'comity', which refers to the deference that the US courts afford to the acts of a foreign sovereign to the extent that they are consistent with the law and policy of the United States: *Allied Bank v. Banco Credito Agricola de Cartago*, 757 F.2d 516 (2d Cir. 1985) (en banc); cert. dismissed, 473 US 934 (1985). For an analysis of these cases, *see* Christopher C. Wheeler and Amir Attaran, 'Declawing the Vulture Funds: Rehabilitation of a Comity Defense in Sovereign Debt Litigation' (2003) 39 Stanford J Int'l L 253, 268–70.

[58] The distressed debt purchasers that specialize in holding out and enforcing their claims through litigation have gained considerable notoriety over the past ten years. For a discussion of their tactics and success rates, *see* Wheeler and Attaran (n. 57). *See* also Samuel E. Goldman, 'Mavericks in the Market: The Emerging Problem of Hold-Outs in Sovereign Debt Restructuring' (2000–01) 5 UCLA J Int'l L & Foreign Aff 159, 169–71; G. Mitu Gulati and Kenneth N. Klee, 'Sovereign Piracy' (2001) 56 Bus L 635.

[59] In the United States, for example, the Foreign Sovereign Immunity Act (FSIA) of 1976 enables a court to exercise jurisdiction over a sovereign where it has waived explicitly or implicitly its immunity from suit, or where the action is: (i) based on commercial activity carried on in the United States by the foreign state; (ii) based on an act in the United States in connection with commercial activity outside the United States; or (iii) taken in connection with commercial activity carried on outside the United States that causes a direct effect in the United States. Bonds issued by emerging market sovereigns that are governed by New York law typically provide for a comprehensive waiver of sovereign immunity, including immunity from suit, prejudgment attachment, attachment in aid of execution, and execution. Moreover, where an express waiver of immunity from suit is absent, the commercial activity exception has been interpreted to include circumstances in which the sovereign has issued debt in a public marketplace and in which its breach of a US dollar debt obligation has caused a direct effect in the United States.

[60] Under the FSIA, only property of a foreign state 'used for a commercial activity in the United states' is available for attachment. It has generally been understood that diplomatic property is protected, even where the waiver contained in the contract is very broad. Third, under the FSIA, the assets of an agency or instrumentality of the sovereign will normally not be available to satisfy a judgment against the sovereign. Most importantly, perhaps, the reserves of the central bank—a potentially attractive target for a judgment creditor—will normally not be available for attachment unless the central bank is also liable under the terms of the debt instrument.

have developed alternative strategies to enforce their claims. In particular, they have sought injunctive relief to interrupt the servicing of debt by the debtor to other creditors—including creditors who have agreed to the restructuring and who are receiving payments on the restructured debt. The legal basis for this strategy has been the *pari passu* provision contained in standard bond documentation, which—according to the plaintiff creditors—precludes the debtor making payments to certain creditors without making rateable payments to all other creditors.

23.68 While the *pari passu* strategy is not new,[61] it has gained recent momentum—and notoriety—as a result of the decision of the New York courts, at the request of a creditor (NML) to prohibit Argentina from making payments on its restructured bonds unless it pays NML the full amount owed on the original unrestructured claims.[62] The injunction has also ensnared the trustee of the restructured bondholders, the Bank of New York Mellon, which is responsible for receiving payments on the restructured bonds from Argentina and distributing them to the bondholders. As a means of enforcing the court order against Argentina, the Court has prohibited the trustee from distributing to the bondholders any payments that might be made in violation of the injunction—that is, any payment that is made without NML being paid in full. The court order has left Argentina with little room for manoeuvre. Even if it were willing to pay NML in full so that it can continue to service its restructured debt, the government enacted a law at the time of the restructuring that precludes it from making any payments to the holdouts.[63]

23.69 Upon appeal, the Second Circuit Court of Appeals upheld the legal theory that provided the basis for the District Court's order.[64] More recently, it also affirmed the District Court's decision regarding the amount that needed to be paid to the holdout creditors and the effect of the injunction on third parties. However, it stayed the enforcement of the injunction pending the resolution by the US Supreme Court of a petition for a writ of certiori filed by Argentina.[65]

23.70 The interpretation of the *pari passu* provision that has been accepted by the Second Circuit is at odds with the views of a number of legal scholars—and at odds with the view of the United States, which filed a statement of interest as *amicus*.[66] In particular, the Court's view that this provision precludes selective payments has been heavily criticized by those who have argued that it is simply designed to prevent involuntary subordination (hence the use of the term 'ranking').[67] What is clear is that these decisions—if they stand—will have an

[61] Prior to the *NML* case, the most celebrated—or notorious—case in this regard involved a successful collection effort by a distressed debt purchaser (Elliott) against the Republic of Peru. In that case, Elliott relied on a *pari passu* provision in the debt to obtain an *ex ante* order from a Brussels court preventing Euroclear from accepting an interest payment from Peru on its Brady holders of the bonds, thereby preventing Peru from servicing its restructured debt: *Elliott Assoc*. No. 2000/QR/92 (Court of Appeals of Brussels, 8th Chamber, 26 September 2000).

[62] *NML Capital, Ltd v. Republic of Argentina* (SDNY 7 December 2011) (No. 1:08–cv–06978–TPG), ECF No 353.

[63] *See* Law 26,017 (the 'Lock Law'), *Boletin Oficial de la Republica Argentina*, CXIII, No. 30.590, 2005.

[64] *NML Capital, Ltd v. Republic of Argentina*, 699 F. 3d 246 (2d Cir. 2012).

[65] *NML Capital, Ltd. v. Republic of Argentina*, No. 12-105 et al., 2013 US App. LEXIS 17645 (2d Cir. NY, 23 August 2013).

[66] Brief for the United States of America as *Amicus Curiae* in Support of the Republic of Argentina's Petition for Panel Rehearing and Rehearing *En Banc, NML Capital Ltd v. Republic of Argentina* (n. 64).

[67] *See* L. Buchheit and Jeremiah Pam, 'The *Pari Passu* Clause in Sovereign Debt Instruments' (2004) 53 Emory LJ 763.

important impact on the debt restructuring process. Holdouts will not have to find assets to satisfy their judgments; rather they will able to use the US courts to exercise a form of financial extortion ('Either repay me in full using whatever resources you have, or I may force you to default on your restructured debt'). This is very likely to make the debt restructuring process far more complicated for at least two reasons. First, by giving holdout creditors of sovereigns greater leverage and by offering the prospect that such holdout creditors will be able to extract preferential recovery outside of a voluntary debt exchange, the decision increases the risk that holdouts will multiply. For intercreditor equity reasons, creditors who are otherwise inclined to accept the terms of a restructuring offer may be less likely to do so. Second, because the Court's decision increases the risk that holdout creditors will be able to interrupt the flow of payments to those creditors who have participated in a consensual debt restructuring, that risk will create an even greater disincentive for creditors to participate in the voluntary restructuring.

In its opinion, the Second Circuit expressed the view that it is unlikely that its decision will enhance the leverage of holdouts in future debt restructurings because, in the future, '[c]ollective action clauses—which effectively eliminate the possibility of "holdout" litigation—have been included in 99% percent of the aggregate value of New York-law governed bonds'.[68] **23.71**

Many observers have been particularly concerned by the Court's view that collective action clauses (CACs) will be a panacea to the problem of holdout creditors. For the past ten years, the IMF has actively supported the inclusion of CACs because they do, in fact, reduce the leverage of holdouts, by enabling a qualified majority of creditors to make a debt restructuring binding on all creditors. However, experience demonstrates that they are not a panacea, particularly since CACs typically bind bondholders only within the same issuance. Provided that a holdout creditor acquires a sufficient percentage of a particular bond issuance, it can effectively neutralize the operation of the CAC in that issuance. In these circumstances, creditors holding other issuances may not be willing to restructure their own instruments because of their inability to ensure that the 'holdout issue' will be bound by the same terms. **23.72**

The recent sovereign debt restructuring in Greece demonstrates the limits of CACs in this respect. Of the thirty-six English-law-governed bond issuances with CACs that were eligible to participate in the Greek restructuring, only seventeen were successfully restructured. The result was a roughly €5 billion holdout creditor population in the Greek restructuring that closed in March of 2013. **23.73**

As a result of these developments, there is renewed discussion—including within the IMF—regarding the need for further reform of the legal framework to ensure that holdouts do not have the leverage to undermine the restructuring process. Between 2001 and 2003, the IMF actively discussed the merits of amending its Articles of Agreement to establish the Sovereign Debt Restructuring Mechanism (SDRM).[69] In essence, the SDRM would have provided the legal basis for a qualified majority of creditors (75 per cent of creditors) to make decisions—including the decision to reach agreement with the debtor on the terms of a restructuring—that would be binding on the entire creditor body. Although this majority voting framework is similar to that relied upon by CACs, the key difference is that while the **23.74**

[68] *NML Capital, Ltd v. Republic of Argentina* (n. 64), 27.

[69] For a comprehensive discussion of the objective and design of the SDRM, *see* generally Hagan (n. 45).

voting provisions of CACs apply on a series-by-series basis, the voting rules envisaged under the SDRM would 'aggregate' claims for voting purposes. The advantage of aggregation is that it avoids the risk of holdout creditors being able to neutralize the CAC of a particular issue through the acquisition of a blocking position.[70] This advantage is illustrated in the Greek debt restructuring: most of the debt owed by Greece was governed by the laws of Greece and did not have CACs. Relying on the fact that the bonds were governed by Greek law, the authorities enacted legislation with respect to these bonds that enabled a qualified majority of bondholders to bind all holders of domestic debt to restructured debt. As with the SDRM, it aggregated the claims of these domestic law instruments for voting purposes. In contrast with the foreign-law-governed debt, all of the domestic-law-governed debt was restructured.

23.75 Notwithstanding the advantages of the type of aggregation that the SDRM would have, there is currently insufficient support for its adoption. An amendment of the Fund's Articles requires the approval of three-fifths of the members, holding 85 per cent of the total voting power. When the SDRM was considered in 2003, it had broad support, but not enough to meet this threshold. In particular, the United States was not supportive, a key reason for its resistance was the fact that the SDRM would require a limited surrender of national sovereignty: under the SDRM, the aggregation process would require the existence of claims verification and a dispute resolution process that would be administered by an international body, the Dispute Resolution Forum (DRF). While the jurisdiction of the DRF would be very limited, it would still supersede that of the US courts during the restructuring process.[71] There is no evidence that, ten years later, the concerns of the United States have abated on this issue.

23.76 In light of these matters, the question arises as to whether the benefits of aggregation could be achieved through contract. There is some limited experience with this approach: several issuers have bonds that give them the option of amending key terms on the basis of aggregated voting across affected bonds where the amendment would affect two or more series of bonds. In these cases, two thresholds must be met: the aggregate threshold (either 75 per cent or 85 per cent) applicable to the principal of all of the bonds; and the series-by-series threshold (66⅔ per cent) applicable to each series.[72] While this series-by-series threshold is lower than the typical 75 per cent threshold, it still enables a holdout to take a blocking position—albeit with greater difficulty. One possible area of reform that has been discussed would be to eliminate the series-by-series threshold entirely. While such a step would greatly reduce the potential leverage of holdouts, it may give rise to intercreditor equity concerns where the claims being aggregated have different maturities—which may be the case where the debt is restructured in a pre-default context.

6. Conclusion

23.77 At the time of writing, there is an ongoing public debate about the benefits and pitfalls of economic austerity. Predictably, the soundbites that have been seized upon by the press tend

[70] *See* Hagan (n. 45), 336.

[71] Hagan (n. 45), 382–90.

[72] For a discussion of these types of clause, *see* Michael Bradley and G. Mitu Gulati, *Collective Action Clauses for the Eurozone: An Empirical Analysis* (March 2013), available online at <http://papers.ssrn.com/sol3/papers.cfm?abstract_id=1948534>, 21.

to oversimplify the positions of the participants and obscure the fact that, among policymakers and academics, there is a general consensus on at least two points. First, for a country with a high debt-to-GDP ratio, the adoption of a credible fiscal consolidation package that seeks to bring down this ratio over the medium term is necessary in order to eliminate economic uncertainty and regain the confidence of capital markets. Second, the pace of fiscal consolidation needs to be tailored to the circumstances of the member. In particular, where growth is very weak, an overly ambitious austerity programme can push the economy back into recession. Although it receives far less attention, there is also broad agreement that there is another instrument that can address the problem of overindebtedness, but one that is currently being underutilized: debt restructuring.

In that context, this chapter has sought to identify specific features of the relevant debt **23.78** restructuring frameworks that require reform. In the corporate context, while there is convergence on the appropriate design of liquidation and rehabilitation legislation, the key problem lies in implementation—particularly where the problem of corporate indebtedness in an economy has become systemic. Addressing this weakness will not only require institutional reform—including within the judiciary—but also a more active role by the government in creating incentives for debtors and creditors to negotiate. While these incentives will vary among countries (for example some countries may have the fiscal space to provide financing incentives, while others will not), experience demonstrates that banks will not have an interest in agreeing to meaningful debt reduction for insolvent corporations unless they are forced by the regulators to write down their loans to these corporations to their true value. With respect to bank restructuring, there has been progress in the development in legal frameworks that resolve financial institutions in a manner that both preserves financial stability and ensures that unsecured creditors and shareholders bear the costs of the resolution process. However, the resolution process will not be effective—or credible—unless further steps are taken to put in place a framework that ensures adequate international cooperation. While the FSB's *Key Attributes* represent an important step forward, it will be important that a core set of jurisdictions adopt these recommendations. Regarding the household sector, a glaring weakness in the existing legal frameworks—including in the United States—is the absence of the ability of the court to restructure mortgages to reflect the true value of the homeowners' property. Allowing this to occur would catalyse the restructuring process without undermining the availability of credit in this area. Finally, notwithstanding reforms that were introduced over ten years ago to improve the way in which sovereign debt should be restructured, recent experience has shown that deficiencies persist. The most significant problem is the delay in the restructuring process. Addressing this problem will require further reform in the Fund's lending policies, given the fact that a sovereign normally initiates a restructuring only if the Fund makes it a condition for its financial support.

24

CORPORATE BANKRUPTCY LAW AND STATE INSOLVENCIES

Philip R. Wood QC (Hon)

1. Introduction

State insolvencies are bankruptcies without a bankruptcy law. Unlike corporations, and unlike banks in particular, there is a completely open regime in the case of a state insolvency. There are no stays, or freezes, or standstills on creditor actions, no petitions for bankruptcy before a court, no revocation of preferential transfers, no liability of managers for deepening the insolvency, no direct control by a creditor representative, no stays on collateral enforcement, no compulsory disclosure, no realization of assets, no formal bankruptcy ladder of priorities, no mandatory equality of creditors on the same rung of priorities, and no discharge of the debtor. **24.01**

The key question therefore is whether a regime under which there is no law, except free contract law, is workable. If the conclusion is that law is not necessary, then it would mean that one of the most important principles of the rule of law is that there should not be too much law. **24.02**

Before decisions can be made as to whether or not a bankruptcy law of some kind is desirable or necessary to cope with state insolvencies, it is first necessary to understand what the differences are between the corporate bankruptcy regime and the position of states. This chapter does not set out to answer the question as to whether there should be an international bankruptcy law for sovereigns, but rather to examine what the differences are. Those who make the policy decisions on whether there should be an international bankruptcy law for sovereign states should have the benefit of a comparison, however modest. **24.03**

Many of the concepts developed in this chapter were raised in a paper, *State Insolvency: Options for the Way Forward*, by the Sovereign Insolvency Study Group of the International Law Association (ILA), chaired by the author and presented at an ILA conference in August 2010. **24.04**

2. How Do Sovereign Bankruptcies Work?

The mechanisms for the resolution of sovereign debt problems are much simpler than those in the case of corporate groups. **24.05**

In the ordinary case, the sovereign offers to exchange existing bonds held by bondholders for new bonds that are worth less and have a longer maturity than the existing bonds. For **24.06** example, a sovereign state may offer to exchange bonds worth 100 for new bonds worth 60 and payable, not in five years, but in thirty years. It is then up to bondholders whether or not they will accept. The sovereign debtor usually makes it clear that the sovereign debtor will not pay out bondholders who do not accept—the holdout creditors.

24.07 The result is that sovereign bankruptcies are resolved by the bargaining position of the parties, not by any prescriptive law. In fact, it is probably the case worldwide that 90 per cent or more of all bankruptcies in relation to corporations are resolved not by recourse to a bankruptcy law, but by an agreement between creditors and the debtor—that is, a private workout. It generally makes no sense for a debtor to be forced into a liquidation, which is a mutually assured destruction for everybody concerned, for the debtor as well as creditors. Even a modern rehabilitation, or rescue, or reorganization law tends to be clumsy, and weighed down by rigid rules and court procedures. It is almost universally considered to be far better, if at all possible, to deal with financial problems out of court. Liquidation is an absolute last resort where everything else has failed. Even reorganization proceedings, where they are available, are often used rather as a rubber stamp for a deal already agreed between creditors and debtor in order to strengthen the validity of the plan that has been agreed, and to give it better recognition in foreign countries.

24.08 If insolvencies at the corporate level are generally resolved by private agreement and contract, why should a bankruptcy law be necessary at all? Apart from the fact that it may be impossible to reach agreement, one reason sometimes advanced is that a private workout agreement between creditors and the debtor is usefully played out against the background of the shadow of the bankruptcy regime. This shadow plays a significant role in the determination of the position of the parties in workout negotiations because, if the workout negotiations fail, then the corporation has to be put into a judicial bankruptcy, at which point the position of creditors is determined by the law, such as the bankruptcy ladder of priorities. Creditors who would be on a higher rung in a court bankruptcy are unlikely to yield this privilege on a private workout. But the question remains as to whether there needs to be a bankruptcy law in the background to provide a framework.

24.09 There are some much more basic considerations that need to be considered. The main purposes of statutory bankruptcy laws for individuals and corporates are to achieve a fair balance between protection of creditors and protection of the debtor, as well as protection of society as a whole. Jurisdictions differ hugely on whether the bankruptcy law should be debtor-friendly or creditor-friendly and the same bank dispute arises in the case of sovereign states. If the outcomes are determined by the bargaining position of the parties and by free contract, is it generally true that the outcomes are reasonably ordinary and fair, and strike a reasonable balance in protecting creditors and the debtor in the case of sovereign bankruptcies? In order to examine this question, one has to analyse the basic unchangeable differences between a sovereign state and a corporation.

24.10 Another issue is whether the time, cost, and disruption of a bankruptcy can be ameliorated by a statutory regime. In this context, it is worth noting that virtually all major corporate bankruptcies are colossally litigious, fraught with dissension between one creditor group and another creditor group, and between creditors and the debtor, enormously costly and time-consuming. Ten years would not be unusual for a very big corporate bankruptcy and some go on for even longer than this, such as the twenty-year bankruptcy proceedings involving Bank of Credit and Commerce International that began around 1991. On current estimates, it would seem unlikely that the bankruptcy of the Lehman Group will be concluded within a decade of its commencement. So it would seem that the law is not a magic wand with which to banish away dissension, to banish away delay. Often, in fact, the opposite may be the case. In practice, it is probably true that major state bankruptcies are resolved much more quickly than corporate bankruptcies.

Nevertheless, it is not the task of this chapter to argue one side or the other. This chapter will make some suggestions or points that need to be considered, but overall it aims to offer an unbiased perspective on what the policy should be. **24.11**

3. What Rights Do Creditors Have?

Since most financial difficulties are resolved by private agreement between creditors and the debtor, the contents of that agreement will be determined by the bargaining position of the parties, which in turn involves a consideration of what the rights of the parties would be if they fail to agree. **24.12**

In the case of a sovereign state, it is generally true that creditors have extremely limited legal rights as against the defaulting sovereign state, compared to the rights that creditors have ultimately against a defaulting corporation. In the case of a corporation, creditors can attach assets and ultimately petition to put the corporation into a liquidation and terminate its existence completely, subject to any reorganization statute. **24.13**

As to sovereign states, in the first place, it is almost invariably the case that sovereign states do not permit creditors to attach publicly owned assets located within the territorial domain of the sovereign state itself. Commonly, creditors have a right to sue their government and to obtain a judgment, but not a right to realize upon the judgment by levying execution. **24.14**

Although it is true that most international bonds and bank loan agreements contain wide waivers or immunity, these do not apply to assets located within the territorial domain of the state because, as mentioned, local assets are almost always immune or could be immunized by local statute. Hence it is only external assets that are de-immunized by these waivers. However, in practice, most modern sovereign states have very few external assets in their own name. The main foreign reserves are located in the central bank, where typically the veil of incorporation prevents creditors from attaching the external foreign reserves. The central bank is not responsible for the debts of the state, which is a separate legal creature, and commonly central bank assets are not held by the central bank as trustee or agent for the state itself and so are not beneficially the assets of the state. **24.15**

As regards other public assets abroad, most other foreign investments will typically be held by sovereign states via state-owned corporations, so that again the assets concerned are protected by the veil of incorporation from attachment by creditors of the sovereign state. State-owned corporations are usually incorporated within the sovereign state itself and so their shares are covered by the immunity of domestic assets. **24.16**

There may be other external assets, such as diplomatic bank accounts and diplomatic premises, but these either do not add up to much or are exempted in immunity clauses. **24.17**

On the other hand, creditors of a state who are determined to hold out against exchange offers can create some disruption if the state seeks to borrow abroad. This is because the **24.18** proceeds of a new issue, and the proceeds of servicing the issue by way of payments of principal and interest, have to touch down somewhere. Theoretically, they can therefore be reached by attachments by unpaid creditors and this can be a nuisance factor in relation to capital-raising efforts of the sovereign state going forward. However, even these assets can be protected either by virtue of immunity provisions in clearing systems, such as the Belgian Euroclear, or by virtue of contract arrangements to ensure that payments reach the new bondholders beneficially within the territory of the sovereign state. These can then be protected by the general immunity accorded by sovereign states to assets within their territorial domain.

24.19 It would follow from this that the one supreme right that creditors of a corporation have against a state—that is, to attach its assets or to ensure that they are realized and sold for the benefit of creditors in the liquidation process—is not available either by law or in practice to creditors of sovereign states. This is probably the most important factor to be taken into account in assessing the bargaining power of the parties.

24.20 If the debt contract is governed by the law of the sovereign state itself, then the rights of creditors are even worse. This is because most developed countries will, if the debt is governed by the local law of the state, recognize a moratorium on exchange control, a rescheduling or the like, which is deliberately introduced by a statute of the sovereign state, subject to some very basic thresholds of unconscionability, oppression, penalty, or gross unfairness. If a creditor and a debtor contract under the law of debtor, then this is the law of the debtor state from time to time, including changes. It is not thought possible to stabilize or freeze the law at a specific date by contract. Even if the contract is governed by a foreign law, then in some circumstances and some jurisdictions it can be overridden by the international recognition of exchange controls required by Article VIII(2b) of the International Monetary Fund (IMF) Articles of Agreement.

24.21 Creditors do, however, have an important practical right that needs to be taken into account. This is that creditors can withhold future credit from the debtor and can, in addition, refuse to provide new money to tide the debtor over the downturn in its financial fortunes. The weight of this factor tends to differ according to the particular circumstances.

4. Moratorium on Payments and Attachments

24.22 One of the most important objectives of a corporate bankruptcy regime is to impose a moratorium on payments by the debtor, so as to enable a resolution to be worked out, and also a stay or freeze on attachments by creditors individually, so as to avoid the piecemeal seizure of assets by creditors, to avoid a race for the courthouse door, and to avoid a lack of equality between creditors once the debtor is insolvent. This moratorium therefore protects both debtor and creditors. The question here is whether a moratorium is necessary in the case of sovereign states to enable negotiations to proceed.

24.23 In the case of a sovereign, it has already been shown that typically there are no assets that creditors can attach, so that a freeze on piecemeal creditor attachments would seem to be of limited utility. The question of whether a moratorium on creditors is needed during the initial phase of negotiations depends upon one's evaluation of the historical experience. It seems to be the case, with both corporate and sovereign workout negotiations, that creditors very often allow negotiations to proceed without taking action so long as the debtor is negotiating in good faith and progress is being made. For example, many workout negotiations involving the financial difficulties of very large corporations can go on for years without being upset by legal action by individual creditors.

Restraints on creditor action could be achieved by contract, such as by no-action clauses in bonds, which provide that no bondholder will take individual action after an event of default or a non-payment unless, say, 15–20 per cent of the bondholders by resolution permit it. These no-action clauses are on an issue-by-issue basis rather than universal and they do not cover other creditors, including official creditors. Syndicated credit agreements typically provide that a majority of more than 50 per cent or two-thirds is required to accelerate a loan, but this does not prevent individual banks from suing for amounts already unpaid without acceleration. **24.24**

As pointed out already, if the debts are governed by a local law, then the debtor can normally implement a moratorium or impose exchange controls by its own statute, and have them absorbed into the debt contract and hence recognized by many other foreign countries, subject to basic standards of fairness. **24.25**

Similarly, if the debt is denominated in the local currency, then a state can inflate that currency by increasing the money supply and other means, and in that way pay the creditors a dividend. **24.26**

5. Bankruptcy Ladder of Priorities

At the heart and central core of corporate bankruptcy regimes is the bankruptcy ladder of priorities. This determines the hierarchy of claimants on final liquidation and hence determines what they can agree on a private workout. **24.27**

The idea that bankruptcy involves equality of creditors is nowhere true. In every developed bankruptcy law in the world relating to corporations, creditors are paid according to a scale of priorities, often in a ladder of forty or fifty intricate steps. **24.28**

The concept of the 'ladder of priorities' is so potent that there is sometimes a basic ladder by consensus in relation to state insolvency, even though state insolvency is not governed by any mandatory bankruptcy laws and even though there is no compulsory ladder of priority. **24.29**

The issue therefore is whether an international statute is necessary or desirable in order to regulate the ladder of priorities. **24.30**

In the case of corporate bankruptcies, a liquidator collects the assets of the bankrupt, sells them, and then uses the proceeds to pay the creditors in the prescribed order of priority. In other words, the priorities are an order of payments out of a pool of assets already realized. **24.31**

Since there is no liquidation and there is no realized pool of assets in the case of a sovereign, priorities must be achieved in a different way. In practice, the priority is realized by the order of payment in time. For example, a creditor who is paid in full on Monday will often, in practice, rank prior to a creditor whose debt is due on Tuesday because, after the payment on Monday, there may be nothing left to pay the creditor on Tuesday. Thus the priority achieved by the IMF results from the fact that the IMF debt is kept current, without any delay or **24.32** haircut, even though other creditors are rescheduled. Once the IMF is paid on its due date, then the sovereign may have less cash to pay other creditors whose rescheduled debts mature on some future date.

24.33 In state bankruptcies, this priority depends on the agreement of all of the creditors involved. It is not laid down in any statute. If, say, bondholders were not to agree to the IMF preferred status, then the remedy of the bondholders would be not to accept the rescheduling and simply to accelerate their debts if the sovereign state defaulted.

24.34 Priority according to maturities is only a de facto priority and applies only if an earlier payment makes it impossible for the debtor to pay a later maturity. This is one reason why a priority order that tries to arrange medium-term or long-term debts according to the priority of maturities is doubtful, because debt that is payable far in the future is not really material to priorities.

24.35 The priority ladder can decide who will survive and who will be drowned, and determines the degree of risk. The predictability of the bankruptcy ladder is of crucial importance to creditors.

24.36 It is worth comparing the sovereign and corporate ladders. In the case of bank and ordinary non-financial corporations, the typical ladder has six basic categories. Each is divided into a multitude of subcategories, especially near the top of the ladder, where there are some finely graded mini-steps, taut and stretched.

24.37 The main corporate categories are as follows.

(a) *Super-priority creditors*
These are typically creditors with collateral, set-offs, and beneficial property rights under trusts, such as custodianship. Trusts are not recognized in many jurisdictions. In the corporate field, jurisdictions differ in their attitude to bankruptcy set-off and to security interests. The result is that set-off and collateral are generally super-priority in the sovereign ladder. The super-priority of trust property depends on the jurisdiction.

(b) *Priority creditors*
In the case of corporations, there is often a long list of preferred unsecured creditors, which can sometimes include depositors at banks, insurers with insurance companies, the tax authorities, employees for their remuneration and benefits, post-commencement new money to finance the reorganization, and post-commencement expenses. These are tracked in the case of sovereign bankruptcies by, for example, the preferred status of the IMF and other multilaterals, the priority of any sovereign deposit insurance schemes (which take over any depositor preference by subrogation), and the preferred status of loans by the European Stability Mechanism (ESM) proposed in paragraphs 13 and 14 of the Recitals to its constitutive treaty. In the case of the Greek debt reorganization of 2012, most of the official loans had a priority by maturity over private sector bonds.

(c) Pari passu
These are typically banks, bondholders, and suppliers. Suppliers are not large claimants in sovereign bankruptcies. In corporate bankruptcies, banks and bondholders may convert into equity. In both corporate and sovereign bankruptcies, banks and bondholders, or both, are typically by far the largest class of creditors, plus official sector loans. They expect to rank equally between themselves, and both the private and official sectors seek to ensure comparable treatment (which did not happen in the case of Greece 2012).

(d) *Subordinated creditors*
These are creditors who agree to be subordinated in their original documents. Typically, there are no subordinated creditors in formal terms in the case of sovereigns, but the same effect can be achieved by postponing the rescheduled debt for, say, twenty years.

(e) *Equity*
If a corporate is insolvent, then the equity is not paid. The shares may be diluted by a conversion of senior *pari passu* debt into equity, thereby wiping out the existing equity, which would in any case receive nothing.
There is no equity in the case of sovereign states, but effectively an exchange into notes of anything over, say, twenty years renders the notes effectively equity in priority terms, because they are similar to perpetual claims. It does not really make sense to talk about priority if maturities are over ten years.

(f) *Expropriated claimants*
In corporate bankruptcies, expropriated claimants are claimants whose claims are not recognized or are otherwise demoted to such a degree as to be worthless. An example is the compulsory conversion of foreign exchange debt into local currency at the commencement of the corporate bankruptcy—a near-universal rule. If the local currency is depreciating, as it often is, the effect is that foreign currency creditors are not paid. Other expropriated claimants are those for foreign taxes or penalties. These expropriated claimants are often not exactly replicated in sovereign bankruptcies, but one can get a similar effect.

What therefore is surprising is how closely the corporate model, with all of its sophisticated refinements, is reproduced in very crude and primitive terms in the case of a sovereign bankruptcy. However, the corporate model has the certainty that the priorities are clear and binding. **24.38**

One of the most contentious priorities is the priority of the official sector for bailout money, as in the case of Greece. **24.39**

Bond and loan contracts do sometimes regulate priorities in a rather basic way, for example *pari passu* clauses in bonds, comparability clauses in Paris Club rescheduling, pro rata sharing clauses in syndicated bank credits, and, in sovereign insolvency bank rescheduling agreements, most favoured debt agreements, which provide that if any other foreign currency debt eligible for the rescheduling is paid out more quickly, then the borrower must repay the rescheduled debt. **24.40**

It would be perfectly possible to draft priority clauses in bonds and loan agreements, but there would be many issues about acceptability and how they would be enforced amongst all creditors. **24.41**

Similar issues apply to the equality of payments that are on the same rung in the ladder. **24.42**

6. Control of the Debtor's Financing

In a corporate insolvency, control of the debtor's business after a formal insolvency has commenced is typically enjoyed or shared by an administrator on behalf of creditors, a creditors committee, the court or a government official, and the debtor's existing management. Where the debtor has exclusive control over the business, subject to major matters, this is called **24.43** 'debtor in possession' (DIP). In the case of corporate liquidations, the debtor's management is invariably displaced.

24.44 The affairs of insolvent states cannot be taken over and managed by a creditor's representative for political reasons. The 'management' of the debtor stays in possession. Instead, the IMF or other official creditors impose austerity or other programmes on the sovereign debtor as a condition of new official finance—typically called 'conditionality'.

24.45 It follows that, in a sovereign insolvency, the restraints on operations, on budgets, on tax policy, or on asset disposals tend to be limited. The conditionality of official creditors typically includes a ceiling on expenditures and the budget deficit, a limit on the incurrence of further borrowings, the privatization of state-owned companies, a reduction in the number and pay of civil servants, a limitation on subsidies, and the like.

24.46 In corporate insolvencies, most jurisdictions give exclusive power to the insolvency administrator to put forward a draft reorganization plan. An exception is the United States, where management has the exclusive right to prepare a plan for a period.

24.47 The terms of a restructuring plan by sovereign debtors is typically significantly influenced by the IMF, the Paris Club, or other official sector creditors—but mainly the IMF.

24.48 It would seem politically impracticable to enhance existing creditor methods of intervention in the finances of a sovereign state by the passage of an international bankruptcy statute to the degree of intervention by administrators in corporate insolvencies.

24.49 In the case of sovereign insolvency, there is no legal provision for the establishment of committees to act as a conduit with, for example, private sector bondholders. Although some sovereigns do appoint trustees on behalf of the bondholders, trustees are not suited for negotiations on the commercial terms of an exchange offer involving a haircut on bondholders or a reprofiling, or the like. Trustees are useful for carrying out the administrative tasks of monitoring the issuer, convening and holding bondholding meetings, liaising with the issuer and other activities, but not decisions about a rescheduling, such as the haircut.

24.50 Nevertheless, it is usually important for bondholders to have a steering committee of some kind to negotiate with the debtor. They can examine the economics of the deal and reflect bondholder opinion. They can endorse a deal, or at least state that its members intend to participate.

24.51 Steering committees do not have to be appointed by the issuer or receive a mandate from the issuer, nor is it necessary for them to receive specific mandates from bondholders or to represent the majority of the bondholders. If they are self-appointed with the tacit consent of the major bondholders, what matters is that the members of the steering committee have sufficient clout with the issuer and the official sector to make it necessary for the issuer and other creditors to treat them as the main negotiating party for bondholders.

24.52 Some English law bond issues do contain a clause for appointing a representative committee of bondholders at the cost of the issuer. Although these are on an issue-by-issue basis, these clauses are considered helpful. The eurozone model collective action clauses (CACs) discussed later in this chapter do not contain a clause for appointing a committee.

24.53 Syndicated bank credit agreements also do not contain provisions for the appointment of negotiating committees, but the practice shows that the major bank creditors commonly do form a steering committee without difficulty, probably because the number of creditors is much smaller than in the case of bond issues.

7. Reorganization Plans

Most modern reorganization statutes in the corporate realm provide for a reorganization plan that is voted on by creditors and approved by the court, whereupon it becomes binding on all creditors, including those who dissent. 24.54

In addition, many countries in the civil code camp have introduced bondholder community statutes conferring powers on bondholders to change the terms of bonds by majority voting, but sometimes limiting the issues on which they can vote. Thus there are bondholder community statutes in Germany, France, Italy, Spain, Belgium, Luxembourg, Switzerland, Japan, Mexico, Brazil, Chile, Argentina, and many other countries. These bondholder statutes typically apply only to issues by local corporations and not to issues by sovereign states. 24.55

The original practice for sovereign bonds governed by New York, German, or Japanese law was not to include bondholder voting to change the terms of the payment of principal or interest. In the case of New York bonds, this resulted from adherence to the policies of the US Trust Indenture Act of 1939, as amended. Section 316 of this Act governing a bond issue provides that the right of a bondholder to receive payments of principal or interest of the bonds on the due dates is not to be impaired or affected without the consent of each bondholder, subject to a minor exemption for interest. Hence the position in the United States is that CACs are outlawed for corporates and banks, so far as their impact on principal and interest is concerned—the only things that really matter. But the 1939 Act does not apply to sovereign issuers. 24.56

The rationale of voting is to bind holdouts or dissenting creditors to a reorganization plan decided by a majority. 24.57

In the case of sovereign issues, there is one view that the best way in which to get paid is not to permit the issuer to bind creditors. The other view is that it is in the interests of creditors that holdouts should be bound since, for example, if the holdouts continue to launch legal attacks against the sovereign issuer, then not only might they get priority if their attacks are successful, but also threats to attach the proceeds of new issues and the repayment proceeds could chill the future access of the sovereign issuer to capital markets, and hence reduce the likelihood that new issues could be used to retire the existing debt. 24.58

The main attempt by the private sector to replicate the effects of a corporate reorganization plan is via CACs, which prescribe that a majority of bondholders, such as two-thirds or three-quarters, can bind dissenting minorities to a reorganization plan, or exchange, or rescheduling approved by the majority. It follows that CACs, at least if they have an aggregation provision allowing voting across all issues, replicate some of the effects of a corporate insolvency reorganization statute. 24.59

In 2004, the International Capital Markets Association (ICMA) published a form of CAC for sovereign issues governed by English law where there is a fiscal agent. In 2002, the G-10 recommended the adoption of a form of CAC for sovereign bonds issued under a foreign system of law, as opposed to local law debt. The G-10 and ICMA forms do not contain the 24.60

aggregation clauses (see paragraph 24.62). In 2012, eurozone states agreed to adopt a form of model CAC for almost all sovereign issues by members of the euro area as from the beginning of 2013.

24.61 Under traditional English practice, and indeed the practice elsewhere if there were CACs, bondholders voted issue by issue. The result is that one or more of the issues could vote against a resolution that had, in fact, been approved by sufficient bondholders of other issues to amount to a two-thirds or three-quarters majority, as required. The result would be to disrupt a plan that enjoyed the support of the majority of the holders. Holdout creditors could buy blocking majorities in small issues at no great expense, and in that way hold the issuer and also the other bondholders to ransom, even if their legal rights are slight. Argentina in 2002 had 152 bond issues outstanding.

24.62 This problem can be countered by the use of aggregation clauses whereby, if a majority of all of the bondholders vote in favour, then all of the issues would be bound, notwithstanding that one or more issues dissented. In order to protect the holders of particular issues, there is usually a double voting requirement that, say, three-quarters of all of the bondholders vote in favour and that at least, say, 50 per cent of the bondholders of each issue vote in favour—that is, less than a supermajority, but still a majority. If less than the majority vote in favour, then the aggregation fails. This principal of aggregation has been adopted by the eurozone model clauses.

24.63 There are also typically provisions for the disenfranchisement of the issuer and sovereign-controlled entities.

24.64 Minority protections are dealt with either by drafting or legal principles preventing discrimination against, or oppression of, a minority, or secret fees or other measures that are severally prejudicial to the interests of a minority.

8. Discharge of a Debtor

24.65 Another of the most important differences between an ordinary bankruptcy—at least of an individual—and sovereign bankruptcy is that, in the case of a sovereign bankruptcy, a state cannot obtain a discharge for debts that it cannot pay unless creditors are willing to cancel the debt, or where the debt is governed by the state's own law. Creditors can keep the claim alive potentially forever, provided that they take appropriate action to toll the debt under prescription or limitation legislation.

24.66 By contrast, in most countries, a bankrupt individual can secure a discretionary discharge. A company can be dissolved and liabilities wiped off, even though unpaid.

9. Other Differences between Corporate and Sovereign Insolvencies

24.67 The following are some miscellaneous differences between a corporate and a sovereign insolvency.

- *Disclosure*—The disclosure and financial statements regime applying to ordinary corporations is much more detailed and prescriptive than that in the case of states.

- *Interest*—In the corporate bankruptcy regime, post-insolvency interest is not usually claimable or (the same thing in practice) is subordinated to other creditors. In state insolvencies, interest continues to run and is typically capitalized by contract. As a result, the interest piles up and can massively increase the defaulted capital.
- *Preferences* —Corporate insolvency laws typically provide for the recapture or revocation of transfers by the debtor in the twilight suspect period prior to the commencement of formal insolvency proceedings in order to achieve equality of creditors. For states, there are no statutory rules for the recovery of preferential payments or transfers to a creditor while the state is insolvent. Whether this is, in fact, a problem is a point that requires a debate in the light of experience.
- *The government's failures*—In the case of corporate bankruptcies, many jurisdictions impose liability on directors and managers for violation of corporate law, and of their duties, including (sometimes) personal liability for deepening an insolvency. In some jurisdictions, directors are required to file for a judicial insolvency proceeding if the company is in fact insolvent.
  In the case of states, there is generally no regime for holding government officials to account, either by retributive sanctions or by the disgorge of assets into the insolvency state.
- *Bankruptcy consolidation*—Under many corporate insolvency regimes, it is permissible, subject to stringent conditions, to consolidate a group of companies by merging its assets and liabilities. This would typically happen if the corporate form had not been observed. Because it has an adverse impact on creditors, bankruptcy consolidation is unusual.
  There is no regime for the consolidation of state-owned companies, central banks, and other controlled entities into the state.

10. International Bankruptcy Court

In the case of ordinary corporate insolvencies, the courts having jurisdiction typically have functions to order the commencement of proceedings if the eligibility criteria are met, so appoint a provisional administrator pending any selection by creditors, to decide disputes, to approve motions for the implementation of stays or freezes, to settle disputes and to approve a reorganization plan to ensure that fairness is observed and in order to enhance recognition of the plan abroad. The courts do not decide the commercial terms of a plan, subject to very basic rules about fairness and compliance with the law, for example observance of the ladder of priorities. **24.68**

In the case of states, there is no international bankruptcy court to undertake these functions. Nevertheless, national courts can and do resolve disputes regarding sovereign debt, and they also give judgment in favour of creditors. Creditors may potentially bring arbitration claims against states based on debt, notably proceedings under bilateral investment treaties. **24.69**

The question here is whether it is desirable to have a collective proceeding that centralizes all claims and oversees all aspects of the case under the control of a single court. **24.70**

A crucial question would be whether or not the insulation achieved by a foreign governing law would be upheld by a central court: this insulation is considered essential for sovereign and other major debt commitments. **24.71**

11. General Differences in Status

24.72 There are some other general differences in the status of sovereign borrowers and private corporate borrowers, including the following.

- *Number of sovereign debtors*—There are millions of corporations; by contrast, the number of sovereign states is fewer than 200. But the number of people affected by sovereign insolvency may be very large. The issue here is whether the very low number of potential debtors affects the management of the problem.
- *Amount of debt*—The amounts of sovereign debt in the case of the largest countries is massive, for example the sovereign debt of the United States and Japan. The amount of the sovereign debt of most other countries is individually small compared to the world's largest corporations. Thus the Greek sovereign debt was around the same size as that of Lehman Brothers, which collapsed in 2008, but six times as much as the previous biggest sovereign insolvency, Argentina in 2001.
- *Banks and other contingent liabilities*—The balance sheets of sovereign states potentially include, for example, banks within their territorial domain. Those states may be obliged effectively to guarantee the liabilities of their banks in the event of systemic banking collapse. This can substantially add to the public debt. Of course, corporations can also have off-balance-sheet liabilities, but accounting rules are severe in their inclusion of these in financial statements. Many sovereigns have other huge contingent liabilities, for example for pensions, which are not usually reflected in government debt statistics.
- *Creditor identity*—Creditors of corporations include not only banks and bondholders (who are typically the largest creditors), but also employees, trade suppliers, pension claimants, tort claimants, and a huge diversity of others. Although sovereign states may have tort liabilities, for example for expropriation and the like, and may also have some trading creditors, the normal case is that most of their creditors are either bondholders or, to a much lesser extent, banks or official sector loan creditors. This means that the conduct of a workout is much simpler than in the case of a large corporation.
- *Geopolitics*—It is a matter for consideration whether the geopolitical importance of sovereign states is much greater than that of very large corporations and how this should affect the resolution of financial difficulties.

12. Conclusion

24.73 It is clear, from this brief comparison, that there is a world of difference between the bankruptcy regime applying to corporations and that applying to sovereign states. It is also clear that the status of sovereign states will always be different from that of corporations, for example as regards the ability of creditors to realize assets and the ability of creditors to control the finances of the debtor. The arguments for and against the introduction of an international bankruptcy procedure should focus in detail on whether the lessons learned from the history of the bankruptcy of individuals and corporations are relevant to sovereign states.

25

EUROPEAN COLLECTIVE ACTION CLAUSES

David Billington

1. What is a Collective Action Clause?

For most of the twentieth century, the collective action clause (CAC) was regarded by many in the sovereign debt community as one of the less glamorous provisions of a sovereign bond—a purely mechanical clause that deals with the hoops through which the issuer must jump in order to amend its terms and conditions. Many sovereign bonds did not include them. Those that did were not exactly bulging with terms and conditions to which the CAC could be applied. Yet, by late 2010, CACs were deemed so important that the European authorities decided to make their use in sovereign debt issuances mandatory for all euro area member states from June 2013 onwards, and CACs made news around the world when Greece retroactively included them in its domestic law bonds in order to complete its restructuring. This chapter explores how and why CACs have gone from optional extra to standardized mainstay so quickly, and examines the constituent provisions of CACs and their use in sovereign debt issuance to date. **25.01**

The term 'collective action clause' refers to a range of contractual terms, all designed to deal with the problem of holdout creditors. CACs exist because of the collective nature of certain contracts, the parties to which include a large number of different entities whose rights and obligations may be the same, but whose economic interests may differ. The classic collective contract is a bond, under which there is one issuer, but potentially hundreds or even thousands of bondholders whose identity can change on a daily basis through trading in the secondary market. These contracts must legislate not only for the rights and obligations owed between the issuer and the bondholders, but also for the rights and obligations owed by the bondholders to each other. **25.02**

2. The Holdout Creditor Problem

In the context of a sovereign bond, the problems will arise when the issuer encounters financial difficulties and it becomes clear that a restructuring of its obligations will be required. To achieve that goal, the sovereign will need to come to some form of agreement with its bondholders, usually with a view to significantly reducing the amount that the sovereign must repay. This is when holdout creditors can emerge. **25.03**

Holdout creditors can create two problems. First, they can create deadlock situations in restructuring negotiations. In the absence of a CAC, any modification to a bond's terms **25.04** would require the consent of every bondholder. That confers on every bondholder the ability to prevent a restructuring that has the support of the vast majority of the issuer's creditors, or to hold the issuer to ransom and extract unwarranted concessions as the 'price' for its support. CACs introduce an element of democracy to deal with this by allowing an issuer to modify the terms of its bonds without having to obtain the consent of every single bondholder—the consent of a 'supermajority' will be sufficient to bind all bondholders, even those who object to the proposed modification.

25.05 Second, holdout creditors that are free to act in their own interests can often precipitate a 'rush for the exit', by taking enforcement action in an attempt to recover some value immediately rather than waiting for the rest of the bondholders to come to an agreement with the issuer on a restructuring plan. In 2002, Buchheit and Gulati expressed the issue as follows:

> It is when the bond issuer runs into financial difficulties that the actions of one bondholder can dramatically affect the interests of all the other lenders. For example, if each holder has the unfettered discretion to accelerate its bonds following an event of default…the other bondholders may find that their own options in dealing with the situation are dangerously curtailed.[1]

In addition to providing a means for resolving deadlock, CACs can also operate to restrain a creditor's instinctive urge to take individual enforcement action by allowing bondholder action only if a requisite majority (by principal amount) are in favour of it, and allowing a supermajority to rescind that action.

25.06 Each investor in a bond that contains a CAC is implicitly accepting that:

- the fundamental legal and economic rights associated with that investment can be altered without his consent if the alteration is supported by enough of his fellow bondholders; and
- he may not be able to take enforcement action in respect of his own bond in circumstances where a majority of the bondholders wish to restrain him.

Put like that, why would anybody buy a bond that contained a CAC and give up the right to control his own destiny? The simple answer is that the benefit of being able to act individually is outweighed by the costs involved in allowing fellow bondholders the same freedom. Each bondholder may be worried that harmful modifications could be made to the terms of their bonds against their will. But they should be equally worried that they could get stuck in a situation in which they wish to accept whatever is being offered to them in a restructuring, and a small holdout creditor causes deadlock or precipitates a disorderly situation by bringing proceedings against the issuer.

3. Are CACs the Only Way?

25.07 In the absence of a CAC, there are ways in which to implement a debt restructuring. One popular method is an exchange offer coupled with what is commonly referred to as an 'exit consent'. This involves the issuer offering its existing bondholders a trade. New bonds are offered to them in exchange for their existing bonds, but the new bonds would, of course, have a lower face amount. Because this is not exactly a great deal for the bondholders, they

[1] Lee C. Buchheit and G. Mitu Gulati, 'Sovereign Bonds and the Collective Will' (2002) 51 Emory LJ 1317, 1324–5.

need to be given an incentive to participate. That incentive is provided by an 'exit consent'. Historically, bonds issued under New York law would typically require unanimity to modify payment terms, but they do usually permit other provisions of the bond to be modified by a simple majority. The purpose of an exit consent is to strip the existing bond of certain of its terms and conditions in order to make it less attractive. By tendering bonds in the exchange, bondholders are deemed to vote in favour of the amendment to the terms of the bonds they are about to relinquish. Unless sufficient numbers of bondholders decide to work together and decline the offer, they each run the risk of getting 'left behind' in a bond that retains its original face amount, but is stripped of its key contractual provisions and may therefore be worth less on the secondary market.

There are two key disadvantages of exchange offers and exit consents, as follows. **25.08**

(a) Exchange offers do not deal with the holdout creditor problem unless 100 per cent of the bondholders agree to the exchange. Those bondholders who do not participate in the exchange are still entitled to be paid the full face value of their bonds. This creates a dilemma for the sovereign issuer: continue to pay the holdouts in full; or default on the old bonds (which may lead to litigation and cause cross defaults in its other obligations). Neither option is palatable.
(b) At least for English-law-governed bonds, there are, at the time of writing, question marks over whether modifications implemented through 'coercive' exit consents are enforceable. It has been a general principle of English law since the late nineteenth century that a contractual power of a majority of creditors to bind a minority must be exercised bona fide and for the purpose of benefiting the class of creditors as a whole. Over the years, this basic principle was gradually eroded as litigants in the English courts increasingly sought (and won) judgments that affirmed the primacy of the terms of the contract as governing the interactions between the parties.[2] As a result, exit consents became relatively common as a liability management technique for bonds and loans governed by English law. It took until 2012 for the High Court to remind us all that the general principle still exists, in a case involving an exit consent conducted by the nationalized Anglo Irish Bank.[3] This was a classic exchange offer with an exit consent, but with one crucial wrinkle: in addition to the usual deletion of the key terms and conditions that participating bondholders were asked to approve, the issuer also asked that they vote in favour of the inclusion of a call option. That call option would allow the issuer to redeem any non-participating bondholders' bonds for 1 cent per €1,000 of face value. A disgruntled bondholder (who had subsequently had its €17 million worth of bonds redeemed for just €170) brought proceedings claiming that the exit consent was invalid as an abuse of the majority's voting power. The High Court agreed with the bondholder. Had this been solely on the basis that the inclusion of the call option was, essentially, an expropriation of the non-participating bondholders' rights, the decision would not have had such broad-reaching implications. But the judge made several comments that suggest that the very idea of an exit consent, regardless of the substance of the proposed changes, offends the general principles of English law that govern majority voting rights. In a much-quoted passage of the judgment, he said 'oppression of a minority is of the

[2] The most recent example in this line of cases is *Redwood Master Fund v. TD Bank Europe Ltd and ors* [2002] All ER (D) 141.

[3] *Assenagon Asset Management SA v. Irish Bank Resolution Corporation Ltd* [2012] EWHC 2090 (Ch).

essence of exit consents of this kind, and it is precisely that at which the principles restraining the abusive exercise of powers to bind minorities are aimed'.[4] At the time of writing, the case is the subject of an appeal. The hope is that the higher courts in England will provide some more definitive guidance on the application of these general principles. Until they do, the validity of exit consents under English-law-governed bonds and credit agreements is open to question.

25.09 CACs, therefore, are the only way in which to deal comprehensively with a holdout creditor problem, because a modification to the terms and conditions of the affected bonds will bind every bondholder, not only those who vote in favour.

4. Collective Action Clauses in Sovereign Debt

25.10 Whilst CACs became commonplace in bonds issued by private sector corporations from the late nineteenth century onwards, their use in bonds issued by sovereign states was, until the early 2000s, patchier. Broadly, a dichotomy had emerged whereby sovereign bonds issued under New York law generally did not contain a CAC and sovereign bonds issued under English law did. Why did the two regimes diverge in this way? The answer is that New York and English law developed different tools to deal with the holdout creditor problem. The English fashion for CACs never really caught on in the United States, initially because of concerns that if a bond could be altered with a majority vote, it would cease to be a negotiable instrument under the Negotiable Instruments Law.[5] As a result, New York law initially developed more sophisticated court procedures for imposing a debt restructuring on all creditors if supported by the majority, and later legislation (in the form of the Trust Indenture Act of 1939) requiring unanimity for modifications to fundamental economic terms in response to concerns that CACs could be manipulated by corporate insiders at the expense of ordinary 'mom and pop' investors. Even though the 1939 Act did not apply to sovereign issuers and the more sophisticated bankruptcy procedures were not available to sovereign states, the custom was entrenched enough to be replicated in the terms of sovereign debt issuances.

25.11 There were also enforceability issues with CACs in other jurisdictions. For a long time, there was uncertainty in Germany about whether CACs were consistent with the Civil Code. The statutory regime for modification of bond terms in Germany was set out in the Act on the Joint Rights of Bondholders of 1899. It applies to issuers resident in Germany, but not to sovereign debt. Like the US Trust Indenture Act, it does not allow a waiver of the bondholders' right to receive principal (which can be achieved only through an insolvency proceeding), although interest rates can be reduced or interest payments postponed by a majority. In addition, the German Civil Code contains consumer protection principles that require a standard of fairness that a CAC may not meet.

25.12 However, it was not only historical custom or local law concerns that perpetuated the reluctance to use CACs in sovereign debt. Many investors held the view that the use of CACs in sovereign bonds should not be encouraged. Forcing a sovereign state to repay its creditors is often difficult or impossible. So the appropriate response for a bondholder is to make

[4] *Assenagon Asset Management* (n. 3), para. 86.

[5] Section 3–104, para. (1)(b). The concern was that a CAC would stop the instrument from being an unconditional promise to pay. The full history is told elegantly by Buchheit and Gulati (n. 1).

defaulting costly and renegotiation of bond terms as difficult as possible. The thinking goes that if sovereign debt contains a CAC, the sovereign state is more likely to borrow recklessly, safe in the knowledge that it can cut a deal with bondholders later on. The prevalence of this investor sentiment led many sovereign issuers themselves to develop an allergy to CACs on the basis that investors would charge a premium to compensate them for the extra risk involved in subscribing for a bond that contains a CAC.

Proponents of CACs take a different view. They argue that sovereigns already have strong **25.13** incentives to avoid a default. Apart from the severe economic hardship for all of the sovereign's citizens that a default would cause, perhaps the strongest incentive for a sovereign to avoid a default is its need to maintain access to the market. As Sönke Häseler points out in a 2009 working paper: 'In a debt situation with practically no collateral and no international institution that can enforce creditor claims, considerations of reputation are of the utmost importance.'[6]

In 1995, after the Mexican crisis, the ministers and governors of the G-10 countries estab- **25.14** lished a working party to consider how sovereign debt crises could be resolved in a more orderly fashion. This working group concluded that CACs were the appropriate tool for the task, but also concluded that, to be successful, their introduction would need to be a market-led process.[7] Effectively, they concluded that 'You can lead a horse to water, but you cannot make it drink.' Little changed—even though the International Monetary Fund (IMF) was a vociferous supporter. It was not until Argentina's default in 2001 that investor sentiment began to shift and, in early 2003, Mexico began including a CAC in its bonds issued under New York law. Within a short period of time, Uruguay, Brazil, and other emerging market sovereigns had adopted the same practice, so that by 2004 CACs were gradually becoming a standard feature in emerging market sovereign bonds issued under New York law. European issuers then began to follow suit, with Italy and Hungary using CACs for the first time in their New York law bonds.

What was it about the Argentina default that suddenly made CACs acceptable to issuer and **25.15** investor alike? In 2012, Michael Bradley and Mitu Gulati[8] suggested that the change was down to two key factors, as follows.

- The defaulted Argentinian bonds did not contain CACs. This led to extreme difficulty in putting a restructuring solution in place, with more than a year passing before a proposal could be made.
- English law sovereign bonds (which typically would include a CAC) were trading at lower spreads than New York law sovereign bonds (which would typically not contain a CAC), showing issuers that there was no price penalty involved in CAC usage.

In addition to these two factors, a more general shift in the landscape had been taking **25.16** place since the 1980s. That shift was the result of a change in the composition of sovereign debt investors, which had grown from relatively small syndicates of large banks to large and

[6] Sönke Häseler, *Collective Action Clauses in International Sovereign Bond Contracts: Whence the Opposition?* (May 2009), available online at <http://ideas.repec.org/p/pra/mprapa/6314.html>.

[7] G-10, *The Resolution of Sovereign Liquidity Crises* (May 1996), available online at <http://www.bis.org/publ/gten03.pdf>.

[8] Michael Bradley and Mitu Gulati, *Collective Action Clauses for the Eurozone: An Empirical Analysis* (May 2012), available online at <http://scholarship.law.duke.edu/faculty_scholarship/2455/>.

broadly dispersed groups of bondholders with a variety of different investment strategies. The Argentina experience confirmed that obtaining unanimous approval from such a diverse group was almost impossible.

5. The Move towards Standardization: Model CACs pre-2013

25.17 The Argentina default prompted action from the official sector too. In 2002, some six years after their first report, the ministers and governors of the G-10 countries formed another working group to look at CACs, this time chaired by Randy Quarles of the US Treasury. Its task was to develop a set of model CACs for sovereign bond issues. In September 2002, the working group's model clauses were published, together with an explanatory memorandum.[9]

25.18 The key G-10 recommendations were that the following provisions be included in sovereign bonds:

- a majority amendment clause permitting amendments of payment terms with the approval of a supermajority of bondholders;
- a mechanism for disenfranchising bonds directly or indirectly owned or controlled by the sovereign issuer;
- a provision requiring a 25 per cent bondholder vote for acceleration and a majority or supermajority of up to 66⅔ per cent vote for rescission of acceleration;
- a provision for a permanent bondholder representative (for example a trustee) and the option for bondholders to elect a negotiating representative;
- a provision allowing bondholders holding at least 10 per cent of the outstanding amount of the bonds to convene a bondholders' meeting; and
- provisions requiring the issuer to distribute appropriate information to the bondholders over the life of the bond, and additional information following an event of default.

25.19 In parallel with the work undertaken by the G-10 working group, a number of private sector trade associations[10] developed their own model CAC. The main differences between the G-10 recommendation and the trade association recommendations were that:

- the voting thresholds proposed by the trade associations were higher than those proposed by the G-10;
- the list of reserved matters proposed by the trade associations was broader than proposed by the G-10; and
- the trade associations recommended a fiscal agent structure rather than a trustee structure (allowing bondholders to litigate individually).

Whilst the trade associations clearly bought into the idea of using a CAC, they (unsurprisingly) wanted a CAC that made it more difficult for the sovereign to restructure and easier for bondholders to sue.

[9] G-10, *Report of the G-10 Working Group on Contractual Clauses* (September 2002), available online at <http://www.bis.org/publ/gten08.pdf>.

[10] The Institute of International Finance, the International Primary Market Association, the Emerging Market Creditors Association, the Trade Association for the Emerging Markets, the Securities Industry Association, the International Securities Market Association, and the Bond Market Association.

Market practice post-2002 has not preferred one model over the other, with issuers and investors preferring to pick and choose from the two menus of recommendations. All of the G-10 recommendations found some traction in the market, with the exception of the requirement to use a trust structure. It seems that, in their dealings with sovereign issuers, investors do not wish to get 'stuck' behind a neutral third party. And, generally speaking, sovereign issuers are not comfortable with the extra level of cost and administration that a trust structure requires. **25.20**

6. The European Sovereign Crisis and Response

By the mid-2000s, following the G-10 and trade association efforts, CACs in sovereign debt had already achieved a degree of standardization. But their use was, with a few exceptions, confined to emerging market issuers or to bonds issued in the context of a restructuring. With Europe's economies booming and only distant memories of a European sovereign default (the most recent was Austria in 1945), there was little incentive for a European sovereign to pre-emptively offer up a CAC in its debt issuances: the very idea that a European sovereign could default seemed outrageous. **25.21**

Fast forward to 2009 and the effects of the financial crisis that started in 2007 began to leak from the private sector into the public sector. Suddenly, the possibility of a European sovereign defaulting on its obligations was no longer fanciful, with the Republic of Ireland requiring assistance from the European Central Bank (ECB) and the IMF in November 2010. This experience confirmed the European authorities' fears that most domestic-law-governed European sovereign debt did not contain a CAC of any kind in its terms and conditions. This situation left a troubled sovereign with two options: **25.22**

- a government bailout (clearly not something the European authorities wished to encourage); or
- a quasi-consensual exchange offer, with the resulting 'freerider' problem.

This state of affairs led the Eurogroup (comprising the finance ministers of the eurozone countries) to issue a statement on 28 November 2010,[11] setting out its proposed approach to future eurozone sovereign debt crises. This approach consisted of a *quid pro quo*: the European Stability Mechanism (ESM), the conduit for European governmental money, would provide 'liquidity assistance' to a sovereign only if that sovereign were to negotiate a 'comprehensive restructuring plan' with its private sector creditors. Stripping away the euphemism, the Eurogroup was really saying that private sector creditors would, in future, have to share the pain in order for a troubled sovereign to obtain governmental assistance. To facilitate this pain sharing, the Eurogroup also announced that standardized and identical CACs would be mandatory in the terms and conditions of all new euro area government bonds, starting in June 2013. **25.23**

The task of coming up with the actual model CAC was delegated to a subcommittee of the Economic and Financial Committee (EFC) of the European Union. The final text of the **25.24**

[11] Eurogroup, *Statement by the Eurogroup* (November 2010), available online at <http://www.consilium.europa.eu/uedocs/cms_data/docs/pressdata/en/ecofin/118050.pdf>.

proposed mandatory CAC (the 'Model CAC') was published on 18 November 2011,[12] following receipt by the subcommittee of feedback from market participants, trade organizations, and other bodies in a public consultation process.

7. The Model Clause in Detail

A. Approval thresholds: reserved matters

25.25 For the draftsman, the approval threshold in a CAC is both the most important and the most difficult part. It is important, because it is the key driver of the clause's effectiveness—the draftsman faces a 'Goldilocks dilemma'.[13] Set the threshold too high and the usefulness of the CAC is diluted; set it too low and investors may be reluctant to subscribe for fear of the ease with which the other bondholders could approve changes to the terms of the bond.

25.26 The challenge is not limited to deciding on the appropriate numerical percentage of bondholders required to approve a reserved matter amendment (that is, the numerator). Careful consideration needs to be given to the appropriate denominator. There are two approaches to the denominator commonly seen in the market today:

- it is set as the aggregate principal amount of *all* outstanding bonds; or
- it is set as the aggregate principal amount of all outstanding bonds that are represented at a bondholder meeting.

25.27 As with many other areas of a CAC, there is a divergence in practice between CACs governed by New York law (which tend to opt for the percentage of *all* outstanding bonds formulation) and English law (which tend to opt for a quorum formulation). One reason for this is that bondholder action under New-York-law-governed CACs tends to happen via written resolutions rather than meetings.

25.28 Many investors (particularly in the United States) are wary of the quorum formulation, because typically a quorum mechanic will reduce the percentage of outstanding bonds required to vote in favour in order to pass a reserved matter modification at a bondholder meeting. The classic example is a quorum level, relatively common in English-law-governed CACs, of 25 per cent of the outstanding bonds for an adjourned meeting. With that level of attendance and a 75 per cent consent threshold, a reserved matter modification could be implemented with support from the holders of only 18.75 per cent of the outstanding amount of the bonds.

25.29 In practice, bondholder meetings called to implement a sovereign restructuring are likely to be well attended and (it has been suggested) bondholders with strong negative views are more likely to attend than those who are ambivalent. In fact, some commentators have suggested that a bondholder meeting mechanic could actually make an amendment more difficult than if the same amendment were effected by a written resolution, because when bondholders meet they may be able to persuade each other that holding out is likely to be a

---

[12] EFC, *Euro Area Model CAC 2012* (November 2011), available online at <http://europa.eu/efc/sub_committee/cac/cac_2012/index_en.htm>.

[13] For those not familiar with the phrase (or the children's tale), Goldilocks was a rather fussy eater when it came to the temperature of her porridge.

successful strategy. The G-10 did not express a preference on this point, although its report did contain passages that suggested support for a quorum mechanic.

For the numerator, the G-10 working group considered 75 per cent support to be an acceptable threshold and cautioned against levels higher than this. Crucially, the G-10 report said that issuers could choose whether or not to adopt a quorum approach, and that the use of one or the other of these approaches should depend on which had gained acceptance by the market. Unsurprisingly, the trade association's model CAC adopted the percentage of all outstanding bonds formulation with a consent threshold of 75 per cent. In addition, the trade association's model continues to make some matters the subject of a unanimous consent requirement (for example changes to the governing law and jurisdiction clauses). **25.30**

As to consent thresholds seen in the market, Mexico's 2003 issuance required 75 per cent and the market settled on that number relatively quickly, with other issuers following suit.[14] **25.31**

A further challenge to drafting this part of a CAC is that, increasingly, bondholder meetings are seen as clunky and old-fashioned; a modern CAC needs to legislate for written resolutions by the bondholders too. While it is true that many recent emerging market sovereign debt restructurings have been implemented by actions in writing, bondholder meetings are the norm in the euro area for corporate restructurings. **25.32**

The Model CAC adopts *both* approaches, and specifies different consent thresholds for each of the following: **25.33**

- for resolutions passed at a bondholder meeting, 75 per cent of the principal amount of the outstanding bonds represented at that meeting; and
- for written resolutions, 66⅔ per cent of the aggregate principal amount of the outstanding bonds.

The stated[15] rationale for this bifurcated approach is as follows. **25.34**

(a) The chosen method of passing a resolution (meeting or written) should not make it easier or harder to pass that resolution.
(b) It is likely that bondholder attendance at a meeting will almost always be less than 100 per cent.
(c) If the meeting approval threshold were set by reference to the aggregate principal amount of the bonds (and not by reference to those represented at a meeting), it would be substantially more difficult in practice for the same proposed modification to be approved at a bondholder meeting than by an action in writing.[16] This is because every bondholder who fails to attend the meeting would automatically be treated as a vote in opposition (rather than an abstention). The result is that a determined investor (or

[14] Brazil's issuance shortly after Mexico's in 2003 specified 85 per cent, but was seen as a symptom of Brazil's poorer credit quality at the time—with other sub-investment grade issuers (Belize, Guatemala, and Venezuala) following suit. Some have suggested that this was to signal a commitment to avoiding future restructurings, but it seems counter-intuitive for an issuer that is more likely to require a restructuring to be choosing a CAC that would make a restructuring more difficult.

[15] *See* EFC Subcommittee on EU Sovereign Debt Markets, *Collective Action Clause: Explanatory Note* (July 2011), available online at <http://europa.eu/efc/sub_committee/pdf/explanatory_note_draft_on_the_model_cac_-_26_july.pdf>.

[16] For example, if the approval threshold is 75 per cent of all of the bonds outstanding and only 80 per cent of the bondholders attend the meeting, the issuer would need 83 per cent of the attendees to vote in favour for the resolution to pass.

group of investors) holding a relatively small principal amount of bonds could frustrate a proposed modification. This would make it too easy to undermine an orderly restructuring and undermine the effectiveness of the Model CAC.

25.35 That deals with the different denominators, but why are the numerators different too (66⅔ per cent versus 75 per cent)? Again, this comes down to the problem of bondholder truancy when resolutions are to be passed at a meeting. Bonds are, by their nature, easily transferable and often issued in relatively small denominations. So the number of bondholders can be very high. As noted already, it is unrealistic to expect 100 per cent attendance at a bondholder meeting. A quorum mechanism allows meetings to proceed without full attendance. Again, the draftsman faces a Goldilocks dilemma, because a quorum mechanic distorts the voting power of a bond at a meeting at which the approval threshold is set by reference to the principal amount of outstanding bonds represented at that meeting. Set the quorum too low and fundamental modifications to the bonds can be passed with the votes of only a small cadre of investors; set the quorum too high and a holdout investor can effectively veto the proposed resolutions simply by not showing up to the meeting.

25.36 Even high quorums can theoretically result in a reserved matter being approved by a relatively small percentage of the total affected bonds then outstanding, especially in the case of a vote held at an adjourned meeting (when quorum levels are usually lowered).

25.37 The Model CAC sets the quorum for a reserved matter modification at 66⅔ per cent of the outstanding bonds, for *both* the initial and any adjourned meeting. This unusual feature ensures parity of treatment between meetings and written resolutions because the holders of 33⅓ per cent + 1 of the outstanding bonds can veto a proposed reserved matter modification regardless of method. However, with this quorum level in place, the approval threshold for resolutions proposed at meeting needs to be adjusted upwards, otherwise a reserved matter modification could theoretically be passed by the holders of less than half of the principal amount of the bonds.[17]

B. Approval thresholds: non-reserved matters

25.38 The Model CAC sets the required approval threshold in the case of a non-reserved matter modification at a simple majority of the outstanding principal amount of the affected series of bonds represented at a duly called meeting of bondholders, or a simple majority of the principal amount of all outstanding bonds if the modification is approved by a written resolution. The quorum for a bondholder meeting to pass a non-reserved matter is set at 50 per cent of the outstanding bonds for the initial meeting and 25 per cent of the outstanding bonds for any adjourned meeting. This means that a non-reserved matter modification could be passed by the holders of just over a quarter of the principal amount of the bonds at the initial meeting, or the holders of just over 12.5 per cent of the outstanding bonds at an adjourned meeting.

C. Aggregation

25.39 The aggregation provision in a CAC seeks to address a practical problem, summarized by Sönke Häseler as follows:

> Collective action clauses are in the first instance issue-specific; their purpose is to solve collective action problems among the bondholders of a particular issue. Once this has been

[17] That is, 66⅔ per cent of 66⅔ per cent works out at 44.4 per cent.

achieved, the problem reappears at the next higher level. By agreeing to debt relief, the majority of bondholders of one issue improves the chances of full repayment for another, and thus creates incentives for holdouts at the level of bond issues.[18]

Put another way, the bondholders of a number of different issues may all be willing to offer debt relief to the sovereign issuer in respect of their own bonds, but each class will be reluctant to 'go first' without any guarantee that the holders in the other classes will provide similar relief.

An aggregation clause seeks to resolve the deadlock by allowing an issuer to group different series of bonds together and propose one set of amendments to the holders of all of those bonds. The underlying rationale for an aggregation mechanic is that it is fair for holders of a single series of bonds to be bound by a proposed modification if the modification is approved by a supermajority of all other affected investors. A cross-series modification provision binds the holders of all affected bonds, even if the holders of one series of bonds have not voted (overwhelmingly) in favour of the modification, so long as a supermajority of the holders of all of the other series of bonds have approved the cross-series modification. **25.40**

For such a proposal to be effected, typically the consent of two constituencies would need to be received: **25.41**

(a) the holders of a requisite percentage of bonds in *each* affected series, taken individually; and
(b) the holders of a requisite percentage of bonds in *all* of the affected series when aggregated together.

It is, of course, possible to draft a CAC with just one aggregated voting threshold—that is, only limb (b). However, that has so far not been a popular construction because it could theoretically allow the terms of a series of bonds to be amended even in the face of objection by a majority of the holders of the bonds in that series. This could lead to some unfair incentives for issuers to group certain series in a tactical manner in order to propose that one series of bonds be modified at the expense of another series.

The G-10 report did not make a specific recommendation on aggregation, expressing the view that an aggregation mechanic could help to facilitate a comprehensive restructuring, but would not be practicable within a contractually based mechanism. The trade association's model CAC similarly did not include a cross-series modification provision. It was left to Uruguay to break new ground by being the first sovereign to include an aggregation clause in its bonds issued as part of a broader restructuring in 2003. It was followed by Argentina in 2004 and the Dominican Republic in 2005. One interesting feature of the Uruguay aggregation clause was that it contained an anti-manipulation feature, in the form of a covenant preventing the issuer from issuing additional bonds with the intention of placing such securities with holders expected to support any modification proposed by Uruguay. At the time of writing, only four nations[19] have included an aggregation provision in their sovereign bonds. **25.42**

The Model CAC contains an aggregation option. The consent thresholds required are 75 per cent (meeting) or 66⅔ per cent (written resolution) on an aggregate basis, and 66⅔ per cent **25.43**

[18] Häseler (n. 6), 121.
[19] Argentina, the Dominican Republic, Uruguay, and Greece.

(meeting) or 50 per cent (written resolution) on an individual series basis. The aggregation clause in the Model CAC contains two unusual features, as follows.

(a) It allows for a partial use of the aggregation mechanic in the event that some, but not all, of the affected series of bonds approve the requested modification. An issuer may implement the proposed modification in relation to those series of bonds the modification of which would have been approved if the cross-series modification had initially been proposed only in respect of the bonds of those series.
(b) It goes some way to preventing manipulation by the issuer by:
    (i) requiring the issuer to make available to the holders of all affected series the full menu of modification options, so that all of the investors are voting on the same set of proposed modifications; and
    (ii) requiring the issuer to notify investors in advance of the conditions under which a partial cross-series modification will come into effect (that is, to prevent the issuer from cherry picking the affected series after the fact).

D. Disenfranchisement: does everyone get to vote?

25.44 In a bond without a CAC, it does not really matter to a prospective investor who the other bondholders are because everybody has a veto over proposed modifications to the terms. But once a CAC is introduced, the dynamics change. If the requisite majority of bondholders agree to a modification, all bondholders are bound. Suddenly, the identity of the other bondholders takes on a new significance to the prospective investor. It is commonplace for CACs contained in the terms and conditions of bonds issued by private sector entities to legislate for the circumstance under which the issuer purchases its own bonds. It is accepted wisdom that an issuer itself should be disenfranchised from voting on a proposed modification, and disenfranchisement provisions have become typical in many sovereign bonds.

25.45 The tentacles of the state in most countries stretch far and wide, and in fact the sovereign state itself is unlikely to be a holder of its own debt directly. So it is logical that the disenfranchisement provision in a sovereign CAC should not allow the issuer to subvert its purpose by procuring that a state-controlled entity purchase and vote its sovereign bonds. It is for this reason that the application of most disenfranchisement provisions in sovereign CACs extends to withdraw voting power not only from bonds held by the issuer itself, but also from those held by 'public sector instrumentalities',[20] or bonds that are, directly or indirectly, controlled by the issuer.

25.46 The G-10 recommended a disenfranchisement provision that would deny voting rights in respect of bonds 'directly or indirectly owned or controlled by the sovereign issuer and its public sector instrumentalities', but states that the definition of public sector instrumentality should be negotiated on a case-by-case basis. Disenfranchisement provisions have been widely adopted in the market post-2003, although there is a variety in breadth of formulation.[21] Many of these formulations were crafted at a time when the idea of a sovereign state taking ownership of large commercial banks headquartered in its jurisdiction was unthinkable.

---

[20] This is actually a misnomer. The term is usually defined deliberately broadly to pick up not only public sector entities, but also private sector companies controlled by the government.

[21] For a broad formulation, *see* the 5.125 per cent notes due March 2022 issued by Turkey, summarized in Keegan S. Drake, *Disenfranchisement in Sovereign Bonds* (February 2012), available online at <http://papers.ssrn.com/sol3/papers.cfm?abstract_id=2007294>.

Now that eventuality has come to pass, it will be interesting to see if any of those entities would be disenfranchised from voting sovereign bonds issued by the 'sponsoring' state.

From a drafting perspective, disenfranchisement can be achieved in a number of ways, including by means of: 25.47

(a) a bespoke stand-alone provision;
(b) a provision that immediately cancels bonds purchased by the issuer (or its public sector instrumentalities); or
(c) a provision that deems bonds held by the issuer (or its public sector instrumentalities) to be not 'outstanding' for the purposes of calculating whether a consent threshold has been reached.

Historically, English-law-governed bonds have favoured the latter formulation, and this is the approach adopted by the Model CAC.

The Model CAC disenfranchises government bonds held by the issuer, by any of its ministries, departments, or agencies, and also by any corporation, trust, or other legal entity that is controlled by the issuer. 'Control' is defined broadly for these purposes as the power to direct the management of or to appoint a majority of the board of directors of the relevant entity, whether through ownership of securities, by contract or otherwise. This is consistent with broad disenfranchisement provisions seen in other sovereign bonds. Where the Model CAC breaks new ground is in *en*franchising entities that would otherwise be disenfranchised if they have 'autonomy of decision', and provides three 'safe harbours', which describe specifically what is meant by the term. 25.48

The logic for the autonomy of decision exception is that the purpose of the disenfranchisement provision, at least as it applies to public sector instrumentalities, is to prevent an issuer from directing the voting of bonds that, although not held directly by the issuer, are held by an entity over which the issuer is able to exercise de facto control. If that de facto control is absent, the entity would have been disenfranchised unfairly. The Model CAC uses 'autonomy of decision' as a proxy for identifying whether the requisite de facto control is present, and is best illustrated by looking at each of the safe harbours described in the Model CAC in turn. 25.49

The first safe harbour is available to government-controlled companies that may not take instruction from their supposedly 'controlling' government. This would cover most, if not all, euro area central banks because Article 130 of the Treaty on the Functioning of the European Union (TFEU) and Article 7 of the Statute of the European System of Central Banks (ESCB) and of the ECB expressly prohibit euro area national central banks and members of their decision-making bodies from seeking or taking instruction from European Union institutions or bodies, from any government of a member state of the European Union, or from any other body. As a result, a central bank's decision to vote for or against the proposed modification of securities must, as a matter of law, be made by the bank acting in its own interest, even though the bank may well be owned or controlled by its government (for example the government may have the right to appoint the bank's governor or a majority of its directors). 25.50

The second safe harbour is available to a government-controlled company that is required by law to act in accordance with an objective prudential standard, in the interest of all of its 25.51

stakeholders (and not only its shareholders) or in its own self interest. This is really a variation on the first safe harbour: if the entity is required by law to act independently of government instruction, it will not be disenfranchised.

25.52 The final safe harbour is available to entities that owe fiduciary (or similar) duties to third parties independently of any obligation that it may owe to its controlling parent. This safe harbour is intended to enfranchise, for example, entities such as government-sponsored pension funds, in which the trustee or manager acts solely for the benefit of the pensioners or beneficiaries.

25.53 The Model CAC has been criticized in some quarters because the autonomy of decision exceptions allows entities that are perceived to be not 'genuine' investors to distort the voting. A further criticism is that it enfranchises entities that may, as a formal matter, be independent, but which are susceptible to 'nods and winks' from the government, which would make their voting on any proposed modification all too predictable. But it is very difficult to legislate to address these criticisms. If the Model CAC were to restrict voting only to 'genuine' investors, it would need to define what qualifications such a person would need to possess. This approach would create two problems, as follows.

(a) First, it involves a level of subjectivity that would be impossible to police. Any test of genuineness implies an attempt at capturing the motivations that the investor had in its mind when acquiring the bond and exercising its voting right. Even if it were possible to establish such motivations in an objective way, how should one decide which motivations are acceptable and which are not? Should voting rights be given only to investors who, in deciding whether to buy the bond and how to vote, take into account only their direct financial returns as bondholders and not their broader economic interests?

(b) Second, it is not only government-owned entities that are likely to vote in a predictable way in a sovereign debt restructuring. One could argue that any privately owned creditor headquartered in and regulated by the sovereign issuer is more likely than not to support a debt restructuring for a variety of reasons. Predictability of action is not a sound basis on which to disenfranchise a bondholder, and even if a construct based on actual control or pressure exerted by the sovereign issuer could be drafted satisfactorily, it would have to be self-policing and therefore ineffective as a bondholder protection.

25.54 The alternative would be to simply disenfranchise all state-owned entities on the basis that if there is any connection with the issuer that could raise doubts about a bondholder's true allegiances, that bondholder should not be allowed to contaminate the voting. But this approach would be draconian in the extreme, particularly in a world in which many financial institutions are currently in (hopefully temporary) state ownership, but essentially act independently of their government masters.[22]

E. Is every bondholder's vote given the same weight? Zero-coupon and index-linked obligations

25.55 Most CACs set their consent thresholds for reserved matter and non-reserved matter modifications by reference to the principal amount of the outstanding bonds. The

[22] If the press is to be believed, the British government does not seem to be able to get the nationalized banks to control their pay or to increase their lending, so it seems like a stretch that it would be able to get them to vote a bond one way or the other.

disenfranchisement provision tells the reader what is meant by 'outstanding', but what is meant by 'principal amount'? The answer may seem obvious, but there are certain types of bond in relation to which the answer is necessarily more complex. These instruments include:

(a) *inflation-linked bonds*, under which the principal amount of the bond is adjusted periodically upwards and downwards based on published inflation figures, which instruments are relatively common in the sovereign debt world, offering investors an inflation-protected investment in addition to the interest, which compensates them for credit risk; and
(b) *zero-coupon obligations*, which can take two forms:
   (i) bonds that do not by their terms provide for the payment of interest (original issue discount, or OID, bonds);[23] and
   (ii) bonds that formerly constituted a part of an interest-bearing bond (stripped component bonds).[24]

When it comes to calculating whether a modification has received the requisite level of consent, these inflation-linked and zero-coupon bonds can have a distorting effect. For example, if the principal amount of an inflation-linked bond is deemed to be the value of the bond on the last adjustment date prior to the date of the modification, the votes attributable to those bonds could be significantly out of proportion to their current 'value'. If inflation has risen since the last adjustment date, then the votes would be under-allocated. Conversely, if inflation had fallen, the votes would be over-allocated. Admittedly, the fluctuations in value are not necessarily permanent until the next adjustment date, because any increase or decrease in inflation could, of course, be undone after the effective date of the modification. The best way in which to describe the problem is that an inflation-linked bond is likely, as of the date of a modification, to have potentially significant uncrystallized adjustments to its principal amount. The question is whether a CAC should allocate voting rights based on the crystallized or uncrystallized value. **25.56**

A similar problem arises with OID bonds. The economic return on these instruments will start to accrue immediately on issuance, but will not crystallize until maturity. If votes are accorded to OID bonds based on their stated principal amount, their holders would enjoy preferential voting rights as compared to the holder of an interest-bearing bond. **25.57**

With stripped component bonds, there would also be an over-allocation of votes. An example is the best way in which to illustrate the problem. Imagine a bond is issued with a principal amount of €100, a coupon of 10 per cent per annum, and a five-year maturity. For voting purposes, the original bond would be allocated €100 worth of votes. But if the bond is stripped of its coupons and those coupons themselves become stand-alone bonds, they will each have a principal amount of €10. So the sum of the stripped components would be entitled to €150 worth of votes. **25.58**

[23] Usually because they are issued at a discount to their face amount. Economically, these bonds do, of course, provide for a return on the investment, but that return is not realized until maturity.

[24] For the uninitiated, in many jurisdictions the stripping of bonds into their component parts is a common practice. It involves the removal and sale (separately) of the coupons from an interest-bearing bond. Each coupon effectively becomes a separate bond (without interest accruing on it).

25.59 The Model CAC is the first to attempt to resolve the potentially distorting effect of these instruments.

25.60 For inflation-linked bonds, the Model CAC allocates by assuming that the principal amount of the bond is adjusted on the date of the amendment to reflect any changes in the relevant index since the prior adjustment date. As noted earlier, this could have the effect of increasing the voting power of inflation-linked bonds by giving them 'credit' for increases in inflation or penalties for decreases in inflation that are subsequently reversed. This would not affect a single-series modification (because all of the bonds in that series would be affected to the same extent), but it could affect a cross-series modification.

25.61 OID bonds and stripped component bonds have their votes allocated not on the basis of their face amount, but based on their 'present value' as of the record date for the proposed modification. The present value is worked out by applying a discount rate to the face amount of the bonds.

(a) For OID bonds, the discount rate is the yield to maturity (that is, the 'implied' interest rate over the life of the bond based on the face amount and the issuance price).
(b) For stripped component bonds, the discount rate is the coupon on the underlying debt security, unless it is not possible to identify that underlying debt security. In that case, the discount rate is taken to be the weighted average of the coupons on the issuer's debt securities that have the same stated maturity date as the stripped component bond.

25.62 The idea behind these complex provisions is that votes should be allocated to bondholders based on the principal amount that they invest; no votes are allocated to the interest portion. If they were, holders of lower-yielding bonds would be disadvantaged. In the case of OID bonds and stripped component bonds, the problem is that the terms and conditions do not shed any light on which part of the payment due to the bondholder is principal and which is interest, because it is all paid in one go at maturity. These provisions of the Model CAC attempt to identify and exclude the part of the bondholder's entitlement that is economically their return on principal invested.

F. Reserved matters

25.63 The list of reserved matters included in a CAC is intended to capture all of the 'key' terms the modification of which should be subject to the more stringent voting and quorum requirements. There has been a degree of convergence in this area, with most CACs following the G-10 recommendations, but many also include additional reserved matters as a response to investor demand, with changes to the governing law and waiver of immunity provisions being frequent additions.

25.64 Broadly, the typical list of reserved matters will include:

(a) changing the timing or amount of any payment due;
(b) changing the currency of any payment due; and
(c) changing the consent thresholds, quorum provisions, or disenfranchisement provisions.

25.65 The Model CAC does not break new ground here and the reserved matter list is broadly consistent with the list of reserved matters found in other CACs currently in the market.

25.66 One interesting feature of the Model CAC is that it treats a change in the law governing a bond as a reserved matter only if a bond is governed by a law other than the law of the issuer.

The rationale here is that there is no need to treat a change from the issuer's own domestic law as a reserved matter because the issuer already has the power, at least in theory, to adopt any desired modification by means of domestic legislation without changing the law governing its bonds. It is only if the bond is originally governed by a foreign law (for example New York law) that a change to the governing law would be a reserved matter. This is obviously to prevent an issuer from changing the governing law to its own law and thereby gaining the ability to subvert the CAC entirely.

G. Calculation agent/bondholder representative

As noted earlier in the chapter, sovereign bonds typically use a fiscal agency structure, whereby payments to the bondholders are channelled through a financial institution that acts as the agent's issuer. The G-10 recommended a trust structure, but this has failed to catch on in the market. A notch down from a trust structure is a separate bondholder representative, who could be elected by a majority of bondholders to negotiate for them in any restructuring. Hungary used a variant of this structure in a 2004 issuance that allowed for a committee of representatives to be appointed to be the mouthpiece of the bondholders. That committee would be able to hire legal and financial advisers (at the issuer's cost). But these clauses are rare and, although popular with some trade associations, arguably not necessary. Bondholders can organize themselves into a committee on an ad hoc basis whenever they choose. **25.67**

The Model CAC follows the weight of market precedent by not requiring a bondholder representative. However, it does provide for a third party to act as a 'calculation agent', in order to determine whether a proposed modification has been approved or not. The calculation agent's role is purely administrative; it will not represent bondholder interests in any way, nor will it be the conduit for communications between bondholders and a sovereign issuer. **25.68**

H. Acceleration and rescission of acceleration

As mentioned in the introductory paragraphs of this chapter, many view a provision restricting bondholders from taking enforcement action after a default to be a critical part of a CAC. The basic format of these clauses is well settled: acceleration of the bonds is not permitted unless at least 25 per cent of the bondholders agree, and that acceleration action can be rescinded by a subsequent vote of the holders of more than half the bonds. So why does the Model CAC not include one? The supplemental explanatory note that accompanies the Model CAC provides two reasons. **25.69**

(a) Since the Model CAC is mandatory, it must be included in both international and domestic obligations. Since many domestic bonds will not have events of default, the concept of acceleration would be meaningless.
(b) The inclusion of a restriction on acceleration would raise serious legal concerns in some euro area jurisdictions. This presumably refers to entrenched legal rules regarding access to justice.

Accordingly, the Model CAC itself does not prescribe a provision restricting the bondholders' rights to accelerate, but does provide a template that follows the form described above and can be included on a voluntary basis. **25.70**

I. Consistency

25.71 If the idea behind a mandatory standardized CAC is that all euro area sovereigns should be subject to the same contractual modification regime for their private sector debt, then ideally all of the CACs would be governed by a single law and would be subject to adjudication in the same forum. That would be the only way in which to ensure absolute consistency of application. Unsurprisingly, the practicalities of such a goal proved challenging. It is expected that each sovereign state will implement the Model CAC in its own jurisdiction either as a contractual matter or by changing the law. It remains to be seen whether this approach will lead to conflicting decisions regarding the effect of the Model CAC.

25.72 If total consistency in application post-June 2013 is the objective, an additional problem is that many outstanding bonds with maturities that go beyond June 2013 do not contain the Model CAC. Enacting some European legislation with direct effect to retrospectively introduce the Model CAC into all outstanding bonds would have been the ideal solution, but very complex and possibly unworkable as a legal matter. Instead, the old bonds will be allowed to run off as they mature and sovereigns will even be able to reopen them in a tap issue, if required, in order to preserve liquidity in those bonds. The extent to which a sovereign will be permitted to tap existing bonds that do not contain the Model CAC will be limited to a certain percentage of the total face amount of all of that sovereign's debt issuance for that year, and that percentage will decline to 5 per cent in 2023.[25]

8. Conclusion

25.73 The CAC has come a long way in a (relatively) short time. Its use in Greece's 2012 restructuring, in which a variant of the Model CAC was introduced into Greece's domestic-law-governed bonds by way of a change in Greek law, is evidence of its usefulness as a tool to effect a consensual debt restructuring on a massive scale. Whether that is a good thing or not will depend on perspective; what is clear is that virtually all market participants have now recognized the general principle that a consensual sovereign debt restructuring need not be unanimous. The CAC, in sovereign debt, is here to stay.

[25] *See* EFC Subcommittee on EU Sovereign Debt Markets, *Model Collective Action Clause: Supplementary Explanatory Note* (March 2012), available online at <http://europa.eu/efc/sub_committee/pdf/supplemental_explanatory_note_on_the_model_cac_-_26_march_2012.pdf>.

26

EUROZONE FINANCIAL RESCUE AND STABILIZATION MEASURES, AND THEIR LEGAL FOUNDATIONS

Andrew Yianni and Nikita Aggarwal[1]

1. Introduction

The 'eurozone crisis' is the product of several, interdependent challenges that have coincided in the euro area, or eurozone, the single currency area of the European Union (EU). It is characterized by high levels of sovereign debt and elevated sovereign borrowing costs in the mostly southern, peripheral euro area member states and Ireland;[2] hence it is often referred to as the eurozone 'sovereign debt crisis'. However, it also impacts euro area member states that do not have a sovereign debt problem, but which, through concurrent political, financial, and economic challenges, share the causes and consequences of the 'sovereign debt crisis' in the mostly southern euro area periphery.[3] 26.01

Following a brief outline of the eurozone crisis, this chapter discusses the emergency financial rescue and stabilization measures that have been taken by the EU institutions and member states in response, as well as key future measures that have been proposed, and explores the EU law considerations associated with them. It will note that whilst the existing measures have, in general, been crafted to fall within the limits on financial assistance to member states under EU law, many of the key future measures under consideration are likely to require changes to this framework. 26.02

This chapter is organized as follows. The next section discusses briefly the background to the eurozone crisis; the chapter then sets out the legal regime for financial assistance by the 26.03

---

1 In relation to the issues raised in this chapter, the position is stated as at 31 May 2013. The views expressed in this chapter are the authors' own and do not represent the views of any organization with which they are associated.

2 The principal affected countries are Greece, Ireland, Italy, Portugal, and Spain (often referred to as the 'GIIPS', or 'PIIGS'). Cyprus has recently joined this group, largely as a result of the effects of the Greek debt restructuring on the Cypriot banking sector. At the time of writing, Slovenia was also in a vulnerable position. France, although not at immediate risk, could suffer if economic and political policies to reduce its fiscal deficit and increase competitiveness were not effective; it would also be particularly vulnerable to a deterioration of the situation particularly in the southern euro area periphery, owing to large sovereign and bank exposures. Effective deficit reduction has improved Belgium's position, although it too remains vulnerable.

3 The effects of the eurozone crisis also extend to non-euro-area member states (in particular the United Kingdom), as well as non-EU countries (in particular the United States). This chapter focuses on the causes of the 'crisis' specific to, and the rescue measures taken within, the euro area.

EU and member states under EU law. In the fourth section are described the key financial rescue and stabilization measures that have been taken by the EU institutions and member states vis-à-vis other member states, including discussion of the legal considerations associated with them. The chapter then looks at key proposals for longer-term financial rescue and stabilization measures, and their legal implications, before concluding.

2. Background to the Crisis

26.04 On 1 January 1999, eleven member states of the EU formed a monetary union with a single currency (the euro) and common central bank with sole responsibility for monetary policy in the euro area (the European Central Bank, or ECB). The euro was introduced in physical form on 1 January 2002, fully replacing national currencies thereafter. The creation of the 'euro area', or 'eurozone', which currently comprises seventeen member states, represents the third stage of economic integration in the Economic and Monetary Union (EMU) established under the Treaty on the European Union (TEU, or Maastricht Treaty).[4] In contrast to full monetary union, EMU creates only partial economic union, in which economic policy is coordinated between the twenty-seven member states and institutions of the EU.

26.05 Thus the euro area remains one stage removed from full economic integration, which would include the complete harmonization of economic and fiscal policies between member states.[5] Moreover, it is not supported by full political union. Whilst the Maastricht Treaty introduced political integration between member states for the first time, this is limited to specific policy areas (inter alia, foreign and security policy, and consumer protection). As areas of shared competence between the EU and member states, political and economic integration is further constrained by the principle of subsidiarity under EU law.[6]

26.06 In many ways, it is this asymmetric integration of the euro area that sowed the seeds for the eurozone crisis. That is not to deny the important role played by national factors specific to each member state, or external factors such as imbalances in the global economy. Nonetheless, the eurozone crisis is characterized by interdependencies and mutually reinforcing cross-border effects that would not have arisen but for the integration of certain member states under monetary union.

26.07 There are principally four underlying problems that have coalesced in the crisis: a banking sector problem; a balance-of-payments problem; a fiscal problem; and the political economy problem of EMU. They have come together to produce a uniquely European crisis that is

[4] The Maastricht Treaty was signed on 7 February 1992 and entered into force on 1 November 1993. It has subsequently been amended by the Treaties of Amsterdam (1997), Nice (2001), and Lisbon (2007). The other treaty governing the EU is the Treaty on the Functioning of the European Union (TFEU), formerly the Treaty on the European Community (TEC and together with the TEU, the treaties).

[5] Full economic union was contemplated by member states, and expressly proposed under the Werner and Delors reports, but was not ultimately incorporated into the Maastricht Treaty: *see* European Commission, 'The Road to EMU', available online at <http://ec.europa.eu/economy_finance/euro/emu/road/werner_report_en.htm>.

[6] Article 5(3) TEU. This provides that, in areas that are not within its 'exclusive competence', the EU may act only if and in so far as the objectives of the proposed action cannot be sufficiently achieved by the member states, but can be better achieved at the EU level. Inter alia, the EU has 'exclusive competence' to act in the area of monetary policy for the euro area member states; on the other hand, economic policy and consumer protection (inter alia) are areas of 'shared competence' with member states (Arts 3 and 4 TFEU).

characterized by a 'sovereign debt crisis' in the mostly southern, peripheral euro area member states. The brief outline in this chapter of the background to the eurozone crisis seeks to highlight both the inherent interconnectedness of these underlying problems and the unique ways in which they have interacted in each euro area member state.

The hallmark of the euro area balance-of-payments problem is the growing divergence between the current account positions of member states since the formation of EMU and subsequent adoption of the euro. Whilst the predominantly northern euro area member states accumulated increasingly large current account surpluses, the predominantly southern euro area member states and Ireland accumulated increasingly large current account deficits.[7] This divergence is in no small part attributable to the design of the euro area, which has united heterogeneous economies under a single monetary policy with a fixed external exchange rate, without the support of sufficient political and economic union.[8] **26.08**

In very broad terms, the mostly northern economies benefited from a weaker currency, which, with lower unit labour costs resulting from wage repression and productivity gains, allowed them to boost their competitiveness. In contrast, the mostly southern economies struggled to maintain competitiveness in the face of a stronger currency and wage inflation exceeding gains in labour productivity. The differences in productivity gains are largely attributable to country-specific factors, in particular structural rigidities such as inflexible labour, and product and services market regulation. The constraints of the single currency and a 'one size fits all' monetary policy meant that these external imbalances could not be accommodated through real external exchange rate adjustments. **26.09**

At the same time, convergence to a single currency had the effect of lowering external borrowing costs for many member states (in particular, the 'deficit' countries of the southern euro area periphery), as markets presupposed a single credit risk for all members of the euro area. Access to cheap funding, combined with dwindling competitiveness, encouraged these countries to borrow heavily and to rely on consumption-led economic growth. Public debt stocks increased rapidly, although this did not reflect increased investment in productive capital. In turn, the 'surplus' countries fed much of their growth directly from demand in 'deficit' countries, given the predominance of trade between euro area member states. **26.10**

The problems in the EU banking sector can be attributed to weaknesses at the international, national, and EU levels. The liberalization of Western financial markets from the early 1990s onwards set the stage for excessive borrowing and credit expansion by banks. Access to a more liquid funding market following the introduction of the euro further encouraged credit growth. At the same time, the creation of a single market in financial services, whilst **26.11**

[7] This compares with a mostly balanced current account position for the euro area member states around 1990, prior to the introduction of EMU: *see* Florence Jaumotte and Piyaporn Sodsriwiboon, *Current Account Balances in the Southern Euro Area*, IMF Working Paper No. WP/10/139 (June 2010), available online at <http://211.253.40.86/mille/service/ers/20000/IMG/000000019454/wp10139.pdf>, 33, Figure 2. The euro area as a whole has a small current account surplus.

[8] For these reasons, many have argued that the euro area is not an 'optimum currency area': *see* Robert A. Mundell, 'A Theory of Optimum Currency Areas' (1961) 51(4) Am Econ Rev 657. For a discussion of the euro area, *see* Barry Eichengreen, *Is Europe an Optimum Currency Area?*, National Bureau of Economic Research (NBER) Working Paper No. 3579 (January 1991), available online at <http://papers.ssrn.com/sol3/papers.cfm?abstract_id=226815>; Marjan Petreski, *Is the Euro Zone an Optimal Currency Area?* (May 2007), available online at <http://papers.ssrn.com/sol3/papers.cfm?abstract_id=986483>.

facilitating cross-border financial intermediation supporting economic growth in the euro area, also increased the scope for negative spillover effects between national banking systems.

26.12 Yet, against this backdrop of heightened risk, national authorities failed to exercise adequate oversight over their banking sectors, in particular by failing to strengthen regulation and take prompt corrective action to address unsound practices. Missing links in the framework for financial regulation and supervision at the EU level, in particular the lack of a common supervisor with a mandate for macroprudential oversight, contributed to the systematic failure to detect and mitigate the build-up of risk. As a result, levels of household and corporate indebtedness rose rapidly in several member states, with particularly pronounced real estate asset price bubbles developing in Ireland and Spain.

26.13 The fiscal problem is, in some ways, a symptom of the balance-of-payments and banking sector problems. At base, it is a result of inadequacies in fiscal policy at the member state and, to a lesser extent, EU levels. There are two observable trends in the changing fiscal positions of the euro area member states, as follows.

26.14 On the one hand, member states such as Greece have run large budget deficits and high levels of public debt relative to gross domestic product (GDP) for the most part of their participation in EMU, and indeed the euro single currency area. This was caused primarily by inadequacies in fiscal policy at the domestic level, in particular unsustainable government spending including the failure to decrease entitlement expenditure in the light of rapidly ageing populations, as well as an inefficient tax system. Low competitiveness and access to cheap financing following the adoption of the euro encouraged the Greek government to borrow externally in order to fund its budget and current account deficits. At the EU level, the Excessive Deficit Procedure (EDP) under the Stability and Growth Pact (SGP) did not effectively control or sanction Greece for its excessive deficit (in excess of 3 per cent of GDP) in the years leading up to the eurozone crisis.[9]

26.15 On the other hand, the vast majority of euro area member states, including Ireland and Spain, had run small budget deficits or budgetary surpluses since their entry into EMU. It was not until the onset of the global financial crisis between 2007 and 2008 that they would incur large fiscal deficits and high levels of public debt. These resulted principally from the failure to anticipate contingent liabilities that had been accumulating in their foreign and private sectors (in Greece's case, these contingent liabilities would cause its budget deficit to balloon).

26.16 The onset of the global financial crisis triggered a retrenchment in cross-border financing and caused widespread shortage of liquidity in global financial markets. This had a particularly pronounced effect on EU banks, which were heavily dependent on financing from US money markets, and countries such as Ireland, which were most dependent on external financing. EU banks had also invested heavily in the US housing market, thus exposing them to large losses when the bubble burst. In turn, the appearance of liquidity strains exposed the macroeconomic imbalances that had been developing within the euro area, causing investors to reassess asset prices and growth prospects of the most vulnerable member states (namely, the 'GIIPS').

[9] *See* n. 21.

However, many member states were reluctant to let their banks suffer large losses given the size and importance of the financial sector for their economies. Within the EU, there was widespread fear that large losses in the financial system of one member state would spread rapidly to other member states, owing to the high degree of financial integration in the EU single market. As a result, bank losses migrated from private to public balance sheets as governments implemented asset protection and guarantee schemes, as well as outright nationalizations of banks deemed to be systemically important for the EU and global financial markets.[10] **26.17**

This strategy had unintended consequences. Above all, it created a negative feedback loop between sovereigns, incurring even higher levels of public debt through bank bailouts, and banks, incurring even larger losses on their exposures to those same sovereigns. Moreover, the fear of 'contagion' was not averted, as losses in the banking systems of one member state quickly spread to other member states through sovereign and/or bank exposures. As a result, fiscal deficits and public debt levels rose sharply, above all in the GIIPS countries. **26.18**

The coincidence of balance-of-payments, banking sector, and fiscal problems that had led to high levels of public debt soon triggered a 'sovereign debt crisis' for several euro area member states. In October 2009, Greece revealed that its estimated deficit for 2009 was significantly higher than had previously been reported to Eurostat.[11] In the context of a widespread deterioration of public finances throughout the EU, higher than previously estimated budget deficits were also reported in Spain and Ireland. Markets reacted negatively, and fears of sovereign default led to higher borrowing costs, first for Greece, followed by the other GIIPS countries, and, most recently, Cyprus. **26.19**

3. EU Financial Rescue and Stabilization Measures, and Legal Foundations

The response to the eurozone crisis has focused on emergency stabilization and rescue measures, as well as strengthened economic governance. In this chapter, we discuss the financial stabilization and rescue measures that have been taken by the EU institutions and member states, and the legal considerations associated with them. Analysis focuses primarily on the EU law considerations associated with these measures, but also takes into account certain decisions taken by national courts to the extent that they could influence the practical scope of action under EU law. These measures have been supported, inter alia, by programmes of assistance from the International Monetary Fund (IMF) and also by private sector measures, particularly the restructuring and recapitalization of banks, including through loss sharing by bank creditors (most recently, in Cyprus). These latter measures are not the focus of discussion in this chapter. **26.20**

[10] Banks that have been fully or partially nationalized in the EU, including through central bank-funded vehicles, include: Northern Rock, Bradford and Bingley, Royal Bank of Scotland, Lloyds TSB and Dunfermline Building Society (UK); ABN Amro and SNS Reaal (Netherlands); Fortis and Dexia (Belgium, Netherlands, and Luxembourg, known as the 'Benelux' countries); KBC Bank (Belgium); Anglo Irish Bank (Ireland); and Bankia (Spain).

[11] This was revised from around 5.6 per cent of GDP to above 12.5 per cent of GDP when a new government came into power. Eurostat is the statistical office of the EU, responsible for providing the EU with statistics at the European level that enable comparisons between countries and regions.

26.21 The EU financial rescue and stabilization measures have been shaped fundamentally by the design of EMU. In particular, member states have sought to avoid sovereign debt default and restructuring out of concern for possible 'contagion' effects to other member states. In this regard, the restructuring of Greek sovereign debt has been treated as an 'exception'.[12] The high level of economic and monetary integration within the euro area has also emboldened member states and the ECB to safeguard the survival of the euro,[13] because the costs of break-up are perceived to be significantly higher than the costs of remaining together.[14] Politically, the euro is a key stage in economic integration and an essential part of 'ever-closer union' in Europe, as enshrined under the Maastricht Treaty.[15]

26.22 At the same time, the limits of EMU as a monetary union with only partial economic and limited political union have constrained the scope for financial assistance by EU institutions and member states. Any attempt to take measures that exceed these limits would risk undermining the democratic basis upon which EMU was agreed. However, treaty change is not seen as an easy option, given that it would require the unanimous agreement of all twenty-seven EU member states, and parliamentary referenda in several of these.[16] Every effort has therefore been made to craft rescue measures in a manner consistent with the existing scope of the treaties.

A. Financial assistance under EU law

26.23 The regime for financial assistance to euro area member states under EU law is set out in Articles 122(2), 123, 124, 125, and 136(3) of the Treaty on the Functioning of the European Union (TFEU), and Protocol 19 annexed to the TFEU and the TEU (see the boxed matter below).[17] In this chapter, the financial rescue and stabilization measures are analysed on the basis of a literal, as well as a teleological, interpretation of these provisions. This reflects the approach of the Court of Justice of the European Union (CJEU), as the ultimate interpreter

[12] European leaders have reiterated that 'Greece is the exception' for sovereign debt restructuring in the euro area. There have been two phases in the Greek debt restructuring, both focusing on loss sharing by private sector bondholders (private sector involvement, or PSI). Under PSI-1 (March 2012), private bondholders took a nominal haircut of around 53.5 per cent under a debt exchange offer. Under PSI-2 (December 2012), Greece bought back bonds from private bondholders at around 33.8 per cent of their nominal face value, as a condition for the release of the next tranche of financing under the second EU–IMF programme for Greece (*see* paragraphs 26.29ff). There have also been adjustments to the EU and IMF exposures to Greece in the transition from the first to the second rescue programme.

[13] In a statement dated 6 September 2012 following the ECB's announcement of outright monetary transactions (OMTs), Mario Draghi, Governor of the ECB, stated that the ECB would 'do whatever it takes within our mandate... to have a single monetary policy in the euro area': *see* <http://www.ecb.int/press/pressconf/2012/html/is120906.en.html>.

[14] This is calculated on the basis of the large, unsettled liabilities of the GIIPS within the Eurosystem (made up of the ECB and the national central banks of the euro area), resulting from their increased share of ECB liquidity support (which in turn reflects their balance of payments positions, whereby deficit countries have a claim and surplus countries a liability against the ECB). This imbalance is reflected in the relative net positions of each national central bank in 'TARGET2', the interbank payment system for the euro area.

[15] Article 1 TEU.

[16] There are two procedures for amending the treaties, which are set out in Article 48 TEU. The *ordinary revision procedure* must be used for any amendment that would increase or decrease the EU's competences and requires *ratification* by all member states 'in accordance with their respective constitutional requirements'. The *simplified revision procedure* can only be used for revisions to Part 3 TFEU (inter alia, this includes the provisions on economic and monetary policy), and cannot be used to increase the EU's competences; this requires *approval* by national parliaments in accordance with their respective constitutional requirements. Some member states have elected to apply lighter ratification requirements to amendments adopted under the simple revision procedure.

[17] These provisions apply to financial assistance by all EU member states and the EU institutions, although those relating to financing by the ECB necessarily apply within the euro area only.

of EU law,[18] to consider 'not only its wording but also the context in which it occurs and the objects of the rules of which it is a part'.[19]

The founding objectives of EMU, as enshrined in the Maastricht Treaty, were to create an economic union that ensures financial and budgetary discipline, and a monetary union that ensures price stability and respect for the market economy.[20] These objectives were to be achieved through fiscal controls, as well as restrictions on financial assistance to member states by the EU and other member states. The regime for fiscal control is governed primarily by Articles 121 and 126 TFEU, and measures agreed on its basis—in particular, the SGP (as subsequently enhanced).[21] The key restrictions on financing are set out under Article 125 TFEU (the 'no bailout' clause) and Article 123 TFEU (the 'no monetary financing' clause). **26.24**

It is important to recognize that the treaties do not create an outright prohibition on financial assistance by EU institutions or member states to other member states. In particular, Article 122(2) grants express permission for EU financing to member states 'in exceptional circumstances'. Moreover, this regime must be interpreted holistically; thus Article 125 could not have the effect of prohibiting financing outright, because this would render Article 122(2) redundant. **26.25**

However, it is clear from both the wording and the objectives of the treaties that the scope of financing is intended to be limited. This means that any financial assistance provided should be limited in quantum, structured on a temporary basis, and subject to market terms, and strict fiscal and economic conditionality. In this way, the treaty-contracting parties believed that the incentives for overborrowing arising from convergence to a common currency would be constrained. Indeed, the emergence of the eurozone crisis has, in many ways, illustrated the shortcomings of this belief. Nonetheless, analysis must be based on the current design of EMU—namely, the explicit language of the existing treaties and the stated objectives upon which they were agreed. **26.26**

The regime for financial assistance was recently enhanced by the addition of Article 136(3) TFEU.[22] This amendment does not create a new power, or otherwise alter the scope of the **26.27**

---

[18] Article 267 TFEU. The CJEU consists of three courts: the Court of Justice (commonly referred to as the European Court of Justice, or ECJ), the General Court; and the Civil Service Tribunal. The ECJ is the highest court of the CJEU.

[19] *Merck v. Hauptzollamt Hamburg-Jonas*, Case 292/82 [1983] ECR 1-3781, 3792. *See* also *Bosphorus v. Minister for Transport*, Case C-85/95 [1996] ECR I-3953, 1-3982. The original formulation of this approach was established by the ECJ in *Van Gend en Loos v. Nederlandse Administratie der Belastingen*, Case 26/62 [1963] ECR 1, to consider 'the spirit, the general scheme and the wording' of EU law.

[20] This is reflected both in the criteria for adoption of the euro ('convergence criteria' under Article 140 TFEU) and ongoing conditions for membership of the euro area (for example Article 126 TFEU and the SGP, amongst other secondary laws). 'Price stability' is enshrined in Articles 119(2) and 127 TFEU.

[21] The SGP is established by two Council Regulations: Regulation 1466/97 on the strengthening of the surveillance of budgetary positions and the surveillance and coordination of economic policies, as amended by Regulations 1055/2005 and 1175/2011 (the 'preventative arm'); and Regulation 1467/97 on speeding up and clarifying the implementation of the Excessive Deficit Procedure, as amended by Regulations 1056/2005 and 1177/2011 (the 'corrective arm'). Under the EDP, member states will be sanctioned if their budget deficit exceeds 3 per cent of GDP or public debt exceeds 60 per cent of GDP (as set out under Protocol 12 TFEU). Reforms to the SGP have been adopted in the wake of the eurozone crisis. The reforms to the SGP in 2011 are referred to as the 'six-pack'; an additional 'two-pack' of reforms, which increase EU oversight over national member state budgets, was adopted in May 2013. Fiscal governance is further enhanced by the Treaty on Stability, Coordination and Governance (TSCG), an intergovernmental treaty between twenty-five member states (excluding the UK and Czech Republic). It includes the 'Fiscal Compact', which requires national budgets to be in balance or surplus, and member states to incorporate key SGP provisions into national law.

[22] Council Decision 2011/199, adopted on 25 March 2011, amending Article 136 of the Treaty on the Functioning of the European Union with regard to a stability mechanism for member states whose currency is the euro. This entered into force on 1 May 2013, following notification to the EU Council of ratification by all member states.

financial assistance regime under the treaties; rather, it was designed to clarify the scope of the existing regime and thereby provide a sounder legal basis for the interpretation of that regime that the EU institutions and member states have adopted in practice.[23] In particular, it was driven by the need to dispel any doubts over the legality of the financial rescue and stabilization measures in the light of mounting legal challenges before national courts (in particular, the *Bundesverfassungsgericht*, or BVerfG—that is the German Federal Constitutional Court[24]), and thereby to allay concerns over Europe's ability to resolve the eurozone crisis.

26.28 This chapter explores the contours of this regime as it applies to each of the financial rescue and stabilization measures in turn.

Regime for financial assistance to euro area member states under EU law

Article 122

2. Where a Member State is in difficulties or is seriously threatened with severe difficulties caused by natural disasters or exceptional occurrences beyond its control, the Council, on a proposal from the Commission, may grant, under certain conditions, Union financial assistance to the Member State concerned. The President of the Council shall inform the European Parliament of the decision taken.

Article 123

1. Overdraft facilities or any other type of credit facility with the European Central Bank or with the central banks of the Member States (hereinafter referred to as 'national central banks') in favour of Union institutions, bodies, offices or agencies, central governments, regional, local or other public authorities, other bodies governed by public law, or public undertakings of Member States shall be prohibited, as shall the purchase directly from them by the European Central Bank or national central banks of debt instruments.
2. Paragraph 1 shall not apply to publicly owned credit institutions which, in the context of the supply of reserves by central banks, shall be given the same treatment by national central banks and the European Central Bank as private credit institutions.

[23] *See* the ECJ's judgment in *Thomas Pringle v. Government of Ireland* Case C-370/12 [2012] ECR I-000, [184]:

> The amendment of Article 136 TFEU by Article 1 of Decision 2011/199 confirms the existence of a power possessed by the Member States.... Accordingly, that decision does not confer any new power on the Member States. Consequently... the right of a Member State to conclude and ratify the ESM Treaty is not subject to the entry into force of Decision 2011/199.

This is also the approach taken under Council Decision 2011/199 amending Article 136: *see* European Council, *European Council Meeting, 28–29 October 2010, Conclusions*, EUCO 25/1/10 REV 1 (November 2010), available online at <http://www.consilium.europa.eu/uedocs/cms_data/docs/pressdata/en/ec/117496.pdf>, para. 2, agreeing to establish a permanent stability mechanism and to undertake consultations with the members of the European Council 'on a limited Treaty change required to that effect, not modifying Article 125 TFEU ("no bail-out" clause)'.

[24] There have been two challenges before the BVerfG: (1) 'constitutional complaints challenge German and European legal instruments and further measures which are related to attempts to solve the current financial and sovereign debt crisis in the area of the European monetary union' (2 BvR 987/10, the '2011 judgment'); and (2) 'applications for the issue of temporary injunctions to prevent the ratification of the ESM Treaty and the Fiscal Compact' (2 BvR 1390/2012, the '2012 judgment').

Article 124

Any measure, not based on prudential considerations, establishing privileged access by Union institutions, bodies, offices or agencies, central governments, regional, local or other public authorities, other bodies governed by public law, or public undertakings of Member States to financial institutions, shall be prohibited.

Article 125

1. The Union shall not be liable for or assume the commitments of central governments, regional, local or other public authorities, other bodies governed by public law, or public undertakings of any Member State, without prejudice to mutual financial guarantees for the joint execution of a specific project. A Member State shall not be liable for or assume the commitments of central governments, regional, local or other public authorities, other bodies governed by public law, or public undertakings of another Member State, without prejudice to mutual financial guarantees for the joint execution of a specific project.
2. The Council, on a proposal from the Commission and after consulting the European Parliament, may, as required, specify definitions for the application of the prohibitions referred to in Articles 123 and 124 and in this Article.

Article 136

[...]

3. The Member States whose currency is the euro may establish a stability mechanism to be activated if indispensable to safeguard the stability of the euro area as a whole. The granting of any required financial assistance under the mechanism will be made subject to strict conditionality.

B. Financial rescue and stabilization measures, and legal foundations

i. Bilateral loans: Greece and Ireland

Structure and operations In May 2010, the EU and IMF agreed the first of two joint financial rescue packages for Greece. Under the three-year Greek Loan Facility (GLF), the euro area member states would provide bilateral loans to Greece for a total amount of €80 billion, administered and coordinated by the European Commission.[25] The loans are non-concessional and extended for a maximum term of five years from the date of disbursement. Member states are liable only for their share of the loan commitments, determined on the basis of the ECB capital contribution key.[26] Alongside this, the IMF made available **26.29**

[25] The terms and conditions of the GLF were agreed between the lending member states and Greece, as borrower, under the Greek Loan Facility and Intercreditor Agreements signed on 8 May 2010, available (in Greek) online at <http://www.minfin.gr/content-api/f/binaryChannel/minfin/datastore/30/2d/05/302d058d2ca156bc35b0e268f9446a71c92782b9/application/pdf/sn_kyrwtikoimf_2010_06_04_A.pdf>. Germany participates through KfW (*Kredietanstalt fur Wiederaufbau*), a financial institution wholly guaranteed and acting on the instructions of the Federal Republic of Germany. The size of the facility was eventually reduced by €2.7 billion, as Slovakia, Ireland, and Portugal stepped down from the facility.

[26] Article 2(1) GLF. The ECB capital key reflects each member state's share in the total population and GDP of the EU.

€30 billion of financing under a three-year standby arrangement and economic adjustment programme.[27]

26.30 Under the joint rescue package for Ireland, agreed in December 2010, €85 billion of funding was made available from external sources (€67.5 billion) and Ireland's own resources (€17.5 billion). External funding was provided through the European Financial Stabilization Mechanism (EFSM) and European Financial Stability Facility (EFSF) (discussed later in the chapter), the IMF, and bilateral loans from Denmark, Sweden, and the United Kingdom (all non-euro-area member states). Disbursements under each of the programmes for Greece and Ireland are subject to strict conditionality agreed with the 'troika' comprising the European Commission, the ECB, and the IMF.

26.31 **Legal considerations** As financial assistance provided by member states, the GLF and the bilateral loans to Ireland are subject to Article 125 TFEU; they are not subject to Article 122(2) TFEU, which applies only to financing by the EU. The scope of financing permitted under Article 125 turns on the meaning of 'liability for or assumption of commitments of Member States [*sic*]', as well as the conditions upon which it is provided. In its recent judgment in *Pringle v. Ireland*, in which the compatibility of the European Stability Mechanism (ESM) with EU law was challenged, the CJEU held that:

> Article 125 TFEU does not prohibit the granting of financial assistance by one or more Member States to a Member State which remains responsible for its commitments to its creditors provided that the conditions attached to such assistance are such as to prompt that Member State to implement a sound budgetary policy.[28]

26.32 In turn, the CJEU held that a member state remains responsible for its commitments provided that another member state does not 'act as guarantor' for its debts. Thus Article 125 does not prevent a member state from mobilizing funds on behalf of another member state—for example in the event that the latter is unable to make a payment that has fallen due—provided that the defaulting member state remains liable for its debt.

26.33 The approach taken by the CJEU, as the institution with ultimate authority to interpret EU law, must be accepted and applied for the purposes of analysis. On this basis, the bilateral loans to Greece and Ireland are within the scope of financing permitted under Article 125, as the borrowing member states remain liable to repay their creditors, who in turn do not provide any form of guarantee for their debts. The strict conditionality, limited duration, and market terms upon which financial assistance is provided are consistent with the objectives of market and budgetary discipline underlying Article 125, as confirmed by the Court in *Pringle*.[29]

[27] The first programme was terminated in March 2012, following agreement on a second EU–IMF programme for Greece. This makes available a total of €164.5 billion until the end of 2014, comprising the undisbursed commitments of the GLF and an additional €130 billion in financing. The commitments of the euro area member states under the second programme are financed by the EFSF. IMF funding is provided under a four-year Extended Fund Facility, approved in March 2012 (the three-year Stand-By Arrangement for Greece agreed in May 2010 was cancelled at the same time).

[28] *See* n. 23, [137].

[29] *See* n. 23, [142] and [143].

ii. The European Financial Stabilization Mechanism (EFSM)

Structure and operations In May 2010, the euro area heads of state and government agreed upon a package of measures to safeguard financial stability in the EU.[30] This included an EFSM and an EFSF. Under the EFSM,[31] the Commission may borrow up to a total of €60 billion[32] in the financial markets on behalf of the EU, under an EU budget 'guarantee'. These funds are on-lent to EU member states by the Commission, acting on behalf of the EU, in the form of either a loan or credit line.[33] The EFSM can be activated only for member states 'experiencing, or... seriously threatened with, a severe economic or financial disturbance caused by exceptional occurrences beyond its control', in the context of a joint EU–IMF economic and financial adjustment programme, and subject to strict conditionality. EFSM funding has been provided to Ireland and Portugal, for a combined total of up to €48.5 billion to be disbursed over three years. 26.34

Legal considerations The stated legal basis for the EFSM is Article 122(2) TFEU.[34] The deepening of the global financial crisis, the deterioration in borrowing conditions of several member states and the ensuing threat to financial stability in the European Union constitute the 'exceptional situation beyond the control of the member states' justifying EU financial assistance thereunder. This approach has been challenged, inter alia, on the grounds that the cited conditions were not truly 'beyond the control' of member states. However, this objection is not easily supported by the text of Article 122(2), which does not specifically limit financial assistance to circumstances that are *exclusively* beyond a member state's control. 26.35

Indeed, as was discussed earlier, the eurozone crisis has resulted from the interaction of multiple political, economic, and financial challenges. Thus it could reasonably be argued that the predicament of individual member states has been aggravated by certain factors beyond their control, for example the deteriorating situation in Greece, Ireland, and Portugal were key triggers for increased yields on Spanish and Italian sovereign debt. In addition, the EFSM seeks to achieve the objectives of the treaties by extending loans based on strict conditionality, limited duration, and market terms, as well as a requirement for the Commission to review regularly whether the exceptional circumstances threatening the financial stability of the EU continue to exist.[35] 26.36

However, the financial assistance regime must be interpreted holistically. Thus financing under Article 122(2) TFEU is permissible only if it complies with the other restrictions on financing under the treaties, including Article 125 TFEU. As already discussed, Article 125 has been interpreted by the CJEU as prohibiting the assumption of responsibility by the EU or member states for another member state's debt in the sense of a guarantee. 26.37

---

[30] *See* Council of the European Union, 'Extraordinary Council Meeting: Economic and Financial Affairs, Brussels, 9–10 May 2010', Press Release 9596/10 (Presse 108) (May 2010), available online at <http://www.consilium.europa.eu/uedocs/cms_data/docs/pressdata/en/ecofin/114324.pdf>.

[31] Council Regulation 407/2010 of 11 May 2010 establishing a European financial stabilization mechanism.

[32] Funding under the EFSM is limited by the Union budget ceiling (Article 2(2) of Commission Regulation 407/2010).

[33] Operationally, the EFSM effectively replicates for all EU member states (including the euro area) the balance-of-payments facility available to non-euro-area member states under Article 143 TFEU.

[34] *See* n. 31, Preambles 1–5.

[35] *See* n. 31, Preamble 8.

26.38 In this regard, the precise legal status of the 'guarantee' under the EFSM is somewhat unclear. Although it is not specifically mentioned in Council Regulation 407/2010 establishing the EFSM, it has been described informally as an 'implicit' guarantee.[36] On the other hand, the 2010 EU Budget includes a budget line for the EFSM, as well as a token entry for commitment and payment of appropriations under the budget line if required; in this sense, it appears to be an 'explicit' guarantee.[37]

26.39 The EFSM has not been challenged before the CJEU and, as such, it is unclear how the Court would interpret its compatibility with Article 125. It is worth noting that the BVerfG has interpreted the EFSM as compatible with the German constitutional principles of budgetary autonomy and parliamentary prerogative, on the basis that there is a limit on the total amount of the liability of member states; however, it declined jurisdiction to consider questions of EU law, including the compatibility of the EFSM with Article 125.[38] Certainly, the strict conditionality and exceptional circumstances by which funding under the EFSM is constrained are consistent with the CJEU's interpretation of Article 125 in *Pringle*, as well as its underlying objectives of achieving market and budgetary discipline.

iii. The European Financial Stability Facility (EFSF)

26.40 **Structure and operations** The EFSF was introduced to provide a more credible crisis response mechanism, with a larger capacity than the EFSM. It was established in June 2010 by an intergovernmental agreement[39] between the euro area member states, and incorporated as a limited liability company under the laws of Luxembourg.[40] Financing under the EFSF is subject to strict conditionality agreed with the troika and must be provided in conjunction with an IMF-supported programme of assistance. It has been activated for Greece (under its second programme), Ireland, and Portugal.

26.41 The EFSF finances itself by issuing bonds, notes, commercial paper, debt securities, or other financing arrangements[41] backed by explicit guarantees from euro area member states, who are its sole shareholders. The total value of the guarantee commitments is €780 billion, giving the EFSF an effective lending capacity of €440 billion.[42] The guarantee commitments of

---

[36] *See*, e.g., European Commission, 'European Financial Stabilisation Mechanism (EFSM)', available online at <http://ec.europa.eu/economy_finance/eu_borrower/efsm/>.

[37] Draft Amending Budget No. 7 to the 2010 EU Budget (adopted 13 September 2010).

[38] *See* 2011 Judgment n. 24, [139]. The BVerfG also considered the legality of the GLF/bilateral loans and the EFSF (and the Securities Markets Programme, or SMP, of the ECB), in each case finding no violation of the German Constitution on the basis that Germany's liability is quantitatively limited.

[39] EFSF Framework Agreement dated 7 June 2010, as amended with effect from 18 October 2011, available online at <http://www.efsf.europa.eu/attachments/20111019_efsf_framework_agreement_en.pdf>. The amendments reflect the agreement of the euro area heads of state and government to enhance: (i) the lending capacity of the EFSF through an increase of the guarantee commitments up to 165 per cent of the value of funding instruments issued after the date of amendment; and (ii) the forms of financial assistance that may be provided by the EFSF in addition to loan facilities.

[40] The EFSF Framework Agreement, financial assistance facility agreements, and funding instruments are governed by English law.

[41] Each a 'funding instrument'. 'Other financing arrangements' include treasury operations, debt management office (DMO) lines, committed and uncommitted credit lines, sale and repurchase agreements, and reverse sale and repurchase agreements, amongst others.

[42] This is the effect of the credit enhancement measures adopted in October 2011 (*see* n. 39).

each member state are limited to an amount calculated on the basis of the ECB capital key.[43] The funds raised are on-lent to euro area member states by means of:[44]

- loan disbursements;
- bond purchases in primary debt markets, or secondary debt markets subject to the ECB's assessment of exceptional financial market circumstances and risks to financial stability;
- precautionary facilities;[45]
- loans to member states to finance the recapitalization of financial institutions;
- partial risk protection certificates for bonds newly issued by member states; and
- purchases of member state bonds through a co-investment fund.[46]

Since October 2012, the activities of the EFSF have been carried out by the ESM, the permanent financial stability fund for the euro area (discussed later in the chapter). The EFSF will be liquidated on the earliest date after 30 June 2013 on which financial assistance to euro area member states, funding instruments issued by EFSF, and any reimbursement due to guarantors are no longer outstanding. **26.42**

Legal considerations In accordance with the EU doctrine of consistency, as well as the principles of sincere cooperation[47] and primacy of EU law, any measures agreed by member states outside the treaties in areas of 'shared competence'[48] must comply with EU law. This applies in particular to the EFSF and ESM, having been agreed outside the treaties on an intergovernmental basis. **26.43**

The principal legal issues to address in connection with the EFSF arise under Article 125 TFEU, the 'no bailout' clause. As has been discussed in the context of both the bilateral loans and the EFSM, based on the interpretation of the CJEU, there is an 'assumption of **26.44**

---

43 *See* Article 2(3) and Annex 1 of the EFSF Framework Agreement (n. 39). If a guarantor makes a payment that causes it to exceed its required proportion of the guarantee, it will be indemnified by the other guarantors on a pro rata basis: Article 7 EFSF Framework Agreement ('Contribution between Guarantors'). If a guarantor itself requests a financial rescue programme, it becomes a 'stepping out guarantor': its guarantee commitments will be suspended and the total guarantee commitments under the EFSF reduced accordingly: *see* Article 8(2) EFSF Framework Agreement. Their *percentage* share of the contribution key will increase, but the *nominal* amount of guarantee commitments of the remaining guarantors remains unchanged (as set out under Annex 1 of the EFSF Framework Agreement).

44 Financial assistance is granted in the form of a 'financial assistance facility agreement'. Repayment (or prepayment) of financial assistance by the beneficiary member state may be in cash, or other forms of consideration as agreed between the parties, for example securitization notes in repayment of the 'debt-buyback instalment' funded by the EFSF under the second programme for Greece: *see* Master Financial Assistance Facility Agreement between EFSF and Greece, as amended, available online at <http://www.efsf.europa.eu/attachments/efsf_greece_fafa.pdf>.

45 The precautionary facilities that are available for non-programme countries and which are modelled on the IMF's credit lines are: the precautionary credit line (PCL); the enhanced conditioned credit line (ECCL); and the enhanced conditioned credit line with sovereign partial risk protection (ECCL+).

46 On 29 November 2011, the euro area heads of state and government reached an agreement to maximize the capacity of the EFSF through the provision of partial risk protection and the creation of a co-investment fund. The EFSF can provide a partial protection certificate for newly issued bonds of a member state, giving the holder fixed credit protection of 20–30 per cent of the principal amount of the bond. This is designed to be used primarily under precautionary facilities with the aim of increasing demand for member state bonds and lowering borrowing costs. The co-investment fund (CIF) can provide funding directly to member states through the purchase of bonds in the primary and secondary markets. The EFSF will bear first losses incurred by the CIF; this is designed to attract investors in senior debt instruments and in turn encourage a market for the member state's debt.

47 Article 4(3) TEU.

48 *See* n. 6.

commitments' for the purposes of Article 125 if any member state—whether as beneficiary or co-'guarantor'—benefits from a financial guarantee from another member state.

26.45 As for the EFSM, although the EFSF uses the language of 'guarantees', these do not amount to legal guarantees within the meaning of the Court's judgment in *Pringle*: whilst so-called 'guarantor' member states might be required to mobilize funds in the event that a borrower member state defaults on a payment to the EFSF, the EFSF remains liable to reimburse the guarantors in respect of any claim paid and to indemnify them for any losses or liabilities incurred in respect of a guarantee. The borrower member state in turn remains liable to repay the full amount of its debt to the EFSF.

iv. European Stability Mechanism (ESM)

26.46 **Structure and operations** The ESM is the permanent financial stabilization mechanism for the euro area. It was established under an intergovernmental treaty between the euro area member states, in the form of an international financial institution (IFI) subject to public international law.[49] It has a maximum lending capacity of €500 billion, and an effective combined lending capacity with the EFSF of €700 billion. The ESM has thus far been activated for Spain and Cyprus.

26.47 Financing through the ESM is funded by the issuance of debt instruments or entry into financial or other arrangements with ESM members, financial institutions, or other third parties. In contrast to the EFSF, the ESM is not backed by a 'guarantee' structure; instead, it relies upon paid-in capital of €80 billion and on-demand callable capital of €620 billion. The liability of euro area member states under the ESM, who are its sole shareholders, is limited to their share of the authorized capital, as set out under the capital contribution key, which is based on the ECB capital key.

26.48 The ESM uses the same financial assistance instruments as the EFSF, with the exception of credit enhancement measures (partial credit protection and the co-investment fund).[50] Financial assistance under the ESM may be granted only to members experiencing, or threatened by, severe financing problems, if indispensable to safeguard the financial stability of the euro area. Furthermore, the grant of assistance is subject to conditionality agreed with the troika, and close cooperation between the ESM and the IMF.

26.49 **Legal considerations** From both a legal and political standpoint, the introduction of the ESM marks a significant departure from the status quo: first, as a permanent stability mechanism, it contrasts fundamentally with the temporary mechanisms that preceded it; and second, it is accompanied by an amendment to the treaties that explicitly recognizes the possibility of establishing a permanent financing mechanism for the euro area.[51] This

---

[49] The ESM Treaty entered into force on 27 September 2012 and the ESM became fully operational on 8 October 2012, following ratification by all of the euro area member states. During the transition period, the EFSF will finance only programmes that started before the ESM Treaty was signed (Ireland, Portugal, and Greece); all new programmes of assistance will be financed by the ESM (including assuming the assistance for Spain, which was initiated under the EFSF). *See* the text of the Treaty, available online at <http://www.european-council.europa.eu/media/582311/05-tesm2.en12.pdf>.

[50] For Spain, financial assistance for bank recapitalization has been provided through the transfer of ESM-issued notes to the *Fondo de Reestructuraction Ordenada Bancaria* (FROB), the Spanish bank restructuring agency. For Cyprus, financial assistance has been provided in the form of a loan facility under a macroeconomic adjustment programme.

[51] *See* paragraph 26.27.

amendment was inevitably influenced by the various legal challenges that have been brought against the EFSF and ESM, notably before the BVerfG.

The principal legal issues to consider in relation to the ESM arise under Article 125 TFEU, the 'no bailout' clause. The ESM was the subject of the challenge in *Pringle*, as well as the 2012 judgment of the BVerfG. As already discussed, the Court in *Pringle* held that the ESM did not breach Article 125, on the grounds that there was no 'assumption of commitments' by member states in the sense of a guarantee.[52] Similarly to the EFSF, member states may be required, under the ESM, to mobilize funding to cover losses resulting from another member state's failure to pay (whether a beneficiary or co-lending member state). In particular, this may result from the capital call procedure, by which the ESM shall call unpaid authorized capital in order to avoid it being in default on any payment due to its creditors.[53] In turn, ESM members 'irrevocably and unconditionally undertake to pay on demand any capital call made on them'; however, in each case, the debtor member state remains liable to repay its debts. **26.50**

The strict conditionality and exceptional circumstances to which financing under the ESM is limited are consistent with the CJEU's interpretation of Article 125 in *Pringle*, as well its underlying objectives of achieving market and budgetary discipline. **26.51**

v. Eurosystem financing: 'non-standard' measures by the ECB

In response to the eurozone crisis, the ECB has implemented a series of 'non-standard' monetary policy measures. These complement the application of standard Eurosystem[54] measures, in particular the lowering of interest rates by the ECB and the provision of emergency liquidity assistance (ELA) to market participants by national central banks. For the most part, the non-standard measures vary the terms and conditions of the ECB's standard monetary policy tools, yet remain comfortably within the scope of its existing powers and objectives under the treaties. However, they also include entirely new measures that may not have been anticipated by the powers and objectives of the ECB, based on both a literal, as well as purposive, reading of the treaties. This chapter discusses the key 'non-standard' measures taken by the ECB and their implications under EU law. **26.52**

Legal regime The ECB's powers to carry out monetary operations are defined under Protocol 4 annexed to the TEU and TFEU, on the Statute of the European System of Central Banks (ESCB) and the ECB. This sets out the types of operation that the ECB may carry out (primarily under Articles 18, 20, and 21), the scope of which is further defined by the objectives, tasks, and institutional structure of the ECB (primarily under Articles 2, 3, and 7) (see boxed matter below). These provisions must be interpreted in accordance with the objectives of market and budgetary discipline that underlie the treaties. Pursuant to Articles 18(2) and 20 of the Statute, the ECB has issued guidelines on the monetary policy instruments and **26.53**

[52] In its 2012 Judgment (*see* n. 24), the BVerfG found that there was a potential breach of the principle of budgetary autonomy under the German Constitution through the ESM, because the liability of ESM members was not clearly limited with respect to revised capital calls (based on a combined reading of Articles 8(5) and 25(2) ESM Treaty). Therefore a quantitative limit on Germany's liability had to be inserted in the German legislation implementing the ESM in order to comply with the Constitution.

[53] *See* Articles 9(2), (3), and 25(2) ESM Treaty.

[54] The Eurosystem comprises the ECB and the national central banks of only euro area member states. It coexists with the European System of Central Banks (ESCB), which comprises the ECB and national central banks of *all* EU member states.

procedures of the Eurosystem (the 'General Documentation'), which it regularly amends.[55] The ECB has also developed a substantial body of jurisprudence interpreting the scope of the Eurosystem's powers, which includes opinions on draft national legislation and general reports such as the annual convergence report.[56]

Key provisions of Protocol 4 on the Statute of the ECB and ESCB

Article 2—Objectives

In accordance with Article 127(1) and Article 282(2) of the Treaty on the Functioning of the European Union, the primary objective of the ESCB shall be to maintain price stability. Without prejudice to the objective of price stability, it shall support the general economic policies in the Community with a view to contributing to the achievement of the objectives of the Community as laid down in Article 3 of the Treaty on European Union. The ESCB shall act in accordance with the principle of an open market economy with free competition, favouring an efficient allocation of resources, and in compliance with the principles set out in Article 119 of the Treaty on the Functioning of the European Union.

Article 3—Tasks

3.1. In accordance with Article 127(2) of the Treaty on the Functioning of the European Union, the basic tasks to be carried out through the ESCB shall be:
- to define and implement the monetary policy of the Community;
- to conduct foreign-exchange operations consistent with the provisions of Article 219 of that Treaty;
- to hold and manage the official foreign reserves of the Member States;
- to promote the smooth operation of payment systems.

[...]

3.3. In accordance with Article 127(5) of the Treaty on the Functioning of the European Union, the ESCB shall contribute to the smooth conduct of policies pursued by the competent authorities relating to the prudential supervision of credit institutions and the stability of the financial system.

[...]

Article 7—Independence

In accordance with Article 130 of the Treaty on the Functioning of the European Union, when exercising the powers and carrying out the tasks and duties conferred upon them by the Treaty and this Statute, neither the ECB, nor a national central bank, nor any member of their decision-making bodies shall seek or take instructions from Community institutions or bodies, from any government of a Member State or from any other body.

55 Guideline ECB/2011/14 of the European Central Bank of 20 September 2011 on monetary policy instruments and procedures of the Eurosystem (recast), (OJ L 331/1, 14 December 2011), available online at <http://www.ecb.int/ecb/legal/pdf/l_33120111214en00010095l.pdf>. Pursuant to section 1.6 of Annex I to the Guideline, the Governing Council may, at any time, change the instruments, conditions, criteria, and procedures for the execution of Eurosystem monetary policy operations.

56 *See* Article 17 of the Rules of Procedure of the ECB setting out the legal instruments of the ECB: ECB, *Institutional Provisions* (November 2012), available online at <http://www.ecb.int/pub/pdf/other/ecbinstitutionalprovisions2012en.pdf>.

The Community institutions and bodies and the governments of the Member States undertake to respect this principle and not to seek to influence the members of the decision-making bodies of the ECB or of the national central banks in the performance of their tasks.

[...]

Article 18—Open market and credit operations

18.1. In order to achieve the objectives of the ESCB and to carry out its tasks, the ECB and the national central banks may:

- operate in the financial markets by buying and selling outright (spot and forward) or under repurchase agreement and by lending or borrowing claims and marketable instruments, whether in Community or in non-Community currencies, as well as precious metals;
- conduct credit operations with credit institutions and other market participants, with lending being based on adequate collateral.

18.2. The ECB shall establish general principles for open market and credit operations carried out by itself or the national central banks, including for the announcement of conditions under which they stand ready to enter into such transactions.

[...]

Article 20—Other instruments of monetary control

The Governing Council may, by a majority of two thirds of the votes cast, decide upon the use of such other operational methods of monetary control as it sees fit, respecting Article 2. The Council shall, in accordance with the procedure laid down in Article 41, define the scope of such methods if they impose obligations on third parties.

Article 21—Operations with public entities

21.1. In accordance with Article 123 of the Treaty on the Functioning of the European Union, overdrafts or any other type of credit facility with the ECB or with the national central banks in favour of Community institutions or bodies, central governments, regional, local or other public authorities, other bodies governed by public law, or public undertakings of Member States shall be prohibited, as shall of the purchase directly from them by the ECB or national central banks of debt instruments.

21.2. The ECB and national central banks may act as fiscal agents for the entities referred to in Article 21.1.

21.3. The provisions of this Article shall not apply to publicly owned credit institutions which, in the context of the supply of reserves by central banks, shall be given the same treatment by national central banks and the ECB as private credit institutions.

There are two key constraints on Eurosystem financing under this regime. In the first place, **26.54** there are limitations under Article 21(1) of the Statute (Article 123(1) TFEU) on Eurosystem financing to the governments or public sectors of member states (the 'no monetary financing' clause). This prohibition applies expressly to: (i) any type of credit facilities with the ECB; and (ii) direct purchases of a member state's debt. Article 123(1) does not expressly prohibit the purchase of a member state's debt on secondary markets; the ECB and European Council have interpreted this to mean that secondary market purchases are permitted to the extent that they do not 'circumvent' the underlying objectives of Article 123.[57] With reference to the preparatory work on the Statute, the objectives of Article 123 are:

(1) to ensure that the Eurosystem can achieve its primary objective of price stability;
(2) to preserve the independence of the ECB and national central banks; and
(3) to safeguard the objectives of the restrictions on financial assistance under the treaties—namely, to impose market and budgetary discipline on member states.

26.55 The second key constraint under this regime arises from the ECB's primary price stability mandate. Under Article 2 of the Statute (Article 127(1) TFEU), the achievement of price stability is given explicit priority over the ECB's broader mandate to support 'general economic policies' in the EU. The Statute does not explicitly address the ECB's objectives with respect to financial stability. Arguably, financial stability falls within the scope of 'general economic policies' under Article 127(1). In addition, Article 127(5) TFEU provides that the ESCB shall 'contribute to the smooth conduct of policies pursued by the competent authorities relating to the prudential supervision of credit institutions and the stability of the financial system'.

26.56 The precise definition of financial stability—in particular its interaction with, and distinction from, price stability—naturally give rise to considerations of an economic and quantitative nature that are not within the scope of discussion in this chapter. For present purposes, it is sufficient to observe that there is room for interpretation under the treaties, on the basis of which the ECB has interpreted its price stability mandate as including (extreme) financial instability where it is deleterious to the 'effective conduct of monetary policy oriented towards price stability in the medium term'. This interpretation of Article 127(1) gives the ECB broad scope for action, including with respect to its operations with public entities under Article 123(1).[58]

26.57 **Non-standard measures** Since 2008, the ECB has implemented a series of temporary, 'enhanced credit support measures' to support bank lending and money market activity in the euro area. Open market and credit operations play an important role in steering interest rates, managing the liquidity situation in the market, and signalling the ECB's monetary policy stance.[59] There are four types of open market operation: main refinancing operations (MROs); longer-term refinancing operations (LTROs); fine-tuning operations; and structural operations.[60] Pursuant to Article 18(1) of the Statute, these operations must be based on 'adequate' collateral.

---

[57] Council Regulation (EC) No. 3603/93 of 13 December 1993 specifying definitions for the application of the prohibitions referred to in Articles 104 and 104b (1) of the Treaty (OJ L 332/1, 31 December 1993), available online at <http://eur-lex.europa.eu/LexUriServ/LexUriServ.do?uri=CELEX:31993R3603:EN:HTML>, Preamble.

[58] *See* ECB Decision 2010/5 of 14 May 2010 establishing a securities markets programme (OJ L 124/8, 20 May 2010), available online at <http://www.ecb.int/ecb/legal/pdf/l_12420100520en00080009.pdf>, Recital 2.

[59] ECB, 'The Eurosystem's Instruments', available online at <http://www.ecb.europa.eu/mopo/implement/intro/html/index.en.html>.

[60] There are five types of instrument available for performing open-market operations: reverse transactions (through repurchase agreements or collateralized loans); outright transactions; issuance of debt certificates; foreign exchange swaps; and collection of fixed-term deposits. Reverse transactions are the most commonly used instrument.

Liquidity management measures The ECB has taken several non-standard measures to ease the liquidity constraints facing credit institutions. Most prominently, it has increased the frequency and size of LTROs by progressively extending their maturity from three months to six, twelve, and thirty-six months.[61] It has also eased the eligibility standards for collateral pledged by credit institutions as security for credit operations. Other measures include: providing unlimited liquidity to credit institutions in the euro area on an overnight basis; 'front-loading' the supply of liquidity to the first half of the month to facilitate the assessment of liquidity demands, without increasing the total amount of liquidity supplied; suspending the tendering process; and offering funding in US dollars and Swiss francs through foreign exchange swaps. **26.58**

These measures were adopted as changes to the general conditions for credit operations under Article 18(2) of the Statute and the General Documentation. It could be debated whether such extended provision of liquidity strictly observes the ECB's primary price stability mandate, although there is no direct evidence of inflationary effects. In other respects, these measures appear to fall within the remit of the ECB's powers and objectives under the treaties. In particular, because they extend to credit institutions only, they do not breach the prohibition on monetary financing to member states under Article 123(1) TFEU (Article 21(1) of the Statute). **26.59**

Collateral requirements The principal non-standard measures taken by the ECB with respect to collateral requirements are as follows. **26.60**

(1) *Waiver of credit rating threshold*—The ECB has waived (or 'suspended') the minimum credit rating threshold requirement for debt instruments issued or guaranteed by any member state eligible for outright monetary transactions (OMT), or which is under an EU–IMF programme of assistance and complies with the applicable conditionality as assessed by the ECB.[62] Where a waiver applies, debt instruments are deemed to fulfil the credit eligibility standards for credit operations by the ECB (the risk eligibility standards continue to apply in the normal way). The waiver has not been extended to member states in selective default on their public debt, except in exchange for 'collateral enhancement'.[63]
(2) *Reduction of credit rating threshold*—The ECB has progressively lowered the rating eligibility threshold for certain asset-backed securities (ABSs) to further support the provision of credit to households and non-financial companies.[64]

---

[61] In March 2008, the ECB announced the first LTRO with a six-month maturity. The first twelve-month LTRO was announced in October 2011; this was replaced by two LTROs of maturities up to three years announced by the ECB as part of the package of additional enhanced credit support in December 2011.

[62] These measures were taken in July 2011, March 2011, and May 2010/March 2012/December 2012 for Portugal, Ireland, and Greece respectively. In each case, the suspension was based on a positive assessment of the EU–IMF programme (note that the use of Greek bonds as collateral was temporarily suspended for the duration of each debt exchange/buyback (PSI(1) and PSI(2)). On 6 September 2012, the waiver was extended to all member states that are under an EU–IMF programme or eligible for OMT, subject to conditionality as assessed by the ECB: *see* ECB, Press release, 6 September 2012, available online at <http://www.ecb.int/press/pr/date/2012/html/pr120906_2.en.html>.

[63] This has been applied to Greece. Greek government bonds were ineligible for use as security between February and March 2012 (pending activation of 'collateral enhancement' agreed with the ECB in the first Greek debt exchange), and between July and December 2012 (following the expiry of the buyback scheme under the first Greek debt exchange). Greek government bonds were reaccepted as collateral in December 2012, with a waiver of credit eligibility standards, on the basis of a positive assessment under its economic adjustment programme.

[64] Note that national central banks have also lowered their collateral requirements for ELA.

(3) *Changes to valuation 'haircuts'*[65]—To offset the increased credit risk resulting from the reduction or suspension of credit eligibility standards, the calculation of haircuts has been amended by:
   (a) imposing higher haircuts for certain assets, including ABSs that are subject to the lower credit ratings threshold;
   (b) introducing graduated valuation haircuts for lower-rated (investment grade) assets,[66] replacing the previously fixed haircut of 5 per cent; and
   (c) applying 'special haircuts' to debt issued or guaranteed by Greece.[67]
(4) *New eligible asset categories*—The categories of assets eligible as collateral have been expanded to include:
   (a) Japanese yen, US dollar, and pound sterling debt instruments issued and held in the euro area;[68] and
   (b) additional performing bank loans that satisfy specified eligibility criteria.

26.61 The changes to the collateral eligibility criteria were adopted as part of the process of amendment to the general conditions for credit operations under Article 18(2) of the Statute and the General Documentation. Whilst certain measures provide an ostensible benefit to member states by supporting a market for their debt, they appear to be accompanied by adequate safeguards for market and budgetary discipline to satisfy the literal and teleological requirements of the 'no monetary financing' clause. In particular, the suspension of credit eligibility standards for pledged collateral is temporary and conditional upon a 'positive assessment' of the adjustment programmes in the relevant member state.

26.62 These measures are currently the subject of a challenge before the CJEU brought by a group of Italian retail investors in Greek government bonds.[69] Inter alia, they claim that the suspension of the collateral requirements and 'collateral enhancement' for Greece are in breach of Articles 123 and 127 TFEU. In the latter case, they argue that these measures have no connection to monetary policy or price stability. It remains to be seen whether the Court accepts the ECB's more expansive interpretation of its primary price stability objective as including extreme financial instability, upon which it has relied thus far.

26.63 **Covered bond purchases** Through its covered bond purchase programmes (CBPPs), the ECB has sought to provide additional support to a specific segment of the financial market deemed important for bank funding and which was particularly affected by the global financial crisis. The first programme (CBPP) commenced in July 2009 and was fully implemented

[65] As a risk control measure, the value of the underlying collateral asset is calculated as the market value of the asset less a certain percentage ('haircut'). *See* further General Documentation (n. 55).

[66] BBB+ to BBB–, or Step 3 on the ESCB ratings scale.

[67] *See* ECB Decision ECB/2012/32 of 19 December 2012 on temporary measures relating to the eligibility of marketable debt instruments issued or fully guaranteed by the Hellenic Republic (OJ L 359/74, 29 December 2012), available online at <http://www.ecb.int/ecb/legal/pdf/l_35920121229en00740076.pdf>.

[68] This measure applied between October 2008 and December 2010, and was reintroduced on 6 September 2012.

[69] *Accorinti and ors v. ECB* Case T-224/12 (OJ C 243/37, 11 August 2012) (action brought on 23 May 2012, pending date before ECJ), seeking to annul the ECB's decision of March 2012 suspending the credit threshold standards for Greek sovereign bonds in return for 'collateral enhancement' to the ECB and national central banks in the form of a buyback scheme.

by end of June 2010, with a total nominal value of covered bonds purchased of €60 billion.[70] The second programme (CBPP2) took place between November 2011 and October 2012,[71] with a total nominal purchase value of €16.418 billion.[72] Covered bonds purchased under both programmes will be held until maturity.[73]

This is a 'non-standard' measure in the sense that the ECB had not previously initiated the purchase of eligible covered bonds. However, it appears consistent with the boundaries of the ECB's objectives, to the extent that it does not undermine price stability in the euro area and supports the general economic policies in the EU. Because participation in the CBPP and CBPP2 was expressly limited to credit institutions, these measures also do not breach the prohibition on member state financing under Article 123(1) TFEU, the 'no monetary financing' clause. **26.64**

Secondary market sovereign debt purchases Under the Securities Market Programme (SMP) and OMTs, the ECB may purchase: (i) on the secondary market, eligible debt instruments issued by member states; and (ii) on the primary and secondary markets, eligible marketable debt instruments issued by private entities incorporated in the euro area.[74] The SMP was launched in May 2010 and has been used to assist all of the GIIPS countries. It was terminated in September 2012 following the announcement of OMTs; debt purchased under the SMP will be held to maturity. **26.65**

OMTs will also be used to carry out secondary market debt purchases, although they make some important changes to the SMP. In particular, there is no *ex ante* quantitative limit on the size of OMTs.[75] Furthermore, purchases will be conditional on the requesting member state receiving financial assistance from the ESM under an EU–IMF programme of assistance.[76] **26.66**

As discussed, based on a literal and teleological interpretation of the treaties, secondary market debt purchases are permitted under Article 123(1) to the extent that they do not undermine its objectives. The ECB treats the SMP as consistent with this interpretation, emphasizing the 'exceptional circumstances in the financial markets' that call for such measures to be taken, as well as their temporary nature and the commitment made by member states to comply with their fiscal targets 'this year and in the years ahead', thus ensuring market and budgetary discipline.[77] **26.67**

---

[70] Decision ECB/2009/16 of the ECB Governing Council of 2 July 2009 on the implementation of the covered bond purchase programme, available online at <http://www.ecb.europa.eu/ecb/legal/pdf/en_decision_ecb_2009_16.pdf>.

[71] Decision ECB/2011/17 of the ECB Governing Council of 3 November 2011 on the implementation of the second covered bond purchase programme, available online at <http://www.ecb.europa.eu/ecb/legal/pdf/en_ecb_2011_17__f_sign.pdf>.

[72] CBPP2 initially targeted a total of €40 billion, but this was reduced to reflect increasing demand from investors for covered bonds and (consequently) the decline in supply.

[73] At the time of writing, the nominal value of outstanding bonds under CBPP was €45.618 billion (CBPP) and €16.077 billion (CBPP2): *see* ECB, 'Liquidity Analysis', available online at <http://www.ecb.int/mopo/liq/html/index.en.html>.

[74] ECB Decision 2010/5 (n. 58).

[75] ECB, 'Technical Features of Outright Monetary Transactions', Press release, 6 September 2012, available online at <http://www.ecb.int/press/pr/date/2012/html/pr120906_1.en.html>:

> The Governing Council will consider Outright Monetary Transactions to the extent that they are warranted from a monetary policy perspective as long as programme conditionality is fully respected, and terminate them once their objectives are achieved or when there is non-compliance with the macroeconomic adjustment or precautionary programme.

[76] OMTs may also be considered for member states currently under an adjustment programme when they are regaining market access. Sterilization operations will be used to reabsorb excess liquidity.

[77] *See* (n. 58), Recitals 2 and 4.

26.68 Concerns about the possible impact of the SMP on price stability, one of the key underlying objectives of the 'no monetary financing' clause, are addressed through the use of SMP-sterilization operations to reabsorb excess market liquidity. With regard to OMTs, conditionality was inevitably introduced in an attempt to offset the moral hazard concerns arising from 'unlimited' purchases, and thereby ensuring compliance with the objectives of Article 123(1).

4. Future Financing Measures: Longer-Term Solutions

26.69 The financial rescue and stabilization measures taken by the EU institutions and member states in response to the eurozone crisis that this chapter has discussed so far are essentially firefighting measures that respond to the immediate effects of the crisis; they are not generally longer-term solutions that seek to address its underlying causes. The ESM bears features of a longer-term solution: by creating a 'permanent' financial safety net to dissipate doubts concerning the financial health of the eurozone and its ability to rescue itself, it seeks to reduce the risk of a crisis arising.[78] This section reviews briefly two of the key longer-term proposals that could alter the scope and design of future financial rescue and stabilization measures: Eurobonds; and an EU deposit insurance and resolution fund.

A. Eurobonds

i. Main proposals and key features

26.70 The term 'eurobonds'[79] encapsulates a broad range of proposals for the issuance of common debt by euro area member states. It should be noted that eurobonds are not in themselves a crisis management tool, but an instrument for ordinary financing of euro area governments. Their principal aim is to delink debt issuance from member states—and therefore their respective public debt profiles—in order to level out the existing variations in borrowing costs within the euro area. In turn, this should minimize the risk of countries being priced out of capital markets, thereby reducing or eliminating the need for costly rescue and stabilization measures,[80] provided that fiscal risks are adequately controlled.

26.71 The proposals for eurobonds fall into three principal categories,[81] differentiated by the proportion of common debt issuance and mutualization of debt. These proposals are not mutually exclusive, and would most likely be introduced jointly or in sequence.[82]

---

[78] Indeed, the future shape of the ESM will need to be re-evaluated in light of any new and permanent financing mechanisms. It is possible that the ESM is adapted, so that it becomes a European Debt Agency (EDA; for the purposes of eurobonds) or (and more likely) an EU Resolution and Deposit Insurance Fund. This would require significant changes to the ESM Treaty, as well as the treaties more generally. Proposals for more limited mutualization of debt—for example backed by 'several', but not 'joint', guarantees—would likely require only minimal amendment to the ESM Treaty and no change to the EU treaties.

[79] Other labels include 'stability bonds': European Commission, *Green Paper on the Feasibility of Introducing Stability Bonds*, COM(2011) 818 (November 2011), available online at <http://ec.europa.eu/europe2020/pdf/green_paper_en.pdf>. Note that 'eurobonds', in this sense, are distinct from the term 'Eurobonds', which refers to international bonds issued in a foreign currency.

[80] *See* European Commission (n. 79), para. 1.2.2.

[81] *See* European Commission (n. 79), section 2 ('Options for issuance of stability bonds'). The EC Green Paper surveys all options for eurobonds or 'stability bonds'; they reflect various proposals made by European academics and commentators.

[82] *See* Stijn Claessens, Ashoka Mody, and Shahin Valée, *Paths to Eurobonds*, IMF Working Paper no. 12/172, available online at <http://www.imf.org/external/pubs/cat/longres.aspx?sk=26034.0>, 'Section V. Possible Paths'.

(1) The theoretical starting point for 'eurobonds' is the full substitution of national debt issuance by common euro area issuance, backed by 'joint and several' guarantees[83] of the member states. Debt issuance could be carried out on a coordinated, decentralized basis, or through a centralized debt management agency. In practice, this would be achievable only in a fully fledged fiscal union with a centralized budget.

(2) In the second category, national debt issuance would be partially substituted by common euro area bonds backed by joint and several guarantees of the member states. This structure has gained most traction, and includes proposals for 'blue–red bonds', 'euro bills' and a 'redemption pact'.

   (a) Under the blue–red bond proposal,[84] eurobonds ('blue bonds') would be issued for the debt of each member state only up to a maximum of 60 per cent of GDP.[85] Member states would continue to issue bonds on a national basis for the remainder of their debt ('red bonds'). An independent stability council would be established to manage the allocation of blue bonds, subject to fiscal conditionality.

   (b) The redemption pact, or 'safe bonds', proposal[86] is the inverse of the blue–red bond proposal. Member states would transfer debt *in excess of* 60 per cent to a European Debt Redemption Fund (EDRF), which in turn would issue 'safe bonds' backed by the joint and several guarantees of euro area member states. Safe bonds would rank senior to all other debts of member states. Participation in this mechanism would be subject to strict conditionality, including debt ceilings, collateral pledges, and the hypothecation of tax revenue. Member states would also be required to repay their debt to the EDRF within a clearly defined period of time. This is envisaged as a temporary financing tool: the redemption fund and safe bonds would be liquidated once the debt of all euro area member states is brought below 60 per cent of GDP.

   (c) Under the eurobills proposal,[87] short-term debt of member states would be mutualized up to 10 per cent of GDP. Eurobills would be issued by a euro area Debt Management Office (DMO), and would fully replace short-term bond issuance by euro area member states. Debt issuance would be subject to strict fiscal conditionality.

(3) In the third category, national debt issuance would be partially substituted by the issuance of eurobonds, backed by *several*, but not joint, guarantees from the euro area member states. The principal proposal in this category is to pool and divide euro area sovereign debt up to 60 per cent of GDP into a senior tranche (the 'European safe bond', or ESBie) and a junior tranche (the 'European junior bond', or EJB).[88] The issuance of ESBies and EJBs would be carried out by a European Debt Agency (EDA).

---

[83] Under a 'joint and several', or unlimited, guarantee, each member state is individually liable for the total guaranteed amount. By contrast, under a 'several', or limited, guarantee, each member state would be liable only for its share of the total guarantee commitments, as specified.

[84] Jacques Delpla and Jakob von Weizsäcker, 'The Blue Bond Proposal', *Bruegel Policy Brief*, 21 March 2011, available online at <http://www.bruegel.org/publications/publication-detail/publication/509-eurobonds-the-blue-bond-concept-and-its-implications/#.UTOR7h32-So>.

[85] The debt limit under the SGP (*see* n. 21).

[86] Peter Bofinger, Lars P. Feld, Wolfgang Franz, Christoph M. Schmidt, and Beatrice Weder di Mauro, 'A European Redemption Pact', *Vox*, 9 November 2011, available online at <http://www.voxeu.org/article/european-redemption-pact>.

[87] Thomas Philippon and Christian Hellwig, 'Eurobills, not Eurobonds', *Vox*, 2 December 2011, available online at <http://www.voxeu.org/article/eurobills-not-euro-bonds>.

[88] Markus K. Brunnermeier, Luis Garicano, Philip R. Lane, Marco Pagano, Ricardo Reis, Tano Santos, Stijn Van Nieuwerburgh, and Dimitri Vayanos, 'ESBies: A Realistic Reform of Europe's Financial Architecture', *Vox*, 25 October 2011, available online at <http://www.voxeu.org/article/esbies-realistic-reform-europes-financial-architecture>.

ii. Legal considerations

26.72 The main issue from an EU law perspective is the compatibility of eurobonds with Article 125 TFEU, the 'no bailout' clause. As discussed, this prevents the *assumption of commitments* by a member state in the sense of a guarantee. On this basis, an amendment to the treaties would seem to be required for all of the eurobond proposals, with the exception of the ESBies, in order to comply with the clause.[89] In practice, the introduction of eurobonds would most likely form part of a more general move towards deeper integration in the euro area, including the creation of a fiscal union. This would involve a paradigm shift in the objectives of EMU and therefore a fundamental reassessment of existing restrictions on financing such as the 'no bailout' clause.[90]

B. EU deposit insurance and resolution funding

26.73 In its first section, this chapter described the origins of the eurozone crisis as lying in multiple challenges that have coincided in the euro area. Amongst these, banking sector problems have played a leading role. Indeed, many of the financing measures that have been discussed in this chapter are designed to provide indirect assistance to the banking sector: ESM assistance for Spain is a notable example. A medium to longer-term solution to the banking sector problems will need to address, inter alia, issues relating to the fundamental design of the EU single market for financial services. In particular, this includes the creation of a 'banking union', with a single financial supervisor, harmonized resolution laws, a common resolution authority, and a common resolution and deposit insurance fund for (at minimum) banks operating in the euro area.

26.74 As with eurobonds, these proposals aim to break the adverse feedback loop between the balance sheets and borrowing costs of banks and sovereigns. This effect could be achieved if funding for bank resolution and deposit insurance were not conditioned upon the financial health of any single member state. To the extent that this relies upon an unlimited or 'joint and several' fiscal backstop from member states, it would be difficult to reconcile with the 'no bailout' clause and is therefore likely to require amendment to the treaties (as well as national laws) in order to be implemented. The creation of a strong and autonomous supranational resolution authority will also require amendment to the treaties.

26.75 In the longer term, treaty amendment will also likely be required to provide an explicit legal basis for the ECB to assume the role of single financial supervisor for the euro area. Thus far, reliance has been placed on Article 127(6) TFEU (Article 25(2) of the Statute); this refers only to 'supervisory tasks' of the ECB,[91] and it may be debated whether it was intended to support a full supervisory role for the ECB in the long run, rather than the performance

[89] *See* further European Commission (n. 79), para. 1.3.2: 'Issuance of Stability Bonds under joint and several guarantees would a priori lead to a situation where the prohibition on bailing out would be breached.'

[90] Eurobonds would also likely require amendment to national law; based on the BVerfG's ESM/EFSF jurisprudence (n. 24), a joint and several guarantee may be difficult to reconcile with the principle of budgetary autonomy enshrined in the German Constitution if the quantum of liability is not precisely defined. Some proposals claim to address these constraints, although it is uncertain how they would be interpreted by the BVerfG or other national courts. For example, it is suggested that eurobills would satisfy the requirement of 'defined liability', because they are limited in time and quantum. The redemption pact would guarantee budgetary autonomy and parliamentary prerogative, because the Bundestag would be required to renew the guarantees as part of its annual budgetary approval process.

[91] Council of the European Union, Proposal for a Council Regulation conferring specific tasks on the European Central Bank concerning policies relating to the prudential supervision of credit institutions (consolidated text), Brussels, 14 December 2012, available online at <http://register.consilium.europa.eu/pdf/en/12/st17/st17812.en12.pdf>.

of discrete tasks only. As discussed in the third section of this chapter, whilst there is room for interpretation under the treaties, the ECB does not appear to have been granted a fully fledged financial stability mandate, including, inter alia, the exercise of macroprudential powers.[92]

5. Concluding Observations

The discussion in this chapter has focused on the question of whether the EU financial rescue and stabilization measures have a firm basis in EU law, based on both its literal wording and the objectives of EMU, as enshrined in the Maastricht Treaty. As has been seen, the measures taken to date have generally been crafted to fall within the formal limits of the treaties and have been upheld by the CJEU. However, it seems likely that several key, long-term measures that are currently proposed will require treaty change in order to ensure that they are supported by a clear and sound legal basis. **26.76**

This chapter has not focused on the political or economic analysis of whether the financial rescue and stabilization measures *should* have been taken, or whether the original design of EMU and the limitations on financial assistance to member states were appropriate. Yet, from this perspective too, there are strong arguments for treaty amendment to support a broader evolution of EMU into full economic, monetary, and greater political union. Above all, this transition will be needed to remedy some of the imbalances that have contributed to the eurozone crisis, and to remove limitations on action by EU institutions and member states in response to a crisis. **26.77**

The unique nature of the EU as a regional union of independent nation states implies that there are inherent limitations to the achievement of this transition, even for the euro area member states. It is questionable whether they will overcome these limitations, and if not whether the future of the EU involves less integration, rather than more. Yet regardless of the precise course that history takes, any material development in the scope of the European project should be supported by—and indeed would be facilitated by—a firm and clear basis in law as derived from the EU treaties. **26.78**

---

[92] The proposal for an EU/euro area banking union, and the designation of the ECB as single financial supervisor, gives rise to several additional legal issues that are not discussed in detail in this chapter. In particular, there is a possible threat to the independence of the ECB enshrined under Article 7 of the Statute, given that the Governing Council, as the ultimate decision-making body of the ECB, would be responsible for both monetary policy and supervisory decisions. There are also various concerns relating to the participation of non-euro-area member states in supervisory decision-making by the ECB. There are further issues relating to the interaction with the EBA (for example the latter's 'binding mediation' procedure), within the European System of Financial Supervisors.

27

UNCTAD PRINCIPLES ON RESPONSIBLE SOVEREIGN FINANCING

Juan Pablo Bohoslavsky and Yuefen Li[1]

1. Introduction[2]

As the co-editors of this book have preliminarily explained in Chapter 1, facing sovereign debt problems implies an unpredictable process and outcome. The main reasons for this are both the lack of incentives to promote cooperative collective actions,[3] and accepted or imposed limits to behaviours of sovereign debtors and their creditors in both good and bad times. This is exacerbated by the specific lack of a formal sovereign bankruptcy mechanism that affects financial behaviours long before insolvency begins to manifest.[4] **27.01**

One might argue that, for some countries, national laws are rather specific in regulating debt contracting;[5] therefore the lack of limits is not actually a problem. However, the existence of national laws regulating sovereign debt does not address two fundamental characteristics **27.02**

---

[1] The authors wish to extend their gratitude for the comments to the drafts of this chapter received from Kristine Forslund, Nicolas Maystre, Marcin Menkes, Alessandro Missale, Marie Sudreau, and Thomas Weiss. They also wish to thank Carla Bellota from the Library of the United Nations Office at Geneva for her efficiency and dedication, and Thomas Colon for his careful editorial work. The views and conclusions reflected in this chapter are those of the authors and do not necessarily represent those of UNCTAD.

[2] Because this book is in honour of Lee Buchheit and this chapter studies the Principles on Responsible Sovereign Lending and Borrowing (PRSLB), it is apt to explain the crucial role played by Lee Buchheit as a member of the Expert Group entrusted with drafting these principles. His intellectual input, his active—and indeed intensive—participation as co-chair of the Expert Group meetings in discussing and drafting the PRSLB, his search for trade-offs between justice and efficiency, his sense of what is politically feasible, and his pro bono commitment to the United Nations made a significant contribution to the process and the outcome of this initiative. More specifically, Lee's frank and passionate discussions with all of the stakeholders on precisely what the PRSLB should be helped to consolidate the legitimacy of the process—a crucial element when thinking of the implementation of soft law instruments. In addition, considering that legality consists not only of statutes, but also of general principles of justice and fairness—yes, even in financial law—the horizontal and robust discussions stimulated by Lee within the Expert Group and with governmental officials strengthened the normative degree of the PRSLB.

[3] Joseph Stiglitz, 'Sovereign Debt: Notes on Theoretical Frameworks and Policy Analyses', in Barry Herman, Jose Ocampo, and Shari Spiegel (eds) *Overcoming Developing Country Debt Crisis* (New York: Oxford University Press, 2010), 53.

[4] Lee Buchheit, 'A Quarter Century of Sovereign Debt Management: An Overview' (2003–04) 35 Georgetown J Int'l Law 637; Christoph Ohler, 'The European Stability Mechanism: The Long Road to Financial Stability in the Euro Area' (2011) 54 GYBIL 50.

[5] Matthias Goldmann, *Responsible Sovereign Lending and Borrowing: The View from Domestic Jurisdictions. A Comparative Survey Written for the United Nations Conference on Trade and Development*, UNCTAD Working Document (February 2012), available online at <http://www.unctad.info/upload/Debt%20Portal/RSLB_MGoldmann_02-2012.pdf>.

of modern financing. First, because we are dealing with *sovereign* debt, states are disposed to use (even abuse) their sovereignty when dealing with debt issues.[6] Second, because debt in general, but debt crises in particular can have broad and deep global implications on financial stability and economic growth, what one national law orders and effectively enforces will likely have repercussions beyond that country. Debt crises induce national decisions that have global implications. Hence financial global problems cannot be tackled only by unilateral strategies, but must also involve global and coordinated actions,[7] and international law should have a say in this matter.[8]

27.03 This was the institutional and legal diagnosis made by the United Nations Conference on Trade and Development (UNCTAD) in 2009 when launching its initiative, 'Promoting Responsible Sovereign Lending and Borrowing'.[9] The explicit 'purpose of the Principles is to fill in a crucial gap in international sovereign financing—the non-existence of a set of essential principles, for all types of sovereign debt contracting, that is globally agreed on'.[10]

27.04 UNCTAD's identification of this legal void was no revelation. While most proposals on regulating sovereign debt argued for the need of some kind of global standards,[11] they failed to garner the necessary political support and/or to be implemented. Was that because there is no need for such global regulation? Was it because these normative proposals promoted the wrong rules? Were their normative approaches not politically feasible? Or were they elaborated or proposed by the wrong actors, or through inadequate procedures?

27.05 This chapter will not try to answer these fundamental questions, which would help to explain recent world financial history; instead, it will use them to frame and assess the desirability and viability of the UNCTAD Principles on Responsible Sovereign Lending and Borrowing (PRSLB), focusing on the following questions.

(i) Are global principles promoting responsible sovereign lending and borrowing really needed?
(ii) Are the contents of the PRSLB adequate to guide sovereign lending and borrowing, to prevent debt crises, and to channel restructurings?
(iii) Does the decision-making process leading to the adoption of the PRSLB reinforce their legitimacy?

---

[6] *See* Jill Fisch and Caroline Gentile, 'Vultures or Vanguards? The Role of Litigation in Sovereign Debt Restructuring' (2004) 53 Emory LJ 1048; Sean Hagan, 'Designing a Legal Framework to Restructure Sovereign Debt' (2005) 36 Georgetown J Int'l Law 299.

[7] Thomas Weiss, 'Fundamental UN Reform: A Non-Starter or Not?' (2011) 2(2) Global Policy 196.

[8] Juan Pablo Bohoslavsky and Carlos Esposito, 'Principles Matter: On the Legal Status of the Principles on Responsible Sovereign Financing', in Carlos Esposito, Yuefen Li, and Juan P. Bohoslavsky (eds) *Sovereign Financing and International Law: The UNCTAD Principles on Responsible Sovereign Lending and Borrowing* (New York: Oxford University Press, 2013), 73–4. Explaining the international community's interest in sovereign (in)solvency, *see*, e.g., United Nations, *Report of the Commission of Experts of the President of the United Nations General Assembly on Reforms of the International Monetary and Financial System* (September 2009), available online at <http://www.un.org/ga/econcrisissummit/docs/FinalReport_CoE.pdf>.

[9] UNCTAD, 'Panel Discussion: Debt Crises Prevention and Management', UNCTAD XIII, Doha, 22 April 2012, available online at <http://unctad.org/meetings/en/SessionalDocuments/uxiiicn2012d15_en.pdf>.

[10] *See* UNCTAD, *Brochure on Responsible Sovereign Lending and Borrowing* (August 2011), available online at <http://www.unctad.info/en/Debt-Portal/News-Archive/Our-News/UNCTAD-Brochure-on-Responsible-Sovereign-Lending-and-Borrowing-Principles/>.

[11] For instance, the proposed International Monetary Fund (IMF) Sovereign Debt Restructuring Mechanism (SDRM), the Institute of International Finance (IIF) Principles for Stable Capital Flows and Fair Debt Restructuring, and the Fair and Transparent Arbitration Procedure proposed by social movement *Jubilee.*

(iv) Can the legal approach of the PRSLB promote their endorsement and/or compliance?
(v) Are the PRSLB consistent with the United Nations' role in the global economic agenda?

These five questions form the structure of this chapter, which concludes with some remarks framed within the general discussion on the legitimacy and deformalization of international law.[12]

2. The Need for Global Principles to Promote Responsible Sovereign Financing

The landscape of financial market has changed tremendously since the 1970s. Capital markets have become globalized and increasingly interdependent. With financial deregulation and changing debt composition, banking and sovereign debt problems could trigger financial instability more quickly and more deeply. These changes provide opportunities, as well as risks, making responsible sovereign financing a necessity. **27.06**

Public debt of both developed and developing countries have increased tremendously since the 1990s. For the former, it increased from around US$10 trillion in 1991 to US$40 trillion in 2010; for the latter, from US$2 trillion in 1992 to US$7 trillion in 2010.[13] The size of the public debt itself implies that the way in which countries handle public debt could be of great significance to the financial stability of the world. **27.07**

Unfortunately, instances of overborrowing and overlending abound, as evidenced by various debt crises. The temptation to overborrow is strong for policymakers, because debt borrowed will often be paid back by future governments and future generations, while the administration contracting the debt can bind over pressing social and economic demands in the short term with the borrowed money. Incentives for overlending originate from desires for higher profit margins or to achieve certain foreign relationship goals. Lack of transparency, imperfect information, and the mismanagement of debt structure and composition can also be reasons for wrong decisions in contracting debt.[14] **27.08**

In light of this physiognomy of modern sovereign financing, in the past decades, deregulation, in a world of financial innovation, has encouraged excessive risk taking from both lenders and borrowers, and has accentuated herd behaviour, making sovereign financing even more treacherous than before. The repeal of the US Glass–Steagall Act in late 1999[15] was the epitome of the deregulation trend. The repeal effectively removed the previously existing separation between investment banks and depository banks. **27.09**

---

[12] UNCTAD and Universidad Autónoma de Madrid co-organized an academic conference entitled 'Responsible Sovereign Financing: The Search for Common Principles', held in Madrid on 2 March 2012. The purpose of this conference was to reflect on the legal and economic implications of the PRSLB. The articles presented and discussed at this conference are collected together in Esposito et al. (n. 8). This chapter directly benefits from these academic insights.

[13] UNCTAD calculation available online at <http://unctad.org/en/Pages/Home.aspx>, based on World Bank, *Global Development Finance 2012* (Geneva: World Bank, 2011).

[14] For further reading on the economic rationale of the PRSLB, *see* Yuefen Li and Ugo Panizza, 'Economic Rationale for the Principles on Promoting Responsible Sovereign Lending and Borrowing', in Esposito et al. (n. 8), 15–37.

[15] The US Glass–Steagall Act of 1933 had provisions prohibiting a bank holding company from owning other financial companies. However, the Act was repealed on 12 November 1999 by the Gramm–Leach–Bliley Act.

27.10 UNCTAD's *Trade and Development Report 2011* identified this phenomenon as one of the main causes for the global financial crisis. The report lamented that:

> ... traditional banking shifted from reliance on deposits to financing from capital markets, and from lending to trading. The loss of diversity of the financial system and uniformity of agents' behaviour fuelled destabilizing speculation, accentuated pro-cyclical trends and eventually led to systemic crises.[16]

27.11 The more intensified herd behaviour for risk taking and risk aversion has made boom-and-bust cycles deeper and more severe. As Crockett[17] notes: '[T]he received wisdom is that risk increases in recessions and falls in booms. In contrast, it may be more helpful to think of risk as increasing during upswings, as financial imbalances build up, and materializing in recessions.'

27.12 With globalization, the world has become more interdependent and interconnected. The benefits and opportunities carried by improved connectedness have been acknowledged by all. However, opportunities are often accompanied by risks. Although the academic world has not unanimously agreed, many are of the view that the financial interconnectedness has made contagion swifter, more severe, and larger in scale.[18] The current global financial and economic crisis, which started with the collapse of Lehman Brothers, is a case in point.

27.13 In addition, the changing composition of debt from predominantly syndicated bank lending to bond financing since the 1980s, aided by a computerized and globalized financial market, has made the capital market more volatile. As a paper by the Bank of International Settlements (BIS) vividly pointed out, 'bond traders are notoriously short-sighted...: their time horizons are days or weeks, not years or decades'.[19] This means that changes of sentiments in the market may lead to sudden reversals of capital flows. Exacerbated by herd behaviour, a crisis could be triggered at lightning speed.

27.14 Debt crisis is the ultimate punishment for erroneous policies and irresponsible behaviour in sovereign lending and borrowing. Since the onset of the global financial crisis in 2008, discussions about the cost of a debt crisis have picked up intensity. It has been generally agreed that the long-lasting output losses of a debt crisis to countries are significant and that its detrimental impact on the banking system is even more damaging.[20] Behind such a loss is immense human suffering.[21] The high cost is infinitely related to the increasing magnitude

16 UNCTAD, 'UNCTAD Says Comprehensive Financial Reform Needed More than Ever: Unambitious Efforts Initiated after the Crisis Have Failed', Press release UNCTAD/PRESS/PR/2011/040, 6 September 2011, available online at <http://unctad.org/en/pages/PressReleaseArchive.aspx?ReferenceDocId=15577&Product_x0020_Taxonomy=1566>.

17 Andrew Crockett, 'Marrying the Micro- and Macro-Prudential Dimensions of Financial Stability', Remarks made before the 11th International Conference of Banking Supervisors, Basel, 20–21 September 2000, available online at <http://www.bis.org/speeches/sp000921.htm>.

18 Marina Primorac, 'The Global Village: Connected World Drives Economic Shift, Finance & Development', *IMF Survey Magazine*, 30 August 2012, available online at <http://www.imf.org/external/pubs/ft/survey/so/2012/NEW083012A.htm>.

19 Stephen Cecchetti, Madhusudan Mohanty, and Fabrizio Zampolli, *The Future of Public Debt: Prospects and Implications*, Bank of International Settlement Working Papers No. 300, (March 2010), available online at <http://www.bis.org/publ/work300.htm>, 1.

20 Davide Furceri and Aleksandra Zdzienicka, *How Costly are Debt Crises?*, IMF Working Paper No. WP/11/280 (December 2011), available online at <http://www.imf.org/external/pubs/ft/wp/2011/wp11280.pdf>.

21 Kunibert Raffer, *Debt Management for Development. Protection of the Poor and the Millennium Development Goals* (Cheltenham: Edward Elgar, 2010).

of sovereign lending and borrowing for different purposes. Scholars consider these, together with the lack of a debt workout mechanism, to be sufficient economic rationale for formulating a universally agreed set of principles guiding sovereign financing.[22]

In 2009, on the heels of the worst global financial crisis since the Great Depression, UNCTAD launched the initiative to formulate a set of global principles to promote more responsible behaviour, and to introduce a pertinent institutional set-up and necessary procedures to backstop responsible culture from the sides of sovereign lenders and borrowers. Behind this initiative was the realization of the asymmetry between regulations governing international trade and those guiding sovereign financing. For the former, there are hard laws; for the latter, laws and regulations are sparse and play a negligible role,[23] and relevant soft instruments are very fragmented, narrow in scope, mostly ad hoc, and have a limited efficacy. **27.15**

Finance is the life blood of economic development, and sovereign debt finance is an important and powerful instrument which is globalized and undertaken in astronomical amounts. This means that sovereign financing is of great significance to the financial stability of a country and to the world, as one country's problem could be the problem of other countries through transmission channels of financial, trade, and other economic linkages. **27.16**

In this context, global principles can set out the framework or boundaries to which actors in sovereign lending and borrowing should adhere in implementing their responsibilities, and should specify unacceptable behaviours. It is equally important to lay out required procedures and institutions for debt crisis prevention and resolution (what is expected and what should be prohibited). This is a step forward to promote a more responsible culture in the world of sovereign financing, which was much neglected in the years leading to the global financial crisis. In addition, more effective regulations are needed to maintain financial stability and market confidence, so as to enable economic growth.[24] This would include greater integrity on the parts of creditors and borrowers, a more transparent environment, less excessive risk taking and fraudulent behaviour, and appropriate institutional set up. **27.17**

From a transnational administrative law perspective, the establishment of global principles would ultimately help to harmonize and facilitate transactions between public and private actors, and contribute to the management of the global market for sovereign debt.[25] **27.18**

3. The PRSLB Tackle Global Debt Problems with Well-Rooted and Tested Principles

The PRSLB not only shape the few rules existing in international law dealing with debt problems (see paragraphs 27.01–27.04), but also seek to learn from concrete sovereign experiences. In more technical terms, the PRSLB were conceived to reflect best practices and **27.19**

[22] Lee C. Buchheit and G. Mitu Gulati, 'Responsible Sovereign Lending and Borrowing' (2010) 73 Law & Contemp Probs 66.

[23] Chris Brummer, 'Why Soft Law Dominates International Finance—and not Trade' (2010) 13 J Int'l Econ L 623.

[24] *See* generally Inge Kaul and Pedro Conceição (eds) *The New Public Finance: Responding to Global Challenges* (New York: Oxford University Press, 2006).

[25] Stephan Schill, 'Transnational Legal Approaches to Administrative Law: Conceptualizing Public Contracts in Globalization', NYU Jean Monnet Working Paper Series (2012) (on file with the authors).

basic principles already existing in most legal domestic orders in the areas of financial, constitutional, administrative, insolvency, and contract law.[26]

27.20 The PRSLB applied to lenders and borrowers are presented separately in the UNCTAD's document. Each principle is accompanied by bullet points that clarify and specify its meaning, and highlight relevant implications. The guidelines for the implementation of the PRSLB that, at time of writing, are being drafted will surely go into more detail when explaining concepts, rules, and concrete implications.

27.21 The PRSLB are conceptualized in a comprehensive way and are thus meant to be applied to sovereign borrowers at the national and subnational levels, and to developed and developing countries alike, as well as their lenders, be they bilateral, multilateral, or private. They are also based on the notion of co-responsibility of lenders and sovereign borrowers. They aim to promote more responsible behaviour, supporting institutional setup and procedures, for the economic benefits to both lenders and borrowers. Because debt crisis prevention should start before the contracting of the debt, the PRSLB deploy a range of rules to be applied before funds are disbursed.

27.22 The PRSLB establish and systematize standards on due diligence (Principles 3, 4, 5, and 10). Concretely, what this means is that while lenders should make informed decisions based on realistic assessments, and determine whether the financing is duly authorized and valid under relevant jurisdiction, borrowers should weigh costs and benefits when seeking loans in order that negative incidences of overborrowing are avoided (Principle 14).

27.23 There should be due authorization and a transparent decision-making process when borrowing, and a broad disclosure of the contractual terms and the economic situation should be made (Principles 10 and 11). Project financing demands, from lenders and borrowers alike *ex ante* and *ex post* investigations of the effects of the projects (Principles 5 and 12).

27.24 In spite of the recent controversy around the Ecuadorian debt audit,[27] the PRSLB found that periodic post-disbursement audits are carried out in most countries[28] and that, under certain conditions,[29] they serve as a useful administrative tool that can promote transparency (Principle 13).[30] Disclosure and publication of information also seek to contribute to more transparency (Principle 11). Strengthening the focus on crisis prevention, the PRSLB establish (and provide some technical guidance for that purpose) that borrowers should implement adequate management strategies and monitoring systems (Principles 10 and 13).

27.25 Two of the more significant principles incorporate the notion of fiduciary relation in the context of sovereign debts. Lenders and borrowers should acknowledge the duty of government

---

[26] *See* generally Goldmann (n. 5).

[27] *See* broadly the material available online at <http://www.auditoriadeuda.org.ec/index.php?option=com_content&view=frontpage&Itemid=1>.

[28] Goldmann (n. 5), 31.

[29] Kristian Jahren Øvretveit (ed.) *The Norwegian Debt Audit from an International Perspective* (Oslo: The Norwegian Coalition for Debt Cancelation, 2011); Yvone Wong, *Sovereign Finance and the Poverty of Nations: Odious Debt in International Law* (Cheltenham: Edward Elgar, 2012), 89–100.

[30] This is what the Norwegian Minister of International Development expressed when he announced that Norway will review its loans to developing countries using the PRSLB as a basis: *see* Norwegian Ministry of Foreign Affairs, 'Norway First in the World to Review Loans to Developing Countries', Press release, 17 August 2012, available online at <http://www.regjeringen.no/en/dep/ud/press/news/2012/loan-review-developing-countries.html?id=697585>.

officials to protect public interest (of both the state and its citizens) (Principles 1 and 8). These principles are based on an *outcome orientation* in sovereign debt contracting, which requires that sovereign actions (such as borrowing) be in the interest of the state's needs.[31]

This principle has deep implications in debt issues.[32] Fiduciary responsibility not only frames the relationship between the government and the legal fiction of the state, but it also provides the legal tools to identify responsibilities more clearly in sovereign financing. Through the implementation of this rich concept, governments and their officials are allocated ethical and performance-related duties in the service of the state. As agents of the state, public officials thus have a direct legal responsibility not only to their constituency, but also to both present and future citizens, as embodied by the state.[33] **27.26**

Principle 6 establishes that lenders must not participate in transactions that violate, evade, or hamper UN sanctions. While this principle may seem obvious considering other international law norms, it is worth recalling here the political and academic discussion on whether multilateral financial organizations are bound by the United Nations Security Council (UNSC) resolutions.[34] **27.27**

As a general principle (according to Principle 9), debts should be honoured, unless the economic circumstances of the borrower prevent its full or timely repayment, or if a judicial authority rules that a legal defence occurred. Two examples of these defences are insolvency and corruption.[35] This principle, while establishing the medullar *pacta sunt servanda* in international economic law, should be read in the light of a dynamic and contemporary notion of sovereignty,[36] the principal–agent fiduciary relationship, and the fact that states repeatedly go bankrupt.[37] **27.28**

In terms of debt restructuring specifically, the PRSLB establish that lenders should behave in good faith and with a cooperative spirit to reach a consensual, speedy, and orderly debt restructuring (Principle 7). From the borrowers' side, if a restructuring becomes unavoidable, it should be undertaken promptly, efficiently, and fairly, seeking a consensual agreement supported by a supermajority of creditors, avoiding opportunistic and discriminatory behaviour, respecting seniority of debts, and ensuring that all stakeholders share an equitable burden of losses (Principle 15). **27.29**

In any case, because the establishment of a financial assistance mechanism does not fully reduce risks of state defaults and systemic implications,[38] the omnipresent question of **27.30**

---

[31] Odette Lienau, *Rethinking Sovereign Debt: Debt and Reputation in the Twentieth Century* (Cambridge, MA: Harvard University Press, 2013).

[32] Buchheit and Gulati (n. 22), 75, 87.

[33] Jose Oyola and Marie Sudreau, 'Fiduciary Relations: Legal Framework and Implications for Responsible Sovereign Debt Management', in Esposito et al. (n. 8), 213–35.

[34] Samuel Bleicher, 'UN v. IBRD: A Dilemma of Functionalism' (1970) 24(1) International Organization 31; Eisuke Suzuki, 'Responsibility of International Financial Institutions under International Law', in Daniel Bradlow and David Hunter (eds) *International Financial Institutions and International Law* (The Hague: Kluwer, 2010), 69.

[35] On this specific issue, *see* Juan Justo, 'The Links between the UN Convention against Corruption and the UNCTAD Principles on Responsible Sovereign Lending and Borrowing', in Esposito et al. (n. 8), 189–211.

[36] *See* Odette Lienau, 'Who is the "Sovereign" in Sovereign Debt? Reinterpreting a Rule-of-Law Framework from the Early Twentieth Century' (2008) 33(1) Yale J Int'l L 63.

[37] A historical overview of sovereign defaults in Carmen Reinhart and Kenneth Rogoff, *This Time is Different: Eight Centuries of Financial Folly* (Princeton, NJ: Princeton University Press, 2009).

[38] Ohler (n. 4), 52.

whether an orderly sovereign debt restructuring is possible at all remains.[39] Because Principles 7 and 15 explicitly deal with procedural issues applied to debt restructurings, UNCTAD has at least broken the inertia of global institutional passivity around the need for building global consensus on a debt workout mechanism, as was recently emphasized during the special event on sovereign debt restructuring organized by the Second Committee of the United Nations General Assembly.[40]

27.31 There are, however, at least two important topics that the PRSLB have *not* addressed: secondary markets and credit rating agencies. These two issues are intrinsically linked to sovereign financing. One possible explanation for these absences in the PRSLB might be related to the fact that domestic laws are not really developed in these two realms, which obviously has implications for a body of principles that tries to mirror domestic legal systems.

4. Injecting Legitimacy into the PRSLB through its Decision-Making Process: Representation, Consultation, and Deliberation

27.32 In 2009, UNCTAD initiated a project under the broad heading 'Promoting Responsible Sovereign Lending and Borrowing'. This involved, inter alia, acting as a discussion forum, with the aim of developing a set of principles and best practices to promote responsible sovereign lending and borrowing. UNCTAD established an Expert Group in 2009 composed of world-renowned experts in law and economics, private investors, and non-governmental organizations (NGOs). Senior representatives from the International Monetary Fund (IMF), the World Bank, and the Paris Club participated as observers of this group.[41] After several formal meetings and intense idea exchanges, the first draft of the PRSLB emerged in May 2011.[42]

27.33 During 2011 and 2012, six regional consultative meetings with countries took place in Buenos Aires, Bangkok, Luanda, Geneva, Jeddah, and Punta Cana,[43] in order to get governmental feedback from UN member states on the design and the possible implementation process. Around seventy-five countries provided their views. After a series of bilateral and high-level regional governmental consultations and subsequent refinements introduced by the project's Expert Group, the consolidated version of the PRSLB[44] was launched in Doha

---

[39] Rosa Lastra, *Legal Foundations of International Monetary Stability* (Oxford: Oxford University Press, 2006), 425.

[40] UNCTAD, 'UNCTAD's Pioneer Work on Sovereign Debt Restructuring Widely Recognized by World-Renowned Experts and Policy Makers', Press release, 29 October 2012, available online at <http://unctad.org/en/pages/newsdetails.aspx?OriginalVersionID=339&Sitemap_x0020_Taxonomy=Globalization%20and%20Development>.

[41] Of course, there is always room for broader participation. In future discussions (*see* n. 94) taxpayers, unions, parliamentarians, public employees, credit rating agencies, public auditors, institutional lenders, and pensioners may also be considered as stakeholders to engage in this forum.

[42] UNCTAD, 'UNCTAD Unveils Principles to Guide Responsible Sovereign Lending and Borrowing', Press release, 4 May 2011, available online at <http://www.unctad.info/en/Debt-Portal/News-Archive/Our-News/UNCTAD-Launches-Principles-on-Responsible-Sovereign-Lending-and-Borrowing-3052011/>.

[43] *See* information on these meetings available online at <http://www.unctad.info/en/Debt-Portal/News-Archive/Our-News/>.

[44] UNCTAD, 'UNCTAD Releases Consolidated Principles on Responsible Sovereign Financing', Press release, 30 January 2012, available online at <http://www.unctad.info/en/Debt-Portal/News-Archive/Our-News/UNCTAD-Releases-Consolidated-Principles-on-Responsible-Sovereign-Financing-310112/>.

on the occasion of UNCTAD XIII, initiating the phase of endorsement and implementation.[45] To date, twelve countries have explicitly endorsed the PRSLB.

UNCTAD did not provide any pre-elaborated proposal on the text of the PRSLB, but it offered the platform to make stakeholders engage in horizontal, active, inclusive, and transparent discussions guided by the UNCTAD Secretariat. In line with new governance features, these procedural definitions seemed to have made a big difference in terms of the legal, political, and institutional outcomes of this project. The inclusiveness of the process of drafting and endorsing the PRSLB is indeed a source of input legitimacy.[46] **27.34**

In addition, the fact that stakeholders with different (even contradictory) interests openly debated the PRSLB not only improved the information available on debt problems and possible remedies,[47] but also forced them to debate and argue their positions, and to look for feasible and balanced criteria to be accepted[48] as contents of the PRSLB. This intense deliberation not only reinforces the legitimacy of the PRSLB,[49] but also potentially generates new ways in which to advance the stakeholders' goals through cooperation.[50] In other words, given that coercion is not available at the international level, a more participatory global law-making process would presumably contribute to provide global public goods more efficiently.[51] **27.35**

In turn, because debates that were taking place during the drafting were eventually translated into a (presumably) final improved legal and more formal discourse, which is a powerful form or argumentation with a manifest impact on state conduct,[52] the PRSLB drafting process has probably strengthened their own influence. **27.36**

5. Soft Law Facilitates Endorsement and Implementation[53]

The Preamble to the PRSLB states that: **27.37**

> ... the normative contribution of these Principles lies not in the creation of new rights nor obligations in international law but in identifying, harmonizing, and systematizing the basic

45 UNCTAD, 'Principles on Sovereign Lending and Borrowing: UNCTAD Kick Starts Endorsement Process', Press release, 22 April 2012, available online at <http://www.unctad.info/en/Debt-Portal/News-Archive/Our-News/Principles-on-sovereign-lending-and-borrowing-UNCTAD-kick-starts-endorsement-process-Doha-22-April-/>.

46 Anna Gelpern, 'Hard, Soft, and Embedded: Implementing Principles on Promoting Responsible Sovereign Lending and Borrowing', in Esposito et al. (n. 8), 347–82; Helen Keller, 'Codes of Conduct and their Implementation: The Question of Legitimacy', in Rüdiger Wolfrum and Volker Röben (eds) *Legitimacy in International Law* (Heidelberg: Springer, 2008), 297.

47 On this implication, *see* Joshua Cohen, 'Deliberation and Democratic Legitimacy', in James Bohman and William Rehg (eds) *Deliberative Democracy: Essays on Reason and Politics* (Cambridge, MA: MIT Press, 1997), 67.

48 Jürgen Habermas, *Teoría de la Acción Comunicativa* (Madrid: Taurus, 1999).

49 *See* generally Bernard Manin, 'On Legitimacy and Political Deliberation' (1987) 15(3) Political Theory 338.

50 Peter Haas and Ernst Haas, 'Learning to Learn: Improving International Governance' (1995) 1(3) Global Governance 255.

51 Inge Kaul, 'Global Public Goods: Explaining their Underprovision' (2012) 15(3) J Int'l Econ L 729.

52 Ian Johnstone, *The Power of Deliberation: International Law, Politics and Organizations* (New York: Oxford University Press, 2011), 3.

53 This section is based on the elaborations made in Bohoslavsky and Esposito (n. 8), and Yuefen Li and Juan Pablo Bohoslavsky, 'Filling a Legal Gap in Sovereign Debt Crisis Prevention and Restructuring', in Matthias Audit and Stephan Schill (eds) *The Internationalization of Public Contracts* (Brussels: Bruylant Editions, 2014), forthcoming.

> principles and best practices applied to sovereign lending and borrowing and in elaborating the implications of these standards and practices for lenders and borrowers at the international level.... The first step of this initiative has been to shape a robust and well grounded set of principles and build consensus around them respecting the sovereigns' priorities and preferences.

More explicitly, according to a brochure released by UNCTAD in August 2011:

> Every principle has an intrinsic vocation of being applied and enforced. The first step of this project has been to shape a robust and well grounded soft law set of principles. The prudent path adopted from the outset has been a gradual process following and respecting the sovereigns' priorities and preferences.[54]

27.38 Therefore the PRSLB are, prima facie, a soft law instrument with the theoretical potential to be persuasive enough to influence the interpretation, application, and development of other rules of law,[55] to become recognized as legal rules by themselves (stabilizing normative expectations), or simply to be followed *as usual*,[56] but with a legal international sense. All of these possible implications are part of the more general phenomenon: the so-called 'politics of deformalization of international law'.[57]

27.39 There is a contractarian explanation for the use of soft instruments in international financial law. Costs of contracting are lower (than international treaties, for example) because soft law provides a cheaper means of agreement-making.[58] Sovereignty constraints limiting the ability of a state to follow its own prerogatives are also fewer than those required by hard law instruments.[59] Treaties are also hard to amend,[60] which, in a field of speedy changes such as financing, can be a serious problem.[61] Soft law instruments can also encourage the international community to resolve global problems over the objections of a few states causing them, while fostering the idea that these same states should be bound by this instrument regardless of their consent.[62]

27.40 Coordination problems in international finance are bolstered by distributive tensions. This is why promoting win–win behaviour in macroeconomic cooperation is so crucial.[63] Why should

---

54 *See* UNCTAD (n. 10).

55 *See* Alan Boyle and Christine Chinkin, *The Making of International Law* (New York: Oxford University Press, 2007), 223. On this discussion, *see* generally Chris Brummer, *Soft Law and the Global Financial System: Rule Making in the 21st Century* (New York: Cambridge University Press, 2012); also Mario Giovanoli, 'A New Architecture for the Global Financial Market: An Outline of Legal Issues', in Mario Giovanoli (ed.) *International Monetary Law: Issues for the New Millennium* (Oxford: Oxford University Press, 2000), 3–59; Lastra (n. 39), 462.

56 Some countries have already adopted and implemented some of the PRSLB. For example, periodic post-disbursement audits (Principle 13) are constitutional accountability mechanisms that are already conducted in most countries: Goldmann (n. 5), 31.

57 Jean d'Aspremont, 'The Politics of Deformalization in International Law' (2011) 3(2) Goettingen J Int'l L 528.

58 Kenneth Abbott and Duncan Snidal, 'Hard and Soft Law in International Governance' (2000) 54 International Organization 434.

59 David Epstein and Sharyn O'Halloran, 'Sovereignty and Delegation in International Organizations' (2008) 71 Law & Contemp Probs 89.

60 Laurence Helfer, 'Exiting Treaties' (2005) 91 Virginia L Rev 1579.

61 Roberta Karmel and Claire Kelly, 'The Hardening of Soft Law in Securities Regulation' (2009) 34 Brook J Int'l L 885.

62 Dinah Shelton, 'Normative Hierarchy in International Law' (2006) 100(2) Am J Int'l L 319.

63 On this argument, *see* Eric Posner and Alan Sykes, *International Law and the Limits of Macroeconomic Cooperation*, University of Chicago Institute for Law & Economics Olin Research Paper No. 609/University of Chicago Public Law Working Paper No. 396/Stanford Law and Economics Olin Working Paper No. 431 (July 2012), available online at <http://papers.ssrn.com/sol3/papers.cfm?abstract_id=2120890>.

a country that has *softly committed* to follow certain borrowing standards not backtrack on its promises if this leads it to a better position? The same question can be posed regarding lenders: why would a lender make the sacrifice of refraining from granting loans (and generating profits) to help the country to borrow beyond its economic repayment capacity, when he speculates, for example, with being paid first in the case of default or being bailed out in the future?

PRSLB compliance could be propelled by showing concrete opportunity costs that might result from not helping to prevent undisciplined, ineffective, abusive, or non-cooperative behaviour on the part of both creditors and sovereign debtors in order to minimize sovereign insolvencies and their negative consequences. Because there is no effective disciplinary mechanism in the global financial arena, it is vital that lenders and (more importantly) sovereign borrowers perceive themselves to be better off by respecting soft law commitments. The ultimate constituency of the PRSLB is the global economic system.[64] **27.41**

Another aspect of this typical international law cost–benefit analysis[65] is reputation.[66] Endorsing a rule while being part of an institutional and legal project, which is centred in global public goods and sponsored by the United Nations, can actually trigger both financial and non-financial benefits for the country participants in this international law machinery: for example accessing lower interest rates because of the commitment made to implement the PRSLB, or elaborating moral discourses in international relations based on accepted legal principles that might help to establish a better position from which to argue or negotiate new agendas. **27.42**

The moral force and economic implications of soft law are of key significance in international financial law. Because the PRSLB constitute an instrument the degree of normativity (legal binding) of which depends on its persuasiveness,[67] the fact that they mainly encompass principles that have been broadly adopted, implemented, and successfully tested at the domestic level of many countries[68] can promote their global implementation. This widespread adoption and implementation (public 'buy-in') might, of course, take time, because the PRSLB need to prove their reasonableness, practicability, and actual win–win effects. **27.43**

Yet even when the PRSLB themselves express in their Preamble that they are a soft law instrument, a few of these principles are actually backed by international treaties and customs. More specifically, lenders and borrowers are not allowed to violate UN sanctions (Article 25 of the UN Charter) nor *jus cogens* norms (Articles 53 and 71(1) of the Vienna Convention on the Law of Treaties 1969).[69] International customary law is even more sparing in providing rules to sovereign financing.[70] One case in point is *pacta sunt servanda*,[71] limited by the **27.44**

64 Gelpern (n. 46), 40.

65 *See* generally Andrew Guzman, *How International Law Works* (New York: Oxford University Press, 2008).

66 Michael Tomz, *Reputation and International Cooperation: Sovereign Debt across Three Centuries* (Princeton, NJ: Princeton University Press, 2007).

67 Bohoslavsky and Espósito (n. 8).

68 *See* generally Goldmann (n. 5).

69 Sabine Michalowski and Juan PabloBohoslavsky, '*Ius Cogens*, Transitional Justice and other Trends of the Debate on Odious Debts: A Response to the World Bank Discussion Paper on Odious Debts' (2010) 48 Colum J Transnat'l L 67.

70 Michael Waibel, 'Out of Thin Air? Tracing the Origins of the UNCTAD Principles in State Practice', in Esposito et al. (n. 8), 87–112. On the connection between the Principles and customary international law, see a first exploratory research in Juan Pablo Bohoslavsky, Yuefen Li and Marie Sudreau, 'United Nations Enhancing Customary International Law in Sovereign Debt Governance' (2013) Capital Markets Law Journal (forthcoming).

71 Article 26, Vienna Convention on the Law of Treaties (general state practice with a sense of obligation; general principle existing in most domestic legal orders; prohibition of unjust enrichment). On the legal basis of

defence of necessity based on the economic or political circumstances that make impossible the full or timely repayment of the debts,[72] and cases of blatant violation of applicable fiduciary duties, such as corruption.[73] Also, the Paris Club supports the idea of parity among creditors since it works on the basis of equitable burden-sharing among the members of this group.[74]

27.45 More importantly, most of the PRSLB might be considered to be general principles of law—one of the legal sources of international law, according to Article 38, Statute of the International Court of Justice.[75] In this particular case, there is one crucial question that future practice and academic development will have to answer. Having crystallized and systematized a number of general principles, are these specific PRSLB already binding? This is a very difficult question, because it requires identifying the precise instant in which instruments well rooted in domestic orders crack the soft law shell and become a legal source of international law. From a practical point of view, general principles are established when courts and tribunals recognize them, since, before that point, they are unknown. However, from a theoretical standpoint, it is possible to argue that these principles exist before a court so decides; they are actually the basis of its decision.

27.46 Arriving at an accurate answer to the main question posed by this section necessarily means fragmenting the PRSLB and tracking down the legal basis of each of them.[76] The interplay of different legal sources, together with the innate persuasiveness of the economic and political soundness[77] of the principles, could indeed reinforce their overall degree of normativity.

6. The Role of the United Nations in the Global Economic Agenda and the PRSLB

27.47 While Bretton Woods institutions have been dominating the global financial agenda for decades,[78] more multipolar world and global financial and economic crises have been challenging that paradigm. Global economic problems and their remedies that require a certain degree of coordination (thus making decisions on how to distribute profits and losses among stakeholders) need a rather horizontal, democratic, inclusive, and still effective institutional platform to be planned, discussed, negotiated, and implemented.

27.48 Therefore it is not surprising that the United Nations was ahead of the curve in analysing the effects of global economic crises, while suggesting major reforms of the international

the *pacta sunt servanda* rule, *see* Waibel (n. 70); Robert Howse, 'Concluding Remarks in Light of International Law', in Esposito et al. (n. 8), 385–9. Specifically on unjust enrichment, *see Jackson v. People's Republic of China* (1982) 550 F Supp 869 (11th Cr). *See* generally Christoph Schreuer, 'Unjustified Enrichment in International Law' (1974) 22 Am J Comp L 281.

[72] Article 25, International Law Commission, Draft on Articles on State Responsibility.

[73] Articles 9, 15*ff*, 34, UN Convention against Corruption. On this specific issue, *see* Justo (n. 35).

[74] Paris Club, *Annual Report 2009* (Paris: Paris Club, 2009), Annex 3; Giovanni Vitale, 'Multilateral Sovereign Debt Restructuring: The Paris Club and the London Club', in Einchengreen and Portes (eds) *Crisis? What Crisis? Orderly Workouts for Sovereign Debtors* (London: Centre for Economic Policy Research, 1995), 123.

[75] *See* Goldmann (n. 5).

[76] For this task, *see* Antonis Bredimas, Anastasios Gourgourinis, and Georges Pavlidis, 'The Legal Contours of Sovereign Debt Restructuring under the UNCTAD Draft Principles: Antagonism and Convergence between Standards of Domestic Insolvency Law and International Investment Protection Law', in Esposito et al. (n. 8), 135–60; Goldmann (n. 5); Waibel (n. 70).

[77] Jaye Ellis, 'General Principles and Comparative Law' (2011) 22(4) Eur J Int'l L 971.

[78] Louis Emmerij, Richard Jolly, and Thomas Weiss, *UN Ideas that Changed the World* (Bloomington, IN: Indiana University Press, 2009), 76, 98, 106.

financial architecture.[79] The Monterrey Consensus (2002), the follow-up Conference in Doha (2008), and the Conference on the World Financial and Economic Crisis and its Impact on Development in New York (2009) are examples of those efforts. The outcomes from the Group of 20 (G-20)[80] help to explain why, during recent years, the United Nations has been reinforced as an important forum in which the causes and necessary remedies for the world economic crisis are to be discussed.

However, this UN role is far from being universally accepted. In 2009, in the context of the Commission of Experts of the President of the United Nations General Assembly on Reforms of the International Monetary and Financial System (the so-called 'Stiglitz Commission'), the political differences around the UN competency to engage in matters of financial systemic reform reappeared. While several developed countries opposed this idea, the G-77 and China strongly suggested that the UN should be involved in discussing and making recommendations on the global economy.[81] **27.49**

Yet a gradual, smooth political shift towards conceding an increasing role to the UN in global financial issues is taking place, as is reflected in the wording of the last annual UN General Assembly resolutions that repetitively and explicitly have recognized the UN competencies to deal with global debt problems. More concretely, the 2011 Debt Resolution called for: **27.50**

> ... the consideration of enhanced approaches to sovereign debt restructuring and debt resolution mechanisms, based on existing frameworks and principles, with the broad participation of creditors and debtors, the comparable treatment of all creditors and an important role for the Bretton Woods institutions and other relevant organizations within the United Nations system, and in this regard calls upon all countries to promote and contribute to the discussions, *within the United Nations and other appropriate forums*, on the need for and feasibility of a more structured framework for international cooperation in this area.[82]

UNCTAD also addressed the issue in its sixth, seventh, and eighth Debt Management Conferences in November 2007, November 2009, and November 2011, respectively. More recently, it was in April 2012, during UNCTAD XIII, that the issue of the UN competency to tackle specifically sovereign debt problems forcefully emerged. Frantic negotiations among states and also NGOs[83] took place in Doha while drafting the mandate, discussing, among other relevant issues, whether UNCTAD should or should not be managing the PRSLB initiative.[84] **27.51**

---

[79] José A. Ocampo, 'Introduction: The United Nations and Global Finance', in Joachim Mueller and Karl Sauvant (eds) *Annual Review of United Nations Affairs 2008/2009* (New York: Oxford University Press, 2010), i–xxxi.

[80] Jakob Vestergaard and Robert Wade, 'Establishing a New Global Economic Council: Governance Reform at the G20, the IMF and the World Bank' (2012) 3(3) Global Policy 257–69; Robert Wade, 'Emerging World Order? From Multipolarity to Multilateralism in the G20, the World Bank, and the IMF' (2011) 39(3) Politics & Society 354.

[81] United Nations, *Report of the Commission of Experts of the President of the United Nations General Assembly on Reforms of the International Monetary and Financial System* (September 2009), available online at <http://www.un.org/ga/econcrisissummit/docs/FinalReport_CoE.pdf>, 9.

[82] Emphasis added. UN General Assembly Resolution 65/144 on external debt sustainability and development, of 20 December 2010.

[83] Mary Donahue, 'A Present Day Victory for the Future of Debt Relief and Development', *Jubilee blog*, 17 May 2012, available online at <http://jubileeusa.typepad.com/blog_the_debt/2012/05/a-present-day-victory-for-the-future-of-debt-relief-and-development.html>.

[84] *See* Robert Wade, 'West Strikes Back against New World Order', *The Guardian*, 2 April 2012, available online at <http://www.guardian.co.uk/business/economics-blog/2012/apr/03/west-strikes-back-new-world-order-unctad/print>:

> The western governments are mounting a determined attempt to amend the text to exclude Unctad from virtually all these issues. They say that these issues are beyond Unctad's 'comparative

27.52 The final outcome of these negotiations is particularly interesting for two reasons. First, the UNCTAD mandate, eventually unanimously approved by state members, explicitly highlighted that 'promotion of responsible sovereign lending and borrowing can play important roles with regard to promoting financial stability as well as with respect to crisis prevention and resolution mechanisms'.[85] Second, the first group of countries explicitly supporting the consolidated version of the PRSLB[86] comprised not only developing countries, but also developed ones.[87]

27.53 These interesting outcomes probably reflect a variety of novel facts, including the following.

(i) The idea that the UN should be actively engaged in the debate and search for remedies on global financial issues is gaining political support.[88]
(ii) A purely South–North theatre does not accurately describe the current state of international relations in which the distribution of material power in the intestate system has become quite dynamic and is being replaced by a more multipolar system.[89]
(iii) The dramatic increase of public debt in the advanced economies with systemic financial crises and/or sovereign debt problems[90] is leading to a change in the way of dealing with (or at least thinking of) global finance;.
(iv) Related to the last point, and judging from the experience of past crises, the fact that it would take at least a decade, if not longer, to absorb high levels of debt would certainly have its negative impact on global economic growth.[91]
(v) Greater financial interconnectedness makes contagion swifter, increasing the potential for crises to be more severe and larger in scale, pushing global financial crises into the select group of vital interests on which to make global commitments.
(vi) The undeniable fact that the market does not possess a self-correcting magic power means that some guidelines become more and more necessary.
(vii) Sovereign borrowers are also becoming sovereign lenders and vice versa,[92] so their views on global financial issues are growing more nuanced and comprehensive.

---

advantage', that they are the prerogative of the IMF, World Bank and WTO, that having different international organisations saying different things about them only causes confusion.

[85] UNCTAD, *The Doha Mandate*, TD/500/Add.1 (May 2012), available online at <http://unctad.org/meetings/en/SessionalDocuments/td500_Add_1en.pdf>, para. 30.

[86] UNCTAD (n. 44).

[87] In the context of UNCTAD XIII, representatives of Brazil, Germany, Italy, Nepal, Norway, and Morocco expressed support for the Principles on behalf of their countries: *see* UNCTAD (n. 45). Also Argentina, Gabon, Honduras, Mauritania, and Paraguay expressed their support for the initiative: *see* UNCTAD, 'Second Draft of Principles on Responsible Sovereign Financing', Press release, 14 November 2011, available online at <http://www.unctad.info/en/Debt-Portal/News-Archive/Our-News/-Second-Draft-of-Principles-on-Responsible-Financing-is-released/>.

[88] Besides the PRSLB, there are other UN initiatives working in debt issues, such as Draft General Guidelines on Foreign Debt and Human Rights, elaborated in 2008 for the UN Office of the High Commission for Human Rights (OHCHR) by Independent Expert Bernards Mudho, and more recently the Guiding Principles elaborated by Independent Expert Cephas Lumina and endorsed by the Human Rights Council.

[89] Wade (n. 80), 347; Thomas Weiss, *Thinking about Global Governance: Why People and Ideas Matter* (New York: Routledge, 2011), 87–100.

[90] Carmen Reinhart and Kenneth Rogoff, *A Decade of Debt*, CEPR Discussion Paper Series No. DP8310 (April 2011), available online at <http://papers.ssrn.com/sol3/papers.cfm?abstract_id=1810275>.

[91] Carmen Reinhart and Kenneth Rogoff, 'Growth in a Time of Debt' (2010) 100(2) AERPP 573.

[92] Wong (n. 29), 100–2.

The PRSLB initiative is part of the current political and institutional progression of increasing partnership of the UN with other stakeholders in working together on debt issues.[93] Within this tendency, the new UNCTAD project for designing a debt restructuring mechanism should be highlighted.[94] 27.54

In addition, the UN Charter works as a normative umbrella for these specific competences, because one of the purposes of the UN is to achieve international cooperation in solving international problems of an economic character, while promoting solutions of international economic and related problems (Articles 1(3) and 55(2)). This raises the question of whether UNCTAD should have this specific role, the reasons being the universal and equal basis of its membership, its technical capacity, and the fact that it is not a financial actor in global markets, which puts it in a unique institutional position to promote financial behavioural changes. 27.55

In fact, the PRSLB are not the first UNCTAD incursion in global debt issues. At its very first session, in 1964, UNCTAD already dealt with debt issues.[95] In almost fifty years, UNCTAD has worked on proposals on debt relief, guidelines on debt rescheduling, and reforms of the international monetary system and development finance.[96] 27.56

7. Concluding Remarks. The PRSLB in the Progression of International Law

Economic ideas cannot be understood if examined divorced from historical and social circumstances. In particular, ideas within the UN are contingent upon world politics and the global economy.[97] The astronomical size of the public debt of countries implies that the responsible handling of sovereign financing is of great importance to financial stability. However, there are various incentives and systemic weaknesses that can lead to overborrowing and overlending. Financial deregulation in a world of financial innovation, the changing composition of sovereign debt from predominantly syndicated bank loans to bonds, increasing financial linkages, and modern communication, despite their benefits and opportunities, have provided fertile soil for excessive risk taking and have also made possible sudden risk aversion actions, thus increasing financial volatility in the capital market, with the economic and social losses that this entails. 27.57

Global principles on promoting responsible sovereign borrowing and lending to sovereigns could help to build a more responsible culture in sovereign financing *ex ante* and *ex post* debt contracting; thus they will be an important instrument for debt crisis prevention. With its two principles on debt restructuring, the PRSLB also help to remove the stigma associated 27.58

[93] Ocampo (n. 79), i–xxxi.

[94] UNCTAD, 'Norway Pledges Financial Support for UNCTAD's Project on Responsible Sovereign Financing', Press release, 9 November 2012, available online at <http://www.unctad.info/en/Debt-Portal/News-Archive/Our-News/Norway-Pledges-Financial-Support-for-UNCTADs-Project-on-Responsible-Sovereign-Financing-25102012>. *See* also Bhumika Muchhala, 'UN General Assembly Special Event on Sovereign Debt and Debt Resolution Mechanisms' (2013) 70 South Bulletin 6–11.

[95] UNCTAD, *The History of UNCTAD: 1964–1984*, (New York: United Nations, 1985), 75.

[96] UNCTAD (n. 95), 94–7, 100.

[97] Weiss (n. 89), 47.

with debt restructuring and open doors to timely, fair, orderly, and transparent debt crisis resolution. Therefore popularization of the PRSLB would enhance lending security and thus lower credit costs, and probably increase the overall volume of credit.[98]

27.59 The PRSLB impose responsibilities on lenders and borrowers according to those who are best suited to take action to prevent losses, seeking to approach *optimal liability*.[99] In addition, the PRSLB reflect and reinforce the morality involved in each behavioural change that they promote (fiduciary duties are, probably, their best sample). Because norms-based theories indicate that fair laws exert a *compliance pull* on states,[100] while reminding them of the morality of their actions, they are more likely to be honest;[101] the PRSLB seem to have a great potential in terms of implementation.

27.60 In the economic realm, the power of the UN (or one of the countries building majorities) does not lie in its capacity to pass resolutions by majority votes.[102] This is why robust consensus building is not only functional to the reinforcement of the ideas' legitimacy, but also an irreplaceable factor in putting them into practice. The horizontal, inclusive, and transparent development process of the PRSLB reinforces their legitimacy and their legal weight, while it contributes to overcoming collective action problems related to global public goods involved in sovereign financing. The universal membership of the UN demanded and facilitated this kind of debate.

27.61 The general legal approach used by the PRSLB is based on a productive interplay between constructivism and international legal theory. On the one hand, it acknowledges the importance of power, material interests, culture, ideas, institutions, discourse, and social norms in influencing behaviour, while legal sources and mechanisms are understood in the broad context of the international legal enterprise.[103]

27.62 On the other hand, the PRSLB are deliberately and mainly based on a cross-sovereign legal source, while acknowledging the relevance of (implicit and explicit) state consent. More concretely, while being conscious of the empirical (political and economic) constraints existing in the international financial arena, in which the legal dimension actually has been playing a rather limited role, the PRSLB do not batten down weak stakeholders so that they follow the rules made by the most powerful. Because the PRSLB reflect general principles existing in most domestic orders, sovereign equality is not diluted, but indeed reinforced. In addition, the PRSLB are open to endorsement by states.

---

[98] Marcin Menkes, 'Responsible Borrowing and Lending. UNCTAD Principles', Paper presented at the Conference on Europe in the World Economy beyond the Sovereign Debt Crisis, Warsaw School of Economics, 31 May–1 June 2012, available online at <http://www.sgh.waw.pl/instytuty/imsg/europe2012/Menkes.pdf>.

[99] Robert Cooter and Thomas Ulen, *Law and Economics* (Boston, MA: Pearson Addison Wesley, 2007), 322.

[100] Oona Hathaway, 'Between Power and Principle: An Integrated Theory of International Law' (2005) 72 U Chicago L Rev 482–3.

[101] Dan Ariely, *Predictably Irrational: The Hidden Forces that Shape our Decisions* (London: Harper Collins, 2008), 213.

[102] John Toye and Richard Toye, *The UN and the Global Political Economy. Trade, Finance, and Development* (Bloomington, IN: Indiana University Press, 2004), 279.

[103] *See* generally Jutta Brunnee and Stephen Toope, 'Constructivism and International Law', in Jeffrey Dunoff and Mark Pollack (eds) *Interdisciplinary Perspectives on International Law and International Relations: The State of the Art* (Cambridge: Cambridge University Press, 2012), 119–45.

The PRSLB initiated a process of *legalization* in international financial law. That means a 'process of adding to, changing or subtracting from the body of law and the legal system over time'.[104] Because legalization is both a political and a legal process at the same time, the heavy reliance on soft law based on general principles of law implicitly admits extensive politics in global debt issues, while deploying an effective strategy of legalization,[105] without undervaluing the legal and moral forces that common principles bring into the equation. **27.63**

The most immediate impact of this dynamic process could probably be the beginning of a change in both values and interests of stakeholders involved in sovereign financing, believing that responsible financial behaviour has axiological and/or economic win–win comparative advantages (*persuasive argument*). This would be a crucial step towards changing financial behaviours through a legalization strategy based on soft law PRSLB. This is crucial, because UN ideas can exert influence through changing the ways in which issues are perceived and altering the language used to describe them, framing agendas for action, changing the ways in which groups perceive their own interests and correlatively altering the balance of forces, and becoming embedded in institutions that can adopt and implement the new ideas. The spread of norms and ideas potentially have the ability to shape what societies see as legitimate and acceptable.[106] The recent decision of the Norwegian government to adopt the PRSLB as new domestic standards with which to review its own loans to developing countries[107] seems to respond to this legalization strategy. This debt audit was carried out and made public in August 2013.[108] **27.64**

The strength of the soft law approach used by the PRSLB is threefold. First, since the principles are rooted in well-grounded and successfully tested rules already recognized by most domestic legal orders, major benefits for both sovereign borrowers and lenders can be reasonably expected from their compliance. Second, the fact that, through fragmenting and tracking down the legal foundation of each PRSLB, one can find that some of them are already backed by hard law norms that could reinforce the overall normativity of the instrument. Third, the soft law format of the PRSLB already provides countries with an array of implementation options. These flexible institutional and operational linkages could contribute to promoting durable compliance.[109] The PRSLB could act as a precursor to hard law and/or as a supplement to hard law instruments. The widespread adoption and implementation (public 'buy-in') might, of course, take time, because the PRSLB need to prove their reasonableness, practicability, and win–win opportunities. **27.65**

As the Sovereign Debt Restructuring Mechanism (SDRM) experiment has left us with several lessons,[110] it is important to note that the PRSLB do not require amendments to any **27.66**

104 Kenneth Abbott and Duncan Snidal, 'Law, Legalization and Politics: An Agenda for the Next Generation of IR–IL Scholars', in Dunoff and Pollack (n. 103), 33–56.

105 *See* Abbott and Snidal (n. 104).

106 Emilie Hafner-Burton, David Victor, and Yonatan Lupu, 'Political Science Research on International Law: The State of the Field' (2012) 106 Am J Int'l L 54.

107 *See* n. 29.

108 *See* Norwegian Foreign Affairs Ministry, 'Første i verden som gransker u-landsgjeld', Press release, 15 August 2013, available online at <http://www.regjeringen.no/nb/dep/ud/pressesenter/pressemeldinger/2013/revisjon_gjeld.html?id=733680>.

109 *See* UNCTAD, 'Information Note. Endorsing and Implementing the Principles on Responsible Sovereign Lending and Borrowing', UNCTAD XIII, Geneva, 2012. *See* more generally Gelpern (n. 46).

110 Hagan (n. 6), 390–4.

international financial institution statute. Beyond the cases of formal international commitments and competent authorities explicitly interpreting that the PRSLB are already general principles of international law, and therefore applicable to a concrete situation or dispute,[111] there is a variety of more (not mutually exclusive) subtle institutional and operational options that can help to promote durable compliance of the PRSLB.[112] It is also necessary to highlight that collective action clauses (CACs) have demonstrated that, while helpful, they cannot be a substitute for a debt workout mechanism, and finally, far from seeking an increase of the frequency of restructurings, the PRSLB actually pay much attention to crisis prevention.

27.67 As explained, the PRSLB initiative is consistent with the ongoing political shift towards conceding increasing competencies to the UN in addressing global economic problems.[113] The increasing recognition of the UN as authority[114] in the economic global realm can potentially reinforce the normativity of the PRSLB.[115]

27.68 In this same vein, as the UNCTAD competencies have historically reflected the results of the bargaining powers of international relations,[116] the broad mandate in debt issues recently agreed in Doha should not be taken for granted, but as a strong political message of the need to get the international community engaged in global finance debates. At the same time, as power shapes how states (and other stakeholders) conceptualize the problems that are the focus of legal norms,[117] the unanimous states' acknowledgement on the significance of the PRSLB with regard to financial stability, crisis prevention, and resolution mechanisms[118] can be seen as an important sign of the determination of countries to consider debt crisis prevention and resolution to be global public goods to which the UN system could contribute to provide more effectively.

27.69 A more multipolar and economically globalized world is challenging the fixed political typologies that have historically explained the successes and failures of the UN in the economic arena.[119] Financial flows make many countries borrowers and lenders at the same time; thus political blocks in the global financial agenda are much more complex nowadays. This fact contributes to explaining why developed and developing countries alike have already explicitly endorsed the PRSLB.[120]

27.70 Given a conspicuous legal void in global debt issues and an urgent need for minimum standards promoting more responsible behaviours, UNCTAD is seeking to fill this gap through

---

[111] Gelpern (n. 46).

[112] Gelpern (n. 46).

[113] *See* the Conclusions of the Special Event on Sovereign Debt Restructuring organized by the Second Committee of the United Nations General Assembly, 25 October 2012 (*see* n. 94).

[114] On authority as a discursive power through recognition, *see* Matthias Ecker-Ehrhardt, '"But the UN Said So...": International Organisations as Discursive Authorities' (2012) 26(4) Global Society 451.

[115] On this specific discursive power related to the PRSLB, *see*, e.g., the interparliamentary document invoking the PRSLB, UNCTAD, 'Principles on Responsible Sovereign Lending and Borrowing Receive Parliamentary Support', Press release, 16 December 2011, available online at <http://www.unctad.info/en/Debt-Portal/News-Archive/Our-News/Parliamentary-Support-of-the-Principles-on-Responsible-Sovereign-Lending-and-Borrowing-23112011/>.

[116] Toye and Toye (n. 102), 184–275.

[117] *See* generally Alexander Wendt, 'Anarchy is What States Make of It: The Social Construction of Power Politics' (1992) 46(2) International Organization 391.

[118] UNCTAD XIII Mandate (n. 85), para. 30.

[119] Toye and Toye (n. 102), esp. 184–229.

[120] UNCTAD (n. 45).

systematizing best practices and general principles on sovereign financing, and by proposing a coherent, holistic, and well-rooted normative framework. This initiative seems to be a logical step in the evolution of the UN role as an expanding platform for global economic and financial issues.

If countries see preventing undisciplined, ineffective, abusive, or non-cooperative behaviour on the part of both creditors and sovereign debtors as being in their own best interests, some achievements can be expected in consolidating the normative degree of UNCTAD's PRSLB and their implementation. In turn, this would enhance their legitimacy in the exercise of international public authority in the sovereign debt realm.[121] **27.71**

The intrinsic vocation of the PRSLB for ensuring output legitimacy (due provision of global public goods) has not excluded deference to consensual international law making: broad representation, consultation, and deliberation during the drafting of the PRSLB, the explicit appeal to endorse them, and the fact that they mirror domestic legal orders all minimize the risk of consolidating the power of those who have the material and intellectual resources to fill the contents of those same goods and principles. **27.72**

[121] Armin Bogdandy and Matthias Goldmann, 'Sovereign Debt Restructurings as Exercises of International Public Authority: Towards a Decentralized Sovereign Insolvency Law', in Esposito et al. (n. 8), 39–70.

28

SOVEREIGN DEBT IN THE LIGHT OF ETERNITY

Lee C. Buchheit

1. Introduction

Unsustainable sovereign debt was once seen as a unique disorder of emerging market countries. No longer. The developed world has, in the space of just a couple of decades, managed to submerse itself in debt stocks that approach, and in some cases exceed, 100 per cent of gross domestic product (GDP). The legacy of these debts will profoundly alter life and politics in the twenty-first century. **28.01**

How might a philosopher viewing sovereign debt, as Spinoza advises, in the light of eternity derive the first principles governing this exceptionally important aspect of the human condition? **28.02**

2. The Moral Element

> While the observance of that good faith, which is the basis of public credit, is recommended by the strongest inducements of political expediency, it is enforced by considerations of still greater authority. There are arguments for it, which rest on the immutable principles of moral obligation. And in proportion as the mind is disposed to contemplate, in the order of Providence, an intimate connection between public virtue and public happiness, will be its repugnancy to a violation of those principles.[1]

We tend to think of ethics as the rules or standards regulating the behaviour of individuals in their direct dealings with other individuals. Sometimes, we speak about the ethical implications of the behaviour of a group of people—a nation, for example—and ascribe to it a collective morality, something that is more than just the aggregated total of the ethical duties of the individuals comprising that group. Only rarely, however, do we consider in ethical terms the implications of the behaviour of an entire society on people with whom they never have, nor can ever have, direct dealings—future generations of that society not yet born. The despoliation of the environment is one area in which we have recently grown accustomed to thinking in terms of such intergenerational ethics. Sovereign debt should be another. **28.03**

[1] Alexander Hamilton, 'First Report on the Public Credit', in Henry Cabot Lodge (ed.) *The Works of Alexander Hamilton, Vol. II* (New York: G. P. Putnam's Sons, 1904), 227, 230–1.

28.04 By its nature, sovereign debt involves the engagement of the credit of a legal fiction—the state—for the repayment of money at some point in the future. In this context, the state does not mean the government, or even the citizens of the nation, as they exist at the time when the debt is incurred. It means the continuing legal entity of the state, including future governments and future generations of citizens. Therein lies the problem. Sovereign debt involves one group of people—the incumbent generation—borrowing money that must be paid back by subsequent generations. The ultimate payers of the debt are not consulted about the wisdom of, or necessity for, the borrowing. The tardiness of their birth renders them mute, disenfranchised, and powerless.

28.05 Now one might imagine that other legal fictions, such as corporations, are in much the same position. The management of a corporation borrows money today and pledges the credit of the company to repay that money at some point in the future. When the maturity date of the loan arrives, the corporate management may have changed, as indeed may its entire universe of stockholders. But here the analogy breaks down. Successor corporate managers and directors, and successor stockholders, voluntarily associate themselves with the company knowing full well the extent of the legacy debts incurred by their predecessors. Citizens of a debtor state do not have that luxury. A fractional responsibility for repaying the legacy debts of prior generations will be part of the birthright of each new citizen. There is nothing voluntary about it. To this extent, sovereign debt is a congenital affliction.

28.06 Thomas Jefferson famously phrased it this way: '"[T]he earth belongs in usufruct to the living": . . . the dead have neither powers nor rights over it.'[2] Jefferson was invoking the Roman law concept of a usufruct—the right to enjoy property, the legal title to which belongs to someone else. Although entitled to enjoy the property, however, the usufructuary is under a solemn duty not to sell it, not to encumber it, nor to despoil it. In Jefferson's view, each generation inhabits this planet as usufructuaries; their entitlement to enjoy the earth does not extend to the right to deprive their successors of the same entitlement when that generation's tenure commences. Public debts, Jefferson reasoned, are a form of encumbrance that deplete the ability of future generations to enjoy the fruits of their labours. Why? Because those later generations will spend a portion of their income paying back the debts they inherited from their progenitors. '[B]y the law of nature,' Jefferson wrote, 'one generation is to another as one independent nation to another.'[3]

28.07 In the light of eternity, a heavy fiduciary responsibility therefore rests upon the shoulders of those who incur a sovereign debt. The minister of finance who signs a loan agreement or bond issue pledging the full faith and credit of the Republic of Ruritania for the repayment of a debt binds both the current citizenry of Ruritania as well as the country's future citizens. At least the former enjoy the consolation of having been able to vote in the election that brought the minister to office and they will presumably benefit in some fashion from the proceeds of the borrowing. For succeeding generations, however, the minister, the lavish signing ceremony, and the proceeds of the loan will all be historical footnotes; those generations will experience only the distasteful residuum of the debt—the need to pay it back.

[2] 'Letter from Thomas Jefferson to James Madison (6 September 1789)', in Philip B. Kurland and Ralph Lerner (eds) *The Founders' Constitution, Vol. 1* (Chicago, IL: University of Chicago Press, 2001), 68.

[3] 'Letter from Thomas Jefferson' (n. 2).

28.08 In practice, this fiduciary duty should translate into prudence and restraint in sovereign borrowing. Prudence will be reflected in the motivation for the borrowing. Some purposes are more defensible, in an intergenerational sense, than others: borrowing to build or refurbish infrastructure; defending the state against an external military threat; and so forth. Others are less so: financing current government expenses as a more politically palatable alternative to taxing the voting public is an obvious example.

28.09 Restraint means preserving what the economists call 'fiscal space'—that is, the capacity to borrow (at tolerable interest rates) in the future. Fiscal space in this context is the difference between the amount that the sovereign *has* borrowed and the amount that it *can* borrow. However large the appetite of a sovereign debtor, the markets will eventually place an outer limit on the country's ability to sate that appetite. Interest rates will rise as the country approaches its saturation point in the credit market. Eventually, market access will be lost altogether. The sin of gluttony does not begin at the saturation point when fiscal space has been squeezed out altogether. It begins long before, as encroachments incrementally narrow that space and constrain the capacity of future generations to respond to whatever emergencies may face them in their lives—wars, recessions, natural disasters, etc.

3. The Legal Element

> Those who are most commonly creditors of a nation, are, generally speaking, enlightened men; and there are signal examples to warrant a conclusion, that when a candid and fair appeal is made to them, they will understand their true interest too well to refuse their concurrence in such modifications of their claims, as any real necessity may demand.[4]

28.10 Sovereign debts are no longer, as they once were, mere 'engagements of honour'.[5] Since about the middle of the twentieth century, sovereign debt contracts have been enforceable at law. The old doctrine of absolute sovereign immunity (sovereigns could not be sued in foreign courts without their consent) gave way to 'restrictive' immunity—when behaving as commercial actors, sovereigns will be treated (more or less) just like commercial actors and held legally accountable for their contractual undertakings.

28.11 There can be little doubt that this doctrinal shift from absolute to restrictive sovereign immunity played an important role in the huge increase in the amount of private sector lending to sovereigns in the last half of the twentieth century. A few intrepid private sector parties had financed sovereigns before this shift, but never confidently, never in size, and often with remorse. The erosion of sovereign immunity has given the financiers of our era at least a

---

[4] Hamilton (n. 1), 230.

[5] Here is how an English judge summarized the law of sovereign debt, circa 1876:

> The first and most important point we have to decide is what the meaning of the bond of a foreign government given to secure the payment of a loan is. As I understand the law, the municipal law of this country does not enable the tribunals of this country to exercise any jurisdiction over foreign governments as such. Nor, so far as I am aware, is there any international tribunal which exercises any such jurisdiction. The result, therefore, is that these so-called bonds amount to nothing more than engagements of honour, binding, so far as engagements of honour can bind, the government which issues them, but are not contracts enforceable before the ordinary tribunals of any foreign government, or even by the ordinary tribunals of the country which issued them, without the consent of the government of that country.
>
> (*Twycross v. Dreyfus* [1876] T 177, judgment of Jessel MR)

theoretical avenue of redress. Sovereignty (in the sense of being above the law) is a vestigial concept, and so it should remain.

28.12 To say that sovereigns should be accountable in municipal courts for their debt contracts, however, is not to say that municipal courts are an appropriate forum for administering a sovereign debt crisis. Judges, powerful as they may be within the four walls of their own courtrooms, are ill-equipped and ill-positioned to decide how the discomfort of a financial crisis should be apportioned among the citizens of the debtor country and the various classes of its creditors. Judges can only hand down judgments saying that, as a matter of law, the sovereign is bound to pay. They cannot prescribe the nature or the degree of the sacrifices that the sovereign would need to impose on its other stakeholders in order to make those payments or to satisfy those judgments.

28.13 In the light of eternity, we have thus established a framework that makes sovereigns accountable to the judiciary for the performance of their sovereign debt contracts even though everyone recognizes that the judiciary is wholly irrelevant in the face of a large sovereign debt problem. This awkwardness can lead to considerable mischief. The theoretical availability of a legal remedy offers less fraternal creditors an opportunity to extract preferential settlements as the price of the sovereign avoiding the unpleasantries of a lawsuit and an unsatisfied judgment creditor interfering with the sovereign's future commercial dealings.

28.14 Much of the headline commotion in the realm of sovereign debt has its genesis in this awkward situation. On the one side are the sovereign debtors who can, with a degree of justification, portray themselves as the victims of a gang of opportunistic, mercenary, and self-righteous creditors looking to exploit the sovereigns' vulnerability to legal remedies. On the other side are lenders who can, with a degree of justification, portray themselves as the avenging angels that bring discipline and accountability to feckless, corrupt, or incompetent government administrators. And in between sit the large majority of creditors whose sole interest is in preserving as much value as possible for their assets, and the debtor country's official sector sponsors, whose primary interest is in containing the political and economic turbulence that inevitably attends a sovereign debt crisis.

4. The Financial Element

> Persuaded as the [US Treasury] Secretary is, that proper funding of the present debt, will render it a national blessing: Yet he is so far from acceding to the position... that 'public debts are public benefits,' a position inviting to prodigality, and liable to dangerous abuse,—that he ardently wishes to see incorporated as a fundamental maxim, in the system of public credit of the United States, that the creation of debt should always be accompanied with the means of extinguishment....[6]

28.15 Borrowing money can become a hideous addiction. As we all know, the United States eventually ceased heeding the advice of its first Treasury Secretary Alexander Hamilton that the incurrence of public debts should be accompanied by the means of their extinguishment. In modern practice, the normal means of extinguishing a public debt is to incur another public debt, the proceeds of which are used to redeem the maturing obligation. The idea that a

[6] Hamilton (n. 1), 283. In the next paragraph of his report, Secretary Hamilton proposed that revenues from the post office be set aside to provide for 'the discharge of the existing public debt'.

government's general (not borrowed) revenues would be sufficient to retire—often even to service—outstanding debts is risible. Moreover, year after year, government budget deficits require additional borrowings, over and above what is required to repay the maturing outstanding debt. Relentlessly, remorselessly, sovereign debt stocks accumulate.

All of this is well known to both the markets and the politicians. No purchaser of a sovereign debt instrument today does so in the hope and expectation that, when the debt matures, the borrower will have the money to repay it. The purchaser does so in the hope and expectation that, when the instrument matures, the borrower will be able to borrow the money from somebody else in order to repay it. This is a crucial distinction. If by 'sovereign creditworthiness' we mean that a sovereign is expected to be able to generate enough revenue from taxes or other sources to repay its debts as they fall due, then most countries are utterly insolvent. Sovereign creditworthiness today means market access, the ability to tap new (or old) sources of credit in order to refinance existing debt stocks. All derivative terms used in the sovereign debt context must be understood accordingly: 'debt sustainability', 'supportable debt load', indeed even 'solvency' itself must be understood as the capacity to refinance, not the capacity to pay out of current revenues. **28.16**

Therein lies the problem. Market access can be interrupted by many factors, only some of which relate to the sovereign borrower. A general downturn in world markets, an unsettling international political event, a rise in interest rates, a loss of confidence in a currency, the misfortune or misbehaviour of a sovereign elsewhere in the world—any of these can cause markets to turn skittish and arthritic. And when they do, a sovereign's ability to refinance maturing debt can evaporate. The result is a sovereign debt crisis. **28.17**

In the light of eternity, we have allowed a financial system to develop for sovereigns that assumes a more or less perpetual state of benignity—in the debtor country, in the region, in the global economic and political environment, and even in the natural world. A disturbance in any of these areas, if it frightens investors sufficiently, risks interrupting the expectation of refinancing that defines sovereign creditworthiness. Many sovereign borrowers would last only a few months, some only a few weeks, if shut off from the ability to refinance their maturing debts. Denied continued market access, they would burn through their reserves with frightening speed. The last step is, for the fortunate borrowers, an official sector bailout, and for the unfortunate, a debt restructuring. **28.18**

Millennialists aside, true believers in perpetual benignity are rare. Bad things will happen. Market access for sovereigns will occasionally be lost. For a lightly indebted country that *wants* to borrow for some purpose or other, these are inconveniences. For a heavily indebted country that *needs* to borrow regularly and in sizeable amounts in order to refinance maturing obligations, however, these hard facts of life can spell catastrophe. The European debt crisis that began in 2010 shows just how quickly options can narrow. The peripheral European countries that lost market access in that crisis (at time of writing, Greece, Ireland, Portugal, and Cyprus) sat like chicks in a robin's nest in springtime—beaks gaping, yelping for someone to provide the funds needed to refinance their maturing debts. Terrified of letting a eurozone member default on its debts, the other members of the eurozone—together with the International Monetary Fund (IMF)—had no choice but to become themselves the refinanciers of last resort. It was a story of heavily indebted, budget-deficit countries propping up even more heavily indebted neighbours, with the primary objective of camouflaging for a while longer the inherent fragility of the system. **28.19**

5. The Political Element

> ... [T]hese [are] plain and undeniable truths:
>
> That exigencies are to be expected to occur, in the affairs of nations, in which there will be a necessity for borrowing.
>
> That loans in time of public danger, especially from foreign war, are found an indispensable resource, even to the wealthiest of them.
>
> And that in a country, which, like this, is possessed of little active wealth, or in other words, little monied capital, the necessity for that resource, must, in such emergencies, be proportionably urgent.[7]

28.20 Politicians who inherit an outstanding stock of debt that must regularly be rolled over cannot be criticized for authorizing those borrowings. Discretion, and the possibility for criticism, will appear in the decisions to finance new projects or to finance budget deficits. In these areas, politicians have a choice. The choice, however, is likely to be more political than financial.

28.21 Democracies—all of them—struggle with these realities:

- politicians like to be elected and re-elected;
- spending money on public services and entitlement programmes increases the likelihood of being elected or re-elected, even if the aggregate amount of those public expenses exceeds the nation's current income (a budget deficit);
- taxing the electorate to pay for a budget deficit diminishes the likelihood of election or re-election; and therefore
- borrowing to cover a budget deficit is usually the only politically acceptable alternative.

28.22 This is the hard political reality of sovereign debt; borrowing is almost always preferable, in a political sense, to taxation or frugality. Moreover, the time never seems appropriate to rein in these tendencies. In good times, when the economy of Ruritania is booming, only a killjoy worries about the size of the Ruritanian debt. After all, an ever-expanding Ruritanian GDP will be able to support an ever-expanding debt. And in bad times, recessions or depressions, borrowing for economic stimulus programmes will be prescribed as the only way in which to return vibrancy to the economy and employment to the unemployed.

28.23 Various methods have been tried over the years to curb the tendency of politicians to borrow rather than take politically unpopular measures to eliminate budget deficits. These include statutory debt ceilings, legislated 'pay as you go' requirements, deficit limits for countries in a monetary union (backed up by monetary penalties), and so forth. They are the equivalent of a dieter taping shut the refrigerator door. But somehow the tape always seems to be dislodged in the morning.

28.24 Once upon a time in some countries (the United States is one), the main constraint upon this feature of weak political flesh was cultural. Running up debts to pay for current expenditures except in times of emergency just struck most people as wrong; it was a violation of the intergenerational covenant about which Thomas Jefferson wrote in 1789. Our collective willingness to tolerate chronic budget deficits during peacetime is a phenomenon of the last

[7] Hamilton (n. 1), 228.

forty years or so. It is, in truth, just one example of a society that has become inured to heavy debt loads at every level—governmental, corporate, and personal.

Excessive sovereign debt, however, is particularly pernicious. Even a large country like the **28.25** United States will insensibly begin to lose some of its geopolitical influence as its national debt grows. This is in part attributable to a perception by citizens and foreigners alike that the country may be running out of fiscal space—that it may not be able, as it once was, to finance unlimited defence requirements or to offer generous monetary support to allies. In Alexander Hamilton's day, foreign credit was essential to the young American republic. His First Report on the Public Credit, portions of which have been liberally quoted in this chapter, had as one of its principal goals the shoring up of the credit standing of the new nation in the eyes of foreign lenders. Secretary Hamilton would no doubt be appalled to learn that, some 225 years later, the prosperity of the United States is once again heavily dependent on the generosity of foreign creditors. It is doubtful that he would renew the title of 'a national blessing' upon a debt stock, the continued servicing of which is critically dependent upon that generosity.

APPENDIX: DEFINING DEFAULT

In its simplest form, a debt contract entered into at time $t = 1$ is a commitment to make a sequence of non-contingent contractual payments $\bar{c}_t \geq 0, t = 1, 2, ...,T$. Although they do not depend on the state of nature, the contractual (coupon) payments $\bar{c}_t$ can vary over time. For instance, the final contractual payment $\bar{c}_T$ could include the final coupon and the repayment of the principal. A simple, but too restrictive, definition of default would be that at some time in the life of the debt contract (between periods 1 and T)—say in period k, with $1 \leq k \leq T$—the remaining sequence of contractual payments $\{\bar{c}_t; T \geq t \geq k\}$ is changed by the borrower to another sequence $\{\bar{\bar{c}}_t; T \geq t \geq k\}$ that is dominated by the original sequence, in the sense that:

$$\begin{aligned} &\bar{\bar{c}}_t \leq \bar{c}_t \text{ for all } t \geq k \\ &\bar{\bar{c}}_t < \bar{c}_t \text{ for at least one } t \geq k \end{aligned} \tag{A1}$$

This definition of default is extended here to include the substitution at time 1 by the borrower of an alternative contractual sequence that has lower net present discounted value (NPV) than the original sequence, if the discount rates used are taken to be the risk-free (that is, free of credit risk or default risk) rates.

Let I_{t_1,t_0} be the nominal stochastic discount factor between periods t_1 and t_0, defined recursively by:

$$\begin{aligned} I_{t_1,t_0} &= \prod_{n=t_0+1}^{t_1} I_{n,n-1} \quad \text{for } t_1 > t_0 \\ &= 1 \qquad\qquad \text{for } t_1 = t_0 \end{aligned} \tag{A2}$$

The interpretation of I_{t_1,t_0} is the price in terms of period t_0 money of one unit of money in period $t_1 \geq t_0$. There will, in general, be many possible states in period t_1, and period t_1 money has a period t_0 (forward) price for each state. Formally, therefore, the stochastic discount factor has the state of the world, s, say, as an argument, and should be written as $I_{t_1,t_0}(s)$, but here this is suppressed, because it does not lead to ambiguity. Let E_t be the mathematical expectation operator conditional on information available at the beginning of period t. Provided that earlier dated information sets do not contain more information than later dated information sets, these stochastic discount factors satisfy the recursion property:

$$E_{t_0}\left(I_{t_1,t_0} E_{t_1} I_{t_2,t_1}\right) = E_{t_0} I_{t_2,t_0} \text{ for } t_2 \geq t_1 \geq t_0$$

Finally, the one-period risk-free nominal interest rate in period t, i_t—that is, the money price in period t of one unit of money in every state of the world in period $t+1$—is defined by:

$$\frac{1}{1+i_{t+1,t}} = E_t I_{t+1,t}$$

Likewise, the risk-free j-period discount factor ($j \geq 1$) in period t is defined by:

$$\begin{aligned} &\left(\frac{1}{1+i_{t+j,t}}\right)^j = E_t I_{t+j,t}, \; j \geq 1 \\ &\frac{1}{1+i_{t,t}} = 1 \end{aligned} \tag{A3}$$

So the definition of default amounts to the statement that the offer of the sequence of contractual payments $\{\bar{\bar{c}}_t; T \geq t \geq k\}$ in lieu of the original sequence of contractual payments $\{\bar{c}_t; T \geq t \geq k\}$ represents a default if, and only if:

$$\sum_{t=k}^{T} \bar{\bar{c}}_t \left(\frac{1}{1+i_{t,k}} \right)^{t-k} < \sum_{t=k}^{T} \bar{c}_t \left(\frac{1}{1+i_{t,k}} \right)^{t-k} \tag{A4}$$

Note that if a contract is in default according to the (A1) criterion, it will also be in default according to the (A4) criterion. The converse does not hold.

Of course, the actual stream of payments that will be made to the creditor(s) by the debtor $\{c_t; 1 \leq t \leq T\}$ is uncertain and will depend on the willingness and ability of the debtor to pay. The NPV of the debt contract at time *k* that is actually priced in the market, P_k, involves the use of the appropriate stochastic discount factors and is given by:

$$P_k = E_k \sum_{t=k}^{T} c_t I_{t,k} \tag{A5}$$

For a debt contract at high risk of default at time *k*, $\{\bar{c}_t; \mathrm{T} \geq t \geq k\}$, the market valuation of an alternative or revised contract $\{\bar{\bar{c}}_t; \mathrm{T} \geq t \geq k\}$ can be higher than the market valuation of the original contract—that is, $E_k \sum_{t=k}^{T} \bar{\bar{c}}_t I_{t,k} > E_k \sum_{t=k}^{T} \bar{c}_t I_{t,k}$ —even though the repudiation by the borrower of the original contract by the alternative contract constitutes an act of default in the sense that (A4), or even (A1), holds.

INDEX

Abaclat v. Argentine Republic 12.10, 12.11, 12.15, 12.45
  decision on jurisdiction and admissibility 12.22–12.28
  factual background 12.18–12.21
  implications for European debt crisis 12.33–12.44
  implications for sovereign debt 12.29–12.44
act-of-state doctrine *see* **comity and act-of-state doctrine**
African Development Bank 1.18
  HIPC initiative 6.23, 6.26, 19.27
aggregation
  CAC Model clause 25.39–25.43
  contracts, achieving aggregation through 23.76
Agronovsky, Alexander 7.26
arbitration *see* **sovereign arbitration**
Argentina
  banking crisis (2001) 15.29–15.33
    causes 15.32
  BITS 12.45
  contagion from Mexico 20.24
  currency mismatches, contingent liabilities and 21.21–21.22
  debt restructuring 1.34, 13.36, 22.34
    default on debt 2.27, 15.29, 19.74, 20.16
    delay in restructuring 7.09
    discouraging holdouts 2.12, 3.28
    Lock Law 4.39, 11.35, 11.39
    subordinating claims 4.07
  defying court judgments 11.05, 11.29, 11.34–11.39, 19.08
  good faith negotiations 5.54
  holdout litigation 2.08, 2.20, 2.28, 3.01, 5.02, 5.31, 5.35
    Abaclat see ***Abaclat v. Argentine Republic***
    BIS, and 10.12–10.27
    central bank immunity *see* under **central bank immunity**
    NML Capital Ltd see ***NML Capital v. Argentina***
Arteta, Carlos 7.27
Asia
  credit boom 20.16
  debt crisis 5.11, 15.52, 20.25–20.27
    lessons from 23.05–23.12, 23.20
    IMF's role in resolving 5.11
assurances, implicit sovereign 18.06
see also **sovereign contingent liabilities**
austerity measures 1.43, 2.05
  consequences of 7.10
  domestic distributional effects 7.11

Bagehot, Walter 16.15–16.16
Bangladesh 19.07
Bank for International Settlements (BIS) 10.01–10.30
  CDSs 20.63
  creation 10.03, 10.08
  holdout creditors of Argentina challenging immunities 10.12–10.27
    facts 10.12–10.13
    final decisions 10.19–10.27
    main issues 10.14–10.18
  immunities 10.03–10.11, 10.19
    absolute/full immunity 10.06, 10.19–10.21, 10.25, 10.28
    immunity from compulsory execution 10.10
    immunity from jurisdiction 10.10
    national courts not competent to review 10.19
  purposes/role 10.03, 10.04, 10.09
    'bank to central banks' 10.03, 10.29
banking crises and sovereign debt 15.01–15.46
  Argentina (2001) *see under* **Argentina**
  banks and governments, relationship between 15.05–15.08
    banks and government crises 15.08
    debt problems related but distinct 15.07
  European/Eurozone crisis 15.39–15.42
  see also **Eurozone debt crisis and financial rescue**
  following credit boom 15.09
  government debt in banking system 15.24–15.26
  Iceland *see* **Iceland**
  Korea *see* **Korea**
  policy decisions on losses 15.09
  regulation/supervision obscuring impact of public debt problems 15.27
  Third World debt crisis *see* **Third World debt crisis**
see also **sovereign debt**
bankruptcy law and state insolvencies *see* **corporate bankruptcy law and state insolvencies**
Basel Committee on Banking Supervision 5.16, 23.28
'Basel process' 10.04
  Basel III 19.14
Belgium 18.13
Belize
  CACs 2.32
  debt restructuring 22.34
  discouraging holdouts 2.14, 2.15
  pari passu clauses 4.47
binding holdouts 2.26–2.34
  CACs *see* **collective action clauses (CACs)**
  class action mechanisms 2.33–2.34
  SDRM *see* **sovereign debt restructuring mechanism (SDRM)**
see also **minimizing holdout creditors**
Blanchard, Oliver 7.10
Borchard, Edwin 12.04
Borensztein, Eduardo 7.22, 7.26
Bradley, Michael 25.15
Brady bond debt exchanges 1.14, 3.27, 3.30, 5.25, 7.13
  Ecuador 1.23
  Mexico 1.29–1.30
  Nigeria 1.30

Brady bond debt exchanges (*cont.*):
structural enhancement of instrument 1.15
value recovery rights 1.29–1.31, 1.33
Venezuela 1.30
Brazil
arbitration of disputes 12.06
bailout 5.25
contagion from Mexico 20.24
IMF's role in resolving financial crisis 5.11
Bretton Woods Conference/regime 5.03, 5.08, 5.11
Buchheit, Lee C. 3.02, 3.55, 4.32, 15.01–15.04, 17.42–17.43, 22.81
CACs 22.31, 22.34
courts 11.01
creditors to the same borrower 5.46
holdouts 25.05
immunizing assets of an EAMS 22.75–22.76
odious debts 17.03, 17.09, 17.13, 17.34
pari passu clauses 4.01, 4.37, 4.52
periods of sovereign debt management 5.24
sovereigns 5.22

CDSs 20.57–20.67
central bank immunity 9.01–9.34
Argentina I 9.08–9.18
facts 9.09–9.11
legal analysis 9.12–9.18
Argentina II 9.19–9.32
'held for its own account' 9.23–9.32, 9.35
independence 9.20–9.22, 9.35
scope of central bank immunities 10.06
immunity from jurisdiction and execution 10.11
property used for central bank functions 10.06
central banks
BIS as bank for central banks 10.03, 10.29
BIS, members of 10.05, 10.09
see also **Bank for International Settlements (BIS)**
control 9.21
emergency liquidity assistance 26.52
European Central Bank *see* **European Central Bank (ECB)**
floor of support to preserve flow of private sector funds 16.25–16.32
functions 10.05–10.06
immunity *see* **central bank immunity**
legal personality distinct from the sovereign 1.05, 9.21
organized in different ways 9.21
policy responses to financial crisis 20.94–20.95
champerty 8.20–8.29
nature of 8.05, 8.20
origins 8.21
sovereign debt litigation 8.22–8.29
Chiang-Mai Initiative 16.19
Chile 21.56
China
cheap labour 20.31
economy, size of 20.28
financial sector, size of 20.103–20.104
Greece 20.105
rise of 20.27–20.31
class action mechanisms 2.33–2.34
co-financing 1.15, 1.16–1.17, 1.35
Greece 1.17, 3.07, 3.38–3.39
Cohen, Daniel 22.32
collective action clauses (CACs) 2.29–2.32, 2.37, 4.50–4.51, 5.26, 7.07, 25.01–25.73
alternatives to 25.07–25.09
blocking 3.29
EU 13.36–13.46
European sovereign crisis and response 25.21–25.24
Greece 3.12–3.14, 3.31, 3.41–3.47, 3.48
historically 2.30, 2.31, 2.37, 13.35
holdout creditor problem 25.03–25.06
addressing 23.71–23.73
implications of accepting CACs 25.06
introduction of 13.36
limited use 3.29, 23.72–23.73
Model clause 25.25–25.72
acceleration/rescission of acceleration 25.69–25.70
aggregation 25.39–25.43
approval thresholds: non-reserved matters 25.38
approval thresholds: reserved matters 25.25–25.37
calculation agent/bondholder representative 25.67–25.68
consistency 25.71–25.72
disenfranchisement/voting 25.44–25.54
reserved matters 25.63–25.66
zero-coupon and index-linked obligations 25.55–25.62
nature of 2.29, 3.29, 25.01–25.02
negotiated individually 13.37
purpose 2.30
sovereign contingent obligations, restructuring 18.37–18.44
sovereign debt, in 25.10–25.16
developments after Argentina default 25.14–25.16
standardization 5.38
G-10 recommendations 25.18
pre-2013 Model CACs 25.17–25.20
private sector trade association recommendations 25.19
collective action problems 23.63–23.76
aggregation through contract, achieving 23.76
composition of creditors, changes in 23.65–23.66
further reform, need for 23.74–23.76
legal environment, changes in 23.67–23.71
CACs addressing holdout problem 23.71–23.73
pari passu clauses *see* ***pari passu* clauses**
SDRM proposal 23.74–23.75
market failure, as form of 23.64
comfort letters 18.07
see also **sovereign contingent liabilities**
comity and act-of-state doctrine 8.05, 8.11–8.19
international comity 8.11
origins 8.14
US
act-of-state doctrine, effects of 8.12
application of principle 8.11–8.14
litigation stays 8.38
sovereign debt litigation 8.15–8.19
sovereign immunity principle deriving from 8.07
comparable treatment *see* **parity of treatment**

concentration risk 19.12–19.18
consequences of restructuring *see* **longer-term consequences of sovereign debt restructuring**
contagion
concentration risk, and 19.12–19.18
EU contagion risk 26.17–26.18, 26.21
financial interconnectedness 27.12
increased risk of contagion within members of currency area 13.19
little contagion after financial crises 19.63–19.64
Mexico, from 20.24
contingent liabilities *see* **sovereign contingent liabilities**
corporate bankruptcy law and state insolvencies 24.01–24.73
bankruptcy consolidation 24.67
bankruptcy ladder of priorities 24.27–24.42
equity 24.37
expropriated claimants 24.37
pari passu 24.37
priority creditors 24.37
subordinated creditors 24.37
super-priority creditors 24.37
banks and other contingent liabilities 24.72
control of debtor's financing 24.43–24.53
creditor identity 24.72
creditor rights 24.12–24.21
disrupting new borrowings 24.18
law of debtor state governing debt 24.20
limited against defaulting sovereign 24.13–24.17, 24.19
withholding future credit 2.21
debt, amount of 24.72
discharge of a debtor 24.65–24.66
disclosure 24.67
general differences in status 24.72
geopolitics 24.72
government failure, holding to account for 24.67
how do sovereign bankruptcies work 24.05–24.11
resolved by bargaining position of the parties 24.06–24.07
whether bankruptcy law necessary 24.08–24.11
interest 24.67
international bankruptcy court 24.68–24.71
moratorium on payment and attachments 24.22–24.26
number of sovereign debtors 24.72
other differences between corporate and sovereign insolvencies 24.67
preferences 24.67
reorganization plans 24.54–24.64
state insolvencies, nature of 24.01
credit-ratings agencies 14.14, 21.53
creditors
bankruptcy ladder of priorities 24.27–24.42
equity 24.37
expropriated claimants 24.37
pari passu 24.37
priority creditors 24.37
subordinated creditors 24.37
super-priority creditors 24.37
creditor remedies
creditor litigation against sovereign debtors 5.28
developments from *NML Capital see* ***NML Capital Ltd v. Argentina***
difficulties of creditor enforcement 11.02–11.03
creditor rights 24.12–24.21
disrupting new borrowings 24.18
law of debtor state governing debt 24.20
limited against defaulting sovereign 24.13–24.17, 24.19
pari passu clauses *see* ***pari passu* clauses**
withholding future credit 2.21
holdouts *see* **holdouts**
litigious creditors 1.08, 1.39, 1.41
retail (individual) creditors 1.09
vulture creditors 2.05, 4.17, 8.04
see also **vulture funds**
Crockett, Andrew 27.11
Cuba
default 19.74
trade sanctions 19.09
currency mismatches 21.12–21.23
Cyprus
bank creditors 26.20
banking sector 15.23
'botched bailout' 15.02–15.03, 19.19
euro area tax haven, demise as 19.49
IMF, and 19.69
loans flouting euro's founding treaty 16.50

Das, Udaibir 7.22
de Grauwe, Paul 14.36
debt sustainability
debt sustainability analysis
credit-ratings agencies 21.53
European Commission 19.65, 19.70
HIPC initiative 6.03, 6.08, 6.35–6.37
IMF *see under* **International Monetary Fund (IMF)**
World Bank *see under* **World Bank**
indicators of debt sustainability 21.44–21.54
anticipating market perception of sovereign default risk 21.54
calculation of primary fiscal outcome 21.49
correlation of fiscally responsible behaviour with public debt size 21.49
fiscal forecasts/alternative scenarios 21.50–21.51
public/private sector foreign debt to export earnings 21.44
ratios of public debt to GDP 21.45–21.48
debts
changing composition of 27.13
corporate debt restructuring in context of systemic crisis 23.05–23.20
corporate insolvency and 2008 crisis 23.13–23.20
lessons from Asian crisis 23.05–23.12, 23.20
debt sustainability *see* **debt sustainability**
enforcement of private debt contracts 19.03–19.07
self-enforcement 19.03–19.06
social or collective contract enforcement 19.07
third-party enforcement 19.03, 19.06
enforcement of sovereign debt contacts *see under* **sovereign default**
government default *see* **sovereign default**

debts (*cont.*):
household debt, systemic implications of 23.44–23.52
economic consequences of household debt 23.45
mortgage debt restructuring 23.47–23.51
mortgage industry views 23.51–23.52
legal construct, as 17.01
negotiable and assignable debt, distinguishing 17.15–17.16
restructuring debt
economic recovery, and *see* **economic recovery and debt restructuring**
sovereign debt *see* **sovereign debt restructuring**
rule of law, and *see under* **rule of law**
sovereign contingent liabilities *see* **sovereign contingent liabilities**
sovereign debt *see* **sovereign debt**
unenforceable *see* **odious debt**
default *see* **sovereign default**
defences 8.01–8.48
difficulties for foreign states in financial crisis 8.02, 8.04
vulture creditors 8.04
states avoiding creditor litigation 8.05
champerty *see* **champerty**
comity and act-of-state doctrine *see* **comity and act-of-state doctrine**
contract-based arguments 8.05, 8.30–8.37
litigation stays 8.38–8.45
sovereign immunity *see* **sovereign immunity**
deterring holdouts 2.16–2.25
exit consents *see* **exit consents**
immunizing debtor assets *see* **immunizing debtor assets**
see also **minimizing holdout creditors**
developing countries 15.25, 21.33
least developed countries
HIPC initiative *see* **Heavily Indebted Poor Countries (HIPC) initiative**
onerous debt 17.07–17.08, 17.38–17.41
sovereign debt restructuring, IMF role in 5.11
see also **Heavily Indebted Poor Countries (HIPC) initiative**
documentation improvements *see* **structural/ documentation improvements**
Dominican Republic
good faith negotiations 5.54
private inflows after restructuring 7.27

economic recovery and debt restructuring 23.01–23.78
challenges for economic policymakers after financial crisis 23.01–23.04
coordination procedures 23.36–23.40
cooperation agreements 23.38
crisis management groups 23.37
recovery and resolution plans/resolvability assessments 23.39
sharing of information 23.40
corporate debt restructuring in context of systemic crisis 23.05–23.20
corporate insolvency and 2008 crisis 23.13–23.20
lessons from Asian crisis 23.05–23.12, 23.20
harmonization of resolution frameworks 23.32–23.35
bailing-in unsecured creditors 23.34
broad resolution power 23.32
creditor safeguards 23.32
early intervention 23.32
harmonization of creditor priorities 23.35
non-discrimination 23.32
household debt, systemic implications of 23.44–23.52
economic consequences of household debt 23.45
mortgage debt restructuring 23.47–23.51
mortgage industry views 23.51–23.52
resolution of financial institution in cross-border context 23.21–22.43
coordination procedures 23.36–23.40
empowering national authorities to cooperate 23.30–23.31
financial burden sharing 23.41–23.43
harmonization of resolution frameworks 23.32–23.35
restructuring sovereign debt: an unresolved problem 23.53–23.76
how should restructuring happen/collective action 23.63–23.76
when should sovereigns restructure debt 23.55–23.62
Ecuador
attracting investment after default 1.23
debt restructuring 1.23, 1.30, 5.53, 22.34
exit consents 2.17
El Salvador 12.06
Elliott-Peru saga 4.17–4.26, 8.22–8.29
Enderlein, Henrik 3.51–3.52
Eurobonds 26.70–26.72
legal considerations 26.72
main proposals and key features 26.70–26.71
meaning of 26.70
European Central Bank (ECB) 5.63
economic assessments 19.70
ESM 22.60
euro area, efforts to reform 20.79
eurosystem financing: 'non-standard' measures by ECB 26.52–26.68
changes to valuation 'haircuts' 26.60
collateral requirements 26.60–26.62
covered bond purchases 26.63–26.64
enhanced credit support 26.57
key constraints on financing 26.54–26.55
legal regime 26.53–26.56
liquidity management measures 26.58
new eligible asset categories 26.60
OMTs 26.65–26.66, 26.88
reduction of credit rating threshold 26.60
secondary market sovereign debt purchases 26.65–26.68
waiver of credit rating threshold 26.60
Greek creditor, as 3.06, 3.07
lender of last resort, as 4.16, 5.63, 19.64
floor of support to preserve flow of private sector funds 16.25–16.32

see also **international lender of last resort**
liquidity assistance
euro areas periphery economies 20.73–20.78
manufacture of eligible collateral 18.16–18.17
methods of providing 18.15
monetary financing to governments forbidden 14.33
outright monetary transaction (OMTs) 16.25, 19.64, 20.80, 26.65–26.68
price stability mandate 26.55–26.56
moving beyond inflation-fighting mandate 16.50
public nature of ECB's portfolio 13.25
Securities Market Programme 3.06
avoiding taking losses on Greek exposure 19.73
troika, member of *see* **troika**
European Commission 5.63, 12.35
debt sustainability analysis 19.65, 19.70
ESM 22.60
European Convention of Human Rights (ECHR) 10.19
European Financial Stability Facility (EFSF) 1.17, 22.50
co-financing agreement with Greece 3.07
Greek restructuring: EFSF bills 3.32–3.40, 13.16
Ireland 20.12
legal considerations 26.43–26.45
nature of 22.42
Portugal 20.12
structure and operations 26.40–26.42
European Financial Stabilization Mechanism (EFSM) 22.42, 22.50
legal considerations 26.35–26.39
structure and operations 26.34
European Free Trade Area (EFTA) 15.20, 15.22, 15.23
European Stability Mechanism (ESM) 2.25, 5.63, 13.15–13.16, 22.36–22.69
CACs 5.38, 22.63
capital 22.49–22.50, 22.56
CJEU interpreting 13.45
critical analysis of 22.64–22.68
financing capacity 22.65
private lender funds 22.67
role of ESM with IMF's role 22.68
scope for action 22.66
dispute resolution 22.61
governing structure 22.51–22.54
ILOLR, and 16.19
IMF, and 22.68
IMF preferred creditor status 5.42
immunizing assets of an EAMS by Treaty add-on 22.74–22.76
legal considerations 26.49–26.51
nature of 22.45
'no bailout' clauses of Art 125 TFEU 5.63, 13.13–13.16
ESM loans not contradicting 13.15–13.16, 26.50–26.51
non-EAMS providing financial assistance 22.58–22.59
private creditors involved in providing relief 14.40
seniority of debt 20.81
structure and operations 26.46–26.48
Treaty establishing 5.38, 5.42, 22.44–22.46
modelled on IMF 5.63
use of 22.47–22.48
nature of financial assistance 22.55, 22.58
procedure for granting financial assistance 22.62
European Union
bailouts 1.17, 2.25
contingent liabilities, treatment of 18.11
euro introduction, effects of 22.39
Eurozone/European debt crisis *see* **Eurozone debt crisis and financial rescue**
Greek creditor, as 3.07
intra-EU BITS 12.35
monetization of government debt prohibited by Art 123 TFEU 5.63
'no bailout' clauses of Art 125 TFEU 5.63, 13.13–13.16
ESM loans not contradicting 13.15–13.16, 26.50–26.51
policy changes/waverings 5.63
restructuring in a monetary union
economic aspects *see* **monetary union, economic aspects of restructuring in**
legal aspects *see* **monetary union, legal aspects of restructuring in**
Stability and Growth Pact 20.69–20.71
debt sustainability, failure to strengthen 21.57, 26.14
enforcement failures 21.58
troika, member of *see* **troika**
Eurostat 26.19
sovereign contingent liabilities, treatment of 18.11, 18.22
Eurozone debt crisis and financial rescue 2.28, 7.13, 15.39–15.42, 22.38
Abaclat, implications of 12.33–12.44
background to the crisis 26.04–26.19
access to cheap funding increasing borrowing 26.10
bank losses migrating to public balance sheets 26.17–26.18
divergence of current account positions 26.08
fiscal deficits 26.14–26.15
lack of adequate oversight of banks 26.12
liquidity shortage in global financial markets 26.16
problems in EU banking sector 26.11, 26.13, 26.16
productivity differences between northern and southern economies 26.09
underlying problems coalescing 26.01, 26.07, 26.19
CACs 25.21–25.24
concentration risk 19.13–19.16
contagion risk 26.17–26.18, 26.21
little actual contagion 19.63–19.64
future financing measures: longer-term solution 26.69–26.75
EU deposit insurance and resolution funding 26.73–26.75
Eurobonds *see* **Eurobonds**
single currency, implications of 13.01, 26.04, 26.09
EMU design shaping financial rescue 26.21–26.22
stabilization measures and legal foundations 26.20–26.68
bilateral loans: Greece and Ireland 26.29–26.33

Eurozone debt crisis and financial rescue (*cont.*):
EFSF *see* **European Financial Stability Facility (EFSF)**
ERSM *see* **European Financial Stabilization Mechanism (EFSM)**
ESM *see* **European Stability Mechanism (ESM)**
eurosystem financing *see under* **European Central Bank (ECB)**
financial assistance under EU law 26.23–26.28
IMF's role 5.11, 26.20
initial responses 22.41–22.43
exit consents 2.17–2.25, 7.07
method 2.18–2.20
disadvantages of exchange offer/exit consent 25.08
exchange offer/exit consent 25.07–25.08
objective of defacing instruments 2.17
see also **minimizing holdout creditors**

financial crisis, global 5.11, 5.30, 5.57, 13.01, 20.01–20.02, 20.12, 23.01
economic recovery after *see* **economic recovery and debt restructuring**
explosion of sovereign-guaranteed bonds after 18.01, 18.12
little contagion after 19.63
Financial Stability Board 5.16
Key Attributes of Effective Resolution Regimes 23.28–23.30, 20.33–20.40
financial sweeteners 1.20–1.21, 1.35
France
AAA rated 18.13
involuntary legal subordination 4.05
pari passu clauses 4.28
freeriding *see* **holdouts**
Frieden, Jeff 7.11
Fuentes, Miguel 7.27

Gelpern, Anna 22.72
Germany 14.21
AAA rated 18.13
bailouts 5.63
bank secrecy 19.49
BITS 12.08, 12.36–12.37, 12.44
CACs 25.11
defaults 19.21, 19.22, 19.36, 19.63, 19.74
public debt share 14.24
globalization 19.47, 27.06, 27.12–27.13
Goodhart, Charles 5.60
government default *see* **sovereign default**
Greece
Abaclat decision, implications of 12.33–12.37
austerity measures 7.10, 13.02
BITS 12.36–12.37, 12.38, 12.44
CACs 3.12–3.14, 3.31, 3.41–3.47, 3.48, 12.33
co-financing 1.17, 3.07, 3.38–3.39
concentration risk 19.14
creditor committee 3.06–3.07
creditor incentives/success of restructuring 3.24–3.53
collective action 3.41–3.47
disorderly default without participation 3.25, 3.26
EFSF bills and de facto seniority upgrade as carrots 3.32–3.40
freerider problem, mechanisms for dealing with 3.27–3.31
private investors experiencing heavy losses 14.39
threatening holdouts 3.48–3.53
debt restructuring 3.01–3.55, 5.48, 12.01
defaults 19.22, 19.36, 19.63, 19.74, 21.19
EU loan 26.29–26.33
legal considerations 26.31–26.33
structure and operations 26.29
euro's existence threatened by sovereign debt problems 5.30
fiscal policies, inadequacies in 26.14
GDP-linked warrant 1.34
haircuts on creditors, size of 3.01, 13.03
holdouts 3.22
paid in full 2.36, 3.23
IMF, and *see under* **International Monetary Fund (IMF)**
'invitation', components of 3.09–3.12
Lee Buchheit's role 3.02
legal issues *see* **Greece debt restructuring, legal issues in**
loans flouting euro's founding treaty 16.50
maturity mismatches 21.34–21.41
outcome of the restructuring 3.18–3.23
ownership of outstanding debt 3.05
participation level 3.22
polarized society, as 19.45
public debt, home bias in holdings of 14.21, 14.23
'reprofiling' of Greek bonds 13.03
restructuring process 3.04, 20.12
sovereign bonds/guarantees 18.13
debt restructuring, and 18.22–18.23
tax evasion 19.48
terms and conditions 3.08–3.17
Greece debt restructuring, legal issues in 13.20–13.33
Greek PSI 13.03–13.05, 13.23–13.24, 19.81
negative pledge clauses/keeping bonds as central bank collateral 13.21–13.22
participation in public sector involvement, against 13.25–13.28
consistency of stance 13.28
monetary financing considerations 13.27
public nature of ECB's portfolio 13.25
public sector involvement meant to address private sector 13.26
participation in the exchange, in favour of 13.29–13.33
bonds fungibility 13.29
jurisdictional limits 13.32–13.33
no preferred creditor status 13.30
subordination 13.31
voluntary Eurosystem participation in CAC process 13.28–13.33
Grenada
restructuring and contingent liabilities 18.21
gross domestic product (GDP)
benchmark of return to financial health, as 1.31, 1.34
GDP-linked warrants 1.34
ratios of public debt to GDP 21.45–21.48

guarantees *see under* **sovereign contingent liabilities**
Gulati, Mita 4.32, 15.01–15.04, 22.34
CACs 22.31, 22.34, 25.05, 25.15
holdouts 25.05
odious debts 17.03

Haiti 19.27
Hale, Galina 7.27
Haseler, Sonke 25.13
Hausmann, Ricardo 20.98
Heavily Indebted Poor Countries (HIPC) initiative 5.23, 6.01–6.37, 7.07, 19.27
debt relief, amounts of 6.30
debt sustainability analyses 6.03, 6.08, 6.35–6.37
Enhanced HIPC debt initiative 6.01, 6.12–6.24
developments banks providing debt relief 6.23–6.24, 19.27
floating completion points 6.14
IDA responsible for providing debt relief 6.21–6.22
increasing eligibility 6.13
new proposals 6.12–6.13
poverty reduction objective 6.15–6.16
sunset clauses extensions 6.20
'topping up' debt relief at completion point 6.17–6.19
guiding principles of HIPC 6.02
initial HIPC debt initiative 6.03–6.11
adjustment programmes 6.04–6.06
aim of framework 6.01
completion point 6.03
creditor participation in assistance 6.01, 6.09
debt sustainability analysis/decision point 6.03, 6.08
eligibility 6.08
IMF assistance at completion point 6.10
introduced 6.01
largely completed 6.29–6.32
process 6.07
sunset clauses 6.06
total cost of debt relief to creditors 6.31
Multilateral Debt Relief Initiative (MDRI) 6.01, 6.25–6.28
criteria for debt cancellation 6.28
Millennium Development Goals, supporting 6.25
total cost of debt cancellation for creditors 6.32
odious debt; UK legislation 17.02, 17.07–17.08, 17.38–17.41
placing limits on enforceability of foreign sovereign debt 17.39
scope of legislation 17.40–17.41
ongoing challenges 6.33
SDRM 22.21–22.22
holdouts
discouraging *see under* **minimizing holdout creditors**
holdout creditor problem 2.03–2.08, 3.27, 25.03–25.06
CACs *see* **collective action clauses (CACs)**
emotions about holdouts 2.05
incentives to holdout 5.26
intercreditor equity 2.06
litigation, drawbacks of 2.08
money/financial predicates 2.04
overestimated 22.02
publicity, adverse effects of 2.07
leverage from *pari passu* clauses *see* ***pari passu* clauses**
minimizing *see* **minimizing holdout creditors**
spectre of holdouts 2.09
tending to be repaid in full 3.27
Hungary 23.13

Iceland
banking crisis (2008) 15.15–15.23, 15.33, 15.41
causes 15.15–15.16, 15.18, 15.22
failed recovery by UK/Netherlands 15.19–15.22
restructuring the banks 15.17
debt repayment referendum 7.11
immunity *see* **Bank for International Settlements; central bank immunity; sovereign immunity**
immunizing debtor assets 2.23–2.25, 2.35
ESM, financial support from 2.25
Iraq 2.23–2.24
see also **minimizing holdout creditors**
indemnities 18.07
see also **sovereign contingent liabilities**
Indonesia 5.55, 23.05
bailout 5.25
currency crisis 15.10
default 20.16
insolvencies, state *see* **corporate bankruptcy law and state insolvencies**
Inter-American Development Bank 6.24
International Centre for Settlement of Investment Disputes (ICSID) 12.01
enforcement of arbitral awards 12.05, 12.17
directly enforceable 12.16
investor-state arbitration 12.16
International Development Association (IDA)
HIPC initiative 6.08, 6.10, 6.21, 6.23, 6.26, 21.27
international financial institutions *see under* **international organizations**
international investor agreements (IIAs) 12.08–12.13
clauses excluding/limiting protection of sovereign debt 12.45–12.51
defaulting sovereigns 12.10–12.13
denial of benefits clauses 12.40
excusing events 12.12, 12.13
first BITS 12.08
investor, definition of 12.40
need to establish more than breach of contract 12.10, 12.12, 12.13
protecting eligible investments 12.09–12.10
international lender of last resort 16.01–16.55
fixed rules for the future, need for 16.05–16.07
floor of support to preserve flow of private sector funds 16.21–16.32
floor of support to restore private sector investment flows 16.33–16.41
factors creating the leverage 16.39
liquidity demands, monitoring 16.40
floor of support to underpin an orderly restructuring 16.42–16.48
IMF, as *see under* **International Monetary Fund (IMF)**

international lender of last resort (*cont.*):
incentives, discipline and control of risk 16.15–16.20
ILOLR, coalitions of government/central banks forming 16.19
official sector floor of support 16.16–16.20
repeated interventions, effects of 16.04
third party in a two-party game 16.08–16.14
towards a credible international lender of last resort 16.49–16.55
International Monetary Fund (IMF) 1.24, 2.27, 5.01–5.64, 7.07
bailout programmes, participating in 5.02
conditionality 5.15, 5.19–5.21, 23.57
financial assistance consistent with Articles of Agreement 5.39
logic of 5.47
meaning of 5.19
purposes 5.20
debt sustainability analysis 5.39, 19.65, 19.66–19.70, 21.52
approach to 19.66
Cyprus 19.69
Debt Sustainability Framework of World Bank/IMF 6.35–6.37
Greece 5.02, 5.32, 5.39, 19.67–19.69
Portugal 19.67
economic reform/adjustment programmes 23.10, 23.15, 23.57–23.58
see also **economic recovery and debt restructuring**
exchange rates 5.07, 5.09, 5.12
flexible 5.13
government-controlled 5.13
Financial Sector Assessment Programmes 23.06
functions 5.11
financial assistance 5.14, 5.15, 5.17, 5.39
regulatory rule-making role 5.16
surveillance 5.12, 5.14, 5.15, 5.18
technical assistance 5.14
Greece 3.16, 21.40, 23.15
debt sustainability analysis 5.02, 5.32, 5.39, 19.67–19.69
Greek creditor, as 3.07
reports on 5.02, 5.32, 5.39, 21.39
HIPC initiative *see* **Heavily Indebted Poor Countries (HIPC) initiative**
history 5.03–5.13
Articles of Agreement 5.06, 5.07, 5.09, 5.11, 5.12, 5.14
establishment 5.03
least developed countries 5.11
mandate to maintain 'oar value regime' 5.06–5.08, 5.10
new roles 5.10
par value regime, abandonment of 5.09–5.10, 5.12
international lender of last resort, as 4.16, 5.17, 5.22, 5.55–5.63
'bailout packages' 5.56
compared with central bank as lenders of last resort 5.59–5.60
drawbacks to official sector bailout packages 5.61–5.62
emergence as de facto lender of last resort 5.55
Flexible Credit Line 5.57
Precautionary and Liquidity Line 5.58
resources no longer sufficient for global marketplace 16.19
SDRM 22.17–22.20
Supplemental Reserve Facility 5.56
mortgage debt restructuring 23.49–23.50
preferred creditor status 5.02, 5.40–5.48, 20.81–20.82
'burden sharing' concept 5.41, 5.46
ESM Treaty 5.42
fundamental to Fund's financial responsibilities 5.44
justification for 5.43
members giving priority to Fund obligations 5.45
role of IMF as 'referee' 5.47
private sector debt, and 5.02
SDRM proposal *see* **sovereign debt restructuring mechanism (SDRM)**
sovereign debt, and *see* **International Monetary Fund and sovereign debt**
tools 5.14–5.22
conditionality 5.15, 5.19–5.21
surveillance and assistance 5.12, 5.14, 5.15, 5.17, 5.18
national tools 5.15
International Monetary Fund and sovereign debt 5.23–5.63
creditor litigation against sovereign debtors 5.28
debt sustainability analysis *see under* **International Monetary Fund (IMF)**
financial assistance
consistent with Articles of Agreement 5.3
incentives to help countries resolve problems 22.04
remedying temporary problems 5.39
IMF lending into arrears policy 5.49–5.54
burden sharing 5.41, 5.46
conditions for Fund support on case-by-case basis 5.51
member's good faith effort to reach agreement 5.52–5.53
modification of arrears policy 5.50
not to lend into arrears policy 5.49
rules for conducting negotiations with creditors 5.53–5.54
IMF paper on sovereign debt restructuring 5.31
IMF preferred creditor status *see under* **International Monetary Fund (IMF)**
international lender of last resort *see under* **International Monetary Fund (IMF)**
periods of sovereign debt management
1982–1985/IMF as 'master of ceremonies' 5.24
1990–1993/Brady initiative 5.25
2000– restructuring sovereign bonds in orderly fashion 5.26
sovereign debt crises, problem with 5.29–5.30
statutory and contractual solutions 5.33–5.40
ad hoc resolution criticized as inefficient 5.34
Articles, creative interpretation of 5.36
four policy options 5.33
SDRM adoption, consideration of 5.35
voluntary 'code of conduct' 5.37
stricter assessment of debt sustainability before support provided 5.32

troika, member of *see* **troika**
types of debt crises 5.23
international organizations
BIS 10.09
independence 10.19
immunities 10.07, 10.19
absolute/full immunity 10.06, 10.19–10.21, 10.25
immunity from jurisdiction and execution 10.11
international financial institutions (IFIs) 7.01
creditors, as 7.05
financial crisis *see under* **economic recovery and debt restructuring**
HIPC debt initiative 6.12, 6.15, 6.25
immunities 10.07
national courts not competent to review 10.19
Iraq 2.23–2.24, 2.25, 22.69–22.73
Ireland
banking crisis 15.40–15.42
OSI 19.81
UK financial support 22.58
BITS 12.38
EU loan 26.29–26.33
legal considerations 26.31–26.33
structure and operations 26.30
fiscal deficits 26.15
IMF, and 20.12
loans flouting euro's founding treaty 16.50
mortgage foreclosure processes 19.73
public debt, home bias in holdings of 14.21
sovereign bonds/guarantees 18.13
Italy 20.12
BITS 12.38, 12.45
mortgage foreclosure processes 19.73
public debt 19.68, 20.20
sovereign bonds/guarantees 18.13
tax evasion 19.48

Japan
downgrading of debt 15.05
government debt 15.25
Jefferson, Thomas 28.06

Kazakhstan 20.64–20.67
keepwells 18.07
see also **sovereign contingent liabilities**
Keynes, John Maynard 5.04, 5.05
Kopf, Christian 14.36
Korea 5.55, 23.05
bailout 5.25
banking crisis (1997) 15.10–15.14, 15.33
outcome 15.12, 15.13
poor decisions by banks as cause 15.13
restructuring 15.11
Kreuger, Anne 2.27

Lastra, Rosa 13.16, 22.18, 22.32
Latin America 20.22
credit boom 20.16
debt crisis 3.05, 7.11, 7.13, 7.19
Latvia 23.13
League of Nations 12.03, 12.04, 12.54–12.56
least developed countries
HIPC initiative *see* **Heavily Indebted Poor Countries (HIPC) initiative**
onerous debt 17.07–17.08, 17.38–17.41
sovereign debt restructuring, IMF role in 5.11
Liechtenstein 19.49
liquidity 19.54 19.64
illiquidity 19.56–19.63
litigation defences, sovereign debt *see* **defences**
Lokey, Houlihan 18.14
London Club 3.04, 5.34, 7.07
longer-term consequences of sovereign debt restructuring 7.01–7.31
avoiding conflation in key terms 7.04–7.07
future capital market borrowing 7.17–7.23
excusable default, idea of 7.21
existence/degree of impact of restructuring 7.19–7.20, 7.23
higher cost of accessing external capital 7.22, 7.23
reputational judgments 7.18
restructuring affecting ability to borrow 7.17–7.18
longer-run ramifications of debt restructuring 7.15–7.28
broader domestic effects 7.28
externally imposed economic cost for payment interruption 7.15
future capital market borrowing 7.17–7.23
trade and capital flows to private sector 7.24–7.27
portrayal of consequences as negative 7.01–7.02
possible consequences of selective emphasis 7.08–7.14
austerity measures, consequences of 7.10
domestic distributional effects from avoiding/delaying restructuring 7.11
'emphasis framing effects' 7.08, 7.14
emphasis on cost and avoided/delayed restructuring 7.09
systemic distributional effect 7.13
transnational distributional effects 7.12, 7.13
trade and capital flows to private sector 7.24–7.27
creditor countries imposing explicit sanctions 7.25
distinctions between effects during crisis and longer term 7.26
flow of capital to private enterprise 7.27
loss reinstatement features 1.22–1.24
low income countries, debt relief for *see* **Heavily Indebted Poor Countries (HIPC) initiative**
Luxembourg 15.23

Martinez, Jose Vicente 7.26
maturity mismatches and high coupons *see under* **sovereign debt**
Mexico 5.55, 20.05
debt restructuring 20.23
bailout 5.25
Brady bonds 1.29–1.30
IMF's role 5.02, 5.11
value recovery rights 1.29–1.30
default 5.24
maturity mismatches 21.28–21.30

MFN clauses 12.48–12.50
minimizing holdout creditors
holdout creditor problem *see under* **holdouts**
implications of offering inducements 1.35–1.43
'floats all boats' argument 1.35–1.36
futility 1.38–1.42
political dimension 1.43
utility 1.37
infectious nature of holdout behaviour 2.36
negotiated workouts
creditor participation rate goal 1.40–1.42
creditors intending legal action 1.08, 1.39, 1.41
holdouts, nature of 1.08–1.10
importance of minimizing holdout creditors 1.10
logic of 1.08
retail creditors not agreeing need for debt relief 1.09
sovereigns uniquely vulnerable to/protected from creditors 1.02–1.06
resulting in negotiated sovereign debt workouts 1.07–1.10
spectre of holdouts leading to delays 2.09
techniques to discourage holdouts 2.10–2.34
binding holdouts *see* **binding holdouts**
deterring holdouts *see* **deterring holdouts**
exit consents *see* **exit consents**
frightening holdouts 2.11–2.15, 2.16
immunizing debtor assets *see* **immunizing debtor assets**
index of government coerciveness 3.51–3.52
techniques to encourage creditor participation 1.11–1.34
assurances of parity of treatment *see* **parity of treatment**
financial sweeteners 1.20–1.21, 1.35
loss reinstatement features 1.22–1.24
menu of restructuring options 1.13–1.14
more creditor-friendly restructuring terms generally not possible 1.11
structural improvements *see* **structural/documentation improvements**
value/effectiveness of 1.36, 1.37, 1.39–1.42
value recovery rights *see* **value recovery rights**
monetary union, economic aspects of restructuring in 14.01–14.54
sovereign debt in a monetary union 14.10–14.20
strengthening financial market resilience 14.30–14.51
basis for determining capital requirements for sovereign debt 14.41–14.51
euro not controlled by individual state, implications of 14.35–14.37
who holds sovereign debt in Europe 14.21–14.29
home bias 14.21–14.23
monetary union, legal aspects of restructuring in 13.01–13.52
differentiation vis-à-vis other sovereign debt restructurings 13.06–13.19
impossibility of being bailed out by other Union members 13.12–13.16
impossibility of devaluing the currency 13.07–13.08
impossibility of imposing restrictions on movements of capital 13.09
impossibility of monetizing the sovereign's debt 13.10–13.11
impossibility of redenominating sovereign debt 13.17–13.18
increased risk of contagion within members of currency area 13.19
Greece debt restructuring *see* **Greece debt restructuring, legal issues in**
legal framework for debt issuance by participating states in EMU 13.34–13.46
CACs 13.35–13.46
statutory framework for debt restructuring in regional monetary union 13.47–13.49
necessary elements 13.48
Multilateral Debt Relief Initiative *see* **Heavily Indebted Poor Countries (HIPC) initiative**

national authorities 23.30–23.31
National Bankruptcy Conference 23.50
negotiated workouts *see under* **minimizing holdout creditors**
New York Convention 12.05, 12.16
Nigeria 1.30
NML Capital Ltd v. Argentina 11.06–11.44, 23.68–23.72
background 11.06
implications for sovereign debt markets 11.04–11.05, 11.09–11.27
outlier, *NML Capital* as 11.27–11.42
Argentina as uniquely defiant debtor 11.35–11.39
court's relevance in sovereign debt litigation 11.29, 11.33
straddling border of law and politics 11.30–11.34
unique remedy for a unique case 11.40–11.42
pari passu clauses 4.01, 4.38–4.49
chaos in the market 4.46–4.49
contract pathology, *pari passu* as 11.21–11.26
different versions of *pari passu* over time 11.20
historical context 11.14–11.17
prevalence of Argentina's version of *pari passu* 11.18–11.20
promise not to restructure, as 11.10–11.13
third parties, enforcement against 11.07–11.08
North American Free Trade Agreement (NAFTA) 12.46–12.47

odious debt 17.01–17.44
assignee of the debt, position of 17.09–17.18
assignee in no better position than original creditor 17.17
fraudulent accessory doctrine 17.09–17.11
improperly advanced debt to good faith assignee 17.12–17.16
negotiable and assignable debt, distinguishing 17.15–17.16
private law providing means of challenging 17.09
properly advanced debt 17.18–17.19
suspecting wrongdoing 17.14
Donegal International Ltd v. Zambia 17.20–17.37
facts 17.20–17.33
lessons from 17.34–17.37
prompting UK legislation 17.38–17.39

meaning 17.04
no doctrine of international law vitiating odious debt 17.06
states' responsibility to succeed to predecessors' debts 17.01, 17.05, 17.43
statutory unenforceability 17.02
UK Debt Relief (Developing Countries) Act 17.02, 17.07–17.08, 17.38–17.41
placing limits on enforceability of foreign sovereign debt 17.39
scope of legislation 17.40–17.41
US defences addressing odious debt 17.06, 17.09–17.10

Pakistan 5.53, 22.34
Panizza, Ugo 7.22, 7.26, 7.27, 20.98
Papaioannou, Michael 7.22
Paraguay 19.75
***pari passu* clauses** 4.01–4.52, 5.27
concise language 4.03
contract pathology, *pari passu* as 11.21–11.26
Elliott-Peru saga 4.17–4.26
equal payment 4.15–4.16
classic narrow interpretation 5.15
new broad interpretation 4.16
prevalence of Argentina's version of *pari passu* 11.18–11.20
equal ranking 4.02–4.09
injunctive relief 23.67
migration from private to sovereign debt instruments 4.09
NML Capital Ltd see ***NML Capital Ltd v. Argentina***
origins 4.04, 4.32–4.45, 4.52
different versions of *pari passu* over time 11.20
historical context 11.14–11.17
nineteenth century 4.34
mid twentieth century 4.35
late twentieth century 4.36
promise not to restructure, as 11.10–11.13
targeting third parties 4.27–4.31
pari passu clauses turned into sharing clauses 4.28
Paris Club 4.29, 5.34, 6.03, 7.07, 13.12
Cologne terms for debt relief 6.13
Comparable Treatment Clause 1.26
HIPC *see* **Heavily Indebted Poor Countries (HIPC) initiative**
IMF's preferred creditor status 5.41
Naples terms 6.03
SDRM 22.16
parity of treatment 1.25–1.27
earmarking of assets 4.10–4.14
holdouts, effects on 1.27
intercreditor equity 2.06
most favoured creditor provisions 1.27
Paris Club Comparable Treatment Clause 1.26
rateable treatment of similarly situated creditors, principle of 2.37
reasons for demanding 1.25–1.26, 2.05
Peru 19.75
Portes, Richard 22.32
Portugal
BITS 12.38
government debt 15.26
IMF, and 19.67, 20.12, 23.15
loans flouting euro's founding treaty 16.50
OSI 19.81
sovereign bonds/guarantees 18.13

Rose, Andrew 7.26
rule of law
contract sanctity/debt enforcement 8.02, 17.02, 17.10, 19.03, 22.76
odious debt 17.05
courts, and 11.44
crisis, in 16.50
default and rule-of-law externalities 19.19–19.22
long-term social cost of weakening rule of law 19.21
rule of law harmed by sovereign default 19.20
principle of not too much law 24.02
Russia 5.25, 20.22
credit boom 20.16
debt exchange 3.30, 7.13
default 7.13, 20.16
Tsarist debt repudiated 7.21, 19.74
IMF's role in resolving financial crisis 5.11
maturity mismatches 21.31–21.32

Sachs, Jeffrey 22.06
St Kitts and Nevis
debt restructuring 1.18, 1.24
discouraging holdouts 2.13
good faith negotiations 5.54
Sandleris, Guido 7.26
Saravia, Diego 7.27
Schwarcz, Steven L. 22.06
Seychelles
debt restructuring 1.18, 1.24
good faith negotiations 5.54
Sgard, Jérôme 22.33
Social Science Research Network 15.01
South Korea *see* **Korea**
sovereign arbitration 12.01–12.56
arbitration clauses in sovereign debt contracts 12.02–12.07
current practice 12.05–12.07
general 12.02
historic use 12.03–12.04
investor-state arbitration of sovereign debt disputes 12.08–12.51
Abaclat decision *see* ***Abaclat v. Argentine Republic***
background 12.08–12.17
IIA clauses excluding/limiting protection of sovereign debt 12.45–12.51
IIAs 12.08–12.13
investor-state arbitration 12.14–12.17
sovereign contingent liabilities 18.01–18.51
camouflaging debt 18.01–18.02, 18.09
contingent obligations, balance sheet treatment 18.09–18.11, 18.15
Eurostat approach 18.11, 18.22
contingent obligations, contingent nature of 18.09
contingent obligations, structure 18.09

sovereign contingent liabilities (*cont.*):
currency mismatches, contingent liabilities and 21.12–21.23
explicit sovereign guarantees 18.04–18.05
explosion in 2008–12 of sovereign-guaranteed bonds 18.12–18.17
bonds/guarantees for countries in eurozone crisis 18.13
manufacturing eligible collateral for liquidity programmes 18.16–18.17
reason for rise 18.15
less-than-voluntary offers in restructuring 18.36–18.50
CACs 18.37–18.44
governing law 18.45–18.48
waiver of immunity 18.49–18.50
precedents 18.18–18.23
earlier sovereign debt restructuring 18.20
Greece 18.22–18.23
Grenada 18.21
need to address significant contingent obligation 18.19
restructurer's dilemma 18.24–18.32
creditor of guaranteed bond, position of 18.30
difficulties of dealing with contingent liabilities 18.31
dishonour guarantee/attempt to restructure liability 18.24, 18.28
honour guarantee if called 18.24, 18.27
no call on guarantee, hope for 18.24, 18.25
voluntary rollover of debt at maturity 18.24, 18.26
restructuring sovereign contingent obligations 18.33–18.50
CACs 18.37–18.44
less-than-voluntary offers 18.36–18.50
voluntary offers 18.34–18.35
risk of contingent liabilities eventuating 21.04, 21.12, 26.15
sovereign comfort 18.03–18.08
comfort letters 18.07
explicit sovereign guarantees 18.04–18.05
implicit sovereign assurances 18.06
implicit sovereign guarantees 18.08
indemnities 18.07
keepwells 18.07
partial guarantees 8.07
sovereign debt 21.01–21.59
amount of public debt that should be issued 21.02–21.03
banking crises, and *see* **banking crises and sovereign debt**
budgetary outcomes/deficits 21.07–21.11
deficit bias, reasons for 21.10–21.11
deficit as the norm 21.07–21.09
CACs, in 25.10–25.16
see also **collective action clauses (CACs)**
currency mismatches, contingent liabilities and 21.12–21.23
disintermediated 7.05
domestic debt 14.02–14.05
financial element 28.15–28.19
financing expenditure from public debt issuance 21.01
foreign-held debt 14.06–14.07
IIA clauses excluding/limiting protection of 12.45–12.51
IMF, and *see* **International Monetary Fund and sovereign debt**
indicators of debt sustainability 21.44–21.54
anticipating market perception of sovereign default risk 21.54
calculation of primary fiscal outcome 21.49
correlation of fiscally responsible behaviour with public debt size 21.49
fiscal forecasts/alternative scenarios 21.50–21.51
public/private sector foreign debt to export earnings 21.44
ratios of public debt to GDP 21.45–21.48
intermediated 7.05
legal element 28.10–28.14
litigation defences *see* **defences**
macro drivers of demand for 20.19–20.23
management/structure 14.01–14.08
maturity mismatches and high coupons 21.24–21.43
fiscal prudence, importance of 21.41–21.43
Greece 21.34–21.41
higher fiscal deficits/public debt, effects of 21.42
Mexico 21.28–21.30
Russia 21.31–21.32
monetary union, in 14.10–14.20
moral element 28.03–28.09
nature/meaning of 7.05
odious debt *see* **odious debt**
political element 28.20–28.25
problems, causes of 21.04–21.05
sovereign debt Laffer curve 19.23–19.25
sovereign debt markets *see* **sovereign debt markets**
sovereign immunity waiver *see under* **sovereign immunity**
sovereigns/sovereign borrowers *see* **sovereigns/ sovereign borrowers**
straddling border of law and politics 11.30–11.34
sovereign debt markets 20.01–20.112
emerging market self-insurance /rise of China 20.24–20.28
Europe, microcosm of crises as 20.68–20.85
financial weapons of mass destruction/ CDSs 20.57–20.67
hostages to benchmarks and ratings 20.106–20.108
lessons learned, ignored, forgotten 20.86–20.87
debt management 20.87
macro stabilization policies 20.87
self-insurance 20.87
limits of conflict resolution 20.100–20.105
macro drivers of demand for sovereign debt 20.19–20.23
'original sin'
apparent end of 20.35–20.42
fallen saints of 20.88–20.99
meaning of 20.36
sovereign borrowing: last thirty years 20.11–20.18
sovereign borrowers, emerging markets as 20.04–20.05

surfing the China wave 20.29–20.34
sovereign debt demand dynamic 20.43–20.56
banks' role, changing 20.52–20.56
emerging markets central bank as lenders 20.46
foreign ownership of sovereign debt, increase in 20.50
institutional investors, advent of 20.49
pension schemes 20.51
sovereign wealth funds 20.47
sovereign debt restructuring
basic mechanisms of 7.06, 24.05–24.08
CACs *see* **collective action clauses (CACs)**
consequences of *see* **longer-term consequences of sovereign debt restructuring**
contingent obligations *see under* **sovereign contingent liabilities**
economic recovery, and *see* **economic recovery and debt restructuring**
exit consents *see* **exit consents**
holdout problem overestimated 22.02
IMF's SDRM proposal *see* **sovereign debt restructuring mechanism (SDRM)**
monetary union, restructuring in
economic aspects *see* **monetary union, economic aspects of restructuring in**
legal aspects *see* **monetary union, legal aspects of restructuring in**
nature of 7.07
restructuring sovereign debt: an unresolved problem 23.53–23.76
how should restructuring happen/collective action 23.63–23.76
when should sovereign restructure debt 23.55–23.62
see also **corporate bankruptcy law and state insolvencies**
sovereign debt restructuring mechanism (SDRM) 2.26, 2.27–2.28, 2.35, 5.01, 5.27, 12.53, 12.55, 22.04–22.35, 27.66
backdoor SDRM: UNSC resolutions 22.70–22.73
evolution of IMF proposal and key features 22.13
HIPCs, special treatment of 22.21–22.22
holdout problem, addressing 23.74–23.75
inclusion of other creditors 22.14–22.16
preferred status of Fund 22.17–22.20
shelving of proposal 22.32–22.33, 23.75
IMF proposal
features of SDRM, initial 22.10
initial consideration by IMF 22.05
key objectives on which to build formal SDRM 22.09
objectives of SDRM 22.07–22.08
rateable treatment of similarly situated creditors 2.37
twin track mechanism 22.07
renewed interest in concept 2.28, 22.06
shortcomings and criticisms of SDRM 22.23–22.35
benefit of 22.30–22.31
opposition to 22.29
practical difficulties in implementing SDRM 22.23–22.28
sovereign default 19.01–19.82
default, meaning of 19.01
default and sovereign debt Laffer curve 19.23–19.25
differences between sovereign and private default, effects of 19.11–19.25
default and sovereign debt Laffer curve 19.23–19.25
financial stability and macroeconomic externalities 19.12–19.22
timing of default 19.76–19.79
effects of default 19.02, 19.10, 19.12–19.21, 19.26
enforcement of private debt contracts 19.03–19.07
self-enforcement 19.03–19.06
social or collective contract enforcement 19.07
third-party enforcement 19.03, 19.06
financial stability and macroeconomic externalities 19.12–19.22
contagion and concentration risk 19.12–19.18
rule-of-law externalities 19.19–19.22
political economy of when/how to default 19.71–19.79
political considerations in defaults 19.72
recovery rates after sovereign default high 19.74–19.75
rules of the game changing 19.72, 19.73
timing of default 19.76–19.79
reasons why governments default 19.26–19.70
arithmetic of fiscal sustainability 19.28–19.35
choice aspect of default 19.02, 19.26–19.27, 21.06
demand for public spending, growing 19.44
feasibility of sustainable fiscal-financial-monetary policy 19.50–19.53
globalization 19.47
historical sovereign risk/default 19.36–19.38
liquidity 19.54–19.64
political polarization 19.45
politics of debt sustainability analysis 19.65–19.70
social capital, erosion of 19.46
taxation/evasion 19.38–19.43, 19.46–19.49
types of countries choosing default 19.21–19.22
self-enforcement of sovereign debt contracts 19.08–19.10
sovereign immunity 5.28
central bank immunity *see* **central bank immunity**
principle of 8.05, 8.07, 24.17
special immunity status of foreign state property 1.05
restrictive theory of sovereign immunity 1.05, 5.28, 8.08
absolute state immunity abandoned 11.28
traditional state immunity 10.06
acta iure gestionis 5.28, 10.06, 10.21
acta jure imperii 5.28, 10.06, 10.21
US 2.22, 8.05–8.10
arbitral awards 12.05
exceptions 8.05, 8.09–8.10
foreign states having almost absolute immunity 8.07
FSIA 8.09–8.10, 8.12, 8.48, 9.01, 9.12–9.18
sovereign debt litigation 8.10
'Tate Letter'/restrictive theory 8.08, 8.09
waiver for sovereign debt instruments 1.15, 2.18, 5.28, 8.10, 11.01, 11.33
immunity of local assets 24.15
sovereign guarantees, in 18.49–18.50

sovereigns/sovereign borrowers
arbitration *see* **sovereign arbitration**
assets held abroad having special immunity 1.05
assurances, implicit 18.06
contingent liabilities *see* **sovereign contingent liabilities**
default *see* **sovereign default**
guarantees *see under* **sovereign contingent liabilities**
meaning of 'sovereign' 19.08
national bankruptcy codes, not subject to 1.03, 8.04
'restrictive' theory of sovereignty 1.05, 5.28
sovereign debt *see* **sovereign debt**
sovereign default *see* **sovereign default**
sovereign immunity *see* **sovereign immunity**
state insolvency *see* **corporate bankruptcy law and state insolvencies**
straddling border of law and politics 11.30–11.34
uniquely shielded from creditors 1.02, 1.04–1.06, 11.02, 19.01
uniquely vulnerable to creditors 1.02, 1.03, 8.04
Spain 20.12
BITS 12.38
fiscal deficits 26.15
IMF, and 20.12
involuntary legal subordination 4.06
loans flouting euro's founding treaty 16.50
mortgage foreclosure processes 19.73
public debt, home bias in holdings of 14.21
sovereign bonds/guarantees 18.13
special immunities *see* **Bank for International Settlements; central bank immunity; sovereign immunity**
state insolvencies and bankruptcy law *see* **corporate bankruptcy law and state insolvencies**
state-owned enterprises 18.09
legal personality distinct from the sovereign 1.05, 24.16
structural/documentation improvements 1.15–1.19
co-financing features *see* **co-financing**
documentation improvements 1.15, 1.19, 1.35
full collateralization of principal 1.15
governing law shift to foreign governing law 1.15, 1.19, 3.31, 3.37
instruments offering better protection from future default 3.30
listing new instruments 1.15
partial guarantee of new debt instruments 1.15, 1.18
sovereign immunity, broader waiver of 1.15
tighter financial covenants 1.15
use of new instruments in programmes 1.15
Sturzenegger, Federico 7.15, 7.27
Switzerland
banking sector 15.23
BIS Headquarters Agreement/base 10.08, 10.18, 10.20, 10.22, 10.25
fiscal rules/budget targets 21.56
international organizations based in Switzerland 10.20
tax haven, as 19.49
Taylor, John B. 22.31
Thailand 5.55, 23.05
bailout 5.25
currency crisis 15.10
Third World debt crisis 15.34–15.38
delay in principal reduction 15.38
origins 15.35
policy change on loss allocation 15.37
Thompson, Robert B. 17.03
Tomz, Michael 7.11
Trebesch, Christoph 7.22, 7.26
troika
conditionality 26.48, 13.16
Cyprus 19.19, 19.69
Greece 19.67, 19.69
programme forecasts 19.67
members 5.63, 19.70, 21.40
streamlining process 5.32

Ukraine 23.13
debt restructuring 5.53, 22.34
UNCTAD principles on responsible sovereign lending and borrowing 5.37, 27.01–27.72
need for global principles to promote responsible sovereign financing 27.06–27.18
changing composition of debt 27.13
deregulation encouraging excessive risk taking 27.09
herd behaviour for risk taking 27.09–27.11, 27.13
increased public debt 27.07–27.08
principles tackling global debt problem 27.19–27.31
debts to be honoured 27.28
disclosure and publication of information 27.24
due diligence standards 27.22
lenders to debt restructure in good faith 27.29
management strategies and monitoring systems 27.24
post-disbursement audits 27.24
protection of public interest 27.25–27.26
sanctions, transactions must not violate 27.27
transparent decision-making 27.33
progression of international law, principles in 27.57–27.72
consensus building, importance of 27.60
fair laws exerting compliance pull on states 27.59
legalization process, principles initiating 27.63–27.64
optimal liability, seeking to approach 27.59
state consent 27.62
strength of the soft law approach 27.65
representation, consultation and deliberation 27.32–27.36
soft law facilitating endorsement and implementation 27.37–27.46
advantages of soft law instruments 27.39
international law backing certain of the principles 27.44
opportunity costs of compliance, showing 27.41
principles as general principles of law 27.45
reputational advantages 27.42
UN role in economic global agenda and the principles 27.47–27.56
increasing role for UN 27.50–27.54

United Kingdom (UK)
act-of-state doctrine 8.12
CACs 2.30, 2.31, 25.10
champerty 8.21
financial crisis, response to 20.72
IMF, and 5.05
involuntary legal subordination 4.05
Ireland, financial support to 22.58
odious debt *see* **odious debt**
pari passu clauses 4.21
post-war economy 5.05
tax avoidance 19.49
United Nations
increasing recognition of UN as authority 27.67
role in economic global agenda and the principles 27.47–27.56
conceding competencies to UN 27.67
forum for discussions, as 27.48
role increasing 27.50–27.54
Stiglitz Commission 27.49
United Nations Commission on International Trade Law (UNCITRAL) 12.15, 23.06
United Nations Conference on Trade and Development (UNCTAD)
debt issues, dealing with 27.56
Debt Management Conferences 27.51
principles *see* **UNCTAD principles on responsible sovereign lending and borrowing**
United Nations Convention on Jurisdictional Immunities of States and their Property 10.06
United Nations Security Council
facilitating debt restructuring 2.23–2.24, 2.25, 22.70–22.73
resolutions binding financial organizations 27.27
United States (US)
Argentina litigation *see* ***NML Capital Ltd v. Argentina***
Bankruptcy Code 2.26, 2.27, 5.35
Chrysler debt 16.50
involuntary legal subordination 4.05
mortgage debt restructuring 23.50–23.52
CACs 2.31, 2.32, 25.10
central bank immunity *see* **central bank immunity**
class action mechanism 2.33–2.34
debt 20.11, 20.20, 20.21
defences
champerty *see under* **champerty**
comity and act-of-state doctrine *see under* **comity and act-of-state doctrine**
contracts-based arguments 8.05, 8.30–8.37
litigation stays 8.38–8.45
sovereign immunity *see under* **sovereign immunity**
deregulation 27.09
financial crisis, response to 20.72
General Motors bankruptcy 19.73
government debt 15.25, 15.26
Great Depression 5.04, 12.02, 19.44, 27.15
mortgage debt restructuring 23.48–23.52
national authorities, cooperating with 23.31
odious debt, defences addressing 17.06, 17.09–17.10
see also **odious debt**
pari passu clauses 4.28
polarized society, as 19.45
public debt, home bias in holdings of 14.23
SDRM, opposing 2.27, 23.75
Uruguay
currency mismatches, contingent liabilities and 21.23
debt restructuring 1.31, 22.30, 22.34
aggregation mechanism 5.26
exit consent 2.22, 2.23
private inflows after restructuring 7.27

value recovery rights 1.28–1.34
benchmarks of return to financial health 1.31
difficulties in using in sovereign debt settings 1.29
free-standing/freely tradeable 1.33
future payments 1.33, 1.35
Mexico 1.29–1.30
misprized by the market when first issued 1.32
purpose 1.28
Venezuela
debt restructuring 1.30
payment delay 19.75
vulture funds 4.01, 4.17, 4.38–4.49
Elliott–Peru saga 4.17–4.26, 8.22–8.29
pari passu clauses *see* ***NML Capital Ltd v. Argentina***
targeting third parties 4.27–4.31

Wälde, Thomas 12.10, 12.52
Weidemeier, Mark 12.04, 12.06
Weil, Simone 8.46
White, Harry Dexter 5.04
World Bank
arbitration of disputes 12.06
debt sustainability analysis 19.65, 21.52
Debt Sustainability Framework of World Bank/IMF 6.35–6.37
development projects, financing 5.39
Financial Sector Assessment Programmes 23.06
HIPIC initiative *see* **Heavily Indebted Poor Countries (HIPC) initiative**
ICSID *see* **International Centre for Settlement of Investment Disputes (ICSID)**
IDA *see* **International Development Association (IDA)**
lender, as 1.16
World Trade Organization 5.34
Wriston, Walter 19.17, 19.18

Zaire 4.11–4.12
Zettelmeyer, Jeromin 7.15, 7.27